T0217407

Communications
in Computer and Information Science 288

Maotai Zhao   Junpin Sha (Eds.)

Communications and Information Processing

International Conference, ICCIP 2012
Aveiro, Portugal, March 7-11, 2012
Revised Selected Papers, Part I

 Springer

Volume Editors

Maotai Zhao
Xueyuan Road 3, Taiyuan, Shanxi, China 030051
E-mail: zmaotai@163.com

Junpin Sha
Jinhua Road 4, Xi'an, Shanxi, China 710032
E-mail: deepakawal@gmail.com

ISSN 1865-0929   ISSN 1865-0937
ISBN 978-3-642-31964-8   ISBN 978-3-642-31965-5 (eBook)
DOI 10.1007/978-3-642-31965-5
Springer Heidelberg Dordrecht London New York

Library of Congress Control Number: 2012942224

CR Subject Classification (1998): I.2, C.2, H.4, H.3, I.4-5, D.2

Typesetting: Camera-ready by author, data conversion by Scientific Publishing Services, Chennai, India

Printed on acid-free paper

Springer is part of Springer Science+Business Media (www.springer.com)

Preface

It is our pleasure to welcome you to the proceedings of the 2012 International Conference on Communications and Information Processing (ICCIP 2012) held in Aveiro, Portugal. ICCIP 2012 was the first conference dedicated to issues related to communications and information processing. A major goal and feature of ICCIP 2012 was to bring academic scientists, engineers, and industry researchers together to exchange and share their experiences and research results about most aspects of communications and information processing, and discuss the practical challenges encountered and the solutions adopted.

The conference was both stimulating and informative with a wonderful array of keynote and invited speakers from all over the world. Delegates had a wide range of sessions to choose from and many had a difficult time deciding which sessions to attend.

The program consisted of invited sessions, technical workshops, and discussions with eminent speakers covering a wide range of topics in communications and information processing. This rich program provided all attendees with opportunities to meet and interact with one another.

We would like to thank the organization staff, the members of the Program Committees, and the reviewers. They worked very hard in reviewing papers and making valuable suggestions for the authors to improve their work. We also would like to express our gratitude to the external reviewers, for providing extra help in the review process, and the authors for contributing their research result to the conference. Special thanks go to Springer.

We look forward to seeing all of you next year at the ICCIP 2013. With your support and participation, ICCIP will continue its success for a long time.

Zhenli Lu

Organization

General Chair

Lu Zhenli   IEETA, University of Aveiro, Portugal

Program Committee

Lorenzo Bruzzone	University of Trento, Italy
Hans du Buf	University of the Algarve, Portugal
Tiberio Caetano	NICTA and Australian National University, Australia
Javier Calpe	Universitat de València, Spain
Rui Camacho	Universidade do Porto, Portugal
Gustavo Camps-Valls	University of València, Spain
Ramon A. Mollineda Cardenas	Universitat Jaume I, Spain
Xavier Carreras	UPC, Spain
Marco La Cascia	Università degli Studi di Palermo, Italy
Rui M. Castro	Eindhoven University of Technology, The Netherlands
Zehra Cataltepe	Istanbul Technical University, Turkey
Javier Ortega Garcia	Universidad Autnoma de Madrid, Spain
Marco Parvis	Politecnico di Torino, Italy
Kostas Plataniotis	University of Toronto, Canada
Fabio Roli	Università degli Studi di Cagliari, Italy
Arun Ross	West Virginia University, USA
Bulent Sankur	Bogazici University, Turkey
Gabriella Sanniti di Baja	CNR, Italy
Carlo Sansone	University of Naples Federico II, Italy
Bhavesh Patel	Shah & Anchor Kutchhi Polytechnic, India
Xu Ning	Wuhan University of Technology, China
Cao Jian	Shanghai Jiao Tong University, China
He Jin	Peking University, China
Sun Pengtao	University of Nevada, USA
Wong Pak Kin	University of Macau, Macau

Table of Contents – Part I

Table of Contents – Part II

Research on Taper Tension Control Theory Apply in Material Rolling Up Procedure

Jincao Hu, Zhengfeng Jiang, and Hong Lu

School of Mechanical and Electronic Engineering, Wuhan University of Technology,
Wuhan, Hubei, P.R. China, 430070

Abstract. In the process of producing strip steel, fiber, plastic material, reeling up is a necessary technical procedure. However, the traditional reeling up that applies constant tension usually causing problems of unstable rolling tension, and it makes the coil edge irregular, coil core protruding, and collapse coil. Aiming at solve these problems this article researches the new control method that use the taper tension adjust theory, using a strip steel factory as an experiment object, the author establishes the control algorithm and specific program. Finally the experiment result had test and verify the research finding: the taper tension control theory successfully apply in the rolling up procedure; and through this research we have deepen the academic field of taper tension theory.

Keywords: taper tension, strip material, reeling up, control.

1 Introduction

In reeling up procedure of strip material producing process, it is usually applying the constant tension control proposal, that is, the reel machine running with a stable tension during the whole reeling procedure: winding、 reeling、 ending and bundling. However, because most reeling up procedure demands installing the sleeve on the mandrel of reeling machine and the sleeve will effecting a relative strong counterforce, and in this situation it will cause the problems that coil edge irregular, coil core protruding and collapse coil, it even will cause damage to the reel machine[1]. A new control model that applying the method of taper tension reeling up will solve the problems to a great extent: the curve of taper tension presenting as a spire cone shape, it can formatting a relative greater winding force to the coil core at beginning of reel up, and with the coil diameter's increasing the winding force will decrease, and this will meet the material reel up technical demand. In past, there is example that taper tension applying in Mill machine in Japan[2], in recent years, taper tension control method had more and more applied on the strip material reeling up procedure such as strip steel, glass cloth producing[3].

In the case which this research base on, the tradition constant tension control mode always cause the strip over strain, and strip coil get blocking in following anneal process, it cause huge damage and inconvenient to production. Aiming at solving the exist problem in the case, we bring forth new idea that applying taper tension control method, we draw up the control algorithm and program and using the reeling up machine of a continues annealing production line in a steel factory as the experimental

M. Zhao and J. Sha (Eds.): ICCIP 2012, Part I, CCIS 288, pp. 1–8, 2012.
© Springer-Verlag Berlin Heidelberg 2012

subject, through collecting and analyzing the experimental data signal, and compare the product quality before and after applying taper tension control proposal, finally we successful verify the practicability of the research.

2   Taper Tension Control Proposal on Reel Machine

2.1   Technological Requirement to the Design of Tension Adjust System

Generally speaking, in the reel up procedure, the production technological requirements the coil tensioning tighten in the core and relative looser on the outer layer, a ideal coil can show as the fig.1.

Fig. 1. Example of an ideal coil

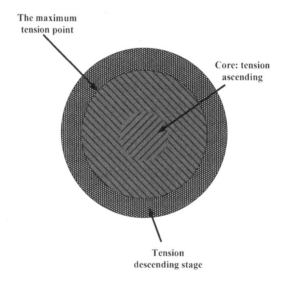

Fig. 2. Reel up tension requirement

It demands the reel up machine running with a relative greater tension at the beginning of winding a coil, and when the coil diameter reaches a certain value, the tension get the maximum and not ascend any more, and the reel up procedure comes into the wrapping region[4], and in this stage, the tension keep falling, the reel machine running with descending tension, the whole technological requirement to the tension adjust system as the fig.2 showed.

According the requirement, we draw up the designed reeling tension curve, as the fig.3 showed: firstly we define an initial tension (A point); then with the coil diameter's increasing, the tension ascending linearity, till it reaches the maximum tension point (C point); after get the maximum value, the tension descending linearity and finally the reel up procedure accomplished (D point). It should notice that the maximum tension point can adjust and it the tension curve's linear ratio, the operator could adjust the maximum tension value to control the tension ascending and descending process, but the maximum tension value should no less than the initial tension value.

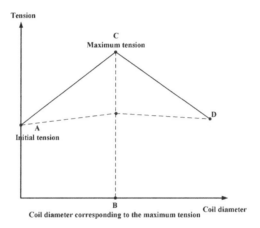

Fig. 3. Designed tension curve

2.2   Control Algorithm Design

We took the linearity adjust tension combined with double logic channels mode to design the control algorithm, as the fig.4 shows: assuming the real diameter as the input and the tension setting value to the reel up machine as the final output, ordering Qmax= tension max value (C point in fig.3), Qmin= initial tension value (A point in fig.3), Imax= coil diameter value corresponding the max tension (B point in fig.3), Imin= initial coil diameter (diameter corresponding to A point in fig.3), and assuming

$$a = \frac{Q_{max} - Q_{min}}{I_{max} - I_{min}} \ , \ b = \frac{Q_{min} \bullet I_{max} - Q_{max} \bullet I_{min}}{I_{max} - I_{min}} \ ;$$ the real coil diameter had been

adjusted by the $\times a + b$ function, we get the control algorithm of the tension linear ascending control function in reel up initial procedure.

By the same rule, assuming Q'max= tension corresponding to the final coil diameter (D point in fig.3), Q'min= tension max value (C point in fig.3), I'max= final coil diameter (diameter corresponding to the D point in fig.3), I'min= coil diameter corresponding to the max tension (B point in fig.3), ordering the $a' = \dfrac{Q'_{max} - Q'_{min}}{I'_{max} - I'_{min}}$,

$b' = \dfrac{Q'_{min} \bullet I'_{max} - Q'_{max} \bullet I'_{min}}{I'_{max} - I'_{min}}$; the real coil diameter had been adjusted by the $\times a' + b'$ function, we get the control algorithm of the tension linear descending control function in rolling-up procedure.

Then, we designed a logic module to completing the chosen the final function from the two tension control module as the tension output to the reel machine: when the real coil diameter value less than diameter value corresponding max tension, module chose the tension ascending function as the output; when the real coil diameter value more than diameter value corresponding max tension, module chose the tension descending function as the output.

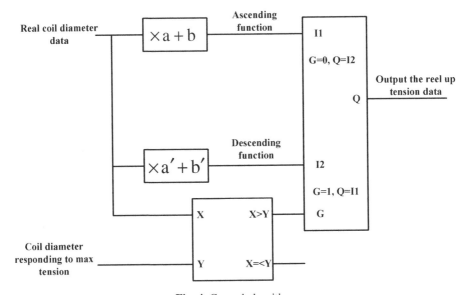

Fig. 4. Control algorithm

2.3   Control Program Design

Based on the algorithm, we programming as the following fig.5 shows: first filtered the real coil diameter data, then the data were processing by the two linear calculation module and choosing by a logic judgment module, finally output the reel up tension data.

Except the main control program, considered the safety element of the reel up machine and the whole device, we had programming the additional safety alarm sector, in this sector we had set a security limit value to the reel up tension data, if the output tension value exceeding the limitation, the program will forcing output the limit data as the final output tension value.

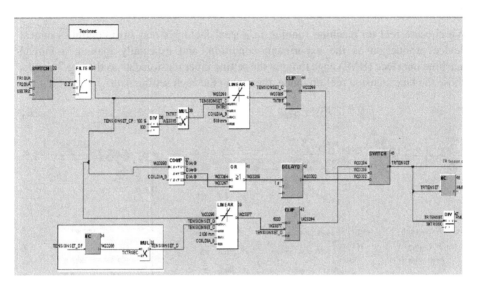

Fig. 5. Main control program

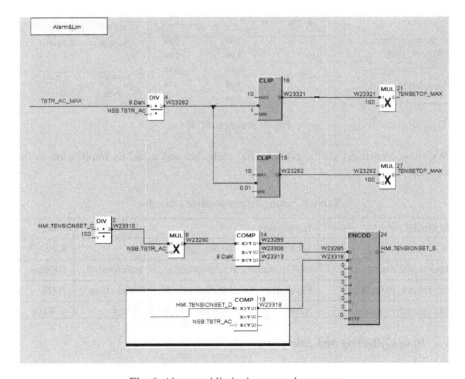

Fig. 6. Alarm and limitation control program

3   Experiment and Application

3.1   Experiment Setting

We chose a reel up machine running in a steel factory's real strip continues anneal device production as the experiment condition, and especially making a human machine interface (HMI) page to input the setting taper tension data as the Fig.7 shows: chose the taper tension reel up mode, then input the each setting data.

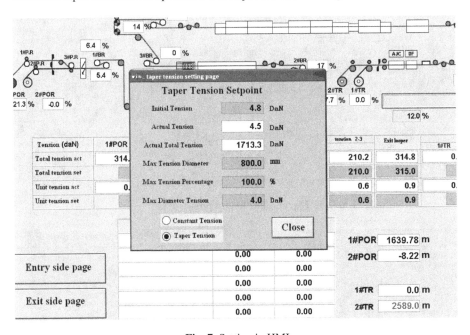

Fig. 7. Setting in HMI

We chose a coil and set the proper data, each data value and its implication as the table.1 shows:

Table 1. Setting data implication and value

Data name	Implication	Value
Initial tension	Unit tension on the beginning of reel up	4.8 DaN
Max tension diameter	Coil diameter Corresponding to the max tension	800mm
Max tension percentage	Percentage of tension max value to initial value	100%
Max diameter tension	Tension value during the ending of reel up	4.0DaN

3.2   Data Collecting and Analyzing

During the taper tension reel up procedure, we monitored and collected the coil diameter, reel up motor torque and reel up tension data, the data shows as the Fig.8: the

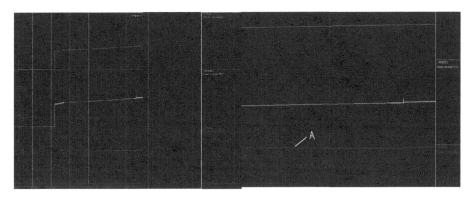

Fig. 8. Data collecting

red curve symbols the coil diameter data, the green curve symbols the reel up machine motor torque data, the blue curve symbols the reel up tension data.

As the coil diameter increasing (red curve ascending), the steel coil getting heavier and it made the motor loading more, so the motor torque output value ascending; the setting tension percentage was 100%, so the tension value was the maximum when the beginning or reel up procedure, till the A point in the Fig.8 shows, the coil diameter achieved the 800 mm (setting coil diameter value corresponding to the max tension), the tension value begin descending linearly till the end of reel up. Considered the device running speed was not a constant value when real production, we had changed the device running speed during the experiment, the motor torque data and tension data had fluctuated but it was not beyond the limit scope[5].

3.3   Application Achievement

Fig.9 shows the achievement of the taper tension application:

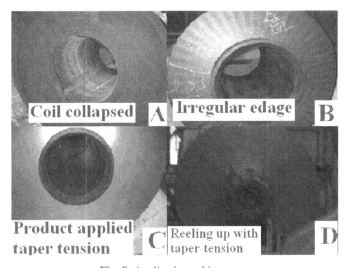

Fig. 9. Application achievement

A, B in Fig.9 shows the coil collapse and irregularity problem in constant tension reel up mode; and by applying the taper tension reel up, the finish product shows as the C and the reel up machine running with taper tension control as D shows in Fig.9----it had solved the problem and the reel up machine running good.

4   Conclusion

The research of taper tension control reel up theory accord with the technical demand of the reel up procedure, the algorithm and program control the taper tension reel up successfully; the experiment result confirmed the research had successfully applied in the strip coil reel up production. But it remains sufficient on coordinate with PID inertia compensate algorithm[6] and accommodate with reel up angle adjust function design[7], it is the further research direction in this research field.

References

1. Dick, M.G., Wilson, M.G.: The Effect of Sustained Wheel Impacts on Tapered Roller Bearing Cages. In: Proceeding of JRC 2006 Joint Rail Conference, Atlanta, pp. 189–195 (2006)
2. Zhang, B.: Application of Taper Tension Control in Coiling of Hot Strip Mill. Electric Drive 40(8), 67–70 (2010)
3. Wu, D.H., Tan, Z.X., Yang, H.Q.: Taper rolling - up and parameter determination in glass fabric packaging. Packing Engineering 40(8), 8–11 (2005)
4. Wang, R., Liu, H.K., Li, J.: Winding tension rotational inertia compensation control. Journal of Wuhan University of Science and Technology 32(3), 305–308 (2009)
5. Wu, S.Y.: Determination of the Maximum Value of Recoiling Tension within a Rolling Pass. Nonferrous Metals Processing 31(1), 54–62 (2002)
6. Wang, Z., Fang, Y.M., Nie, Y.: Design Based on the Quantitative Feedback Control for Coiler Tension Controller of Tandem Cold Rolling Mill. Metallurgical Equipment, Total No.157, 13–17 (2006)
7. Cui, X.Y., Hua, F.A., Zhang, D.H., Liu, X.H., Wang, G.D.: Tension control system of continuous annealing simulator for cold rolled strip. Metallurgical Industry Automation 34(3), 39–42 (2010)
8. Lee, C.W., Shin, K.H.: A Study on Taper-Tension Control Considering Telescoping in the Winding System. IEEE Transactions on Industry Application 46(2), 687–693 (2010)
9. Huang, B., Zhou, H., Qi, Q.: Application of adaptive speed control to tension coiler. Engineering Journal of Wuhan University 37(5), 101–104 (2004)
10. Ning, Y.: A Practical Technique to Improve the Precision of Rolling Tension Control. Non-ferrous Metallurgical Equipment, 11–13 (February 2000)

Research on Active Vibration Isolation Based on Chaos Synchronization

Zhixing Li, Shijian Zhu, Qianghong Zeng, Shuyong Liu, and Aibo Yang

College of Naval Architecture and Power, Naval University of Engineering,
Wuhan, 430033, China

Abstract. To improve warship capability of concealment, the key problem of the design of the chaotic vibration isolation system is how to keep the chaotic response in different working condition. The existing isolation systems, however, are designed based on linear system theory, and thus it is difficult to generate chaos; but if the isolation system is designed according to nonlinear theory, it is difficult to realize in practical engineering. The main reason is that the element of isolation system should be calculated accurately. The controller based on the Lyapunov stability theory is designed, and the aim is to make the output variable of the isolation system track the output variable of the chaos system, i.e. the output of two systems are synchronized by choosing the output matrix of chaos system suitably. Results show that the response of the double layer vibration isolation can track the output of the Duffing driven system, and the force transferred to base is reduced effectively. The performance of the vibration isolation is improved.

Keywords: Chaos synchronization, Active control, Double layer vibration isolation system, Duffing system.

1   Introduction

Chaos exists abroad in nature and human society, and its wide application in biological engineering, chemical engineering, information disposal and mechanical engineering is glory. Cha studied the chaos in neural system[1]; Kiss J et al studied the chaos in electrochemistry[2]; Aihara K et al studied the chaotic characteristic in NN information disposal system[3]; the chaotic behavior in car system was discussed in reference[4]; Lou et al presented using the chaos theory to isolate equipment in machine to decrease or avoid the characteristic line spectrum, which is on the basis of the characteristic that the power spectrum is successive when chaos is produced in nonlinear vibration isolation system. The parameter range of a nonlinear vibration isolation system is small and hard to be searched when the system is designed directly, and precision process to isolation elements is requested at the same time [5], and thus the question that   how to keep the isolation system exhibiting chaotic response and increase the isolation capability must be taken into consider.

Chaos synchronization has been attracting much attention because of its essential application in secret communication, life science and so on since the realization project

M. Zhao and J. Sha (Eds.): ICCIP 2012, Part I, CCIS 288, pp. 9–19, 2012.

of chaos synchronization was presented firstly by L. M. Pecora and T. L. Carroll in 1990, and research on chaos synchronization is progressed greatly, which has been become a hotspot on nonlinear science research [6]. A generalized chaos synchronization method is presented in reference [7], that is chaos signal is used to drive a isolation system to keep the chaotic response for a long time, which, however, can improve isolation only on a determined condition and is strict quietly in parameters chosen which decrease the robust of the system to keep chaotic; controllers of a disturbed chaotic system are designed to realize two chaotic systems synchronization on the basis of Lyapunov stability theory in reference [8], but they are hard to be determined due to the number of controllers need to be equal to the number of state variable, and uncertainty existing. A method of the output of chaotic system which is tracked by the output of a disturbed linear system to realize two systems export synchronized controllers is presented in this paper, pre-requirement of the established designed method is cleared to make a linear system produce chaotic vibration, and the controlled method is applied in double-stage vibration isolation system, all of these are on the basis of the reference [8].The results show that the isolation system is chaos and can reduce the force to the base effectively, the isolation capability can be improved effectively if the output matrix of the chaotic system is chosen reasonably.

2   Design of Chaos Synchronization Controller

The state equation of disturbed linear system:

$$\begin{cases} \dot{X}_r = AX_r + BU + EW \\ Y_r = C_r X_r \end{cases} \tag{1}$$

where $X_r \in R^n$ is the state vector of the linear system, $U \in R^m$ is the intended controller vector, $Y_r \in R^m$ is the output of the linear system; $A \in R^{n \times n}$, $B \in R^{n \times m}$, $E \in R^{n \times l}$, $C_r \in R^{m \times n}$. $W \in R^l$,is the vector of a disturbing system outside, and the external disturbance W is continuously differentiable, the vibration characteristic of which is determined by the following ecosystem[8]

$$\begin{cases} \dot{\xi}(t) = G\xi(t), t > 0 \\ W = H\xi(t) \end{cases} \tag{2}$$

Chaos driven system:

$$\begin{cases} \dot{X}_d = f_d\left(X_d(t),t\right) \\ Y_d = C_d X_d \end{cases} \tag{3}$$

where $X_d \in R^p$ is the state vector of the driven system, f_d is a function of the nonlinear system, $Y_d \in R^m$ is the output of the nonlinear chaotic system, $C_d \in R^{m \times p}$.

Tracked error is:

$$e(t) = Y_r - Y_d \tag{4}$$

Error dynamic system is obtained:

$$\dot{e}(t) = \dot{Y}_r - \dot{Y}_d \tag{5}$$

If Eq. (6) is satisfied:

$$\lim_{t \to \infty} |e(t)| = \lim_{t \to \infty} \|Y_r - Y_d\| = 0 \tag{6}$$

Then system synchronization export can be defined.

Theorem 1. If ① Y_r and Y_d are continuously differentiable in the state vector sets X_r and X_d ; ② $\begin{bmatrix} A & C_r \end{bmatrix}$ is observed, $C_r B$ is reversible, B is the linear transformer of C_r^T ; ③the controller meets the equation $\dot{U} + KU = -\phi$;

$$U = e^{-K(t-t_0)} U(t_0) + e^{-K(t)} \int_{t_0}^t e^{K(\tau)} \left[-\phi(\tau) \right] d\tau;$$

where

$$K = (C_r B)^{-1} (C_r AB + C_r B);$$

$$\phi = (C_r B)^{-1} [(C_r + C_r A + C_r A^2) X +$$

$$(C_r EH + C_r AEH + C_r EHG)\xi - C_d (\ddot{X}_d + \dot{X}_d + X_d)]$$

Then the output of system (1) and system (3) are synchronized.
Proved: the Lyapunov function is constructed as follows

$$V(e(t), \dot{e}(t)) = e^2(t) + \dot{e}^2(t)_,$$

Then the Eq.(7) is written as:

$$\dot{V} = 2e\dot{e} + 2\dot{e}\ddot{e}$$
$$= 2(\dot{Y}_r - \dot{Y}_d)(Y_r - Y_d + \dot{Y}_r - \dot{Y}_d) \tag{7}$$

Let:

$$
\begin{aligned}
& C_r X_r - C_d X_d + C_r A^2 X_r + C_r ABU + C_r B\dot{U} \\
& + (C_r AEH + C_r EHG)\xi - C_d \ddot{X}_d \\
& = -C_r \dot{X}_r + C_d \dot{X}_d \\
& = -C_r A X_r - C_r BU - C_r EW + C_d \dot{X}_d
\end{aligned}
\tag{8}
$$

Then the equation above can be transformed as:

$$
\begin{aligned}
& -C_r B\dot{U} - (C_r AB + C_r B)U = (C_r + C_r A + C_r A^2)X_r \\
& + (C_r EH + C_r AEH + C_r EHG)\xi - C_d(\ddot{X}_d + \dot{X}_d + X_d)
\end{aligned}
\tag{9}
$$

$-(C_r B)^{-1}$ is multiplied to both sides of Eq. (8) at the same time, then

$$
\dot{U} + KU = -\phi
\tag{10}
$$

where:

$$
K = (C_r B)^{-1}(C_r AB + C_r B),
$$

$$
\begin{aligned}
\phi = (C_r B)^{-1} [(C_r + C_r A + C_r A^2)X \\
+ (C_r EH + C_r AEH + C_r EHG)\xi - C_d(\ddot{X}_d + \dot{X}_d + X_d)]
\end{aligned}
$$

Eq. (10) is nonhomogeneous linear differential equation, whose solution is:

$$
U = e^{-K(t-t_0)}U(t_0) + e^{-K(t)}\int_{t_0}^t e^{K(\tau)}\left[-\phi(\tau)\right]d\tau
\; ;
$$

Assume

$$
t_0 = 0, U(0) = 0,
$$

then

$$
U = e^{-K(t)}\int_{t_0}^t e^{K(\tau)}\left[-\phi(\tau)\right]d\tau
\tag{11}
$$

Substitute Eq. (11) into Eq. (7), then can get

$$
\dot{V} = -2(C_r \dot{X}_r - C_d \dot{X}_d)^2 < 0
\tag{12}
$$

Multiform synchronization such as chaos antisynchronization and umbriferous chaos synchronization can be realized through the output matrix C_d of driven system and C_r of response system being chosen.

3 Mathematic Model of Double-Stage Vibration Isolation System

As is shown in Fig.1, the model of vibration isolation system is:

$$\begin{cases} m_1\ddot{x}_1 + c_1(\dot{x}_1 - \dot{x}_2) + k_1(x_1 - x_2) = F \\ m_2\ddot{x}_2 + c_1(\dot{x}_2 - \dot{x}_1) + k_1(x_2 - x_1) + c_2\dot{x}_2 + k_2x_2 = F_u \end{cases} \tag{13}$$

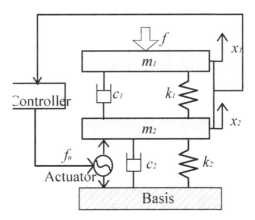

Fig. 1. Sketch map of active control of double-stage vibration isolation system

Assume $\mu = \dfrac{m_1}{m_2}$, $\omega_1 = \sqrt{\dfrac{k_1}{m_1}}$, $\xi_1 = \dfrac{c_1}{2\sqrt{m_1k_1}}$, $\omega_2 = \sqrt{\dfrac{k_2}{m_2}}$, $\xi_2 = \dfrac{c_2}{2\sqrt{m_2k_2}}$,

$f = \dfrac{F}{k_1}$, $f_u = \dfrac{F_u}{k_1}$, the equation of the system after dimensionless method written as:

$$\begin{cases} \ddot{x}_1 + 2\xi_1\omega_1(\dot{x}_1 - \dot{x}_2) + \omega_1^2(x_1 - x_2) = \omega_1^2 f \\ \ddot{x}_2 + 2\mu\omega_1\xi_1(\dot{x}_2 - \dot{x}_1) + \mu\omega_1^2(x_2 - x_1) \\ + 2\xi_2\omega_2\dot{x}_2 + \omega_2^2 x_2 = \mu\omega_1^2 f_u \end{cases} \tag{14}$$

Sketch map of initiative control of double-stage vibration isolation system is shown in Fig.1. Assume $X = \begin{bmatrix} x_1 & \dot{x}_1 & x_2 & \dot{x}_2 \end{bmatrix}^T$, then Eq.(14) can be written as the matrix form:

$$\dot{X} = AX + BU + Ef \tag{15}$$

where:

$$A = \begin{bmatrix} 0 & 1 & 0 & 0 \\ -\omega_1^2 & -2\xi_1\omega_1 & \omega_1^2 & 2\xi_1\omega_1 \\ 0 & 0 & 0 & 1 \\ \mu\omega_1^2 & 2\mu\xi_1\omega_1 & -(\mu\omega_1^2 + \omega_2^2) & -(2\mu\xi_1\omega_1 + 2\xi_2\omega_2) \end{bmatrix},$$

$$B = \begin{bmatrix} 0 \\ 0 \\ 0 \\ \mu\omega_1^2 \end{bmatrix}, \quad E = \begin{bmatrix} 0 \\ \omega_1^2 \\ 0 \\ 0 \end{bmatrix},$$

Output of the system is taken as:

$$Y_r = C_r X \tag{16}$$

What can be known from condition (2) of Theorm.1 is the choice of C_r should make $C_r B$ reversible, $\begin{bmatrix} A & C_r \end{bmatrix}$ observed and B be the linear transformation of C_r^T. If $C_r = \begin{bmatrix} 0 & 0 & 0 & 1 \end{bmatrix}$ can be chosen to meet the conditions mentioned above, then $Y_r = \dot{x}_2$.

4   Driven Chaotic System

Duffing system is a typical nonlinear dynamic system, Duffing equation is chosen as follow:

$$\begin{cases} \dot{x}_{d1} = x_{d2} \\ \dot{x}_{d2} = -ax_{d2} - bx_{d1} - x_{d1}^3 + q\cos(\omega t) \end{cases} \tag{17}$$

when assume $a = 0.4$, $b = -1.1$, $\omega = 1.8$, $q = 1.498$, the system is chaos, whose chaos attractor is shown in Fig.2.

Assume the output of driven system is: $Y_d = C_d X_d$ where, $C_d = \begin{bmatrix} c_d & 0 \end{bmatrix}$, $X_d = \begin{bmatrix} x_{d1} & x_{d2} \end{bmatrix}^T$, then $Y_d = c_d x_{d1}$.

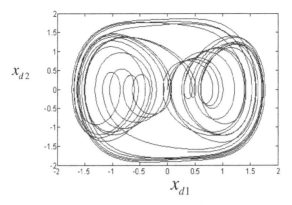

Fig. 2. Phase diagram of $x_{d1} - x_{d2}$ in Duffing system

5   Simulation Results

The parameters of the double-stage vibration isolation system are taken as $\mu = 2$, $\omega_1 = 3.2113$, $\xi_1 = 4.9038$, $\omega_2 = 10.7529$, $\xi_2 = 4.8978$, $f = 0.9091\cos(6t)$, $C_d = \begin{bmatrix} 10^{-3} & 0 \end{bmatrix}$. It is simulated as the controller designed according to Theorem.1. The velocity $\dot{x}_2$ of middle mass of the isolation system before being controlled is periodic, which is shown in Fig.3; Y_d can be tracked by Y_r absolutely after the chaos synchronization control being added to the vibration isolation system, and the error between Y_r and Y_d is shown in Fig.4. Time history of $\dot{x}_2$ is shown in Fig.5 after control being added, and vibration of $\dot{x}_2$ is not periodic any longer after control being added. The amplitude of $\dot{x}_2$ is influenced directly by the value of c_d ,which can be known from Theorem.1 mentioned above, the smaller c_d the smaller $\dot{x}_2$; but the robust from the controller to initial disturbance will be bad due to smaller c_d .

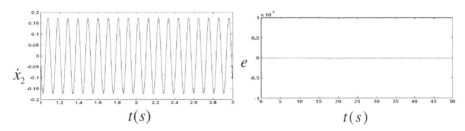

Fig. 3. Time history of $\dot{x}_2$ when passive vibration isolation being used

Fig. 4. Error curve

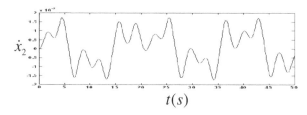

Fig. 5. Time history of $\dot{x}_2$ when synchronization control being used

6   Analysis of Vibration Isolation Efficiency

The vibration isolation efficiency of the system can be reflected directly by the force to the base because the outside exciting force of passive vibration isolation and active vibration isolation is equal.

The force from passive vibration isolation to the base is:

$$F_{base} = k_2 x_2 + c_2 \dot{x}_2 \tag{18}$$

Eq. (18) can be transformed as the follow after dimensionless method being used to it:

$$f_b = F_{base}/m_2 = \frac{1}{m_2}\left(k_2 x_2 + c_2 \dot{x}_2\right)$$

$$= \omega_2^2 x_2 + 2\xi_2 \omega_2 \dot{x}_2 \tag{19}$$

The force passed to the base is uniform amplitude and periodic. Force on the base of the vibration isolation is shown in Fig.6 when active control without being used.

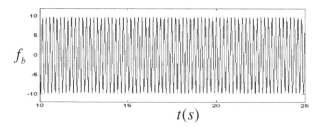

Fig. 6. Force on the base of passive vibration isolation

The force f_b passed to the base through spring and damping of vibration isolation system can be expressed as Eq. (18) when chaos synchronization is come out, its time history is shown in Fig.7, and its power spectrum is shown in Fig.8, and f_b is chaos at the time and the characteristic line spectrum is not happened in its power spectrum, which can be known in Fig.7 and Fig.8.

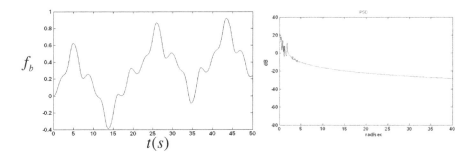

Fig. 7. Time history of f_b at chaos synchronization

Fig. 8. Power spectrum of f_b at chaos synchronization

Reacting force of the actuator should be added to the force passed to the base when active vibration isolation is taken duo to the actuator is fixed between m_2 and the base, here the force on the base is:

$$F_{base} = k_2 x_2 + c_2 \dot{x}_2 + F_u \tag{20}$$

Where F_u is the output force of the controller; the following expression can be gotten after Eq.(20) being transformed with dimensionless method:

$$f_z = F_{base}/m_2 = \frac{1}{m_2}\left(k_2 x_2 + c_2 \dot{x}_2 + f_u k_1\right)$$
$$= \omega_2^2 x_2 + 2\xi_2 \omega_2 \dot{x}_2 + \mu \omega_1^2 f_u$$

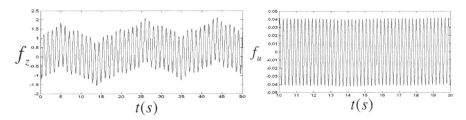

Fig. 9. Force on the base at chaos synchronization   **Fig. 10.** The output curve of controlled force

Amplitude of the force passed to the base is reduced after active control of the chaos synchronization being taken which can be known from the comparison between Fig.6 and Fig.9; vibration isolation capability of the vibration isolation system can be increased greatly after less energy being imported to the actuator, which can be realized because of the output amplitude of the actuator smaller than the amplitude of the outside exciting system which can be known from Fig.10 at the same time.

The force on the base is decreased greatly and the value of power spectrum at the linear spectrum of exciting frequency is reduced by 25dB after active control of the chaos synchronization being taken, but the characteristic linear spectrum is not removed by active vibration isolation system, the main causes are the actuator is fixed between the bottom mass and the base and the characteristic linear spectrum of the force on the base is produced by the actuator, all of which can be known from Fig.11 which shows the power spectrum of the force on the base.

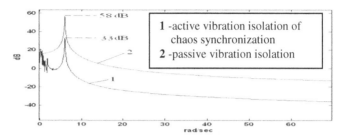

Fig. 11. Power spectrum of the force on the base

7   Conclusions

A controller designed theorem which can make the output of disturbance linear system synchronized to the output of a chaotic system is presented on the basis of Lyapunov stability theory and is proved in this paper, from which conclusions can be drawn as follows: (1) the theorem is applied to double-stage vibration isolation system to make active control be added to the system, which makes synchronization chaotic system be exported from the system and the chaos be produced from vibration isolation system; (2) the characteristic power spectrum of the system is continuous spectrum and avoiding the features of characteristic linear spectrum which are validated after chaos being produced from double-stage vibration isolation system; because the actuator is fixed between the bottom mass and the base the reacting force of the actuator is also passed to the base which gains linear component of the power spectrum belongs to the base force, which can be known from the analysis to the power spectrum of the base force; however, the vibration isolation effect is improved much relative to passive vibration isolation system. (3) the driven chaotic systems of double-stage vibration isolation system not only contain Duffing system but also other chaotic system according to the theorem presented in this paper.

Acknowledgement. This project is supported by the Youth Foundation of the National Science Foundation (Grant No.51009143), State Key Laboratory of Ocean Engineering (Shanghai Jiao Tong University)(Grant No.1009), and FANEDD in 2009 (Grant No.201057).

References

1. Cha, Y.T.: Chaos in a three variable model of an excitable cell. Physica D 16, 233–274 (1985)
2. Kiss, I.Z., Gaspar, V.: Controlling electrochemical chaos in the copper-phosphoric acid system. Phys. Chem. A 101, 8668–8674 (1997)

3. Aihara, K., Takabe, T., Toyoda, M.: Chaotic neural networks. Phys. Lett. A 144, 333–369 (1990)
4. Wu, G., Sheng, Y.: Review on the Application of Chaos Theory in Automobile Nonlinear System. Journal of Mechanical Engineering 10, 87–93 (2010)
5. Lou, J.-J., Zhu, S.-J., He, L., Yu, X.: Application of chaos method to line spectra reduction. Journal of Sound and Vibration 286, 3645–3652 (2005)
6. Xiaoning, L., Yunwen, S., Sanmin, W., Zhiying, G.: Chaos Control for a Gear System with Clearance Nonlinearity Based on The Ott-Grebogi-Yorke Method. Journal of Mechanical Engineering 41(11), 26–31 (2005)
7. Yu, X., Zhu, S.-J., Liu, S.-Y.: A new method for linear spectra reduction similar to generalized synchronization of chaos. Journal of Sound and Vibration 306, 835–848 (2007)
8. Pi, H.-H., Liu, H.: Tracking Control and Synchronization of Any Continuous Chaotic System in the Presence of Perturbation. Journal of Chuzhou University 10(6), 47–48 (2008)

Research on the Demodulation Technique of Waterjet Pump Cavitation Characteristic

Jizhong Song, Yongbao Liu, and Qingchao Yang

College of Naval Architecture and Power, Naval University of Engineering,
Wuhan, 430033, China

Abstract. As the influence of rotation effect, the frequency of cavity creating and bursting is modulated by the shaft frequency, blade frequency and double blade frequency when the cavitation is given birth to impeller machine. The cavitation measurement of a certain real ship's waterjet pump is performed in this paper. The inlet underwater acoustic pressure signals (direct effect) and the shell vibration signals (indirect effect) of cavitation are obtained in the test. The demodulation techniques including time-delay, correlation and envelope are studied and the cavitation modulation characteristic of waterjet pump is successfully extracted by this means. Also, the introduction of time-delay technology is greatly increasing signal to noise ratio. The results show that the cavitation signal is of modulation characteristic, which can be made use of for on-line monitoring of cavitation.

Keywords: waterjet pump, cavitation feature, demodulation technique, on-line monitoring.

1 Introduction

The pump characteristic of a ship's propulsion unit is greatly changed after using waterjet. The former limitation in the system of "ship-propeller-machine" which used propeller impetus is the mainframe, but now the limitation in the system of "ship-pump-machine" which uses waterjet is waterjet pump [1]. Only if the cavitation is given birth to the waterjet pump, its' thrust and efficiency will decrease, its' noise will increase, and the cavitation will also lead to the metal on the surface of the impeller, the guide vane and the runner denudated at the same time. Research on the cavitation of waterjet pump can improve the performance of waterjet pump and prolong its using life which is essential on the realistic and the military value. Because of commercial secrets and technology blockade, foreign manufacturers say little about the cavitation feature of waretjet pump. The demodulation techniques including time-delay, correlation and envelope are used to demodulate the cavitation modulation characteristic of waterjet pump, and the modulation characteristic of blade frequency and double blade frequency of a certain real ship's waterjet pump is successfully extracted by this means on the basis of the research on the cavitation of impeller machine[2~7] which combined with the cavitation measurement of a certain real waterjet pump. This provides some ideas for monitoring of cavitation of waterjet pump and makes it possible for on-line monitoring of cavitation at the same time.

M. Zhao and J. Sha (Eds.): ICCIP 2012, Part I, CCIS 288, pp. 20–29, 2012.

2   Theoretical Basis

(1) The demodulation method of envelope of correlation and envelope of correlation with time-delay

The demodulation method of correlation [8] is firstly to progress the signal with correlation analysis to get the correlation function and then to demodulate the function using the Hilbert.

Assumed the modulated signal is $x(t) = Ae^{j\omega t}e^{j\Omega t}$, here ω is modulation frequency; Ω is carrier frequency; A is a constant.

The autocorrelation function of $x(t)$ is $R_x(\tau) = \lim_{T \to \infty} \int_0^T x^*(t)x(t+\tau)dt$.

Where $x^*(t)$ is the conjugate function of $x(t)$. After the former function being taken into the latter, the function $R_x(\tau) = A^2 e^{j\omega \tau}e^{j\Omega \tau}$ can be gotten.

It can be seen that the autocorrelation function of the modulated signal still modulated signal, and the modulation frequency and the carrier frequency will never change. Make the autocorrelation function of vibration signal $R_x(\tau)$ to be transformed using the Hilbert, that is to say $\tilde{R}_x(\tau) = \frac{1}{\pi}\int_{-\infty}^{\infty} \frac{R_x(\tau)}{\tau - t}dt$, and then the envelope function $p(\tau) = \sqrt{R_x^2(\tau) + \tilde{R}_x^2(\tau)}$ is created, after which the spectral analysis of $p(\tau)$ can be undertaken. The correlation demodulation spectrum of the signal can be gotten from it.

The correlation function not only has the feature of decreasing noise which has been applied extensively in handling and analyzing the signal but has the feature of not changing modulated characteristic of the signal. The features are the very theoretical basis of decreasing noise and demodulation of the demodulation method of correlation.

Its' autocorrelation function is attenuated to zero quickly with the increasing of τ for broadband random signals. At the beginning segment of the correlation function, the signal segment which is affected by noise may be occurred, so a delay is needed before the Hilbert transformation of correlation function in order to decrease the influence of noise further. The result of decreasing noise of correlation analysis will be more obvious for it. In addition, it's suitable to choose the sample length of vibration signal longer. Take a sure delay to avoid the influence of noise and to make full use of sample signals which can ensure the resolution ratio of spectrum high enough. Finally, get the correlation demodulation spectrum through spectral analysis of envelope function. What mentioned above are the basic principle of time-delay correlation demodulation method.

(2) The demodulation method of correlation of envelope and correlation of envelope with time-delay

As its name indicates, the achievement steps of the demodulation method of correlation of envelope and envelope of correlation are exchanged, that is make the operation of envelope to remark the modulation elements at first, and then analysis the correlation to decrease the noise of the modulation elements, get the spectral analysis of the signals to get the period elements at last, from the steps the demodulation spectrum of correlation of envelope of signals can be gotten. The demodulation method of correlation of envelope with time-delay which is on the basis of correlation of envelope takes a sure time-delay when the spectral analysis of the correlation signal is undertaken at last to avoid the influence of noise which can influence the correlation analysis of the initial segment, which can lead to the modulation characteristic stand out.

Envelope the signals the modulated elements included is the basic of its demodulation analysis, no matter do the correlation analysis first or latter to decrease noise or gain the time-delay to eliminate the signal segment which is influenced by noise, all of this is to increase the signal to noise ratio of signals of modulation characteristic. The basic idea is the same with the traditional resonance demodulation technique of rolling bearing, which is to get a better the signal to noise ratio of characteristic signals through the signal processing technology and to get its modulation characteristic at last.

3   Experimental Studies

According to the given rotating characteristic curve of a certain real ship's waterjet pump, the curve is shown in the Fig.1. Three working sections and three cavitation limited lines are corresponded in Fig.1. KaMeWa Company divides the working section of waterjet into three. Section I is limited section of no-working hours in which the waterjet can working at the condition of non-cavitation. Section II is mild-section in which the waterjet is enabled the annual work hours no more than 500. Waterjet working in this section has produced mild harmful cavitation already due to larger loads. Section III is heavily cavitation section in which the enabled annual working hours are no more than 50. Waterjet working in this section lies in a heavy cavitation condition; the decreasing of hydraulic performance and denudated ruin are serious, so it is controlled tighter for annual working hours in section III. Experiment study is to get the characteristic of outline of cavitation performance while waterjet is working in different sections. The experiment study is to obtain the inlet underwater acoustic pressure signals (direct effect) through testing hydrophone located in opercle (the standard hydrophone RHS-30 manufactured by 715 in Zhejiang Faying, as is shown in Fig..2), the shell vibration signals (indirect effect) through testing the accelerated speed signals which obtained from the accelerated transducer (PCB608-A11, as is shown in Fig.2)fixed pump case of waterjet, the rpm of waterjet through the HE-01 Hall tachometric transducer fixed on drive shaft, the speed signal elicited by log indicator through serial 422, all of these signals are collected by corresponding NI collecting card, after being preprocessed corresponding the signals get into the system of NI data collecting. And all of these signals can be real time display and saved on-line by the signal collected and analyzed program and save the program through LabVIEW software, where the sample frequency of hydrophone is 102.4kHz, the sample frequency of the accelerated transducer is 51.2kHz, the collected time is controlled by the compiled programs and the data saved as excel which can be loaded to Matlab directly and be offline analyzed and handled.

4   Results Analysis

Analysis each five seconds data of three working section points as is shown in Fig.1 in order to analysis different corresponding cavitation feature of waterjet pump working at different sections consequently. These three points correspond to the three sections waterjet working at respectively, that is non-cavitation section I, cavitation section II and III. Time-domain characteristic and frequency-domain characteristic of the inlet underwater acoustic pressure signals and the shell vibration signals are obtained as are shown in Fig.3 (a) and Fig.3 (b) through dealing with experimental data. As are shown in the Fig.3 the amplitude of time-domain becomes higher and higher with the rpm and speed rising, while the characteristic of blade frequency and double blade frequency corresponded in frequency-domain is obvious, and the corresponding peak becomes higher and higher at the same time. Obtain the demodulation spectrum as are shown in Fig..4 and Fig.5 through demodulating the modulation characteristic of initial signals using correlation of envelope, correlation of envelope with time-delay, envelope of correlation and envelope of correlation with time-delay which mentioned in the text, here takes one of five of total time as time-delay, that is one second. What shown clearly in these two Figures are both the inlet underwater acoustic pressure signals and the shell vibration signals appear to be modulated by blade frequency and double blade frequency when waterjet working in the cavitation section II and III, and the inlet underwater acoustic pressure signals is more sensitive than the shell vibration signals for cavitation. Also, the introduction of time-delay technology is greatly increasing signal to noise ratio which can be seen qualitatively. In order to research the demodulation techniques suggested above quantitatively, a peak factor [2] is defined as follows to measure demodulation results of modulation characteristic.

$A = Peak(f_1) / Average(f)$, here A is peak factor, $Peak(f_1)$ is the peak of points of characteristic frequency, $Average(f)$ is the average of spectrum whose bandwidth is given.

The points chosen of characteristic frequency correspond to their blade frequency and double blade frequency in this experiment (the impeller of the waterjet pump has six blades), blade frequency in three sections is 39Hz, 73 Hz and 82 Hz respectively, double blade frequency is 78 Hz, 146 Hz and 164 Hz. Ignore the peak factor of blade frequency and double blade frequency when working in section I due to modulation does not appear when waterjet pump working in the section of non-cavitation.

Bandwidth are given respectively at $\frac{1}{2} \sim \frac{3}{2}$ of blade frequency and double blade frequency, calculate the peak factor respectively when waterjet pump working in the three sections using the demodulation method of correlation of envelope, correlation of envelope with time-delay, envelope of correlation and envelope of correlation with time-delay, the results are shown in Table.1.

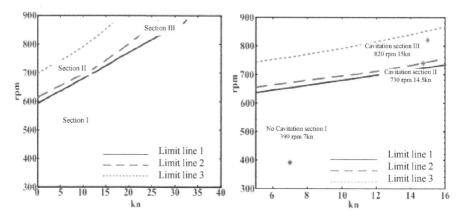

Fig. 1. rpm characteristic curve of a waterjet pump and locations of operating points in different cavitation condition

Fig. 2. Locations of the accelerated transducer and the hydrophone

It is obvious that the modulation characteristic at blade frequency and double blade frequency that correspond to their characteristic frequency. The peak factor of the inlet underwater acoustic pressure signals who reflects direct effect of cavitation is almost greater than the peak factor of the shell vibration signals. It shows the conclusion that the inlet underwater acoustic pressure signals is more sensitive than the shell vibration signals for cavitation quantitatively. Also, the results through the peak factor defined with the introduction of time-delay technology show that the technology is greatly increasing signal to noise ratio. All of these can be known from the results as table 1 shows.

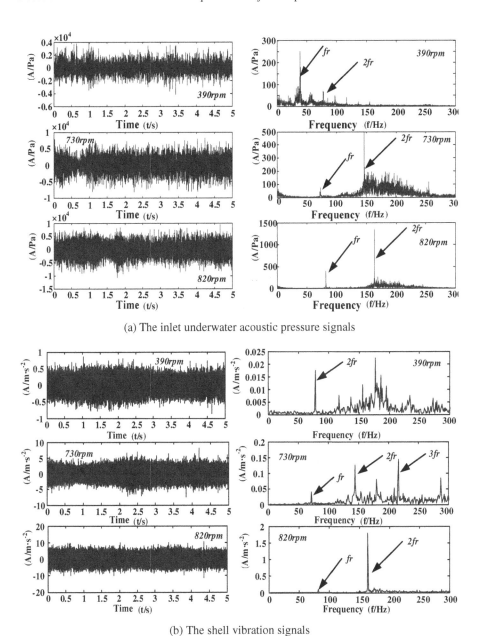

(a) The inlet underwater acoustic pressure signals

(b) The shell vibration signals

Fig. 3. Time-domain and frequency-domain of signals

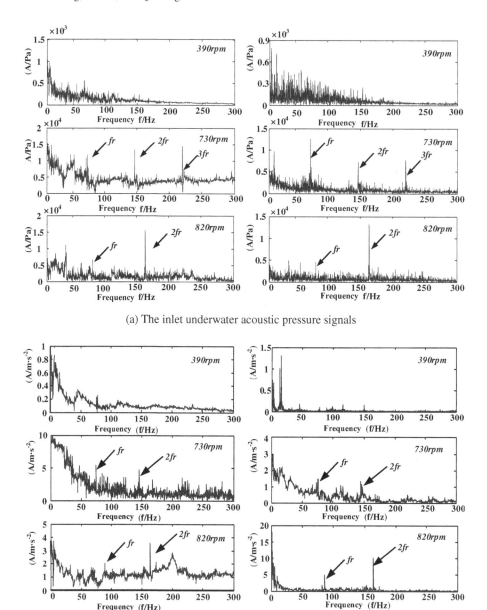

(a) The inlet underwater acoustic pressure signals

(b) The shell vibration signals

Fig. 4. The demodulation spectrum of correlation of envelope and correlation of envelope with time-delay

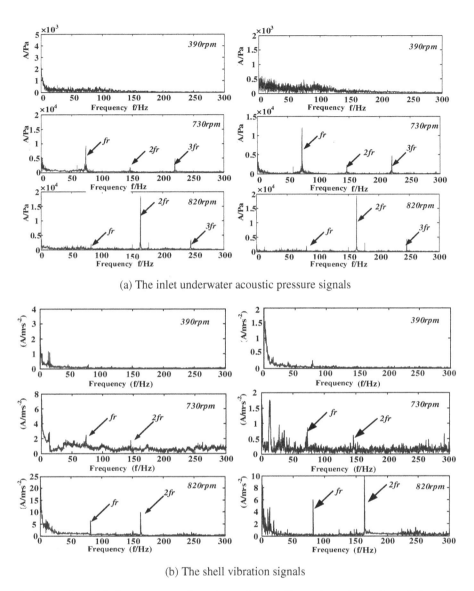

(a) The inlet underwater acoustic pressure signals

(b) The shell vibration signals

Fig. 5. The demodulation spectrum of envelope of correlation and envelope of correlation with time-delay

Table 1. The peak factor of modulation characteristic at different demodulation techniques

Signal types	Operation condition	demodulation techniques	peak factor of blade frequency	peak factor of double frequency
the underwater acoustic pressure signals	Cavitation section II (the shaft speed is 730rpm,the sailing speed is 14.5kn)	correlation of envelope	2.4374	3.7208
		correlation of envelope with time-delay	9.3393	8.2833
		envelope of correlation	4.0554	7.6795
		envelope of correlation with time-delay	7.1831	12.6084
	Cavitation section III (the shaft speed is 820rpm,the sailing speed is 15kn)	correlation of envelope	2.7857	2.7991
		correlation of envelope with time-delay	3.1531	3.6391
		envelope of correlation	3.0965	2.4900
		envelope of correlation with time-delay	4.2752	4.4140
the shell vibration signals	Cavitation section II (the shaft speed is 730rpm,the sailing speed is 14.5kn)	correlation of envelope	1.1729	1.6272
		correlation of envelope with time-delay	1.3787	3.6452
		envelope of correlation	2.4380	2.3565
		envelope of correlation with time-delay	3.5763	4.6212
	Cavitation section III (the shaft speed is 820rpm,the sailing speed is 15kn)	correlation of envelope	1.1411	1.3306
		correlation of envelope with time-delay	1.1811	2.0034
		envelope of correlation	1.4340	1.7646
		envelope of correlation with time-delay	1.9793	1.8181

5   Conclusions

According to the inlet underwater acoustic pressure signals and the shell vibration signals obtained from measuring a certain ship's waterjet pump, the signals can character the cavitation. The results show conclusions through researching on the demodulation techniques of modulation characteristic of the cavitation signals as follows:

① Waterjet pump is modulated by its blade frequency and double blade frequency when working in the cavitation sections;

② The modulation characteristic of waterjet pump is demodulated well through using the demodulation techniques of correlation of envelope, correlation of envelope with time-delay, envelope of correlation and envelope of correlation with time-delay which mentioned above;

③ The introduction of time-delay technology is greatly increasing signal to noise ratio;

④ The inlet underwater acoustic pressure signals is more sensitive than the shell vibration signals for cavitation quantitatively through calculating the peak factor of characteristic frequency points respectively;

⑤ It is possible to make use of modulation characteristic of the cavitation signal for on-line monitoring of cavitation with the cavitation measurement database of a certain ship enriched and improved.

References

1. He, J., Wang, Y., Ding, J.: Study on principles and methods of cavitation prediction of a waterjet pump. China Shiprepair 19(2), 24–26 (2004)
2. Kaye, M.: Cavitation Monitoring of Hydraulic Machines by Vibration Analysis. Laboratoire de Machines Hydrauliques (LMH), Switzerland (2000)
3. Osterman, A., Hocevar, M., Sirok, B., et al.: Characterization of incipient cavitation in axial valve by hydrophone and visualization. Expermental Thermal and Fluis Science (33), 620–629 (2009)
4. Cudina, M., Prezelj, J.: Detection of cavitation in situ operation of kinetic pumps:effect of cavitation on the characteristic discrete frequency component. Applied Acoustics (70), 1175–1182 (2009)
5. Wu, D.: Study on the technique of hydro-turbine's condition monitoring based on acoustic. Huazhong University of Science and Technology, Wuhan (2006)
6. Su, Y., Wang, Y., Yan, F., et al.: Study on the analysis and extracted methods of modulation characteristic which belongs to the cavitation vibration signals. Journal of Vibration Measurement and Diagnosis 30(5), 570–572 (2010)
7. Xavier, E., Mohamed, F., Eduard, E., et al.: Dynamics and intensity of erosive partial cavitation. Transactions of the ASME (129), 886–893 (2007)
8. Meng, T., Liao, M.: Diagnose rolling bearing fault with the demodulation method of time-delay correlation. Acta Aeronautica et Astronautica Sinica 25(1), 41–44 (2004)

Study on the Evaluation of Phase Space Reconstruction Based on Radial Basis Function Network Prediction

Shuyong Liu, Qingchao Yang, Xiulei Wei, and Aibo Yang

College of Naval Architecture and Power, Naval Univ. of Engineering,
Wuhan, 430033, China

Abstract. The radial basis function neural network model was applied to characterize the nonlinear dynamical behavior of the chaotic attractor neighborhood evolution, and the key problem of how to ensure the reconstructed dynamical system is identified with original one topologically by the calculated reconstruction parameters was solved effectively. The proposed method characterizes the nonlinear dynamics more accurately than the traditional linear model prediction. Simulation results show that the original phase space can be reconstructed by the suitable embedding dimension and delay time, and the short-term prediction of chaotic time series is realized by the radial basis function network. The method was reasonable for proving the availability of phase space reconstruction.

Keywords: phase space reconstruction, radial basis function, chaotic attractor, prediction model.

1 Introduction

The evaluation of phase space reconstruction parameters is a key problem in chaos identification, such as LE exponent calculation, fractal dimension extraction. However, the topic is neglected because of scarce of corresponding reconstruction criterion. In fact, the important characteristic of chaos is the short-term prediction. When the reconstruction parameter is reasonable, the basic features of chaotic system are described objectively with the proposed mathematic model [1]. The traditional linear prediction methods are on the basis of fast steepest algorithm, Kalman algorithm etc., but these algorithms cannot be applied to characterize the chaos nonlinear dynamics freely [2]. Furthermore, the system parameters are varied with the external environment, such as working condition, temperature, in the process of chaotification or chaos anti-control, and thus the prediction model should be adjusted according to the prediction error.

The nearest orbits prediction model is a classic algorithm in the chaos analysis. The mathematic model is established on the basis of neighborhood evolution, and then the function relation is used to calculate the prediction values conveniently. However, for a reference point, there exist same neighbor points on the trajectories of attractor, and

M. Zhao and J. Sha (Eds.): ICCIP 2012, Part I, CCIS 288, pp. 30–36, 2012.
© Springer-Verlag Berlin Heidelberg 2012

then the prediction error is obvious, i.e., those methods depend on the phase space geometrical structure closely. A kind of Radial-Basis Function (RBF) prediction model in which a group of basic function is applied to fit the nonlinear dynamical system is presented by Powell [3], and the chaos prediction is carried out accurately if the phase space reconstruction is effective.

2   Prediction Theory of Radial Basis Function

Because the intrinsic law of chaos orbit evolution is not reflected in the nearest point prediction model, the results depend on the attractor structure [4]. And thus, the local neighbourhood evolution behavoiur should be described with mathematic model. In general, the dynamic equation is,

$$\mathbf{x}(t+\tau) = f(\mathbf{x}(t)) \tag{1}$$

where the $\mathbf{x}(t+\tau)$ is map of $f(\mathbf{x}(t))$, and as far as arbitrary point $\mathbf{x}(t)$ in the space is concerned, the mapped point after time τ is obtained,

$$\mathbf{x}(t+\tau) = f\left(x(t), x(t+\tau), \cdots, x(t+(m-1)\tau\right) \tag{2}$$

In order to find the mathematic model f of time series according to the phase space attractor, the neighborhood evolution of predicted point P is considered to fit the basic motion trend. Then, the next location vector on the trajectory is obtained. Finally, the prediction point value is extracted on the basis of last vector component.

The evolution law of the phase space trajectories in short time is characterized as

$$\mathbf{x}(i+1) = \mathbf{A}\mathbf{x}(i) + \mathbf{b} \tag{3}$$

where $\mathbf{A}$ is matrix with elements a_{ij}, and $\mathbf{b}$ is the constant vector with elements b_j, $j=1,2,\ldots N_p$, ,and N_p is the number points. The Eq. (3) is used to fit the evolution behavior of all the points in the neighborhood, which is applied to determine the matrix A and vector $\mathbf{b}$. Because the process is described by the linear approximation, the serious errors may occur in the algorithm [6]. A group of basic function has to be applied to approach the nonlinear dynamical behavior.

Assume that the dynamic of f can be described by the radial basis function, and thus

$$f(\mathbf{x}(t)) = \sum_{i=0}^{s} \zeta_i \varphi_i(\mathbf{x}(t)) = \zeta^{\mathbf{T}} \varphi \tag{4}$$

where $\zeta = [\zeta_0, \zeta_1, \zeta_2, \cdots, \zeta_s]^T$, $\varphi = [1, \varphi_1, \varphi_2, \varphi_3 \cdots\cdots \varphi_s]$. The basis is chosen as Guassian function

$$\varphi_i = \exp\left(-\frac{\|\mathbf{x} - \mathbf{c}_i\|^2}{2\sigma_i^2}\right) \qquad (5)$$
$$i=1, 2\ldots s$$

As far as the state $\mathbf{x}(t)$ in the space is concerned, the nature of the phase space flow and attractor are required to predict the next point, and the $\mathbf{x}(t+1)$ are determined by the neighborhood around $\mathbf{x}(t)$. If the nearest points are $\mathbf{x}_{nb}^j(t)$, $j=1,2,\ldots,N_p$, the next time is $\mathbf{x}_{nb}^j(t+\tau_p)$. Here, the performance function is defined as

$$J = \sum_{j=1}^{N_p}\left(x_{nb}^j(t+\tau_p) - \sum_{i=0}^{s}\zeta_i\varphi_i(\mathbf{x}_{nb}^j(t))\right)^2 \qquad (6)$$

when Eq.(6) is minimum, the system dynamics is described effectively by this equation. In order to improve the prediction efficiency, the effect of the nearest distance is considered in the function.

$$J = \sum_{j=1}^{N_p}\left(\frac{(\delta_{nb}^j)^{-1}}{\sum_{j=1}^{K}(\delta_{nb}^j)^{-1}}\left\{ x_{nb}^j(t+\tau_p) - \sum_{i=1}^{s}\zeta_i\varphi_i(\mathbf{x}_{nb}^j(t))\right\}\right)^2 \qquad (7)$$

where the δ_{nb}^j is the distance between the nearest point $\mathbf{x}(t)$ and referenced one $\mathbf{x}_{nb}^j(t)$. According to the analysis above, the main process of the phase space reconstruction parameters evaluation is listed. Firstly, the phase space reconstruction is carried out from the single variation time series. The embedding dimension and time delay are obtained, and the original dynamic characteristic is recovered. Then, the neighborhood of referenced point $\mathbf{x}$ (p) is searched with kd tree method. Thirdly, the radial basis function is chosen, and the prediction model coefficients are calculated according to the minimal performance function value.

3   Simulation Results

The radial basis function is applied to chaos prediction on the basis of phase space reconstruction. This method is different from the local linear prediction method, and the center points should be selected according to the feature of basis function. The k mean value clustering method is chosen, because the total number of the neighborhood is low in the algorithm.

(1) When the embedding dimension is 5, and delay time is 11, the phase space reconstruction is obtained. For a predicted point, the neighborhood size are 14, and clustering center number is 8. The prediction results are shown in Fig.1, where original signal curves are represented with "—", the reference curves is "—*—", and predicted one is "—°—". Seen from this figure, the time series are predicted in the range of 15 steps. And then, the prediction error is increased greatly after 45 steps, which illustrates the short-term predictability of chaos.

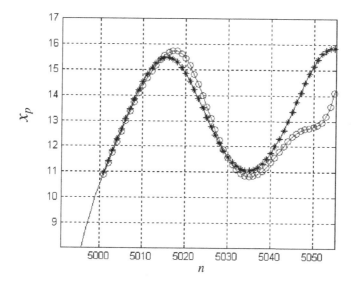

Fig. 1. Local nonlinear prediction curve and reference one of chaotic signal

(2) The effect of reconstruction parameters on prediction results. When the embedding dimension is 5, and the delay time parameter is 6 or 3, the predicted curves are shown in Fig.2. As it is shown, the prediction error is obvious. Furthermore, the prediction is serious in the first stage, and the main reason is the unsuitable phase space reconstruction.

(3) Effect of radial basis function center points on the prediction results. When the embedding dimension is 5 and delay time is 11, the prediction curves stray from the reference one at the first stage under the condition of neighborhood size 14 and center points number 2, as shown in Fig.3 (a). The main reason is that the nonlinear characteristics of the system cannot be described with few basis functions, and the evolution behavior of the phase space trajectories is reflect scarcely. When the number of the center is increased to 8, the prediction results are effective, as shown in Fig.3 (b). Thus, many center number points of the basis function are required in this algorithm.

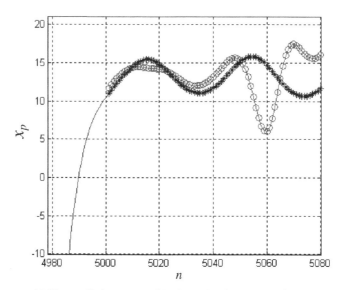

(a) The prediction curve with dimension 5 and delay time 6

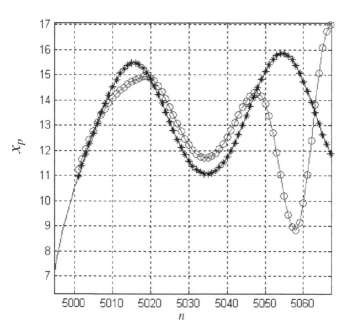

(b) The prediction curve with dimension 5 and delay time 3

Fig. 2. Prediction curves affected by reconstruction parameters

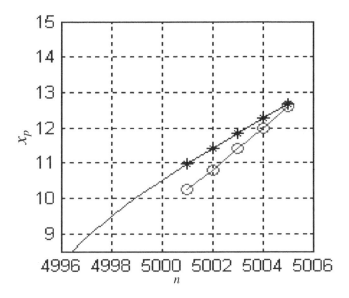

(a) Prediction results when center number is 2

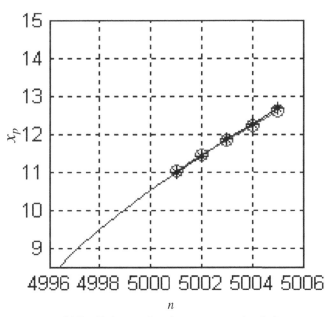

(b) Prediction results when center number is 8

Fig. 3. Prediction curves affected by number of radial base function center points

4   Conclusions

The radial basis function model prediction is applied to evaluation the phase space reconstruction in the paper, and the nonlinear evolution process of the neighoubour on the attractor is characterized by this algorithm. Compared with the local linearization method, this prediction is more effective. Results show that when the reconstruction parameters are suitable, the short-term prediction is completed correctly. The algorithm is also affected by the basis function center number and neighbourhood size. When the number of the center point is few, the nonlinear process cannot be discovered objectively with the basis function. At the same time, the effect of external environment variation should be further studied.

Acknowledgement. This project is supported by the National Science Foundation (Grant No.51179197), and State Key Laboratory of Ocean Engineering (Shanghai Jiao Tong University)(Grant No.1009).

References

[1] Jayawardena, A.W., Li, W.K., Xu, P.: Neighbourhood Selection for Loca Modeling and Prediction of Hydrological Time Series. Journal of Hydrology 258, 40–57 (2002)
[2] Navone, H.D., Ceccatto, H.A.: Forecasting chaos from Small data sets: a comparison of different nonlinear algorithms. Phys. A:MathGen. 28(12), 3381–3388 (1995)
[3] Che, Z., Feng, T.-J., Zhang, H.-Y.: Chaotic time series analysis and phase space reconstruction based on wavelet neural network. Journal of Computer Research &Development 38(5), 591–596 (2001)
[4] Linsay, P.S.: An efficient method of forecasting chaotic Time series using linear interpolation. Phys. Lett. A 153(6,7), 353–356 (1991)
[5] Meng, Q.-F.: Nonlinear dynamical system time series analysis method and its application, ShangDong University (2008)
[6] Farmer, J.D., Sidorowich, J.J.: Predicting chaotic time series. Phys. Rev. Lett. 59(8), 845–848 (1987)

An Improved Algorithm for Estimating
the Largest Lyapunov Exponent

Aibo Yang, Ji Wang, Shuyong Liu, Xiulei Wei, and Qingchao Yang

College of Naval Architecture and Power, Naval University of Engineering,
Wuhan, 430033, China

Abstract. The largest Lyapunov exponent is an essential criterion to judge whether the time series are chaos or not. But traditional methods have some disadvantages such as calculated amount is large and calculated time is long, which lead to these methods have limitations in engineering application. An improved algorithm based on space grid method for estimating the largest Lyapunov exponent is presented in this paper. The whole reconstructed phase space is divided into many small spaces in the algorithm. Only the points locating in the subspace are the reference point exist are searched when needed, and thus the fast searching speed is gained. Simulation results show that neighborhoods can be searched quickly by the suggested algorithm. At the same time, the algorithm is robust and easy to be programmed.

Keywords: chaos, Lyapunov exponent, space grid method.

1   Introduction

Lyapunov exponents quantify the average rate of convergence or divergence of nearby trajectories, in a global sense. In order to judge a time-series chaos or not, the largest Lyapunov exponent (LLE) needs to be computed, and a positive exponent implies chaos. Wolf et al [1] put forward the trajectory tracked method firstly in1985, the Lyapunov exponents were estimated on the basis of evolvement of trajectory, plane and volume in the phase directly in the long term. Rosenstein et al [2] improved the Wolf method based on the idea of the trajectory tracked method and put forward a practical method from small data sets to compute the LLE, which can make full use of data sets and is used widespread.

However, methods of searching nearest point of a reference point are complex calculate and low efficiency when the characteristic exponents of a chaotic vibration are calculated, which limits the whole calculating speed. Actually, the points that are far away from the reference point needn't to be searched when the nearest point is being searched; hence, when the whole reconstructed phase space is divided into many small spaces the searching speed and calculating speed can be improved clearly.

The algorithm for phase space division is based on Friedman et al [3] article, where the whole phase space is divided into spaces with different sizes, and the whole phase space is divided into spaces with the same size in N. N. Oiwa et al [4] article. An algorithm based on space grid method [5] is suggested to divide the whole space into spaces with the same size to improve the calculating speed in this paper.

M. Zhao and J. Sha (Eds.): ICCIP 2012, Part I, CCIS 288, pp. 37–44, 2012.
© Springer-Verlag Berlin Heidelberg 2012

2   Selects the Reconstructed Parameters

The C-C method [6] is a better method relatively which can estimates embedding dimension and delay time at the same time, but the embedding dimension is larger which will gain the computation greatly. The MTBP as time window [7] is suggested to calculate the reconstructed parameters m and τ at the same time which can improve the undulate situation with the embedding dimension.

Assume the time series is $\{x_1, x_2, \cdots\cdots, x_N\}$, the reconstructed phase space is calculated with the Takens embedding theory:

$$X(i) = \left(x_i, x_{i+\tau}, \cdots\cdots, x_{i+(m-1)\tau}\right), (i = 1, 2, ..., M) \tag{1}$$

where τ is time delay, m is embedding dimension, and $M = N - (m-1)\tau$. The expression $\tau_\omega = (m-1)\tau$ is used to calculate m and τ, one of them can be known after another being known.

The minimum of the attractor's out-of-order degree is suggested as the optimization target [8] to judge the quality of the phase space being reconstructed.

3   Search the Nearest Point Based on Space Grid Method

Phase points are m dimensions and out of order after the phase space being reconstructed. Searching the nearest point indicates to find the nearest point of a reference point in the whole reconstructed phase space. It wastes time greatly if traditional methods are used to calculate the nearest point due to the data is usually large. An algorithm based on algorithm for finding k-nearest neighbors which based on space grid method [5] is suggested to find the nearest point of a reference point, which considers the data range, the number of points and the number of the k-nearest neighbors.

Store every coordinate value of every phase point into a one-dimensional array, the maximum and the minimum of every coordinate value of all the phase points can be gotten; then the equation

$$L = \beta \sqrt[m]{\frac{k}{M}(x_{1\max} - x_{1\min})(x_{2\max} - x_{2\min})...(x_{m\max} - x_{m\min})} \tag{2}$$

is used to calculate side length L of all hyper cubes, here β is an adjustment parameter which is used to adjust the length of hyper cubes, k is the number of neighbors being searched, and $M = N - (m-1)\tau$ is the number of whole phase points.

After the side length L being determined, the resolutions at every coordinate where the minimum hypercube locates are:

$$\begin{cases} L_1 = \lceil (x_{1\max} - x_{1\min})/L \rceil, \\ L_2 = \lceil (x_{2\max} - x_{2\min})/L \rceil, \\ \dots \\ L_m = \lceil (x_{m\max} - x_{m\min})/L \rceil \end{cases} \quad (3)$$

Hence, the structure of hypercube is $[x_1][x_2]...[x_m]$, here $x_1 = 1,...,L_1$; $x_2 = 1,...,L_2$;...; $x_m = 1,...,L_m$. And all phase points are classified into their hypercube subspaces at last.

Find the subspace which the reference point belongs to when k-nearest neighbors is searched firstly; then calculate the shortest distance d_{short} between the reference point and the wall of its subspace loop; thirdly, search the k-nearest neighbors in the subspace loop, record the distance between the reference point and the points searched in ascending order and its ordinal number, mark the searched subspace at the same time; if the k-nearest neighbors are found in the present subspace loop and the distance between the reference point and the kth point is shorter than d_{short}, ends the searching program, record their ordinal number and reset the marked subspace which will be convenient for next searching of next reference point. Otherwise, the subspace loop extends a circle outward and does the loop mentioned above again.

Index of every reference point can be transformed to the index of grid (subspace) and the coordinate value of every phase point can be transformed to the coordinate value of grid when the neighbors are searched based on space grid method. So the relationship between points can reference the coordinate relationship of the grid which they locate in, only need to find the grid when the neighbors are searched and positioned through the coordinate instead of searching the whole reconstructed phase space, which increases calculating speed greatly. The calculating speed can be improved $\dfrac{L_1 L_2 ... L_m}{3^m}$ times in theory.

4   Calculate the LLE

The estimating equation from small data sets [2] is

$$d_j(i) = C_j e^{\lambda_1 (i\Delta t)}, C_j = d_j(0) \quad (4)$$

where $d_j(i)$ is the distance between the jth pair of nearest neighbors after i discrete-time steps. Take logarithm of the Eq. (4):

$$\ln d_j(i) = \ln C_j + \lambda_1 (i\Delta t), (j = 1, 2,..., M) \quad (5)$$

where $i = 1, 2,..., \min(M - j, M - \hat{j})$.

The largest Lyapunov exponent is easily and accurately calculated using a least-square fit to the "average" line defined by

$$y(i) = \frac{1}{n\Delta t} \sum_{j=1}^{n} \ln d_j(i) \qquad (6)$$

5   Simulation Results

Simulation study is done to some typical chaotic systems in order to check the efficiency of the algorithm suggested. Take the Lorenz system as the example and the equation is:

$$\begin{cases} \dot{x} = 16.0(y - x) \\ \dot{y} = x(45.92 - z) - y \\ \dot{z} = xy - 4.0z \end{cases} \qquad (7)$$

The method of forth Runge-Kutta is used to solve the equation to obtain the original data sets, the period of sample time is $\Delta t = 0.01\text{s}$. Remove the former transition points when simulated. The broken line in figures is theory value of the system.

(a) Influence of the embedding dimension. The number of data sets N is three thousand, time delay J is eleven and nearest point is one. The influence is shown in Fig.1 when data without being polluted. The influence of the embedding dimension is little which is shown in Fig.1, and the results tend to the theory value and tend to be steady with the embedding dimension increasing. The influence is shown in Fig.2 when the data is polluted by noise (SNR=-10), the computing results are still in efficiency range and robust to the embedding dimension with high noise level, which are shown in Fig.2. The algorithm suggested is robust to the embedding dimension whether the data is polluted by noise or not.

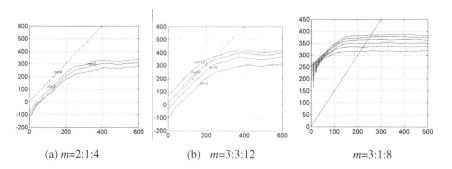

(a) m=2:1:4   (b) m=3:3:12 m=3:1:8

Fig. 1. Influence without noise   **Fig. 2.** Influence with noise (SNR=-10)

(b) Influence of the time delay. The number of data sets N is three thousand, time delay J is eleven and nearest point is one. The influence is shown in Fig.3 when the data without being polluted, and the influence is shown in Fig.4 when the data is polluted by noise (SNR=-10).Fig. (a) shows the influence of the time delay in the range from eight to twelve; Fig. (b) shows the influence of the time delay in the range of J=15:5:30. The results show the algorithm suggested is robust to the time delay either the data polluted or not. And noise only influences the separated initial value.

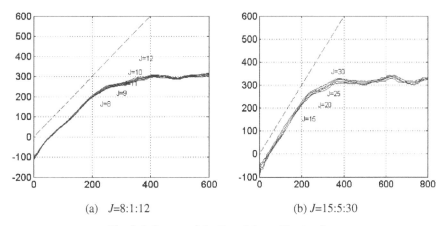

(a) J=8:1:12   (b) J=15:5:30

Fig. 3. Influence of the time delay without noise

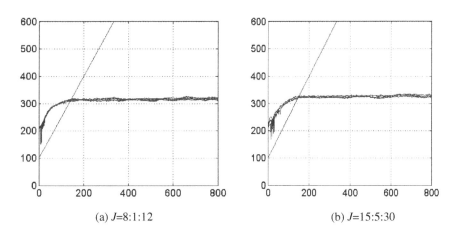

(a) J=8:1:12   (b) J=15:5:30

Fig. 4. Influence of the time delay with noise (SNR=-10)

(c) Influence of the number of neighbors. The number of data sets N is three thousand, time delay J is eleven and nearest point is one. The influence is shown in Fig.5 when data without noise. Fig.5 (a) shows the influence of the number of neighbors in the range from one to five; Fig.5 (b) shows the influence of the number of neighbors in the range of k=10:10:50. The results are closest to the theory value when the number is one and results increase with the number increasing, but the results are almost the same when the number of neighbors in the range of $k=10\sim50$, which show the algorithm is robust to the number of neighbors. The influence is shown in Fig.6 when the data is polluted by noise ($SNR=-10$), the computing results show that the algorithm is more robust and more accurate when the data is polluted. It's convenient to the application in engineering.

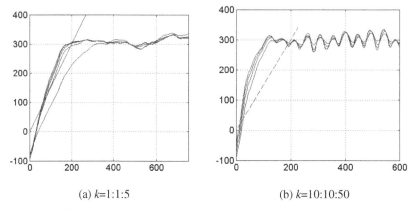

(a) $k=1:1:5$ (b) $k=10:10:50$

Fig. 5. Influence of the number of neighbors without noise

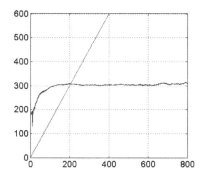

Fig. 6. k=5:5:60 (the noise level is $SNR=-10$)

(d) Influence of the number of data sets. The number of embedding dimension m is three, time delay J is eleven and nearest point is one. Fig.7 shows the different influence as different number of data sets. Fig.7 (a) shows that the maximum error occurs when the number of data which without being polluted is five hundred. The results become more and more accurate with the number of data increasing, but the results tend to be steady when the number beyond three thousand; Fig.7 (b) shows that the results are more steady and the robustness to the number of t=data sets is better when the data is polluted by noise ($SNR=-10$), which indicates that a satisfactory result can be obtained without large data set.

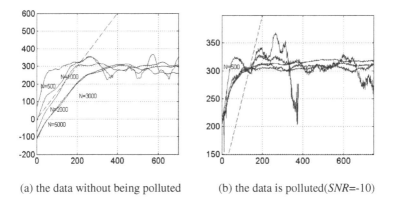

(a) the data without being polluted   (b) the data is polluted(*SNR*=-10)

Fig. 7. Influence of different number of data sets

(e) Influence of different level noise. The number of data sets *N* is three thousand, time delay *J* is eleven. The results are shown in Fig.8 when nearest point is one and shown in Fig.9 when the number of nearest points is ten. The results are shown in Fig.9 (a) of the two figures when the signal to noise ratio is *SNR*=-50:10:0; the results are shown in Fig.9 (b) of the two figures when the signal to noise ratio is *SNR*=10:10:50.What can be indicated from the results are the algorithm can judge data sets is chaos or not with the number of nearest points increasing in a high noise level, the results tend to be the same in different noise level with the number of nearest points increasing and the algorithm is good at robustness to noise.

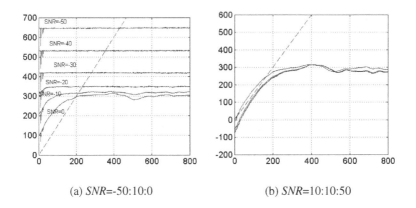

(a) *SNR*=-50:10:0   (b) *SNR*=10:10:50

Fig. 8. Influence of different noise level (*k*=1)

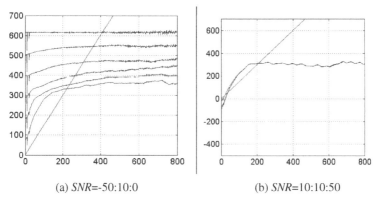

(a) *SNR*=-50:10:0   (b) *SNR*=10:10:50

Fig. 9. Influence of different noise level (k=10)

6   Conclusions

Methods of searching nearest point of a reference point are complex calculate and low efficiency when the characteristic exponents of a chaotic vibration are calculated, which limits the calculating speed, so an improved algorithm based on space grid method is suggested in the text. The algorithm can search the neighbors of a reference point in chaotic attractor quickly and effectively, which can improve the calculating speed of Lyapunov exponents greatly. The simulation results indicate that the improved algorithm can reach the goal, the algorithm is robust whether data sets is polluted by noise or not and easy to be programmed. All of these are good references to quick extract the characteristic exponent of chaos signal.

Acknowledgement. This project is supported by the National Science Foundation (Grant No.51179179), and State Key Laboratory of Ocean Engineering (Shanghai Jiao Tong University) (Grant No.1009).

References

1. Wolf, A., Swift, J.B., Swinney, H.L., Vastano, J.A.: Determining Lyapunov exponents from a time series. Physica 16D, 285–317 (1985)
2. Rosenstein, M.T., Collins, J.J., De Luca, C.J.: A practical method for calculating largest Lyapunov exponents from small data sets. Physica D 65, 117–134 (1993)
3. Friedman, J.H., Bentley, J.L., Finkel, R.A.: ACM Trans. Math. Soft. 3, 209 (1977)
4. Oiwa, N.N., Fiedler-Ferrara, N.: A fast algorithm for estimating Lyapunov exponents from time series. Physics Letters A 246, 117–121 (1998)
5. Xiong, B., He, M., Yu, H.: Algorithm for Finding k-Nearest Neighbors of Scattered Points in Three Dimension. Journal of Computer-aided Design & Computer Graphcis 16(7), 909–917 (2004)
6. Kim, H.S., Eykholt, R., Salas, J.D.: Nonlinear dynamics, delay times, and embedding windows. Physica D 127, 48–60 (1999)
7. Yang, S., Zhang, X., Zhao, C.: A steady algorithm to estimating the largest Lyapunov exponent. Acta Physica Sinica 49(4), 636–640 (2000)
8. Liu, S., Zhu, S., Yu, X.: Study on Phase Space Reconstruction Optimization. Journal of Data Acquisition & Processing 23(1), 65–69 (2008)

Research on Gear Assembly Interference Check Based on Virtual Technology

Xiangyang Jin, Tiefeng Zhang, and Hanlin Yang

School of Light Industry, Harbin University of Commerce, Harbin 150028, China

Abstract. Specific structure of reducer can be designed through the application of thickened gear into reducer. Transmission ratio of the reducer can be calculated by relative velocity method. Then constraint of each element is being matched, assembly path and process is being designed. Coordinate Transformation Method and Matrix Method are adopted for interference check of virtual assembly. It turns out that no interference phenomena occur during engagement process of thickened gear. Sectional views of meshing in different time points testify the correctness of interference check method and serves as the theoretical reference for virtually assembling reducer.

Keywords: Coordinate Transformation, Virtual Assembly, Interference Check.

1   Introduction

Due to linear changes of modification coefficients along the axial, tooth thickness of thickened gear contracts just like the bevel gear along the axial in geometrical view. Thickened gear is a kind of transformative bevel gear drive in nature [1]. Owing to flexible drive method, thickened gear pair possesses unmatched advantages compared with ordinary bevel gear drive.

These advantages of thickened gear stimulate more and more research and application. Ordinary straight tooth planetary gear drive is conducted in the first class of special reducer of certain type. Internal gear drive with less teeth differences is used in the second class. Its drive principle is shown in Fig.1.

In the new reducer with high accuracy, input gear axial delivers electromechanical gyroscopic motion to two equal-spaced planet wheels z_2 through straight gear z_1. And under drive of first class is realized. Then, planetary gear z_2 stimulates eccentric motion of thickened external gear z_3 through double eccentric shaft H; Thickened internal gear z_4 in the shell is fixed, and thickened external gear z_3 experiences revolution and rotation simultaneously. And finally, by means of gear stand ω the output of rotation movement is achieved. In such case, under drive of second class is realized. The structure shaped like a parallelogram composed of two double eccentric shafts and thickened gear guarantees balanced force and steady motion [2]. And relocatable form adopted for sun gear in the first class is used to compensate manufacturing deviation caused by gear drive and parallelogram drive mechanism as well as to eliminate loads maldistribution between the two planet wheels and the sun gear.

M. Zhao and J. Sha (Eds.): ICCIP 2012, Part I, CCIS 288, pp. 45–52, 2012.
© Springer-Verlag Berlin Heidelberg 2012

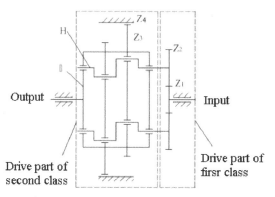

z_1- Gear Shaft z_2- Planetary Gear z_3-Thickened External Gear z_4-Thickened Internal Gear   H- Double Eccentric Shaft ω-Gear Stand

Fig. 1. Drive Principle of Special Reducer

Transmission ratio of the reducer can be worked out by relative velocity method. Suppose that absolute angular velocities of each component in the following figure are ω_1 、 ω_2 、 ω_H 、 ω_3 、 ω_4 、 ω_ω , and formula for transmission ratio can be worked out according to Relative Movement Principle:

$$i_{1\omega} = \frac{\omega_1}{\omega_\omega} = 1 + \frac{z_2}{z_1} \cdot \frac{z_4}{z_4 - z_3}$$ (1)

Second class drive equals to two-tooth difference drive, which means $z_4 - z_3 = 2$, and the following formula can be worked out:

$$i_{1\omega} = 1 + \frac{z_2 \cdot z_4}{2 \cdot z_1}$$ (2)

It can be seen that in such kind of drive method, bigger reduction ratio with high practical utility can be worked out by making use of several components. As for the reducer discussed here, z_1 is 14, z_2 is 48, z_4 is 70, and the correspondent reduction ratio is 121.

2   Virtual Assembly Scheme for Special Reducer

The most important procedure of component assembly is to restrain components appropriately. Assembly methods of components provided by Pro/E are as follows: matching, aligning, insertion, coordinate system, tangency, point on line, point on curved surface, edge on surface and so on. The first three assembly methods are used mainly in assembling the reducer. That is to say matching and aligning are mainly adopted for each component in different surfaces, and insertion is adopted between axial and aperture. As for two surfaces, those which are defined as matched have their normal modules oppositely, and those which are defined as aligned have synclastic normal modules. A certain model can be selected from superposition, offset and orientation after restrained in these two ways. And superposition here means putting the two surfaces into one surface; when offset is selected, a fixed numerical setover exists between the two surfaces.

Research on generating assembly order and its geometric feasibility analysis is mainly discussed in designing assembly path. In this way, geometric interference of assembly units during assembly operation is avoided. Aiming at realizing non-collision and non-interference assembly, the design for assembly motion trail contributes to protecting components and accelerating assembly [3].

Under virtual environment, manual assembly process is simulated in this article. By taking advantage of this virtual method, research on dismounting process of new-pattern adjustable reducer is conducted, the direction and order for component motion is decided when assembling and disassembling [4]. Relevant assembly procedure is shown in Fig.2.

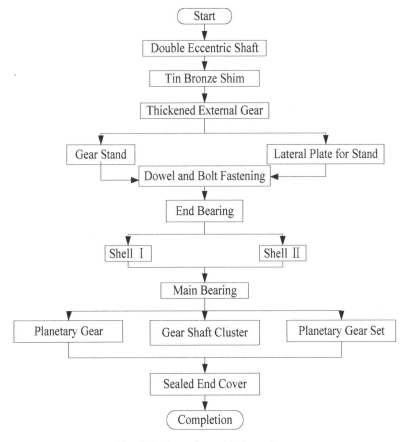

Fig. 2. Reducer Assembly Procedures

When assembling gear shaft, bearing and circlip for shaft are installed along the direction of gear shaft. Then end cover assembled with seal ring is added. And finally, circlip for hole is installed. The correspondent assembly procedures are shown in Fig.3.

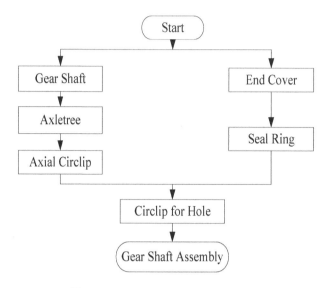

Fig. 3. Gear Shaft Assembly Procedures

3   Interference Check on Virtual Assembly

Interference check is an important procedure for virtual assembly. Dynamic interference check can be conducted according to correctly assembled model which means that interference phenomenon between different components is checked during the reducer movement. Dynamic interference check on thickened gear meshing is conducted in this article. Thickened gear mesh is an important innovative component of the new-pattern reducer. The detailed method of dynamic interference is as follows: sub-function of Pro/E is invoked for obtaining necessary data, and matlab order is adopted for processing data so that task of checking dynamic interference can be accomplished[5].

Possessed with the function of dynamic data recording, motion analysis of Pro/E can obtain coordinate values of a certain point in output objects between different predetermined time intervals and can draw out geometric locus as well. Loca for point A on the surface of external gear are shown in Fig.4. Dynamic recording function of Pro/E data is mainly adopted in this article for obtaining coordinate values of the points in external tooth profile of thickened gear. And then Penetration Testing Method is used for checking whether the panel points that left measured can penetrate internal tooth profile.

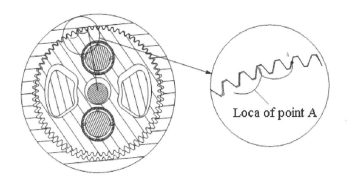

Fig. 4. Locus Recording Diagrammatic Sketch for Pro/E

Main skill of interference check is penetration detection algorithm. In this article, two kinds of algorithms are put forward: Coordinate Transformation Method and Matrix Method. Easier for realizing programming, Coordinate Transformation Method is simpler and faster. But confined by functions, it only applies for penetration judgment from point to line. Although Matrix Method can measure any circumstances precisely, it is difficult to realize programming with very complicated calculation.

Applied mainly under the circumstances of penetration from point to line, Coordinate Transformation Method chiefly transforms panel points coordinates left judged to local polar coordinates with the line segment being the horizontal axis. Whether line segment penetration is realized can be told by panel point values of local polar coordinates. That is to say in this case interference occurs. Internal gear profile should be dispersed into line segment in the first place and penetration inspection should be conducted when adopting Coordinate Transformation Method. If every line segment can pass penetration inspection, it means that at certain moment interference phenomenon doesn't occur at the point that left unchecked.

Due to the frequent use of coordinate transformation, coordinate transformation formula used in this article is put forward in the first place. It is easier to transform point of polar coordinate into that of world coordinate. And formulas for transforming coordinates are as follows:

$$\begin{cases} x = x_0 + R_{new} \cos \theta_{new} \\ y = y_0 + R_{new} \sin \theta_{new} \end{cases} \tag{3}$$

In the formulas, x and y are Cartesian coordinate values for panel points in world coordinate. x_0 and y_0 are Cartesian coordinate values for original points in polar coordinate. θ_{new} is the polar angle in local polar coordinate formed by newly generated panel point.

For the fact that inverse trigonometric function isn't univalent function, it is difficult to transform local polar coordinates into world Cartesian coordinates. Therefore, value of angle for panel point should be judged according to correspondent quadrant. Coordinate transformation formula is shown as follows:

$$\begin{cases} R = \sqrt{x^2 + y^2} \\ \theta = \begin{cases} \theta_0 + a\cos\left(x/R\right) & y > 0 \\ \theta_0 + 2\pi - a\cos(x/R) & y <= 0 \end{cases} \end{cases} \qquad (4)$$

In this formula, θ_0 is the angle of local polar coordinate in world coordinate (it is prescribed that anticlockwise direction is positive).

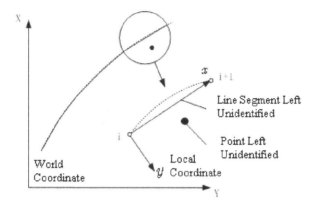

Fig. 5. Coordinate Transformation Method

As shown in Fig.5, after transforming point coordinate into local polar coordinate, if conditions of formula 5 can be satisfied, then it can tell that the point doesn't penetrate line segment. If the second formula can't be satisfied, it can tell that this point is beyond the range of this line segment and thus unnecessary for judgment.

$$\begin{cases} 0 \le \theta \le \pi \\ 0 \le R \le D \end{cases} \qquad (5)$$

In this formula, θ, R is the local coordinates for the point, and D is the length of line segment which suggests inner radius of point $i+1$.

Based on numerical manifold, Matrix Method makes use of determinants to judge whether penetration is taken place. With fine functions, Matrix Method which is suitable for any circumstances can figure out the location where the penetration takes place. As shown in Fig.6, the entry-distance from P_1 to $P_2 P_3$ can be worked out by the following formulas:

$$d = \frac{1}{l}\Delta = \frac{1}{l}\begin{vmatrix} 1 & x_1 + u_1 & y_1 + v_1 \\ 1 & x_2 + u_2 & y_2 + v_2 \\ 1 & x_3 + u_3 & y_3 + v_3 \end{vmatrix} \qquad (6)$$

$$l = \sqrt{\left(x_2 + u_2 - x_3 - u_3\right)^2 + \left(y_2 + v_2 - y_3 - v_3\right)^2} \tag{7}$$

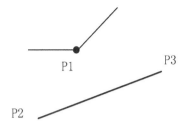

Fig. 6. Matrix Method

In the above-mentioned formulas, x_i, y_i is coordinates of the point, d is the distance from point to line, l is the length of the line segment and u_i, v_i is movement speed respectively of the point.

If penetration doesn't take place within the time step but rather does take place at the end of the time step, the penetration phenomenon and its location can be worked out. Suppose that $t = 1$ when the time step ends, and the following formula can be worked out:

$$\Delta(t) = \frac{1}{l} \begin{vmatrix} 1 & x_1 + tu_1 & y_1 + tv_1 \\ 1 & x_2 + tu_2 & y_2 + tv_2 \\ 1 & x_3 + tu_3 & y_3 + tv_3 \end{vmatrix} \tag{8}$$

And $\Delta(0) > 0 \quad \Delta(1) < 0$ can be known.

Time t_c satisfies the following formula:

$$\Delta(t) = \begin{vmatrix} 1 & x_1 + t_0 u_1 & y_1 + t_0 v_1 \\ 1 & x_2 + t_0 u_2 & y_2 + t_0 v_2 \\ 1 & x_3 + t_0 u_3 & y_3 + t_0 v_3 \end{vmatrix}$$

$$= \begin{vmatrix} 1 & x_1 & y_1 \\ 1 & x_2 & y_2 \\ 1 & x_3 & y_3 \end{vmatrix} + \begin{vmatrix} 1 & t_0 u_1 & y_1 \\ 1 & t_0 u_2 & y_2 \\ 1 & t_0 u_3 & y_3 \end{vmatrix} + \begin{vmatrix} 1 & x_1 & t_0 v_1 \\ 1 & x_2 & t_0 v_2 \\ 1 & x_3 & t_0 v_3 \end{vmatrix} + \begin{vmatrix} 1 & t_0 u_1 & t_0 v_1 \\ 1 & t_0 u_2 & t_0 v_2 \\ 1 & t_0 u_3 & t_0 v_3 \end{vmatrix} = 0 \tag{9}$$

This formula suits to situations where internal tooth profile moves as well.

Coordinate Transformation Method and Matrix Method are both adopted for inspecting gear engagement process. It can be found through dynamic inspection that no interference phenomenon takes place during thickened gear engagement process. Sectional views of engagement process in different time points are selected in this article in order to testify the correctness of the methods. As shown in Fig.7, no interference phenomenon occurs during engagement process can be testified by inspecting sectional views, and thus the correctness of the methods adopted by the article can be testified.

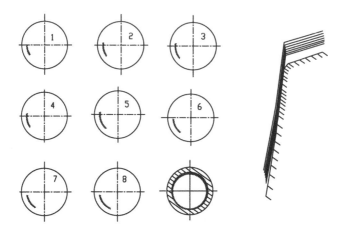

Fig. 7. Sectional View Intercepted and Interference Check

4   Conclusions

Procedures like determining assembly order and path of each component in a reducer, establishing a complete virtual prototype by assembling all the three-dimensional component models, dynamically simulating dismounting process for reducer and inspecting the feasibility of assembly path can be used for instructing actual products assembly.

Successful interference check and motion simulation is conducted on reducer's working process and thus testify the correctness of transmission motion mode for reducer's virtual prototype.

References

1. Bahgat, B.M., Osman, M.O., Sankar, T.S.: On the Spur Gear Dynamic Tooth Load under Consideration of System Elasticity and Tooth Involute Profile. Transactions of ASME, Journal of Mechanisms, Transmissions, and Automation in Design (105), 302–309 (1983)
2. Kahraman, A., Singh, R.: Non-linear Dynamics of A Spur Gear Pair. Journal of Sound and Vibration (142), 49–75 (1990)
3. Perret-Liaudet, J.: An Original Method for Computing the Response of A Parametrically Excited Forced System. Journal of Sound and Vibration (196), 165–177 (1996)
4. Lin, H.-H., Huston, R.L., Coy, J.J.: On Dynamic Loads in Parallel Shaft Transmissions: Part–Modeling and Analysis. Transactions of ASME, Journal of Mechanisms, Transmissions, and Automation in Design 110(6), 221–225 (1988)
5. Lin, H.-H., Huston, R.L., Coy, J.J.: On Dynamic Loads in Parallel Shaft Transmissions: Part–Parameter Study. Transactions of ASME, Journal of Mechanisms, Transmissions, and Automation in Design 110(6), 221–225 (1988)

Research on Dynamic Assembly and Kinematics Simulation of Speed Reducer Based on Three-Dimensional Model

Xiangyang Jin, Tiefeng Zhang, and Hanlin Yang

School of Light Industry, Harbin University of Commerce, Harbin 150028, China

Abstract. In view of the existing situation that, the high cost of speed reducer designing, the long term for research cycle, and the reducer working process is impossible to understand, the following analysis is made by the use of virtual technology in the process of disassembling the speed reducer on a computer, planning the assembling route, assembling the virtual machine parts into virtual prototype, doing dynamic simulation of the reducer working process and completing the design program verification and demonstration. The researches in this thesis are mainly focused on these things: analyzing the kinematics performance of the gear in detail, working out the gear motion route in any period of time, and verifying the speed reduction ratio through calculating the motion period, which can provide useful reference for the optimization design of the reducer.

Keywords: Dynamic simulation, virtual prototype, path planning.

1   Introduction

A reducer contains many spare parts, so the assembly and disassembly of the reducer are complicated. The dynamic simulation of the virtual assembly is of great importance, which can verify the correctness of the assembly path planning and provide a foundation for the following real work on assembling, disassembling and adjusting gear clearance. Meanwhile, the dynamic simulation can illustrate the assembling and clearance adjusting process directly and vividly, being easy to be understood, so the dynamic simulation plays an important role in further reducer promotion.

2   Dynamic Simulation in the Process of Assembly, Disassembly and Clearance Adjustment

During the process of assembly simulation, people should use mouse directly to remove the components and parts in terms of the assembly path plan, and then the decomposition chart is generated. All the constraints are removed in the process to avoid the hampering of mouse drag for parts removing. Pro/E can be used to make

M. Zhao and J. Sha (Eds.): ICCIP 2012, Part I, CCIS 288, pp. 53–60, 2012.

point drag and part body drag, and the locations of parts can be changed by encapsulation movement methods, and the parts can even translate or revolve along the direction of a certain axis through the high-level drag in Pro/E. During the assembly and disassembly process of a reducer, the parts generally move along with the direction of the middle axis of the reducer, so the high-level removal is used. Then, imitating the process of animation, people can take snapshot in each key location and produce key frame, arranging the key frames in order and defining the time. The computer can figure out the general pictures through the method of linear or smooth interpolation and finally continuously play these frames like a film, so a complete animation is created [1]. The above process is illustrated in Fig. 1 as follows.

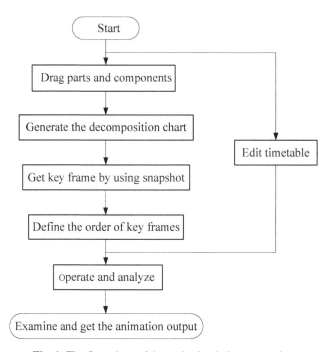

Fig. 1. The flow chart of dynamic simulation generation

The virtual reducer prototype as shown in the paper is a model, completely assembled. In fact, it comes from the snapshot that generated according to the parts disassembling sequence. One or more key frames are required to be set when each part is disassembled [2]. Firstly, the sealed end cap and its O-ring should be disassembled, then, on the side of the sealed end cap, the planetary gear and the planetary gear module should be disassembled, and on the other side, the gear shaft module should be disassembled, as shown in Fig. 2.

When disassembling the gear shaft module, people should dismantle the circlip for hole in the first, and draw out the gear shaft from the end cap hole, then remove the sealing ring from the end cap slot, and finally dismantle the circlip for shaft and the back-up bearing of the gear shaft, as shown in Fig. 3.

Fig. 2. The disassembly of planetary gear, planetary gear module and gear shaft module

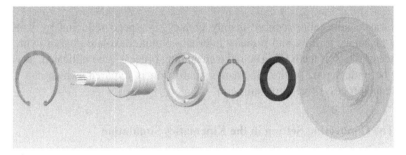

Fig. 3. The disassembly of gear shaft module

After that, people should firstly dismantle the circlip for hole from casing I, and dismantle the back-up bearings of casing I and casing II, then remove four small bearings which supporting the double eccentric shaft, gear brackets and bracket sideboard, and finally dismantle the bevoloid gear and tin bronze gasket[3]. The assembly process is similar to the disassembly process, only reversing the key frames sequence. Therefore, the generated dynamic simulation can illustrate the process of assembly and disassembly obviously.

During the process of clearance adjusting, people should firstly dismantle the screw which connecting the two casings, and remove the adjusting gasket between the flanges from both sides, then, adjust the thickness of the special gasket and put it into the original place again, and finally assemble the connecting screw[4]. Its key frames are shown in Fig. 4 as follows.

According to the sequence adjustment, all the key frames are generated into the key frame sequence. Then, people should adjust the timetable for the continuous playing, thus, the dynamic assembly and disassembly process of the new type of the clearance adjustable reducer.

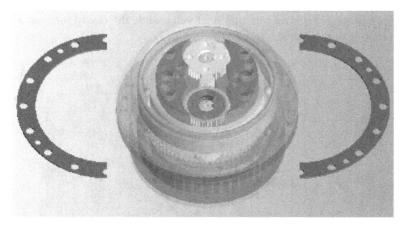

Fig. 4. The key frames of removing the adjusting gasket

3   The Kinematics Simulation during the Reducer Running

The clearance adjustable reducer mainly creates the speed reducing by using the primary planetary gearing and primary internal involute bevoloid gearing with small difference of the gear teeth [5]. The reducer running process is complicated, as well as hard to be understood, so the kinematics simulation is required, which can clearly illustrate the process of gear transmission.

3.1   The Connecting Setting in the Kinematics Simulation

In Pro/E, people cannot use the complete constraint model to make the kinematics analysis and simulation of the reducer, so the placement constraint is changed into connection constraint in this paper. The placement constraint totally defines the location relationship among the parts, and the relative movement cannot be generated, while the "connecting" method can be used to define the relationship of the parts with relative motion, as well as the moving pair in the assembly. Each kind of connection is related to a group of independent geometric constraints, and those constraints and traditional assembly constraints in Pro/E are identical in meaning, which make a group of constraints of each connection be related to the designated degree of freedom.

The pin connection restricts the axis alignment and translation along the direction of the axis, so it contains one rotation degree of freedom and 0 shifting degree of freedom, which means that the components with pin connected can rotate around its attached component, but cannot move from the component. Most of the moving pairs of the reducer are rotation pair, so the relation of the components with apparent relative rotation are all defined as pin connection, such as shaft and bearing, bearing and the bearing hole of the bevoloid gear, bearing and the bearing hole of the gear bracket and so on[6]. In order to verify the efficiency and correctness of the connection in time, people should make an examination through the method of dragging the component body when setting up a connection, which can revise each possible error in time.

3.2   The Realization of the Kinematics Simulation

On the basis of the model, several steps are required in the kinematics analysis as follows: firstly, connection should be set in the model; secondly, the transmission mechanism of the gear pair should be defined; thirdly, the servo motor should be added to the model as a power; finally, people should make an operating analysis and output the results. The flow is as shown in Fig. 5.

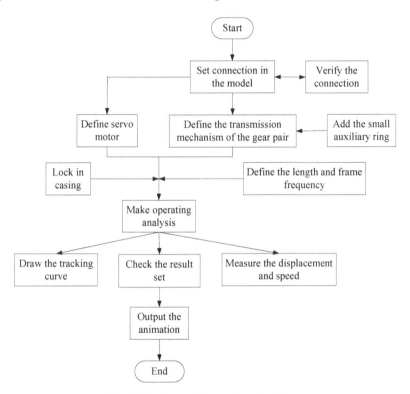

Fig. 5. The flow of kinematics simulation

There are four gear pairs in the reducer. In the planetary gear pair, there are connections in the center of the gear rotation, so the connection shaft can be defined here. In the bevoloid gear pair, the outer bevoloid gear is driven by two bearings and there is no connection in the gear-rotating center, so the rotation axis of the gear cannot be found and the gear pair cannot be directly defined. A scheme is proposed in this paper as shown in Fig. 6. In the scheme, an auxiliary part such as a small ring, is assembled in the rotating center of the gear, aligning its axis with the gear axis, which can be defined as pin connection, and the relation of the small ring and the back-up bearing of bevoloid gear can be defined as rigid body connection. It is obvious that the bevoloid gear driven by bearings rotate around the rotating shaft of the pin connection, which successfully resolves the problem of being unable to define the connecting shaft. The highlighted part is the small auxiliary ring in Fig. 6.

Fig. 6. The solution to the definition of the rotating shaft of bevoloid gear

So far, people can make the operating analysis. Firstly, people should create an object for analysis and define the length and frame frequency. Then, because the reducer casing body is connected with the base, people should fix it by the method of body locking. At last, people can make the operating analysis, which means the movement can be coped with in several steps with the help of the analysis. In order to get the kinematics simulation animation easily, people make a subroutine with the above content by using the secondary development module of Pro/E in the paper. When people input the machinery revolution, simulation operating time and simulation step into the subroutine, the kinematics simulation can be generated automatically. The picture of kinematics simulation is shown in Fig. 7.

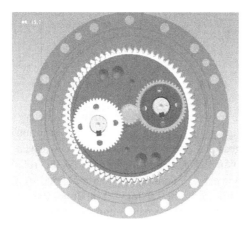

Fig. 7. The kinematics simulation of reducer

3.3   Track and Measurement

The most important mechanism in new type precise reducer is the bevoloid gear pair transmission. In order to inspect the movement of bevoloid gear and verify the correctness of the movement, people build a track curve in this paper by making use of the function of "track curve" and "measurement" in Pro/E. People can firstly choose any point in the profile of the outer bevoloid gear. On the basis of the above operating analysis, people can take the casing part as the paper part, using the point as a pen, and drawing the movement track which is relative to the inner bevoloid gear in casing, and finally the running process of the bevoloid gear pair can be found clearly, as shown in Fig. 8.

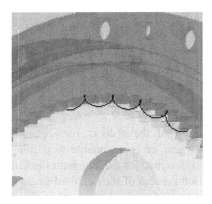

Fig. 8. The track curve of any point in outer bevoloid gear being relative to the inner gear

The paper illustrates the kinematics performance of bevoloid gear in detail with the help of the "measurement" function in Pro/E.

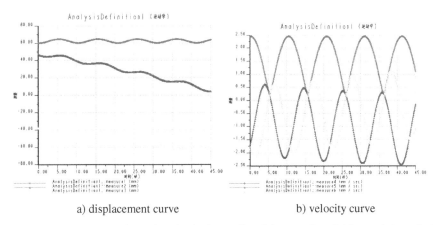

a) displacement curve   b) velocity curve

Fig. 9. The motion curve of certain point in the profile of the outer bevoloid gear, being relative to the reducer axis

A coordinate system, being relative to the casing and stationary in position, should be placed in the cross point of bevoloid gear side and the central axis of reducer.

People can establish the measurement and measure the motion curve of certain point in the outer profile of the bevoloid gear. The motion curve is based on the coordinate system, as shown in Fig. 9. There are three curves in the picture, the top line describing the module of displacement of speed, and the lower two lines showing the displacement and velocity of X and Y in vertical direction.

Seen from the above figure, people can find that the outer bevoloid gear is doing the rotation while it is revolving around the reducer axis. People are able to get the related data in each point for research, as well as the primary motion condition. The speed reduction rate can also be verified through calculating the motion period.

4   Conclusion

The researches in this paper focus on the method of generating three-dimensional dynamic simulation. The dynamic simulation also contains the assembly, disassembly and clearance adjusting process of the new type clearance adjustable reducer. The research provides not only the verification of the assembly path planning, but also the guidance for the actual assembly.

The kinematics simulation of the reducer running process is generated. The problem on outer bevoloid gear of being unable to define the connection shaft is solved and the subroutine is designed for the kinematics calculation.

An analysis on the motion process of the bevoloid gear pair is made in the paper. The analysis illustrates the motion track of the point in the profile of outer bevoloid gear, and the point moves around the inner bevoloid gear, so the motion track of the point is around the inner bevoloid gear. Based on the research, people can get the displacement and velocity curves which are relative to the central axis of the reducer, and the motion pattern of the outer bevoloid gear is verified.

According to the research, people can educe the dynamic assembly pictures and kinematics simulation in the common animation format, and make an arrangement, so that the animation can be viewed and analyzed without Pro/hE at anytime.

References

1. Yang, D.C.H., Sun, Z.S.: A Rotary Model for Spur Gears Dynamics. Transactions of ASME, Journal of Mechanisms, Transmissions, and Automation in Design (107), 529–535 (1985)
2. Han, D.C., Choi, S.H., Lee, Y.H.: Analysis of Vibration Characteristics for a Rotor-Bearing System Using Distributed Spring and Damper Model. International Journal of Rotating Machinery 1(3), 277–284 (1995)
3. Ozguzen, H.N., Houser, D.R.: Mathematical Models Used in Gear Dynamics – A Review. Journal of Sound and Vibration (121), 383–411 (1988)
4. Ozguzen, H.N., Houser, D.R.: Dynamic Analysis of High Speed Gears by Using Loaded Static Transmission Error. Journal of Sound and Vibration (125), 71–83 (1998)
5. Umezawa, K., Sato, T., Ishikawa, J.: Simulation on Rotational Vibration of Spur Gears. Bulletin of JSME (27), 102–109 (1984)
6. Mark, W.D.: Analysis of the Vibratory Excitation of Gear Systems: Basic Theory. Journal of Acoustic Society of America (63), 1409–1430 (1978)

Simulated Mutation in Differential Evolution

Youyun Ao

School of Computer and Information, Anqing Normal University,
246011 Anqing, China
youyun.ao@gmail.com

Abstract. Population-based evolutionary algorithms (EAs) have been widely applied to solve various real-world optimization problems. In essence, they are a type of optimization techniques and traverse the population landscape in whatever direction that can lead to a peak or an optimal solution through climbing hills. The differences between different EAs are operators and combinations. Each EA has its own particular operators and its own particular combination of these operators. Typically, in EAs, there are three operators (i.e., crossover and/or mutation, and selection). Each EA utilizes its crossover operator and/or mutation operator to exploit and/or explore the search space of the problem, and utilizes its selection operator to guide the search towards the optimal region. Differential evolution (DE) and particle swarm optimization (PSO) are two relatively recent branches of EAs, have been successful in solving many real-world optimization problems, and have increasingly attracted researchers' attention. Through comparing and contrasting similarities and dissimilarities between DE and PSO, in this study, we make an attempt to develop some variants of mutation inspired by PSO in DE. Numerical experiments are conducted on a test set of global optimization problems.

Keywords: differential evolution (DE), particle swarm optimization (PSO), evolutionary algorithm (EA), global optimization, mutation.

1   Introduction

Conventional evolutionary algorithms (EAs) can be divided into four kinds including genetic algorithm (GA) [1], evolution strategy (ES) [2], genetic programming (GP) [3], and evolutionary programming (EP) [4]. They have been successfully applied to solve many practical problems and have increasingly received attention from various fields [5]. Lately, some new kinds of EAs have been proposed. The representatives of these new EAs involve differential evolution (DE) [6], particle swarm optimization (PSO) [7], ant colony optimization (ACO) [8], etc. In EAs, there are some operators (typically including crossover, mutation, and selection) which drive the population to evolve and generate new individuals so that they can find the optimal solution to the problem. However, in order to reduce the search blindness, some researchers have developed some new operators with heuristic [9], [10], [11] and incorporate some local search techniques into EAs to improve the search performance of an EA. These

M. Zhao and J. Sha (Eds.): ICCIP 2012, Part I, CCIS 288, pp. 61–76, 2012.

local search techniques involve chaos optimization (CO) [12], tabu search (TS) [13], simulated annealing (SA) [14], etc.

It is well known that operators and update strategies of the population play the key roles in the performance of EAs. The relative roles of crossover and mutation have been debated for a long time [15]. John Holland [1] claimed that crossover is a more efficient search operator and more important than mutation in GAs, while Fogel [16] claimed that mutation results in more efficient searches. The debate about the relative roles of crossover and mutation still continues. However, with respect to the relative roles of crossover and mutation, some differences have already been found. The role of crossover is to exploit the search space, while the role of mutation is to explore the search space. Crossover proves less and less effective as the similarities between individuals increase, while mutation becomes more and more important as the variance of the population reduces. Crossover tends to preserve, while mutation tends to destroy. Generally, each operator has two dual roles: constructive and disruptive. The behavior of crossover depends on the population size and influences disruptive effects. Usually, a small population is actually easier to suffer from the premature convergence than a large population. This is due to the fact that a small population has a low information capacity, resulting in inaccurate sampling. Mutation is a more flexible search operator and can be used to mimic operators in other EAs. Some researchers have noted that the optimal mutation rate is much dependent on the state of the population, especially the variance of the population. The relative importance of the crossover and mutation rates usually interrelates [15]. Hence, in order to utilize the roles of crossover and mutation more efficiently, some techniques for adapting crossover and mutation rates have been developed [17], [18].

In EAs, some researchers claimed that operators (typically including crossover, mutation, and selection) are instances of some common "ancestor" operators and are fundamentally the same. Similarly, EAs are instances of some common "ancestor" optimization mechanisms and are fundamentally the same. The same problems are tackled using several different techniques, when one technique produces a solution similar to that produced by another technique. Researchers begin to seek similarities and patterns between different techniques. When one technique provides a better solution, researchers begin to scrutinize differences between different techniques. On the one hand, each operator has its own characteristics, and each EA also has its own characteristics. On the other hand, an operator or a technique can be viewed as sibling or cousins of another operator or another technique with similar mechanisms only implemented different. Hence, the real significance of differences between different operators (or techniques) comes from the analysis of the performance [15], [19]. Differential evolution (DE) and particle swarm optimization (PSO) have been demonstrated to be effective EAs [20], [21], [22], [23]. In this study, through comparing and contrasting similarities and dissimilarities between DE and PSO, in DE, we develop three variants of mutation inspired by PSO, and investigate the relative performances of the developed variants of mutation.

In the remainder of this paper is organized as follows: Section 2 and Section 3 describes the basic ideas of DE and PSO respectively; Section 4 seeks similarities and dissimilarities between DE and PSO, and gives three variants of mutation inspired by mutation of PSO in DE; Section 5 gives some experimental results. Finally, some conclusions and future work are pointed out in Section 6.

2   Differential Evolution (DE)

Conventional DE [6], [24] uses three major operators (typically including mutation, crossover, and selection) to evolve the population so that it can find the optimal solution of the problem. First DE randomly generates the initial population within boundaries of decision variables. Then DE repeatedly uses three operators to generate the next population till the termination criterion is achieved. Conventional DE can generate the offspring according to the following steps. Firstly, DE randomly generates the initial population within the bounds of decision variables. Let us assume that $P(t) = (x_{ij}(t))_{NP \times n}$ denotes the tth generation population, where NP is the population size, n is the number of decision variables, and $x_{ij}(t)$ is the jth variable of the ith individual. Then the initial population is generated by

$$\forall i \leq NP, \forall j \leq n : x_{ij}(0) = L_j + rand_{ij} \times (U_j - L_j) \tag{1}$$

where $rand_{ij}$ is the uniformly distributed number between 0 and 1, L_j and U_j are the lower and upper of the jth decision variable, respectively.

Secondly, DE randomly chooses three individuals from the current population to perform its mutation and generate the new vector $v_i(t)$ by

$$v_i(t) = x_{r_1}(t) + F \times (x_{r_2}(t) - x_{r_3}(t)) \tag{2}$$

where $r_1, r_2, r_3 \in \{1,2,...,NP\}$ are three randomly selected indices, and r_1, r_2, r_3, i are mutually different. The scaling factor $F \in [0, 2]$ is used to control the amplification of the differential vector $(x_{r_2}(t) - x_{r_3}(t))$, and is often set to 0.5. Equation (2) above is called "DE/rand/1/bin". In practical applications, DE has multiple alternative variants of mutation, which can be described in the following.

"DE/best/1/bin": $v_i(t) = x_b(t) + F \times (x_{r_1}(t) - x_{r_2}(t)) \tag{3}$

"DE/current to best/2/bin": $v_i(t) = x_i(t) + F \times (x_b(t) - x_i(t)) + F \times (x_{r_1}(t) - x_{r_2}(t)) \tag{4}$

"DE/best/2/bin": $v_i(t) = x_b(t) + F \times (x_{r_1}(t) - x_{r_2}(t)) + F \times (x_{r_3}(t) - x_{r_4}(t)) \tag{5}$

"DE/rand/2/bin": $v_i(t) = x_{r_1}(t) + F \times (x_{r_2}(t) - x_{r_3}(t)) + F \times (x_{r_4}(t) - x_{r_5}(t)) \tag{6}$

where $x_b(t)$ is the best individual from the tth generation population, and the symbol *bin* denotes binomial recombination. After performing mutation, if one or more of variables of $v_i(t)$ is beyond its corresponding boundaries, the following repair rule is applied:

$$v_{ij}(t) = \begin{cases} L_j, \text{if } v_{ij}(t) < L_j \\ U_j, \text{if } v_{ij}(t) > U_j \end{cases} \tag{7}$$

Thirdly, DE performs its crossover. The aim of crossover is to improve the diversity of the population. The new vector $u_i(t)$ is generated by recombining between $x_i(t)$ and $v_i(t)$ according to the following formula:

$$u_{ij}(t) = \begin{cases} v_{ij}(t), \text{if } rand[0,1] \leq CR \text{ or } j = rand[1,n] \\ x_{ij}(t), \text{otherwise} \end{cases} \tag{8}$$

where $CR \in [0,1]$ is the crossover probability, $rand[0,1]$ denotes the uniformly distributed random number from the range $[0,1]$, and $rand[1,n]$ is the randomly selected index from the set $\{1,2,...,n\}$ to ensure that at least one of variables is changed and $u_i(t)$ doesn't directly duplicate $x_i(t)$.

Finally, DE continues to perform its selection. If $u_i(t)$ is superior to $x_i(t)$, then $u_i(t)$ will survive to be the ith member $x_i(t+1)$ of the next generation population $P(t+1)$. Without loss of generality, for a minimization optimization problem, the following selection rule is applied:

$$x_i(t+1) = \begin{cases} u_i(t), \text{if } f(u_i(t)) < f(x_i(t)) \\ x_i(t), \text{otherwise} \end{cases} \tag{9}$$

where $f(\cdot)$ is the fitness function also called the objective function.

3   Particle Swarm Optimization (PSO)

3.1   The Original PSO Algorithm

Particle swarm optimization (PSO) [22], [25] is an optimization technique originally proposed by Kennedy and Eberhart [7]. The attractive features of PSO include ease of implementation and the fact that no gradient information is required. PSO has been successfully applied to solve various types of optimization problems [26], [27], [28]. The original PSO algorithm is based on the sociological behavior inspired by bird flocking [7]. It is made up of multiple particles, where each particle represents a potential solution to an optimization problem. The basic idea of the original PSO algorithm (also called the *pgbest* model) can be described in the following. Let us assume that s is the warm size, and that each particle i is represented as an individual with some characteristics. These characteristics are assigned the following symbols: 1) x_i: the current position of the particle; 2) v_i: the current velocity of the particle; 3) y_i : the personal best position of the particle; 4) $\hat{y}$: the global best position discovered by any particles so far. The current velocity of particle i is updated by

$$v_{ij}(t+1) = v_{ij}(t) + c_1 r_{1j}(t)(y_{ij}(t) - x_{ij}(t)) + c_2 r_{2j}(t)(\hat{y}_j(t) - x_{ij}(t)) \tag{10}$$

where c_1 and c_2 are two constant numbers and $c_1 = c_2 = 2$ are suggested. c_1 regulates the maximum step size in the direction of the global best position and c_2 regulates the maximum step size in the direction of the personal best position of the particle. The variable w is called *inertia weight*, this value is typically set up to vary linearly from 1 to 0 during the course of a training run. $r_1 \sim U(0,1)$ and $r_2 \sim U(0,1)$ are two random sequences reflecting the stochastic nature of PSO and influence the maximum step size that the particle can take in a single iteration. v_{ij} denotes the jth dimensional velocity of the current velocity of particle i, and usually is clamped to the range $[-v_{max}, v_{max}]$ to prevent the particle from leaving the search space, and $v_{max} = k \times x_{max}$ is suggested, where $0.1 \leq k \leq 1.0$. Then the current position of particle i is updated using the new velocity, by the following equation:

$$x_i(t+1) = x_i(t) + v_i(t+1) \tag{11}$$

The personal best position of particle i keeps the best position that the particle has visited. For a minimization problem, let us assume that the symbol f denotes the objective function. Then, the personal best position is updated by

$$y_i(t+1) = \begin{cases} y_i(t) & \text{if } f(x_i(t+1)) \geq f(y_i(t)) \\ x_i(t+1) & \text{otherwise} \end{cases} \tag{12}$$

The global best position is updated by the following equation:

$$\hat{y}(t+1) \in \{\hat{y}(t), y_1(t+1),..., y_s(t+1)\} \mid f(\hat{y}(t+1))$$
$$= \min\{f(\hat{y}(t)), f(y_1(t+1)),...., f(y_s(t+1))\} \tag{13}$$

The PSO algorithm firstly initializes the parameters and the flying velocity, and generates the initial population. Then it repeatedly applies the update equations above to generate the new swarm and find the optimal solution of the problem.

To interpret the different components in the velocity update equation, Kennedy [29] partitioned the velocity update term into two components consisting of a cognition component and a social component [22]. The term $c_1 r_{1j}(t)(y_{ij}(t) - x_{ij}(t))$ is associated with cognition since it only takes into account the experiences of the individual's own experiences. The corresponding velocity update equation is constructed as follows:

$$v_{ij}(t+1) = v_{ij}(t) + c_1 r_{1j}(t)(y_{ij}(t) - x_{ij}(t)) \tag{14}$$

Kennedy found that the performance of this *cognition only* model is inferior to that of the original *pgbest* model. One of the reasons for the poor behavior of this *pbest* version of PSO is that there is no interaction between the different particles. The term $c_2 r_{2j}(t)(\hat{y}_j(t) - x_{ij}(t))$ is associated with social since it only takes into account the social interaction between the particles. The corresponding velocity update equation is constructed as follows:

$$v_{ij}(t+1) = v_{ij}(t) + c_2 r_{2j}(t)(\hat{y}_j(t) - x_{ij}(t)) \tag{15}$$

Kennedy also found that the performance of this *social only* model (also called the *gbest* model) is superior to that of the original *pgbest* model on the specific problem that Kennedy investigated, and concluded that the social component may be more significant on some problems according to the initial results.

3.2   The Modified PSO Algorithm

Clerc [30] indicated that a constriction factor may help PSO to ensure convergence. He employed a constriction model that describes a way of choosing the values of w, c_1, and c_2 so that convergence is ensured. The modified velocity update equation base on the constriction model is given by the following equation:

$$v_{ij}(t+1) = \chi(v_{ij}(t) + c_1 r_{1j}(y_{ij}(t) - x_{ij}(t)) + c_2 r_{2j}(\hat{y}_j(t) - x_{ij}(t))) \tag{16}$$

where $\chi = \frac{2}{\left|2 - \varphi - \sqrt{\varphi^2 - 4\varphi}\right|}$, and $\varphi = c_1 + c_2$, $\varphi > 4$. Let $c_1 = c_2 = 2.05$, and substitute $\varphi = \varphi_1 + \varphi_2 = 4.1$ into χ to yield $\chi = 0.7298$. Then the following equation is obtained:

$$v_{ij}(t+1) = 0.7298(v_{ij}(t) + 2.05 r_{1j}(y_{ij}(t) - x_{ij}(t)) + 2.05 r_{2j}(\hat{y}_j(t) - x_{ij}(t))) \tag{17}$$

Since $2.05 \times 0.7298 = 1.4962$, this is equivalent to using the values $c_1 = c_2 = 1.4962$ and $w = 0.7928$ in the modified PSO velocity update equation.

4   Simulated Mutation in Differential Evolution

4.1   Similarities and Dissimilarities between DE and PSO

Differential evolution (DE) and particle swarm optimization (PSO) have been widely applied to solve various types of optimization problems, and received increasing interests from various research fields [20], [21], [22], [23]. They have their own characteristics and also have some similar characteristics. Hence, comparing and contrasting similarities and dissimilarities between DE and PSO can help researchers to develop some new techniques such as operators and update strategies of individuals, so that researchers can utilize these refined techniques or combine DE and PSO to improve the search performance of a refined evolutionary algorithm [19]. In the following, we give some similarities and dissimilarities between DE and PSO.

Firstly, DE and PSO begin with and are evolved on their own populations. The initial population is generated within bounds of decision variables of the problem to be optimized. The similarities between DE and PSO are that there are some parameters required to be set before the execution of the population or tuned during the execution of the population. Some common parameters adopted by DE and PSO are the population size and the stopping criterion (usually, the predefined maximum generation number), etc. There also are some different parameters that DE uses the scaling factor F to control the amplification of the differential vector of two randomly selected individuals, and the crossover probability CR, and that PSO utilizes two scaling factor c_1 to control the differential vector between the personal best position and the current position, and c_2 to control the differential vector between the global best position and the current position, respectively. In addition, in PSO, there is another control parameter w called *inertia weight* to control the flying velocity of the current particle. In the initial phase, PSO is required to initialize the flying velocity of the particle. Secondly, in DE, there are three major operators (i.e. mutation, crossover, and selection). DE repeatedly performs its mutation, crossover, and selection successively to generate the offspring of each individual. Selection after mutation and crossover is performed between the current individual and the mutant vector. However, in PSO, there are only two major operators (i.e., mutation and selection). Mutation is similar to the formulation of Gaussian mutation [31]. Firstly, the velocity of the current particle is updated, and then the new particle is generated by the current particle and the updated velocity. Selection is associated with the update of the personal best position and the global position.

4.2   Proposed Variants of Mutation in DE

In EAs, there usually exist some typical operators such as crossover, mutation, and selection. The roles of crossover and mutation are to explore and exploit the search space, respectively, while the aim of selection is to lead an EA to the optimal region. For EAs, in order to guide the search, the selection is a necessary operator, while crossover and mutation are alternative, that is, there are some EAs that utilize crossover and don't utilize mutation to search the solution space, and there are EAs that utilize mutation and don't utilize crossover to search the solution space. In EAs, DE utilizes mutation and crossover to search the solution space, and mutation is a more efficient search operator. Selection is performed between the target individual and the mutant individual. If the resulting individual is superior to its target individual, then the resulting individual becomes a member of the next generation population; otherwise the target individual is retained. However, PSO utilizes mutation to search the solution space. This formation of the mutation is similar to that of Gaussian mutation in evolution strategy (ES) [31]. The procedure of mutation involves two steps: firstly, update the flying velocity of the particle, and then the next position is generated by adding the updated flying velocity to the current position. In the equation of updating the flying velocity of the particle, the personal best position and the global best position are utilized simultaneously and are required to update. If the personal best position is superior to the target position, then the personal best particle becomes a member of the next generation population; otherwise the target position is retained in the next generation population. The global best position keeps the best position of all personal best positions. In DE and PSO, mutation plays an important role in the search performance. The formation of updating the flying velocity of the particle in PSO is similar to the formation of mutation in DE. Hence, according to Equations (14), (15), and (10) or (16) or (17), we make an attempt to develop three similar variants of mutation in DE, which can be formulated as follows:

"DE/pbest to target/2/bin":

$$v_i(t+1) = x_i(t) + F_1 r_{1j}(p_{l,r}(t) - x_i(t)) + F_2 r_{2j}(x_{r_1}(t) - x_{r_2}(t)) \qquad (18)$$

"DE/gbest to target/2/bin":

$$v_i(t+1) = x_i(t) + F_1 r_{1j}(p_g(t) - x_i(t)) + F_2 r_{2j}(x_{r_1}(t) - x_{r_2}(t)) \qquad (19)$$

"DE/pgbest to target/3/bin":

$$v_i(t+1) = x_i(t) + F_1 r_{1j}(p_{l,r}(t) - x_i(t)) + F_2 r_{2j}(p_g(t) - x_i(t)) + F_3 r_{3j}(x_{r_1}(t) - x_{r_2}(t)) \quad (20)$$

where $r_1, r_2 \in \{1,2,...,NP\}$ are two random integers (NP is the population size) and $r_1 \neq r_2 \neq i$, and $r \in \{1,2,...,NP\}$ is a random integer and $r \neq i$, F_1, F_2 and F_3 are three constant numbers. r_{1j}, r_{2j} and $r_{3j} \sim U(0,1)$ are three independent random sequences. $p_l(t)$ is the personal best position, while is updated by the following equation:

$$p_{l,i}(t+1) = \begin{cases} p_{l,i}(t) & \text{if}\,(f(x_i(t+1)) \geq f(p_{l,i}(t))) \\ x_i(t+1) & \text{otherwise} \end{cases} \quad (21)$$

The symbol f denotes the objective function (in this study, we consider the minimization optimization problems), $p_g(t)$ is the best position found so far and is updated by the following equation:

$$p_g(t+1) = \min\{p_g(t), f(x_1(t)), f(x_2(t)),..., f(x_{ps}(t))\} \quad (22)$$

It is important to mention that in Equations (18)-(20), the aim of the most right item added is to prevent the premature convergence.

5   Experimental Studies

5.1   Benchmark Test Functions

To investigate the performance of the proposed approaches, we test them on some well known test functions [13], [32] listed in Appendix A. The characteristics of these test functions are scalable and diverse enough to cover many kinds of difficulties that arise in global optimization problems to be optimized.

5.2   A Feasibility Analysis of Proposed Variants of Mutation

In the experiments, we first study on the feasibility of proposed variants of mutation including "DE/pbest to target/2/bin", "DE/gbest to target/2/bin", and "DE/pgbest to target/3/bin". These variants of mutation are conducted on a randomly selected test Set A given in Table 1. For convenience, the corresponding DE algorithms of "DE/rand/1/bin", "DE/pbest to target/2/bin", "DE/gbest to target/2/bin", and "DE/pgbest to target/3/bin" are called "DE", "DE-pbest", "DE-gbest", and "DE-pgbest", respectively. Among these algorithms, DE is used to compare with other algorithms based on proposed variants of mutation. The corresponding parameters utilized by variants of mutation are given in Table 2. Table 3 gives the experimental results for test functions (Set A). These experimental results involve the mean, best, worst, and "std" (standard deviation) results over 20 runs.

Table 1. Test functions (Set A) for a feasibility analysis of proposed variants of mutation

no.	f	function name	n	no.	f	function name	n
1	Z_2	Zakharov	2	4	R_5	Rosenbrock	5
2	R_2	Rosenbrock	2	5	Z_{10}	Zakharov	10
3	Z_5	Zakharov	5	6	R_{10}	Rosenbrock	10

Table 2. Parameter settings for functions in Set A

method	population size	maximum generation number	scaling factor	crossover probability
DE	50	200	$F = 0.5$	$CR=0.5$
DE-pbest	50	200	$F_1=1.0$, $F_2=1.0$	$CR=0.5$
DE-gbest	50	200	$F_1=1.0$, $F_2=1.0$	$CR=0.5$
DE-pgbest	50	200	$F_1=1.0$, $F_2=1.0$	$CR=0.5$

Table 3. Experimental results (over 20 runs) with respect to Set A

f	optimal	method	mean	best	worst	std
Z_2	0	DE	6.386446e-28	1.758755e-31	1.131094e-26	2.516795e-27
		DE-pbest	1.469772e-26	2.083445e-28	9.007324e-26	2.271381e-26
		DE-gbest	2.246505e-35	2.571179e-37	1.921802e-34	5.387434e-35
		DE-pgbest	3.496637e-35	1.148631e-38	2.050092e-34	5.687264e-35
R_2	0	DE	4.043810e-10	4.073580e-15	2.772325e-09	7.336665e-10
		DE-pbest	6.095435e-04	3.444860e-09	8.225564e-03	1.933000e-03
		DE-gbest	5.721392e-12	9.338300e-19	1.132792e-10	2.531759e-11
		DE-pgbest	3.418620e-12	7.556023e-18	6.663427e-11	1.488025e-11
Z_5	0	DE	4.828193e-07	4.867303e-08	1.477054e-06	3.882830e-07
		DE-pbest	2.402931e-09	1.197717e-10	1.031742e-08	2.735907e-09
		DE-gbest	8.058018e-17	4.462600e-18	5.719185e-16	1.269059e-16
		DE-pgbest	7.253825e-14	4.250352e-15	4.123926e-13	9.366879e-14
R_5	0	DE	5.688557e-01	4.036903e-02	1.177119e+00	3.13825e-01
		DE-pbest	4.260344e-01	1.265806e-01	9.894117e-01	2.82920e-01
		DE-gbest	5.697655e-01	2.621168e-04	3.954726e+00	1.165815e+00
		DE-pgbest	4.473080e-01	3.584614e-04	3.947445e+00	8.568890e-01
Z_{10}	0	DE	6.622624e+00	2.348601e+00	1.277686e+01	2.834790e+00
		DE-pbest	1.164231e-01	3.390072e-02	2.993678e-01	8.409105e-02
		DE-gbest	5.749389e-05	1.005118e-05	1.710637e-04	4.665417e-05
		DE-pgbest	2.462301e-03	5.173298e-04	1.016100e-02	2.686405e-03
R_{10}	0	DE	6.792124e+00	5.732544e+00	8.054731e+00	5.117326e-01
		DE-pbest	6.403195e+00	1.588632e+00	1.097295e+01	2.256358e+00
		DE-gbest	4.418085e+00	3.729706e-01	8.703678e+00	2.257661c+00
		DE-pgbest	4.583725e+00	6.703071e-02	5.881916e+00	1.571484e+00

According to Table 3, we can directly observe that for all functions, the mean, and best results obtained by DE-gbest and DE-pgbest are clearly superior to those by DE and DE-pbest. For Z_2 and R_2, the mean, and best results obtained by DE are better than those by DE-pbest, while for Z_5 and Z_{10}, DE-pbest outperforms DE with respect to the mean, and best results. It is interesting to note that for R_5, among all algorithms, DE-pbest performs best, while for R_{10}, DE-pbest also performs worst. This shows that proposed variants of mutation are feasible and effective. In addition, we also conclude that each variant of mutation has its own advantages and disadvantages, when applied to solve different optimization problems.

5.3   Comparison among Proposed Variants of Mutation

Table 4. Test functions (Set B) for comparison among proposed variants of mutation

no.	f	function name	n	no.	f	function name	n
1	RT_{10}	Rastrigin	10	6	SS_{20}	Sum Squares	20
2	G_{10}	Griewank	10	7	Z_{20}	Zakharov	20
3	SS_{10}	Sum Squares	10	8	L_{30}	Levy	30
4	RT_{20}	Rastrigin	20	9	SR_{30}	Sphere	30
5	G_{20}	Griewank	20	10	AK_{30}	Ackley	30

Table 5. Parameter settings utilized by several methods for functions in Set B

method	population size	maximum generation number	scaling factor	crossover probability
DE-pbest	50	1000	F_1=1.0, F_2=1.0	CR=0.5
DE-gbest	50	1000	F_1=1.0, F_2=1.0	CR=0.5
DE-pgbest	50	1000	F_1=1.0, F_2=1.0	CR=0.5

Table 6. Experimental results (over 20 runs) with respect to Set B

f	optimal	method	mean	best	worst	std
RT_{10}	0	DE-pbest	1.902277e-01	0	1.695898e+00	5.132144e-01
		DE-gbest	8.954632e-01	0	2.984877e+00	7.840963e-01
		DE-pgbest	1.492439e-01	0	9.949591e-01	3.645008e-01
G_{10}	0	DE-pbest	1.377763e-04	0	1.536761e-03	3.488477e-04
		DE-gbest	3.763520e-02	0	8.850457e-02	2.372000e-02
		DE-pgbest	6.403875e-03	0	2.215777e-02	7.468707e-03
SS_{10}	0	DE-pbest	1.005822e-54	7.499897e-57	6.969933e-54	1.759954e-54
		DE-gbest	9.018085e-88	2.129121e-90	5.111028e-87	1.497840e-87
		DE-pgbest	5.035500e-85	1.046825e-86	2.007719e-84	5.893653e-85
RT_{20}	0	DE-pbest	2.460349e+01	1.386501e+01	3.326031e+01	6.026570e+00
		DE-gbest	5.571808e+00	0	8.954632e+00	2.529432e+00
		DE-pgbest	5.571808e+00	0	8.954632e+00	2.529432e+00
G_{20}	0	DE-pbest	8.634492e-04	0	9.857285e-03	2.684819e-03
		DE-gbest	8.863576e-03	0	2.955218e-02	9.221660e-03
		DE-pgbest	8.863576e-03	0	2.955218e-02	9.221660e-03
SS_{20}	0	DE-pbest	1.574687e-28	1.019866e-31	2.771844e-27	6.168592e-28
		DE-gbest	8.620828e-55	1.019811e-56	4.764586e-54	1.109052e-54
		DE-pgbest	8.620828e-55	1.019811e-56	4.764586e-54	1.109052e-54
Z_{20}	0	DE-pbest	6.207022e-03	8.610498e-04	3.710671e-02	8.087983e-03
		DE-gbest	1.870221e-08	3.594251e-10	2.172025e-07	4.755446e-08
		DE-pgbest	2.011221e-06	4.329901e-07	5.904441e-06	1.585290e-06
L_{30}	0	DE-pbest	2.685848e-02	0	8.952825e-02	4.209281e-02
		DE-gbest	1.874892e+00	2.685848e-01	4.811783e+00	1.291529e+00
		DE-pgbest	2.347783e-01	0	5.438523e-01	2.006344e-01
SR_{30}	0	DE-pbest	8.281491e-19	1.304874e-20	2.851701e-18	8.519970e-19
		DE-gbest	1.087464e-25	1.755273e-29	9.533253e-25	2.881606e-25
		DE-pgbest	2.388738e-39	1.542118e-41	3.293399e-38	7.312764e-39
AK_{30}	0	DE-pbest	1.043227e-01	5.445500e-10	1.155149e+00	3.231451e-01
		DE-gbest	2.423414e+00	1.155149e+00	3.835916e+00	7.203066e-01
		DE-pgbest	3.819176e-01	1.000000e-14	1.155149e+00	5.375028e-01

In the following, we investigate the relative performances of proposed variants of mutation "DE/pbest to target/2/bin", "DE/gbest to target/2/bin", and "DE/pgbest to target/3/bin". The behaviors of the corresponding algorithms "DE-pbest", "DE-gbest", and "DE-pgbest" are conducted on another test Set B given in Table 4. The corresponding parameters utilized by these algorithms are given in Table 5. Table 6 gives the experimental results over 20 runs.

According to Table 6, we can first observe that for most of test functions except RT_{20}, three algorithms "DE-gbest", "DE-gbest", and "DE-pgbest" can find or get close to the optimal solution(s). For G_{10}, G_{20}, and L_{30}, the mean performances of DE-pbest are better than those of two other algorithms, while for SS_{10}, RT_{20}, SS_{20}, Z_{20}, and SR_{30}, DE-gbest and DE-pgbest outperform DE-pbest. This seems to validate what Kennedy [29] addressed in PSO, that is, one of reasons for the relatively poor behavior of this version of "DE-pbest" is that there is no interaction between different individuals. For most of test functions except SS_{10} and Z_{20}, the mean results of DE-pgbest are not worse than or superior to those of DE-gbest. Thus, we can conclude that DE-pgbest outperforms DE-gbest in terms of the mean performance. Additionally, it is worth mentioning that DE-pgbest is more stable than DE-pbest and DE-gbest.

5.4   Incorporating Other Techniques into "DE-pgbest"

Conventional differential evolution (DE) only employs one single mutation operator. It may perform well when applied to solve one optimization problem; while it may perform poorly when applied to solve another optimization problem. This is because each variant of mutation has its own characteristics which are suitable to solve some optimization problems and are not suitable to solve some other optimization problems [33]. In order to make up the shortcomings of one single variant of mutation in DE, some researchers often incorporate some search techniques into DE or simultaneously employ multiple variants of mutation to improve the general search performances of the proposed approaches. To show this, we will introduce the following search technique into DE-pgbest to improve the general search performance and this hybrid algorithm is called HDE-pgbest. In HDE-pgbest, after performing each generation, each individual utilizes the following equation similar to non-uniform mutation [10] and variant of mutation "DE/rand/1/bin" to generate the new vector:

$$v_i(t) = \begin{cases} x_i(t) + \Delta(U - x_i(t), t, T, b) \text{ if } \xi \leq 0.5 \\ x_i(t) - \Delta(x_i(t) - L, t, T, b) \text{ otherwise} \end{cases} \tag{23}$$

where ξ is a random number in the range [0,1], t and T are the current generation number and the maximum generation number, and the parameter b is often predefined as 2 or 3. The function Δ is defined as $\Delta(y, t, T, b) = y\xi(1 - \frac{t}{T})^b$. After generating the new vector $v_i(t)$, if $v_i(t)$ is superior to $x_i(t)$, then $v_i(t)$ is taken as the ith member of the tth generation population $P(t)$; otherwise $x_i(t)$ is retained. Accordingly, the personal best position and the global best position are updated. DE-pgbest and HDE-pgbest are conducted on the third test Set C given in Table 7. The corresponding parameters utilized by DE-pgbest and HDE-pgbest are given in Table 8. The experimental results (over 10 runs) are given in Table 9.

Table 7. Test functions (Set C) for comparison between DE-pgbest and HDE- pgbest

no.	f	function name	n	no.	f	function name	n
1	Ak_{100}	Ackley	100	7	RT_{100}	Rastrigin	100
2	DP_{100}	Dixon&Price	100	8	SC_{100}	Schwefel	100
3	G_{100}	Griewank	100	9	SR_{100}	Sphere	100
4	L_{100}	Levy	100	10	SS_{100}	Sum Squares	100
5	PW_{100}	Powell	100	11	Z_{100}	Zakharov	100
6	R_{100}	Rosenbrock	100	--	--	--	--

Table 8. Parameter settings for functions in Set C

method	function	population size	maximum generation num	scaling factor	crossover probability
DE-pgbest	$Ak_{100}, DP_{100}, G_{100}, L_{100}, PW_{100},$ $RT_{100}, SC_{100}, SR_{100}, SS_{100}$	100	5000	$F_1=1.0, F_2=1.0$	$CR=0.2$
	R_{100}	100	50000	$F_1=1.0, F_2=1.0$	$CR=0.2$
	Z_{100}	100	5000	$F_1=1.0, F_2=1.0$	$CR=0.95$
HDE-pgbest	$Ak_{100}, DP_{100}, G_{100}, L_{100}, PW_{100},$ $RT_{100}, SC_{100}, SR_{100}, SS_{100}$	100	2500	$F_1=1.0, F_2=1.0$	$CR=0.2$
	R_{100}	100	25000	$F_1=1.0, F_2=1.0$	$CR=0.2$
	Z_{100}	100	2500	$F_1=1.0, F_2=1.0$	$CR=0.95$

Table 9. Experimental results (over 10 runs) with respect to Set C

f	optimal	method	mean	best	worst	std
AK_{100}	0	DE-pgbest	2.078338e-14	1.509903e-14	2.220446e-14	2.484078e-15
		HDE-pgbest	2.433609e-14	2.220446e-14	2.930989e-14	2.995911e-15
DP_{100}	0	DE-pgbest	1.521863e+00	0	7.081450e+00	2.588281e+00
		HDE-pgbest	2.746358e-22	3.740410e-29	2.729722e-21	8.626451e-22
G_{100}	0	DE-pgbest	1.477978e-03	0	1.477978e-02	4.673776e-03
		HDE-pgbest	1.231608e-03	0	1.231607e-02	3.894684e-03
L_{100}	0	DE-pgbest	2.072515e-01	0	6.333805e-01	2.337717e-01
		HDE-pgbest	6.972935e-32	1.499760e-32	5.623151e-31	1.730770e-31
PW_{100}	0	DE-pgbest	2.382684e-02	1.768633e-02	2.830610e-02	3.329010e-03
		HDE-pgbest	1.253810e-03	1.157127e-04	3.933299e-03	1.319286e-03
R_{100}	0	DE-pgbest	9.727958e+01	3.303956e-01	1.760685e+02	5.895088e+01
		HDE-pgbest	8.875525e+00	1.187580e-09	8.875525e+01	2.806687e+01
RT_{100}	0	DE-pgbest	3.372288e+01	2.984877e+01	4.278322e+01	3.997297e+00
		HDE-pgbest	0	0	0	0
SC_{100}	0	DE-pgbest	1.300988e+04	3.790028e+03	2.055947e+04	6.313565e+03
		HDE-pgbest	1.272757e-03	1.272757e-03	1.272757e-03	0
SR_{100}	0	DE-pgbest	1.118508e-64	3.392121e-65	4.191784e-64	1.141361e-64
		HDE-pgbest	1.540705e-32	3.236388e-33	3.283952e-32	1.110491e-32
SS_{100}	0	DE-pgbest	2.604988e-62	3.470676e-63	8.281143e-62	2.466781e-62
		HDE-pgbest	3.978402e-30	1.733676e-31	1.252258e-29	3.768654e-30
Z_{100}	0	DE-pgbest	1.807821e-25	2.200000e-36	1.807821e-24	5.716832e-25
		HDE-pgbest	5.217734e-16	6.066764e-19	2.766612e-15	1.015614e-15

As shown in Table 9, it can be clearly observed that the mean results obtained by HDE-pgbest are obviously superior to those by DE-pgbest with respect to DP_{100}, L_{100}, PW_{100}, R_{100}, RT_{100}, and SC_{100}, while the mean results produced by HDE-pgbest are slightly worse than those produced by DE-pgbest with respect to other functions. We also find that for each function, HDE-pgbest can find the optimal or near-optimal solution. It is important to mention that R_{100} requires more the number of fitness evaluations to find the optimal solution and there is an obviously deviated solution out of 10 solutions (over 10 runs), and that the suitable crossover probability used for Z_{100} is different from that used for other functions. In summary, the general search performance of HDE-pgbest is improved.

6   Conclusions and Future Work

In this paper, we firstly introduce the basic ideas of differential evolution (DE) and particle swarm optimization (PSO), and compare and contrast the similarities and dissimilarities between them. Then, we develop three variants of mutation in DE, which are inspired by mutation operators in PSO. Through experimental studies, we investigate the feasibility of the proposed variants of mutation and initially compare their relative performances. Finally, we also briefly introduce the application methods to amply exert the efficiency of the proposed variants of mutation. The experimental results show the prospect of the proposed variants of mutation and that they can find the optimal or near optimal solution.

As future work, some research directions are also considered in the following. On the one hand, in order to improve the convergence speed, we can incorporate some local search or heuristic search techniques into DE using the proposed variants of mutation. On the other hand, in the experiments, we also note that DE using the proposed variants of mutation is sensitive to the crossover probability. Hence, in order to improve the adaptive ability of DE using the proposed variants of mutation, some self-adaptation strategies can be introduced during evolution, which can dynamically tune the crossover probability to improve the efficiency of crossover. In addition, in order to reduce the probability of being stuck in the local optimal solutions, we will introduce some explorative operators into DE using the proposed variants of mutation.

References

1. Holland, J.H.: Adaptation in Natural and Artificial Systems. University of Michigan Press, Ann Arbor (1975)
2. Rechenberg, I.: Evolution Strategy: Optimization of Technical Systems by Means of Biological Evolution. Fromman-Holzboog (1973)
3. Koza, J.R.: Genetic Programming: on the Programming of Computers by Means of Natural Selection. The MIT Press, Cambridge (1992)
4. Fogel, D.B.: Applying Evolutionary Programming to Selected Traveling Salesman Problems. Cybernetics and Systems 24, 27–36 (1993)
5. Yao, X., Xu, Y.: Recent Advances in Evolutionary Computation. Journal of Computer Science and Technology 21(1), 1–18 (2006)
6. Storn, R., Price, K.: Differential Evolution- A Simple and Efficient Adaptive Scheme for Global Optimization over Continuous Spaces. Technical Report TR-95-012, International Computer Science Institute, Berkeley, CA (1995)

7. Kennedy, J., Eberhart, R.C.: Particle Swarm Optimization. In: Proceedings of IEEE International Conference on Neural Networks, Perth, Australia, vol. 4, pp. 1942–1948. IEEE Service Center, Piscataway (1995)
8. Duan, H., Yu, X.: Hybrid Ant Colony Optimization Using Memetic Algorithm for Traveling Salesman Problem. In: Proceedings of the IEEE Symposium on Approximate Dynamic Programming and Reinforcement Learning, pp. 92–95 (2007)
9. Tsutsui, S., Yamamure, M., Higuchi, T.: Multi-Parent Recombination with Simplex Crossover in Real Coded Genetic Algorithms. In: Proceedings of the Genetic and Evolutionary Computation Conference (GECCO 1999), pp. 657–664. Morgan Kaufmann Publisher, San Mateo (1999)
10. Michalewicz, Z.: Genetic Algorithms + Data Structures = Evolution Programs, 3rd edn. Springer, New York (1996)
11. Costa, L., Oliveira, P.: An Evolution Strategy for Multiobjective Optimization. In: Congress on Evolutionary Computation (CEC 2002), vol. 1, pp. 97–102. IEEE Service Center, Piscataway (2002)
12. Ammaruekarat, P., Meesad, P.: A Chaos Search for Multi-Objective Memetic Algorithm. In: 2011 International Conference on Information and Electronics Engineering (IPCSIT 2011), vol. 6, pp. 140–144. IACSIT Press, Sinapore (2011)
13. Hedar, R., Fukushima, M.: Tabu Search Directed by Direct Search Methods for Nonlinear Global Optimization. European Journal of Operational Research 170(2), 329–349 (2006)
14. Bertsimas, D., Tsitsiklis, J.: Simulated Annealing. Statistical Science 8(1), 10–15 (1993)
15. Senaratna, N.I.: Genetic Algorithms: The Crossover-Mutation Debate. Degree of Bachelor of Computer Science of the University of Colombo (2005)
16. Fogel, D.B., Atmar, J.W.: Comparing Genetic Operators with Gaussian Mutations in Simulated Evolutionary Processes Using Linear Systems. Biological Cybernetics (1990)
17. Matsui, S., Tokoro, K.I.: Improving the Performance of a Genetic Algorithm for Minimum Span Frequency Assignment Problem with an Adaptive Mutation Rate and a New Initialization Method. In: Proceedings of the Genetic and Evolutionary Computation Conference (GECCO 2001), pp. 1359–1366. Morgan Kaufmann Publishers, San Francisco (2001)
18. Younes, Ghenniwa, H., Areibi, S.: An Adaptive Genetic Algorithm for Multiobjective Flexible Manufacturing Systems. In: Proceedings of the Genetic and Evolutionary Computation Conference (GECCO 2002), pp. 1241–1248. Morgan Kaufmann Publishers, San Francisco (2002)
19. Deb, K., Padhye, N.: Improving a Particle Swarm Optimization Algorithm Using an Evolutionary Algorithm Framework. KanGAL Report Number 2010003, Kanpur Genetic Algorithms Laboratory, Department of Mechanical Engineering, Indian Institute of Technology Kanpur, PIN 208016, India, February 21 (2010)
20. Das, S., Abraham, A., Chakraborty, U.K., Konar, A.: Differential Evolution Using a Neighborhood-Based Mutation Operator. IEEE Transactions on Evolutionary Computation 13(3), 526–553 (2009)
21. Rahnamayan, S., Tizhoosh, H.R., Salama, M.M.A.: Opposition-Based Differential Evolution. IEEE Transactions on Evolutionary Computation 12(1), 64–79 (2008)
22. Bergh, F.V.D., Engelbrecht, A.P.: A Cooperative Approach to Particle Swarm Optimization. IEEE Transactions on Evolutionary Computation 8(3), 1–15 (2004)
23. Coelho, L.D.S.: Gaussian Quantum-Behaved Particle Swarm Optimization Approaches for Constrained Engineering Design Problems. Expert Systems with Applications 37(2), 1676–1683 (2010)

24. Storn, R., Price, K.: Differential Evolution- A Simple and Efficient Heuristic for Global Optimization over Continuous Spaces. Journal of Global Optimization 11(4), 341–359 (1997)
25. Eberhart, R.C., Kennedy, J.: A New Optimizer Using Particle Swarm Theory. In: Proceedings of the Sixth International Symposium on Micro Machine and Human Science, Nagoya, Japan, pp. 39–43. IEEE Service Center, Piscataway (1995)
26. Shi, Y., Eberhart, R.C.: Empirical Study of Particle Swarm Optimization. In: Proceedings of the Congress on Evolutionary Computation, Washington DC, USA, pp. 1945–1949. IEEE Service Center, Piscataway (1999)
27. Helwig, S., Wanka, R.: Particle Swarm Optimization in High-Dimensional Bounded Search Spaces. In: Proceedings of the 2007 IEEE Swarm Intelligence Symposium (SIS 2007), Honolulu, Hawaii, USA, pp. 198–205. IEEE Press (April 2007)
28. Zahara, E., Hu, C.H.: Solving Constrained Optimization Problems with Hybrid Particle Swarm Optimization. Engineering Optimization 40(11), 1031–1049 (2008)
29. Kennedy, J.: The Particle Swarm: Social Adaptation of Knowledge. In: Proceedings of the International Conference on Evolutionary Computation, Indianapolis, IN, USA, pp. 303–308 (1997)
30. Clerc, M.: The Swarm and the Queen: towards a Deterministic and Adaptive Particle Swarm Optimization. In: Proceedings of the Congress on Evolutionary Computation, Washington DC, USA, pp. 1951–1957. IEEE Service Center, Piscataway (1999)
31. Bäck, T., Schwefel, H.: An Overview of Evolution Algorithms for Parameter Optimizations. Evolutionary Computation 1(1), 1–23 (1993)
32. Floudas, C.A., Pardalos, P.M., Adjiman, C.S., Esposito, W.R., Gumus, Z., Harding, S.T., Klepeis, J.L., Meyer, C.A., Schweiger, C.A. (eds.): Handbook of Test Problems for Local and Global Optimization. Kluwer Academic Publishers, Boston (1999)
33. Ao, Y., Chi, H.: Experimental Study on Differential Evolution Strategies. In: 2009 Global Congress on Intelligent Systems (GCIS 2009), vol. 2, pp. 19–24 (2009)

Appendix A: Benchmark Test Functions

1) (AK_n) Ackley Function:

Minimize: $AK_n(x) = 20 + \exp(1) - 20\exp(-\frac{1}{5}\sqrt{\frac{1}{n}\sum_{i=1}^{n} x_i^2}) - \exp(-\frac{1}{n}\sum_{i=1}^{n}\cos(2\pi x_i))$.

Search space: $-15 \leq x_i \leq 30$, $i = 1,2,...,n$. Global minimum: $x^* = (0,....,0)$; $AK_n(x^*) = 0$.

2) (DP_n) Dixon&Price Function: Minimize: $DP_n(x) = (x_1 - 1)^2 + \sum_{i=2}^{n} i(2x_i^2 - x_{i-1})^2$.

Search space: $-10 \leq x_i \leq 10$, $i = 1,2,...,n$.

Global minimum: $x_i^* = 2^{-\left(\frac{2^i-2}{2^i}\right)}$, $i = 1,...,n$; $DP_n(x^*) = 0$.

3) (G_n) Griewank Function: Minimize: $G_n(x) = \sum_{i=1}^{n}\frac{x_i^2}{4000} - \prod_{i=1}^{n}\cos(x_i/\sqrt{i}) + 1$.

Search space: $-300 \leq x_i \leq 300$, $i = 1,...,n$. Global minimum: $x^* = (0,...,0)$; $G_n(x^*) = 0$.

4) (L_n) Levy Function: Minimize: $L_n(x) = \sin^2(\pi y_1) + \sum_{i=1}^{n-1}[(y_i - 1)^2(1 + 10\sin^2(\pi y_i + 1))]$

$+ (y_n - 1)^2(1 + 10\sin^2(2\pi y_n))$, $y_i = 1 + \frac{x_i - 1}{4}$, $i = 1,...,n$.

Search space: $-10 \leq x_i \leq 10$, $i = 1,...,n$. Global minimum: $x^* = (1,...,1)$; $L_n(x^*) = 0$.

5) (PW_n) Powell Function:

Minimize: $PW_n(x) = \sum_{i=1}^{n/4} (x_{4i-3} + 10x_{4i-2})^2 + 5(x_{4i-1} - x_{4i})^2 + (x_{4i-2} - x_{4i-1})^4 + 10(x_{4i-3} - x_{4i})^4$.

Search space: $-4 \le x_i \le 5, i = 1,...,n$.

Global minimum: $x^* = (3,-1,0,1,3,...,3,-1,0,1)$; $PW_n(x^*) = 0$.

6) (R_n) Rosenbrock Function: Minimize: $R_n(x) = \sum_{i=1}^{n-1} [100(x_i^2 - x_{i+1})^2 + (x_i - 1)^2]$.

Search space: $-5 \le x_i \le 10, i = 1,2,...,n$. Global minimum: $x^* = (1,...,1)$, $R_n(x^*) = 0$.

7) (RT_n) Rastrigin Function: Minimize: $RT_n(x) = 10n + \sum_{i=1}^{n} (x_i^2 - 10\cos(2\pi x_i))$.

Search space: $-2.56 \le x_i \le 5.12$, $i = 1,...,n$. Global minimum: $x^* = (0,...,0)$; $RT_n(x^*) = 0$.

8) (SC_n) Schwefel Function: Minimize: $SC_n(x) = 418.9829n - \sum_{i=1}^{n} (x_i \sin\sqrt{|x_i|})$.

Search space: $-500 \le x_i \le 500$, $i = 1,2,...,n$. Global minimum: $x^* = (1,...,1)$, $SC_n(x^*) = 0$.

9) (SR_n) Sphere Function: Minimize: $SR_n(x) = \sum_{i=1}^{n} x_i^2$.

Search space: $-2.56 \le x_i \le 5.12, i = 1,2,...,n$.

Global minimum: $x^* = (0,...,0)$; $SR_n(x^*) = 0$.

10) (SS_n) Sum Squares Function: Minimize: $SS_n(x) = \sum_{i=1}^{n} ix_i^2$.

Search space: $-5 \le x_i \le 10, i = 1,...,n$. Global minimum: $x^* = (0,...,0)$; $SS_n(x^*) = 0$.

11) (Z_n) Zakharov Function: Minimize: $Z_n(x) = \sum_{i=1}^{n} x_i^2 + (\sum_{i=1}^{n} 0.5ix_i)^2 + (\sum_{i=1}^{n} 0.5ix_i)^4$.

Search space: $-5 \le x_i \le 10, i = 1,2,...,n$. Global minimum: $x^* = (0,...,0)$; $Z_n(x^*) = 0$

Application of Smart Handheld Device in Agricultural Product Traceability System

Yi-sheng Miao, Hua-ri Wu[*], Hua-ji Zhu, and Fei-fei Li

National Engineering Research Center for Information Technology in Agriculture,
Beijing 100097, P.R. China

Abstract. The quality and safety of agricultural products is becoming more and more important nowadays. The devices commonly used are POS (Point of Sales) terminals, electronic scales, bar-code scanners, etc. The mismatches among various devices cause a lot of problems during data communication, synchronization, manipulation and flow control. Here a smart handheld device will be introduced, which can resolve these problems. Highly integrated design reduces the total cost of the traceability devices; an overall control makes the cooperation easy and guarantees the traceability flow more reliable and robust. The device hardware mainly consists of an ARM (Advanced RISC Machines) core, a power management block and some functional peripherals. The implementation of the device focused on four issues: 1. power circuit and power management design in multi-power system; 2. peripheral cooperation under CPU control; 3. signal integrity and power integrity in PCB design; 4. transaction model based software design and database synchronization.

Keywords: Agricultural Product, Smart Handheld Device, Traceability System, Electronic Tag.

1   Introduction

The agriculture product safety is extremely important to human health; it is the foundation of disease prevention and human health improving [1]. In recent years, many agricultural product safety problems like mad cow disease, foot-and-mouth disease; avian flu broke out all over the world. In China, there were snails, inferior milk powder, illegal use of clenbuterol and other food quality events, especially in 2008, Sanlu milk powder incidents, did serious harm to the consumer's health and safety [2]. Agricultural product traceability system is an important part of agricultural product safety system. Building on information technology-based quality and safety of agricultural product traceability system can effectively control the nutritional information, production process information, origin information of agricultural products. These advantages play an important role in developing a high quality, efficient, ecological, agricultural products, and promoting a traceability system that covering production, processing and distribution [3]. Many developed countries have

---

[*] Corresponding author.

M. Zhao and J. Sha (Eds.): ICCIP 2012, Part I, CCIS 288, pp. 77–85, 2012.

generally established agricultural product traceability system; various regions and departments in China also worked in the safety of agricultural product traceability system and started many pilot demonstrations. 2003 "863" project set up a "feed and livestock products of digital security monitoring system", Ju-Fang Xie made a study of pork traceability system [4]; Nanjing city deems the agricultural safety signs as the agricultural product quality carrier, and starts agricultural quality IC card management system based on the quality and safety Web site supervising platform [5]. In 2004, under the cooperation of the State Administration of Quality Supervision, Quality and Technical Supervision in Weifang and Shouguang Shandong Province, a vegetable quality and safety traceability system were explored in Shouguang and Luochen vegetable base[6].

The agricultural production and circulation in China has its own characteristics, there are some problems like scattered production space, low level of large-scale operations, non standardized production conditions, dispersed circulations   and relatively poor human factors etc [7]. Currently, the agricultural production and circulation management in China is still relatively weak; the old traceability method is mainly based on handwriting bills or notes which are easy to be forged or to be used from someone else. While the wholesalers and distributors are inspecting the receiving goods, they record all the information of agricultural products each time, such as source, name, size, quantity, flow, etc. mainly by the establishment of accounting. However, in the actual operation, there are non-standard operations, incomplete records or other issues affecting the implementation of agricultural traceability system. This paper introduces a smart handheld device used in the agricultural traceability system making the bills and notes electrically, make it convenient for traceability information recording, searching, supervising and managing. At the same time, the device avoiding the information manual input minimizes the impact of manual mistakes and many other factors.

The agricultural product traceability system in China still remains at the initial stage, and the researches are mainly focusing on the food and livestock field. There are problems like unsuccessful sharing and exchanging of the information, different objectives and principles of system development, non-standard traceability information, non-consistent data flow and non-compatible software [3]. This paper aiming at the shortcoming mentioned above represents a multi-functional device, which avoids manual inspection and input to ensure the encrypted code-bar check, ID card authentication and digital transaction flow online monitoring.

2   Smart Handheld Device Overview

Smart handheld devices generally refer to the battery-powered terminals which have human interface computing power and data storage capability. Furthermore, the smart terminals further integrate operating system, graphic user interface, and second development platform. Smart phone, PDA, IC card terminal and some barcode scanner all belong to this field.

Equipments such as POS terminal, barcode scanners, electronic scales and PDA terminals are mainly used in the agricultural product circulation process. These single functional devices are not appropriate in cooperating, data synchronization, and insufficient network supervision. Especially in the stock, wholesale and retail flow, it is hard to achieve the processing control, market accessing, and trade information sharing and business interaction.

Based on the research of the smart handheld device, this paper presents a design which is based on an ARM core, integrating techniques like bar-code, electronic tag, wireless communication and GPS. This device provides several means and techniques for effective information collection, recording and transmission in traceability system, thereby satisfying the agricultural products traceability requirements in different sectors.

3   Implementation and Application of Traceability Smart Handheld Device in Agricultural Product

Agricultural product traceability smart handheld device functions as a bridge connecting between information carriers and network database server [8, 9]. To integrate all the functions into a single smart handheld device, the following four components must be considered. First, the cooperation of several peripherals under the CPU control; second, the power supply design and power management in the multi-power system; third, power integrity and signal integrity concern during PCB layout; fourth, transaction flow based program design and traceability network database synchronization. These issues will be mainly discussed during the implementation of the agricultural product traceability smart handheld device.

3.1   System Architecture

The agricultural product traceability smart handheld device has a central control module which consists of ARM core, SDRAM, NAND Flash and clock generator circuit. The device uses a 3.5 inches TFT LCD touch panel as the user input and output apparatus. According to the agricultural product traceability needs, the device integrates the functional modules like identification module, which is used to read the transaction user ID card; data communication module, which exchanges data with the database server; code-bar reader module, which is used to scan the product bar code; Geographic positioning module, which collects the real time transaction position information; micro printer module, which is used to print transaction list or traceability bar code. These peripheral modules are all connected to the central control unit and controlled by it to cooperate and communicate. The device also contains some universal port like USB port, TF card connector, extending printer connector. All modules above are powered by a single cell Li-battery, through a power shift and management circuit. The smart handheld device system architecture block diagram is shown as in Fig. 1.

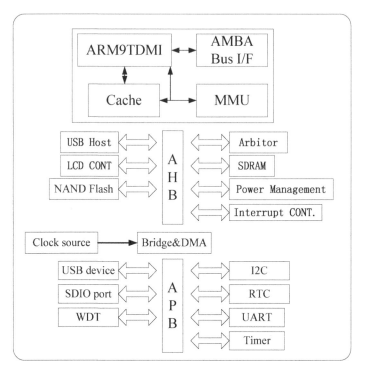

Fig. 1. Block diagram of smart handheld device

3.2   Device Hardware Design

Device hardware consists of three parts, central control block, peripheral modules and power converter and management block. The central control block includes a main processor S3C2410, a 64MB SDRAM, a 512MB NAND Flash and crystals for PLL and RTC. The schematic of central control block is shown as Fig. 2.

The peripheral modules of the device are GPRS module, GPS module, RFID reader/writer module, micro printer module and bar code scanner module. Modularized design can greatly reduce costs and shorten development cycles, and also facilitates embedded system hardware and software cut for different applications. Because of the different functions and sizes, there are different ways of integrating each module. Considering the user custom of the handheld devices, micro-printing module and barcode scanner are usually on the top of or in the upper part of the enclosure, so we design two connectors on the edge of the board and connect the module through a FPC cable when using. GPRS and GPS module has no special requirements on the relative position, because of large number of pins and small volume; it can be integrated directly on the motherboard.

We have to resolve the multi-level power supply and guarantee the battery life time, to integrating several modules into a single device. For the hardware design, this means providing higher power conversion efficiency and more plentiful methods of power management when reaching the multi-level power needs. This paper chooses LTC3577

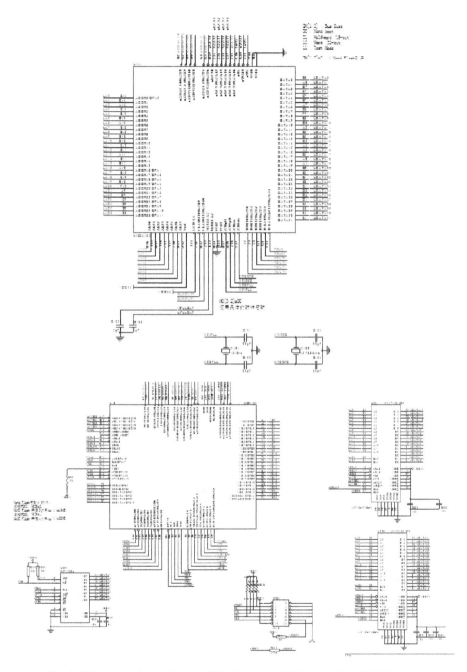

Fig. 2. Schematic of central control block in traceability smart handheld device

from LINEAR as the power shifter and power management, and LTC2941 as the gas gauge. LTC3577 is a highly integrated DC converter which integrates DC-DC, battery charging, LCD backlight driver and power management. It consists of 2 LDOs, 3 high efficiency bucks, LCD backlight driver circuit and IIC port. The power supply schematic is shown as Fig. 3.

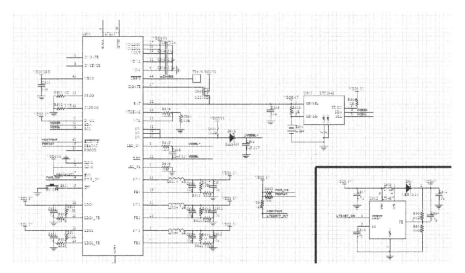

Fig. 3. Schematic of power converter and gas gauge

After the schematic design, it turns to the place and routing on PCB. Placement begins with the main components, especially connectors and those have position requirement. Layout design should hold priority to high-frequency signals, especially clock signal. For a group of high speed signal layout, it is necessary to pay attention to the data synchronization, which means they must have the same transmission delay. The space and integrity of power plane is also important. For this design, the CPU frequency is 200M Hz, SDRAM interface frequency is 133M Hz, the NAND Flash interface frequency is up to 20M Hz. 133M Hz signal should be considered as a high speed signal, the layout design of the SDRAM interface high speed signal trace will impact the overall performance[10,11].

Here we use 6 layers PCB, to ensure the system power integrity and high speed interface signal integrity while minimizing the cost of PCB manufacturing. The second layer of PCB is a complete ground plane, which is the best signal return path and is essential for signal and power integrity. The fifth layer is a large copper power plane, which brings good power supply capacity and power integrity. For the SDRAM high-speed interface signal, the layout design has adopted the following approach to ensure signal integrity. Using termination impedance matching to reduce overshoot and undershoot; using snake-like way to ensure alignment with the group delay between the signal line precisely the same; using minimum line spacing constrain and orthogonal routing in adjacent layers to minimize crosstalk. After debugging and testing, all parts of the board works fine. The system is still stable when CPU frequency up to 266MHz.The PCB layout of the smart handheld device is shown as Fig.4.

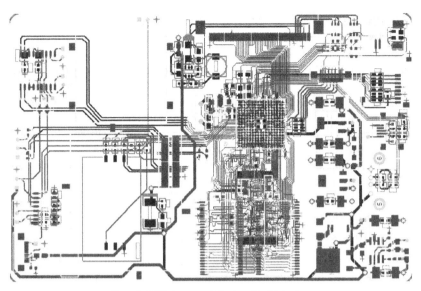

Fig. 4. PCB layout of the handheld device

3.3   Device Software Design

The software of the handheld device consists of 3 layers: operation system layer, database and Function layer. The software architecture is shown as Fig. 5.

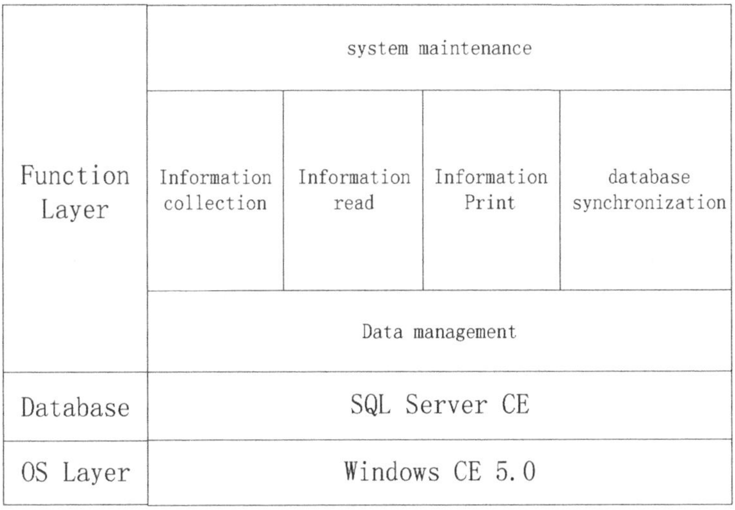

	system maintenance			
Function Layer	Information collection	Information read	Information Print	database synchronization
	Data management			
Database	SQL Server CE			
OS Layer	Windows CE 5.0			

Fig. 5. Agricultural product traceability device software architecture

We choose Windows CE 5.0 as the operation system. Windows CE 5.0 is a 32-bit, embedded, real-time, multi-task and modular operation system developed especially for smart handheld device by Microsoft. The advantages of Windows CE are commercial-supported availability, abundant resources of GUI, efficient management and speculation on the hardware resources and threads.

Here we choose SQL Server 2005 CE as the embedded database which is used to manage terminal data and synchronize with the server. SQL Server CE has two ways to synchronize data: Merge Replication and Remote Data Access (RDA). Compared with the former, RDA is safer and more suitable for simple tables. In the RDA way, users can select some part or all information for data synchronization. Different users will be authorized proper permissions to access the data server.

There are six functional modules: information collection module, information read module, information print module, data management module, system maintenance module, and database synchronization module. The information collection module comprises two sections: manual data entry and GPS information entry. The manual data entry is only opened for producers, who input the product information like product name, farm name, what kind of agricultural chemical have been used during the growing period, and so on. Other users in the transaction flow can only read these information using the Information read module. The GPS information is automatically recorded and added into the database. Information read module is a two-dimension scanner used for reading the information outside the product package. Information print module can print words or two-dimension bar code. The two-dimension bar code is usually attached outside the product package. Data management module complete tasks like add, query, delete and modify information. Data synchronization module is very important, because it synchronizes local device data with database in central server. New information collected by handhold device is uploaded to central database, consumers and sellers use this module to download the up-to-date information.

3.4   Practical Applications

This traceability smart handheld device is very practical, easy using and stable working in the application and demonstration of in Yongning Ningxia and Gaocheng Hebei. During the demonstration, we recorded information in storage, production and distribution and sales more than 4,000 pieces, printed transaction forms more than 400 pieces, generated and printed more than 500 pieces of two-dimensional bar code, scanned bar-code more than 600 batches, found substandard agricultural products more than ten times, achieved the desired design goals.

4   Conclusion

This paper introduces a smart handheld device which makes the note and card electrically and easy in storage, check and supervise. This design resolves the existing problems like single function, hard for several devices to cooperating and data synchronization. At the same time this device avoiding the manual input in the transactions minimizes the impact of human factor and Achieve agricultural products traceability flow control. This design plays a positive role for China to promote the agricultural products traceability system.

Acknowledgment. This paper is supported by two grants from the Ministry of Industry (Grant No. 2010ZX01045-001-004), a grant from National Natural Science Foundation of China (Grant No. 60871042), National Technology R&D Program (Grant No. 2011BAD21B02) and Science Foundation for Young Scientists of Beijing Academy of Agriculture and Forestry Sciences (Grant No. 61102126).

References

1. Chen, H., Shi, Y., Tian, Z.: Game model analysis of agricultural product traceability system in China. China Economist 7, 10–12 (2007)
2. Zheng, L.: Research and Application of agricultural product quality tracking and traceability technique. China Collective Economy 4 (2011)
3. Jin, H., Liu, J.: Status, problems and countermeasures of agricultural product quality fast traceability system. Business Times 25 (2009)
4. Wang, L., Lu, C., Xie, J., Hu, Y.: Review of traceability system for domestic animals and livestock products. Transactions of The Chinese Society of Agricultural Engineering 21(7), 168–174 (2005)
5. Ji, G., He, J., Shi, Z.: Construction progress and thinking of agricultural product quality and safety in Nanjing. Jiangsu Agricultural Sciences (3), 87–89 (2004)
6. Zhou, Y., Geng, X.: Application of Traceability in Food Safety. Research of Agricultural Modernization 23(6), 451–454 (2002)
7. Deng, X., Lv, X., Zheng, S.: GIS-based traceability system of agricultural product safety. Transactions of the Chinese Society of Agricultural Engineering 24(2), 172–176 (2008)
8. Huang, F., Hao, P., Wu, H.: Application of RFID middleware in agricultural product safety traceability system. Transactions of the Chinese Society of Agricultural Engineering 24(2), 177–181 (2008)
9. Li, M., Qian, J.-P., Yang, X.-T., et al.: A PDA-based record-keeping and decision-support system for traceability in cucumber production. Computers and Electronics in Agriculture 70, 69–77 (2009)
10. Deng, B., Wang, W.-Z., Zhang, J.: Signal Integrity Design Based on High-speed Digital Processing Module. Aeronautical Computing Technique 40(2), 101–104 (2010)
11. Eric, B.: Signal Integrity, Translated by Li, Y., Li, L. Electronic Industry Press, Beijing (2005)
12. Xiong, B.-H., Fu, R.-T., Lin, Z.-H.: A Solution on Pork Quality Traceability from Farm to Dinner Table in TianjinCity, China. Agricultural Sciences in China 9(1), 147–156 (2010)
13. Yang, X., Qian, J., Sun, C.: Design and application of safe production and quality traceability system for vegetable. Transactions of the Chinese Society of Agricultural Engineering 24(3), 162–166 (2008)

Model Checking Approach to Real-Time Aspects of Denial-of-Service Attack

Tatsuya Arai and Shin-ya Nishizaki

Department of Computer Science, Tokyo Institute of Technology, 2-12-1-W8-69,
O-okayama, Meguro, Tokyo, 152-8552, Japan
{tatsuya.arai,nisizaki}@lambda.cs.titech.ac.jp

Abstract. Vulnerability of communication protocols can cause several kinds of attacks, which cause significant damage to systems connected to the Internet. Denial-of-service attack (DoS attack) is an instance of them. Analysis of resistance against DoS attacks is considered as significant. We previously proposed a formal framework for DoS attack resistance, the spice calculus. In this paper, we develop a method for analyzing communication protocols from the aspect of DoS attack resistance. In this method, we first formalize a communication protocol in terms of the spice calculus. Then we translate expressions of the spice calculus into timed automata and analyze them using the real-time model checker UPPAAL. We explain the method by showing an example of a simple communication protocol.

Keywords: denial-of-service attack resistance, real-time model checking.

1 Introduction

With the widespread adoption of the Internet, communications among computers have become an important type of infrastructure in modern society. Accordingly, attacks that exploit vulnerabilities in communication protocols are now serious problems. A formal approach to the detection and analysis of the vulnerability of communications protocols is increasingly required.

The Transmission Control Protocol (TCP) [1] is one of the core communication protocols used on the Internet. TCP provides reliable data exchange between two hosts on the Internet. TCP uses a three-way handshake to establish a connection between a client and a server:

1. SYN: The client sends a SYN to the server. It sets the sequence number of the client to a random value, x.
2. SYN-ACK: In response, the server replies with a SYN-ACK. The server's acknowledgment number is set to x+1, and the responder's sequence number is set to another random value, y.
3. ACK: Finally, the client sends an ACK back to the server.

A SYN flood [2] is a type of denial-of-service (DoS) attack in which an attacker sends an enormous number of SYN requests to a target's system over a short period of time although the attacker does not receive the SYN-ACK responses. The server will wait for some time for acknowledgment. These half-open connections consume resources

M. Zhao and J. Sha (Eds.): ICCIP 2012, Part I, CCIS 288, pp. 86–94, 2012.

on the server. Consequently, all resources for half-open connections are sapped and no new connections can be made for a certain period, which results in denial of service. Although the SYN flood is not fatal due to protections such as SYN-cookie, we cite this as a typical example of a DoS attack in this paper.

Formal studies on DoS attacks. In a pioneering study, Meadow [3] reported a formal framework for describing and analyzing protocols with respect to DoS attack resistance. The framework is a type of protocol description in the Alice-and-Bob style, in which a computational cost is annotated with each communication step of the protocol. Although the Alice-and-Bob specification is easy to understand, it lacks accuracy in some cases.

To address these inaccuracies, we propose a formal system for analyzing DoS attack resistance. This system is called the spice calculus [4][5] and is based on Milner's pi calculus [6] and Abadi and Gordon's spi calculus [7]. As a process calculus is more accretive and precise than the Alice-and-Bob style for describing communication processes in protocols, the spice calculus enables an understanding of the dynamism of a protocol. Consequently, it clarifies the cost imbalances between clients and servers.

Another advantage of the spice calculus, in comparison with pi and spi calculi, is its explicit memory management. As memory management features such as memory allocation and de-allocation are implicit in the pi and spi calculi, memory usage cannot be readily traced. Making memory management explicit is indispensable for estimating memory costs.

In addition to our approach, Cervesato developed another technique for correcting this type of inaccuracy using multi-set rewriting (MSR) [8].

Purpose. We propose a formal framework, the spice calculus, for analyzing DoS attack resistance. Although we can describe communication protocols in this framework, we cannot formalize specifications for resistance against DoS attacks. To analyze such resistance, it is necessary to describe conditions related to real-time properties. SYN-flooding is a typical example, in which the number of half-open connections in a certain period of time is crucial.

Here, we propose a method for analyzing DoS attack resistance using the model checker UPPAAL based on timed automata and real-time Timed Computational Tree Logic (TCTL). We provide a model translator from expressions of spice calculus to timed automata and describe DoS attack resistance in TCTL formulae. Background

Spice calculus. The spice calculus is a formal framework based on Milner's pi calculus and Abadi et al.'s spi calculus, and therefore has very similar syntax. A detailed definition of the spice calculus has been presented previously [4]. *Processes* are expressions for program fragments that can be executed in parallel.

processes	P, Q, R,...	replication	repl P
message sending	out n <M>; P	termination	stop
message receiving	inp n(x); P	memory allocation	store x = M; P
parallel execution	(P I Q)	deallocation	free x; P
name generation	new(n); P	matching	match M is N err {P}; Q
		pair decomposition	split $[x_1,...,x_n]$ is M err{R};P

Terms are expressions describing primitive data structures.

terms	M,N,...	integer	...,−2,−1,0,1,2,...
name	m,n,n_1,n_2,...	pairing	[M_1,...,M_n]
variable	X		

The semantics of the spice calculus [4] are given as operational semantics based on transition among processes. The transition relationship between processes in the spice calculus is annotated with a cost consumed by the transition, which is the difference between the pi calculus and spice calculus.

1.1   Real-Time Model Checker UPPAAL

In software engineering, *model checking* is regarded as a genuine breakthrough, especially with regard to the improvement of software design and coding. Model checking is a technique for verifying whether a model satisfies a given specification. Models are extracted from descriptions presented as state-transition diagrams or in concurrent programming languages. The specifications are often represented by temporal logic formulae. A number of model checkers have been developed, including SPIN [5] and UPPAAL [9]. In UPPAAL, models are described in terms of timed automata using a GUI (Graphical User Interface) and specifications expressed by computational tree logic (CTL). The most distinctive feature of UPPAAL is its use of real-time clocks. We can write conditions for the branches of an automaton and verification queries using real-time clock variables to represent real-time constraints. UPPAAL can thus be applied to the verification of real-time systems [10, 11].

2   Translation of the Spice Calculus to Timed Automata

In this section, we present a translation of the spice calculus into timed automata. The timed automaton in UPPAAL is enriched with variables that store primitive values, messages that pass via communication ports, and the parallel composition of automata. Nevertheless, the timed automaton in UPPAAL is less expressive than the spice calculus. The two systems differ in that passing a port name via a message port is possible in the pi, spi, and spice calculi but not in UPPAAL. Nested parallel composition is allowed in the pi and spi calculi, but not in the spice calculus or the timed automaton in the UPPAAL, where parallel composition is only allowed in the top level. This restriction stems from limitations in dynamic process generation. For example, a process (P | (Q | R)) means that the process P is first executed, the control thread is *duplicated*, and the processes Q and R are executed in parallel. The thread duplication causes dynamic process generation. Each process in the spice calculus corresponds to an instance of an automaton template of UPPAAL. Such processes are composed in parallel at the top level without nesting. Here, we omit the formal definition of the translation from the spice calculus to the timed automaton due to a lack of space and only explain the translation with an example. Let us consider a spice calculus term that implements a simple communication protocol,

(repl P1) | P2,
where P1 is
inp c1 (r); match r is **hpswd** err{ free(r); stop};free (r); out c2 <d>; stop
and P2
store x is hash(**pswd**); out c1 <x>;free (x); inp c2 (r);free(r); stop.

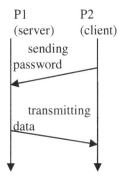

Fig. 1. Simple Com-munication Protocol

The constant **pswd** is a password and **hpswd** is its hash value. The process expression describes the communication as shown in Fig. 1. The sub-processes P1 and P2 are a server and a client, respectively. First, the client sends a hash value of a password **pswd**, which is known as **hpswd** by the server in advance. Second, the server receives the hash value of the password in a memory cell r and compares it to **hpswd**. Third, the server sends a message back to the client.

Translation Step 1: *decomposition of parallel composition processes.*
In UPPAAL, each process is sequentially executed and their parallelism is represented as a juxtaposition of sequential processes. The above-mentioned process ((repl P1) | P2) is decomposed into two processes (repl P1) and P2.

Translation Step 2: *finitely approximate expansion of repetition processes.*
Informally, replication (repl P) means an infinite number of parallel compositions; a congruence that (repl P) ≡ P | (repl P) and therefore (repl P) ≡ P | P | P | ... It bears some resemblance to the Unix™ *fork ()* system call. As such infinite features cannot be handled, we substituted a finite number of parallel compositions for the infinite number. For example, we can replace

repl P
with
(repl P) | (repl P) | (repl P)

where (repl P) is equivalent to P and the annotation symbol repl indicates that it originates from process replication. The spice calculus [4] has a restriction that parallel execution is only allowed in the outermost construct. We call components of the parallel execution *sequential processes.*

Translation Step 3: *global declaration of constants and a clock variable.*
This step is independent of the first step. A model obtained by the translation computes the costs of execution. We declare constants representing units of each type of cost. The cost units are defined as

> const int TC_repl = 0;
> const int TC_store = 1;
> const int TC_free = 1;
>   …
> const int TC_comm = 100;

where TC_*Name* represents the unit of cost *Name*.

Variables for storing costs are provided for the CPU nodes and costs. Although the number of CPU nodes is large in the real world, we assume it to be sufficiently small to enable the model checker UPPALL to verify the model in a realistic time.

Types of cost values are defined as a struct type cost in which each field corresponds to a type of computational cost. The following is an example of such a struct type:

> typedef struct {
> int c_repl;
> int c_store;
>   …
> } cost;

The fields c_repl and c_store represent costs of process replication and memory allocation, respectively.

Variables for recording costs are declared by the struct type. Such variables are prepared for each CPU node. For example, if two CPU nodes a and b are assumed, then we declare two variables a and b:

> cost a, b;

For each CPU node, a clock variable is declared to represent the local time of the CPU node. If we assume two nodes a and b, we declare two clock variables ts_a and ts_b:

> clock ts_a, ts_b;

We adopt the naming convention where the name of a clock variable for a CPU node *NodeName* is ts_ *NodeName*.

Channels for inter-process synchronous communication are also declared. For example,

> chan c1, c2;

Translation Step 4: *generation of process templates.*
A process template T_P of UPPAAL is generated from each process P of the spice calculus. It has two formal parameters ts and c in reference-passing, which are declared as

> clock &ts, &c;

For each type of computation step (reduction steps in the previous paper [4]), a locally defined function is provided to compute its cost value. For example, a function store() is defined for memory allocation:

```
void store () {
ts = 0;
c.c_store++;
}
```

A timed automaton of the process template is defined by induction of the structure of the sequential process. Operations in the sequential process are matched   to pairs of a state node and a transition edge in the timed automaton. A process (store x = M ; P) is translated into a timed automaton.

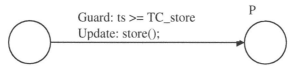

Processes (out *port* <*message*>; P) and (inp *port* (x); P) are translated into the following timed automata, respectively.

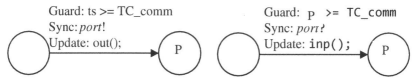

A type of conditional branch matching (match M is N err {P}; Q) is translated into a diverging node as

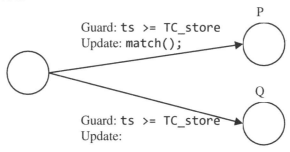

For example, the process P1 shown at the beginning of Section 3 is translated into the following timed automaton.

Translation Step 5: *Instantiation of process templates*
Finally, we instantiate the process templates obtained in the previous step. The process replication is handled statically in this phase. That is, a process to be replicated is duplicated a certain finite number of times as process instantiation, in place of dynamic process duplication in standard pi calculus. For example, if a replication (repl P) is approximated by three copies generated by process instantiation, we write the following description in system declaration as

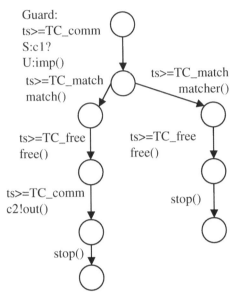

Fig. 2. Automaton of P1

P0 = T_P(ts_a, a);
P1 = T_P(ts_a, a);
P2 = T_P(ts_a, a);

For a non-replication process (say Q), we make a single instantiation as

Q0= T_Q(ts_b, b);

The variables P0, P1, P2, and Q0 are declared as system variables as follows:

system P0, P1, P2, Q0;

We implemented software based on the translation introduced in the previous section. The program is written in the programming language Ruby [11] and uses the parser generator Racc for Ruby. The input file for the translator is a source code file in the spice calculus and the output file is an XML file, which describes a timed automaton and passes to the UPPAAL model checker. We give the number of duplications as an approximation of replication, as a parameter.

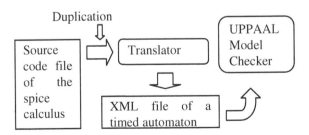

Examples of analysis using the translator and UPPAAL model checker

We applied the translator proposed in the previous section and the UPPAAL model checker to an example of TCP SYN-flooding attack [1]. In this section, we present an example of analysis of the DoS attack resistance by comparing two networking situations with different bandwidths.

We consider a process expression

repl Pi | Pn | Pn | repl Pb

where Pi is an attacker process, Pn is a process modeling a network, and Pb is a victim server process. We have omitted the definitions of the three processes here due to space constraints, but further details are presented in our previous paper [4]. We analyze the process under two types of configuration.

1   Both processes Pn are executed on the same node N1.
2   The two processes Pn are executed on two distinct nodes. The left occurrence of Pn is executed on node N1 and the right occurrence is executed on node N2.

The configurations (1) and (2) represent two networks with different bandwidths. The network of (1) is slower than that of (2).

We analyze the length of time for which the computation cost of the server exceeds a certain limit. If the duration is short, then it costs the attacker more, because the server falls into heavy load more easily. As memory allocation is the primary cost in the server, we focus on the memory allocation cost c_store. We can determine the length of time for which c_store reaches a value n by verifying the query formula

$$E \Diamond b.c\_store \geq n$$

and detecting its counter example with the "fastest" option. The length of time required by the counter example is the duration that we wish to determine. We analyze the query formula assuming the variable n to be several positive integer values. The results of this experiment are as follows.

n	1	2	3	4	5	6	7	8	9
(1)	202	203	203	203	402	403	403	403	false
(2)	202	203	203	203	304	305	305	305	false

(The query formula does not hold in the case n = 0.)

In this table, we know that the length of time in configuration (2) is longer than that in (1). This result indicates that in the faster network the attacker applies a heavier attack on the victim server.

3   Concluding Remarks

We have proposed a method for analyzing communication protocols from the viewpoint of DoS attack resistance. We focused on real-time properties related to resistance. In this method, we first formulated a communication protocol in terms of the spice calculus and then translated the expressions of the spice calculus into timed automata. Then we analyzed the timed automata using the real-time model checker

UPPAAL. Through an example of an SYN-flood attack, we demonstrated the effectiveness of our method. Several issues remain regarding the method proposed in this paper. One such issue is the efficiency of verification, which we did not consider in the translation from the spice calculus to the timed automata. Therefore, the timed automata that can be handled by the model checker are still very limited. Further studies are required to improve the translation from the viewpoint of verification efficiency.

References

1. Comer, E.D.: Internetworking with TCP/IP, vol. 1. Prentice Hall (2005)
2. CERT Advisory CA-1996-21 TCP SYN Flooding and IP Spoofing Attacks (1996), http://www.cert.org/advisories/CA-1996-21.html
3. Meadows, C.: A formal framework and evaluation method for network denial of service. In: Proceedings of the 12th IEEE Computer Security Foundations Workshop, pp. 4–13 (1999)
4. Tomioka, D., Nishizaki, S., Ikeda, R.: A Cost Estimation Calculus for Analyzing the Resistance to Denial-of-Service Attack. In: Futatsugi, K., Mizoguchi, F., Yonezaki, N. (eds.) ISSS 2003. LNCS, vol. 3233, pp. 25–44. Springer, Heidelberg (2004)
5. Ikeda, R., Narita, K., Nishizaki, S.: Cooperative approach to qualitative and quantitative cost analyses of distributed system. In: Proceedings of the 13th International Conference on Software Engineering and Application 2009, pp. 126–132 (2009)
6. Milner, R., Parrow, J., Walker, D.: A calculus of mobile processes, Part I and Part II. Information and Computation 100(1), 1–77 (1992)

Research of Automatic Conversion from UML Sequence Diagram to CPN Based on Modular Conversion

LianZhang Zhu and FanSheng Kong

College of Computer and Communication Engineering, China University of Petroleum,
Qingdao 266555, China

Abstract. Failures which result from performance defects are always fatal to the development of software. The best way to solve this problem is to bring performance evaluation mechanism of software into the process of software development life cycle through the way of modeling and simulation of software. Because of the differences between the semantic of UML and CPN, this paper applies the though of modular conversion, providing an intermediate model to standardize UML sequence diagram and CPN models, which establishes a bridge between the two models. The process is automatic and needs little manual intervention. The converted CPN models can be used in software performance evaluation directly. An example is given to verify the effectiveness and reasonability of this method.

Keywords: CPN, sequence diagram, performance evaluation, automatic conversion, modular conversion.

1   Introduction

The development of large-scale software is based on software development life cycle usually, but performance always comes out accurately after the completion of software, when the failure of software performance means the failure of the whole software. Therefore, the introduction of performance evaluation mechanism during software development cycle is of great significance to ensure the performance quality of software.

From the 1980s, many scientists begin to discuss software performance evaluation. For example, Lazowska using queuing network[1], Lin chuang using Petri net[2], Compare using Stochastic process algebras[3]. All of these can be called solution-based, which can also be applied to evaluate software performance. Although these solutions are reliable and accurate, it becomes very difficult to compute because of the state space explosion when the system reaches a certain size. Marsan, Giovanni, Kurt, Wells, etc. give methods of performance evaluation from the perspective of software modeling and simulation using Petri nets and colored Petri net (CPN)[4-7], which have the advantage of modeling and simulating, and largely avoid the problem of state space explosion. This method is considered to be one of the most suitable ways for system performance evaluation. However, this method requires evaluation

M. Zhao and J. Sha (Eds.): ICCIP 2012, Part I, CCIS 288, pp. 95–102, 2012.

staff to build evaluation models by themselves, which requires to master CPN, and this may be a very great challenge to most general performance evaluation staff.

Given the wide range of applications of the Unified Modeling Language (UML) in software development life cycle, the most effective way to solve the problem of software performance is considered to build performance evaluation models from the pre-established UML documents and simulate, evaluate the models dynamically, which is the key of performance evaluation. Smith also published a book, introducing performance engineering to software engineering firstly[8]. Currently methods applying UML modeling and simulation to performance evaluation all over the world can be divided into three types:

The first type is theoretical exploration. Gherbi, Liehr, etc. focused on discussing how to extend the UML model to the performance evaluation model based on UML-SPT or MARTE specification [9,10] Miga, Liehr discuss the scenario demands activity and accessibility by the means of use-case diagram mapping mechanism (UCM) , activity sequence diagram (LSC) [11,12]; Letichevsky, Harel, etc. research the state space of message sequence chart using tracking technology [12,13]. These works confirm the ability of UML extension mechanisms to express the performance of software, and gives guidance strategies and methods. Unfortunately, these theoretical results have no platforms. There are still lots of work to do from UML diagrams to the output of performance evaluation results.

The second kind of method is largely based on the characteristics of UML performance models, dividing the execution of process into modules, branch, loop firstly, then secondly calculating the entire process or part of the resource utilization, resource consumption time of the process according to the resource utilization, resource consumption time of each module, and computing model throughput, resource utilization and other performance indicators by the method of queuing network (QN) or hierarchical queuing network (LQN). Some typical representatives are Smith, Marzolla, Petriu [8, 14-16]. We call these methods for the static calculation methods. Such methods have the advantages of simple calculation and having the only results, but it is not always easy to express the execution of process using modules in order, branches, and loops. For example, random page-visitor problems, state space explosion, also challenge the calculation of performance indicators.

The third kind of method is mainly focused on converting UML performance models directly into the executable CPN model based on the characteristics of them [17-20], which we call dynamic simulation. Due to CPN has the ability of Turing machines[6], which is considered the most effective methods for software performance evaluation. Shin, Shinkawa study the conversion mechanism from UML system model to CPN [17]. Fernandes figures the conversion from UML use case diagram, sequence diagram to CPN [18]. Staines gives transformation rules from UML activity diagram to CPN [19]. These methods avoid the shortage of the second method through simulation. But because of the semantic differences between CPN and UML, it is difficult to make an effective correspondence between them, and always requires a lot of manual interventions, which is not conducive to achieve the automatic conversion.

The method this article describes introduces an intermediate layer - the "middle model" between the UML and the CPN model, which provides a support similar to the advanced structured programming language, in addition to a programming language's support for the structured process such as order, branches, loops, but also the support of introduction of events-arriving strategy and random responses. This method makes it quite easy to convert UML models to the intermediate model, which features can be well supported in the CPN model. Intermediate model is composed of a variety of types of nodes. In the process of conversion to CPN model, each type of node has a specific corresponding with CPN module, so we can establish a direct correspondence between the intermediate model and the CPN model. The intermediate model can solve the UML / CPN semantic differences, and provides a basis for the automatic conversion from UML to CPN. By this method, performance evaluators can get performance information at any time during development as long as there are enough UML models to use. This is meaningful for understanding the software performance accurately and availability in advance in large-scale software development cycle and avoiding development failure resulted from software performance failure.

2   Automatic Conversion Based on Module

According to the characteristics of current life-cycle in software engineering, the general software development process consists of requirements, design, construction, testing, and maintenance. Each stage will generate the corresponding UML documents, and these UML documentations are not suitable for software performance because of inadequate information. But we can get performance parameters after adding some information to them. This process involves three stages. Firstly, UML models become UML performance evaluation models through extension, then extracting the intermediate model according to some certain specifications from them. And finally transform the intermediate models into CPN performance evaluation model. The CPN models can execute directly. This paper mainly discusses the automatic conversion from UML sequence diagram to CPN.

2.1   Intermediate Model

In the process of Transformation from UML to CPN, we need to analyze the process of UML performance evaluation models and identify input parameters in the process, including the nodes and their characteristics, which are sequence, branch, loop, parallel, etc. and the randomness of the incident response, serving-strategy and the identification of the introduced parameters, etc. The key technology of the operation is the identification and storage of predecessor nodes and subsequent nodes. Given all that above, we need to build some specific node structures, forming the meta-model library.

Since UML models need to be extended before used to evaluate software. This paper standardizes the extended information and classifies the elements needed to be attracted in UML according to characteristics of CPN models after a lot of research. The properties of nodes contain the information needed for automatic conversion and performance evaluation applying CPN models. These nodes are also similar to the stereotype in UML.

1) Simple node: It is a description of the simplest node in the process similar to the basic statements in high-level programming language. It is corresponding to a transaction and a place in CPN. Its attributes are shown in Fig 1:

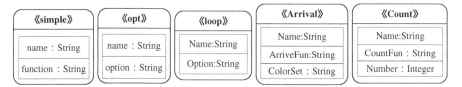

Fig. 1. Structure of simple, opt, loop, Arrical, and Count node

2) Structure Node: a) OPT node is similar to the "if" statement in high-level programming language, depending on a guard condition to determine whether to execute. The structure of OPT and LOOP node is shown in Fig 1. b) PAR node represents that a segment in the process is executed in parallel, and CPN also has its own advantages in describing parallel and concurrent. PAR node's structures as shown in Fig. 2:

3) Functional Node: it is a class of nodes with specific functions which maps a complex CPN module in order to facilitate the realization of automatic conversion, different from the simple node. These nodes are abstract according to some certain functions. For example, Arrival node is designed to represent the event-arriving strategy (arriving-rate, distribution that events are subject to, etc.). Structures are shown in Fig. 1.

4) Resource node represents the information of resources used in the process. Its parameters include the initial number of resources, access time, and default-use time. Structure is shown in Fig.2.

5) Resource-Visit node: It represents the visit to a range of resources, recording the information related to resource uses, including time spent to get and the time spent to use. Structure is shown in Fig 2.

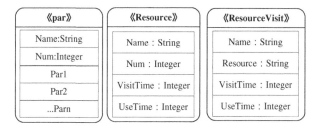

Fig. 2. Structure of Resource node

The identified nodes from UML are stored in the intermediate model in a form similar to high-level programming language. XMI (XML-based Metadata Interchange) provides programmers and other users with the standard methods of metadata information exchange using the Extensible Markup Language (XML). The aim is to help programmers who use the Unified Modeling Language (UML) and different languages and development tools to exchange data model. This intermediate model supports XMI format. By extracting the intermediate model, we convert a two-dimensional UML diagram into a one-dimensional linear model, which becomes very easier to traverse and conducive to realize the goal of automatic conversion.

2.2   The Extension of UML Models

The UML maps generated in general software design cycle are lack of information required for performance evaluation, so we need to introduce the information required for performance evaluation into the UML design model by UML extension mechanism. In detail, according to the UML maps generated in software development life cycle, after performance extensions, Extracting intermediate model from them according to the requirements of performance evaluation through the simplification and analysis, then converting to a CPN model. UML2.0 provides expansion mechanisms: tagged values, constraints and stereotypes, and extended content format references to the UML SPT (UML Profile for Schedulability, Performance and Time Specification) [21].

UML SPT provides a good reference for UML model-based expansion, but the information is insufficient to achieve automatic conversion from UML to CPN. Nodes presented in Fig.1-2 contain enough information for software performance evaluation and automatic conversion, and they are equivalent to stereotypes in the UML.

2.3   The Conversion from Intermediate Model to CPN

After the expansion of UML, the extraction operation of the intermediate mode begins. The methods of extraction are different due to the different output formats of different modeling software. The authors in this paper did a lot of research of the extraction from UML sequence diagram built in StarUML, and develop extracting strategy.

After extraction of the intermediate model, it is the nest step to start conversion from the intermediate model to the CPN model. Due to the fact that in the process of design of intermediate model and nodes, every node is designed to represent one certain CPN module, each node has a corresponding CPN model. The node in intermediate model is linked to CPN module according to functions. The CPN module is compared to a black box, which is not visible to intermediate model and it is also not necessary. The information contained in the attributes of each node are the information the CPN module need to acquire.

For example, the conversion mechanism from structure node in the intermediate model to the CPN model is as followed. The intermediate model is represented as a tree structure by means of XML. Structure node has four kinds of nodes: OPT, PAR, CASE, and LOOP. Figure 3 shows an OPT node and its corresponding CPN model: Option corresponding to the conditions in CPN model, transition T2 is execution sequence after meeting the conditions.

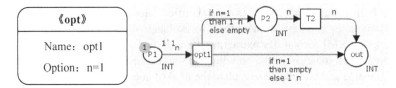

Fig. 3. Example of the opt node and its corresponding CPN

3   Automatic Conversion Instance

This paper further illustrates the automatic conversion theory through an example. Figure 4(a) shows a process of handling user requiring using resource "Server". Sequence diagram use loop symbol to indicate this repeat process. The arrival of user is subject to some strategy.

1) The sequence diagram and its expansion. The expansion in this sequence diagram focuses on the message and object. In this case, the object Server is expanded as resource node, and then the call messages are expanded as resource-visit node. Routing structure loop is extended to structure nodes. After the expansion of sequence diagram, the next step is to extract the intermediate model.

Fig. 4. (a) sequence diagram; (b) intermediate model in xml format

2) Automatic conversion from UML to CPN. The intermediate model extracted is shown in Figure 4(b). Nodes represent the node sequence, Resources represents all the resources used in this process. After extracting the Intermediate model, the next step is to translate every node to its corresponding CPN model following the thought of modular conversion. The transformed CPN model is shown in Figure 5. The resource-visit node and arrival node are represented as Substitution Transitions in order to demonstrate briefly. This CPN model starts with the Arrivals node, and ends with an end node. In order to ensure the transformed CPN model can run correctly, it needs to construct the necessary variable declarations and ML blocks and functions (such as exptime ()). This is no longer described in detail.

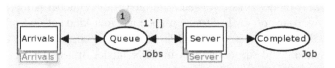

Fig. 5. The converted CPN model

Transformed CPN model can run directly. On this basis of this model, performance evaluator can modify the model with individual needs, such as adding a monitor to a place, which can obtains certain aspects of performance evaluation information after simulation. In this case, we add monitors to this CPN model in order to get information about delay time and queue length. Etc.

After adding monitors, we set simulation steps to 100. When the simulation ends, the LOG file generated by the monitor records all the information needed to be recorded. Performance indicators can be obtained from the output file of simulation. The untimed statistics generated in output file is shown in Table 1.

Table 1. Simulation report

Untimed statistics							
Name	Count	Sum	Avrg	95% Half Length	StD	Min	Max
Count_trans_ occur_Arrival s'Arrive_1	34	34	1.0	0.0	0.0	1	1
Long_Delay_ Times	33	22	0.6666 67	0.17016 7	0.478 714	0	1
Queue_Delay	33	8868	268.72 7273	60.6866 96	170.7 24060	0	588
Server_Utiliz ation_by_Pro cTime	1	0.85403 7	0.8540 37	Insuffic ent	0.000 000	0.8540 37	0.854 037
Total_Process ing_Time	33	2933.0	88.878 788	35.0330 48	98.55 5111	1.0000 00	532.0 00000

4   Conclusion

This paper presents an approach of conversion from the UML sequence diagram into the intermediate model, and then converted to CPN model, which resolves the problem of needing a lot of manual interventions due to the differences between the natures of maps. After the conversion from the UML model to the intermediate model, every type of nodes is organized according to the process. Each node is corresponding to a certain CPN module, thus establishing the correspondence between the CPN and UML. The transformed CPN model can be directly used for performance evaluation, providing the basis for the automation of large-scale software performance evaluation. So in the software development life cycle, performance evaluation can be implemented quickly at any time in order to prevent software failure caused by performance problems. However, the conversion method in this paper still needs improvements in some areas: such as functional class classified, variable declaration in the CPN, ML function block and the establishment of function library.

References

1. Lazowska, E.D., et al.: Quantitative System Performance. Prentice-Hall, Inc. (1984)
2. Lin, C.: Stochastic Petri net and system performance evaluation. Tsinghua University Press, Beijing (2005)

3. Compare, D., et al.: Our experience in the integration of process algebra based performance validation in an industrial context. Tech. Rep. TR SAH/047, MIUR Sahara Project (2003)
4. Marsan, M.A.: On Petri Net-Based Modeling Paradigms for the Performance Analysis of Wireless Internet Accesses. In: PNPM 2001 (2001)
5. Denaro, G., Pezzé, M.: Petri Nets and Software Engineering. In: Desel, J., Reisig, W., Rozenberg, G. (eds.) ACPN 2003. LNCS, vol. 3098, pp. 439–466. Springer, Heidelberg (2004)
6. Kurt, J.: Colored Petri Nets. Basic Concepts, Analysis Methods and Practical Use. Basic Concepts. Monographs in Theoretical Computer Science, vol. 1. Springer, Berlin (1997)
7. Wells, L.: Performance Analysis using CPN Tools. In: Proc. First International Conference on Performance Evaluation Methodologies and Tools (ValueTools 2006), pp. 1–10. ACM Press (2006)
8. Smith, C.U.: Performance Engineering of Software Systems. Addison-Wesley (1990)
9. Gherbi, A., Khendek, F.: From UML/SPT models to schedulability analysis: approach and a prototype implementation using ATL. Autom. Softw. Eng. 16, 387–414 (2009)
10. Liehr, A.W., Buchenrieder, K.J.: Generation of MARTE Allocation Models from Activity Threads, Languages for Embedded Systems and Their Applications. LNEE, vol. 36. Springer Science + Business Media B.V (2009)
11. Miga, A., Amyot, D., Bordeleau, F., Cameron, D., Woodside, C.M.: Deriving Message Sequence Charts from Use Case Maps Scenario Specifications. In: Reed, R., Reed, J. (eds.) SDL 2001. LNCS, vol. 2078, p. 268. Springer, Heidelberg (2001)
12. Harel, D., Kugler, H.-J., Weiss, G.: Some Methodological Observations Resulting from Experience Using LSCs and the Play-In/Play-Out Approach. In: Leue, S., Systä, T.J. (eds.) Scenarios. LNCS, vol. 3466, pp. 26–42. Springer, Heidelberg (2005)
13. Letichevsky, A.A., Kapitonova, J.V., Kotlyarov, V.P., Volkov, V.A., Letichevsky Jr., A.A., Weigert, T.: Semantics of Message Sequence Charts. In: Prinz, A., Reed, R., Reed, J. (eds.) SDL 2005. LNCS, vol. 3530, pp. 117–132. Springer, Heidelberg (2005)
14. Marzolla, M., Balsamo, S.: UML-PSI: the UML performance simulator. In: First International Conference on the Quantitative Evaluation of Systems, QEST 2004, pp. 340–341 (2004)
15. Abdullatif, A.A., Pooley, R.J.: UML-JMT: A Tool for Evaluating Performance Requirements. In: 17th IEEE International Conference and Workshops on Engineering of Computer Based Systems (ECBS), pp. 215–225 (2010)
16. Petriu, D.C., Shen, H.: Applying the UML Performance Profile: Graph Grammar-Based Derivation of LQN Models from UML Specifications. In: Field, T., Harrison, P.G., Bradley, J., Harder, U. (eds.) TOOLS 2002. LNCS, vol. 2324, pp. 159–177. Springer, Heidelberg (2002)
17. Salvatore, D., et al.: From UML to Petri Nets: The PCM-Based Methodology. IEEE Transactions on Software Engineering 37(1), 65–79 (2011)
18. Fernandes, J.M., et al.: Designing Tool Support for Translating Use Cases and UML 2.0 Sequence Diagrams into a Coloured Petri Net. In: Sixth International Workshop on Scenarios and State Machines, SCESM 2007 (2007)
19. Staines, T.: Intuitive Mapping of UML 2 Activity Diagrams into Fundamental Modeling Concept Petri Net Diagrams and Colored Petri Nets. In: ECBS 2008 (2008)
20. Zhang, H., Zhu, L.: Building dynamic model in UML using colored petri nets. In: 1st International Symposium on Computer Network and Multimedia Technology, CNMT 2009 (2009)
21. Object Management Group (OMG). UML Profile for Schedulability, Performance and Time specification. Final Adopted Specification ptc/02-03-02, OMG (2002)

Study and Design of Workflow Model and Modeling Methods in Highway Engineering Measurement and Payment System Based on Workflow

Junqing Liang[1], Shaohua Zhao[2], and Xiaoyun Xiong[1]

[1] School of Computer Engineering,
Qingdao Technological University, Qingdao, China
[2] Qingdao Letong Civil Group, Qingdao, China
{junqingl,zhaoshaohua6167}@163.com

Abstract. In this paper, with the relevant knowledge of workflow, we created the model for these steady business processes in the payment of highway engineering measurement, and brought up an examination and approval workflow in detail; presented a flow nesting modeling method to resolve the question of work order rollback in the examination and approval flow of trust certificate, and did very detailed instance analysis and comparison.

Keywords: Highway engineering, Measurement and Payment, Workflow Model, Modeling.

1   Introduction

Study and design of Workflow model and modeling methods in highway engineering measurement and payment system based on workflow, which realizes information sharing, standardizes control flow. It can meet the requirements of different users from different engineering, improve the management level, and ensure the completion of engineering with high quality and efficient.

The business process in the measurement and payment process of highway engineering can be distributed into two classes: the first class is business of transmission, including the approval of contract, trust certificate, detailed interim measurement, measurement and payment, modification, and so on; second is business of processing, including the confirmation of detailed list, the management of basic data, the calculation of bill quantities, the management of document, etc. the business of transmission is the most important application of workflow in highway engineering measurement and payment system.

In this paper, combined with the establishment method of workflow meta-model, we create the model of trust certificate approval workflow and interim measurement approval workflow, and put forward a flow nesting modeling method to resolve the question of work order rollback in the workflow model of this system. We described in

M. Zhao and J. Sha (Eds.): ICCIP 2012, Part I, CCIS 288, pp. 103–109, 2012.

detail the method of flow nesting modeling and its application in highway engineering measurement and payment.

The rest chapters in this paper are organized as follows: Section 2 introduces the f establishment and analysis of workflow model. The flow nesting modeling method and its application is especially described in Section 3. Finally we summarize this paper in Section 4.

2   The Establishment and Analysis of Workflow Model

In highway engineering construction supervision measurement and payment system, every entire workflow contains task, people, document information and rules. So we can use object, role, routing and rule to analyze workflow. There are different characteristics in different workflow. Analyzed with the above method, every workflow can be present with a directed graph as below.

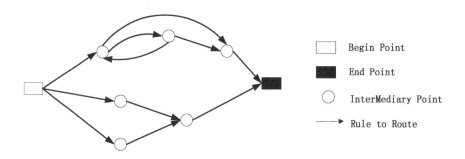

Fig. 1. The direxted graph of workflow

In the directed graph, every node indicates a step in the process. It is used to express that the operator of this step manipulate an object. The operator is a role of the process. Each edge indicates the document object changed from one step to another step with some rules. All nodes from begin of a workflow instance to the end form a possible route.

In highway engineering measurement and payment system, the object refers to the documents, sheets, events, notifications, etc.; role refers to the contractor, supervisor, etc.; route refers these start, middle and end nodes passed through by a workflow object; rule refers to all rules or conditions which impact workflow object. The examination and approval of trust certificate is an important measurement part in the examination and approval of interim measurement, which directly determines the progress of interim measurement. The trust certificate involved the engineering basic information, the examination and approval of bill quantities confirmation sheet, the result of examination and approval, and so on. The trust certificate basic flow chart is shown as follows:

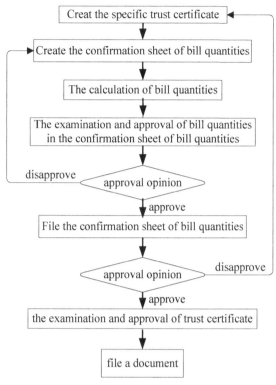

Fig. 2. The examination and approval processes of trust certificate

According to the actual business need of trust certificate examination and approval, we set some authority and rules for the activity of different users accessing workflow to ensure the implementation of the workflow. The design of the process instance is described in detail as table 1.

Table 1. The relationship table of trust certificate examination and approval processes

Activity Name	Activity Roles	Change Condition
Create the specific trust certificate	contractor	begin to do interim measurement
Create the confirmation sheet of bill quantities	contractor	the specific engineering has filled with measurement condition
The calculation of bill quantities in the confirmation sheet of bill quantities	contractor	the specific engineering has filled with measurement condition
The examination and approval of bill quantities in the confirmation sheet of bill quantities	supervisor	the checking of bill quantities
File the confirmation sheet of bill quantities	contractor, supervisor	the examination and approval of sub-process has passed
the examination and approval of trust certificate	Supervisor	the checking of bill quantities and others engineering information
file a document	contractor, supervisor	the examination and approval of whole process has passed

After analyzing the examination and approval of interim measurement and payment in the system, we extract the various elements involved in the examination and approval process of measurement and payment, and adapt the examination and approval workflow diagram of measurement and payment as below.

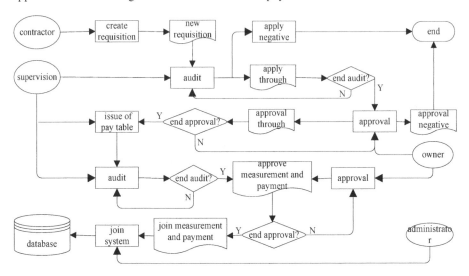

Fig. 3. The examination and approval workflow diagram of measurement and payment

3   The Flow Nesting Modeling Method and Its Application

Modeling workflow is a quantitative description process for Fig. 1. The most common way is to use points, edges in the Fig. as basic element, and to use modeling tools or process modeling and analysis. In the measurement and payment of highway engineering, the modeling process is to do the process modeling and analysis for each of basic elements in Fig. 3. The Specific modeling method will be completed in next work. In this paper, we using the flow nesting modeling method for resolving the question of work order rollback in the examination and approval flow of trust certificate.

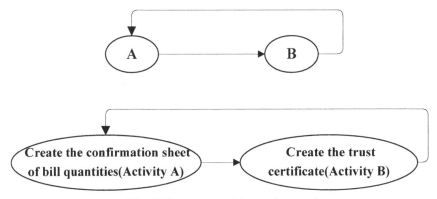

Fig. 4. The instance of the the flow nesting

In above Fig., there two activities: A and B. In the examination and approval process of detailed interim measurement, activity A is creating the confirmation sheet of bill quantities, and activity B is creating the trust certificate. This process is realized by some program. According to Fig. 1, the need of this program is: after activity A (creating the confirmation sheet of bill quantities) processed, activity B (creating the trust certificate) began to process; if the data in the confirmation sheet of bill quantities need to re-calculation, then after activity B processed, the result will be back to the activity A re-processing. In this case, we can use block to process.

Block is a way for looping execution a series of activities. It is usually a part of the process. You can set the condition of exit. Only meeting the exit conditions of the whole block, the block will exit the loop. However, the block does not mean the loops with high performance and high capacity. More important is only when all activities in a block end, the block should end. The end condition of an activity must be one of the following three conditions: an activity ends itself; an activity is forced to terminate; an activities enter into a dead path and cannot be executed.

Combining with the practical application, in the examination and approval processes of trust certificate, the creating end condition of active trust certificate is that the confirmation sheet of active bill quantities is forced to end. Because the bill quantities in the confirmation sheet of active bill quantities still don't be confirmed in that time. So the second action will roll back the work order to the first action, in other words, it needs roll back the confirmation sheet immediately without waiting the process end of other nodes in the block. Therefore, another available method of rolling back process is provided, that is using sub-flow nesting method to resolve above question. For example:

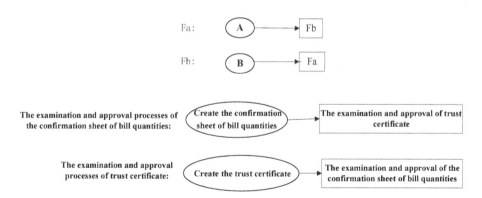

Fig. 5. The instance of the sub-flow nesting

As shown in Fig. 5, two processes are created:

Process a (Fa) is composed of activity A and sub-process Fb,
Process b (Fb) is composed of activity B and sub-process Fa.

When process "a" is executed, first executes activity A, then sub-process F. If we need the operation of rolling back after completion of activity B, with meeting some condition the sub-process Fa of process Fb will be called. That will lead to the execution of activity A once again, and ensure the implementation of rolling back operation. The use of sub-process can greatly improve the reusability of the system. Any process can be reused as sub-processes. When multiple processes need to reuse a more complex processing logic unit, this processing logic unit can be encapsulated as a sub-process. Its advantage is that you can only modify sub-process one time, while using block, you must modify in all place that call this block.

The processing of previous rolling back question is comple te with manual methods. In this case, it usually leads to the cancel of bill quantities confirmation sheet because of the examination and approve question of bill quantities, and finally leads to the cancel of corresponding trust certificate. The trust certificate isn't a common file which can be printed in system; it is a special regular file with a number, tripartite sheets are the important payment evidence. This rolling back incident must lead to the discontinuities and waste of trust certificate, and lead to affect the whole process of measurement and payment.

In the practical modeling process, we introduce the nesting flow approach. The design methods are: process "a" refers to the examination and approval of trust certificate, it is composed of the creating the specific trust certificate and the examination and approval process of bill quantities confirmation sheet; process "b" refers to the examination and approval of bill quantities confirmation sheet, it is composed of the creating the bill quantities confirmation sheet and the examination and approval process of trust certificate. The specific implementation procedures are described as follow. Before creating the trust certificate, we should create the confirmation sheet of bill quantities. After created the confirmation sheet of bill quantities, if we find the bill quantities are not up to standard, must do the operation of rolling back for calling the examination and approval process of bill quantities confirmation sheet. It will ensure the examination and approval process of trust certificate can be called once again. The creating operation of trust certificate can be active and performed again. This method not only meets the needs of flow nesting, but also save resources, increases workflow flexibility.

4   Conclusions

In this paper, using the relevant knowledge of workflow to abstract the stable business process in the measurement and payment of highway engineering with presentation method of the directed graph, we summarize workflow of the trust certificate and interim measurement examination and approval process. By further analysis of these models, we presented a flow nesting modeling method to resolve the question of work order rollback in the examination and approval flow of trust certificate, and do very detailed instance analysis and comparison. In the practical design and applications of system, the method of examination and approval flow and the flow nesting modeling can reduce manual operation, avoid of waste of trust certificate and cost savings. It can provide reliable guarantee for the strict control of all processes in measurement and payment process. Exploring and perfecting the special model and relevant modeling tools is the focus of our work in nest step.

References

1. Liao, Z.X., Gao, F.: Research on integration technology of workflow automatization with GIS in electronic government system. Journal of Hefei University of Technology (Natural Science) 28(3), 35–37 (2005)
2. Sun, R.Z., Shi, M.L.: The meta-model of Supporting dynamic workflow process. Journal of Software 14(1) (2003)
3. Li, W.G.: Study the workflow modeling and control Flow based Execution. Computer Engineering and Applications 44(3), 98–100 (2008)
4. Lin, L., Cai, Z.Y., Zhang, L.: The design and application of the workflow modeling based the extended directed graph. Computer Applications 28(9), 2437–2439
5. WfMC. The Workflow Reference Model (1995)
6. Fan, Y.S.: Fundamentals of workflow management Technology. Tsinghua University Press, Beijing (2001)
7. Georgakopolous, D., Honick, M., Sheth, A.: An Overview of Workflow Management: From Process Modeling to Workflow Automation Infrastructure. Distribute and Parallel Dtabase 3(2), 326–348 (1995)
8. Williams, T.J.: The Purdue Enterprise Reference Architecture. Computer in Industry (1994)
9. Zhang, Z.Y., Tian, Q.J.: A workflow-based software requirements analysis, and application of computer engineering 17, 106–109 (2002)
10. Lin, T., Zhang, Z.H., Li, H.C.: The Research of the Application of the process model in the Workflow system. Computer Applications 22(6) (2002)
11. Rosenstein, M.T., Collins, J.J., De Luca, C.J.: A practical method for calculating largest Lyapunov exponents from small data sets. Physica D 65, 117–134 (1993)
12. Friedman, J.H., Bentley, J.L., Finkel, R.A.: ACM Trans. Math. Soft. 3, 209 (1977)
13. Oiwa, N.N., Fiedler-Ferrara, N.: A fast algorithm for estimating Lyapunov exponents from time series. Physics Letters A 246, 117–121 (1998)
14. Xiong, B., He, M., Yu, H.: Algorithm for Finding k-Nearest Neighbors of Scattered Points in Three Dimension. Journal of Computer-aided Design & Computer Graphcis 16(7), 909–917 (2004)

Formal Framework for Cost Analysis
Based on Process Algebra

Shin-ya Nishizaki and Hiroki Kiyoto

Department of Computer Science, Tokyo Institute of Technology
2-12-1-W8-69, O-okayama, Meguro-ku, Tokyo, 152-8552, Japan
nisizaki@cs.titech.ac.jp

Abstract. Several formal systems have been proposed for reasoning about concurrent systems. The Algebra of Communicating Processes (ACP) is proposed by J. A. Bergstra and J. W. Klop, and an algebraic system for such reasoning. In such formal systems, the equivalence between processes is the fundamental relation for reasoning, and several kinds of equivalence have been investigated in the process algebras. These equivalence relations are based on behavior of processes. Recently, the computational cost in execution of processes is considered to be one of the important factors in concurrent systems and is beginning to interest to us. For example, the denial-of-service attacks are related to it closely. We developed a formal system for reasoning about computational costs of concurrent systems in the previous works, based on the Milner's pi-calculus. In this paper, we investigate another system based on ACP.

Keywords: process algebra, the algebra of communicating systems, ACP, cost analysis, concurrent systems.

1 Introduction

A denial-of-service (DoS) attack is an attempt to make a system resource unavailable to its intended users. Several types of DoS attacks are known, and those that are caused by the vulnerability of a network protocol are known to be serious. A SYN flood attack is a typical example of this, exploiting the vulnerability of TCP's three-way handshake with respect to inappropriate imbalances between the computational costs of clients and server.

Meadow's work [1] is a pioneering study of a formal framework for describing and analyzing protocols with respect to DoS attack resistance. The framework is a kind of protocol description in the Alice-and-Bob style, in which a computational cost is annotated with each communication step of the protocol. Although the Alice-and-Bob-style specification is easy to understand, it lacks accuracy in some cases. To address these inaccuracies, we propose a formal system for analyzing DoS attack resistance. The system is called the spice-calculus [2] and is based on Milner's pi-calculus [3] and Abadi and Gordon's spi-calculus[4]. Because a process calculus is more accretive and more precise than the Alice-and-Bob style for describing

M. Zhao and J. Sha (Eds.): ICCIP 2012, Part I, CCIS 288, pp. 110–117, 2012.

communication processes in protocols, the spice-calculus enables grasping the dynamism of a protocol. Consequently, it clarifies the cost imbalances between clients and servers.

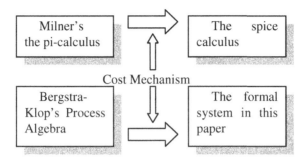

Fig. 1. Overview of our works

In the spice calculus, we know the cost during processes' execution through the annotation which attached to the transition which formulates execution of a process. We therefore say that the approach to the computational cost in the spice-calculus is indirect. The purpose of this paper is to develop an algebraic framework for cost analysis, which gives us more direct approach than the previous one. In order to give an algebraic framework, we adopt another formal system, called ACP, in place of the pi- and spi-calculus. *The Algebra of Communicating Processes*, ACP, is an algebraic approach to reasoning about concurrent systems, which was proposed by Jan Bergstra and Jan Willem Klop [5][6]. In contrast to CSP, CCS and the pi-calculus, the development of ACP focus on the algebra of processes. More concretely, the equation system is built up on the basis of the transition relation between processes. We construct a framework for cost analysis, giving a cost equivalence relation between processes to ACP.

2   Fragments of ACP

The expressions, called *terms,* of ACP is defined as follows:

- a,b,c,...   (atomic actions)
- τ (the silent action)
- s + t   (alternative composition)
- s·t   (sequential composition)
- s ∥ t   (merge)
- s ∥_ t   (left merge)
- s ∣ t   (communication)
- $\partial_H(a)$ (encapsulation)

The axioms of ACP are given as a system of equation. We often consider two subsystems of ACP, BPA(Basic Process Algebra) and PAP (Process Algebra of Parallelism). The axioms of BPA is given as

- x+y = y+x   A1
- (x+y)+z = x+(y+z)   A2
- x+x = x   A3
- (x+y)·z = x·z+y·z   A4
- (x · y) · z = x · (y · z) A5

Actually, this equivalence relation coincides with the bi-simulation relation derived from the transition relation defined by

- $v \to^v \sqrt{}$,
- if $x \to^v \sqrt{}$,   then $x+y \to^v \sqrt{}$,
- if $x \to^v x'$,   then $x+y \to^v x'$,
- if $y \to^v \sqrt{}$,   then $x+y \to^v \sqrt{}$,
- if $y \to^v y'$ then $x+y \to^v y'$,
- if $x \to^v \sqrt{}$ then $x·y \to^v y$,
- if $x \to^v x'$, then $x·y \to^v x'· y$,

where x,y,z run over the set of processes. The axioms of PAP are A1-A5 of BPA and the following rules

- $x \parallel y = (x \parallel\_ y + y \parallel\_ x) + x \mid y$ M1
- $v \parallel\_ y = v · y$ LM2
- $(v · x) \parallel\_ y = v·(x \parallel y)$ LM3
- $(x+y) \parallel\_ z = x \parallel\_ z + y \parallel\_ z$ LM4
- $v \mid w = \gamma(v, w)$ CM5
- $v \mid (w·y) = \gamma(v,w) · y$ CM6
- $(v·x) \mid w = \gamma(v, w) · x$ CM7
- $(v·x) \mid (w·y) = \gamma(v,w) · (x \parallel y)$ CM8
- $(x + y) \mid z = x\mid z + y\mid z$ CM9
- $x\mid(y + z) = x\mid y + x\mid z$ CM10.

These equations are also derived from the transition rules of BPA and

- if $x \to^v \sqrt{}$ then $x \parallel y \to^v \sqrt{}$,
- if $x \to^v x'$ then $x \parallel y \to^v x' \parallel y$,
- if $y \to^v \sqrt{}$ then $x \parallel y \to^v \sqrt{}$,
- if $y \to^v y'$ then $x \parallel y \to^v x \parallel y'$,
- if $x \to^v \sqrt{}$ and $y \to^w \sqrt{}$ then $x \parallel y \to^{\gamma(v,w)} \sqrt{}$,
- if $x \to^v \sqrt{}$ and $y \to^w y'$ then $x \parallel y \to^{\gamma(v,w)} y'$,
- if $x \to^v x'$ and $y \to^w \sqrt{}$ then $x \parallel y \to^{\gamma(v,w)} x'$,
- if $x \to^v x'$ and $y \to^w y'$ then $x \parallel y \to^{\gamma(v,w)} x' \parallel y'$,
- if $x \to^v \sqrt{}$ then $x \parallel\_ y \to^v y$,
- if $x \to^v x'$ then $x \parallel\_ y \to^v x' \parallel y$,
- if $x \to^v \sqrt{}$ and $y \to^w \sqrt{}$ then $x \mid y \to^{\gamma(v,w)} \sqrt{}$,
- if $x \to^v \sqrt{}$ and $y \to^w y'$ then $x \mid y \to^{\gamma(v,w)} y'$,
- if $x \to^v x'$ and $y \to^w \sqrt{}$ then $x \mid y \to^{\gamma(v,w)} x'$,
- if $x \to^v x'$ and $y \to^w y'$ then $x \mid y \to^{\gamma(v,w)} x' \parallel y'$.

Two processes s and t are *bisimular*, denoted $s \leftrightarrow t$,   if s and t satisfies the relation (s R t) defined by the following rules.

If (s R t) and (s $\to^v$ s') then (t $\to^v$ t') and (s' R t').
If (s R t) and (t $\to^v$ t') then (s $\to^v$ s') and (s' R t').

If (s R t) and (s $\rightarrow^v$ $\sqrt{}$) then (s $\rightarrow^v$ $\sqrt{}$).
If (s R t) and (t $\rightarrow^v$ $\sqrt{}$) then (t $\rightarrow^v$ $\sqrt{}$).

As mentioned above, both in BPA and in PAP, the bisimulation relation derived from each transition is equivalent to the equivalence relation defined by the axiom, system respectively, that is, (s = t) $\leftrightarrow$ (s $\leftrightarrow$ t) . The property (s = t) $\rightarrow$ (s $\leftrightarrow$ t) is called *soundness* of the axiom system with respect to the bisimulation and (s = t) $\leftarrow$ (s $\leftrightarrow$ t) *completeness*.

In this paper, we develop formalization of costs focusing on these two sub-systems, BPA and PAP. Hence, we would like to omit details of the full fragment of ACP for lack of space.

3   Algebraic Formalization of Costs

First, we define the notion of cost in the process algebra in the style of Bergstra-Klop. A *summand* of a process s, denotes cost(s), is the set of multisets of actions defined as

$$\text{cost(s)} = \{ a_{11}+a_{12}+...+a_1 n_1, \ a_{21}+a_{22}+...+a_2 n_2..., am_1+a\,m_2+...+a\,m\,n_m\}$$

where the transition paths starting at s is assumed to be

$s \rightarrow a_{11} \ s_{11} \rightarrow a_{12} \ s_{12} \rightarrow... \ \rightarrow a_1 n_1 \rightarrow s_1 n_1$

$s \rightarrow a_{21} \ s_{21} \rightarrow a_{22} \ s_{22} \rightarrow... \ \rightarrow a_2 n_2 \rightarrow s_2 n_2$

$\quad ...$

$s \rightarrow a_{m1} \ s_{m1} \rightarrow a_m \ _2 \ s_m \ _2 \rightarrow... \ \rightarrow a_m n_m \rightarrow s_m \ n_m.$

The expression $a_{11}+a_{12}+...+a_1 n_1$ denotes the multiset whose elements are $a1_1, a_{12},$ ...,and $a_1 n_1$, For example, consider a process P=(send receive || receive send) where send and receive are actions. Then, its summand cost (P) is

{2send+2receive, send+receive+comm, 2comm},

where the action comm is the result of communication between the actions send and receive, that is, comm = γ (send, receive).

We define a binary relation (s $\approx$ t) between processes as cost(s) = cost(t).

The *summand* of a process s, cost(s), means all the possibility of total amount of actions in possible paths. The *cost value equality* between processes, denote s $\approx$ t, is defined as cost(s) = cost(t). We next present basic properties on the cost equality.
In the fragment of BPA, we have the following properties.

Proposition. The cost value equality is an equivalence relation on processes in BPA.

Proof Sketch. This proposition is proved by checking reflectivity, symmetricity, and transitivity, which is straight-forward.

Proposition. The cost value equality is a congruence relation on processes in BPA, that is, if s $\approx$ t then u[s] $\approx$ u[t], where u[ ] means a process with a hole [ ]. and u[s] a process which is obtained by replacing a hole [] in the u [] by s.

Proof Sketch. This proposition is proved by induction on the structure of u[ ].

The cost value equality is axiomatized by the following equality rules

$$x + y \sim y + x, \qquad\qquad\qquad \text{A'1}$$
$$(x+y)+z \sim x+(y+z), \qquad\qquad \text{A'2}$$
$$x+x \sim x, \qquad\qquad\qquad\qquad \text{A'3}$$
$$(x+y)\cdot z \sim x \cdot z + y \cdot z, \qquad\qquad \text{A'4}$$
$$(x \cdot y) \cdot z \sim x \cdot (y \cdot z), \qquad\qquad \text{A'5}$$
$$x \cdot y \sim y \cdot x. \qquad\qquad\qquad\quad \text{A'6}$$

We call the relation $s \sim t$ defined above the *formal cost equality*. The noticeable difference of the formal cost equality from the equivalence relation $s = t$ defined in the previous section is the rule A'6. The relation $s \sim t$ satisfies soundness and completeness with respect to the cost value equality $s \approx t$.

Theorem. The formal cost equality $s \sim t$ is sound with respect to the cost value equality $s \approx t$, in other words, $s \sim t \rightarrow s \approx t$.

Proof Sketch. The proof is proved by structural induction on the relation $s \sim t$.

Theorem. The formal cost equality $s \sim t$ is complete with respect to $s \approx t$, in other words, $s \approx t \rightarrow s \sim t$.

Proof Sketch. We first introduce an inverse function of $\text{cost}(-)$, $\text{cost}^{-1}(-)$ defined as

$$\text{cost}^{-1}(S) = a_{11} \cdot a_{12} \cdot \ldots \cdot a_{1 n_1} + a_{21} \cdot a_{22} \cdot \ldots \cdot a_{2 n_2} + \ldots + a_{n1} \cdot a_{12} \cdot \ldots \cdot a_{1 n_1},$$

where $S = \{ a_{11}+a_{12}+\ldots+a_{1 n_1}, \ a_{21}+a_{22}+\ldots+a_{2 n_2}, \ldots, am_1+am_2+\ldots+am_{n_m}\}$.

We assume some total ordering among the actions, which enable us to arrange actions and sub-terms in order based on the lexicographic ordering. We then show that a property that $s \sim \text{cost}^{-1}(\text{cost}(s))$ for any process s, which is proved by mathematical induction on the length of s.

Next we prove that if $s \approx t$ then $\text{cost}^{-1}(\text{cost}(s)) \sim \text{cost}^{-1}(\text{cost}(t))$.

In PAP, the properties that the cost value relation is an equivalence and congruence relation similarly to the case of BPA.

Proposition. The cost value equality is an equivalence and congruence relation on processes in PAP.

This proposition is proved similarly to the one of BPA. However, the cost value equality is not a congruence relation in PAP. In PAP, the cost value equality satisfies congruence with respect to alternative and sequential compositions satisfies, but not for merge, left merge, and communication.

Proposition. If $s \approx s'$ and $t \approx t'$ then $s+t \approx s'+t'$ and $s \cdot t \approx s' \cdot t'$.

Proposition. There exist s, s', t, t' satisfying that $s \approx s'$ and $t \approx t'$ but *neither* $s \parallel t \approx s' \parallel t'$, $s \parallel\_ t \approx s' \parallel\_ t'$, *nor* $s \mid t \approx s' \mid t'$.

Processes $(a \cdot b)$ and $(b \cdot a)$ have the same cost, that is, $a \cdot b \approx b \cdot a$ since $\text{cost}(a \cdot b) = \{a + b\} = \{b + a\} = \text{cost}(b \cdot a)$. However, $(a \cdot b) \parallel (b \cdot a)$ and $(b \cdot a) \parallel (a \cdot b)$ do not have the same cost. Therefore the pair of these processes is a counterexample for merge. The counterexample for left merge is a pair of processes $(a \cdot b) \parallel\_ c$ and $(b \cdot a) \parallel\_ c$ and the one for communication is a pair of $((a \cdot b) \mid c)$ and $((b \cdot a) \mid c)$.

Theorem. In PAP, the formal cost equivalence is sound with respect to the cost value function, that is, if s ~ t then s ≈ t.

Proof Sketch. We consider a variation of the cost value equivalence, which distinguish of ordering of actions in each execution path. In other words, we consider a variation of the cost function, cost', such that

$$\text{cost'}(s) = \{\ a_{1\,1}\,a_{1\,2}...a_1\,n_1,\ \ a_{2\,1}a_{2\,2}...a_2\,n_2,\,...,\ am_{\,1}a\,m_{\,2}..a\,m\ n_m\}$$

where we distinguish the ordering of actions in each element of the value set . For example, assuming $a_{1\,1} + a_{1\,2} + ... + a_1\,n_1$ to be an element of cost(s), is identified with $a1_2 + a1_{1+} ... + a_1\,n_1$. However, the element $a1_1\,a_{1\,2}...a_1\,n_1$ is distinguished from $a_{1\,2}\,a_{1\,1}...a_1\,n_1$.

We first prove that if s ~ t then cost'(s) = cost'(t). Second we prove that if cost'(s) = cost(t) then cost(s)=cost(t), that is, s ≈ t.

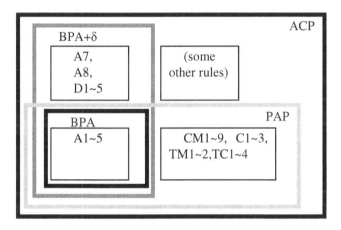

Fig. 2. Relationship among sub-fragments of ACP

The full fragment of ACP is under investigation with respect to cost equivalence. We have another sub-fragment BPA+δ than PAP. ACP is the formal system which is added the mechanism of δ to PAP; on the other hand, BPA+δ is the system which δ is added to BPA.

The axioms for δ are

- x + δ = x,   A7
- δ · x = δ,   A8
- if v∈ H then ∂H(v) = v,   D1
- if v ∉ H then ∂H(v) = δ,   D2
- ∂H(δ) = δ   D3
- ∂H(x+y) = ∂H(x)+∂H(y),   D4
- ∂H(x·y) = ∂H(x)·∂H(y), D5

The constant δ, called deadlock is the action which does not display any behavior. The communication function γ is extended by allowing that the communication of two atomic actions results to δ, that is, $\gamma : A \times A \to A \cup \{ \delta \}$. TH5s extension of γ enables us to express that two actions a and b do not communicate, by defining γ (a, b) = δ.

The behavior of the encapsulation operators is captured by the following rules

if $x \to^v \sqrt{}$ and $v \notin H$,   then $\partial H(x) \to^v \sqrt{}$.
If $x \to^v x'$ and $v \notin H$ then $\partial H(x) \to^v \partial H(x')$.

The formal cost equivalence of BPA is extended by adding the constant action δ and the following rules:

- $x + \delta \sim x$,   A'7
- $\delta \cdot x \sim \delta$,   A'8
- if $v \in H$ then $\partial H(v) \sim v$,   D'1
- if $v \notin H$ then $\partial H(v) \sim \delta$,   D'2
- $\partial H(\delta) \sim \delta$ D'3
- $\partial H(x+y) \sim \partial H(x)+\partial H(y)$,   D'4
- $\partial H(x \cdot y) \sim \partial H(x) \cdot \partial H(y)$,   D'5

The additional rules for formal cost equivalence are similar to the rules for the axioms for δ. The same cost value function as BPA is introduced to BPA+δ.

Then we have the following property.

Proposition. The cost value equivalence $\approx$ in BPA+ δ is an equivalence relation, that is, it satisfies reflexivity, symmetry, and transitivity.

In BPA+ δ, alternative composition satisfies the congruence.

Proposition. In BPA+ δ, if s $\approx$ s' and t $\approx$ t' then s+t $\approx$ s'+t'.

However, the other operators do not satisfy the congruence.

Proposition. In BPA + δ, the following two properties hold.

(a) There exist processes s, s', t, t' satisfying that s $\approx$ s' and t $\approx$ t' but it does not hold that s $\cdot$ t $\approx$ s' $\cdot$ t'.
(b) There exist processes s and s', satisfying that s $\approx$ s' but it does not hold that $\partial H(s) \approx \partial H(s')$.

4   Concluding Remarks

We developed a formal system for reasoning about computational costs of concurrent systems in the previous works, based on the Bergstra-Klop's process algebra. We investigated several fragments of the Algebra for Communicating Processes extending the mechanism of cost equivalence. We firstly gave the cost value function, secondly defined the cost value equivalence, and thirdly studied soundness and completeness for the cost value equivalence and the formal cost equivalence which is obtained by bisimulation of the transition rules.

In future, we should improve the notion of cost equivalence which enjoys congruence and completeness.

Acknowledgement. One of the author, Hiroki KIYOTO, contributed to this paper when he was a student of Tokyo Institute of Technology. Now he belongs to Barclays Captal Japan.

References

1. Meadows, C.: A formal framework and evaluation method for network denial of service. In: Proceedings of the 12th IEEE Computer Security Foundations Workshop, pp. 4–13 (1999)
2. Tomioka, D., Nishizaki, S., Ikeda, R.: A Cost Estimation Calculus for Analyzing the Resistance to Denial-of-Service Attack. In: Futatsugi, K., Mizoguchi, F., Yonezaki, N. (eds.) ISSS 2003. LNCS, vol. 3233, pp. 25–44. Springer, Heidelberg (2004)
3. Milner, R., Parrow, J., Walker, D.: A calculus of mobile processes, Part I and Part II. Information and Computation 100(1), 1–77 (1992)
4. Abadi, M., Gordon, A.D.: A calculus for cryptographic protocols: The spi calculus. In: Fourth ACM Conference on Computer and Communication Security, pp. 36–47. ACM Press (1997)
5. Bergstra, J.A., Klop, J.W.: Process Algebra for Synchronous Communication. Information and Control 60, 109–137 (1984)
6. Fokkink, W.: Introduction to Process Algebra. Springer (2000)

Ontology-Based Web Information Extraction

Qian Mo and Yi-hong Chen

Computer and Information Engineering College,
Beijing Technology and Business University, Beijing 100048
xdrl@163.com

Abstract. This article aims to give introduce to an Ontology-based Web information extraction system and the related content about Web information extraction and Ontology. This paper introduces the modules of the Web information extraction system, including: Web page preprocessing, DOM tree formation, Positioning information domain, Lexical analysis, Ontology construction, Ontology analysis, Keyword management, Rule generation, Information extraction and Information storage. And then, it also describes the experimental results. Finally, it describes the development trends and challenges of Ontology-based Web information extraction.

Keywords: Web information extraction, Ontology, DOM (Document Object Model).

1   Introduction

As the rapid development of Internet, Web pages present information on the explosive growth. To some extent, the growth of the amount of information of Web pages can help people learn more about the world, but its rapid growth also has brought inconvenience to people. Facing a massive amount of information on the Web, how to make full use of Web and how to quickly find interested and really needed information become human must face. Under such a background, Web information extraction has developed and it also has formed a variety of research methods.

When we introduce the Ontology into information extraction, in theory, as long as the building of the Ontology sufficiently comprehensive, then the information extraction system will be able to obtain a higher accuracy rate and recall rate.

The test set used in this Ontology-based Web information extraction system described in this paper is a set of information about the books on the Web pages.

2   Web Information Extraction

Web information extraction is a branch of information extraction. It is also one of the most active areas in information extraction.

Web information extraction is to identify the information that users are interested in, including semi-structured or unstructured information on Web pages, and turn it into a clearer format in structure and semanteme (XML, relational data, object-oriented data, etc.) [1]. Its main object is the text on Web pages, but it can also extract images, audio, video and other media. The process of Web information extraction is shown in Fig. 1.

M. Zhao and J. Sha (Eds.): ICCIP 2012, Part I, CCIS 288, pp. 118–126, 2012.
© Springer-Verlag Berlin Heidelberg 2012

From the above description, we can find that the mathematical description of Web information extraction can be like this: Let D be a collection of massive amounts of data on Web pages. It is an infinite set.

$$D = \{d_1, d_2, d_3 \cdots d_i, \cdots d_n \cdots\}.$$

$$i = 1,2,3 \cdots n, \cdots.$$

Let R be a set that every element in R is an element in the D and is satisfied the condition f (d) =0. This means that R is a subset of D. The condition f (x) = 0 is used to extract the required data.

Fig. 1. Web information extraction

Currently, Web information extraction research methods have a variety of categories. Main categories are as follows:

1, be divided according to the object of Web information extraction: Unstructured text extraction, Semi-structured text extraction, Structured text extraction;

2, be divided according to the degree of automation: Artificial information extraction, Semi-automatic information extraction, Automatic information extraction;

3, be divided according to the existing Web information extraction system and model implementation principle: Inductive learning based information extraction, HTML-based information extraction, Ontology-Based Information Extraction, Information extraction based on natural language processing, Web query-based information extraction

3   Ontology and Related Concepts

3.1   The Concept of Ontology

Ontology was originally a philosophical concept [2], and later was introduced into the computer field. Although the Neches, Gruber, Borst, Studer are respectively proposed the definition of Ontology, it still has no clear and uniform definition about Ontology. In this paper, we can consider that Ontology is the description of the concepts in the objective world. And it also describes the connection between these concepts.

3.2   The Modeling Primitives and Basic Relations of Ontology

There are four basic relationships in the Ontology [2]:

part-of: the relationship between the whole and the part;

kind-of: the inheritance relationship;

instance-of: the relationship between instances and concepts;

attribute-of: one concept is a attribute of another concept;

Ontology is made up of five parts, including: C, R, I, F, A [3]:

C: classes or concepts; It is a collection of objects. And it is an abstract about the objects that has some of the same nature in the real world

R: relationship; It refers to the interaction between concepts in a field. It is formally defined as subsets of the n-dimensional Cartesian product: R: C1*C2*...*Cn.

I: instances; It is an instance of a class, that is, an object

F: function; It is a special kind of relationship, defining the certain conditions that elements is required to meet.

A: axioms; objective laws; correct assertion

4   Ontology-Based Web Information Extraction

Ontology-based Web information extraction is to introduce the technologies related to Ontology into the traditional Web information extraction, and then use the Ontology constructed to extract data from Web pages.

The data source of this system is from information-rich Web pages about books.

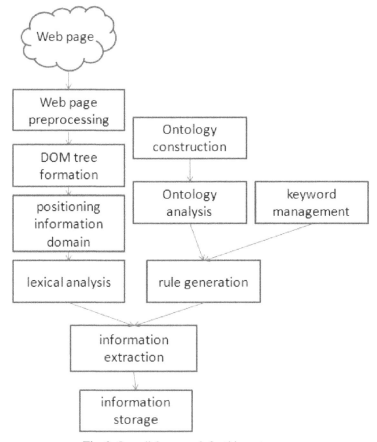

Fig. 2. Overall framework for this system

4.1   System Architecture

This paper describes the overall architecture of Ontology-based Web information extraction system, including: the module of Web page preprocessing, the module of DOM tree formation, the module of positioning information domain, the module of lexical analysis, the module of Ontology construction, the module of Ontology analysis, the module of keyword management, the module of rule generation, the module of information extraction, the module of information storage. The overall architecture is shown in Fig. 3.

Web Page Preprocessing
The information obtained directly from Web pages on the Internet usually contains a number of complex and redundant data. In order to speed up the processing speed and accuracy of other modules, Web page preprocessing is very necessary.

DOM Tree Formation
Any Web page can be viewed as an HTML document. Every HTML element is nested from each other. Based on the nested tags, we can build a DOM tree. In this module, we can use the parser to parse the Web page into a DOM tree. The example of tag tree is shown in Fig. 3.

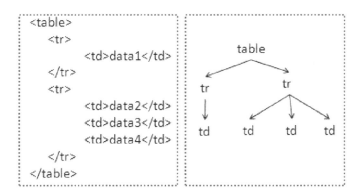

Fig. 3. Tag tree

Positioning Information Domain
In this module, it mainly has three parts, including: looking for data fields, identifying data fields, identifying data items.

In this module, this article uses the MDR algorithm [4], as shown in Fig. 4. There are mainly three steps in MDR algorithm:

1, Traverse the node tree upon layer to find the data fields;
2, Identify the data fields that are found and return the smallest generalized node;
3, Identify data items, in the case of all data fields and all generalized nodes are found;

```
Algorithm MDR(Node, K)
1 if TreeDepth(Node) >= 3 then
2     CombComp(Node.Children, K);
3     for each ChildNode ∈ Node.Children
4         MDR(ChildNode, K);
5 end
```

Fig. 4. MDR general algorithm

Lexical Analysis
In this module, it is mainly to take further processing on the data items that are found in the previous module. Through lexical analysis, it makes the text simpler and more concise, and then easier to be extracted.

Ontology Construction
Ontology construction can be divided into three categories:

1, Ontology entirely created by hand;
2, Ontology created by semi-automatic way;
3, Ontology created by automatic way;

Its methods are mainly: Uschold and King's skeleton law; Methontology methods; Gruninger and Fox's TOVE methods; Berneras methods, etc.

In this paper, this module uses semi-automatic way, builds Ontology according to the information items in the Web page, and uses the open source tool Protégé to build Ontology.

This paper takes information of books as a test case. An instance of books typically includes the basic information (title, author, publisher, publication date, summary, picture, and review), the price of books (price, original price, and discount), etc. Part of the Ontology concept hierarchy about the information of books is shown in Fig. 5.

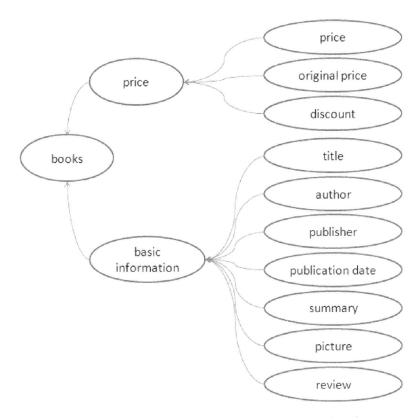

Fig. 5. Part of the Ontology concept hierarchy about the information of books

Ontology Analysis

When Ontology building is completed, in order to be able to apply it, we must parse the Ontology. After parsing the Ontology, we can obtain a series of related concepts, attributes, and instance, etc.

Keywords Management

This keywords management module corresponds to the concepts that are formed by parsing Ontology. It mainly stores the keywords required by the information extraction module. Keywords can be stored into the keywords management module when the Ontology analysis module is parsing the Ontology. And you can also manually operate keywords. These keywords are mainly prepared to match with the data items to be extracted.

Rule Generation

After the Ontology analysis and keywords management, the rule generation module will generate information extraction rules based on the results of the two previous modules. These rules will be applied to the information extraction module to extract the required information

Information Extraction

In this module, it is mainly to apply the extraction rules (are generated by the rule generation module) to the results (are obtained by the lexical analysis module).

Information Storage

Information that is extracted will be stored into the database for the subsequent operations such as query, modify, etc.

4.2   The Results

The evaluation indicators of Web information extraction system are accuracy rate and the recall rate. Accuracy rate means the ratio of the correct results that are extracted to the all results that are extracted. It is shown in Formula 1; Recall rate means the ratio of the correct results that are extracted to all the possible correct results in Web pages. It is shown in Formula 2. The meaning of each variable in Formula 1 and Formula 2 is shown in Table 1.

Table 1. The meaning of variables

	correct	wrong
extracted	EC	EW
not extracted	NEC	NEW

Table 2. The meaning of β values

Value	Meaning
$\beta > 1$	Accuracy rate is more important than recall rate.
$\beta = 1$	Recall rate and accuracy rate are equally important.
$\beta < 1$	Recall rate is more important than accuracy rate.

$$Precision = EC \, / \, (EC \, + \, EW) \tag{1}$$

$$Recall = EC \, / \, (EC \, + \, NEC) \tag{2}$$

In order to evaluate the performance of Web information extraction systems more comprehensively, we generally use a weighted geometric average of the accuracy rate and the recall rate. The weighted geometric average is denoted by F and is shown in Formula 3. The β is the relative weight of the recall rate and the accuracy rate. It is usually set to 1. The meaning of β values is shown in Table 4.2.2.

$$F = \frac{(1+\beta^2) \times Recall \times Precision}{Recall + \beta^2 \times Precision}$$

(3)

The table structure design of the system is shown in Fig. 4.2.1. The part of the extracted results is shown in Fig. 4.2.2. The accuracy rate and recall rate of the Ontology-based Web information extraction system described in this paper is respectively about 0.865 and 0.841.

5   Summary

Ontology-based information extraction can effectively solve the problem of the knowledge bottleneck. The portability of information extraction system is improved to a certain extent, because of introducing the Ontology into information extraction. When applications change, you need only change the related Ontology. Ontology-based information extraction also can extract the relationship between the entities, and the traditional information extraction technology cannot extract it, so the extraction of Ontology-based information extraction is more comprehensive.

However, Ontology-based information extraction technology is still some shortcomings: Due to the construction of Ontology is not perfect enough, there is no fully play the role of Ontology in the information extraction process; Due to the construction of Ontology itself is a difficult job, we still use a semi-automatic way, so the portability of system is not high, etc.

Therefore, there are still many aspects to be studied in Ontology-based Web information extraction: Study on how to simplify the process of Ontology modeling; Study on how to construct the required Ontology comprehensively and accurately; Study on how to construct the Ontology by a automatic way, etc.

Picture	Image
Title	Short Text
Review	Image
Author	Short Text
Time	Date
Press	Short Text
Summary	Long Text
Price	Number
Cost	Number
Discount	Number

Fig. 6. The table structure design

Picture		Title	Author	Time	Price	Cost	Discount
(Binary/...	Kb.	The Amazing Book of Useless Noel Botham	2011-01-01	67.5	90	75	
(Binary/...	Kb.	The Book of Useless Informat Noel Botham	2006-06-01	66	88	75	
(Binary/...	Kb.	ARCHITECTURE.INFORMATION.GR/ Markus S. Bra	2006-09-01	391	460	85	
(Binary/...	Kb.	The Best Book of Useless Inf Noel Botham	2007-12-01	66	88	75	
(Binary/...	Kb.	The Essential Book of Useles Donald A. Voo	2009-10-01	81	90	90	
(Binary/...	Kb.	The Wall Street Journal Guic Dona M. Wong	2010-01-01	159.2	245	65	
(Binary/...	Kb.	Management Information Syste Laudon, Kenne	2003-12-01	75	100	75	

Fig. 7. The part of the extracted results

References

1. Liu, J.-G., Liu, G.-S., He, L.-Y., Chen, S.: Status and development of Web-based information extraction technolog. Fujian Computer (2007)
2. Deng, Z., Tang, S., Zhang, M., Yang, D., Chen, J.: Overview of Ontology. Acta Scientiarum Naturalium Universitatis Pekinensis (2002)
3. Perez, A.G., Benjamins, V.R.: Overview of Knowledge Sharing and Reuse Components: Ontologies and Problem-Solving Methods. In: Stockholm, V.R., Benjamins, B., Chandrasekaran, A. (eds.) Proceedings of the IJCAI 1999 Workshop on Ontologies and Problem-Solving Methods (KRR5), pp. 1–15 (1999)
4. Liu, B., Grossman, R., Zhai, Y.: Mining data records in Web pages. In: Getoor, L., et al. (eds.) ACM SIGKDD Proceedings of the Ninth ACM SIGKDD International Conference on Knowledge Discovery and Data Mining, Washington, DC, USA, pp. 601–606 (2003)
5. Eikvil, L.: Information extraction from world wide web – a survey. Technical Report 945. Norweigan Computing Center, Norway (1999)
6. Chen, J., Zhu, Q.-M., Gong, Z.-X.: Overview of Ontology-Based Information Extraction. Comput ER Technology and Development (2007)
7. Yang, X.-Q., Kong, D.-R., Shi, H., Sun, N., Zhang, Y.: Web information extraction based on domain ontology. Information Technology (2009)
8. Liu, J.-G., Chen, S., Huang, Y.: Improved Ontology-based Web Information Extraction. Computer Engineering (2010)

Research about Image Mining Technique

Xianzhe Cao and Shimin Wang

Beijing Technology and Business University
100048
Cxz0616@gmail.com

Abstract. Image mining is a development potential technology for data mining which involves in multiple disciplines, it is also a challenging field which extends traditional data mining from structured data to unstructured data such as image data. The paper introduces the concepts, mining models and mining technology related with image mining. Although these image mining techniques have not yet developed mature, not long time later, image mining has its own distinctive theoretical system.

Keywords: image mining, mining model, image mining technique.

1   Introduction

The rapid development of Internet multimedia technology and imaging technology leads to the rapid growth of image data. Among the mass of image data hide much useful information. However, traditional data mining based on text can only retrieve the image according to the description about the image, can't retrieve according to content of the image directly and not to say that mine some useful information among the image data based on the image semantic. How to excavate useful information from these unstructured and ambiguous-semantic image data becomes a hot spot attracting researchers. An emerging field, image mining comes into being which solves the problems mentions above. Image mining is an integrated technology combined traditional data mining techniques with image processing techniques, used for the field full of massive image. The first Multimedia Data Mining/Knowledge Data Mining convened in 2000 and the Multimedia Data Mining/Knowledge Data Mining convened in 2001 promote the development of image data mining technology greatly [1].

Image data mining is a technology aims at finding useful information and knowledge from large scale image data [2]. In the process of image data mining it involves in computer vision, image processing and analysis, pattern recognition, image retrieval, machine learning, artificial intelligence and so on. Although all these subjects above study the same object-image, the essential difference between image data mining and the other subjects is that image data mining focus on large scale set of images while image processing and analysis and pattern recognition analysis based on only a single image, image retrieval is simply find out the eligible image among the set of images which can't find the potential useful information and knowledge. Above all these mentioned prove that image data mining is an irreplaceable promising subject. Image

M. Zhao and J. Sha (Eds.): ICCIP 2012, Part I, CCIS 288, pp. 127–134, 2012.

data mining can be used for analyzing remote sensing image, diagnosing medical imaging, managing traffic, forecasting disaster and other fields having massive images.

2   Difference between Image Mining and Traditional Data Mining

Image data mining is a branch of data mining in theory, but it doesn't mean that image data mining simply applies the traditional data mining techniques to images. Image data mining is a multidisciplinary field which is more complex than traditional data mining and its differences from traditional data mining is mainly as the followings [2][3]:

a) Difference of data processing. Before mining among the image data, it doesn't only need to clean the data, but also solve the problems such as how to store the image, compress the image and establish the multimedia database and so on. Besides, the pixel of image can't reflect the image content, so it must use image segmentation, object recognition, target expression and description and so much more image processing techniques to extract the image feature, then transform from these preliminary data to the data that can be understand by computers in semantic.

b) Image data has relative meaning while relational data has absolute meaning. In relation database, each record expresses single meaning without any ambiguities, but in multimedia database, the same image object can convey many different meanings which are determined by the location of image object, so image data has relative meaning.

c) It contains subjective factors when understanding image data. Different people with different interest and purpose will have different understanding with the same image. It is namely that people may have not only one understanding with an image which depends on the representation and application of the image.

d) Image data contains the information of the image object's spatial relationships. The information of the image object's spatial relationships have separation, intersecting, cincture, up, down and including.

3   Process of Image Mining

Image data is different from structured data, it is complex and semantic ambiguity. The image data is expressed by pixel value, while the pixel value of single point can't reflect any meaningful information, as a consequence, the original image can't be applied to image data mining, it must generate high-level image feature database by pretreatment techniques which map low-level pixel into high-level semantic. Briefly, it can divide the process of image data mining into three parts:

First, data preprocess. There are a lot of dirty and noisy data in large image database, and these data will do bad to the resource of image mining algorithm. So in order to guarantee the best resource of image mining algorithm, we need preprocess image data before image mining. At this stage, it will remove noise data and integrate useful data through the pretreatment. What's more, the task in pretreatment still contains expressing the pattern of image.

Second, feature attributes extraction. The basic feature attributes used to describe a picture contain color, shape and texture. During the process of extracting feature attributes it needs to use image processing technologies such as image segmentation, picking up the edge to extract task-related feature vectors and form multi-dimensional feature vectors.

Third, image object identifying, image retrieving, association rule mining and image classification and image clustering among the image feature attributes extracted during the second process in order to find potential knowledge. At this stage, there are various methods being used to mining hidden knowledge such as object recognition, image indexing and retrieval, image classification and clustering, neural network and so on, all these methods are used on feature vectors.

4   Image Mining Model

Despite that computer vision, image processing, image retrieving, data mining, machine learning, database and artificial intelligence all have developed mature as an independent discipline, it is at the initial stage to utilize all these knowledge together in image data mining. Because of the huge difference between image data mining and structured data mining, the models used in traditional structured data mining may not work in image data mining. According to the characteristic of image data mining, there are mainly two mining models:

4.1   Function-Driven Model

Function-driven image mining model is the image mining model organized by modules with different functions. The function-driven model usually contains two modules: data obtaining, pretreatment and saving module and image mining module. The first module is used for image pick-up, original image storage and searching. The second module is used for mining image model and meanings. The Multimedia Miner is the first function-driven model for image data mining which is developed by Simon Fraser University and it is also a system prototype for multimedia data mining. The Multimedia Miner contains four major components: image excavator, a preprocessor, a search kernel, the discovery modules. Image excavator extracts images and videos from multimedia repository. A preprocessor extracts image features and storing precomputed data in a database. A search kernel matches queries with image and video features in the database. The discovery modules exclusively perform image information mining routines to intelligently explore underlying knowledge and patterns within images. Figure 1 shows the system architecture of the Multimedia Miner [3]:

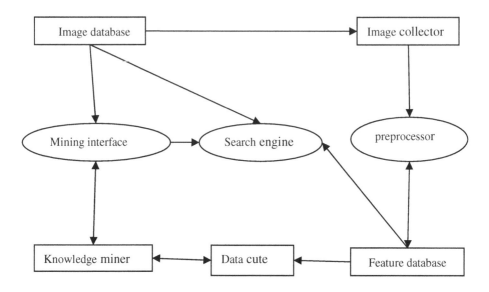

Fig. 1. Function-Driven Model

The majority of image mining system architectures existing later fall under this function-driven image mining framework. For example, Milhai Datcu and Klaus Seidel propose an intelligent satellite mining system that comprises a data acquisition, preprocessing and archiving system and an image mining system [4]. The former is responsible for the extraction of image information, storage of raw images, and retrieval of image. The latter enables the users to explore image meaning and detect relevant events.

4.2   Information-Driven Model

The function-driven model serves the purpose of organizing and clarifying the different roles and tasks to be performed in image mining, while the information-driven model focus on the different meanings of image data in different levels. Zhang et.al. distinguish four levels of information: pixel level, object level, semantic concept level, pattern and knowledge level. And these four levels can be divided into two levels further: low level which contains pixel level and object level and high level which contains semantic concept level and pattern and knowledge level. The low level is mainly responsible for image analysis, image processing and image recognition, while the high level is responsible for extracting semantic concept and knowledge from image collection. Therefore, the high level's information is more meaningful than the low level's.

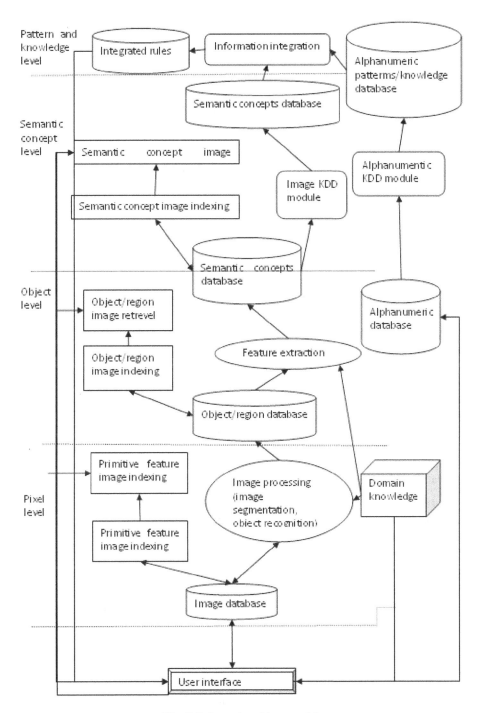

Fig. 2. Information-driven model

Now we will introduce the information-driven model from lowest level at detail. At the Pixel Level, we are dealing with information relating to the primitive features such as color, texture, and shape. At the Object Level, simple clustering algorithms and domain experts help to segment the images into some meaningful regions/objects. At the Semantic Concept Lever, the objects/regions identified earlier are placed in the context of the scenes depicted. High-level reasoning and knowledge discovery techniques are used to discover interesting patterns. Finally, at the Pattern and Knowledge Level, the domain-specific alphanumeric data are integrated with the semantic relationships discovered from the images and further mining are performed to discovered useful correlations between the alphanumeric data and those found in the images. Such correlations discovered are particularly useful in the medical domain.

5   Image Mining Technique

Image data mining doesn't only need suitable mining models, but also needs mining techniques. Only are mining models and mining techniques used together that we can mine useful information among the image data. The followings are some common image data mining techniques:

Similarity Retrieval. Sometimes we need to search some images meeting our demand just like we search for database to find something we interested in, and this leads to the born of similarity retrieval. There are two kinds of similarity retrieval, one is based on the image labels that are appended to image artificially to describe it, the other one is based on the image content which searches the eligible image according to image feature attributes such as shape, color and texture. The first method needs to label images artificially which takes a lot of time and energy as price, so this method is only suitable for the little number of image collection. However, the second method is more intelligent and more suitable for the large scale of image collection. And one typical application is the famous image retrieval system QBIC Virage.

Object Recognition [5]. The main task of object recognition in image data mining is to recognize the objects in the image which we can also find in the actual world such as tree, animal and so on. The most common recognition model is priori model. The object recognition module contains four components: models database, feature detector, hypothesized and hypothesis testing.

Association Rule Mining. Association rule mining is a typical approach used in data mining domain for uncovering interesting trends, patterns and rules in large datasets. Recently, association rule mining has been applied to large image databases. There are two ways to mine out association rules among the image data. One is to mine from large collections of images alone and the other is to mine from the combined collections of images and associated alphanumeric data [5]. Just because that image data contains spatial relationships which structured data doesn't have, so image association rule mining is much more complex than structured data mining. Now people propose many image association rule mining algorithms. For example, jelena Tesic proposes the Perceptual Association rules mining algorithms which is based on the perceptual events in image database. Another typical example is the FP-Trees algorithm proposed by Ankur Teredesai which is proved more effective than Apriori algorithm.

Image Classification and Image Clustering. Both Image classification and image clustering classify the image into groups respectively. But the only difference between them is that image classification is supervised classification but image clustering is unsupervised classification. The problem of image classification is to label newly encountered, unlabeled images according to the collection of labeled image given in advance. While, the problem of image clustering is to group a collection of images without labels into meaningful clusters based on the image content without any priori knowledge. Now the image classification algorithms have Bayesian, Genetic algorithm, Decision tree and Rough set and image clustering algorithms have K-means which is a kind of Hierachical clustering algorithm and Expectation-Maximization which is a kind of Nonhierarhical clustering algorithm. Recently people propose some improved algorithms. Mihai Datcu and Klaus Seidel proposed a new image clustering algorithm which takes advantage of stochastic model to classify the images come from the same sensor [6]. C.Z. Zhu proposes a algorithm called MCFC short for multi-context fuzzy clustering which is applied In medical image mining. RIE HONDA applies two steps SOM short for self organizing map based on EM algorithm to clustering weather images and identifying typhoon pattern to forecast typhoon.

Neural Network. A neural network is a massively parallel distributed processor made up of simple processing units, each of which has a natural propensity for storing experiential knowledge and making the knowledge available for use. Neural networks are fault tolerant and are good at pattern recognition and trend prediction. In the case of limited knowledge, artificial neutral network algorithms are frequently used to construct a model of the data. It worth to mention that G.G Gardner et al developed the Artificial Neural Network (ANN) which applies neural network to image mining and provides a wholly automated approach to image analysis [7]. What's more, W.Strelein develops a mining tool based on fuzzy ARTMAP and Antonie applies neural network in breast cancer image classification which is proved to be low sensitive to unbalancment of image database.

6   Conclusion

Image data mining is a promising and vast field, mature image mining techniques can bring huge benefit to medical, meteorological, aerospace and traffic. Although image data mining is still in the initial stage and the relative techniques are all in the researching time, I strong believe that image data mining will explore its own way in the near future and in that time, image data mining will bring huger benefit to more fields.

References

1. Liu, Z., Jiang, L.: The Research of Image Data Mining. Computer Engineering and Applications 39(33) (2003)
2. Du, L., Chen, Y., Zhu, J.: Overview of Research on Image Data Mining. Computer Applications and Software 28(2) (2011)

3. Yu, X., Li, M.: Models and techniques of image data mining. Journal of Clinical Rehabilitative Tissue Engineering Research 14(35) (2010)
4. Zhang, J., Hsu, W., Lee, M.L.: An Information-Driven Framework for Image Mining. In: Mayr, H.C., Lazanský, J., Quirchmayr, G., Vogel, P. (eds.) DEXA 2001. LNCS, vol. 2113, p. 232. Springer, Heidelberg (2001)
5. Zhang, J., Hsu, W., Lee, M.L.: Image Mining Issues. Frame Works, and Technique. In: Proceedings of the ACM SIGKDD International Conference on Knowledge Discovery&Data Mining, KDD 2001 (2001)
6. Datcu, M., Seidel, K.: Image Information Mining: Exploration of Image Content in Large Archives. In: IEEE Aerospace Conference Proceedings (March 2000)
7. Gardner, G.G., Keating, D.: Automatic detection of diabetic retinopathy using an artificial neural network: a screening tool. British Journal of Ophthalmology (1996)

A Secure Communication System Based on DCSK

Gang Zhang, Li-fang He, and Tian-qi Zhang

Chongqing Key Laboratory of Signal and Information Processing (CQKLS&IP),
Chongqing University of Posts and Telecommunications (CQUPT)
Chongqing, 400065, China

Abstract. Chaotic secure communication has many advantages than traditional communication for its broadband, noise like characteristics. Only after good features of the chaotic system being studied deeply, chaos-based secure communication can be applied. In the traditional secure communication based on Chaos Shift Keying (CSK), synchronization needs to be established between the transmitter and receiver of the system. While due to the extreme sensitivity of initial value of chaotic signal, it is very difficult to achieve synchronization so this method is difficult to be applied practically. Therefore to solve this problem, a new Differential Chaos Shift Keying (DCSK) system was proposed which chaos synchronization is not necessary. The new system was deeply studied and was compared with the Binary Phase Shift Keying (BPSK) modulation. Finally, a new application with DCSK in the image transmission was given.

Keywords: Secure Communication, Chaos Synchronization, DCSK.

1 Introduction

In traditional communication, information has to be digitized firstly, and then can be encrypted. This is because the encryption is based on principles of discrete number theory. As the complexity of the algorithm, encryption on digital signals is a big burden for system. However, the use of chaotic signals do not need digitization, and chaotic encryption devices can be realized with fast devices in addition [1-2]. The chaotic signals have certain characteristics such as broadband spectrum, random distribution, noise like, relatively simple analog hardware realization, etc. which make it the best choice for secure communication technology [3]. Chaotic secure communication has been studied for more than a decade. In recent years, a lot of chaos-based communications have been proposed such as Chaos Synchronization (chaotic mask), Chaos Shift Keying (QCSK, SCSK), Chaos Control, Chaotic Pulse Position Modulation (CPPM), and Chaotic Frequency Modulation (CFM), etc. Although the chaotic secure communication in some ways have better performances than the traditional communication, but after ten years of research, chaotic secure communication has not replaced the traditional communication, and the chaotic secure communication lack of efficiency than the traditional communication.

Nevertheless, the main advantage of such technique is in secure communication. The digital secure communications are mainly achieved by Chaos Shift Keying (CSK)

M. Zhao and J. Sha (Eds.): ICCIP 2012, Part I, CCIS 288, pp. 135–143, 2012.

modulation. The received signal at the receiver is correlated with different reference signals by the chaotic system, and decision is made simply on the basis of the output values of different correlators. This approach requires the transmitter and receiver to be synchronized with each other. But due to the extreme sensitivity on the initial value, the chaotic synchronization is too difficult to achieve, so this approach is very hard difficult to apply practically. On this basis, a new Differential Chaos Shift Keying (DCSK) modulation was proposed, and was in-depth researched [9]. The comparison on performance between DCSK and Binary Phase Shift Keying (BPSK) modulation was also given. Finally, the impact of DCSK on encryption system was also studied and a new application using DCSK modulation in image transmission system was also given.

2   Chaos Shift Keying（CSK）

In Chaos Shift Keying (CSK) communication, the dynamic state of chaotic signals sent by the transmitter converges to a strange attractor. By changing one or more parameters of the system, the location of the attractor can be changed, thus the chaotic signals can carry information. At the receiver, the original information can be restored by estimating the different locations of the strange attractor. Carroll and Pecora proposed a new chaotic communication system based on attractor of 3-dimension Rossler system in [4]. In a symbol period T_s, the amount of information to be transmitted N_b is $N_b = \log_2 M$, where M is the number of strange attractors. T_s must be long enough to ensure that the system's dynamic state can converge to one strange attractor. The receiver needs to determine that the transmission signal $s(t)$ belongs to which strange attractor. $s(t)$ is usually a scalar, and the state of the transmitter can be of high dimension, then the transmitter can detected the signal by coherent or non-coherent technique and make a decision.

In traditional communication, coherent detection technique makes the received signal correlate with the expected signal, so the output of the correlators can achieve maximum Signal to Noise Ratio (SNR). So if the transmitter and receiver are synchronized, the transmitted waveform can be recovered by coherent detection at the receiver. [7] proposed a Binary Chaos Shift Keying (CSK) communication system, shown in Figure 1.

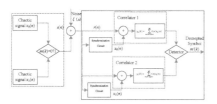 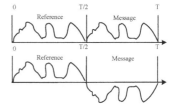

Fig. 1. Binary Chaos Shift Keying communication system

Fig. 2. DCSK Modulation Diagram

$m(k)$ is the information to be transmitted. The transmitter generates two chaotic sequences, $x_0(n)$ and $x_1(n)$ which are generated by two different chaotic maps or by the same map but with different initial states. To transfer a binary symbol, β bits chaotic signals are needed, which is defined as the spread factor. After modulation, the signal $s(n)$ is as Eq.1 shown. If the signals are transmitted in Additive White Gaussian Noise (AWGN) channel, then the received signals is given by Eq.2, where $\xi(n)$ is Additive White Gaussian Noise, the mean is zero and the power spectral density $N_0 = 2$.

$$s(n) = \begin{cases} x_0(n) & m(k) = 0 \\ x_1(n) & m(k) = 1 \end{cases} \quad (1) \quad r(n) = s(n) + \xi(n) \quad (2)$$

If the transmitter and the receiver have been synchronized, then $x_0(n)$ and $x_1(n)$ can be restored at the receiver. The received signal $r(n)$ is correlated with $x_0(n)$ and $x_1(n)$ at the correlators respectively. At the end of each symbol period, the output signals of the correlators are sampled to make decision like Eq.3 and Eq.4.

$$y_0(k) = \sum_{n=(k-1)\beta+1}^{k\beta} r(n)x_0(n) \quad (3) \qquad y_1(k) = \sum_{n=(k-1)\beta+1}^{k\beta} r(n)x_1(n) \quad (4)$$

At the detector, if the original information is "0", then $m(k) = 0$, so the output signals of two correlators are $y_0(k)$ and $y_1(k)$.

$$\begin{aligned} y_0(k) &= \sum_{n=(k-1)\beta+1}^{k\beta} r(n)x_0(n) \\[2mm] &= \sum_{n=(k-1)\beta+1}^{k\beta} [x_0(n) + \xi(n)]x_0(n) \quad (5) \\[2mm] &= \sum_{n=(k-1)\beta+1}^{k\beta} x_0^2(n) + \xi(n)x_0(n) \end{aligned} \qquad \begin{aligned} y_1(k) &= \sum_{n=(k-1)\beta+1}^{k\beta} r(n)x_1(n) \\[2mm] &= \sum_{n=(k-1)\beta+1}^{k\beta} [x_0(n) + \xi(n)]x_1(n) \quad (6) \\[2mm] &= \sum_{n=(k-1)\beta+1}^{k\beta} x_0(n)x_1(n) + \xi(n)x_0(n) \end{aligned}$$

As $x_0(n)$ and $x_1(n)$ are uncorrelated pseudo-random sequences, and $\xi(n)$ belongs to Gaussian distribution with zero mean, then the mean of the latter in Eq.5 is zero, and Eq.6 is zero mean, so $y_0(k) > y_1(k)$; On the other hand, if $m(k) = 1$, then $y_0(k) < y_1(k)$. Therefore, to restore $m(k)$, the rules to make decision is like Eq.7. meaning that the detector only make decision simply according to the output higher value of the correlators.

$$m'(k) = \begin{cases} 0 & y_0(k) > y_1(k) \\ 1 & y_0(k) < y_1(k) \end{cases} \quad (7) \qquad b(k) = \begin{cases} -1 & m(k) = 0 \\ 1 & m(k) = 1 \end{cases} \quad (8)$$

3   Differential Coherent Detection in DCSK

In CSK modulation, synchronization between the transmitter and receiver is required by coherent detection. However, due to the extreme sensitivity of initial values, the noise puts big impact on the synchronization performance on system, then synchronization is extremely difficult to achieve, so this method is difficult to apply practically. Based on DPSK, a Differential Chaos Shift Keying (DCSK) modulation was proposed. Like DPSK, DCSK can transmit the information by the difference on phase of the modulated signals. The synchronization between the transmitter and the receiver is not needed. In DCSK, the chaotic signals are transmitted during the first $T/2$, and the modulated signals are transmitted in the later $T/2$, where T is one symbol period as shown in Figure 2 [5-6]. The advantage of using DCSK is the ability to counter the burst noise which will cause the serious interference to channel.

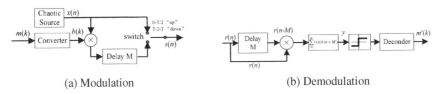

(a) Modulation   (b) Demodulation

Fig. 3. Modulation and Demodulation

DCSK modulator and demodulator are shown in Figure 3. $m(k)$ is useful information represented by binary codes. $b(k)$ is the bipolar codes through the code converter where k is the bit counter. The relationship between $m(k)$ and $b(k)$ is like Eq.8. During the symbol time T, the transmitter generates chaotic sequence $x(n)$ in first $T/2$, the length of which is M. $x(n)$ is delayed $T/2$, then multiplied by $b(k)$, and put it in the second $T/2$ by a switch. So length of sequence is $2M$ in one symbol time. $s(n)$ can be expressed as Eq.9.

$$s(n) = \begin{cases} x(n) & 1 < n \leq M \\ b(k)x(n-M) & M < n \leq 2M \end{cases} \quad (9) \quad y(k) = \sum_{i=1}^{M} r(n)r(n+M) \quad (10)$$

M is defined as spread factor, so that one information symbol will be modulated into $2M$bit. Then the relationship between f_s and f_m is $f_s = 2M f_m$, where f_s is the code rate and f_m is the original information rate. In order to restore the information, the received signal $r(n)$ are multiplied by $r(n-M)$, then summarize from 1 to M. Thus, the output is as Eq.10 shown.

If the received signal $r(n) = s(n) + \xi(n)$, where $\xi(n)$ is the noise on the channel which is a stationary random process. If $i \neq j$, then $\xi(i)$ and $\xi(j)$ are statistically independent, so a good synchronization would be maintained. The output of the correlators is as Eq.11 where the first item is useful signals and the second item are zero-mean random processes. Thus $y(k)$ and $b(k)$ have the same polarity, then decisions can be made by Eq.12.

$$y(k) = \sum_{i=1}^{M} r(n)r(n+M)$$

$$= \sum_{i=1}^{M} [s(n)+\xi(n)][s(n+M)+\xi(n+M)]$$

$$= \sum_{i=1}^{M} \{b(k)x^2(n) + x(n)[\xi(n+M)+b(k)\xi(n)]+\xi(n)\xi(n+M)\}$$

$$= b(k)\sum_{i=1}^{M} x^2(n) + \sum_{i=1}^{M} \{x(n)[\xi(n+M)+b(k)\xi(n)]+\xi(n)\xi(n+M)\}$$

(11)

$$m'(k) = \begin{cases} 0 & y(k) > 0 \\ 1 & y(k) < 0 \end{cases}$$

(12)

4   Simulation Results

Since $f_s = 2M f_m$, in order to maximize the transmission efficiency, M should be minimized under the premise of insurance on system reliability. The chaotic sequence is generated by Logistic map like Eq.12 where $\mu = 2.9$.

$$x(n+1) = \mu x(n)[1-x^2(n)]$$

(13)

To generate chaotic signals, provided the initial value $x(1)=0.1$. After 50 iterations, the chaotic signals can be used to modulate the information. The noise signal power spectrum is assumed zero. If $M = 50$, each symbol are to be modulated with 100 chaotic bits. Because $f_s = 2M f_m$, if the information transfer rate $f_m=1000$ Hz, then $f_s=10$ KHz. The information is randomly selected binary codes $m(k)=\{0\ 0\ 1\ 0\ 1\ 1\ 0\ 1\ 0\ 0\}$, then the output of the converter $b(k)=\{-1\ -1\ 1\ -1\ 1\ 1\ -1\ 1\ -1\ -1\}$ which are shown in Figure 4, and the power spectrum are also shown. It can be seen that the power spectrum concentrated in the vicinity of 120Hz and 380Hz. After DCSK modulation, the signal and the power spectrum are shown in Figure 5. It is shown that modulated signal s_n is chaotic. The original power spectrum has been spread to broadband after modulation, and then security communication can indeed be achieved. After demodulation, the information $b'(k)$ is shown in Figure 6, meaning that the information can be restore perfectly.

  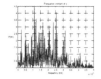

(a) Original information   (b) Power spectrum   (a) Information after   (b) Power spectrum
                                                   encryption

Fig. 4. Original information and its power spectrum

Fig. 5. Information after encryption and its power spectrum

The above simulation did not include the channel noise, and there are two factors affecting system performance. One is the power spectral density of the noise which will put a direct impact on E_b/N_0 (dB). If the noise power becomes smaller, the bit error rate is lower. The other one is the spread factor M, which will affect the randomness of the sequence. M is larger, the greater the randomness, so the lower the bit error rate. However, if M is longer, then the length of the sequence becomes longer which will make the system utilization lower. If the noise added to the channel is only AWGN signal (additive white Gaussian noise), then the simulation results are given jointly with the error rate BER and E_b/N_0 (dB). Where E_b is the bit energy, N_0 is the spectral density of the single sideband noise.

The bit error rate in traditional Binary Phase Shift Keying (BPSK) is as Eq.14. The relationship among BER, E_b/N_0 and M in DCSK is as Eq.15 [9].

$$BER_{BPSK} = \frac{1}{2} erfc(\sqrt{E_b / N_0}) \quad (14) \quad BER_{DCSK} = \frac{1}{2} erfc(\sqrt{\frac{E_b}{4N_0}(1 + \frac{2}{5M}\frac{E_b}{N_0} + \frac{N_0}{2E_b}M)^{-1}}) \quad (15)$$

DCSK and BPSK modulation is compared in Figure 7. It can be seen that, under the same E_b/N_0, the BER in BPSK is 1-2 orders of magnitude lower than in DCSK. With the E_b/N_0 increasing, the gap is more obvious in BER diagram, so the performance of DCSK is worse than BPSK. However the advantages of DCSK than BPSK are in secure communications. For DCSK, the performance when $M=8$ is better than that when $M=4$. Therefore, the larger the M value, the better the performance.

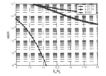

Fig. 6. the restored information $b'(k)$ **Fig. 7.** Comparison between BPSK and DCSK   **Fig. 8.** Performance of DCSK in different M **Fig. 9.** Original image

The relationship between BER and spread factor M is shown in Fig.8. It can be seen from the figure that, with M increasing, the performance of the system has been improved. When E_b/N_0 is very small, M put little impact on the system performance, but when E_b/N_0 become larger, the performance will be greatly improved. For instance, when E_b/N_0 is in the vicinity of 30dB, the system can achieve one order of magnitude improvement. If the BER is the same, the greater the BER is, the greater the improvement of E_b/N_0. When the BER is 10^{-3} and M is 6 and 8, the performance can be improved 10dB.

This secure communication system can be applied in image transmission. The original image to be transmitted is shown in Fig. 9. Suppose the image is transmitted in channel with Additive White Gaussian Noise (AWGN) environment, when the SNR varies from -20dB to 20dB, simulation results under different SNR and M are shown in Fig. 10. It can be seen that when the noise intensity gradually is reduced which makes the signal to noise ratio gradually increase, there is a great improvement of the image quality. And with M increasing, image quality has also been improved to some extent. So it is proved the feasibility to make this system to transmit the image.

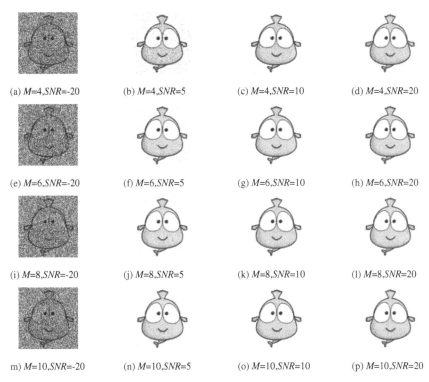

(a) *M*=4,*SNR*=-20   (b) *M*=4,*SNR*=5   (c) *M*=4,*SNR*=10   (d) *M*=4,*SNR*=20

(e) *M*=6,*SNR*=-20   (f) *M*=6,*SNR*=5   (g) *M*=6,*SNR*=10   (h) *M*=6,*SNR*=20

(i) *M*=8,*SNR*=-20   (j) *M*=8,*SNR*=5   (k) *M*=8,*SNR*=10   (l) *M*=8,*SNR*=20

m) *M*=10,*SNR*=-20   (n) *M*=10,*SNR*=5   (o) *M*=10,*SNR*=10   (p) *M*=10,*SNR*=20

Fig. 10. Restored image at different SNR and *M*

5   Conclusion

Digital chaotic secure communication is mainly achieved by CSK, which is difficult to realize for its technological complex in synchronization. However DCSK is more convenient and simple to achieve because it doesn't need synchronization. The principles of DCSK have been deeply studied in detail in order to optimize the modem that can be used in the actual circuit. Also the coherent detection algorithms have been described. The performances of BPSK and DCSK have been analyzed deeply through simulation. An example using DCSK in image transmission has been also introduced, so that DCSK can indeed be applied in secure communication. However its performance remains to be further improved. It is noteworthy that the process of coherent detection algorithm takes time, so there is delay between the transmitter and receiver. The delay put an impact on the system, so the next work is to study how to minimize the delay. Another factor have a significant impact on system performance is noise, which is uncertain in the channel. Because the system is master-slave mode, then there is no feedback from receiver to transmitter, so it is not self adaptive which is also need to be studied in the future.

Acknowledgments. This work is supported by the National Natural Science Foundation of China (No.61071196), the NSAF Foundation (No.10776040) of National Natural Science Foundation of China, the Program for New Century Excellent Talents in University (No.NCET-10-0927), the Project of Key Laboratory of Signal and Information Processing of Chongqing (No.CSTC,2009CA2003), and the Natural Science Foundation of Chongqing (No.CSTC,2009BB2287, CSTC,2010BB2398, CSTC,2010BB2411), and the Research Fund of CQUPT(No.A2010-2).

References

1. Smith, T.F., Waterman, M.S.: Identification of Common Molecular Subsequences. J. Mol. Biol. 147, 195–197 (1981)
2. May, P., Ehrlich, H.-C., Steinke, T.: ZIB Structure Prediction Pipeline: Composing a Complex Biological Workflow Through Web Services. In: Nagel, W.E., Walter, W.V., Lehner, W. (eds.) Euro-Par 2006. LNCS, vol. 4128, pp. 1148–1158. Springer, Heidelberg (2006)
3. Foster, I., Kesselman, C.: The Grid: Blueprint for a New Computing Infrastructure. Morgan Kaufmann, San Francisco (1999)
4. Czajkowski, K., Fitzgerald, S., Foster, I., Kesselman, C.: Grid Information Services for Distributed Resource Sharing. In: 10th IEEE International Symposium on High Performance Distributed Computing, pp. 181–184. IEEE Press, New York (2001)
5. Foster, I., Kesselman, C., Nick, J., Tuecke, S.: The Physiology of the Grid: an Open Grid Services Architecture for Distributed Systems Integration. Technical report, Global Grid Forum (2002)
6. National Center for Biotechnology Information, http://www.ncbi.nlm.nih.gov
7. Chien, T.-I., Liao, T.-L.: Design of secure digital communication systems using chaotic modulation, cryptography and chaotic synchronization. J. Chaos, Solitons & Fractals 24(1), 241–255 (2005)
8. Penaud, S.: Etude des potentialités du chaos pour les systèmes de télécommunication: Evaluation des performances de systèmes à accès multiples a répartition par les codes (CDMA) utilisant des sequences d'étalement chaotiques: Thèse résentée à l'université de Limoges Faculté des Sciences le 06 Mars (2001)
9. Schimming, T., Hasler, M.: Optimal detection of differential chaos shift keying. J. IEEE Trans. Circuits Syst. 47(12), 1712–1719 (2000)
10. Carroll, T.L., Pecora, L.M.: Synchronizing hyperchaotic volume preserving maps and circuits. J. IEEE Trans. Circuits Syst. 45(6), 656–659 (1998)
11. Lau, F.C.M.: Performance of Chaos-Based Communication Systems Under the Influence of Coexisting Conventional Spread-spectrum Systems. J. IEEE Trans. Actions on Circuits and Systems 50(11), 1475–1481 (2003)
12. Lau, F.C.M., Tsey, C.K.: Optimum Correlator-Type Receiver Design For Csk Communication Systems. J. International Journal of Bifurcation and Chaos 12(5), 1029–1038 (2002)
13. Kennedy, M.P., Kolumb, A.N.: Controlling Chaos and Bifurcations in Engineering Systems, pp. 477–500. CRC Press, NY (1999)

14. Han, C.-Y., Bao, X.-L., Wang, G.-Y.: A new digital chaotic cipher sequence and its property. Journal of Chongqing University of Posts and Telecommunications 22(3), 334–338
15. Ben Farah, M.A., Kachouri, A., Samet, M.: Design of secure digital communication systems using DCSK chaotic modulation. In: International Conference on DTIS 2006, pp. 200–204 (2006)
16. Jovic, B., Unsworth, C.P.: Fast synchronisation of chaotic maps for secure chaotic communications. J. Electronics Letters 46(1), 49–50 (2010)
17. Hugues-Salas, O., Shore, K.A.: An Extended Kalman Filtering Approach to Nonlinear Time-Delay Systems: Application to Chaotic Secure Communications. J. Circuits and Systems I 57(9), 2520–2530 (2010)
18. Pisarchik, A.N., Ruiz-Oliveras, F.R.: Optical Chaotic Communication Using Generalized and Complete Synchronization. J. Quantum Electronics 46(3), 279–284 (2010)

Analysis on Application of Fusion Function on Fuzzy Controller for Double Inverted Pendulum

Lian-yun He

Department of Mechanical and Electronic Engineering, Dezhou University, 253023, Shandong, China
helianyun@163.com

Abstract. As a typically fast, multivariable and non-linear unsteady system, the inverted pendulum system has always been the focus of control theory and application, whose control methods and thoughts also have wide applications in the general industrial processes, so the study on the inverted pendulum system has important theoretical and practical application value. The fuzzy controller for double inverted pendulum based on fusion function will convert the fuzzy control for the multivariable system into fuzzy control for two-input variable system, which greatly reduces the number of fuzzy control rule, simplifies the design of fuzzy controller and effectively solves the multivariable problem. It is shown from MATLAB simulation test that the control effect is perfect.

Keywords: Inverted pendulum, non-linear system, fusion function, fuzzy control, MATLAB simulation.

1 Introduction

The double inverted pendulum system is a complicated, non-linear and unsteady high-order system with more control targets. The traditional fuzzy controller adopts system error and error derivative as the input. The design of fuzzy control rule is very complicated and the adjustable parameters are also very many, it is obviously difficult for realization and the increase of computation amount also has influence on the real time of the control system. In order to simply the problem, the fuzzy controller for the double inverted pendulum system is designed with the help of the linear model of the system, i.e. with combination of linear system theory and the fuzzy control technique, the fuzzy control for the multivariable system is converted into the fuzzy control for two input variables, which greatly reduces the number of fuzzy control rules, simplifies the design of fuzzy controller, effectively solves the multivariable problem and improves the performance quality of the fuzzy controller.

2 Mathematical Model of Double Inverted Pendulum System

The double inverted pendulum system is shown as in Fig.1. The double inverted pendulum device is composed of the cart moving along the guide rail and the pendulum fixed on the cart through the mounted shaft[1]. The photoelectric coder is installed at one end of the rail for measuring the cart position. There are rotor shafts

M. Zhao and J. Sha (Eds.): ICCIP 2012, Part I, CCIS 288, pp. 144–151, 2012.

for connection between the pendulum and the cart as well as between the pendulums and there are two photoelectric coders at the connections for separately measuring the angle of lower pendulum and the angle of upper pendulum. The lower pendulum and the upper pendulum can move right and left on the horizontal guide rail around respective rotor shaft thus to make the inverted pendulum stable at the vertical position and be able to move upside down along the rail.

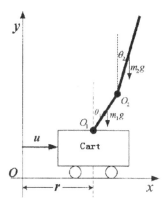

Fig. 1. Schematic diagram of motion analysis on double inverted pendulum

Table 1. Parameter table of double inverted pendulum system

Mechanical parameter	Value
Cart mass m_0	1.32Kg
Pendulum pole mass m_1 of lower pendulum	0.215Kg
Pendulum pole mass m_2 of upper pendulum	0.132Kg
Moment of inertia J_1 of lower pendulum around the centroid G_1	0.008398Kg·m²
Moment of inertia J_2 of upper pendulum around the centroid G_2	0.01825Kg·m²
The distance l_1 from the centroid G_1 of lower pendulum to the rotor shaft O_1	0.13m
The distance l_2 from the centroid G_2 of upper pendulum to the rotor shaft O_2	0.22m
Pendulum pole length L_1 of lower pendulum	0.16m
Pendulum pole length L_2 of upper pendulum	0.40m
Coefficient of sliding friction f_0 between the cart and the guide rail	23.6782N*s/m
Coefficient of friction resistance moment f_1 of lower pendulum rotating around rotor shaft O_1	0.003425N*s*m
Coefficient of friction resistance moment f_2 of upper pendulum rotating around rotor shaft O_2	0.003425N*s*m
Gravity acceleration g	9.8m/s²
Control volume (force) u of inverted pendulum system	N

If $x = \begin{bmatrix} r & \theta_1 & \theta_2 - \theta_1 & \dot{r} & \dot{\theta}_1 & \dot{\theta}_2 - \dot{\theta}_1 \end{bmatrix}^T$, the equation of state can be derived:

$$\begin{cases} \dot{X} = AX + Bu \\ Y = CX \end{cases}$$

$$A = \begin{pmatrix} 0 & 0 & 0 & 1 & 0 & 0 \\ 0 & 0 & 0 & 0 & 1 & 0 \\ 0 & 0 & 0 & 0 & 0 & 1 \\ 0 & 0.9603 & -0.1161 & -15.7642 & 0.0123 & -0.0054 \\ 0 & 35.9660 & -3.3441 & 47.2820 & -0.5526 & 0.2964 \\ 0 & -5.5607 & 12.3138 & 9.6637 & 0.2887 & -0.1885 \end{pmatrix}$$

$$B = \begin{pmatrix} 0 & 0 & 0 & 0.6658 & -1.9969 & -0.4081 \end{pmatrix}^T$$

$$C = \begin{pmatrix} 1 & 0 & 0 & 0 & 0 & 0 \\ 0 & 1 & 0 & 0 & 0 & 0 \\ 0 & 0 & 1 & 0 & 0 & 0 \end{pmatrix}$$

3   Design of Fusion Function

Theoretically speaking, there is great coupling relation between the cart displacement r as well as speed $\dot{r}$ and the pendulum pole angle θ as well as the angular velocity $\dot{\theta}$ of the pendulum pole[2]. Not only the cart motion shall be controlled within the scope of zero position but also the pendulum shall not fall. For the multi-factor problem, the solving process of the problem can be simplified by adopting the method of in-step treatment. This thought can be applied into the design process of multi-input fuzzy controller[3]. For the multi input cases, the single complicated control policy can be converted into multi-level simple control policy. For the nesting function $Y=f_2[f_1(X)]$, i.e. the input variable X is initially treated with algorithm $f_1()$, then the control is carried out with algorithm $f_2()$ according to the output of front-level algorithm. If the dimensions of the output vector of algorithm $f_1()$ is less the dimensions of X, the control work of algorithm $f_2()$ is simplified. It can be seen that many information are synthesized and optimized in algorithm $f_1()$ by using the internal relation of the system state to complete the function of system information combination and extraction, so it is called "fusion function". The algorithm $f_2()$ realizes the function of reasoning according to the contracted factors, so it is called "activation function". The fuzzy controller realizes the fusion function with the linear optimal control theory but the activation function is realized through the fuzzy control.

Firstly, the linear optimal control theory is applied and the state feedback coefficient of system can be derived with lqr function in the Matlab environment to be taken as the initial value of the comprehensive coefficient of system, $K = \begin{bmatrix} k_r & k_{\theta_1} & k_{\theta_2-\theta_1} & k_{\dot{r}} & k_{\dot{\theta}_1} & k_{\dot{\theta}_2-\dot{\theta}_1} \end{bmatrix}$, which can make the linear model of the double inverted pendulum system able to be basically stable.

In order to realize variable fusion, two feedback coefficients are separately selected as the principle component of control and the other input variables can separately be merged into two principle components according to the relation and fusion with the principle component. The state vectors $x = \begin{bmatrix} r & \theta_1 & \theta_2 - \theta_1 & \dot{r} & \dot{\theta}_1 & \dot{\theta}_2 - \dot{\theta}_1 \end{bmatrix}^T$, $\theta = \theta_2 - \theta_1$ and $\dot{\theta} = \dot{\theta}_2 - \dot{\theta}_1$ are selected as the principle components of control of the whole controlled system and its corresponding coefficients can be recorded as $k_\theta = k_{\theta_2 - \theta_1}$ and $k_{\dot{\theta}} = k_{\dot{\theta}_2 - \dot{\theta}_1}$ and the output vector of fusion function is recorded as $\tilde{x} = \begin{bmatrix} \tilde{\theta} & \dot{\tilde{\theta}} \end{bmatrix}^T$, then:

$$u = Kx$$
$$= k_r r + k_{\theta_1}\theta_1 + k_{\theta_2 - \theta_1}(\theta_2 - \theta_1) + k_{\dot{r}}\dot{r} + k_{\dot{\theta}_1}\dot{\theta}_1 + k_{\dot{\theta}_2 - \dot{\theta}_1}(\dot{\theta}_2 - \dot{\theta}_1)$$

$$= k_\theta (\frac{k_r}{k_\theta}r + \frac{k_{\theta_1}}{k_\theta}\theta_1 + \theta) + k_{\dot{\theta}}(\frac{k_{\dot{r}}}{k_{\dot{\theta}}}\dot{r} + \frac{k_{\dot{\theta}_1}}{k_{\dot{\theta}}}\dot{\theta}_1 + \dot{\theta})$$

$$= k_\theta\tilde{\theta} + k_{\dot{\theta}}\dot{\tilde{\theta}}$$

The output equation of fusion function is:

$$f_1(x) = \begin{bmatrix} E \\ EC \end{bmatrix} = \begin{bmatrix} \dfrac{k_r}{k_\theta} & \dfrac{k_{\theta_1}}{k_\theta} & 1 & 0 & 0 & 0 \\ 0 & 0 & 0 & \dfrac{k_{\dot{r}}}{k_{\dot{\theta}}} & \dfrac{k_{\dot{\theta}_1}}{k_{\dot{\theta}}} & 1 \end{bmatrix} \bullet x$$

Six state variables of the system are synthesized into two complex variables through linear combination, i.e. six state inputs are reduced to two-dimension output, then which is provided to the activation function for realizing control, i.e. as the input of fuzzy control. E and EC are obtained after dimension reduction of fusion function as the input value of the controller, so only one two-dimension Mandani-type fuzzy controller is required to de designed, which greatly simplifies the design of fuzzy controller.

In the practical control of system, assumed:

$$Q = diag[10 \quad 50 \quad 250 \quad 0 \quad 0 \quad 0]; \quad R = 0.01$$

According to the parameters of double inverted pendulum, the state feedback matrix K can be derived through Matlab computation:

$$K = [32.000 \quad -215.00 \quad -363.93 \quad 39.000 \quad -70.000 \quad -643.20]$$

The fusion function $f_1(X)$ can be further designed and the comprehensive error E and the change rate of comprehensive error EC can be derived.

$$\begin{bmatrix} E \\ EC \end{bmatrix} = f_1(x) = \begin{bmatrix} -0.0879 & 0.5907 & 1 & 0 & 0 & 0 \\ 0 & 0 & 0 & -0.0606 & 0.1088 & 1 \end{bmatrix} \bullet x$$

4   Design of Fuzzy Controller

One two-dimension Mandani-type fuzzy controller can be designed through the dimension reduction of fusion function. The domains of E and EC are separately taken as $E=[-10,10]$ and $EC=[-10,10]$ and the output domain is taken as $U=[-1,1]$. Both input variable and the output variable adopt the triangular, fully-overlapped and evenly distributed membership function[4-6] and each variable is described with four fuzzy subsets [NB NS ZE PS PB] as shown in Fig.2、Fig.3 and Fig.4.

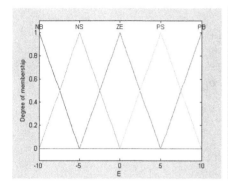
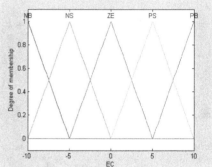

Fig. 2. Membership function of E **Fig.3.** Membership function of EC

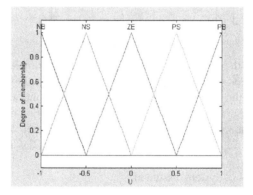

Fig. 4. Membership function of U

According to the division of fuzzy linguistic variables in the input and output domains, the fuzzy reasoning rule can be designed shown as follows.

    1. If (E is NB) and (EC is NB) then (U is NB)
    2. If (E is NB) and (EC is NS) then (U is NB)
    3. If (E is NB) and (EC is ZE) then (U is NB)
    4. If (E is NB) and (EC is PS) then (U is NS)
    5. If (E is NB) and (EC is PB) then (U is ZE)
    6. If (E is NS) and (EC is NB) then (U is NB)
    7. If (E is NS) and (EC is NS) then (U is NB)

8. If (E is NS) and (EC is ZE) then (U is NS)
9. If (E is NS) and (EC is PS) then (U is ZE)
10. If (E is NS) and (EC is PB) then (U is PS)
11. If (E is ZE) and (EC is NB) then (U is NB)
12. If (E is ZE) and (EC is NS) then (U is NS)
13. If (E is ZE) and (EC is ZE) then (U is ZE)
14. If (E is ZE) and (EC is PS) then (U is PS)
15. If (E is ZE) and (EC is PB) then (U is PB)
16. If (E is PS) and (EC is NB) then (U is NS)
17. If (E is PS) and (EC is NS) then (U is ZE)
18. If (E is PS) and (EC is ZE) then (U is PS)
19. If (E is PS) and (EC is PS) then (U is PB)
20. If (E is PS) and (EC is PB) then (U is PB)
21. If (E is PB) and (EC is NB) then (U is ZE)
22. If (E is PB) and (EC is NS) then (U is PS)
23. If (E is PB) and (EC is ZE) then (U is PB)
24. If (E is PB) and (EC is PS) then (U is PB)
25. If (E is PB) and (EC is PB) then (U is PB)

The fuzzy controller realizes fuzzy solution with the centroid method. Compared with the generally adopted maximum degree of membership method, the centroid method has smoother output reasoning control.

5   Simulation of Fuzzy Controller and Analysis

Under the environment of Matlab6.5, the simulation of fuzzy control for the linear fusion of double inverted pendulum is realized with Simulink. the fuzzy controller has two inputs, i.e. comprehensive error E and change rate of comprehensive error EC, one output U ; , two quantitative factors k_e and k_{ec} as well as one scaling factor k_u.

Besides a good fuzzy control rule[7] is required for the design of one fuzzy controller, it is also very important to reasonably select the quantitative factor of the input variable and the scaling factor of output variable of the fuzzy controller. It is shown from the test results that relative relations between the sizes of quantitative factor and scaling factor as well as between the sizes of different quantitative factors have great influence on the control performance of the fuzzy controller[8][9].

The sizes of quantitative factors K_e and K_{ec} have great influence on the dynamic performance of the control system. If K_e is over small, the rise speed of system will be over small, which will probably cause the system to generate vibration and even make the system unstable. If K_e is selected larger, the overshoot of system is also larger and the transition process is longer. If K_e is over large, the rise speed of system is over fast, which will also cause to generate vibration and even make the system unstable. When K_{ec} is selected larger, the overshoot of system is smaller, but the response time of system will become slow. The sizes of quantitative factors K_e and K_{ec} have influence on the different weighting degrees of input variable error and error change. K_e and K_{ec} also have influence on each other [10].

As the overall gain of fuzzy controller, the size of scaling factor K_u of output control value has influence on the output of the controller. if K_u is selected over small, it will make the dynamic response process become longer, but if K_u is selected over large, it will exacerbate the vibration of the system. The input size of the controlled object can be changed through adjusting K_u. Generally speaking, k_u is always determined firstly when determining the quantitative factor and the scaling factor of the fuzzy controller for the double inverted pendulum to make the output value of the fuzzy controller at a more suitable order of magnitude. In order to facilitate the debugging, k_u is taken as the fixed value firstly in the practical application of the controller for double inverted pendulum, then the quantitative factor is debugged. k_e=4, k_{ec}=20 and k_u=0.1875 can be derived according to the simulations of many times.

The simulation curve of the cart position, angle of lower pendulum and angle of upper pendulum of the double inverted pendulum is shown as in Fig.5.

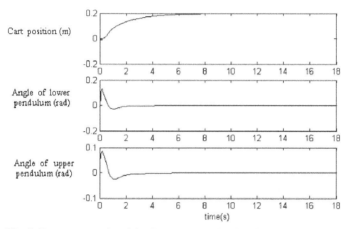

Fig. 5. Response results of the fuzzy control for double inverted pendulum (1)

One disturbing force $\dot{f}$=0.5N is applied to the centroid of the cart when t=10s, the response results are shown as in Fig.6.

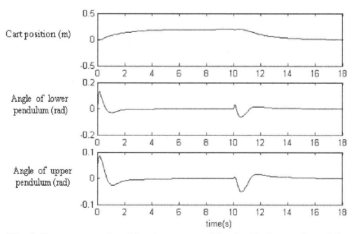

Fig. 6. Response results of the fuzzy control for double inverted pendulum (2)

It can be seen from the running results of simulation that the controller can perfectly control the running of the inverted pendulum and realize the control target. The angle of upper pendulum is approximately within 0.08*rad*, the angle of lower pendulum is around 0.15*rad* and the maximum distance of the deviation from the equilibrium position of the cart displacement is less than 18*cm*. The control value is also within the reasonable scope and the system basically returns to the equilibrium position in short time with fast response speed. After the inverted pendulum reaches the control target, the disturbing force is applied to the centroid of the cart and it will only take 3 seconds or so for the fuzzy controller to recover the inverted pendulum to the original equilibrium state. The fuzzy controller demonstrates perfect dynamic performance, steady state performance and anti-jamming performance in the control.

References

1. Shi, X., Zhang, Z., et al.: Modeling and Application of a Double Inverted Pendulum. Journal of Hebei University of Technology 30(5), 48–51 (2001)
2. Wang, H.: Foundation of Modern Control Theory, pp. 138–145. National Defence Industry Press, Beijing (2004)
3. Xue, D., Chen, Y.: System Simulation Technology and Application Based on Matlab/Simulink, pp. 235–244. Tsinghua University Press, Beijing (2002)
4. Tang, B., Lu, L., et al.: Fuzzy Control Theory and Application Technology, pp. 285–302. Tsinghua University Press, Beijing (2002)
5. Li, S., Wang, J.: Intelligent Control, pp. 168–177. Mechanical Industry Press, Beijing (2005)
6. Li, T., Lin, X., et al.: Application of Fuzzy Control in the Control System for inverted pendulum. Modern Electronics Technique 136(5), 66–68 (2002)
7. Wu, X., Lin, Z., et al.: Design of MATLAB-aided fuzzy system, pp. 169–185. XiDian University Press, Xi'an (2002)
8. Huang, Z.: Computer Simulation of Control System MATLAB, pp. 246–255. National Defence Industry Press, Beijing (2004)
9. Wang, M.: Simulink Modeling and Dynamic Simulation, pp. 68–101. Publishing House of Electronics Industry, Beijing (2002)
10. Cao, C., Wan, N.: Intelligent Control, pp. 375–387. Tsinghua University Press, Beijing (2004)

Research and Improvement of the Algorithm to Extract Association Rules Based on Concept Lattice

Shi-min Zhang

Zibo Vocational Institute
Zibo, Shandong, China, 255314
shimin.zhang81@gmail.com

Abstract. The algorithm is improved to extract association rules based on concept lattice. The algorithm in this paper doesn't extract all rules, but a subset of all rules which is called rule-generating set. Consequently, it can be used to get all rules. Due to the fact that number of the rule-generating set is smaller than all rules, the efficiency of mining is increased. This kind of algorithm can not gain confidence as well as support from each rule while other algorithm can. It only gets all rules those support and confidence is larger than threshold that is given by user.

Keywords: data mining, association rules, concept lattice, rule-generating set.

1   Introduction

Knowledge discovery in databases becomes more and more important in artificial intelligence research field currently, and rule extraction is the core data mining tasks, which has been already studied extensively. Traditional Apriori algorithm is efficient in generating all association rules, while it at the same time brings about redundancy problems. In the process of knowledge mining rules, the rule itself is made manifest by the relationship between sets, and nodes of concept lattice is just the combination of connotation and extension. The relationship between each node reflects the generalization and specialization of concepts. Actually, each node is one of the largest item sets, which makes the concept is perfectly suitable for rule extraction grid data structure. Currently, there are many rule extraction based on concept lattice algorithm.

2   Research of Association Rules Mining Based on Concept Lattice

2.1   A Concept Lattice-Based Idea of Mining Association Rules

The task of Association rule mining is to explore all strong association rules from the database D, and it will be divided into the following two sub-parts:

1. Find all frequent item sets in Transaction database D. In other words, it is to pick out all the item sets in which the minimum user-specified support threshold smaller than any other items.

M. Zhao and J. Sha (Eds.): ICCIP 2012, Part I, CCIS 288, pp. 152–158, 2012.

2. Generate strong association rules by frequent item sets. That is to say, association rule first generate candidate item sets, which is then verify whether its confidence lower than user-specified minimum confidence threshold. If it is not lower, then conclusion can be got that this candidate is the strong association rules.

Because the process of generating association rules from frequent item sets is comparatively simple, this paper mainly analyses how to find out frequent item sets from concept lattice.

2.2   The Traditional Concept Lattice-Based Algorithm to Extract Association Rules

Algorithm 1. Algorithm of extracting association rules from established association rules lattice

```
Input: Established association rules lattice L, Support

threshold θ, Credibility threshold O

  Output: Set of association rules RULES

  begin

      RULES: =O;

      numsup:=θ*|U|;

      Cand_Node:=O

      For each node C in L do     /* Generate all candidate tuples
*/

          If   C.ext_count>=numofsup   then

            numcon:=C.ext_count/O;

            PAIRS[C]:=O;

            queue:=nil;   /* Set the queue is empty */

            push(queue,C);

            while notempty(queue) do

                CC:=pull(queue);

                For each parent CCp of CC do

                  If CCp.ext_count<=numcon then

                    Push(queue,CCp);

                  Endif;
```

```
            Endfor;
        PAIRS[C]:=PAIRS[C]∪{CC};
      Endwhile;
      Cand_Node:=Cand_Node∪{C};
    Endif;
  Endfor;
  For Cand_Node each node C in descending order by number
of content do
    For each child C' of C do /* Eliminating redundant
candidate pair */
        PAIRS[C]:= PAIRS[C]-PAIRS[C'];
    Endfor;
    LH:=O;
    For each C' in PAIRS[C] do
      LH:=LH∪C'.int_red;
    Endfor;
    for each M in LH do
        if LH exist in M 'to meet the M'⊂M then
        LH:=LH-{M};
      Endif;
    Endfor;
    RULES:=RULES∪{red⇒C.intension-red|red∈ LH};
  Endfor;
End;
```

3   Improvement of the Algorithm to Extract Association Rules Based on Concept Lattice

3.1   Overview of the Algorithm

The algorithm in this paper extracts a subset instead of all rules, which is named rule-generating set and can be applied to derivate all rules. The rule-generating set is smaller than all rules, which improves the efficiency of mining. This kind of algorithm is unable to get each rule's support and confidence while other algorithm can. It only gets rules whose support and confidence is higher than threshold given by users. But when the mining data is very large and the confidence threshold is low, our algorithm can get smaller rule-generating set than other algorithm. So if users are provided with smaller rule set, they can choose rules based on their needs. Also this method makes it possible to use smaller memory sizes storing rules and increase the speed of finding rules.

3.2   Description of Algorithm

Algorithm 2. Algorithm to extract rule-generating set based on concept lattice
Input: Established concept lattice L, Minimum support α, Minimum trust β_o.
Output: Minimal rule-generating set Σ.

Step1: Initialize$\Sigma=\phi$; Find the total number of transactions N, Make n=N*α ; Put lattice Vertex into the set M0.
Step2: Find directly subordinate nodes from M0; put them into M1, and remove the node to meet extension number < n.
Step3: If M1=ϕ, turn to step 5(end).else, make C={the first node from M1 }.

① Find extension number of the node C, makes it e.
② Find directly subordinate nodes of C, put it into the set N0, and remove the node to meet extension number < n or remove the node from e*β.
③ Put the 100% most simple rules between the node C and C'(C'$\in$ N0) into Σ.
④ Seek a direct subordinate of each point from N0, put them into N1, remove the node to meet extension number < n or remove the node from e*β.
⑤ If N1=ϕ, turn to ⑥; else each node from N1 and its direct superior node pair, seek the 100% most simple rules, put them into Σ; remove direct superior node of N1 from N0; N0=N0∪N1; turn to ④.
⑥ Node C and I(I $\in$ N0) paired, the rules generated by this method A $\rightarrow$ Intension(I)-A(A$\in$ Gmin (C)) , put rules into Σ.
⑦ If there is not the successor node of C in M1, turn to step 4; else make C= {the successor node of C}, turn to •.

Step4: M1 $\rightarrow$ M0, turn to step 2.
Step5: end.

4   Algorithm of Deriving General Rules Set from Group Rules Set

Algorithm 3. Algorithm of deriving general rules set from group rules set

Input: Established set M of rules list.
Output: Generated set $\Sigma$of rules among all candidate node pairs.
Step1: Initialize $\Sigma=\phi$.
Step2: Remove the first list from the set M, the pointer H points to the list.

Step3: Put it into the set Σ that it is storage rules of the head node of the list pointed to by H.

Make the set G= {storage rules of the head node}, N1=ϕ.

Step4: If the number of lower node of the head node is zero, then turn to step 5, else:

① Take its rules stored in the lower node, if there is an empty node, then further find the lower node of the empty node, until it is a non-empty node, put all nodes into the set N, record the number m of empty nodes before each node.

② If all the rule's consequent in N and the rule's antecedent in G are the same, then turn to ⑥, else next.

③ Find the intersection set and the difference set of the rules, these rules are stored in the node of the set N.

④ Put the rules into the set Σ, these rules satisfy that they are respectively consequent and antecedent in G to lose the intersection set A and they are consequent in G to lose the intersection set A. (The rule's consequent in the set N1) Subtract (The intersection set A),m subtract 1,m is the number of empty nodes ; if m of some rules =0, put the rule of N1 into the set Σ, and remove the rule from the set N1.

⑤ If A ≠ B, put the rules into the set N1, these rules meet they are consequent that they are antecedent in G to lose the difference set B and they are consequent in G to lose the difference set B. (The number of empty nodes) subtract (The number of items in the difference set B).

⑥ The set N is replaced with all subordinate of nodes in N, turn to ②.

⑦ Make the following changes in the rule G: the rule's consequent in the set N is interchanged with the rule's antecedent in the rule G, put the new rules generated into the set Σ. Search the entire list, the rules in the set G are interchanged with the new rules that they are the same with some 100% rule's consequent in list (the original rules of the set G are discarded), turn to step 4.

Step5: If the set M is null, then turn to step 6; else remove the next list from the set M, the pointer H points to the list,   turn to step 3.

Step6: end.

5   Algorithm of Deriving Single Consequent Rules from Rules Set

Algorithm 4. Algorithm of deriving single consequent rules from general rules set

Input: Established concept lattices L, Minimum support α, Minimum confidence β.

Output: The rules set Σ of a single back item (W) to meet the requirements.

Step1: Initialize Σ=ϕ, M=ϕ; Find the total number of transactions N, make n=N*α.

Step2: Search the entire concept lattice L, find all the candidate nodes to meet (αnβ), keep node pair with intension of item W.

Step3: Find simple intension of each node in the candidate node pair and put it into the set M.

① Select a node pair (C1, C2) (C1 $\geq$ C2) from the set M with simple intension.

② Find the basic concepts of each node.

③ Item sets from node C2 that without the item W are regarded as the rule's antecedent, put W into the set Σ as a rule of the rules consequent, and its credibility is 100%.

④ Item sets from node C1 that without the item W are the rule's antecedent, put W into the set Σ as a rule of the rule's consequent, its credibility is 100% or |C2|/|C1|(If the item W is in the node C1, then the rule trust is 100%, else the latter is our choice).

⑤ if the set M=ϕ, then turn to step 4; else remove a node pair with simple intensions from the set M, turn to ②.

Step4: end.

Algorithm 5. Algorithm of generating simple intension group set from intension based on concept lattice

Input: Intension of a concept C and the set of its simple intension group Y.

Output: The concept's set of all the basic content X.

Step1: make X=ϕ;

Step2: Remove a simple intension (item sets) from the set Y which is assigned to C'.

Step3: make M=C-C'; if M=ϕ, ouput C to the set X, turn to step 5; else next.

Step4: Find the set of all subsets of M I={im|im $\subseteq$ I}. Make item sets T=C' $\cap$ im, if T$\not\subseteq$ X, add T to the set X.

Step5: if the set Y=ϕ, turn to step 6; else remove a simple contents from Y is assigned to C', turn to ③.

Step6: end.

Algorithm 6. Algorithm of deriving single consequent rules from group rules set

Input: A set M of group reduction rules generated by the algorithm 2.

Output: The rules set Σ of a single back item (W) to meet the requirements.

Step1: Initialize Σ=ϕ.

Step2: Remove the first list from the set M with a pointer H to the list.

Step3: Make P= storage rules of the head node of the list pointed to by H, if W$\not\in$ antecedent of P and W$\not\in$ consequent of P, turn to step 5; else next.

Step4: If W$\in$ antecedent of P, backward search from the head node, find the node to meet consequent of storage rules equal to W, put storage rules of the node into the set Σ, and the credibility of the rule is 100%; if W$\in$ consequent of P, make P1= consequent of P -W, P2=P1 $\cup$ antecedent of P, then put the rule P into the set Σ, put the rule to satisfy the situation that P2 is antecedent and W is consequent into the set Σ.

Step5: If the set M is null, then turn to step 6; else remove the next list from the set M, the pointer H points to the list, turn to step 3.

Step6: end.

6   Analysis of Experiment Results

This paper applies three data mining algorithms (traditional algorithms, concept lattice (Xie) algorithm and our algorithm) to the rule mining of same database.
The comparison of these three different tests method is shown in Fig. 1:

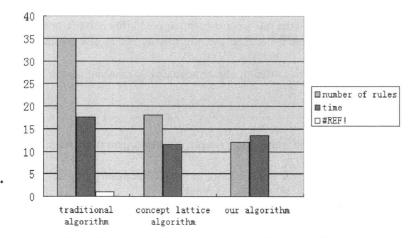

Fig. 1. Performance Comparison between Three Algorithms

Fig. 1 show: Our algorithm gets the least mining association rules, while the traditional algorithm (APRIOR algorithm) gets the largest number with unnecessary redundancy. View from prospect of calculating speed, our algorithm is slower than the general concept lattice mining algorithms, and it may due to the little bit inefficiency in our grid search, which indicates that further improvement is very necessary.

References

1. Zaki, M.: Mining Non-Redundant Association Rules. Data Mining and Knowledge Discovery 9, 223–248 (2004)
2. Deogun, J.S., Raghavan, V.V., Sever, H.: Association mining and formal concept analysis. In: Anita, W., San, C. (eds.) Proceedings of the RSDMGrC 1998. Elsevier Science Publishers, Duke (1998)
3. Ganter, B., Wille, R.: Formal Concept Analysis: Mathematical Foundations. Springer, Heidelberg (1999)
4. Zaki, M.J., Hsiao, C.J.: CHARM:An Efficient Algorithm for Closed Itemset Mining. In: Grossman, R., et al. (eds.) Proceedings of the 2nd SIAM International Conference on Data Mining, pp. 12–28. SIAM, Arlington (2002)
5. Pasquier, N., Bstide, Y., Taoui, R., Lakhak, L.: Closed set based discovery of smallcovers for association rules. In: Proc, BDA Conf., pp. 361–381 (1999)

Study on Prediction Model of Context-Aware Services Technologies for Internet of Things

Bo Deng[1] and Jing Ji[2]

[1] Henan Province Zhongwei Surveying and Planning Information Engineering Co Ltd,
454001 Jiaozuo, China
[2] Pingdingshan Industrial College of Technology,
467001 Pingdingshan, China
zwdengbo@126.com

Abstract. Through all kinds of communication technology, Computing resources around people's living will are networked in the age of Internet of Things .It is possible that the Internet of Things get user's dynamic information of environment related. Context-aware services get collect information of the scene by some sensors, processed the information of perception independently, and provided services to users who want to be serviced. This paper puts forward a kind of combination with Bayesian filter model and dynamic Bayesian network model, which include actor, time, location, the weather, the regional cultural background. It can aware the object's scene changed, predict behavioral tendency, based on which provided service matching user's expectation service. So prediction model of Context-aware services can greatly optimized resources of networking and the optimal allocation of resources, improve the performance of the whole system, with profound academic value and practical meaning.

Keywords: Context-aware services, Internet of Things, Bayesian filter model, dynamic Bayesian network model.

1 Introduction

Along with the development of the computer and communication technology, especially the communication and sensor technology by leaps and bounds, a new generation of internet technology—Internet of Things arises. Internet of Things is a kind of large-scale virtual network in which with various access technology mass electronic equipment through the Internet and heterogeneous information will be interconnected together to complete a specific task [1].Context-aware and fusion is also one of the most important features in the Internet of Things, which include the collection, control, transmission and the upper of the application the whole "content objects connected" process. It is the goal of the context-aware services of Internet of Things that through multi-sensor information fusion and cooperative aware, without users request services what he wants, with independently judges, it will be able to provide a service to users automatically. The context-aware services as a new

M. Zhao and J. Sha (Eds.): ICCIP 2012, Part I, CCIS 288, pp. 159–168, 2012.
© Springer-Verlag Berlin Heidelberg 2012

application can provide to customers personalized service, services for people's work and life, bring great convenience, mobility and security, has great market potential.

Context-aware services technologies for Internet of Things is a relatively new research fields of application, basically is to use all kinds of wireless location and environmental sensors to learn the position and scene information, improves the operation of the application system and service. Due to changes in the environmental and position, the user look forward to get different information service. Context-aware services prediction model of research is in the initial stage, for example, an integrated position information prediction [2] [3], through some prediction algorithm to get the change of customer's position, provide prediction of the services based on the position [4].

At present, the study of Context-aware services prediction is still mainly concentrated in prediction services based on location, not based on the information and forecast. This paper puts forward a kind of combination with Bayesian filter model and dynamic Bayesian network model, which include actor, time, location, the weather, the regional cultural background, and can better judge user information of forecast situation, and can offer a better service.

2   Context-Aware Services and Bayesian Network Model

2.1   Context-Aware Services

The processing of the context-aware is the environment information of object scene. The information of users is usually obvious scenarios, such as the user of the environment, temperature, humidity and the current time. It is quite difficult to give general definition scene information. The definition of Context has many versions. In context is defined as: position[5], the people logo around user, time, season and temperature, etc. In defined context as user the user's position[6], environment, identification and time. At present the context commonly used is Dey in the paper gives the definition[7].Context is any information that can be used to characterize the situation of an entity. An entity is a person, place, or object that is considered relevant to the interaction between a user and an application.

In 1994, B.N. Schilit [8] [9] thought that context-aware was the system which aware the scene and made the corresponding reaction of calculation equipment. The ultimate goal of context-aware is that the computer can acquire scene actively, and further perception scene, improve and enrich the way of traditional man-machine interactive to provide better services.

2.2   Bayesian Network Model[10]

The Bayesian network is based on the probability analysis refers to the graph theory of a kind of uncertainty knowledge expression and reasoning model. Speaking from the intuitive, Bayesian network behaves as a value assignment complex causality network diagram, the network of each one node is a variable, namely one event, all variables in the arc said events between the direct causality. A Bayesian network can be thought of as a binary group $B = <G, P>$. G refers to the network structure, $G = < X, A >$ is a directed acyclic graph *(DAG)*, the node is random variable $X = \{X_1, X_2, and..., X_n\}$, $n \geq 1$, is a collection of arc. P is network parameter; P refers to each of the elements of the condition node X_i represents probability density. The probability of chain rules can be:

$$P(X) = P(X_1, X_2, \cdots, X_{n-1}) = \Pi(X_i / X_1, X_2, \cdots X_{n-1}) \tag{1}$$

2.3   Dynamic Bayesian Network Model[11]

In the context-aware of Internet of Things, all kinds of situation information changes along with the time factor. Context-aware data in the different time reflect change rule of variables. The analysis of this change rule must establish adaptation of the dynamic model. Dynamic Bayesian network will expand to the time evolution of Bayesian network's process; reflect the development and change of the variable law can be used to explain the dynamic data and the future trend analysis and prediction.

To make the Dynamic Bayesian network as study and corresponding model, we first need to do some assumptions that introducing Markov assumption and the transfer of the probability that not change timely. Markov assumption is to point to every state variable set of moment is only associated with the value of the state variables of moment before. In a limited time, time-invariant of transition probability is the change process of conditional probability is steady and consistent for all t, not change over time.

Dynamic Bayesian network can be defined as $<B_0, B \rightarrow>$, which indicates the beginning of B_0 B_N, $B \rightarrow$ indicates the graphics of the B_N fragment consisting in more than two times. With $P(X_t \mid X_{t-1})$ expressed the former variable of any given state at a time and the probability of occurrence of the current state; $X_t(i)$ expressed the *i-th* variable value at time t, $Pa(X_t(i))$ expressed the parent node; N expressed the number of variables. In the $B \rightarrow$, the conditional probability can be over-written:

$$P_{B \rightarrow}[X_{t+1} / X_t] = \Pi P_{B \rightarrow}[X_{t+1}(i) / PaX_{t+1}(i)] \tag{2}$$

The joint probability of entire set variables is defined as:

$$P(X[0], X[1], \cdots [T]) = P(X[0]) P_{B \rightarrow}[X_{t+1} / X_t] \tag{3}$$

3   Construction Context-Aware Dynamic Bayesian Network Prediction Model

According to the architecture description of Internet of Things, the context-aware services are divided into three levels: the current situation aware, the current situation to understand, predict the future trend, shown in Fig. 1.

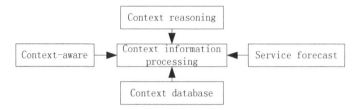

Fig. 1. Context-aware processing of Internet of Things

3.1   Bayesian Network for Context-Aware Model

For example, the following simple scene of everyday life, Context-aware services on the structure of Bayesian network modeling. Context information based on user and device information, the user's basic situation can be learned. For example, the user's preferences, the user's location in tourist attractions or industrial zone, day or night, driving or walking, what is the weather now, regional custom characteristics. The contextual information to provide Context services f include:

1) weather, weather, *WE* (good, medium, poor);
2) geographical factors, location, location, *LC*, customs *CL*;
3) user factors, the role *AC*.
4) Context-aware service events S, including food, clothing, housing, transportation, entertainment, consumer, and so sub-events.

Based on these factors to determine the causal relationship between the structure of Bayesian Network, the establishment of Bayesian network model shown in Fig. 2.

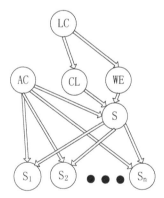

Fig. 2. Bayesian Network models of Context forecasting services

Circular nodes represent perception factors, where S is the target node, which expressed contains many sub-time status of various sub-services. *WE*, *LC*, *AC* as input node, *CL* node for the transition; the line on behalf of the causal links between nodes, can be expressed as:

$$S = \{S_1, S_2, \cdots, S_n\} \tag{4}$$

In formula, S_i $(i = 1,2, ... n)$ expressed perceived service set to give the form of multi-group

$$S_i = <WE, LC, AC, CL, S> \tag{5}$$

In formula: S-Context type of service; S_i-a subset of Context services; WE-the weather; LC-location; CL-customs; AC-the role.

It is main way of determine the probability parameters of each node that experts in the field methods and empirical method, and the combination of both knowledge and data fusion. Empirical method is to rely on experts in the field, given directly impact on the probability distribution of the node, is simple but the error is greater. Integration method is the empirical method used to estimate first, and then re-use learning method to improve the accuracy of which experts in the field of confidence is the key to set the right value.

Under a priori knowledge of $LL = (LL_1, LL_2,...,LL_m)$, the current real-time data $WW = (WW1, WW2, ..., WWn)$, and   context $S= (S_1, S_2, ..., S_n)$,the assumption $P (H/LL, WW)$ is calculated, P represent alternative scenarios for each service which has a probability of uncertainty associated value. Based on knowledge, established the correspondence between the features of services and elements, services of the current situation is classification and identification: context-aware set space $\Omega = \{a, b, c, ...\}$, context space whose elements are all possible classification of scenarios, $\Psi = \{x, y, z, ...\}$ are feature set of situational awareness, are scenario appears in the services space. Solution of context-aware here is actually seeking correspondence between collection of services and the space scene.

$$f : \Psi \rightarrow \Omega \tag{6}$$

As can be seen from the above, services estimation process rely on context-aware space, need to rely on a wealth of knowledge to establish corresponding rules ,solved solution of the application of knowledge-based reasoning algorithm. The establishment of a priori applicable domain knowledge and the template is required.

As not consider the time factor, Bayesian Network can not explain the variable node, as shown in Fig. 2, WE, CL and LC nodes are change over time. The context-aware services is often estimated in the data time-series data. Based on analysis, not only the destination node can predict the probability of future time value, but also the optimal solution for the maximum probability. This context-aware application service estimate is very important.

3.2   Dynamic Bayesian Network Prediction Model Context-Aware

In Fig. 2, the context-aware factors of Bayesian network model: WE, CL and LC are constantly changing. In order to express change, and can predict future scenarios, Dynamic Bayesian network is constructed to solve changes in the Bayesian network along the timeline, Fig. 3 Dynamic Bayesian network model diagram as follow.

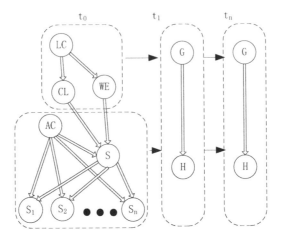

Fig. 3. Dynamic Bayesian prediction model for context-aware service

Fig. 3 is divided into left and right parts. Left part of the Bayesian network structure, similar to Fig. 2; in the right half, *G* refer to the changes of observations, including *WE*, *CL* and *LC* variable node; *H* is impact on hidden variables *G*, including *AC* and *G*-related transition variable; *S* is the target variable, namely the estimated service *{S1, S2 ... Sn}*. Dynamic Bayesian network and Bayesian network are for the same scene, but the structure of Dynamic Bayesian network need to express the time correlation information. In order to express time, combined with Bayesian network and the Bayesian filtering model [12] changes along the time axis are constructing Dynamic Bayesian network model. The difficulty is how to determine the location of observations, because the location information with a non-linear. First, based on the raw data analysis, Defined the probability distribution of Bayesian network, got the relational model between time-series and observations, it is to constructed that the conditions the probability distribution function associated with the time t. Dynamic Bayesian network model can be used to express time-dependent changes in the *LC*. Through a large number of observations based reasoning can be taken to the maximum variable value, to speculate on future scenarios. It not only has the advantage of a static Bayesian network, and can deal with dynamic problems, greatly expanded the scope of use. Reasoning of the Dynamic Bayesian network, the most easily understood method, is to start Bayesian network to Dynamic Bayesian network, and then one by one starting from the beginning of time pieces to calculate. But in the long fragment and more cases, the network model will be very big, very difficult to calculate. Here we use the general Bayesian filtering model reasoning.

3.3   Bayesian Filtering Algorithm [13]

In the dynamic Bayesian prediction model, the position is changing over time and is non-linear, where the use of Bayesian filtering for location estimation. For all the conditional probability distribution of random variables are subject to a linear Gaussian distribution. Bayesian filtering model is as follows:

Formal statistical motion model:

$$X_{K+1} = F_K X_K + V_K \tag{7}$$

Measurement model:

$$Z_{K+1} = H X_{K+1} + W_{K+1} \tag{8}$$

In the above formula, X_K and location that is relevant factors, F_K, said the system state matrix, H denotes the transformation matrix of observations, Z_K that perceived information. From the motion model (9), define a probability density function, Markov transition density, which encapsulates the information contained in this model:

$$f_{k+1/k}(x/x') = N_{Qk}(x - Fx') \tag{9}$$

The state and covariance estimates $x_{k/k}$, $P_{k/k}$ at time step k:

$$f_{k/k}(x/Z^k) = N_{P_{k/k}}(x - x_{k/k}) \tag{10}$$

A likelihood function:

$$f_{k+1}(z/x) = N_{R_{k+1/k}}(z - H_{k+1}x) \tag{11}$$

The state and covariance estimates $x_{k+1/k}$, $P_{k+1/k}$ at time step $k + 1$:

$$f_{k+1/k}(x/Z^k) = N_{P_{k+1/k}}(x - x_{k+1/k}) \tag{12}$$

The corrector step:

$$f_{k+1/k+1}(x/Z^{k+1}) = N_{P_{k+1/k+1}}(x - x_{k+1/k+1}) \tag{13}$$

The state and error covariance:

$$\int x \cdot N_{P_{k+1/k+1}}(x - x_{k+1/k+1})dx = x_{k+1/k+1} \tag{14}$$

$$\int xx^T \cdot N_{P_{k+1/k+1}}(x - x_{k+1/k+1})dx = P_{k+1/k+1} \tag{15}$$

It contains the entire context and location-related information, then through the dynamic Bayesian model calculated context-aware services.

4   Simulation

4.1   Simulation Results of Position

In order to verify the validity and effectiveness of the Bayesian filtering model, data of 100 sets generated to study the results and the actual data error comparison shown in Fig. 4, where the abscissa is forecast time, the vertical axis is the average relative error. Early, the forecast error was greater than the latter part, the Tendency stabilizing over time, the simulation experiments to illustrate the effectiveness of the use of Bayesian filtering algorithm in Dynamic Bayesian network and Bayesian filtering has good generalization.

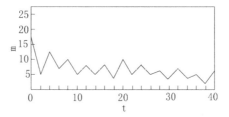

Fig. 4. The estimated error of location information based on Bayesian filtering

4.2   Context-Aware of Dynamic Bayesian Estimation Simulation

In the experiment, with t [i] and e [i] denote the i-th moment and evidence, set the threshold value of 60%, and the following table of values in percent.

In t [0] time, the context-aware elements value as following:

CL[0]	CL_1	CL_2	...	CL_n
Probability	12.3	5.3		12.6

AC[0]	AC_1	AC_2	...	AC_n
Probability	4.7	28.9		2.1

WE[0]	WE_1	WE_2	...	WE_n
Probability	3.3	51.6		1.5

In t [1] time, elements of context-aware as fllowing:

CL[1]	CL_1	CL_2	...	CL_n
Probability	33.5	21.6		3.8

AC[1]	AC_1	AC_2	...	AC_n
Probability	76.9	1.9		2.6

$WE_{[1]}$	WE_1	WE_2	...	WE_n
Probability	45.8	1.9		3.6

In t [0] and t [1] time the context-aware service are shown in Table 1 & 2:

Table 1. t [0] time of context-aware services estimated

value	context-aware services estimated			
	S_1	S_2	...	S_n
True	78.9	43.9		33.8
false	21.1	56.1		66.2

Table 2. t *[1]* time of context-aware services estimated

value	context-aware services estimated			
	S_1	S_2	...	S_n
True	69.2	37.9		15.2
false	30.8	62.1		84.8

Inputted Context-aware, used historical data, the model can be obtained by studying the most appropriate set of services relative to S, and to provide appropriate services to users. If the elements of context as: $CL=$ {user likes to read}, $LC=$ {user in a library near the intersection}, $WE =$ {sunny weather}, $AC =$ {students}, we can estimate point of the user will view the book, then the system will calculated the best path to the library recently, and feedback to the user. If the user does not agree, then the system followed by introduction of Program one and program two.

5   Conclusion

In this paper, the characteristics of data in the context-aware service prediction changes over time, by building Dynamic Bayesian network and Bayesian filtering model to solve the problem of expression of the variable node. Through the analysis of probability parameter and reasoning process, and the use of simulation experiments of Dynamic Bayesian network and Bayesian filtering model, the simulation results show the validity of the model feasible.

References

1. Vermesanet, O., et al.: Internet of Things Strategic Research Roadmap. EPoSS (September 2009)
2. Yavas, G., Katsaros, D., Ulusoy, O.: A data mining approach for location Prediction in mobile environments. Data and knowledge Engineering 54, 121–146 (2005)
3. Tseng, V.S., Lin, K.W.: Efficient mining and Prediction of user Behavior patterns in mobile web systems. Information and Software Technology 48, 357–369 (2006)
4. Abowd, G.D., Atkeson, C.G., Hong, J., Long, S., Kooper, R., Pinkerton, M.: Cyber guide: A mobile contex-aware tour guide. Wireless Networks 3(5) (1997)
5. Brown, P.J., Bovey, J.D., Chen, X.: Context-aware applications: From the laboratory to the market place. IEEE Personal Communications 4(5), 58–64 (1997)
6. Chien, B.-C., Tsai, H.-C., Hsueh, Y.-K.: CADBA: A Context-aware Architecture Based on Context Database for Mobile Computing, pp. 369–372 (July 2009)
7. Dey, A.K.: Providing architectural support for building context aware applications. Georgia Institute of Technology, Atlanta (2000)
8. Schilit, B.N., Adams, N., Want, R.: Context aware computing applications. In: WMCSA 1994, Santa Cruz, CA, USA, pp. 85–90 (1994)
9. Schilit, B.N., Hilbert, D.M., Trevor, J.: Context-aware communication. Wireless Communications, 46–54 (October 2002)

10. Krieg, M.L.: A Tutorial on Bayesian Belief Networks.DSTO Electronics and Surveillance Research Laboratory (2001)
11. Murphy, K.: Dynamic Bayesian Networks: Representation, Inference and Learning. University of California Berkeley (2002)
12. Ivansson, J.: Situation assessment in a stochastic environment using Bayesian network. Linkoping University, Sweden (2002)
13. Mahler, R.: Statistical Multisource Multitarget Information Fusion. Artech House (2007)

A New CFR Approach for OFDM Signals
Using Grouped Pulse Cancellation

Yaqian Huang and Zhibin Zeng

Engineering Research Center of Digital Audio and Video,
Ministry of Education
Communication University of China
Beijing, China
{hyq1006,zhbzeng}@cuc.edu.cn

Abstract. main disadvantage of OFDM systems is the high peak-to-average ratio (PAR) which can result in significant distortion when transmitted through power amplifiers. The common pulse cancellation method (cPCM) is an attractive technique in crest factor reduction, but for OFDM signals, this method is of high complexity. In this paper, a new approach named grouped pulse cancellation method (gPCM) is proposed for OFDM signals. Compared with cPCM, gPCM is of a simple algorithm and comparative performance, hence easy for implementation.

Keywords: OFDM, CFR, pulse cancellation, EVM.

1 Introduction

The orthogonal frequency division multiplexing (OFDM) signal is a predominant technique featuring high spectrum efficiency in current wireless communications. However, the main drawback of OFDM signals is that its time domain representation approximates a Gaussian distribution which causes its peak-to-average ratio (PAR) to be to be very high. High PAR demands enough power back-off of power amplifier (PA) to avoid degrading on radio frequency (RF) performance. Crest factor reduction (CFR) is used to reduce the PAR of signal before amplification by reducing its PAR to be low enough to be transmitted without power back-off.

Numerous literatures have been published in recent years, which provide various methods to solve the PAR problem [1]. Among these diverse CFR techniques, the pulse cancellation method is one of the clipping techniques, which is widely applied due to its high efficiency and easy implementation.

Here, based on the conventional pulse cancellation (cPCM), the grouped pulse cancellation method (gPCM) is proposed for OFDM signals. First, OFDM system model and related CFR Techniques are presented. Then, the principle and details of gPCM for OFDM signals are analyzed. Finally, the performance comparison between gPCM and cPCM is obtained through extensive MATLAB simulations.

M. Zhao and J. Sha (Eds.): ICCIP 2012, Part I, CCIS 288, pp. 169–176, 2012.
© Springer-Verlag Berlin Heidelberg 2012

2   CFR Techniques for OFDM Signals

2.1   OFDM Signals

OFDM is an attractive technique for high data rate transmission in mobile fading channels. The binary information bits are mapped to complex-valued 16-QAM symbols then the OFDM modulation is realized by using an inverse fast Fourier transform (IFFT). With the complex 16-QAM symbol denoted as d_i, the N-th OFDM samples can be written as:

$$x_n = \sum_{i=0}^{N-1} d_i \exp(j\frac{2\pi ik}{N}) \qquad (0 \le k \le N-1) \qquad (1)$$

OFDM characterizes efficient spectrum in that a single data stream is transmitted over some linear independent subcarriers for which the frequency spacing is reciprocal to the symbol period. As mentioned above, one main drawback of OFDM, however, is its high PAR which will result in serious nonlinear distortion and band radiation. PAR is defined as:

$$PAR(dB) = \frac{P_{peak}}{P_{average}} = 10\log_{10}\frac{\max[|x_n|^2]}{E[|x_n|^2]} \qquad (2)$$

Where $\max[|x_n|^2]$ is the peak signal power and $E[|x_n|^2]$ is the average signal power.

For OFDM signals consisting of N subcarriers, its PAR is not bigger than N, in other words, maximum PAR is equals to N. Maximum of PAR increases linearly with N. This places high demands on the linear range of the power amplifier especially for OFDM signal with great number of subcarriers.

2.2   Conventional CFR Techniques

Diverse methods, such as clipping [2], probabilistic [3], and adaptive symbol selection techniques [4], PTS (Partial transmit sequences) techniques, [5] noise shaping method and peak windowing etc. have been proposed to mitigate the CFR problem [1].

Clipping is the simplest method and, since the large peaks occur with a very low probability, clipping could be an effective technique for the CFR. However, there are several problems when applying it: clipping may cause significant in-band distortion of OFDM signals, which degrades the BER performance, and out-of-band noise. Filtering after clipping can reduce the spectral splatter but may also cause some peak regrowth.

The peak windowing algorithm is introduced to compensate for the out-band radicalization caused by amplitude clipping [6]. The key to this method is to choose an appropriate window function to make a balance between performance and complexity.

In noise shaping, the signal is clipped and then subtracted from the original to produce a clipping noise. The clipping noise is filtered to occupy the same frequency bands as the input signal. The spectrally shaped clipping noise is then subtracted from the input signal to produce a PAR reduced signal with minimal out-of-band degradation.

The cPCM is one of the clipping techniques which find its way into practical implementation due to its higher efficiency and better spectral characteristics. Although cPCM does not produce out-of-band interference, it isn't suitable for OFDM signals in that large number subcarrier will always result in too many peaks within equivalent time length. The gPCM we proposed is based on the combination of Grouped Threshold Detection and Target Threshold Detection which obtain a low computational complexity and equivalent performance in peak reduction [7].

Signal CFR is constrained by the EVM (Error Vector Magnitude), PCDE (Peak Code Domain Error) requirements and CCDF (Complementary Cumulative Distribution Function).When attempting to change the PAR performance of the OFDM signals, it is inevitable to alter the signal and lead to the degradation of these signal quality measurements. The algorithm needs to seek the tradeoff between the CFR and degradations in EVM, and PCDE measurements.

3   The Grouped Pulse Cancellation Method for OFDM Signals

3.1   Algorithm Overview

The pulse cancellation is a powerful CFR mechanism. It reduces the PAR of a signal by subtracting spectrally shaped pulses from signal peaks that exceed a specified threshold. However, for OFDM signals, every peak including many near threshold peaks need to be cancelled for multiple iterations will increase the difficulty of the design and introduce more interference.

The gPCM improves the common pulse cancellation method (cPCM) by using a grouped threshold detection. The grouped threshold is slightly higher than the target threshold. In our simulation, the grouped clipping ratio (CR) is larger than the target clipping ratios by 0.5. The input data is divided into groups and only one peak is detected per over-grouped threshold region thus reducing the effects of peak regrowth and improving the cancellation pulse generators allocation statistics.

This allows the algorithm to ignore peaks that are just barely crossing the target threshold and focus on peaks that exceed the target threshold by some delta then update the data and deal with the small peaks with pulse cancellation.

The main reason that gPCM is better than cPCM lies in the fact that gPCM ensures only one peak processed in each group, thus simplifying the algorithm construction, and avoiding some peak regrowth (near target threshold peaks) as well. Allocating the cancellation pulse generator resources to these higher peaks at first and then deal with the smaller peaks would provide better CFR performance for avoid missing higher peaks that mainly influence the performance. The input data is divided into groups and one of the groups is showed in Fig. 1.

Note that the gPCM have two independent thresholds:

1. The grouped threshold: the highest peak A above the grouped threshold is given priority to be cancelled.
2. The target threshold: detected peaks will be reduced to the target threshold.

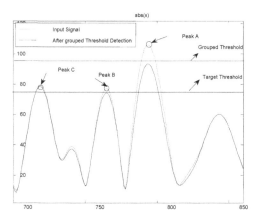

Fig. 1. The principle of gPCM

Three peaks exist in the over target threshold region, but only peak A is selected for cancellation in the grouped threshold detection before peak C is selected for cancellation in the target threshold detection. Peak B doesn't need to be processed because peak B is under the target threshold after the grouped threshold detection. As comparison, the cPCM will deal with peak A, B, C with more iterations, thus leading to unnecessary peak regrowth and interference.

3.2   Algorithm Details

The gPCM is constructed by grouped threshold detection and target threshold detection. The higher peaks are cancelled through the grouped threshold detection while the smaller peaks are cancelled through the grouped threshold detection. The block diagram of gPCM is shown in Fig. 2.

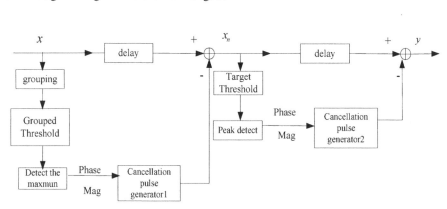

Fig. 2. The block diagram of gPCM

The OFDM signals x is divided into m groups $x_1, x_2, \ldots x_m$ in the grouping block then detect peaks based on finding the highest peak within an over grouped threshold region in each group. This has the advantage that only one peak is detected per over grouped threshold region in each group thus reducing the effects of peak regrowth and improving the cancellation pulse generator 1 allocation statistics.

The cancellation function and peak scaling value is generated according to the grouped threshold for each group in the cancellation pulse generator 1 block. The cancellation signal g_n is band-limited, and can be changed according to the input spectral characteristics. It is expressed by:

$$g_n = \sum_{j=0}^{N} \alpha_j h_j \qquad (3)$$

In equation (3), α is peak scaling value of magnitude equal to the difference between the signal peak and the grouped threshold and the phase is set equal to that of the signal peak. h_n is pulse cancellation function which is designed to occupy the same frequency bands as the input signal x_n.

Add the Cancellation signal g_n to the input signal then update the OFDM signal x_n:

$$\widetilde{x_n} = x_n + g_n \qquad (4)$$

Define all signal peaks in the updated signals $\widetilde{x_n}$ according to the target threshold. It is simple to define a peak as any sample that has magnitude bigger than its neighboring samples. The cancellation pulses are designed to have a spectrum that matches that of the input signal in the cancellation pulse generator 2 block. Add the Cancellation pulse to the signal $\widetilde{x_n}$ then output the result y.

4   Comparison Simulation

The OFDM signals used for performance comparison between gPCM and cPCM consist of 64 subcarriers with 16-QAM modulation. The simulations give detailed comparison results on EVM, PAPR and PCDE.

4.1   Time-Domain View

To demonstrate how the gPCM works, time-domain view before and after the gPCM cancellation is illustrated in Fig. 3. The top waveform in this Fig. shows a part of the input signal magnitude. The horizontal line overlaid on the waveform indicates the target threshold $Th0$. The grouped CR is specified as 1.85 while the target CR is 1.8. The gPCM has reduced the magnitude of samples around three peaks that exceed the target threshold. The middle waveform shows the magnitude of the output signal after subtracting the cancellation pulse from the input signal. The bottom waveform shows the magnitude of the cancellation pulse that is to be subtracted from the input signal.

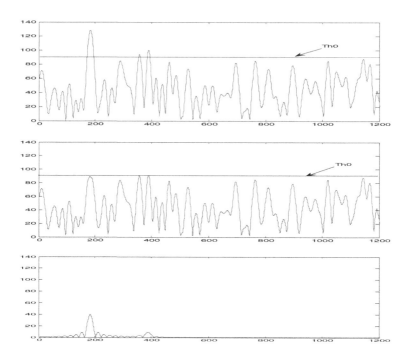

Fig. 3. Time-domain view before and after cancellation

4.2   CCDF Comparison

This part compares the gPCM with the cPCM through MATLAB simulations. Fig. 4 shows the CCDF for the gPCM versus the cPCM with different iterations. The superior performance of the single iteration gPCM is evident. The single iteration gPCM obtains comparable performance with the five iterations cPCM in pulse reduction.

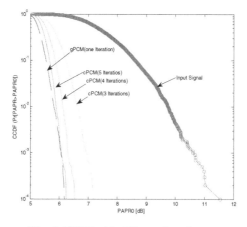

Fig. 4. CCDF with different Iterations

Fig. 5 illustrates the CCDF for the gPCM with the four iterations cPCM based on the 64-subcarrier OFDM signals case with CR set to 1.8 or 2.2. The gPCM outperforms the cPCM with different thresholds. Consider for example the CR=2.2 case, where the PAPR for gPCM is around 7.5 dB and for cPCM around 8.2dB, an improvement of 0.7dB.

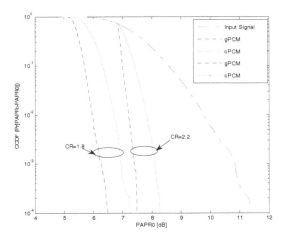

Fig. 5. CCDF with different thresholds

4.3   Other Performance Comparison

PAPR, EVM, PCDE are the main indicators to measure performance of the algorithm. In addition, the number of cancellation is also recorded to compare these two methods.

Table 1. Performance Comparison

	CR	ΔPAPR(dB)	EVM(%)	PCDE(dB)
gPCM	2	4.25	5.35	-48.4964
cPCM	2	4	4.66	-49.7759
gPCM	1.85	4.77	8.2	-45.8896
cPCM	1.85	4.7	7.23	-49.2238

Table 1 summarizes the performance of the single iteration gPCM and the five iterations cPCM. The three performances of single iteration gPCM are close to the five iterations cPCM while gPCM deal with less than half of the number of cancellation.

5   Conclusion

In this paper, the grouped pulse cancellation method (gPCM) is proposed for OFDM signals. Extensive simulations demonstrate the single iteration gPCM is comparative to the five iterations cPCM and deal with less than half of the cancellation number of cPCM. The gPCM is more suitable for OFDM signals, which is of a simple algorithm and equivalent performance.

Acknowledgments. Sponsor by Important National Science & Technology Specific Projects (2010ZX03005-001).M.

References

1. Han, S., Lee, J.: An overview of peak-to-average power ratio reduction techniques for multicarrier transmission. IEEE Trans. Wireless Commnun. 12, 56–65 (2005)
2. Deng, S.K., Lin, M.C.: OFDM PAPR reduction using clipping with distortion control. In: IEEE International Conference on Commum, Seoul, Korea, vol. 4, pp. 2563–2567 (May 2005)
3. Armstrong, J.: Peak-to-average power reduction for OFDM by repeated clipping and frequency domain filtering. Electronics Letters 38(5), 246–247 (2002)
4. Ochai, H., Imai, H.: Performance of the Deliberate Clipping with Adaptive Symbol Selection for Strictly Band-Limited OFDM Systems. IEEE Journal on Selected Areas in Communications 18(11), 2270–2277 (2000)
5. Hong, F., Cimini, L., Sollenberge, N.: Peak-to-average power ratio reduction of an OFDM signal using partial transmit sequence. IEEE Comm. Letters 4, 86–89 (2000)
6. Kuo, H., Cheung, S.: Optimization of windowing and peak-windowing techniques for wcdma systems. In: Proc. IEEE ICASSP 2006, May 14-19, vol. 4, pp. IV 313–IV 316 (2006)
7. Thomas May, H.R.: Reducing the peak-to-average power ratio in OFDM radio transmission systems. In: IEEE Vehic. Tech. Conf. 1998, Ottawa (May 1998)

An Empirical Study on the Efficiency of Information Propagation in Online Social Network

Mo Hai, Shuyun Zhang, Lei Zhu, and Yanlin Ma

School of Information, Central University of Finance and Economics,
Beijing, China
haimozhi@gmail.com

Abstract. In this paper we measure the efficiency of information propagation in online social network from two metrics: the speed and the width. We collect data from Sina microblogging website, and analyze the relation between the speed as well as width and the number of fans as well as interested by the method of correlation analysis. The analysis results show that both the speed and the width of information propagation are highly correlated with the number of fans, but they are not strongly correlated with the number of interested.

Keywords: efficiency, information propagation, speed, width, fans, interested.

1   Introduction

Online social network has become a popular way to share and propagate information among people. Famous online social networks, such as Twitter, MySpace, Facebook, Sina microblogging website, provide different kind of social network service, information are shared and propagate among different users by creating social network based on the relation of friends, acquaintances and families. These sites have huge number of users, for example, Facebook has more than 750 million users, Sina microblog website has more than 200 million users. Different from traditional Web network, information propagation is user-centric and dependent on the relation among people. Users act both as the provider of contents and the propagator of contents. Three kinds of propagation forms: 1 to1, 1 to many and many to many are implemented in social network. The efficiency of information propagation in social network outperforms that of traditional linear propagation.

Because of the high efficiency and influence of information propagation in social network, marketing based on social network has been growing rapidly in recent years. The key value of marketing based on social network is the chain of human relationships. Brand information is penetrated to the user's interpersonal networks and is guided to spread. Depending on active propagation and broad participationof users, information can reach most users in relationship network. To develop a reasonable and efficient strategy of marketing based on social network will bring huge profits to

M. Zhao and J. Sha (Eds.): ICCIP 2012, Part I, CCIS 288, pp. 177–184, 2012.

enterprises, and the key problem of develop marketing strategy is the research on the efficiency of information propagation in social network. The sales and profits of marketing are proportional to the efficiency of information propagation. Therefore, [1]the analysis and empirical study of information propagation efficiency is important and meaningful.

2   Related Work

There are a number of researches focusing on the relation between social structure and information propagation in social network [1-5]. [6-9] measured and analyzed the efficiency of information propagation in online social network by empirical analysis. [6] measured and analyzed Flickr, it found that the social network played a significant role in the propagation of photos, which is confirmed by examining the correlation between the number of fans of 1,500 photos and the indegree of uploaders of those photos. Different from the work of [6], [7] examined the influence of not only the uploaders, but also the neighboring fans. In [7], a large-scale trace of information dissemination in the Flickr social network is collected and analyzed. An in depth study of these data set is conducted to determine how pictures spread through the Flickr social network. The data analysis has several interesting findings about information propagation in Flickr: firstly, most information does not spread widely throughout the network; secondly, information spreads slowly in the network, and there is a significant delay (often several months) in the propagation of information across friend links. These findings are in conflict with initial expectation that information would spread widely and quickly across the Flickr social network. However, this paper doesn't examine how the structure of the social network affects the spread of information. This drawback is solved in the work of [8]. [8] extracts social networks of active users on Digg and Twitter, and track how interest in news stories spreads among them. It shows the network structure affects dynamics of information flow. Digg networks are dense and highly interconnected. A story posted on Digg initially spreads quickly through the network, but afterwards the spread of the story on the Digg slows significantly. Twitter social network is less dense than Digg's, and stories spread through the network slower than Digg stories do initially, but they continue spreading at this rate and generally penetrate the network farther than Digg stories. [9] studies the spread of a kind of health information-Campylobacter in social network. Different from the work of [6-8], in [9] Erd'os-R'enyi and Small World random graphs are used to model a social network. The spread process under different initial configurations of these two graph structures is observed by simulations. The simulations results show that the distributions of vertex characteristics are similar in Erd'os-R'enyi and Small World graphs.

[1] The work is supported by Discipline Construction Foundation of Central University of Finance and Economics and 211 Project for Central University of Finance and Economics (the 3rd phrase).

3   Measurement of the Efficiency of Information Propagation

3.1   Definition of the Efficiency of Information Propagation

At the Sina microblogging website, users can publish his seeing, hearings and thinking, sharing with his friends at any time, and it is a typical SNS network in China. On the webpage of the Sina microblogging website, each user has several properties: (1) user ID, (2) nick name, (3) the number of fans, (4) the number of interested, (5) ID of each micro blog, (6) the number of comments of each micro blog, (7) the number of forwards of each micro blog. In order to measure the efficiency of information spread at the Sina microblogging website, the first step is to collect the data that will be analyzed, and then the speed and width of information propagation are measured separately. This paper mainly analyzes the relationships among the number of fans, the number of interested, the number of comments and the number of forwards of each micro blog. The more the number of times a micro blog is forwarded, the more users will see the micro blog. Therefore, firstly collect the micro blogs published at the same time by a certain number of users, and then compute the width of information propagation by the total number of forwards of a micro blog in a period of time; to analyze the propagation speed of information published by users at the Sina microblogging website, firstly, collect the micro blogs published by a certain number of users at the same time; secondly, monitor the number of comments and forwards of these collected blogs continuously; finally, compute the propagation speed of the published information by the dynamic characteristics of the number of comments and forwards.

3.2   Measurement

The data of this paper is collected by invoking the APIs provided by the Sina microblog website. The information of 10,000 users are obtained. We extract five items from the information of each user: (1) users' ID, (2) user's nick name, (3) the number of fans, (4) the number of interested, (5) the ID of the user's latest micro blog. Then the data is filtered in order to delete the duplicate contents and order it by Excel. The ID of the latest micro blog of each user is extracted from the filtered data. The related APIs are invoked after one week, and the number of comments as well as the number of forwards of these micro blogs is acquired in batch by inputting the ID of the latest micro blog of each user. After collecting the number of comments and the number of forwards of 10,000 micro blogs, the same method as the above is used to delete the duplicate contents and sort the data. Finally, the data of 10,000 users and 10,000 micro blogs are integrated and used in the analysis of the width of information propagation.

When collecting the data which is used for analyzing the speed of information spread, a group of data needs to be monitored continuously. Firstly, collect the data of 10,000 micro blogs by invoking the APIs, which can crawl the latest micro blogs. The data not only contains the ID of a micro blog, but also the number of user's fans and the number of user's interested, etc. After importing the XML documents into Excel, the data set is obtained, which can be used in the correlation analysis. After deleting the duplicate contents and ordering the data, the IDs of the latest published 10,000 micro blogs are extracted. The initial values of the number of comments and forwards of these micro blogs are set to zero. In the process of continuous monitoring of seven days, the APIs, which can collect the number of comments and forwards are invoked at a certain time of each day.

3.3   Analysis of Measurement Results

Among the collected data, there are a total of 535,999,833 fans, 2,590,902 interested, 297,879 comments and 519,756 forwards. Every user has an average of 53,600 fans and 259 interested. Each micro blog has an average of 30 comments and 52 forwards. Fig. 1 and Fig. 2 show the distribution of users with different number of fans and interested respectively. Fig. 3 and Fig. 4 show the distribution of micro blogs with different number of comments and forwards. From these figures, we can see that the distribution of fans is unbalanced: each has no more than 200 fans in 51.24% of all users, while 48.76% of all users have most fans, which is 99.93% of total fans. Meanwhile, the distribution of comments and forwards is also unbalance. The number of comments and forwards of most micro blogs is less than 100. The number of micro blogs whose comments is less than 100 is 93.46% of the total number of micro blogs; the number of micro blogs whose forwards is less than 100 is 91.9% of the total number of micro blogs. However, the number of comments and forwards of some micro blogs is large, even more than 1,000, and the users of these micro blogs have more fans. By Excel, we sort the number of comments in a descending order as shown in Fig. 5 and sort the number of forwards in a descending order as shown in Fig. 6.

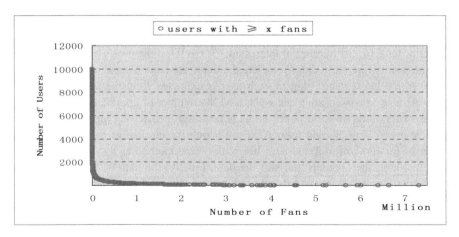

Fig. 1. Distribution of the number of users with a certain number of fans

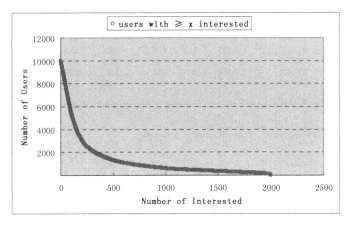

Fig. 2. Distribution of the number of users with a certain number of interested

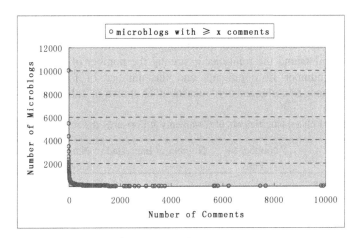

Fig. 3. Distribution of the number of micro blogs with a certain number of comments

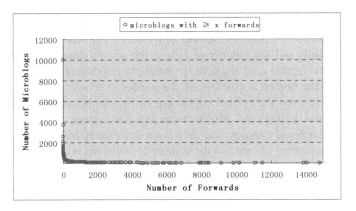

Fig. 4. Distribution of the number of micro blogs with a certain number of forwards

followers_count	friends_count	comments	rt	status_id
1731100	13	28292	14801	6021205661
1624745	36	9931	5530	8618583133
2408577	285	9852	5315	9249426132
2067353	146	7688	3321	8892781348
2995306	154	7455	20533	10262741136
2356012	49	6247	8459	9141462025

Fig. 5. An example of data ordered by the number of comments

followers_count	friends_count	comments	rt	status_id
2995306	154	7455	20533	10262741136
1731100	13	28292	14801	6021205661
396406	7	1457	14094	8872716983
69423	229	2350	13905	8884027610
2899039	113	5706	11518	8400140599
3382736	100	90	11126	8862950367
2342852	20	3290	10192	8858297952

Fig. 6. An example of data ordered by the number of forwards

From Fig. 5 and Fig. 6, we can observe that top users have more followers, and most of them are celebrities. The larger the number of comments and forwards is, the more influential they are on the Sina microblogging website.

In order to understand the relationship among the number of fans, the number of interested, the number of comments and the number of forwards, the related coefficients of these four elements are measured, as shown in Table 1.

Table 1. Related Coefficients of Comments & Forwards & Fans & Interested

	Number of Fans	Number of Interested	Number of Comments	Number of Forwards
Number of Fans	1			
Number of Interested	0.021	1		
Number of Comments	0.361	-0.009	1	
Number of Forwards	0.422	0.012	0.624	1

From Table 1, we can see that the number of comments and the number of forwards have the largest related coefficient-0.62, which means that the more the number of comments, the more the number of forwards. The related coefficient of the number of forwards and the number of fans is the second largest, that is 0.42. The third largest is the related coefficient of the number of comments and the number of fans. However, the related coefficient of the number of forwards and the number of interested is small, even the related coefficient of the number of comments and the number of interested is negative, which means that the number of interested has little influence on the number of comments and the number of forwards. Meanwhile, the related coefficient of the number of fans and the number of interested is also small, so there is no obvious relationship between the number of fans and the number of interested. In summary, the more fans a user has, the more comments and forwards he will receive. Furthermore, the more comments a blog gets, the more forwards this blog will get. That is, the more fans a user has, the broader the information spreads.

The number of comments and the number of forwards of each day in a week are measured, and are shown in Table 2. The relation between the number of comments as well as forwards and the number of days is shown in Fig. 7.

Table 2. Number of Comments and Forwards

No. of Days	1	2	3	4	5	6	7
Number of Comments	27179	29236	29679	29763	29812	29854	29859
Number of Forwards	28045	30153	30635	30896	31085	31236	31397

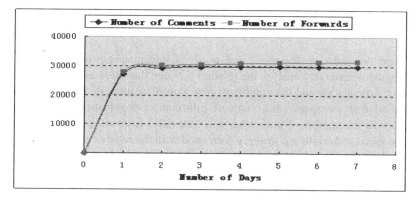

Fig. 7. Number of Comments and Forwards as a function of Number of Days

In Table 2, the number of comments and forwards is the total number of comments and forwards from the day when this micro blog is published to a given day. From Fig. 7, we can observe that the number of comments and forwards increases sharply at the first day after being published. After the first two days the number of comments and forwards keep almost unchanged.

The average number of comments and forwards per day of each blog is computed, and we compare them with the number of fans and interested, the related coefficient of these four items is shown in Table 3. From Table 3, we can observe that the related coefficient of daily incremental of comments and forwards is about 0.99; the related coefficient of daily incremental of comments and the number of fans is about 0.93; the related coefficient of daily incremental of forwards and the number of fans is about 0.94, which means that the daily incremental of comments and forwards are strongly related with the number of fans. However, the related coefficient of daily incremental of comments as well as forwards and the number of interested are 0.005 and 0.004 respectively, which means that the number of interested has little influence on daily incremental of comments and forwards. Therefore, the more fans a user has, the faster the information spreads.

Table 3. Related Coefficients of Daily Incremental Comments & Forwards & Fans & Interested

	Number of Fans	Number of Interested	Daily Incremental of Comments	Daily Incremental of Forwards
Number of Fans	1			
Number of Interested	0.033	1		
Daily Incremental of Comments	0.932	0.005	1	
Daily Incremental of Forwards	0.939	0.005	0.996	1

4   Conclusions

In this paper we measure the speed and width of information propagation at Sina microblogging website and analyze the relation between the speed as well as width of information propagation and the number of fans as well as interested. By the crawled data we find that the speed and width of information propagation is not closely correlated with the number of interested, which deviates from our previous intuition. Indeed the speed and width are strongly correlated with the number of fans. The more fans a user has, the faster and broader the information spreads. In our future work, we will collect more data from Sina microblogging website and try to find other key influencing factors of the speed as well as width of information propagation at Sina microblogging website.

References

1. Anagnostopoulos, A., Kumar, R., Mahdian, M.: Influence and Correlation in Social Networks. In: ACM SIGKDD (2008)
2. Chun, H., Kwak, H., Eom, Y.-H., et al.: Online Social Networks: Sheer Volume vs Social Interaction. In: ACM IMC (2008)
3. Gómez, V., Kaltenbrunner, A., López, V.: Statistical Analysis of the Social Network and Discussion Threads in Slashdot. In: WWW (2008)
4. Kossinets, G., Kleinberg, J., Watts, D.: The Structure of Information Pathways in a Social Communication Network. In: ACM SIGKDD (2003)
5. Leskovec, J., Lang, K., Dasgupta, A., et al.: Statistical Properties of Community Structure in Large Social and Information Networks. In: WWW (2008)
6. Lerman, K., Jones, L.: Social Browsing on Flickr. In: Proc. of Int. Conf. on Weblogs and Social Media (2007)
7. Meeyoung, C., Alan, M., Krishna, P.G.: A measurement-driven analysis of information propagation in the flickr social network. In: Proc. of WWW (2009)
8. Lerman, K., Ghosh, R.: Information Contagion: an Empirical Study of the Spread of News on Digg and Twitter Social Networks. In: Proc. of ICWSM (2010)
9. Charanpal, D., Sandrine, B., Stephan, C., et al.: Dissemination of Health Information within Social Networks. To appear as a chapter in Networks in Social Policy Problems. Cambridge University Press (2010)

Effectiveness Analysis of Data Transmission Strategy Based on Single-Copy

Xiaohua Wu and Jianping Li

School of Computer Science and Engineering, University of Electronic Science and
Technology, China
wxhcshua@126.com

Abstract. We here propose a so-called single-copy-based data transmission
strategy (SCBDTS) by using the history information of the met between nodes
to predict the chance of connection in the future. We also propose details of
the design process of SCBDTS. The most important is that we verify the
effectiveness of the algorithm from algorithm without rings of sex, through
the best relay node forwarding packets, and time complexity three aspects. The
verification conclusions show that SCBDTS is cost effectively and has a high
delivery ratio.

Keywords: Opportunistic network, Data transmission strategy, Effectiveness
analysis, Verification.

1 Introduction

Opportunity network[1] is mainly applied to the lack of communication infrastructure,
wicked network environment and emergency incidents occasion, such as wildlife
monitoring sensor network[2], Moving vehicle nets[3,4], Interstellar network[5],
Tactical communication network[6], Switching pocket network[7], Rural
communication network[8] and so on. Opportunity network is able to deal with a lot
of wireless network's problems which are difficult to solve, and to meet the conditions
of network communication needs, so there are lots of important research and
application value in military and civilian wireless communication field, and the
related study is more and more widely.

Opportunistic Routing (OR) has been investigated in recent years as a way to
increase the performance of multi-hop wireless networks by exploiting its broadcast
nature. In contrast to traditional routing, where traffic is sent along pre-determined
paths, in OR an ordered set of candidates is selected for each next-hop. Upon each
transmission, the candidates coordinate such that the most priority one receiving the
packet actually forwards it [9].

One of the main challenges in building opportunistic network is to guarantee high
performance despite the unpredictable and highly variable nature of the wireless
network. For example, the broadcast nature of the medium can be used to provide
opportunistic transmissions as suggested in. But the network limited resources, the

M. Zhao and J. Sha (Eds.): ICCIP 2012, Part I, CCIS 288, pp. 185–192, 2012.

broadcast nature of the medium will greatly increase the transmission cost. Therefore, it is necessary to design an algorithm to solve in a single copy of the case, the improvement of as much as possible of data transmission reliability and efficiency.

The main focus of this paper is proposing the nodes and the utility of the connection between the goal node calculation models. Based on the models, we propose a so-called single-copy-based data transmission strategy (SCBDTS), and verify the effectiveness of SCBDTS from algorithm without rings of sex, algorithm can through the best relay node to forward packets and algorithm of time complexity three aspects.

2   Algorithm Model

In this paper, we set some assumptions as model, specific as follows:

1. G (V, E) is an undirected unconnected graph including N nodes, V represent node set of the network, E represent link set of the network.
2. In a certain moment, while the node u and node v can take transmission each other, we define the link between the two nodes as (u, v) ∈ E, and all links in set are bidirectional. Link (u, v) is not permanent, which is connected at one time while may be not connected at the other time.
3. The undirected connected graph G contains several connected branches. One single connection can form a sub-graph called clusters. There may be at least one cut vertex and one cut edge in G, through the cut vertex and the cut edge, these connected branches can be joined up. If we delete any one of the cut vertex and the cut edge, the undirected connected graph G will evolve into unconnected graph, and be made up of several connected branch.
4. Every node contains its own local buffer which is not unlimited and has the same size of buffer, moreover for the single-copy data packet, every node can ensure the data forwarding normally and enough buffer operation.
5. The nodes in the network G are moving according to random walk movement model, but their movement speed is not same. In each cluster block, the cut vertex's movement is fast, while the nodes' movement is slow.
6. Due to the nodes are in constant motion, and in the long time the nodes' movements keep a certain regularity, these nodes will meet other nodes constantly, Therefore, we can record some historical information of meeting with other nodes, so as to make assessment and prediction of encounter the next time between nodes, that is to say each node is able to predict the future encounter with the goal through these historical information

3   SCBDTS Algorithm Design

The current OR routing algorithms mainly are based on Dijkstra algorithm or Bellman-Ford algorithm, but these algorithms have common defects, such as the large cost of network resources, a long time delays. Therefore, it is necessary to design a new type of single-copy-based data transmission strategy (SCBDTS), and as far as possible to reduce the consumption of network resources and delay.

In opportunistic network, there is not stable connection between nodes, and the nodes are always in a moving, the topology of the network will change with the mobile node. Therefore, we need to fully consider this factors, and record the history information of the node movement of each cluster in different intervals and the network topology structure change, also need to combine with its own utility values and neighbors around node of the topology information, analyze, thus able to select the optimal neighbor node as relay node, increase the chance of data forwarding on this basis, reduce the network overhead and delay.

The literature[10] proposed by wuxiaohua gave the definition of utility values, SCBDTS is based on the utility values, consists of three parts, firstly calculate nodal overall utility values, secondly collect near neighbor node network topology information, thirdly forward data.

3.1   Collect Node Neighbor Node Table Information of n

The node m needs to send broadcast to all the other nodes within cover area, and set the timer; Neighbors node which received the message sent by m and then send a reply message to m. The specific algorithm process is described as shown in Algorithm 1:

```
Algorithm 1 NeighborNodesTable Algorithm(m)
  begin
    m broadcasts a message to all nodes within cover
area;
    while m receive neighbor node's reply message in
the effective time T do
      begin
        m received neighbor node's reply message;
        extract a part of the field from the reply
message, calculate the utility value;
        update the information in the local neighbor
node table;
        Obtain the routing table information from
corresponding neighbor nodes;
        update the local routing table information;
      end
    end while
  end
```

3.2   Calculate the Utility Values between the Sending Node m and the Goal Node n

First of all, the node m obtains it's neighbor node information and local network topology information through the Neighbor Nodes Table Algorithm (m) Algorithm, and calculate it's connectivity through these information; in a certain period of time, we would traverse all information of the nodes which have interaction history with the goal node n, and observe the movement change information of m; If don't find interactive information recorded of n, it means that utility values of m is only related with node connectivity and mobile connection degree of itself; on the contrary, besides the calculation of the node m connectivity and mobile connection degree, it need to   calculate frequently degree, intimate degree and connection time interval of the node through the history interaction record of m and n, and calculate correlation degree. The next step, traverse the goal node n from the cluster of local topology information, if the goal node's information is existing, the goal node n and the sending node m are in the same cluster block, then calculate the similarity of m and n by they neighbor table's information obtained the last algorithm; If can't find the goal node n or n and m are not in the same cluster block, their similarity is set to 0. According to the above calculation results, we can compute the utility values of the node m.

The specific algorithm process is described as shown in Algorithm 2 (The definition of relevant formula and definition in the algorithm2 has proposed in the literature [10]):

```
Algorithm 2 UtilityComputing Algorithm(m,n)
  begin
    calculate connectivity for m through the algorithm 1;
      in a certain period T, traverse all information of
the nodes which have interaction history with n and the
movement information of m;
        if history information of n does not exist
        then   U(m, n)=CE(m, n)+MC(m)
        else   AP(m, n)=FP(m, n)+CP(m, n)+RP(m, n);
        endif
        traverse all information of n;
        if the information exists && n and m are in the
same cluster block
        then calculate Sim(m, n)
        else Sim(m, n)=0
        endif
        U(m, n)= αAP(m, n)+ βSim(m, n)+ γCE(m, n)+MC(m)
  end
```

3.3   The Specific Algorithm of Forwarding Data

Whether to a sending node m, or a goal node n, or a relaying node, need to process the received data, only the correct treatment of the received data, can get the full accurate information, and provide the basis of correct delivery date quickly.

In this paper, the processed message is set as M, first, Judge m and   n whether for the same node, if it is, the goal node n directly process M; if not, judge whether the goal node n can be the next hop of m, If it is, m directly forward the data packet M to the goal node n, if the goal node n can not be the next hop node of m, then in a certain period T, traverse all effective neighbor nodes of m, choose the maximum utility nodes x as a relay node , and execute the recursion algorithm.

The specific algorithm process is described as shown in Algorithm 3:

```
Algorithm 3 Forwarding Message(m, d, M)
var     m = sending node, n = goal node
    begin
      if m = n
      then n directly process M(message)
      else  if  n is the next hop of m
            then directly forward M to n
             else
               {
               traverse all effective neighbor nodes of m
               (through Algorithm 2);
               choose the maximum utility node X as a
               relay node forward M;
               Forwarding Message(m, d, M);
        }
            endif
      endif

    end
```

4   Effectiveness Analysis of SCBDTS

We will make a theoretically detailed analysis in the correctness of the algorithm of time complexity form three aspects.

4.1   Algorithm without Rings of Sex

The algorithm is to verify whether without rings routing, which can be a very important properties of achieving rapid convergence.

If the network is a ring, then assuming there is a loop (i, j, l, i), as shown in figure 1

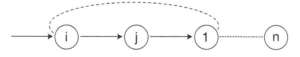

Fig. 1. Loop drawing

Figure 1 shows the process of the data forwarding through the loop (i, j, l, i) to the goal node n.

When data arrives at the node i, as a relay node i, which will traverse the neighbor node list, so as to find the maximum utility node j, namely while U(j, n) > U(i, n), the node i will forward data to the node j;

When data arrives at the node j, j also will make the same treatment, traverse the neighbor node list, so as to find the maximum utility node l, namely while U(l, n) > U(j, n), the node j will forward data to the node l.

Through the above, it is easy to see that U(l, n) > U(j, n) > U(i, n). When the data arrives at the node l, as the existing loop in the network, node l will regard i as the next hop, and therefore in the l neighbors list of the node l, the utility values of i is greater than l, namely U(i, n) > U(l, n), that is to say, U(l, n) > U(j, n) > U(i, n) conflict with U(i, n) > U(l, n), this is not possible.

Therefore, the algorithm by comparing the utility values to determine the next hop, the network does not appear in the loop.

4.2   Through the Best Relay Node Forwarding Packets

First of all, from evidence process of the theorem 1, we can see, each node will traverse its neighbors node table before forwarding, and the data in the table will be analysis and compared, so as to judge whether from the table can find goal node n or the other node which had interactive information recorded history with n, to predict the possibility of interaction with the goal node n in the future. Through the comparison of the utility value of the nodes, we select the largest utility values node which can in the shortest possible time interactive with the goal node as the relay node to forward data. In a certain sense, in end-to-end doesn't exist stable connection network, the algorithm greatly increases the reliability of sending node.

In network, there may be some nodes never connecting with goal node n, so while calculating the utility values, besides using forecasting the historical information, it still needs to analysis the node connectivity. Through the local topology information analysis, we can effectively choose the node having recent distance cut point with the goal node n as the most suitable relay hop, so as to ensure that the current may be connected in the cluster blocks.

To sum up, this algorithm can through the best relay hop to forward packets.

4.3   Time Complexity of Algorithm

Because in Opportunity network, there is not stable connection between nodes, that is to say, the connection may be exist, while in the next moment the connection will be cut off. So in the calculation of the time complexity, we need to begin while overall topology structure of the network, make the of the time complexity analysis according to different network.

In this paper we have already proposed that SCBDTS consists of three parts, firstly calculate nodal overall utility values, secondly collect near neighbor node network topology information, thirdly forward data.

In order to make the complexity analysis of the whole network situation, the first is to make time complexity analysis in extreme cases of network. we make the hypothesis in an extreme case, in Opportunity network, there are connections between nodes, that is to say there are not non-connection each other, at this time, no matter the node is sending node or goal node, there exist connection between them, we can establish direct connection between the sending node and the goal node. In this case, the time complexity of the algorithm is mainly that the other nodes $|V| - 1$ Send data and the process of receiving the response of the neighbor nodes, therefore, the time expenses can be expressed as $O(|V| - 1)$. On this basis, at this time the time expenses of every node in the network can all be expressed as $O(|V| - 1)$, therefore, the total time expenses of the whole network should be $O(|V|(|V| - 1))$, approximately equal to $O(|V|^2)$.

5   Conclusions

Opportunistic network routing appears to be a rich and challenging problem. It requires techniques to select paths, schedule transmissions, estimate delivery performance, and manage buffers. In this paper, we have developed single-copy-based data transmission strategy (SCBDTS). Our contribution is verify the effectiveness of the algorithm from algorithm without rings of sex, through the best relay node forwarding packets, and algorithm of time complexity three aspects. The verification conclusions show that SCBDTS is cost effectively and has a high delivery ratio. Opportunistic networks.

References

1. Xiong, Y.-P., Sun, L.-M., Niu, J.-W., Liu, Y.: Opportunistic network. Journal of Software 20, 124–137 (2009)
2. Juang, P., Oki, H., Wang, Y., Martonosi, M., Peh, L.S., Rubenstein, D.: Energy-Efficient computing for wildlife tracking: design tradeoffs and early experiences with Zebranet. In: 10th Annual Conference on Architectural Support for Programming Languages and Operating Systems, pp. 96–107. ACM Press, New York (2002)
3. Darus, M.Y.B., Bakar, K.A.: Congestion Control Framework for Disseminating Safety Messages in Vehicular Ad-Hoc Networks (VANETs). International Journal of Digital Content Technology and its Applications 5, 173–180 (2011)
4. Wu, H., Fujimoto, R., Hunter, M., Guensler, R.: MDDV: A mobility-centric data dissemination algorithm for vehicular networks. In: Proceeding of the ACM SIGCOMM Workshop on Vehicular Ad Hoc Networks (VANET 2004), pp. 47–56. ACM SIGMOBILE Press, New York (2004)
5. Burleigh, S., Hooke, A., Torgerson, L., Fall, K., Cerf, V., Durst, B., Scott, K.: Delay-Tolerant networking: An approach to interplanetary Internet. IEEE Communications Magazine 41, 128–136 (2003)

6. Krishnan, R., Basu, P., Mikkelson, J.M., Small, C., Ramanathan, R.: The SPINDLE disruption-tolerant networking system. In: Proceeding of the MILCOM 2007, pp. 1–7. IEEE Press, New York (2007)

7. Erramilli, V., Chaintreau, A., Crovella, M., Christophe, D.: Diversity of forwarding paths in pocket switched networks. In: 7th ACM SIGCOMM Conference on Internet Measurement, pp. 161–174. ACM SIGMOBILE Press, New York (2007)

8. Seth, A., Kroeker, D., Zaharia, M., Guo, S., Keshav, S.: Low-Cost communication for rural internet kiosks using mechanical backhaul. In: 12th Annual International Conference on Mobile Computing and Networking, pp. 334–345. ACM Press, New York (2006)

9. Dubois-Ferriere, H., Grossglauser, M., Vetterli, M.: Candidate Selection Algorithms in Opportunistic Routing. In: 5th ACM Workshop on Performance Monitoring and Measurement of Heterogeneous Wireless and Wired Networks, pp. 48–54. ACM SIGMOBILE Press, New York (2010)

10. Wuxiaohua, L.: Utility-Value-Based Data Delivery Scheme for Opportunistic Network and Its Performance Study. International Journal of Advancements in Computing Technology (accept)

Multispectral Image Fusion Based on Contrast Modulation and Weighted Wavelets and Markov Modeling

Haiyan Jin, Shuai Li, Bingbo Wang, and Xueming Sun

School of Computer Science and Engineering, Xi'an University of Technology,
Xi'an, 710048 China
jinhaiyan@xaut.edu.cn

Abstract. This paper presents an improved multisensor image fusion scheme, which is based on the typical geometrical structure of images. Consider the textures, directional and spectral features, the paper modulate and enhance the contrast of the original images in different scales and reduce the time cost at the same time using contrast pyramid; use weighted wavelets and wedgelets to capture the geometrical characteristics of different scales. In wedgelets, employ Markov models to find the best wedgelet orientations at different scales. Results clearly demonstrate the superiority of this improved approach when compared to conventional wavelet-based systems.

Keywords: Multisensor image fusion, Weighted wavelets and wedgelets, Markov modeling, Contrast modulation.

1 Introduction

In the past few years, several researchers have proposed different image fusion methods aimed at multispectral images. Wavelets are very effective in representing objects with isolated point singularities, while they are not the most significant in representing objects with singularities along lines such as edges. Different from wavelets, wedgelet theory presented by Donoho [1] is a concise contour presentation method, which uses multiscale wedgelets to piecewise approximate image contour linearly. Wedgelets are defined in the 2-D space directly, so it can capture surface features in images better.

In this article, an improved image fusion algorithm is presented, which extend existing solutions for multispetral images. Image texture modulation enhances the generalized contrast, which is obtained by applying contrast modulation to the original input data. Further considering the respective predominance of wavelets and wedgelets, we construct effective weighted wavelets and wedgelets to capture the various geometrical features of images. In wedgelets, adopt Markov quad-tree models to search the best wedgelet decompositions. An image fusion approach based on contrast modulation and weighted wavelets and wedgelets Markov models (CM-WWWM) is proposed in this paper.

M. Zhao and J. Sha (Eds.): ICCIP 2012, Part I, CCIS 288, pp. 193–200, 2012.
© Springer-Verlag Berlin Heidelberg 2012

2   Image Fusion Modeling

2.1   Contrast Modulation by Contrast Pyramid

In order to improve the efficiency of algorithm and modulate the contrast of images, contrast pyramid decomposition is introduced. The construction is similar to that of the popular Laplacian pyramid [2]. First a lowpass pyramid is constructed. This is a sequence of images in which each image is a lowpass filtered and subsampled copy of its predecessor. Let G_l present the l-th level of the pyramid decomposition and array G_0 contain the original image. This array G_0 becomes the bottom or zero level of the pyramid structure. Each node of pyramid level l ($1 \leq l \leq N$, where N is the index of the top level of the pyramid) is obtained as a Gaussian weighted average of the nodes at level l-1 that are positioned within a 5×5 window centered on that node.

Convolving an image with a Gaussian-like weighting function is equivalent to applying a lowpass filter to the image. Gaussian pyramid construction generates a set of lowpass filtered copies of the input image, each with a bandlimit one octave lower than that of its predecessor. Because of the reduction in spatial frequency content, each image in the sequence can be represented by an array that is half as large as that of its predecessor. The process that generates each image in the sequence from its predecessor is called REDUCE operation since both the sampling density and the resolution are decreased. Thus, for $1 \leq l \leq N$ we have

$$G_l = \text{REDUCE}(G_{l-1}) \tag{1}$$

meaning

$$G_l = \sum_{m=-2}^{2} \sum_{n=-2}^{2} w(m,n) G_{l-1}(2i+m, 2j+n), \quad 0 < l \leq N, 0 \leq i < C_l, 0 \leq j < R_l \tag{2}$$

where N is the total levels of the pyramid, C_l and R_l are column number and row number of the level l, respectively, and $w(m, n)$ is a weighting function, which satisfies the following conditions:

(a) Separable, that is $w(m, n) = w(m)w(n)$, $m \in [-2,2]$, $n \in [-2,2]$;

(b) Unitary, that is $\sum_{n=-2}^{2} w(n) = 1$;

(c) Symmetry, that is $w(n) = w(-n)$;

(d) Equal contribution of odd and even item, that is $w(-2)+w(2)+w(0)=w(-1)+w(1)$.

The restriction of above conditions is to assure the property of lowpass and also retain the smoothness of images. Therefore, we choose $w(0)=2/5$, $w(1)=w(-1)=1/4$, $w(2)=w(-2)=1/20$. A common window width is 5×5, and according to the restriction conditions we can get the weighting function as

$$w = \frac{1}{400}\begin{bmatrix} 1 & 5 & 8 & 5 & 1 \\ 5 & 25 & 40 & 25 & 5 \\ 8 & 40 & 64 & 40 & 8 \\ 5 & 25 & 40 & 25 & 5 \\ 1 & 5 & 8 & 5 & 1 \end{bmatrix} \tag{3}$$

It is well-known fact that the human visual system is sensitive to local luminance contrast. Contrast pyramid analysis scheme is based on local luminance contrast. This scheme computes the ratio of the lowpass images at successive levels of the Gaussian pyramid. Since these levels differ in sample density, it is necessary to interpolate new values between the given values of the lower frequency image before it can divide the higher frequency image. Interpolation can be achieved simply by defining the EXPAND operation as the inverse of the REDUCE operation.

Let G_l* be the image obtained by applying EXPAND operation. Then

$$G_l^* = \text{EXPAND}(G_l) \tag{4}$$

Corresponding to the formula (2), EXPAND operator is defined as

$$G_l^*(i,j) = 4\sum_{m=-2}^{2}\sum_{n=-2}^{2} w(m,n)G_l'\left(\frac{i+m}{2},\frac{j+n}{2}\right), \qquad 0 < l \le N, 0 \le i < C_l, 0 \le j < R_l \tag{5}$$

where $\quad G_l'\left(\dfrac{i+m}{2},\dfrac{j+n}{2}\right) = \begin{cases} G_l\left(\dfrac{i+m}{2},\dfrac{j+n}{2}\right) & \text{when } \dfrac{i+m}{2},\dfrac{j+n}{2} \text{ are integer} \\ 0 & \text{otherwise} \end{cases}$

A sequence of ratio images R_i is defined by

$$\left. \begin{aligned} R_i &= \frac{G_i}{\text{EXPAND}(G_{i+1})}, & \text{for } 0 \le i \le N-1 \\ R_N &= G_N & \text{for } i = N \end{aligned} \right\} \tag{6}$$

Thus, every level R_i is a ratio of two successive levels in the Gaussian pyramid.

Luminance contrast is defined as

$$C = (L - L_b)/L_b = L/L_b - I \tag{7}$$

where L denotes the luminance at a certain location in the image plane, and L_b represents the luminance of the local background, and I is the unit gray image, that is $I(i,j)=1$, for all i, j. When C_i is defined as

$$\left. \begin{aligned} C_i &= \frac{G_i}{\text{Expand}(G_{i+1})} - I & 0 \le i < N \\ C_N &= G_N \end{aligned} \right\} \tag{8}$$

Combining with (6), we have

$$R_i = C_i + I \tag{9}$$

Therefore, we refer to the sequence R_i as the contrast modulation pyramid. The contrast modulation is a complete representation of the original image. G_0 can be recovered exactly by reversing the above steps as (10)

$$
\left.
\begin{aligned}
G_N &= R_N & i &= N \\
G_i &= (C_i + I)\,\mathrm{Expand}(G_{i+1}) = R_i\,\mathrm{Expand}(G_{i+1}) & 0 &\leq i \leq N-1
\end{aligned}
\right\} \quad (10)
$$

2.2 Representations Based on Weighted Wavelets and Wedgelets

2.2.1 Wedgelet Approximations

Wedgelet analysis is a kind of directional information detection model presented by David L. Donoho [1]. A wedgelet w is a function on a square S that is piecewise constant on either side of a line l through S. Four parameters $(S; v_1, v_2, m_a, m_b)$ are needed to define w: two parameters (v_1, v_2) for l, where l intersects the perimeter of S, and the values w of the two sides of l are m_a, m_b, respectively (see Fig.1) [3] [4]. A function that is constant over all of S is called a degenerative wedgelet.

There are two components in the multiscale wedgelet analysis: multiscale wedgelet decomposition (MWD) and multiscale wedgelet representation (MWR). The MWD divides the image into dyadic blocks at different scales and projects these image blocks onto wedgelets at various orientations. Once we have calculated the projection in the MWD, we can use the results to choose a representation of the image. A MWD is constructed by choosing a set of dyadic squares that partition $[0, 1]^2$ and a wedgelet contained in each. In fact, the wedgelet representation has been shown to have near optimal non-linear approximation and rate-distortion properties for images consisting of piecewise constant regions separated by smooth boundaries [1].

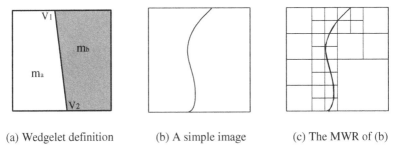

(a) Wedgelet definition   (b) A simple image   (c) The MWR of (b)

Fig. 1. The sketch map of wedgelets

2.2.2 Constructions of Multiscale Weighted Wedgelet with Wavelets

The process of wedgelet transform is approximating images self-adaptively using wedgelet basis function. The formation of wedgelet basis function is explained as Fig.2 (a). In the dyadic square, the left area of edgelet m_a constructs the wedgelet basis function of constant c_a, while the right area of edgelet m_b does the c_b. The constant c_a and c_b can be attained by

$$c_a = Average(I(S_{j,k})|m_a) \tag{11}$$
$$c_b = Average(I(S_{j,k})|m_b)$$

where I is the dyadic square $[0, 1]^2$, and $S_{j,k} \subset [0,1]^2$, c_a and c_b is the mean value of all pixels in corresponding wedgelet field [3] [4], which shows that wedgelets can be used in grey image by the linear combination of constant function with wedgelet function.

In general, for a dyadic image of size $n \times n$, we define an object function as $f(x_1, x_2)$. Wedgelet transform can be noted as

$$W_f(w) \equiv \langle f, w \rangle, \quad \forall w \in W \tag{12}$$

Accordingly, the result of recursive partition for an image (wedgelet inverse transform) is as follows:

$$f = \sum_{w \in W} W_f w \tag{13}$$

where W_f is the coefficients of wedgelet transform, and w is the basis function of wedgelets.

In [1], the CART algorithm is used to find a MWR with an optimal tradeoff between the approximation and parsimony criteria. Given a weighting parameter λ, we can exploit the quad-tree structure (described in section 2.3) of the representation to find a fast solution to the following optimization problem and further to find the wedgelet basis function w:

$$\min_W D(W) + \lambda |W| \tag{14}$$

where $D(W)$ is the mean-square error between the image f and the MWR W, and $|W|$ is the number of terms (namely leaves of quad-tree) in W. The parameter λ is usually defined as (15):

$$\lambda = \sqrt{4 * \log(n)} \sigma \tag{15}$$

where σ is the standard deviation and n is the size of image.

Wedgelets have good approximation performance for multi-variable function with linear discontinuity and can retain the linear structure effectively and smooth the flat field at the same time. It is well-known that wavelets can approximate the texture field with point singularities effectively. We expect to make the best use of the advantages of wedgelets and wavelets respectively and weigh them together in the image fusion processing.

Firstly, sample the original image and partition as four matrixes, for each matrix, wavelet approximation and wedgelet approximation are executed, respectively as follows.

$$x_1[n,m] = x[2n, 2m] \tag{16}$$
$$x_2[n,m] = x[2n, 2m+1]$$
$$x_3[n,m] = x[2n+1, 2m]$$
$$x_4[n,m] = x[2n+1, 2m+1]$$

Considering the respective predominance of wedgelets and wavelets in different image field, we weigh and average the results of two approximations to capture the variety of geometrical features of images. If we continue to partition each matrix, we can get to next scale. When reconstruct, only need to do inverse transform to (16).

2.3   Wedgelet Domain Markov Modeling

In order to process the images efficiently, by imposing a geometric model for smooth contours using the relationships between MWRs of increasing resolutions, we will be able to quantify how well a particular arrangement of wedgelets fits our notion of edge structure. To capture these dependencies, our geometry model will describe how we expect the orientations in the MWR to change as we increase the resolution. It is to make the MWR less parsimonious but a better approximation to original images.

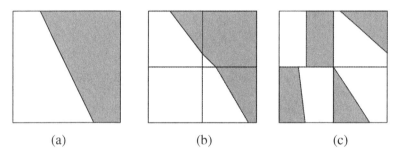

(a)   (b)   (c)

Fig. 2. Wedgelet representation. (a) The coarse scale wedgelet representation, (b) Wedgelet representation at next scale, (c) Another wedgelet representation.

Therefore, the inter-scale relationships between the wedgelets can be captured using a quad-tree structured finite Markov model [5] [6]. The state at each node represents the orientation of the best wedgelet fit in the corresponding dyadic square. A state transition matrix is used to score different wedgelet refinements. For example, the transition from the parent state in Fig.2 (a) to the child states shown in Fig.2 (b) would receive a high score, while the transition to the child states shown in Fig.2 (c) would receive a much lower score.

The probabilities are assigned based on the distance $d(l_{parent}, l_{child})$ between the lines l_{parent} and l_{child} that define the parent and child wedgelet orientations. In this paper, for example, we use $\Pr(l_{child} | l_{parent}) \sim e^{-d(l_{parent}, l_{child})^2}$. It is notable that the distance between lines is just the Euclidean distance between their representative points in $\mathbb{R} \times [0, 2\pi)$ [3].

Now that we have geometry model, we can use it regularize our choice of MWR. We can again exploit the quad-tree structure of the wedgelet representation along with the Markov nature of the model to find an exact solution to

$$\min_W D(W) + \lambda \left[-\log_2 P(W) + |W| \right] \tag{17}$$

where $D(W)$, $|W|$ and λ are the same as in formula (11) and $P(W)$ is the likelihood of W under our geometry models.

2.4   Image Fusion Algorithm Based on the CM-WWWM

Step1. Initialize parameters. We use window function of formula (3) in section 2.1.

Step2. Decompose two original input images respectively using contrast modulation, and we can obtain two decomposed images— "$m1$" and "$m2$".

Step3. Using weighted wavelets and wedgelets with Markov modeling to decompose the low-pass images "$m1$" and "$m2$", respectively, we can get two groups of results— "$y1$"and "$y2$", respectively.

Step4. According to the fusion rule of pixel gray maximal solute value (MS), we construct a set of new coefficients "y" by finding maximal absolute value of corresponding position of "$y1$" and "$y2$".

Step5. Inverse transform of weighted wavelets and wedgelets.

Step6. Reconstruction and we can get the final fused image.

3   Experiments

In experiments, "Sym4" wavelets are used in wavelet-based fusion, which is a family of near symmetry wavelets. The number of wavelet decomposition level is 3.In addition to visual analysis, we use information entropy (IE), average grads (AG) and standard deviation (STD) to analyze fused results [7].

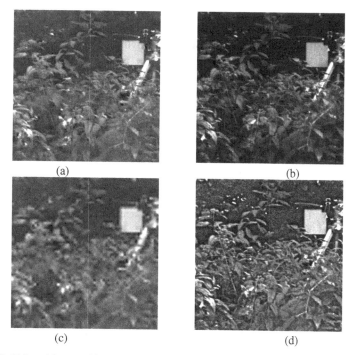

Fig. 3. 512×512 multispectral images of fusion products. (a) (b) Original images by 30 channel DRA hyper-spectral scanner. (c) Processed by wavelets. (d) Processed by CM-WWWM.

Table 1. Comparisons of quantitative results for Fig.3

Images	IE	AG	STD	Execution time (s)
Original image (a)	4.8186	5.2740	40.2334	——
Original image (b)	4.5149	5.5323	42.2116	——
Wavelet-based fusion result (c)	4.7978	3.0985	37.5534	1389.7024
CM-WWWM fusion result (d)	5.1199	11.6290	53.8869	4.6422

4   Conclusion

In our analysis of the spectral and spatial quality of the fused image, we found some statistical differences between the original and synthesized images. From these differences, we conclude that the CP-WWWM method of image fusion provides more detailed spatial information than the wavelet-based image fusion and, simultaneously, preserve the richer spectral content of the images.

We have presented an improved method of image fusion based on CM-WWWM. Contrast modulation has proven itself to be promising for multispectral image fusion of data. The proposed fusion procedure allows homogenous data to be effectively integrated with the physically heterogeneous backscatter by weighted wavelets and wedgelets through realizing respective preponderances.

Acknowledgment. This work has been supported by Science Research Program Project of Educational Committee of Shaanxi Province under grant No. 11JK1028 and Science and Technology Key Program Project of Xi'an City under grant No. CXY1127(3).

References

1. Donoho, D.L.: Wedgelets: Nearly-Minimax Estimation of Edges. Annals of Statistics 27, 859–897 (1999)
2. Do, M.N., Vetterli, M.: Framing pyramids. IEEE Transactions on Signal Processing 51, 2329–2342 (2003)
3. Romberg, J.K., Wakin, M.B.: Multiscale Wedgelet Image Analysis: Fast Decompositions and Modeling. In: International Conference on Image Processing, vol. 3, pp. 585–588 (2002)
4. Romberg, J.K., Wakin, M.B.: Multiscale Geometric Image Processing. In: SPIE Visual Communications and Image Processing (2003),
   http://hdl.handle.net/1911/20302
5. Spence, C., Parra, L.C., Sajda, P.: Varying complexity in tree-structured image distribution models. IEEE Transactions on Image Processing 15, 319–330 (2006)
6. Romberg, J.K., Choi, H., Baraniuk, R.G.: Bayesian tree-structured image modeling using wavelet-domain hidden Markov models. IEEE Transactions on Image Processing 10, 1056–1068 (2001)
7. Jin, H.-Y., Yang, X.-H., Jiao, L.-C., Liu, F.: Image Enhancement via Fusion Based on Laplacian Pyramid Directional Filter Banks. In: Kamel, M.S., Campilho, A.C. (eds.) ICIAR 2005. LNCS, vol. 3656, pp. 239–246. Springer, Heidelberg (2005)

Efficient Interval Query of Genome Alignment and Interval Databases in Cloud Environment

Zhiqiong Wang, Ke Gong, Shikai Jin, Wenjun Li, and Zixi Liu

Sino-Dutch Biomedical and Information Engineering School
Northeastern University, Shenyang 110819, P.R. China
wangzq@bmie.neu.edu.cn

Abstract. Interval overlap query has become a fundamental tool for biomedical researches. However, existing methods are either not efficient or hardly to extend. In this paper, cloud computing is applied to solving the limited speed and scalability problems of interval overlap query. First, the NCList algorithm based on centralized environment is applied to cloud computing in order to improve the query efficiency, and the CNCList algorithm is presented. Second, two optimization strategies are proposed to further enhance the query efficiency of CNCList and an advanced algorithm named CNCList⁺ is formed. Third, detailed comparison experiments between CNCList⁺ and CNCList prove the better performance of CNCList⁺ both on query time and scalability, thus demonstrating the excellent capability of CNCList⁺ on solving the limited query speed and scalability problems of interval overlap query.

Keywords: Interval query, Genome alignment, Cloud computing, Massive data.

1   Introduction

Interval overlap query has proved to be a fundamental and necessary tool in the discovery of genomics data mining and it is of great importance to biomedical researches and applications. For example, if biomedical researchers find a gene sequence interval that related to cancer, the interval overlap query tool can be used to examine which person has that overlapping sequence interval, and then prediction can be made that this person may have the risk of getting cancer. In this case, it will make a great contribution to cancer research. Similarly, by examine the correlation (overlap level) between the aimed sequence query interval and sequences among different types of species will accelerate the pace of discovery of biological science and medical science. Thus, interval overlap query is a very important method in modern biomedical area.

However, many problems arise from executing interval overlap query. The most remarkable problems are the limited query speed and scalability of traditional interval overlap query methods. While a new interval overlap query algorithm named NCList was created aimed at accelerating interval query of genome alignment and interval database. In their tests, the query speed of NCList algorithm was 5-500-fold faster

M. Zhao and J. Sha (Eds.): ICCIP 2012, Part I, CCIS 288, pp. 201–209, 2012.

than other indexing methods, such as MySQL multi-column indexing, MySQL binning and R-Tree indexing. And NCList data structure appears to provide a useful foundation for highly scalable interval database applications [1]. Nevertheless, what they did was based on single computer, which is not a good choice in face of a large amount of data in biomedical field nowadays because of its disadvantage of processing large amounts of data, thus limiting the potential of improving the interval overlap query speed and scalability further. Fortunately, with the cloud computing technology coming up, we can address this problem properly.

The major contributions of this paper can be summarized as follows:

1. The NCList algorithm is transplanted to cloud computing environment to improve the query efficiency, and a new algorithm called Cloud Nested Containment List (CNCList) is presented.
2. Based on deep analysis of CNCList, two optimization strategies are proposed to futher enhance the efficiency of CNCList, which form the CNCList$^+$ algorithm.
3. The extensive simulations demonstrate that CNCList$^+$ performs better than CNCList in both query speed and scalability.

2   Related Work

The annotation and determination of complete genomic DNA sequences offer a good chance for unprecedented advances in our understanding of genetics, evolution and physiology. An excellent browser named the human genome browser (HGB) at UCSC [2] provides an access to the sequence and annotations of the human genome. However, browser shows a single gene or region at a time. They are not able to support complex queries across multiple forms of information simultaneously or multiple genes. In this context, a database of genomic DNA sequence alignments and annotations called GALA [3] was developed to address this problem.

Many approaches has been attempted on interval overlap query. Segment R-tree [4] was created as an indexing technique for interval data in multiple dimensions. The Relational Interval Tree [5] was designed for any relational or object-relational table containing intervals. Based on the Relational Interval Tree, a new join algorithm [6] was proposed for interval data. And MV3R-Tree [7] was presented as a structure to utilize the concepts of multi-version B-trees and 3D R-trees. However, all the approaches are based on single computer, thus both limiting speed and making them hardly to extend, in this paper, we adapt the cloud computing technology to improve the efficiency and scalability of interval overlap query.

3   CNCList: NCList in Cloud Environment

NCList [1] is based on this idea that it makes all the sequences into several groups, and all the sequences within a same group must obey the rule that they do not have containment relationship with each other, which means they are both in ascending start order and ascending end order. In this case, when querying sequences in a group and encountering the first non-overlapping interval, it can stop scanning the rest of that group, thus reducing the query complexity and enhancing the query speed.

Cloud computing technology can improve the efficiency of NCList, and NCList on cloud named CNCList. In CNCList, all the sequences are assigned into several big groups as the NCList does (see Fig. 1). Nevertheless, the difference of CNCList is that the tasks of querying result sequences inside each big group are distributed to several common computers. In this case, the query processes of each group are executed simultaneously, which will improve the query efficiency remarkably.

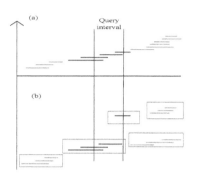

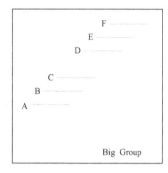

Fig. 1. Illumination of CNCList

Fig. 2. The sequences inside a big group are both in ascending start order and end order

4   CNCList⁺: Improved NCList

In this section, the CNCList+ algorithm is proposed by integrating the CNCList algorithm and two additional new subalgorithms named subgroup formation and boundary interval filter.

Algorithm 1. Map of CNCList	**Algorithm 2.** Reduce of CNCList

Void map(Vector key, Vector value)
 //key: serial number of big group
 //value: all the sequences inside one big group
 	
 ReduceCollector(key.bigGroupSerial Number, value);
	Void reduce (Vector key, Vector value)
	 //key: serial number of big group
	 //value: all the sequences inside one big group
	 FOR EACH geneInterval IN value.thisBigGroup
	 IF (geneInterval $\cap$ queryInterval $\neq \emptyset$)
	 ResultCollector (value.geneInterval)
	 ELSE IF (geneInterval.start > queryInterval.start)
	 Break;

4.1   Process of CNCList

All the sequences are assigned into several big groups, and Map (see Algorithm 1) passes the information of the serial number and inner sequences of every big group to

Reduce. In the process of Reduce (see Algorithm 2), every big group will be checked one by one. When scanning all the sequences inside one group, and if there is an intersection between a sequence and query interval, the sequence will be the result sequence. The scanning process of one big group continues until it encounters the first non-overlapping sequence inside that big group. Then the sequences inside another big group will be scanned, and the whole scanning process stops until all the big groups are checked.

4.2   Subgroup Formation

The process of subgroup formation happens after all the original big groups are formed, in which all the sequences are both in ascending start and end order, and whether the subgroup of a big group can be formed is based on two rules we set.

Maximum Efficiency Length Rule. The first rule is the maximum efficiency length rule. Maximum efficiency length is the length that when the total sequences' length of a subgroup equals to this length, the execution of the algorithm will be the most efficient and the speed of execution will be the fastest compared to other values of length. In this rule, subgroup should satisify two properties. Firstly, the total length of all the sequences in a same subgroup is no greater than the maximum efficiency length. Secondly, when next adjacent sequence is added into this subgroup, the total length of all the sequences in the new formed subgroup will top the maximum efficiency length.

Figure 2 show that sequences A, B, C, D, E and F are in the same big group. When a new subgroup within one big group needs to be formed, the scanning process shoud be executed from the first sequence in that big group, which is A in this example. If A's length does not reach the maximum efficiency length, the next one will be checked, which is B. If the total length of A and B does not reach the maximum efficiency, then next one C will be checked. In this example, we assume that the total length of A, B and C is less than the maximum efficiency length, so the checking process continues to the next one, D. Finally, when D is taken into account, the total length of A, B, C and D is greater than the maximum efficiency length. So the first subgroup formation process stops between C and D, making A, B and C into a same subgroup, which is shown in Figure 3. Then another subgroup formation process starts from checking D.

Adjacent Gap Rule. The second rule is called adjacent gap rule. It means that if there is a gap between two adjacent sequences (the gap between two sequences exists when the location of the end of the former is ahead of the location of the start of the latter), For example, sequence H is the former and sequence I is the latter (see Fig. 4), and if the total length of all the sequences before H has reached the two thirds of the maximum efficiency length, the subgroup formation will stop between H and I, making H in one subgroup and forming the next subgroup from I even if the total length of the subgroup do not top the maximum length when both H and I are made into this subgroup.

Figure 4 shows that sequences G, H, I, J, K and L are in the same big group. When forming the subgroup as maximum efficiency length rule does, the subgroup result will be like that shown in Figure 5, which means that the total length of G, H and I is no greater than the maximum efficiency length while the total length of G, H, I and J is longer than the maximum efficiency length. However, the real result of subgroup formulation is not like what Figure 5 shows when adjacent gap rule is taken into account. As Figure 4 shows, there is a gap between two adjacent sequences, H and I. In the process of subgroup formation, we find that the total length of G and H is less than the maximum efficiency length while greater than the two thirds of it. And when the next sequence I is scanned, a gap between H and I is detected, so the process of subgroup formation stops between H and I, making G and H into a same subgroup (see Fig. 6) and forming the next subgroup from checking the sequence I, even if the total length of G, H and I is no greater than the maximum efficiency length.

If any of the two rules (maximum efficiency length rule and adjacent gap rule) is satisfied, the subgroup formation will be executed.

Fig. 3. Subgroup formation process

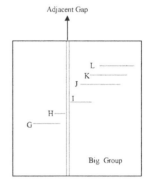

Fig. 4. The adjacent gap between H and I

4.3   Boundary Interval Filter Rule

After forming the original big groups and subgroups, the boundary of every big group and subgroup will be stored as interval, and when querying an aimed query interval, first step is to check the containment relationship between every big group's boundary interval and query interval. If the boundary interval of one big group is completely contained by query interval, then all the sequences inside that big group are the result sequences. Otherwise, the next check which is whether there is an intersection between the boundary interval of that big group and query interval will be executed. If there is no intersection, all the sequences inside that big group will be discarded. If there is, then the relationship between the boundary interval of subgroup within that qualifying big group and query interval will be examined with the same method. If subgroup's boundary interval is completely contained by query interval, all the sequences within that subgroup are result sequences. If there is no intersection, subgroup will be discarded. If part of intersection exists, scanning process inside that subgroup will be executed until encountering the first non-overlapping sequence within that subgroup.

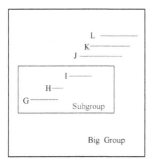

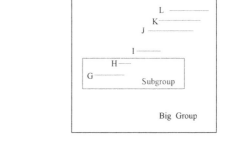

Fig. 5. Maximum efficiency length rule   **Fig. 6.** Adjacent gap rule

Figure 7 shows that the query interval is [1959713, 1966104], when checking the group 20 of which the boundary interval is [351991, 900708] it turns out that there is no intersection between the boundary interval of the big group 20 and query interval. Therefore, the big group 20 will be discarded and other big groups will be checked. As a result, the boundary interval of the big group 28 has an intersection with the query interval. Then the boundary interval of its subgroups need to be examined, when it is found that subgroup 1-28 has no intersection with query interval, it can be discarded and the process continues to the next subgroup. As as result, it turns out that only the subgroup 2-28 has the intersection with the query interval, so what we need to do next is to check the sequences inside the subgroup 2-28 and find the result overlapping sequences, which are marked in black lines in this example.

Algorithm 3. Map of CNCList⁺	**Algorithm 4.** Reduce of CNCList⁺

Void map(Vector key, Vector value)
  //key: serial number and boundary of big group
  //value: all the sequences inside one big group and the data of its m subgroups
  Vector bigGroupBoundary = key.boundary
    IF (bigGroupBoundary $\subset$ queryInterval)
      ResultCollector (value.thisBigGroup)
  ELSE   IF   (bigGroupBoundary $\cap$ queryInterval $\neq \varnothing$)
    ReduceCollector (key.bigGroupSerialNumber, value)
  ELSE
    Discard (key, value);
    Return;
	Void reduce (Vector key, Vector value)
	  //key: serial number of big group
	  //value: all the sequences inside one subgroup and the information of its boundary
	  Vector subGroupBoundary = value.subBoundary;
	  FOR EACH boundary IN subgroupBoundary
	  IF (boundary $\subset$ queryInterval)
	    ResultCollector (values.thisSubgroup)
	  ELSE IF (boundary $\cap$ queryInterval $\neq \varnothing$)
	    FOR EACH geneInterval IN values.thisSubgroup
	    IF (geneInterval $\cap$ queryInterval $\neq \varnothing$)
	      ResultCollector (values.thisSubgroup)
	    ELSE IF (geneInterval.start > queryInterval.start)
	  Break;
	  ELSE
	    Discard (key, value);
	  Return;

4.4   Process of NCList⁺

The Map (see Algorithm 3) store all the serial number and boundary of every big group. Then whether the boundary interval of a big group is fully contained in query interval will be examined at first, if it is completely contained, then all the sequences inside that big group are the result sequences. Otherwise, whether there is an intersection between the boundary interval of that big group and query interval will be inspected. If there is not, all the sequences inside that big group will be discarded. If there is, Map will pass the information of qualifying big groups and their subgroups to Reduce. In the Reduce process (see Algorithm 4), the containment relationship between the boundary interval of subgroup and query interval will be checked first. If subgroup's boundary interval is completely contained by query interval, all the sequences within that subgroup are result sequences. Then the intersection relationship between subgroup boundary interval and query interval will be examined. If there is no intersection, all the sequences inside the subgroup will be discarded. If intersection exists, scanning process toward sequences inside that subgroup starts until encountering the first non-overlapping sequence.

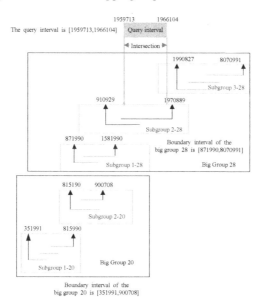

Fig. 7. Illumination of boundary interval filter rule

5   Experimental Evaluation

In our experiments, we use Ubuntu 10.04, Linux 2.6.32-31-generic as operating system. The environment is Hadoop 0.21, RAM is 2.0 GB and the switch is net-core NSD1016D (16 port Fast Ethernet Switch, 10M/100M). CPUs and their remaining disk spaces are listed below.

5.1   Results

Different Number of Machines. The number of machines is a key factor to the final query time. The following experiment will test the relationship between the final query time and the number of machines. In this experiment, the variable is the number of machines and the amount of test data is set to be 10GB.

Result analysis: 1) Fig. 8 shows that for both CNCList and CNCList$^+$, the more of the number of the machine, the less query time will be used; 2) For the same number of machine, the query time of CNCList$^+$ is shorter than the query time of the CNCList.

CNCList$^+$ demonstrates superior query speed ability over CNCList under the same amount of machine. Moreover, as the amount of machines has reached a level, the degree of the reduction of query time is not that remarkable. Therefore, we can set the proper number of machines according to the size of data and computation.

Different Amount of Data. When the configuration of platform and the amount of the machines is fixed, we consider the increase of data would not optimize the finished time. Hence, the final experiment is going to test the influence from the amount of data to the final query time. The variable is the amount of data and we set the number of machines as eight. What's more, the other configuration would be the same, which guarantee the accuracy. The result is shown on Figure 9.

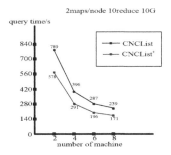
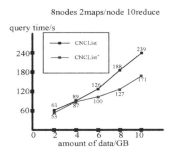

Fig. 8. Relationship between number of machine and query time

Fig. 9. Relationship between amount of data and query time

Result analysis: according to the tendency of the experiment curve, we can see that: 1) for both , the larger the amount of data, the longer final query time will be used; 2) for the same amount of data, the query time of CNCList$^+$ is shorter than that of CNCList; 3) when the amount of data reaches a level, about 4 GB in our test, with the amount of data increasing, the increase speed of query time of CNCList$^+$ is less than that of CNCList, which demonstrate the better scalability of CNCList$^+$.

5.2   Summary

The above experiments shows that CNCList$^+$ have superior query speed ability over CNCList for both the same amount of machine and data. In addition, we can enhance the query time by increasing the number of machines. Thus, for biomedical researchers, the CNCList$^+$ algorithm based on cloud computing will be an excellent choice to improve the query efficiency and reduce the query speed when they make the overlap interval query researches which contain a large amount of data.

6   Conclusion

In this paper, the cloud computing is applied to the NCList algorithm and make it a new algorithm named CNCList. Furthermore, two optimization strategies are proposed on CNCList, thus an advanced overlap interval query algorithm CNCList$^+$ is created. Elaborate experiments demonstrate the better performance of CNCList+ than the CNCList on both query speed and scalability. Hence, the CNCList$^+$ algorithm will provide much help for biomedical researchers on data mining and make interval overlap query a more convinent tool in biomedical area.

Acknowledgement. The paper was supported by Liaoning Provincial Natural Science Foundation of China(No. 201102067) and Overseas Distinguished Foreign Expert Project of Universities directly under the Ministry of Education (No. MS2011DBDX021).

References

1. Alekseyenko, A.V., Lee, C.J.: Nested Containment List (NCList): a new algorithm for accelerating interval query of genome alignment and interval databases. Bioinformatics 23(11), 1386–1393 (2007)
2. Kent, W.J., Sugnet, C.W., Furey, T.S., et al.: The human genome browser at UCSC. Genome Res. 12, 996–1006 (2002)
3. Giardine, B., Elnitski, L., Riemer, C., et al.: GALA, a database for genomic sequence alignments and annotations. Genome Res. 13, 732–741 (2003)
4. Kolovson, C.P., Stonebraker, M.: Segment indexes: dynamic indexing techniques for multi-dimensional interval data. SIGMOD, 138–147 (1991)
5. Kriegel, H.P., Pötke, M., Seidl, T.: Managing intervals efficiently in objcct-relational databases. VLDB, 407–418 (2000)
6. Enderle, J., Hampel, M., Seidl, T.: Joining interval data in relational databases. SIGMOD, 683–694 (2004)
7. Tao, Y., Papadias, D.: Mv3r-tree: a spatio-temporal access method fortimestamp and interval queries. VLDB, 431–440 (2001)

The Method on Improving the Adaptability of Time Series Models Based on Dynamical Innovation

Wei Wang

Department of Mathematics, Information School,
Renmin University of China, Beijing, 100872, P.R. China
wwei@ruc.edu.cn

Abstract. It is well known that time series analysis is the method to build a model and to make statistical inference based on historical records. Therefore the model will be dependent on the choice of sample data and the modeling method. Owing to the complexity and uncertainty of practical problems, the characteristics of time series will probably be variant in coming periods. So in order to make a proper prediction, improving the adaptability of the model is necessary.

The paper considers the method of improving the adaptability of time series models based on introducing dynamic innovation mechanism to the model. Firstly, the time series model is translated into the form of state space, and the controllability of the model is analyzed. Secondly, based on the error feedback principle, an error innovation term is introduced into the time-series model to improve the adaptability of the model. The theoretical result is obtained. Finally, some case studies are shown to demonstrate the efficiency of the method.

Keywords: time series, adaptability, dynamic innovation, error feedback.

1   Introduction

In many of the study for social or economic problems, it is often necessary to deal with future trends of certain variables relevant to the changing situations. The inference to the evolution is very important for the decision or management under the given uncertain circumstances. Time series analysis is one of the essential tools to the technical analysis of such kind of problems ([1]).

Since the publication of the seminal book Time Series Analysis: Forecasting and Control ([2]), a number of books and a vast number of research papers have been published in this area. Time series analysis and its applications have become increasingly important in various fields of research, such as business, economics, engineering, medicine, environ-metrics, social sciences, politics, and so on ([1], [3]).

The emphasis in time series analysis is on studying the dependence among observations at different points of time ([2]). Therefore, the model will be different because of the choice of sampled data and the modeling method. At the same time, because of the complexity and uncertainty of practical problems, the characteristics of

M. Zhao and J. Sha (Eds.): ICCIP 2012, Part I, CCIS 288, pp. 210–217, 2012.
© Springer-Verlag Berlin Heidelberg 2012

the time series will probably be different in coming periods ([4], [5], [6], and [8]). Therefore, we need to find some ways to improve the adaptability of the model and to enhance the predictive ability of the model. By now, the improvement of time series model has been performed by increasing the order of models, or by choosing the proper forms of fitness functions. There also have methods such as adaptive method, natural network, etc. ([4]). There has nearly nothing been done by using the method of error feedback to improve the model.

This paper proposes the dynamic error regulation method to improve the adaptability of time series models. Some theoretical results are obtained. In the end of the paper, we will demonstrate the specific application of this method through some cases studies. It indicates the efficiency of the method.

2   The Statement of the Problem

In the theory of time series analysis, the fundamental type is the stationary time series. There have been almost completely results on it. For stationary time series, the common models are the ones such as: auto-regression (AR) model, moving average (MA) model, and the synthetic form of AR and MA, i.e. the ARMA model. For the $ARMA\,(p,q)$ model, its general form can be described as:

$$X_t - \phi_1 X_{t-1} \cdots - \phi_p X_{t-p} = \alpha_t - \theta_1 \alpha_{t-1} - \theta_2 \alpha_{t-2} - \cdots - \theta_q \alpha_{t-q} \tag{1}$$

where $\phi_1, \phi_2, \cdots, \phi_p, \theta_1, \cdots \theta_q$ are $p+q$ weighted coefficients. The definition of the forms and the coefficients can be found in [2] and [7].

For the non-stationary time series, however, by choosing the proper way to preprocess the data, we can obtain a stationary time series and find a model for the stationary series. Then, from the inverse transformation of the first step, we can obtain the model on the original non-stationary time series. One of such kind of time series models is known as autoregressive integrated moving average (ARIMA) models. It is shown that the model has been used widely in the modeling of some complex processes, such as financial processes ([6]).

Time series analysis is the method that based on the historical records to build a model and then make statistical inference for future evolution. The emphasis in time series analysis is on studying the dependence among observations at different points of time. The model will be different because of the quality of sampled data and the effectiveness of the modeling method. Because of the complexity and uncertainty of the practical world, the characteristics of time series will change probably in coming periods. So improving the adaptability of the model is necessary. This paper will consider the problem to improve the adaptability of time series models by introducing dynamical innovation term into the model. It will also have a great impact on the predictive results.

3   The Improvement of the Adaptability of Time Series Models

In this section, we will propose the method of improving time-series models by introducing error feedback to innovate the model to revise the adaptability of the model.

3.1   The State Space Form of Time Series Models

For the sake of simplicity, we consider only the form of ARMA model, the general form of ARMA can be described as follows:

$$
\begin{aligned}
&y(i+n) + p_{n-1}y(i+n-1) + \cdots + p_1 y(i+1) + p_0 y(i) \\
&= q_{n-1}u(i+n-1) + \cdots + q_1 u(i+1) + q_0 u(i)
\end{aligned}
\tag{2}
$$

where $y(k)$ can be regarded as the output, $u(k)$ can be regarded as the input, $p_1, p_2, \cdots, p_n$ and $q_1, q_2, \cdots, q_n$ are given constants. In order to obtain the state space form of time series model (2), we should choose the state variables as follows ([9]):

$$
x_1(i) = y(i) - c_0 u(i)
\tag{3a}
$$

$$
\begin{cases}
x_1(i+1) = x_2(i) + c_1 u(i) \\
\quad \vdots \\
x_{n-1}(i+1) = x_n(i) + c_{n-1}u(i) \\
x_n(i+1) = -p_0 x_1(i) - \cdots - p_{n-1}x_n(i) + c_n u(i)
\end{cases}
\tag{3b}
$$

where $c_1, c_2, \cdots, c_n$ are coefficients needed to be chosen.

Using (3a) (3b) for the variables in (2), and comparing the coefficients of $u(k), u(k+1), \cdots, u(k+n)$, we can obtain the following results about the coefficients,

$$
c_0 = q_{n-1}
$$

$$
\begin{cases}
c_1 = q_{n-2} - p_{n-1}c_0 \\
c_2 = q_{n-3} - p_{n-2}c_0 - p_{n-1}c_1 \\
\quad \vdots \\
c_n = q_0 - p_0 c_0 - p_1 c_1 - \cdots - p_{n-1}c_{n-1}
\end{cases}
\tag{4}
$$

So, we can translate (2) into the following form of a difference equation

$$
\begin{bmatrix} x_1(k+1) \\ \vdots \\ x_{n-1}(k+1) \\ x_n(k+1) \end{bmatrix}
=
\begin{pmatrix} 0 & 1 & & \\ \vdots & & \ddots & \\ 0 & & & 1 \\ -p_0 & -p_1 & \cdots & -p_{n-1} \end{pmatrix}
\begin{bmatrix} x_1(k) \\ \vdots \\ x_{n-1}(k) \\ x_n(k) \end{bmatrix}
+
\begin{pmatrix} c_1 \\ \vdots \\ c_{n-1} \\ c_n \end{pmatrix}
u(t)
\tag{5a}
$$

and

$$
y(k) = \begin{pmatrix} 1 & 0 & \cdots & 0 \end{pmatrix}
\begin{pmatrix} x_1(k) \\ x_2(k) \\ \vdots \\ x_n(k) \end{pmatrix}
+ c_0 u(t)
\tag{5b}
$$

where (5a) is the state space of (2), (5b) is the output equation, $c_1, c_2, \cdots, c_n$ can be decided by (4).

3.2   The Characteristics of Error Feedback and Some Related Results

From the viewpoint of control theory, we know that the proper use of error feedback can improve the performance of the closed-loop system, such as the tracking results or stability, etc.

Now, we consider the following general form of linear system

$$X(k+1) = AX(k) + Bu(k) \tag{6}$$

in which $X(0)$ is given.

We intend to choose the control series $u(k)$ such that, as $k \to \infty$, the error vector $X(k) - X^*(k)$ will converge to zero, where $X^*(k)$ is the controlled or the required one. In such a circumstance, the error of real output and the required output will also converge to zero. In doing so, here we use the conclusion about pole assignment ([9]).

Theorem 1. Consider the following linear system

$$X(k+1) = AX(k) + Bu(k) \tag{7}$$

where $X(t) \in R^n$. If there exists a feedback control law which has form of from state to input as follows:

$$u(k) = KX(k) + w(k) \tag{8}$$

such that the following closed-loop system

$$X(k+1) = (A+BK)X(k) + Bw(k) \tag{9}$$

has the poles at the given positions of the complex plane, if and only if the system of (7) is controllability.

3.3   The Implementation of Improving Adaptability of Time Series Models

It is the advantage of the error feedback that we can use certain error feedback as the innovation information to improve the adaptability of the model.

As a matter of fact, for a time series model, such as (2), we can always introduce the variable $\varepsilon_t = X_t - X_t^*$, in which X_t^* is the estimated one by using the model (2) and x_t is the observed one. And we can obtain the error system about ε_t. In such a case, we can turn the problem of revising the model into the problem of regulating of error system. That is to say, we should find the regulation way to revise the error system, such that $\varepsilon_t \to 0$.

For the given model such as (2), we obtain the following error system

$$\varepsilon_t - \phi_1 \varepsilon_{t-1} \cdots - \phi_p \varepsilon_{t-p} = \alpha_t - \theta_1 \alpha_{t-1} - \theta_2 \alpha_{t-2} - \cdots - \theta_q \alpha_{t-q} \tag{10}$$

Under certain circumstances, we can mend the system in following ways.

Firstly, we change the model (10) into the model (5), and obtain the state equation and its output equation like (5a) and (5b).

Secondly, we judge the controllability of system (5), that is, the rank of the controllability matrix of $P_c = [B \quad AB \quad A^2B \quad \cdots \quad A^{n-2}B \quad A^{n-1}B]$ is n or not.

Thirdly, we introduce the feedback control to the system (5) if it is controllable. Let $u(k) = KX(k) + w(k)$, where $K = (k_1, k_2, \cdots, k_n)$. Calculate the characteristic roots of characteristic equation: $p(s) = |sI - (A+BK)| = 0$. And suppose that the coefficients of $p(s) = 0$ are equal to the required coefficients of the characteristic equation determined by the given poles, we can obtain the gains matrix $K = (k_1, k_2, \cdots, k_n)$. Then the original system (5) is changed into

$$X(k+1) = (A + BK)X(k) + Bw(k) \tag{11}$$

The new system of (11) is the revised one. And it is stable. That is the model we want.

It is the introduction of error regulation that the model has the adaptability, and it can also improve the prediction ability of the model. When the original system (5) is observability, the revised problem can also be solved in the similar way.

4   Some Cases Studies

In this section, we intend to demonstrate the efficiency of the method by providing some of the actual cases studies. We will consider the modeling of time series about the Gross Domestic Product (GDP) by the method given above ([5]). The sample data can be found from the main page of the Statistics Bureau of Chinese Government, and the sample period of GDP is from 1978 to 2006.

4.1   The Modeling of the Time Series

From the scatter diagram of the sample data, we can see that the series on the GDP of per person ($GDPP_t$) has the tendency in an exponential form. Therefore, by taking the logarithm, we can obtain the new series about the sample data, $i.e.$ $\ln(GDPP_t)$. From its scatter diagram we know that, $\ln(GDPP_t)$ will increase in linear form. So, here we build the regression model for $\ln(GDPP_t)$ related with time. And then we consider the time-series model on the error (ε_t) of $\ln(GDPP_t) - \ln(GDPP_{t-1})$. In order to compare the difference between the method given above and the common time series method, we will use the data of 2006 for comparison.

From the graph of the auto-correlative function (ACF) and the partial auto-correlative function (PACF) of ε_t, we know that the PACF of ε_t is truncated after $t = 2$. And its auto-correlative function is with certain tailed. Therefore, we choose $AR(2)$ as the model of the series of ε_t.

Using the software of E-Views ([10]), we can obtain the estimation results shown in Table 1.

Therefore, we can obtain the model of $AR(2)$ as follows:

$$\varepsilon_t = 1.573\varepsilon_{t-1} - 0.795\varepsilon_{t-2} + \upsilon_t \tag{12}$$

The predict model is the one as follows:

$$GDPP_t = \exp(5.651 + 0.144t + 1.573\varepsilon_{t-1} - 0.795\varepsilon_{t-2} + \omega_t) \tag{13}$$

Based on the calculation we know that the characteristic roots of the characteristic equation of (12) are all in the unit circle. So the model of (12) is more stationary than the model of AR (2).

Table 1. The estimation results of parameters in $AR(2)$ of ε_t

Sample(adjusted): 1980--2004
Included observations: 25 after adjusting endpoints
Convergence achieved after 3 iterations

Variable	Coefficient	Std. Error	t-Statistic	Prob.
AR(1)	1.573143	0.124011	12.68549	0.0000
AR(2)	-0.795453	0.123491	-6.441375	0.0000
R-squared	0.914576	Mean dependent var		-0.005456
Adjusted R-squared	0.910862	S.D. dependent var		0.132703
S.E. of regression	0.039620	Akaike info criterion		-3.542357
Log likelihood	46.27946	Durbin-Watson stat		1.731761
Inverted AR Roots	.79 -.42i	.79+.42i		

4.2 The Revision of the Model

We can translate the form (12) into the following form. From the time series model

$$y(k+2)-1.573y(k+1)+0.795y(k)=u(k+2)$$

Let

$$x_1(k) = y(k) - c_0 u(k)$$
$$\begin{cases} x_1(k+1) = x_2(k) + c_1 u(k) \\ x_2(k+1) = -0.795\,x_1(k) + 1.573\,x_2(k) + c_2 u(k) \end{cases}$$

Comparing the coefficients of $u(k)$, we obtain the coefficients c,

$$\begin{cases} c_0 = 1 \\ c_1 = 1.573 \\ c_2 = 1.679 \end{cases}$$

Therefore, we can obtain its state space form as follows:

$$\begin{pmatrix} x_1(k+1) \\ x_2(k+1) \end{pmatrix} = \begin{pmatrix} 0 & 1 \\ -0.795 & 1.573 \end{pmatrix}\begin{pmatrix} x_1(k) \\ x_2(k) \end{pmatrix} + \begin{pmatrix} 1.573 \\ 1.679 \end{pmatrix} u(k) \qquad (14a)$$

$$y(k) = \begin{pmatrix} 1 & 0 \end{pmatrix}\begin{pmatrix} x_1(k) \\ x_2(k) \end{pmatrix} + u(k) \qquad (14b)$$

It is easy to know that the controllable matrix of system (14) is as follows:
$P_c = \begin{pmatrix} B & AB \end{pmatrix} = \begin{pmatrix} 1.573 & 1.679 \\ 1.679 & 1.39 \end{pmatrix}$. Because $\det(P_c) \neq 0$, P_c is a matrix with full rank.
Therefore, the states of model (14) are controllable.

From the linear system theory, we obtain the feedback in the following form
$u(k) = KX(k) + w(k)$, where $K = (k_1 \quad k_2)$, then the state space form of the closed loop system is as follows:

$$X(k+1) = (A+BK)X(k) + Bw(k) \qquad (15)$$

Then the characteristic equation is

$$|\lambda I - (A + BK)| = \begin{vmatrix} \lambda - 1.573\,k_1 & -1 - 1.679\,k_2 \\ 0.795 - 1.679\,k_1 & \lambda - 1.573 - 1.679\,k_2 \end{vmatrix} = 0 \tag{16}$$

Suppose that the poles are $\lambda_1 = 0, \lambda_2 = 0.795$, then $p(\lambda) = \lambda^2 + 0.795\lambda$. Let the relevant coefficients of the two characteristic equations are equal, we obtain the result as follows: $k_1 = 0.573, k_2 = -1$. Let $K = (0.573 \quad -1)$, and instead it into equation (15), we can obtain the following new system

$$\begin{pmatrix} x_1(k+1) \\ x_2(k+1) \end{pmatrix} = \begin{pmatrix} 0.901 & -0.573 \\ 0.167 & -0.106 \end{pmatrix} \begin{pmatrix} x_1(k) \\ x_2(k) \end{pmatrix} + \begin{pmatrix} 1.573 \\ 1.679 \end{pmatrix} u(k) \tag{17a}$$

$$y(k) = \begin{pmatrix} 1 & 0 \end{pmatrix} \begin{pmatrix} x_1(k) \\ x_2(k) \end{pmatrix} + u(k) \tag{17b}$$

Because of the poles of matrix $\begin{pmatrix} 0.901 & -0.573 \\ 0.167 & -0.106 \end{pmatrix}$ are $\lambda_1 = 0, \lambda_2 = 0.795$, which are all in an unit circle, then the system is stable. We can obtain the new revised model of (14) in the following input and output form:

$$y(k+2) - 1.007\,y(k+1) - 0.263\,y(k) = w(k+2)$$

Then the revised model of (12) can be expressed in the following form:

$$\varepsilon_t = 1.007\varepsilon_{t-1} + 0.263\varepsilon_{t-2} + \omega_t \tag{18}$$

From some calculation we know that the characteristic equation of (18) is $\phi(B) = 1 - 1.007B + 0.263B^2 = 0$, and its roots will be in an unit circle. Then the $AR(2)$ model described by (18) is stable. Therefore, we obtain the predict equation as follows:

$$GDPP_t = \exp(5.651 + 0.144t + 1.007\varepsilon_{t-1} + 0.263\varepsilon_{t-2} + \omega_t) \tag{19}$$

Now, we predict the result of 2006' GDPP. Replace the value into the model (13) we obtain $GDPP_t = 16789.3$. The error is $4.38\% < 5\%$. And put the value into model (19) we obtain $GDPP_t = 16627.14$. The error is $3.38\% < 5\%$. Therefore, the model (19) is better than the model (13). The new model can be more precise to simulate the real sinuous of ε_t.

4.3   The Comparison Analysis for the Prediction Results

In order to compare the results between before and after the revision, we calculate $\Delta_1 = \varepsilon' - \varepsilon$ and $\Delta_2 = \varepsilon'' - \varepsilon$, the first one is the prediction error of before revision, the second one is the prediction error of after the revision, and the figures are shown in Fig. 1 and Fig. 2.

From the comparison we know that, the revised model (19) is more precise than the model (13) in simulating the sinuous of ε_t. It should be noted that for the same kind of sample data we can use different time series methods for the model. In this example, we use the difference of $\ln(GDPP_t) - \ln(GDPP_{t-1})$ to build the model. We can also build the model by using other time-series methods, and then to revise the model. For other kinds of models, we can also use the method discussed above.

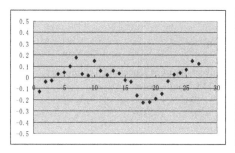
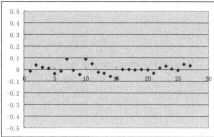

Fig. 1. The scatter diagrams of Δ_1 **Fig. 2.** The scatter diagrams of Δ_2

5   Conclusion

The adaptability of time-series models is an important aspect for time series analysis. This paper provides an useful method for improving ARMA models by using error feedback. For other time-series models we can also revise the models by using the method above. It needs further consideration when the system is uncontrollable.

References

1. Chatfield, C.: The Analysis of Time Series. Chapman & Hall (2004)
2. Box, G.E.P., Jenkins, G.M., Reinsel, G.C.: Time Series Analysis: Forecasting and Control, 3rd edn. Pearson Education, Inc. (1994)
3. Thoma, M.A., Wilson, W.W.: Market adjustments over transportation networks: a time series analysis of grain movements on the mississippi inland waterway system. Journal of Transport Economics and Policy 41(Part 2), 149–171 (2007)
4. Tang, X.: Time series forecasting of quarterly barge grain tonnage on the McClellan-Kerr Arkansas River navigation system. Journal of the Transportation Research Forum 40, 91–108 (2001)
5. De Jong, D.N., Liesenfeld, R., Richard, J.F.: A nonlinear forecasting model of GDP growth. Review of Economics and Statistics 87, 697–708 (2005)
6. Engel, J., Haugh, D., Pagan, A.: Some methods for assessing the need for non-linear models in business cycles. International Journal of Forecasting 21, 651–662 (2005)
7. Zhang, S., Qi, L.: The Concise Course on Time Series Analysis. Tsinghua University Press, Beijing Jiaotong University Press, Beijing (2003)
8. Wang, W.: The novel reconstruction strategy for signals with uncertain dynamical properties. In: Proc. of 2011 4th Int. Congress on Image and Signal Processing, pp. 2526–2530. IEEE Press, New York (2011)
9. Gong, D.-E.: The Introduction on Economics Control. Renmin University of China Press, Beijing (1988)
10. Gao, T.: The Method and Modeling on Metrieconomics Analysis——EViews Applications and Examples. Tsinghua University Press, Beijing (2005)

A File System Framework Independent of Operating Systems

Ilhoon Shin

NowonGu GongleungDong, Seoul National University of Science and Technology,
Building 3,207, Seoul 139-743, South Korea
ilhoon.shin@snut.ac.kr

Abstract. The goal of this work is to share file system code between multiple operating systems (OSs). Existing file systems have been implemented under OS-subordinate file system frameworks, such as Linux Virtual File System Switch, using OS-subordinate interfaces, data structures, and functions. Thus, the sharing of file system code between different OSs is almost impossible. In order to eliminate this OS dependency and enable the sharing of file system code, we isolate the OS-subordinate code to OS-adaptation modules and design a file system framework that provides OS-neutral interfaces, data structures, and library functions for file systems. File systems implemented under the OS-neutral framework are independent of OSs and can be deployed to multiple OSs via OS-adaptation modules without modifying the source code. In order to test the feasibility of our approach, we implement a Linux adaptation module and port the Linux VFAT file system to the OS-neutral framework. The Linux Test Project result and performance evaluation results with iozone and fileop benchmarks show that an OS-neutral framework is feasible.

Keywords: OS-independency, File System Framework, Operating Systems.

1   Introduction

Various forms of embedded systems such as mobile phones, MP3 players, and digital TVs are now widespread in daily life, and the market for such systems is rapidly growing. Traditionally, small-sized real-time operating systems (OSs) such as Vxworks, pSOS, and Rex have dominated the embedded OS market, because they guarantee timely constraints of such systems and can be performed by low-speed controllers with small-sized RAMs. However, with the emergence of complex embedded systems such as smart phones and digital TVs with various applications, the embedded versions of general-purpose OSs such as WinCE, iOS, and Embedded Linux are becoming more useful because they provide various file systems, network protocols, and graphic libraries. Accordingly, various OSs are now competing in the embedded system market. This phenomenon is likely to continue because it is in the interest of manufacturing companies not to be subordinate to any dominant OS.

File system providers for embedded devices should support various embedded OSs. Although it is best to apply a file system implementation to multiple OSs

M. Zhao and J. Sha (Eds.): ICCIP 2012, Part I, CCIS 288, pp. 218–225, 2012.

without modifying the source code, this is not straightforward at the present time. Functionally rich OSs such as Linux, WinCE, and Symbian have unique file system frameworks to support multiple file systems in an efficient manner. For example, file systems in Linux are implemented under the virtual file system switch (VFS) using the data structures and functions provided by the VFS. The implemented file systems are linked to the VFS via an interface defined by the VFS. Unfortunately, the data structures, functions, and interfaces provided by file system frameworks are not standardized, and hence the file systems become subordinate to the OS. Currently, file system providers implement them in a redundant manner according to the file system frameworks of different Oss.

Our goal is to share file system code between OSs. For this purpose, we design an OS-neutral file system framework (OSN) that isolates OS-dependent data structures and functions to OS adaptation modules, and provides file systems with OS-neutral data structures, functions, and interfaces. File systems are implemented using the OS-neutral data structure and functions, and linked to the OSN framework via OS-neutral interfaces. Thus, the implemented file systems are not dependent on a specific OS. They can be deployed to any OS without modifying the source code, so long as an adaptation module is developed for the target OS. In this work, we implement the Linux adaptation module and investigate the feasibility of our approach. The results of the Linux Test Project (LTP) [1] show that our approach is feasible at least for the Linux OS. Thus far, there has been no failed case caused by the OSN framework among 1221 total cases tested. In addition, we find that the range of the performance overhead for the OSN framework is less than 1% in case of read and write.

This paper is organized as follows. In section 2, we explain the design of the OSN framework in detail, and implement the Linux adaptation module in section 3. Section 4 presents the test and performance evaluation results of the OSN framework. In section 5, we draw conclusions and discuss future work.

2   OS-Neutral File System Framework

2.1   OS-Neutral Interface between OSN Framework and File Systems

In OSs that support multiple file systems with a file system framework, the file service requests are handled by the cooperation of file system framework and the target file system. The file system framework first performs the jobs that are not subordinate to a specific file system and then calls the appropriate file system functions to process the file system-dependent jobs. Thus, the prime file system functions to handle file service requests should be linked to the file system framework. For this purpose, the file system framework defines and exports the interface with file systems as a form of function pointers. The file systems implement the exported interface function and are linked to the framework via this interface.

Currently, the names, formats, and contents of the interface functions differ according to the OS. For example, the name of the interface function for creating a directory is mkdir() in Linux. The mkdir() interface has three parameters, the parent directory, the name of the new directory, and the mode of the new directory—similar to access permission [2]. However, in WinCE, the name of the same interface is MyFSD_Create DirectoryW(), and the parameters are the volume, the entire path that includes the new directory name, and a security attribute that is not currently used [3]. In addition, the amount of jobs that file system should perform is also different. The basic principle of Linux is to make the file system code compact. A job is performed by the file system framework if it is able to do so. In WinCE, however, most jobs are done by the file system. The file system framework simply forwards the request to the file system. These inconsistencies in the names, parameters, and contents of the interfaces make it difficult to share file system code.

In order to address these inconsistencies, the OSN framework standardizes the name, parameters, return value, and content of each interface to an OS-neutral form. In the case of creating a directory, the standard interface name is CreateDir(). The parameters are the parent directory, the name of the directory to create, access permission, and a pointer to the new directory created by the interface. The CreateDir() interface should allocate a block for the new directory, add the new directory entry to the data block of the parent directory, and create an in-memory object of the new directory that contains the metadata of the directory. The OS-dependent code is implemented in the OS adaptation module. For example, in the case of Linux, the mkdir() interface is implemented in the Linux adaptation module. It performs several Linux-dependent jobs such as handling dentry structures and transforming the original request to the standard form. The CreateDir() is called by mkdir(). The OS-subordinate code is completely removed from CreateDir() and is isolated within mkdir(). As for other interfaces, the OSN framework defines the standard formats and contents in a manner similar to those for creating a directory. We eschew a detailed description of other interfaces for space constraints.

2.2   OS-Neutral Data Structures of OSN Framework

In order to handle file service requests efficiently, file systems generally define several primary in-core objects: Inode, OpenFile, PathCache, Volume, and BufferCache. Inode contains the metadata of a file. OpenFile has the information related to the open file such as current offset. PathCache links the path to a file and the appropriate inode. Volume contains the metadata of an entire volume. BufferCache has the recently accessed file data. Given that most file systems require implementing these in-core objects, the file system framework provides the common in-core objects that contain the information commonly needed by file systems. File systems can define their unique in-core objects that have file system-specific information. These in-core objects are linked to the in-core objects of the file system framework. The names and member variables of the in-core objects provided by the file system framework differ depending on the OS. This is another factor that makes sharing file system code difficult.

Given that member variable names vary depending on the OS, if a file system accesses the member variables directly using the "." operator, it becomes subordinate to a specific OS. To avoid this, the OSN framework prevents file systems from directly accessing the member variables of the OSN framework in-core objects.

Instead, the OSN framework provides the standard interface that accesses the member variables of the OSN framework in-core objects. File systems should use the standard interface to access member variables. The name and format of each interface are defined in OS-neutral form, and thus the file system code is not dependent on the OS.

For example, the in-core object that functions as inode is Vnode in the OSN framework. Vnode has file-related metadata such as file ID, size, access information, attributes, and time-related information. Given that member variable names differ depending on the OS, the OSN framework exports the standard interface to access member variables. For example, the OSN framework provides the VnodeGetID() interface that returns the file ID. In order to know the ID of a file, file systems should use this interface instead of directly accessing the member variable using ".". The VnodeGetID() interface is implemented in the OS adaptation module because its code should differ depending on the OS. For other in-core objects, the OSN framework defines and exports the standard interface for member variables in a similar way. As a result, the OS dependency of file systems is eliminated within the OSN framework.

2.3   OS-Neutral Library Functions of OSN Framework

OSs provide several library functions to help implement file systems. Representative libraries are the list management, synchronization, memory allocation, endian handling, string management, time management, and unicode handling libraries. The OSN framework defines the standard name and format of each library function. File systems should be implemented using the standard library functions provided by the OSN framework. Each library function is implemented in the OS adaption module using the appropriate library functions provided by the target OS.

2.4   Other Hurdles

OSs deploy different encoding methods. For example, WinCE and Symbian use UTF16, whereas Linux generally uses UTF8. In order to conceal differences in the encoding method, the OS adaptation module transforms a passed string to UTF16 format, and then passes the UTF16 string to the OSN framework. Thus, the OSN framework and file systems are implemented under the assumption that the strings are always encoded in UTF16 format.

OSs use different time formats. For example, Linux expresses time with the time elapsed from the first day of 1970. In the other hand, for WinCE, the reference date is the first day of 1980. The OSN framework follows the Linux time format. Thus, the WinCE adaptation module should transform time to the Linux format.

3   Implementation of Linux Adaptation Module

File systems in the OSN framework can be deployed to multiple OSs via OS adaptation modules. Here, we implement the Linux adaptation module. We describe the module in detail in this section.

3.1   Interface

Existing file systems in Linux are directly linked to the Linux VFS through the interface exported by the VFS. However, in our approach, file systems are linked to the OSN framework by the interface exported by this framework. The Linux adaptation module connects the OSN framework to the Linux VFS by implementing the exported VFS interface to call the appropriate OSN function. The VFS interface processes Linux-subordinate jobs such as handling dentries and inodes, transforming Linux-subordinate data to the OSN standard format, and calling the appropriate OSN functions. Fig. 1 shows the pseudo code of the mkdir() interface. Other VFS interfaces are implemented in a similar way.

```
int OSN_CreateDir (struct inode pDir, struct dentry pDentry, int dwMode)
{
  - transform the new directory name to UTF32 format using NLS module;
  - call the CreateDir() function of the OSN framework passing the directory name, access mode,
    and parent directory;
  - add the created directory to the inode hash of VFS (by insert_inode_hash());
  - link the inode of the created directory to the dentry passed with the argument (by d_instantiate();
}
```

Fig. 1. Pseudo code of mkdir() interface

3.2   Data Structures

The Linux VFS provides various in-core objects such as inode, file, dentry, super_block, and buffer cache to help implement file systems. A file system can have its unique in-core objects to maintain additional information that the VFS in-core objects do not have. The in-core objects of file systems are linked to the appropriate VFS objects.

The Linux VFS in-core objects already have the member variables that must be defined by the OSN in-core objects. Thus, the OSN in-core objects are implemented using Linux VFS objects. For example, a file object of the Linux VFS has all the member variables that the OSN OpenFile must define. Thus, OpenFile is defined by redefining the file object as seen in Fig. 2. For Vnode, we need to define additional member variables to the VFS inode. We thereby let Vnode contain stInode in the VFS inode as the member variable, much as the EXT3 inode contains the VFS inode (Fig. 2). The Vnode has pFops and pVnops, which have interface function pointers with file systems. Fig. 2 also shows the definition of Volume and BufferCache. The Volume object points to the VFS super_block with pSb. The Volume object of the file system is linked to the OSN Volume with pPrivate. The interface functions of the file system are linked to the OSN framework with pVops.

In order to hide the implementation details of the OSN objects, the OSN framework prevents file systems from directly accessing the in-core objects as described in section 2. File systems should access the member variables of the OSN objects with the standard interface. The interface name and format are the same regardless of the OS. However, the implementation is different depending on the OS.

For example, in Linux, VnodeGetSize() is implemented to get the file size (Fig. 3). Given that the VFS inode has the member variable of file size, VnodeGetSize() accesses the appropriate VFS inode and returns the i_size variable, which contains the file size. Similarly, OpenfileGetOffset(), which gets the current file offset, returns the f_pos variable of the appropriate VFS file object (Fig. 3).

```
typedef struct file                  OSN_OPENFILE;
struct osn_vnode {
        OSN_INT64                    lwID;
        …
        struct osn_file_ops*         pFops;
        struct osn_vnode_ops*        pVnops;
        struct inode                 stInode;
};
typedef struct osn_vnode             OSN_VNODE;
struct osn_volume {
        struct super_block*          pSb;
        …
        struct osn_volume_ops*       pVops;
        void*                        pPrivate;
};
typedef struct osn_volume            OSN_VOLUME;
typedef struct buffer_head           OSN_BUF_ENTRY;
```

Fig. 2. Definition of OSN in-core objects

```
static inline int VnodeGetSize (OSN_VNODE      *pVnode) {
        return pVnode->stInode.i_size;
}
static inline OSN_INT64   OpenfileGetOffset (OSN_OPENFILE *pFile) {
        return ((struct file*) pFile)->f_pos;
}
```

Fig. 3. Implementation example of standard interface for OSN objects

3.3   Library Functions

The library functions of the OSN framework, which are needed to implement file systems, are implemented using the appropriate Linux kernel functions. For example, MiscLockSem(), which acquires a semaphore, is defined using the mutex_lock() function of the Linux kernel (Fig. 4).

```
#define MiscLockSem          mutex_lock
```

Fig. 4. Implementation example of library functions

4   Experiment

In order to evaluate the feasibility of the OSN framework, we ported the Linux VFAT file system to the OSN framework and performed the Linux Test Project (LTP) [1] on the ported VFAT file system. We chose the VFAT as the target file system. Table 1 shows the result. Among the 1221 tests, 133 tests resulted in failure. Most failures occurred because the VFAT file system does not support symbolic link and access permissions. In order to distinguish such failures from those that resulted from VFAT limitations, we executed the LTP on the original VFAT file system and filtered out redundant failures. As a result, there was no remaining failure. The LTP test result shows that the OSN framework correctly functions within the Linux OS.

Table 1. LTP Result

Total Tests	1221
Total Failures	133
Additional Failures	0

The OSN framework causes the computational overhead of transforming a string to UTF16 format and an original request to the OSN standard format. In order to assess the overhead of the OSN framework, we compared the read/write throughputs and the various system call throughputs of the ported VFAT with those of the original VFAT. The iozone [4] and the fileop benchmarks were used to measure the read/write and other system call throughputs.

Fig. 5 shows the read and write throughputs. In order to filter out the temporary effects of background jobs, we performed the iozone benchmark 10 times on a cleanly

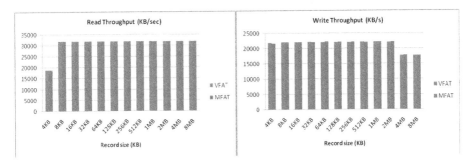

Fig. 5. Read & Write throughputs (iozone benchmark)

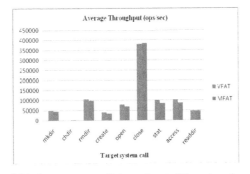

Fig. 6. Various system call throughputs (fileop benchmark)

formatted storage and depicted the average throughput. The effect of buffer cache was also removed with the umount option (-U). The X-axis denotes the read/write unit (record size) and the Y-axis denotes the throughput in KB/s. We denote the ported VFAT file system as MFAT. The results show that the MFAT delivered almost the same read and write throughput with the VFAT. The overhead of the OSN framework was negligible. Fig. 6 shows other system call throughputs. The experiment was performed on 8,000 files, which are 10 KB in size, and 8,000 directories. The X-axis denotes the target system call and the Y-axis denotes the average throughput in operations/s. From fig. 6, we see that the VFAT delivers a slightly better performance in most system calls. The overhead of the OSN framework was -5~16%. These system calls need to transform file name and directory name to UTF16 format, and thus the overhead of the OSN framework was relatively conspicuous.

5   Conclusion

In this work, we presented an OSN file system framework that enabled the sharing of file system code between OSs. The OSN framework isolated the OS dependency within the OS adaptation module and provided OS-neutral interfaces, data structures, and libraries for file systems. Thus, file systems that are implemented under the OSN framework are not subordinate to a specific OS and can be deployed for multiple OSs via adaptation modules. In order to investigate the feasibility of the OSN framework, we performed the LTP test on the ported VFAT file system and evaluated the computational overhead of the OSN framework with iozone and fileop benchmarks. The LTP test result showed that there was no failure, which was caused by the OSN framework, among 1221 test cases. The benchmark execution results showed that the OSN framework could be realized in Linux OSs.

Acknowledgments. This work was supported by the Korea Research Foundation Grant funded by the Korean Government (KRF- 331-2008-1-D00466) and by Basic Science Research Program through the National Research Foundation of Korea (NRF) funded by the Ministry of Education, Science and Technology (2011-0005542).

References

1. Linux Test Project, http://ltp.sourceforge.net/
2. Linux manuel page, http://www.linuxmanpages.com/man2/mkdir.2.php
3. MSDN, http://msdn.microsoft.com/en-us/library/aa910530.aspx
4. Iozone benchmark, http://www.iozone.org/

Design and Implementation of Catastrophic Emergency Rescue System Based on GIS

Zhuowei Hu[1,2,3], Lai Wei[1,2,3,*], and Changqing Liu[1,2,3]

[1] College of Resources Environment and Tourism,
Capital Normal University 100048 Beijing, China
[2] Key Lab of Resources Environment and GIS 100048 Beijing, China
[3] Key Lab of Integrated Disaster Assessment and Risk Governance of the Ministry of Civil
Affairs 100048 Beijing, China
mitsubishisony@163.com

Abstract. This paper mainly considers the disaster reduction business in China. We using development kit, such as ArcEngine, C#, IDL and oracle, to develop system, and design the catastrophic emergency rescue system. It can integrate multi-source data, such as remote sensing image, basic geographic data, socio-economic data and etc for synergy analysis. It is good for disaster reduction business of our country.

Keywords: disaster, system, ArcEngine, emergency, rescue.

1 Introduction

China is one of the most serious natural disaster countries in the world. In recent year, Wenchuan earthquake in 2008 is the biggest impact disaster. It brings heavy losses of life and property to us. During the disaster rescue, the Chinese Government and Chinese People actively join earthquake relief. It makes significant contribution, and powerful protects life and property of Chinese people. However, there are some problems in earthquake relief. These are impending problem, because it can reflect ability of earthquake relief in China.

At present, the capability of integration and synergy by multi-source data is weak. The accurate disaster analysis and loss assessment can provide important information for disaster rescue. It can help us to identify the epicenter, magnitude, degree of damage and etc. These are important guarantee in efficient rescue. It needs a lot of data. But we lack the support of data in disaster information extraction, loss assessment and disaster analysis. Such as① The data type is single. It can`t provide comprehensive information for disaster rescue; ②Selection in massive data lack support of technology and solution; ③ Every data has different data structure, such

---

* Corresponding author.

M. Zhao and J. Sha (Eds.): ICCIP 2012, Part I, CCIS 288, pp. 226–233, 2012.

as metadata, name, spatial characteristic and property. These make some barriers for data using. So we need to solve the integration and synergy of multi-source data.

2   System Overall Design

2.1   System Logical Framework

This system mainly includes three tiers, which are data tier, business tier and presentation tier. Data tier is catastrophic emergency rescue data, which includes basic geographic information data, field collection data, remote sensing data, metadata, socio-economic data and etc. Business tier is the service that provided by system, such as catastrophic emergency geographic information service, disaster information integrated display, instant-messaging and etc. Presentation tier includes basic geographic information integration and quick service and etc.

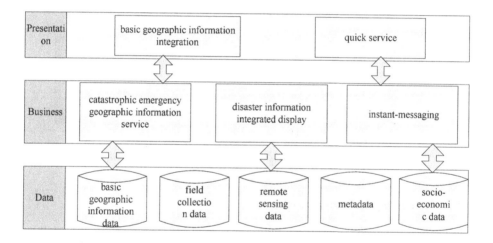

Fig. 1. System logical framework

2.2   System Data Framework

This system mainly provides support for disaster application, such as data collection, storage, processing and integration display. There is the system operation process. Firstly, user sends request to the server. Secondly, server receives it to analysis. A component plays broker role. It does the parameter matching through the parameter of query. Then we divide a single query statement into many sub-query statements. After that, another component plays wrapper role. It sends the sub-query statement to local database for processing. If it wasn't local data, it will enter index library or access other relational database for processing through the registered server. Thirdly, we deal the query result by integrated mode, put relational information into one record, and convert the data structure. Finally, we present complete result to user by browser.

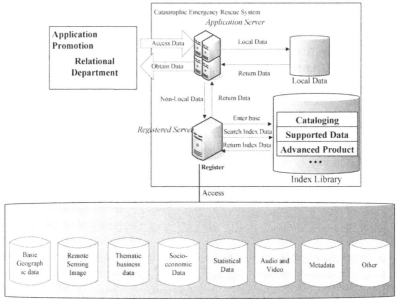

Fig. 2. System operation flow charts

2.3   System Physical Framework

The hardware operation environment of catastrophic emergency rescue information system includes server, switch, router, RAID and etc. The database provides basic geographic information data, disaster data, socio-economic data and etc. Then it can manage the server service. Switch mainly uses for data exchange between the each server and workstation. It can achieve the data collection and instant-messaging by wireless.

2.4   System Development Framework

Catastrophic emergency rescue information system is based on C#, ArcEngine, ArcSDE, ArcGIS Server IDL. The development environment is Visual Studio 2005. The database adopts the Oracle. The system accesses database by ADO.NET. The remote sensing image processing and spatial data analysis can use ArcEngine and

IDL to achieve. The spatial database can construct by ArcSDE. The B/S framework can use ArcGIS Server to achieve the geographic information service. The development framework is shown in figure.

2.5   System Function Design

This system mainly provides integrated data for disaster analysis, such as data collection, processing, integrated display and etc. It should have capacity of integration analysis, quick acquisition and quick processing in multi-scale basic geographic information and disaster information.

1) Multi-scale Basic Geographic Information Integration and Quick Service Module
Multi-scale basic geographic information integration and quick service module can provide the show of basic geographic data and catastrophic emergency rescue data, property query of geographic element, query of place name, buffer analysis, metadata query and etc.

2) Analysis and Display of Disaster Information Data Module
This module mainly includes three functions. There are field collection planning of disaster data, analysis and export of reported disaster data, and display of disaster data.

3) Catastrophe Information Integrated Display in Field and Background Module
Catastrophe information integrated display in field and background module can provide image loading, vector loading, DEM loading, map loading by WMS, line marking, polygon marking and so on. The specific function is shown in table.

4) Fusion and Integration of Multi-source Spatial Data Module
Fusion and integration of multi-source spatial data module can provide some function, such as acquisition of space multi-source data, acquisition of near-surface multi-source data and integration of multi-source information.

5) Quick Processing of Disaster Abnormal Area Module
Quick processing of disaster abnormal area module can provide some functions, such as quick geometric correction, quick level 0 aerial image mosaic, remote sensing merge and quick recognition of disaster abnormal area.

6) Quick Mapping of Remote Sensing Thematic Disaster Module
This module mainly include seven functions, such as earthquake disaster impact mapping, assessment of housing damage quick mapping, remote sensing monitoring of housing damage quick mapping, distribution of housing structure mapping, assessment of traffic damage mapping, assessment of distribution of tent mapping and disaster ground survey mapping.

After function module started, the system automatically call template of earthquake impact. Then user can input epicenter, magnitude, distance and other information into system, it will make scope of earthquake disaster, count and display object features within earthquake impact scope.

3   System Implementation Technology

3.1   Cooperative Analysis of Comprehensive Information

Catastrophic emergency rescue system is using for many different disaster. Therefore, the data has different kinds, such as remote sensing image, basic geographic information data, field collection data, socio-economic data and etc. With the difference of relief demand, decision and data are different. During the disaster rescue, different data can provide different information. So we need to integrate these data for decision and support of rescue.

3.2   Integration of Different Data

Integration of different data is associates with different kinds of remote sensing image, basic geographic data, field collection data, metadata and etc. It can solve some problems, such as store, processing, transmission of catastrophic emergency rescue data. Then it can provide decision and support for disaster analysis and risk analysis.

1) Difference of Data Spatial Characteristic
- Difference of Coordinate System. Because of the diversity of data source, spatial coordinate system may be different. In general, spatial coordinate has two kinds. One is spherical coordinate system. Its location is described by longitude and latitude, such as Beijing 1954. Another is plane coordinate system. Its location is (x,y) relative to origin. Uniform coordinate system framework is precondition for integration of disaster spatial data.
- Difference of Project. Spatial characteristic of spatial data usually distribute in 3D spherical space. But spatial data often is planar data. We can use project transmission ways to convert coordinate system.
- Difference of Data Scale. Catastrophic emergency rescue data has a lot of kinds. So the acquisition of a certain scale data is very difficult. Then we need to consider the difference of data scale.
- Difference of Entity Measurement Unit.Because of difference of data scale, the data measurement unit may be different. Some is meter, kilometer and etc.
- Difference of Geometric Characteristic.The expression form of same entity is different. For example, the same feature can remark by point, polygon and etc in same scale and different database, because of importance of feature. But in different scale dataset, it can express different geometric characteristic because of need of map generalization.
- Difference of Data Format.Data format is an organization record way of spatial characteristic and attribute in data file. Dataset must consider difference of data format.

2) Difference of Data Attribute

- Different of Data Encoding.Geo-spatial entity usually uses code to recognize. The standard, method and principle of encoding is different, therefore, same feature has different code, It is bad for data integration.
- Different of Attribute.The data type of same data in different dataset may be different. For example, we can use number to express district code. Its type may be string or numeric. It lacks a uniform standard.

3) Synthesis Information Integrated Display

- Integration of Multi-resource Remote Sensing Data. According to different characters of aviation and spaceflight remote sensing, we merge multi-spatial resolution, radiation resolution, Spectral resolution and temporal resolution by invoking data from each orbit of satellite platform, technical indices, sensor's characters, fitness of weather and reliability of image. The merged data is a set of spatial information and integrated image.
- It includes following parts: 1. Mergence of qualitative and quantitative data; 2. Mergence of data of identical resolution from different platform; 3. Mergence of data of different resolution from different platform; 4. Mergence of radar and optical data.
- Integration of Multi-scale basic geographic data. According to spatial entities from different scales which are with multiple meaning including semantic relation, expression method, connection mechanism and conversion method, we design the data model of organization, storage and management of multi-scale information. It reconstructs and transforms the original and updated basic geographic data with identical format and structure of database, and objectifies geographic features of the different scales physically and logically based on distinct demands of application. We build the coding rules of different scales and develop auto coding software of core features and transform the codes of core features based on analysis of geographic entities and rules of transform. After transforming, we build relationship of mapping with different scales and switch data of different scales with spatial indices. We explore the method of maintain consistency of those features to avoid error when display and analyze in different scales. All in all, we realize the spatial link and integrated management of geographic features which are in different scales.
- Integration of non-spatial data. Non-spatial data is descriptive or attribute data which reflects non-spatial characters, such as literature report and video files. These data include structured and unstructured. Structured data have structure which can divide basic features and be displayed by table or graph; unstructured data have unclear structure, such as document and multimedia data.
- Integration of spatial and non-spatial data. We use the relational model database management system to integrate them. This management model takes full advantage of RDBMS to manage, process, control and store mass data through SQL Language.

4   Implementation of System Function

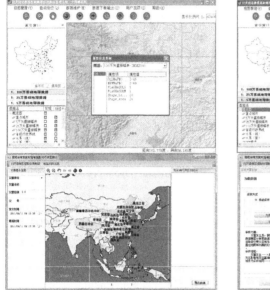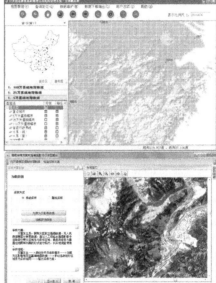

Fig. 3. System Implementation Effect

5   Conclusion

This paper does a research of data of type, characteristic, application and etc. We design the synergy technology of multi-source data in flow of data and disaster reduction business. We use this system to achieve intended function. Research result can provide support for data using in Chinese disaster reduction business. In future, we can ceaselessly consummate relational fruit.

Acknowledgments. Project supporting: National Technology Supporting Program Collaborative analysis of comprehensive information and world integrated data integration (2008BAK49B07-2); National Technology Supporting Program (2007BAH15B02, 2006BAC08B02003).

References

1. Hoshiya, M., Ohno, H.A.: Quantitative Functional Evaluation Model of Lifeline by System Dynamics in the Earthquake Disaster. In: Proc. of the 1st East Asian Conf. on Structual Engineering and Construction, Bangkok (1986)
2. Isoyama, R., Itawa, T., Watanabe, T.: Optimization post-Earthquake Restoration of city gas systems. In: Proc. of th Trilateral Seminar-Workshop on Lifeline Earthquake Engineering, Taibei, China, pp. 3–7 (1984)

3. Hoshiya, M., Ohno, H.A.: System Dynamics Model in Seismic Performance Assessment on Electric and Water Supply Networks. In: Proc.Trilateral Seminar-Workshop on Lifeline Earthquake Engineering, Taipei, China (1985)
4. Taleb-Agha, G.: Seismic Risk Analysis of Networks. SDDA Report NO.22 MIT Dept. of Civel Eng. (1975)
5. Shinozuka, M., Takada, S., Kawakami, H.: RiskAnalysis of Underground Lifeling Network Systems. In: US-South East Asia Symposium on Engineering for Natural Hazards Protection, Manilla (1977)
6. Anshel, J.S.: Northridge Earthquake Lifeline Performance and Post-Earthquake Response. American Society of Civil Engineers, New York (1995)
7. Duke, C.M., Moran, D.F.: Guidelines for Evaluating of Lifeline Engineering. In: Proc. of the U.S. National Conference on Earthquake Engineering (1975)
8. Medina, A.M., Krawinkler, H.: Evaluation of Drift Demands for the Seismic Performance Assessment of Frames. Journal of Structural. Engineering 131(7), 1003–1013 (2005)
9. Krawinkler, H., Alavi, M.A.: Seismic Drift and ductility demands and their dependence on ground motionsw. Engineering Structure 25(5), 637–653 (2003)
10. Gordon, P., Moole, J.E., Richardson, H.W., Shinozuka, M.: An integrated model of bridge performance, highway netweoks, an the spatial metropolitan ecomomy: towards a general model of how losses due to earthquake impacts on lifelines affect the ecomomy. In: Proceedings of the Workshop on Earthquake Engineering Frontiers in Transportation Facilities, National Center for Earthquake Engineering Research, NCEER-97-0005, Buffalo, N.Y, August 29 (1997)

GPU-Based Aggregation of On-Line Analytical Processing

Guilan Wang[1] and Guoliang Zhou[2]

[1] Infomation and Network Management Center, North China Electric Power University,
071003 Baoding, Hebei, China
[2] Information of Department, Baoding Electric Power Voc. &Tech. College
071051 Baoding, Hebei, China
{wang.guilan,yu_bing_2000}@163.com

Abstract. OLAP (On-Line Analytical Processing) is data and compute intensive application, how to improve the performance of OLAP are researchers always pursued goal. Aggregation is one of high frequently used operations which have a great impact on OLAP performance. Modern GPU (Graphic Process Units) have more raw computing power and higher memory bandwidth, so utilizing GPU accelerating aggregation computation is straight forward. But now GPU equipment does not supports float atomic operation and incremental memory allocation, so GPU algorithm need to be well-designed. In this paper, we discuss real-time aggregation in OLAP based on dense and sparse dataset, which fully utilize the high parallelism and high memory bandwidth and achieve performance improvements approximately 20X over CPU-based algorithms. On dense dataset, source data are chunked based on shared memory size, each thread block processes one chunk, each thread in block computes one cell in chunk cuboid. Algorithms adapts to GPU architecture and high parallelism which ensure high performance of algorithms. But on sparse dataset, there is a complex relationship between the compression dataset and the unknown size of result cuboid, it is impossible to define a straightforward parallelization. So we utilize sort, map and prefix sum primitive finishing source data partition, and reduction primitive aggregation data. At last, we introduce prototype system GPUOLAP (GPU-based OLAP) architecture which is under development now. Our work is a good attempt to real-time OLAP using new hardware.

Keywords: Real-time Aggregation, OLAP, CUDA, GPUOLAP.

1 Introduction

OLAP is one of the most important data analysis tools and widely used in business circle. But based on BI Survey 8 performance is a topic of most concerned [1]. How to improve performance is a hot spot. There are mainly three solutions: fast and efficient cube algorithm [2-5], materialized view [6, 7] and parallel cube algorithm [8-10].

M. Zhao and J. Sha (Eds.): ICCIP 2012, Part I, CCIS 288, pp. 234–245, 2012.

Traditional OLAP is based on historical data and pre-computation, but in the highly competitive commercial society, decision-maker need to analyze real-time data. Driver-based forecasting and planning becomes more important, such as what-if analysis [11] which requires strong real-time computing power. So the real-time OLAP [12] appears. Real-time OLAP only stores the lowest level data, which prevent data explosion and materialized view maintenance. But OLAP is data and compute intensive application, real-time OLAP faces two major challenges: one is processing user's query on demand—real-time computing; the other is OLAP data synchronization with production database simultaneously—real-time ETL (Extract-Transform-Load). In this paper, we focus on real-time aggregation computation.

Real-time aggregation requires more computing resource, but general multi-core CPU are limited and memory stall prevent further performance improving [13]; on the contrary modern GPU has more raw computing power and higher memory bandwidth, and its massive thread parallelism can effectively hide memory latency. CUDA (Compute Unified Device Architecture) and other related development tools are accelerating the use of GPU for general purpose (GPGPU). Through GPU accelerating aggregation computation is straight forward. For example, sum is one of frequently used aggregate functions, comparing executing time between multi-core CPU (Intel Core2 Quad CPU 2.66GHz) and GPU (GTX275) of summation 100 millions numbers. GPU algorithm obtains approximate 20-fold speedup than Open MP-based [14] algorithm. GPU provides hardware support for real-time aggregation.

GPU is a special hardware which highly parallel and programmable. The latest GPU like NVIDIA's GTX275 contain 240(30*8) processing cores and theoretical performance beyond 1 TFLOP. Current GPU supports 4G global memory and one computer can assemble several GPU cards, while 64-bit GPU support more memory. So we hypothesize cube data can be wholly resident in GPU global memory. GPU executes in a SIMD (Single Instruction Multiple Data) mode, the inside has thousands of simultaneous execution threads, and these threads are organized as grid and block structure [17]. The simplified architecture of CUDA is shown in Fig. 1.

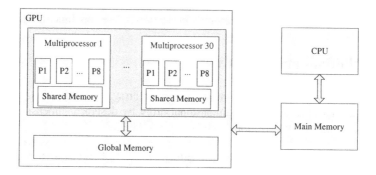

Fig. 1. GPU Architecture of GTX275

Generally GPU algorithms require carefully optimization. Two core principles are multiple threads accessing continued memory (coalesced access) and fully using shared memory for reducing memory latency.

Utilizing GPU accelerating data management applications received widespread attention. Join is an important and time-consuming operation in relational database. So GPU joins [15] are proposed. Several join algorithms are revised to fit GPU architecture and acquire about 2-7 times speedup. Based on these work, relational query processing on GPU (GDB) is developed and cost estimation for GPU is discussed [23]. In contrast, we focus on GPU-based OLAP aggregation, but some primitives of GDB can be used in our algorithm. GPU sort algorithm gets extensively study, several GPU sorts [15, 18, 20, 21] are proposed, which mostly based on bitonic sort and acquire high speedup. Data mining applications also can be accelerated by GPU [22], but writing GPU code for data mining algorithm need great effort. A translation system for enabling data mining applications on GPU is proposed [16]. CUDPP (CUDA Data Parallel Primitives) [19] is a library of data-parallel algorithm primitives including parallel prefix-sum ("scan"), parallel sort and parallel reduction. CUDPP is widely used.

In this paper, we discussed real-time aggregation on GPU. Aggregation algorithms on dense and sparse dataset are purposed. On dense dataset, source data are chunked based on shared memory size, each thread block processes one chunk, each thread in block computes one cell in chunk cuboid. Algorithms adapts to GPU architecture and high parallelism which ensure high performance of algorithms. But on sparse dataset, there is a complex relationship between the compression dataset and the unknown size of result cuboid, it is impossible to define a straightforward parallelization. So we utilize sort, map and prefix sum primitive finishing source data partition, and reduction primitive aggregation data. Our work is a useful attempt to improve the efficiency of OLAP using new hardware and provide a basis for the realization of real-time OLAP.

The rest of the paper is organized as follows. In Section 2, we give definition and some primitive for GPU-based aggregation. In Section 3, we discuss GPU-based aggregation algorithm. We give an overview of GPUOLAP system in Section 4. The results from our experiments are presented in Section 5. We conclude in Section 6.

2   Definitions and Primitive

In most cases, OLAP data model is multidimensional array (MOLAP, Multidimensional OLAP). But data linearize to one-dimensional array by designed dimension order for storage. One common linearization formula is defined below.

Linearization: Suppose $(d1,...,dn,m1,...,mm)$ is a cell in multidimensional array, so the position in one-dimensional array is defined by:

$$\text{LINEAR}(d_1,...,d_n)=d_1+d_2|D_1|+d_3|D_2||D_1|+...+d_n|d_{n-1}|...|D_1|. \tag{1}$$

This function is reversible, the inverse linear: suppose R is one-dimensional array from Linearization multidimensional array, so position P is decomposed as $(d_1, d_2, \ldots, d_n)$ through the formula:

$$R\text{-}LINEAR(P) = (d_1, d_2, \ldots, d_n) \ . \tag{2}$$

Where $d_1 = P \% |D_1|$, $d_2 = [P/|D_1|] \% |D_2|$, ..., $d_n = [[[[[P/|D_1|]/|D_2|]/]L/]/|D_{n-1}|] \% |D_n|$, [x] is integer operator, % is modulus operator.

In some cases, high dimensional array are very sparse. A commonly used compression technology is offset storage which only stores the offset and value of valid cells.

In order to conveniently describe aggregation algorithm, we utilize a set of parallel primitives simplifying algorithm like [15, 23].

Map: map operation is a transformation process. Defined as

$$O[i] = fun(I[i]), \tag{3}$$

where I is input array, O is output array and fun is transition function.

Scan: prefix scan is a useful building block for many parallel algorithms including sorting and building data structures. Defined as

$$O[i] = \oplus j < i I[j], \tag{4}$$

where $\oplus$ is any binary operator. We use the prefix sum implementation from CUDPP.

Scatter and Gather: scatter operation is index write and gather operation is index read. Defined as below, Scatter:

$$O[P[i]] = I[i], \tag{5}$$

where write input array I[i] to output array with position P[i];

Gather:

$$O[i] = I[P[i]], \tag{6}$$

where read input array with position P[i] to output array with position i.

Filter: Filter operation is selecting cells which satisfying user's condition. If data is dense, we can easily define the size of result. For example, if we want to find the cells of A=2, we first define the size of result, then inverse linearization get the A=2 cells to B position. Specially, each thread is responsible for one cell in AB, inverse linearization subscript get A and B, if A satisfying the condition then scatter the value to position B.

On sparse data set, we need carefully define the size of result and the position of cells in result. First we use map and prefix sum scan primitive getting the size and position of cells meeting query's requirement; second fetch the meeting condition cells to result (scatter).

Reduction: Give a set of values and output one value. It merges together input values to form an output value.

3   GPU-Based Aggregation

3.1   Aggregation on Dense Data

In this Section, we introduce GPU-based aggregation algorithms. The main ideas are below:

Firstly, the multidimensional array is chunked based on shared memory size. The size of chunk is defined by shared memory size and the aggregated dimension. The formula is below:

$$|chunk| = |SM| * |D_i| \tag{7}$$

where $|SM|$ is the size of shared memory, $|D_i|$ is the cardinality of dimension Di.

Each chunk is processed by each thread block and some block mapped to multiprocessors. Process is shown in Fig. 2(a).

Secondly, each thread computes one element of sub result cuboid. Process is shown in Fig. 2(b). Number of threads in block defined as below:

$$|threads| = |C_i * C_{i-1} \ldots * \ldots C_1| \tag{8}$$

where $|C_i|$ is the size of chunked Ci dimension.

Last, we merge each sub result into final result.

In this way, we can utilize high parallelism and shared memory computing aggregation and high performance.

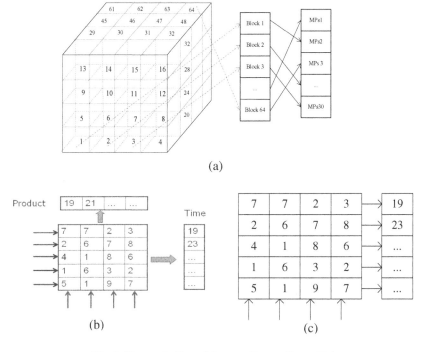

(a)

(b)   (c)

Fig. 2. Demonstration of Aggregation on Dense Data

But most multidimensional array stored as one-dimensional array based on designed dimension order and aggregation can be completed by two ways. Given a two dimensional array AB, if we compute A from AB and AB is linearized by A then B, this kind of aggregation is straight forward. We should only create |A| threads, in which every thread compute one cell in A, and every thread execute |B| times. But if we compute B from AB, we need carefully determine which cell in base cuboid aggregate to B cuboid. For utilizing coalesced access we compute A and B adopts different strategy. When we compute B from AB, we create |B| block, each block compute one element in B. Each block includes |A| threads and we utilize reduction primitive computing B cell value. Execution process is shown in Fig. 2(c).

When the cuboid includes limited cells, parallelism is low. We first calculate one cuboid which ensures full use of GPU high bandwidth and computing capability. In GTX275, one warp is composed of 32 threads; memory access latency is 500 cycles, each thread executes needing 16 cycles. Hide memory latency need Minimum number of threads $500/16 \approx 32$ warps. That is to say, the result contains at least 32*32 cells to full capacity of GPU.

Based on our aggregation algorithm, we give a GPU-based cube algorithm. Cube computation is a core problem in OLAP fields which is fast computing all cuboids. Our GPU-based cube algorithm adopts top-down and depth-first approach to take full advantage of high bandwidth and SIMD features of GPU. Each time compute one cuboid using GPU-based aggregation algorithm. We show the algorithm through an example. We compute a three dimensional cube. First, we compute AB, then from AB to A and from A to ALL. Second, we create |C| block, each block include |A| threads, each thread execute |B| times; and each block process |AB| cells beginning from position bid* |AB| for computing AC from ABC, where bid is index of thread block. We put |A| in shared memory and ensure coalesced access for high performance. Third, we create |BC| block and each block reduction |A| cells beginning position at bid*|A| for BC computation, then we compute from BC to B and C. In this way, we complete the calculation of cube.

An example of processing tree of four-dimension cube is shown in Fig. 3, the number in round parentheses denotes the computing order. Heavy black line is the most costly computing process.

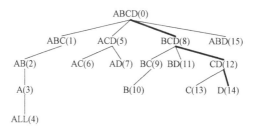

Fig. 3. Processing Tree (ABCD)

There is a pattern for creating blocks and threads from computing from $D_{i1}D_{i2}...D_{in}D_{i(n+1)}D_{i(n+2)}...Dik$ to $D_{i1}D_{i2}...D_{in}D_{i(n+2)}...Dik$. We create $|D_{i(n+2)}...D_{ik}|$

blocks and each block including $|D_{i1}D_{i2}...D_{in}|$ threads. Each thread executes $|D_{i(n+1)}|$ times. We put $|D_{i1}D_{i2}...D_{in}|$ cells in shared memory and all threads in one block coalesced access beginning from bid $|D_{i1}D_{i2}...D_{in}D_{i(n+1)}|$ position $|D_{i1}D_{i2}...D_{in}|$ cells. That is to say, we can utilize prefix of cuboid to improve efficiency.

3.2 Aggregation on Sparse Dataset

Because the size of result cuboid is not known beforehand, we can't define the thread number in each block straight forward. The technology of aggregation on dense data is not applicable. Aggregation on compression data requires well-designed. We adopt a completely different manner on compression data. We apply a few steps to complete this algorithm. As shown in Figure 4, OLAP data is stored as two arrays, one for offset, and the other for vakid values. Dimension information hides in offset array. Through series of sorting, prefix sum scanning and mapping operations, we finish data partition and determine the size of result cuboid. Finally obtain the final result by the reduction primitive. Algorithm is described as follows:

```
Program of Aggregation
Input:
    const n_tuples; The effective number of cells
    const BLOCK_NUM;
    const THREAD_NUM;
    float value[n_tuples];
    int     offset[n_tuples];
    int     bit[n_tuples];
    int     scan[n_tuples];
    int     output;
    int     tid,bid; thread index and block index
Output:
    float*  o_value;
    int*    o_offset;
    begin
    for i=tid; i < n_tuples ; i += BLOCK_NUM* THREAD_NUM
do
        R-LINEAR(offset[i])=(A,B,C))
        LINEAR(A,B)
        end do
    sort based on cuboid offset
    bit[0]=1;
    for i= tid+1;i< n_tuples;i += BLOCK_NUM* THREAD_NUM
do
        if(offset[i]>offset[i-1])
            bit[i] =1 ;
        else
            bit[i] = 0;
        end if
    end for
    scan = prefixsum(bit);
    output = scan[n_tuples-1];
```

```
    o_value = mollac(output);
    o_offset = mollac(output);
    t_position = mollac(output);
    for i= tid+1; i<n_tuples ;i += BLOCK_NUM* THREAD_NUM
do
        if(scan[i]>scan[i-1])
            t_position[scan[i]] = i;
        end if
    end for
    t = bid;
    for                            i=tid;i<t_position[t+1]-
t_position[t];i+=THREAD_NUM do
        block_reduction();
    end for
```

An example of algorithm is shown in Fig. 4. We first obtain AB linearization (1) and sort the AB offset array (2). Then we get a bit vector (3) for prefix sum scan(4), utilizing bit array and prefix sum array, we obtain the size of result and the position which cells aggregate to in result (5). At last, each block computes one element in results which is a reduction process.

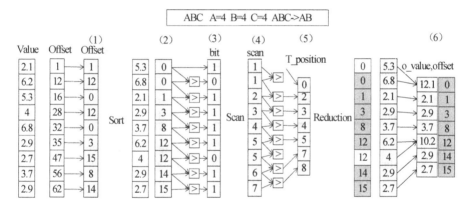

Fig. 4. Demonstration of Aggregation on Sparse Data

4   Architecture of GPUOLAP

In this section, we introduce prototype system GPUOLAP under development simply. GPUOLAP distribute data storage into CPU main memory and GPU global memory. Cube data stored in GPU, for scalability system support multi-GPUs; Meta data stored in CPU. When user's query request is parsed and the conditions are sent to GPU, GPU filter the cube data and is responsible for aggregate computation. At last, aggregation result transferred back to CPU and capsulated data to client. A simple architecture of GPUOLAP is shown in Fig. 5.

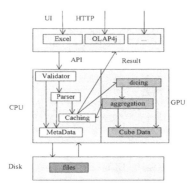

Fig. 5. Architecture of GPUOLAP

5   Evaluations

In this section, we evaluate the performance of aggregation algorithms integrated with GPU in comparison with aggregation algorithms based on CPU. We implement and test our aggregation algorithms on a PC with GTX275 and Intel Core2 Quad CPU 2.66GHz. GPU and CPU hardware configuration is shown in following Table 1.

Table 1. Hardware Configuration

	GPU	CPU
Processors	1404MHz*30	2.66GHz*4
Cache	16K*30	L2:3M*2, L1:32K*4*2
DRAM	1.8G	4G
Bus width(GB/sec)	127	10.67

We used synthetic data sets for evaluation. The data sets include dense and sparse data. Dense data is multi dimensional array. Sparse data is offset-value array. Our tests focus on filter and aggregation algorithms.

5.1   Data Transfer Time

Although our cube data is always resident in GPU global memory, the query results need transfer from GPU to CPU. We evaluate data transmission efficiency. GPU

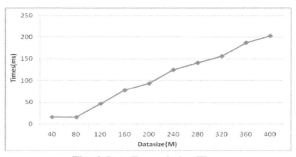

Fig. 6. Data Transmission Time

connected to CPU through PCI-EXPRESS and the theoretical bandwidth is 4GB/s. Fig. 6 shows the time cost when copy data from GPU to CPU. The figure indicates that with the data volume increasing, transmission time linearly grows.

5.2   Filter Primitive

We only evaluate filter primitive on sparse dataset. We carefully change data size and dimension number for comparing algorithm efficiency. Cardinality of all dimensions is 100. Filter condition is 0<=B<=50 and 50<=C<=100. Test results are shown in Fig. 7, which indicates GPU-based filter primitive is far superior to CPU-based.

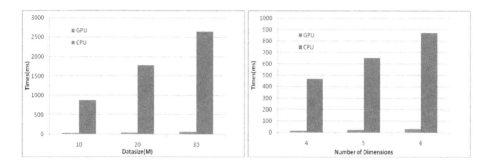

Fig. 7. Execution Time of filter primitive

5.3   Aggregation Algorithm

We first estimate aggregation algorithm on dense dataset. The datasets is a 4-dimentions array with size of 128*128*128*128(ABCD). To be fair, we respectively computer ABCD→ABC, ABCD→AB, ABCD→A and ABCD→BD. In GPUOLAP, we use shared memory and coalesced access to optimize algorithms. At the same time OPEMMP is used to accelerate algorithms on CPU. In most cases, the result of aggregation algorithm is relatively small, so we only compare the executing time, not including data transmission time which can be evaluated as Figure 6. Test results are shown in Fig. 8.

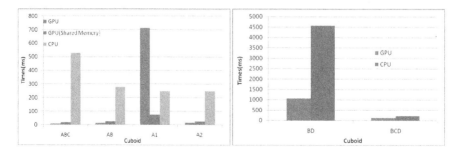

Fig. 8. Execution Time of Aggregation on Dense Dataset

As we can see, some aggregation algorithm on GPU is 20X corresponding to CPU, and the other has limited speedup. When we calculate A cuboid (A1), the GPU is slower because of low parallelism. In that case, we first calculate AB then from AB to A, the result is shown in Figure 8(A2).

Next we evaluate aggregation algorithm on sparse dataset. Sparse datasets is 4-dimentions; with cardinality 100. We change dataset size from 1 million to 10 million and number of dimensions from 4 to 6, the comparison of GPU and CPU calculating time is shown in Fig. 9. From the figure we can see that GPU algorithm is approximately 40 times faster than CPU.

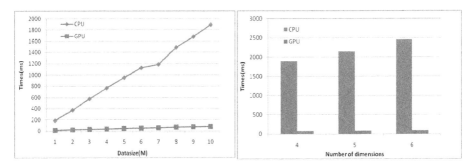

Fig. 9. Execution Time of Aggregation on Sparse Dataset

6   Conclusions

GPU received extensive attention in solving data and compute intensive applications. With GPU hardware continual development, more applications can benefit from GPU. In this paper, we discuss GPU-based aggregation algorithms in OLAP fields. Based on dataset feature, dense and sparse based aggregation algorithms are proposed. We also give a cube algorithm based on aggregation technology. The experimental results show high speedup than CPU algorithms.

In this paper, we focus on aggregation algorithms on GPU. GPUOLAP is a beneficial attempt for real-time OLAP. But GPUOLAP still has a great gap to real-time OLAP and practical system. There is a lot of work to be done. Our next research direction is to fulfill GPUOLAP system in more applications and more features. Our final target is a full-fledged GPUOLAP system.

Acknowledgments. Supported by National 863 Grant No. 2008AA01Z120; the Ph.D. Programs Foundation of Ministry of Education of China under Grant No.20090004110002.

References

1. The BI Survey Analyzer, http://www.bi-survey.com/
2. Zhao, Y., Deshpande, P.M., Naughton, J.F.: An Array-based Algorithm for Simultaneous Multidimensional Aggregates. In: SIGMOD 1997, pp. 159–170. ACM Press, New York (1997)
3. Beyer, K., Ramakrishnan, R.: Bottom-up Computation of Sparse and Iceberg CUBEs. In: SIGMOD 1999, pp. 359–370. ACM Press, New York (1999)

4. Xin, D., Han, J.W., Li, X.L., Wah, B.W.: Star-Cubing: Computing Iceberg Cubes by Top-down and Bottom-up Integration. In: 29th International Conference on Very Large Data Bases, pp. 476–487. Morgan Kaufmann Publishers, San Francisco (2003)
5. Shao, Z., Han, J.W., Xin, D.: MM-Cubing: Computing Iceberg Cubes by Factorizing the Lattice Space. In: 16th International Conference on Scientific and Statistical Database Management, pp. 213–222. IEEE Computer Society, Washington (2004)
6. Hurtado, C.A., Mendelzon, A.O., Vaisman, A.A.: Maintaining Data Cubes Under dimension Updates. In: 15th International Conference on Data Engineering, pp. 346–355. IEEE Computer Society, Washington (1999)
7. Lee, K.Y., Kim, M.H.: Efficient Incremental Maintenance of Data Cubes. In: 32th International Conference on Very Large Data Bases, pp. 823–833. ACM Press, New York (2006)
8. Dehne, F., Eavis, T., Hambrusch, S., Rau-Chaplin, A.: Parallelizing the Data CUBE. Distributed and Parallel Databases 11(2), 181–201 (2002)
9. Dehne, F., Eavis, T., Rau-Chaplin, A.: Cluster Architecture for Parallel Data Warehousing. In: IEEE International Conference on Cluster Computing and the Grid, CCGrid 2001, Brisbane, Australia, pp. 161–168 (2001)
10. Ng, R., Wagner, A., Yin, Y.: Iceberg-cube Computation with PC Clusters. In: Proceedings of the 2001 ACM SIGMOD International Conference on Management of Data, SIGMOD 2001, pp. 25–36. ACM Press, California (2001)
11. Lakshmanan, L.V.S., Russakovsky, A., Sashikanth, V.: What-if OLAP Queries with Changing Dimensions. In: 24th International Conference on Data Engineering, pp. 1334–1336. IEEE Press, Cancun (2008)
12. Real-time OLAP, http://www.sia.com.br/rtolap.htm
13. Ailamaki, A., DeWitt, D.J., Hill, M.D.: Data Page Layouts for Relational Databases on Deep Memory Hierarchies. The VLDB Journal 11(3), 198–215 (2002)
14. OpenMP, http://www.openmp.org/
15. Bingsheng, H., Ke, Y., Rui, F.: Relational Joins on Graphics Processors. In: SIGMOD 2008, pp. 511–524. ACM Press, New York (2008)
16. Ma, W., Agrawal, G.: A Translation System for Enabling Data Mining Applications on GPUs. In: 23th International Conference on Supercomputing, pp. 400–409. ACM Press, New York (2009)
17. Programming Guide NVIDIA CUDA Compute Unified Device Architecture Version 2.0 (July 6, 2008)
18. Govindaraju, N., Gray, J., Kumar, R., Manocha, D.: GPUTeraSort: High Performance Graphics Coprocessor Sorting for Large Database Management. In: SIGMOD 2006, pp. 325–336. ACM Press, Chicago (2006)
19. CUDPP: CUDA Data Parallel Primitives Library, http://www.gpgpu.org/developer/cudpp/
20. Satish, N., Harris, M., Garland, M.: Designing Efficient Sorting Algorithms for Manycore GPUs. In: 23rd IEEE Intel Parallel & Distributed Processing Symposium. IEEE Press, Rome (2009)
21. Govindaraju, N.K., Raghuvanshi, N., Henson, M., Tuft, D., Manocha, D.: A Cache-Efficient Sorting Algorithm for Database and Data Mining Computations using Graphics Processors. Technical report, TR05-016 (2005)
22. Fang, W., Lu, M., Xiao, X., He, B., Luo, Q.: Frequent Itemset Mining on Graphics Processors. In: 5th International Workshop on Data Management on New Hardware, pp. 34–42. ACM Press, New York (2009)
23. He, B., Lu, M., Yang, K., Fang, R., Govindaraju, N.K., Luo, Q., Sander, P.V.: Relational Query Coprocessing on Graphics Processors. ACM Transaction, Database System, 1–39 (2009)

Sequences Modeling and Analysis Based on Complex Network

Li Wan[1], Kai Shu[1], and Yu Guo[2]

[1] Chongqing University, China
[2] Institute of Chemical Defence People Libration Army
{wanli,shukai}@cqu.edu.cn

Abstract. In this paper, we present a method to model frequent patterns and their interaction relationship in sequences based on complex network. First, an algorithm NOSEM is proposed to find non-overlapping pattern instances in sequence. Then, we give a new way to construct state model of sequence formed by non-overlapping patterns, namely pattern state model. The proposed pattern state model of sequence is a graph-like model. We discover that the graph formed by non-overlapping frequent patterns and their interaction relationship is a complex network. Experiments on real-world datasets and synthetic datasets show that the pattern sate models formed by the frequent patterns of sequences in almost all the domain are complex network. However, models in different domains have distinct power-law values, which are used to classify various types of sequence.

Keywords: Complex network, Frequent pattern, Power-law.

1   Introduction

Sequence analysis, discovering knowledge in the structure of sequences, is an important problem in various domains, such as sensor network, biological informatics, natural disasters prediction, and so on.

In the decades, abundant literatures has been dedicated to discovery frequent patterns in sequence [1, 2, 3, 4, 5, 6].Most of them focus on the speed of the algorithm and generative model of sequences based on the discovered frequent patterns [2, 3, 4, 5, 6]. Studying the features of sequences by subsequences they included is a new trend. Lei Zhou etc. [1] try to use symbol state to divided sequences to study weather system, and analyze sequence features based on complex network. However, Lei Zhou etc. formulated the state model by subsequences occur successively in a sequence. In this paper, we consider frequent patterns in sequences and generate a new model based on the patterns. As illustrated inFig.1, if the minimum support is set as 2, we can get frequent patterns (i.e. "RR","RD","RdD") from the sequence listed in Fig. 1(a). As shown in Fig.1 (b), the occurrence of a pattern is represented as a time interval. Then, we can model the patterns and their relationships by a graph-like model. Suppose each pattern as a vertex, if two instances of different patterns are *overlapping*(i.e. the corresponding time interval intersect with each other), then an edge exists between the corresponding vertices of the patterns. Finally, we formulate the patterns in the sequence given in Fig.1 (a) into a pattern-state-model which is shown in Fig.1(c).

M. Zhao and J. Sha (Eds.): ICCIP 2012, Part I, CCIS 288, pp. 246–252, 2012.

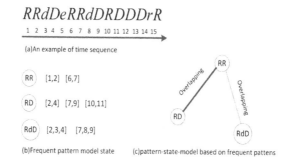

Fig. 1. An example of pattern-state-model

So the aim of this paper is to use frequent patterns to construct *pattern state model* of sequences and study the features of sequences through the features of pattern state model. We find and prove that the pattern state models of sequences generated in many domains are complex network (see details in Sec. 5).

Generally, frequent patterns are subsequences with frequency no less than a user-defined threshold (i.e. minimum support). According to the position occurring in sequences, there are various types of frequent patterns. Therefore, selecting a proper type of pattern plays an important role in formulating our model. One type of frequent pattern that are usually chosen to form generative model of sequence is non-overlapping pattern [3]. If any two instances of a pattern are non-overlapping (i.e. the corresponding time intervals of instances are not intersected with each other) then it is a non-overlapping pattern. For example, the patterns in Fig.1 (b) are all non-overlapping patterns. We also choose *non-overlapping frequent patterns* to construct pattern state model, such that the vertices in pattern sate model do not have self-loop edges.

2   Related Work

Lei Zhou etc. [1] analyze temperature sequence and found its complex feature. They divide the sequence to subsequences with the same length successively and formulate them into a complex network model. However, Lei Zhou etc. does not consider frequent patterns of sequence in their model.

S. Laxman etc. [3] defined non-overlapping episode and proposed the first algorithm to discovery non-overlapping episodes. Meger and C. Rigotti. [2] proposes a complete algorithm (i.e. WinMiner) to find frequent episode pattern in a single long sequence. J. Pei and J. Han [7] presented the first algorithm discovering sequential patterns.

3   Problem Formulation

3.1   Notations and Basic Concepts

Definition1 (Sequence). A sequence of objects, $T = \{<o_1,t_1>,<o_2,t_2>,...,<o_i,t_i>\}$, Where $O = \{o_1,o_2,...,o_i\}$ represents the symbols of different types of objects and t_i the time of occurrence of the i th object.

Definition2 (Serial Episode). Given a sequence and a minimum support γ. A sequence occurs once in this sequence contributes 1 to its support. If a sequence's support is larger than γ, it's a serial episode. We also use episode as a short form of serial episode. If no specific instructions, serial episode and episode are equal.

Definition 3 (Non-overlapping episode). Suppose an episode occurs in the sequence twice, if any object associated with either occurrence doesn't occur between the objects associated with theother occurrence, then these two instances of the episode are called non-overlapping episode.The frequency of an episode is defined as the maximum number of non-overlapping occurrences of the episode in sequence.

Definition 4 (Minimum Occurrence). Let $[t_s, t_e]$ be an occurrence of an episode ∂ in the sequence S If there is no other occurrence $[t_s', t_e']$ such that $(t_s < t_s' \wedge t_e' \le t_e) \vee (t_s \le t_s' \wedge t_e' < t_e)$ (i.e. $[t_s', t_e'] \subset [t_s, t_e]$), then the interval $[t_s, t_e]$ is called a minimum occurrence of ∂. As shown in Fig.1, [2,3,4] is a minimum occurrence of "RdD",while [1,3,4] is not.

3.2   Problem Formulation

Definition 5 (Overlapping relation). Serial episode α overlaps β, if and only if $\alpha.begin < \beta.begin \le \alpha.end < \beta.end$, where $e.begin$ and $e.end$ denotes the begin time and end time of episode e respectively. The overlapping relationship of α and β is donated as $\alpha\_overlap\_\beta$. As shown in Fig.1, [1,2] and [2,4] are overlapping.

Definition 6 (pattern-state-model). An undirected graph with vertices state frequent pattern instances and edges present the overlapping relationship of vertices. If two pattern vertices are overlapping, an edge between them is added. As shown in Fig.1(c), it's a pattern-state-model. Pattern "RR" and "RD" are overlapping, so an edge is connected between them.

Problem: To represent a sequence by a pattern-state-model and study the features of sequences by the features of their corresponding pattern-state-model.

Sub-problem 1: discovering all the non-overlapping episode in sequences
Sub-problem2: constructing pattern-state-model and analyze the feature of the sequences by the degree distributions in pattern-state-models.

4   From Frequent Pattern to Complex Network

In this section, we first present our method to generate model state: non-overlapping pattern. Then the algorithm NOSEM is given to discovery non-overlapping patterns.

Based on the model states, we build network graph and analyze its topological characteristics. Finally, we discover the complex network feature in sequences.

4.1   Frequent Pattern Discovery

The algorithm NOSEM is used to discovery non-overlapping patterns with episode rules of window sizes. We first introduce the algorithm NOSEM using the example in Fig.2,the detail description of NOSEM will be present later.

For the sequence in Fig.2, we definite the minimum min-support γ =2and gap-max ω =3,the main algorithm steps are as follows:

Step1: Scan the whole sequence, finding size-1 frequent patterns. There are 5 types of size-1 patterns, <R>, <r>, <D>, <d>, <e>.

Step2: Join existing frequent patterns with every size-1 patterns, getting frequent patterns with size greater than 1 with non-overlapping instances.

Step3: Iterate the join process, finding all non-overlapping frequent patterns.

4.2   Pattern-State-Model

In this section, we construct pattern-state-model based on all non-overlapping patterns discovered from sequence. Then we analyze the model and found it's a complex network through power-law distribution. Based on complex network features, for example degree distribution, shortest path of graph, clustering coefficient and power-law, we analyze the characteristics of sequence. In this paper, we focus on power-law value because it's the core feature of complex network.

We consider the sequence in Fig.1 with minimum non-overlapping min-support γ =2,and gap-max ω =3. Through algorithm NOSEM we can get all the non-overlapping instances of frequent patterns. If two instances are overlapping, a direct edge is added between them (e.g. illustrated in Fig.2).

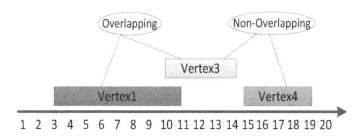

Fig. 2. Examples of pattern relations: overlapping and non-overlapping

The degree distribution of complex network follows power-law distribution. Different sequence may have different network model, therefore analyzing the degree distribution is an important step to discovery complex feature.

We analyze accumulated distribution graph of degrees and discovery sequence system's complex feature through power-law values. Various complex systems can be distinguished with different power-law values.

5   Experiments

We do experiments on sensor network dataset of temperature, gene sequence (splice), Lorenz system simulation dataset and synthetic datasets. We use exponential function to fit the accumulated distribution of degree. If the *fitting correlation*, which means similarity between real data and target function, is above 90%,we accept the complex feature. The result shows that all the datasets accord with complex feature to a very high probability.

All the datasets are generated as follows: Intel Lab Sensor Dataset [10] (using IL Sensor for short) has been collected from 54 sensors from February 28th to April 5th, 2004. We only select continuous 50000 data and discretize them using equal probability thoughts with symbols in {R, r, d, D}; we also evaluate Lorenz System and discretize it with the algorithm SAX [11].

All the experiments are performed on a 2.10GHZ Intel Core 2 PC machine with 2.00GB main memory, running Microsoft Windows 7.All algorithms are implemented in Java. Data fitting is completed in Matlab2010.

5.1   Experiments on Real-World Sequences

We use the algorithm NOSEM to discover non-overlapping pattern instances from the sequence.Every instance has been treated as vertex. If any two vertices are overlapping, both degree of them increase by 1.We use exponential function to fit degree's accumulative degree distribution.Result is acceptable when fitting correlation is above 90%. Finally we get Power Law Value Distribution (PLVD for short) graph.

5.1.1   IL Sensor Network Dataset
Fig.3 illustrate 46 of 48 sequences (with probability of 95.83%) accord with power-law distribution. The average value is approximately equal to -0.242.

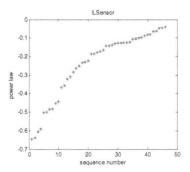

Fig. 3. The power law value distribution of 46 IL Sensor dataset sequences

5.1.2   Real Gene Sequence (Splice)
Fig.4 shows that the accumulation distribution of degree accords with power-law distribution to a high probability. The fit correlation is greater than 90%, which means this sequence is a complex network.

Fig.5 illustrate nearly all 100 sequences (with the probability of 99%) accord with complex feature (i.e. power-law distribution).While the power-law value is concentrated between -0.15 and -0.25.The average value isapproximately equal to-0.389.

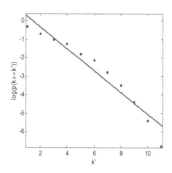
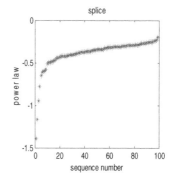

Fig. 4. Accumulation distribution of degree in a sequence: splice

Fig. 5. The powerlaw value distribution of 100 splice sequences

5.2   Experiments on Synthetic Dataset

Fig.6 shows the power-law value distribution of sequences generated from synthetic datasets with length 500.They illustrate that all the synthetic sequences accord with complex feature with the probability 100%.

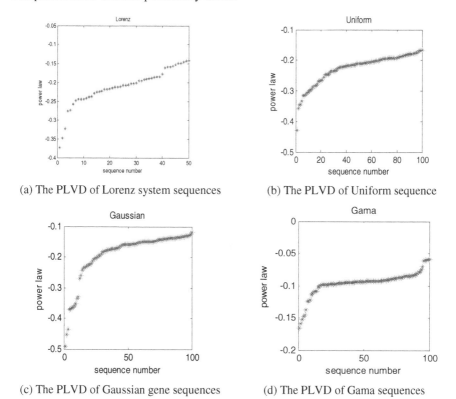

(a) The PLVD of Lorenz system sequences

(b) The PLVD of Uniform sequence

(c) The PLVD of Gaussian gene sequences

(d) The PLVD of Gama sequences

Fig. 6. The power law value distribution of 4 kinds of synthetic sequences (Lorenz, Uniform, Gaussian, Gama)

In summary, our performance study proved that all the datasets in this experiment are complex network system. We use frequent pattern instances to state sequence model and build complex network model. Power-law value can be significant approach to predict different system.

6   Conclusions

In this paper, we present complex network features in sequences using frequent pattern mining method. We first present that using non-overlapping frequent pattern to construct pattern state model, and we propose the algorithm NOSEM to mining non-overlapping pattern instances from sequence. We state the pattern network distribution and find various sequence including gene sequence, sensor network and synthetic dataset are complex network systems. While these systems has different inner feature (i.e. power-law value) so we can use this to predict and separate them.

References

1. Zhou, L., Gong, Z.-Q., Zhi, R., Feng, G.-L.: An Approach to Research the Topology of Chinese Temperature Based on Complex Network. Acta Physica, Sinica (2008)
2. Méger, N., Rigotti, C.: Constraint-Based Mining of Episode Rules and Optimal Window Sizes. In: Boulicaut, J.-F., Esposito, F., Giannotti, F., Pedreschi, D. (eds.) PKDD 2004. LNCS (LNAI), vol. 3202, pp. 313–324. Springer, Heidelberg (2004)
3. Laxman, S., Sastry, P.S., Unnikrishnan, K.P.: Discovering Frequent Episodes and Learning Hidden Markov Models: A Formal Connection. IEEE Computer Society 17(11), 1505–1517 (2005)
4. Mannila, H., Toivonen, H.: Discovering Generalized Episodes Using Minimal Occurrences. In: Proceedings of SIGKDD (1996)
5. Laxman, S.: Stream Prediction Using A Generative Model Based On Frequent Episodes In Event Sequences. In: Proceeding of KDD 2008 (2008)
6. Carl, H.M., John, F.R.: Mining: Relationships Between Interacting Episodes. SIAM (2004)
7. Pei, J., Han, J., Pinto, H., Chen, Q., Dayal, U., Hsu, M.-C.: PrefixSpan: Mining Sequential Patterns Efficiently by Prefix-Projected Pattern Growth. In: 17th Int' l Conference Data Eng., pp. 215–224 (2001)
8. Newman, M.E.J.: The Structure and Function of Complex Network. SIAM 45(2), 167–256 (2003)
9. Newman, M., Barabasi, A.L., Watts, D.J.: The Structure and Dynamics of Networks. Proceeding of Journal of Statistical Phicsics 126(2), 419–421 (2007)
10. Intel Lab Data, http://db.csail.mit.edu/labdata/labdata.html
11. SAX (Symbolic Aggregate approXimation),
http://www.cs.ucr.edu/~eamonn/SAX.htm

Performance Analysis of an Improved 4-Order Chebyshev Chaotic Sequence

Xiang Li, Liyong Bao, Dongfeng Zhao, Dongdan Li, and Weijie He

School of Information Science and Engineering, Yunnan University
Kunming, 650091, P.R. China
lybao@ynu.edu.cn

Abstract. Based on the idea of 32 bits integer quantization, this paper presents a efficient method to generate an improved 4-order Chebyshev chaotic sequence. The mathematical model and probability density analysis have been carried out with the sequence. Compared with m sequence in the autocorrelation and cross-correlation characteristics property, the findings of theoretical analysis and the experiments show that the improved sequence maintains good performance.

Keywords: spread spectrum communication, Chebyshev chaotic sequence, 32 bits integer quantization, the autocorrelation property, the cross-correlation property.

1   Introduction

The spread spectrum communication, as one of the most important techniques has very well confidentiality and stronger anti-interference ability in the 21st century, receives a universal attention to the research on its key techniques. The spread spectrum sequence plays a decisive role in spread spectrum communication. At present the spread spectrum Sequence mainly includes m sequence, Gold code, R-S code, and so on.

With the development of the next generation communications system, a solution is urgently expected to meet the requirements of a fairly large number and good performance of spread spectrum sequences. Because the traditional spread spectrum sequences have some problems with low complexity, poor confidentiality and small amount, so the traditional spread spectrum sequences will hard to meet above high demands.

The Chaotic sequences have the randomness, broadband frequency spectrum and are sensitive to the initial value, etc. Therefore, the chaotic sequences are drawing attention to applying in communication system. Most discrete chaotic sequences are generated by maps. The Chaotic sequences are generated by discrete dynamic chaotic system. Because the accuracy of computer is limited, the chaotic sequences generated by discrete dynamic chaotic system, which are sensitive to the initial value and have pseudo random. The sequence always shows periodic [1-2]. Some scholars have provided suggestions on the mathematical theory analysis and computer simulation about the chaotic sequence [3-6].

M. Zhao and J. Sha (Eds.): ICCIP 2012, Part I, CCIS 288, pp. 253–260, 2012.
© Springer-Verlag Berlin Heidelberg 2012

This paper introduces the 32 bits quantization into Chebyshev chaotic map and generates the improved 4-order Chebyshev spread spectrum sequence. The 32-bit quantization reduce effectively the loss of accuracy. The quantization also reduce the iteration times and the amount of computation. This research carries out theoretical analysis and simulation experiments with the improved sequence. The sequence is compared with m sequence in the autocorrelation and cross-correlation characteristics property.

2   The Mathematical Model and Probability Density Analysis

2.1   The 4-order Chebyshev Map Mathematical Model

The Chebyshev map definition is shown as following:

$$x_{n+1} = f(x_n) = \cos(k \cdot \cos^{-1} x_n) \qquad -1 \le x_n \le 1 \qquad k \in Z^* \tag{1}$$

The deformation form is exended as following:

$$
\begin{aligned}
x_{n+1} &= \sum_{i=0}^{\left[\frac{k}{3}\right]} (-1)^i \cdot \binom{k}{2i} \cdot \cos^{k-2i}(\cos^{-1} x_n) \sin^{2i}(\cos^{-1} x_n) \\
&= \sum_{i=0}^{\left[\frac{k}{3}\right]} (-1)^i \cdot \binom{k}{2i} \cdot \cos^{k-2i}(\cos^{-1} x_n)(1 - \cos^2(\cos^{-1} x_n))^i \\
&= \sum_{i=0}^{\left[\frac{k}{2}\right]} (-1)^i \cdot \binom{k}{2i} \cdot (\cos(\cos^{-1} x_n))^{k-2i}(1 - \cos(\cos^{-1} x_n))^i(1 + \cos(\cos^{-1} x_n))^i \\
&= \sum_{i=0}^{\left[\frac{k}{3}\right]} (-1)^i \cdot \binom{k}{2i} \cdot x_n^{k-2i}(1 - x_n)^i(1 + x_n)^i \qquad -1 \le x_n \le 1 \qquad k \in Z^*
\end{aligned}
\tag{2}
$$

When k=4, equation (2) changes to 4-order Chebyshev map model. It can be derived as:

$$
\begin{aligned}
x_{n+1} &= \sum_{i=0}^{2} (-1)^i \cdot \binom{4}{2i} \cdot x_n^{4-2i} \cdot (1 - x_n)^i \cdot (1 + x_n)^i \\
&= x_n^4 + (1 - x_n^2)^2 - (2^1 + 2^2) \cdot x_n^2 \cdot (1 - x_n^2) \\
&= 8x_n^4 - 8x_n^2 + 1 \qquad\qquad -1 \le x_n \le 1
\end{aligned}
\tag{3}
$$

Where

$$\binom{4}{2i} = \frac{4!}{(4 - 2i)! \cdot (2i)!}$$

2.2   The Chebyshev Map Probability Density Analysis

As is well-known, the equation (1) is a nonlinear map from line segment $I = (-1,1)$ to itself. As long as x_n falls within I, x_{n+1} will also fall within I. If $x = \cos(t)$, equation (1) can be transformed to the following form:

$$\cos t_{n+1} = \cos(k \cos^{-1}(\cos t_n))$$
$$= \cos(kt_n) \qquad k \in Z^* \tag{4}$$

So

$$t_{n+1} = 2n\pi + kt_n \qquad n \in N \tag{5}$$

Along with recursive algorithms, t_n can be representation as the following form:

$$t_n = 2n\pi + k^n t_0 \qquad n \in N \tag{6}$$

In view of the relation between t_n and x_n, equation (6) can be derived as:

$$x_n = \cos(k^n \cos^{-1} x_0) \qquad k \in Z^* \tag{7}$$

When k=4, formula (7) can denote 4-order Chebyshev map:

$$x_n = \cos(4^n \cos^{-1} x_0) \qquad k \in Z^* \tag{8}$$

According to equation (8), the distribution function can be derived as:

$$p(x) = \frac{1}{2\pi} \cdot 2 \cdot \frac{d\theta}{dx} = \frac{1}{\pi\sqrt{1-x^2}}, \quad -1 \le x_n \le 1 \tag{9}$$

3   The Performance Analysis

General 2-phase spreading codes mainly generate by binary quantization, the binary spread sequence only has two values +1 and -1. In this paper the Chebyshev chaotic sequence (Abbrev. C sequence) is generated by taking 32 bit binary quantization. Assume sequence $\{x_n, n = 0,1,\cdots, N-1\}$ is obtained by Chebyshev recursive map, the produced sequence is a real number valued in (-1,1). The x_n is taken into absolute value with its distribution within (0, 1). Further more, the value is converted into a binary form:

$$x_n = \sum_{i=0}^{\infty} b_i(x_n) \cdot 2^{-(i+1)} = b_0(x_n)b_1(x_n)\cdots b_{i+1}(x_n) \qquad b_i(x_n) \in [0,1] \tag{10}$$

$b_i(x_n)$ can be denoted as:

$$b_i(x_n) = \sigma_{1/2}(2^{i-1}|x| - \left[2^{i-1}|x|\right]) \tag{11}$$

Where $|x|$ represents the largest integer which is not exceeding x. $\sigma_c(x)$ is a threshold function.

$$\sigma_c(x) = \begin{cases} 0, & x < c \\ 1, & x > c \end{cases} \tag{12}$$

Choosing the first L bits to present, equation (12) can be transformed to the following form.

$$x_n = 2^{-L} \sum_{i=0}^{L-1} b_i \cdot 2^{L-1-i} = 2^{-L} \cdot X_n \tag{13}$$

The formula $X_n = \sum_{i=0}^{L-1} b_i \cdot 2^{L-1-i}$ is a L-bit binary integer, which is one to one mapping with x_n. When L=32, $|X_n - x_n| < 2^{-32}$, X_n could express sequence x_n accurately.

3.1   Autocorrelation Characteristics Property

In the range-finding, radar, communications and other fields , the researchers hope that the signal which carries the information and its own time phase shift signal can easily distinguish. In the real-time target detection, measurement and terminal system identification, multi-access communication, etc, the researchers also hope that the signal and other signals can easily distinguish. Here, the former sentence means applications need an outstanding autocorrelation performance sequence, and the latter sentence means applications need a good cross-correlation[7]. For 4-order Chebyshev chaotic sequences, autocorrelation is

$$R_x(m) = \lim_{N \to \infty} \frac{1}{N} \sum C(x_i x_{i+m})$$
$$= \lim_{N \to \infty} \frac{1}{N} \sum C[xf^m(x)] = \int_{-1}^{1} C[xf^m(x)]\rho(x)dx \tag{14}$$

When $m = 0$, there is

$$R_x(0) = \int_{-1}^{1} C[x^2]\rho(x)dx = \int_{-1}^{1} \frac{1}{\pi\sqrt{1-x^2}}dx = 1 \tag{15}$$

When $m \neq 0$, there is

$$R_x(m) = \int_{-1}^{1} C[xf^m(x)]\rho(x)dx \tag{16}$$

Because $C[xf^m(x)]\rho(x)$ is an odd function, so $R_x(m) = 0$

Cross-correlation function is:

$$R_{xy}(m) = \int_{-1}^{1}\int_{-1}^{1} C(xf^m(x))\rho(x)\rho(y)dxdy - x^{-2}$$

$$= \int_{-1}^{1} C(x)\rho(x)dx \bullet \int_{-1}^{1} C[f^m(y)]\rho(y)dy = 0$$

(17)

In the simulation, the length of the sequence must be limited. So the limited length sequence's correlation is part correlation. Part correlation function is described as:

$$R_{xy}(m) = \begin{cases} \dfrac{1}{(N-m)} \sum_{i=0}^{N-1-m} x_i y_{i+m} & 0 \le m \le N-1 \\ \dfrac{1}{(N+m)} \sum_{i=0}^{N-1-m} x_{i-m} y_i & 1-N \le m \le 0 \end{cases}$$

(18)

Where x, y denotes 2 sequence, N denotes the sequence's length. When $x = y$, the equation (17) become part of autocorrelation[8].

This article choose $x_{01} = 0.89999$, $x_{02} = 0.9$ as the initial parameters in the chaotic sequence model with a sequence's length 8192 and relevant interval 2000 .The m sequence in this article is a sequence of 12-order with a initial value [1 0 1 1 0 1 1 0 0 0 1], [1 0 1 1 0 1 0 0 0 0 1]. Along with the simulation experiments , the results of the sequence's autocorrelation and mutual correlation can be acquired. Experimental results was shown as the Fig.1 and Fig.2:

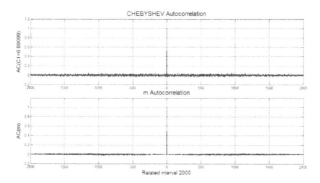

Fig. 1. Chebyshev and m sequence autocorrelation comparition

Through the simulation we can discover, Chebyshev chaotic sequences and m sequence both have a peak value of autocorrelation, which means the autocorrelation produced is a correct autocorrelation.Through calculating, the mean value of autocorrelation of the C sequence is 0.0125, while the mean value of autocorrelation of the m sequence is 0.0073, and C sequence has a peak value of autocorrelation is 0.0239, while the m sequence is 0.0239. According to the performance criterion of the

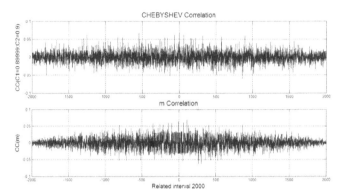

Fig. 2. Chebyshev and m sequence correlation comparition

sequence spread-spectrum autocorrelation peak criterion and the related average interference standards .Autocorrelation performance of the two sequences can meet the requirements of spread spectrum sequence[9].

According to Fig.2, according to analyzing the data, the C sequence has the cross-correlation mean value 0.0123, its cross-correlation absolute value has reached a peak 0.0681; meanwhile, the m sequence has the cross-correlation mean value 0.0077, its cross-correlation absolute value has reached a peak value 0.0688. Along with above analysis, it conclude that the cross-correlation performance of the m sequence is slightly better than the C sequence with a very small distinction. And according to the cross-correlation average interference criterion and cross-correlation peak criterion raised in literature [10], It is found the mutual correlation of the m sequence and the C sequence both meet the spectrum communication requirements.

A sequence generated by Chebyshev chaotic model has a very good autocorrelation, of which the peak in 0 point is very apparent. In terms of the mutual correlation, two sequences have not obviously even with a difference of 0.00005 . It is concluded sequences generated by this model can not only easily distinguish with their own time-shift signal, but also have no relation to other signals.

3.2   Cross-Correlation Characteristics Property

Autocorrelation side-lobe and cross-correlation mean square value are indispensable performance index of correlation analysis. Autocorrelation side-lobe represents the sequence's spread-spectrum anti-multipath interference ability.Cross-correlation mean-square represents the sequence's multi- access interference ability. The two abilities in the spread spectrum communication system is very important.

About calculation of autocorrelation side-lobe and cross-correlation mean square value, a formula is as follows:

$$\sigma_{R_{xx}} = \sqrt{\frac{1}{M}\sum_{m=1}^{M}[R_{xx}(m)]^2} \tag{19}$$

$$\sigma_{R_{xy}} = \sqrt{\frac{1}{2M+1} \sum_{m=-M}^{M} [R_{xy}(m)]^2} \tag{20}$$

Formula (19) is the side-lobe expression, where $\sigma_{R_{xx}}$ denotes sequence of autocorrelation side-lobe value, is a sequence of autocorrelation value, and M is related intervals. Formula (20) is the cross-correlation of the mean square value of expression, where $\sigma_{R_{xy}}$ dennotes cross-correlation mean square value.

Along with the above-mentioned method, the experiment produced some C sequence , which length from 256 to 16384. The research also analysis the autocorrelation side-lobe value and cross-correlation mean square value of the C sequence. The experimental results are shown in table 1:

Table 1. The relationship between correlation and sequence length

The relationship between autocorrelation side lobe value and sequence length						
sequence length	256	512	1024	2048	4096	8192	16384
m sequence	0.01276	0.01316	0.01300	0.00884	0.00491	0.00254	0.00138
C sequence	0.02209	0.02122	0.02160	0.01923	0.01595	0.01251	0.01062
The relationship between correlation side lobe value and sequence length						
sequence length	256	512	1024	2048	4096	8192	16384
m sequence	0.02574	0.02594	0.02586	0.02404	0.02289	0.02250	0.02240
C sequence	0.03143	0.03082	0.03108	0.02948	0.02746	0.02562	0.02475

Table 1 indicates that autocorrelation side-lobe value and cross-correlation mean square value of the C sequence and the m sequence are small. Because its value is below 0.1 in all situations. These characteristic satisfy the requirements of spread spectrum system against multipath, multi- access interference. So the C sequence is an excellent sequence of anti-jamming performance without influence of the sequence's length.

4   Conclusion

This paper provides 32 bits integer quantization method to generate the 4-order Chebyshev chaotic spread spectrum sequence is proposed. This efficient method improves the precision of qualification and decreases the amount of calculation. It feasible to the C sequence code realize with hardware circuit system. Furthermore, compared with m sequence in the autocorrelation and cross-correlation characteristics property, the improved sequence is described that has good performance.

Acknowledgments. Our sincere thanks to Professor Zha Guangming of UESTC. The authors would like to give their sincere thanks to the financial support by the Nation Natural Science Foundation of China (No.61072079) and National Innovation Experiment Program for University Students of Yunnan University (No. 101067309).

References

1. Palmore, J.: Chaos and Fractal. Computer Arithmetic. Physics 42, 99–110 (1990)
2. Jie, G., Lin, W., Zhi, L.: Analysis and comparison of Chebyshev chaotic sequence and m sequence. Journal of Chongqing University of Posts and Telecommunications (December 1999)
3. Zhang, X., Fan, J.: Extended Logistic chatic sequence and its performance analysis. Tsinghua Science and Technology, 156–161 (July 2007)
4. Hai, W., Hu, J.: The improved Logistic-Map chaotic spread spectrum sequences. Journal of China Institute of Communications 18(8), 71–77 (1997)
5. Yan, S., Chen, Y.: Performance analysis of full mapping chaotic sequence about Logistic. Modern Electronics Technique 3, 194–199 (2010)
6. Zhu, Z., Wu, Y., Liu, X., Zhu, W.: Chaotic spread spectrum sequence by Mid Multi-Bit quantifying and its properties. Journal of Northeastern University 23(8), 733–737 (2002)
7. Zhu, J.: Spread Spectrum Communication and Its Application. China University of Technology Press, Hefei (1993)
8. Lei, L., Ma, G., Cai, X., Shi, X.: Study of chaotic squence based on Chebyshev mapping. Computer Engineering 35(24), 4–6 (2009)
9. Sun, Y., Zhao, D., Yu, J., Li, J.: The implementation and application of chaotic sequnce code. Journal of Circuits and Systems, 50–53 (August 2003)
10. McGillem, C.D., Heidari-Bateri, G.: A chaotic direct-sequence spread spectrum communication system. IEEE Trans. on Communications 42(2), 15324–1527 (1994)

A New Adaptive Method for Digital Predistortion Using NLMS and RLS

Dian Xie and Zhibin Zeng

Engineering Research Center of Digital Audio & Video,
Ministry of Education
Communication University of China
Beijing, China
xietian-888@163.com

Abstract. In this paper, a joint adaptive algorithm combining normalized least mean square (NLMS) and recursive least squares (RLS) is presented for digital predistortion to compensate nonlinearity of power amplifier (PA). NLMS features stability and less calculation amount, while RLS characterizes precision and fast convergence speed. The simulation results show that this joint method can achieve not only a desirable linearization performance, but the rapid convergence and better stability.

Keywords: power amplifier, digital predistortion, normalized least mean Square, recursive least squares.

1 Introduction

Power amplifier (PA) plays an important role in contemporary wireless communication system. Today, almost all kinds of non-constant envelope modulation and the multi-carrier modulating techniques are easy to cause signal distortion through PA, make a high requirement on linearity of PA. For the sake of effectiveness and the linearity, linearization technology should be used to suppress spectral regrowth, especially in-band distortion. Among various linearization techniques, the digital adaptive predistortion has the fine performance, therefore is widely used.

The digital predistortion performance is influenced considerably by memory effect. If the input signal bandwidth is enough small, then the memory effect is negligible, but for broadband transmission signal, the PA memory effect cannot be neglected. The nonlinear system with memory effect is usually expressed by Volterra series which is of high complexity. However, the large number of coefficients in Volterra series makes it unattractive for practical application and then appeared some improved model. The memory polynomial is one of the simplified Volterra series, which is easy to implementation.

The predistortion architectures of power amplifier can be classified into two types, the direct learning structure and the indirect learning structure. The direct learning structure needs to determine the exact model of PA; while the indirect learning

M. Zhao and J. Sha (Eds.): ICCIP 2012, Part I, CCIS 288, pp. 261–268, 2012.
© Springer-Verlag Berlin Heidelberg 2012

structure does not need to determine the PA model, but depend on the input and output data through PA. The predistortion coefficients can be calculated by perform data training for iterations.

Adaptive algorithm is used to calculate coefficients of PA model, the literature[1] proposed for instance the classics LMS algorithm. Although NLMS algorithm is sensitive to initialization parameters, NLMS algorithm [2] is influenced by the relevance of input data, compared to LMS, it bears smaller steady-state misadjustment, features faster convergence speed and less calculation amount. But the The RLS algorithm [1] also is one classical algorithm, has the quick convergence rate and the accuracy, but large amount of calculation is its limitations. Using NLMS algorithm combined with RLS algorithm to apply in the predistortion adaptive algorithm module. Simulation in this paper shows that desirable linearization performances can be obtained.

2   Power Amplifier Modelling

2.1   Volterra Series

Volterra series [3] is always used to model the PA nonlinearity with memory effect, whose expression is given by:

$$z(t) = \sum_{n=1}^{\infty} \frac{1}{n!} \int_{-\infty}^{\infty} du_1 ... \int_{-\infty}^{\infty} du_n g_n(u_1,...,u_n) \prod_{r=1}^{\pi} x(t-u_r) \qquad (1)$$

where $x(t)$ and $z(t)$ denote the input and output of PA, respectively; $g_n(u_1,...,u_n)$ is the nth-order Volterra kernel.

The main disadvantage of Volterra series is the high computational complexity and can hardly be utilized for application. For the purpose of implementation, the simplified forms of Volterra series, such as Hammerstein model and memory polynomial, are developed for implementation.

2.2   Memory Polynomial

Memory polynomial [4] is one of the simplified models of Volterra series, whose expression is as below:

$$z(n) = \sum_{k=1}^{K} \sum_{m=0}^{M} a_{km} x(n-m) |x(n-m)|^{k-1} \qquad (2)$$

In this equation, $a_{k,m}$ is the complex coefficients of polynomial term, K is the polynomial order, Q is the memory depth.

Memory polynomial is widely used to describe PA nonlinearity with memory effect due to its simplicity and effectiveness.

3 DPD Algorithm Theory

3.1 DPD Overview

The PA nonlinearity is represented by their amplitude modulation to amplitude modulation conversion (AM/AM) and amplitude modulation to phase modulation conversion (AM/PM).The predistorter, in which the kernel adaptive algorithm is performed, is responsible for producing anti-phase and anti-amplitude curves to the PA model, i.e. inverse to the AM/AM and AM/PM characteristics of PA, thus compensating for the PA nonlinearity.

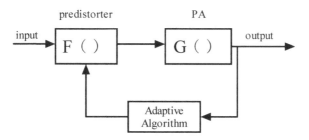

Fig. 1. DPD block diagram

As seen in Fig. 1, $G(\ )$ and $F(\ )$ represent the nonlinearity characteristics and its inverse characteristics of PA, respectively. The predistorter carries out transfer function $F(\ )$ before $G(\ )$. Adaptive algorithm is in charge of making $F(\ )$ be inverse to $G(\ )$, thus make these two functions complementary to achieve linear amplification.

3.2 Joint Algorithm Based on NLMS and RLS

In fact, PA features gradient change in its nonlinear characteristic, and the coefficients updating of the memory polynomial could be performed by combing the NLMS and RLS. During the adaptive algorithm operation period, quick convergence and precision is obtained in initial stage by RLS; for later stage, the main purpose is stability and simplicity which can be achieved by using NLMS.

NLMS algorithm is expressed as

$$w(n+1) = w(n) + 2\frac{\mu}{\left\|x(n)\right\|_2^2} e^*(n)x(n) \tag{3}$$

where

Tap-weight vector : $w = [w_0,...,w_{N-1}]^T$

Input vector : $x(n) = [x(n), x(n-1),..., x(n-N+1)]^T$

Output vector : $y(n) = w^T x(n)$

Error signal : $e(n) = d(n) - y(n)$

By dividing the step size by the norm of the data vector $x(n)$, the NLMS algorithm is equivalent to employing a variable step size in the form as shown below:

$$\Delta(n) = \frac{\mu}{\|x(n)\|_2^2} \tag{4}$$

In order to solve the estimation problem which the gradient noise causes, the recursion expression revision is:

$$w(n+1) = w(n) + 2\frac{\mu}{\|x(n)\|_2^2 + \varepsilon}e^*(n)x(n) \tag{5}$$

Where: $\varepsilon > 0$, ε is the adjustment factor.

The major advantage of NLMS algorithm lies in its computational simplicity. However, the cost paid for this simplicity is the slow convergence. To obtain faster convergence, it is necessary to devise more complex algorithm, which involve additional parameters.

RLS algorithm is based on least squares (LS) algorithm, which is given by the following equations :

Compute the filter output: $\hat{z}(n) = U^H(n)a(n)$

Compute the Kalman gain vector: $K(n) = \dfrac{P(n-1)U(n)}{\lambda + U^H(n)P(n-1)U^H(n)}$

Compute the error: $e(n) = z(n) - \hat{z}(n)$

Updata the inverse of the correlation matrix: $P(n) = \dfrac{P(n-1) - K(n)U^H(n)P(n-1)}{\lambda}$

Updata the coefficient vector: $a(n+1) = a(n) + K(n)e^*(n)$

Where λ is forgetting factor.

As mentioned above, NLMS should be carried out after RLS during predistortion of joint algorithm to get desired balance between performance and complexity.

3.3   Predistorter Architecture

Both NLMS and RLS are performed in the following adaptive predistorter architecture [5] as showed in Fig. 2

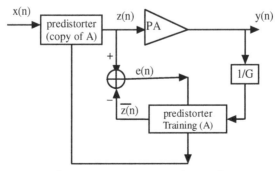

Fig. 2. Block diagram of adapative predistorter

And the procedure of the joint algorithm is as follows:

1. Set the initial coefficients of the predistorter;
2. Compare the input $z(n)$ and output $y(n)$ of PA;.
3. Calculate coefficients of predistorter using RLS until convergence. As long as the system meets the linearization requirements, then put the present coefficients as the initial value of NLMS algorithm.
4. If the linearization requirements is not met, i.e., e(n) is not equal to or approximates to zero, then jump to step2.

4   Simulation and Analysis

Memory polynomials and 16-QAM signal are used as the PA model and input vector in our Matlab simulation based on this joint adaptive algorithm.

4.1   Error Curve

Error curve is most direct-viewing to observe the erroneous value and the convergence rate.

Simulations are carried out on error curve using the NLMS algorithm and the RLS+NLMS joint algorithm, respectively.

It is clear from Fig. 3 that stable converge is obtained through around 500 iterations with NLMS algorithm. At the same time, as seen in Fig. 4, the joint algorithm only needs some 200 operations to get stables state. Furthermore, the latter bears a smaller erroneous value than the former.

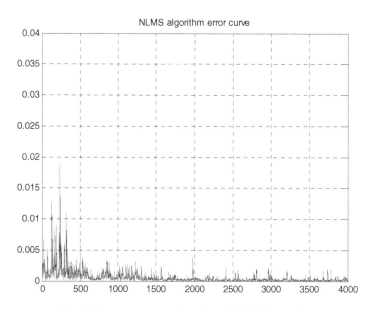

Fig. 3. The error curve only using the NLMS algorithm

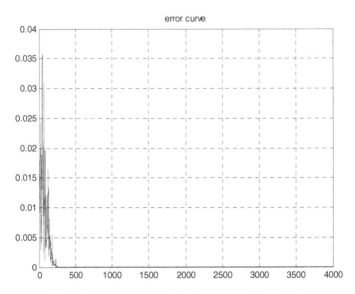

Fig. 4. The error curve using the NLMS+RLS algorithm

4.2   PSD Performance with Adaptive Joint Algorithm of DPD

Simulation demonstrates that about 40 dB improvement is obtained in PSD with the joint algorithm of DPD as shown in Fig. 5.

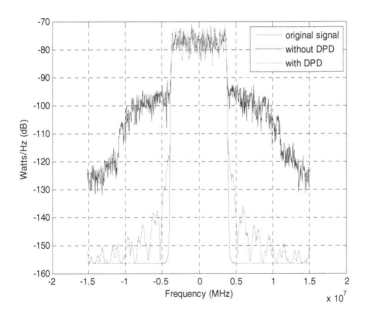

Fig. 5. PSD performance by joint algorithm of DPD

4.3   AM-AM and AM-PM Performance

In simulation on AM-AM and AM-PM performance, a desirable result is achieved by using joint algorithm of DPD, as is illustrated in Fig. 6 and Fig. 7.

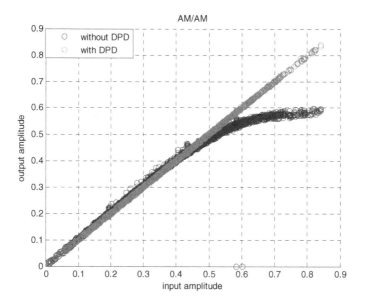

Fig. 6. AM-AM using joint algorithm of DPD

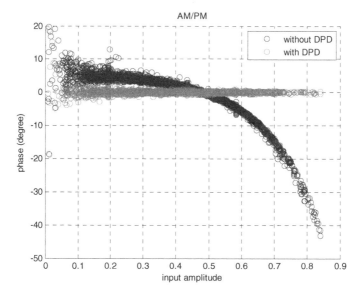

Fig. 7. AM-PM using joint algorithm of DPD

4.4   Constellation Performance

The simulation on constellation performance is shown in Fig. 8. It is obvious that the amplitude diffusion and phase rotation are also improved significantly.

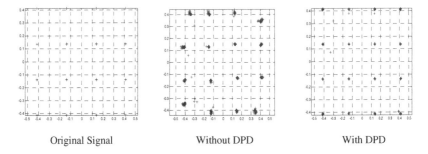

Original Signal   Without DPD   With DPD

Fig. 8. Constellation with and without DPD

5   Conclusion

In comparison to the traditional adaptive algorithm, this joint method can not only reduce the calculation, but also enhance convergence stability. Simulations show that this joint algorithm contributes about 40dB of PSD improvement for memory polynomial model, at the same time, the AM-AM and constellation performance are also significantly improved, hence obtaining desirable linearization performances.

Acknowledgment. Sponsor by Important National Science & Technology Specific Projects (2010ZX03005-001).

References

1. Proakis, J.G., Manolakis, D.G.: Digital Signal Processing, Principles, Algorithm, and Applications. 4th edn. (June 2007) ISBN 978-7-121-04042-9
2. Rupp, M.: The behavior of LMS and NLMS algorithm in the presence of spherically invariant processes. IEEE Transaction on Signal Processing 41(3), 1149–1160 (1993)
3. Isaksson, M.: Behavioural modeling of radio frequency power amplifiers// An Evaluation of Some Block Structure and Neural Network Models, Uppsala (2005)
4. Ding, L., Zhou, G.T., Morgan, D.R., et al.: A robust digital baseband predistorter constructed using memory polynomials. IEEE Transaction Comunication 52(1), 159–164 (2004)
5. Ai, B., Zhong, Z.D., Zhu, G., et al.: A Novel Scheme for Power Amplifier Predistortion Based on Indirect Leaning Architecture. Wireless Personal Communications 46(4), 523–530 (2008)

Monitoring Wildlife Conservation Using Networked RFID for Secure Positioning

Fan Yang, Fengli Zhang, Jiahao Wang, and Dady Seble Hailu

School of Computer Science and Engineering,
University Electronic Science and Technology of China,
610054 Sichuan Chengdu, China
yangfan126cn@yahoo.com.cn, {fzhang,wangjh}@uestc.edu.cn,
seble.hailu1@gmail.com

Abstract. As RFID systems are becoming more common in many application areas, managing the associated privacy and security concerns has become an important part of our lives. Although there are many RFID-based monitoring schemes, current solutions for target tracking and reminding either lack needed functionality or are much too costly to be used. A new model for secure positioning in networked RFID systems is introduced, and a novel identification protocol based on distance-bounding protocols for target tracking is proposed. By integration the above model and protocol with Wireless Sensor Networks, the classical approach in which all RFID distance-bounding protocols make reader infer an upper bound of distance to the tag is avoided. On the same time, the tag deduces the distance to the reader with WSNs.

Keywords: RFID (Radio Frequency Identification), WSNs (Wireless Sensor Networks), secure positioning, target tracking.

1 Introduction

Security is quickly becoming important in all devices, not only personal computers or mobile phones, but also many in RFID applications. Since RFID tags are primarily used for authentication purposes, 'security' in this context means that it should be infeasible to 'fake' a legitimate tag. 'Privacy', on the other hand, means that adversaries should not be able to identify, trace, or link tag appearances [1].One of the main drawbacks of most of RFID applications is that tags answer indiscriminately to reader queries, compromising the privacy of tag's holder. Similarly, RFID technology is being used for inventory control, stock security and quality management by manufactures in the food industry, textile industry, etc.[2] Focus should be on security technologies, application technologies and sourcing options that enable applications that are secure, but less tightly tied to specific devices and platforms. Now PUFs (Physical Unclonable Functions)[18] which significantly increase physical security by generating volatile secrets that only exist in a digital form when a chip is powered on and running are introduced, and WISP(Wireless Identification and Sensing Platform) is also a new RFID tag technology which is different to standard passive or active

M. Zhao and J. Sha (Eds.): ICCIP 2012, Part I, CCIS 288, pp. 269–276, 2012.

tags. WISPs are similar to passive tags in the sense that they only use power harvested from the reader's RF signals, and like active tags they can continue collecting data away from readers [19]. We believe that the current research works about PUFs and WISPs will extend further developments of security technology in RFID applications.

An RFID system contains four components: Tags, Reader, Antenna and Manager which contains a back-end database about the tagged object. A Reader can use tag contents as a look-up key into a back-end database storing product information, tracking logs and key management of data. For example a bottle of wine may have 2D-code or a RFID/NFC tag for fetching producer information. In this era, mobile augmented reality has a huge potential to become the users digital eye to the World [17]. We could know where and when the wine comes from. But distributed applications do not require separate security tools to be installed on the client. This will enable delivering applications that can run on a wider range of devices. In these cases, an adversary can disclose the state of the tagged object that represents some private valuable information.

To understand this better, let us consider a simple example. We tag a Panda with a collar which keeps its private information. Suppose that this tagged Panda is in the field of its nature protection and that we create wireless sensor networks for tracking the Panda's actions. If the Panda goes outside of WSNs, a system raises an alarm whether the Panda is detected basically with its tag. A Panda has a real-time inventory of the content of its field, what can be very useful. For example this real-time inventory in the RFID system could describe when and where the Panda moves away.

Yet, the level of security of an RFID system's protocol does not reply exclusively on the cryptographic primitives used, but sometimes on whether an adversary can successfully (in time and from a certain distance) break the RFID system. For instance, in the RFID context if an attacker can run a brute threat to disclose a Panda's static identifier but as he needs a plenty of time, the attack becomes impossible. Moreover, the reader should note that the key length used in many RFID applications is shorter than what we can find in standard cryptographic applications. There is a viewpoint in the paper of Kenneth P. Fishkin et al [3], titled "Distance Implies Distrust". They assume a scenario in which some "dishonest" RFID reader tries to interrogate (or even change) the information on an RFID tag. This is because the closer the reader is, the more it is subject to be monitored by the users of the tagged object.

1.1 Contribution

The contribution of this paper is twofold. Firstly, an identification protocol based on distance-bounding protocols is introduced. Secondly, we twist the above protocol combining it with WSNs (Wireless Sensor Networks). However, the classical approach in which all RFID distance-bounding protocols make reader infer an upper bound of distance to the tag is not used. On the contrary, in this issue, the tag deduces the distance to the reader with WSNs. This article is organized as follows. Section 2 introduces the basic definitions for RFID system and WSNs or some notation. Section 3 discusses a selection of distance-bounding protocols existing models, their underlying assumptions, their usability, and some further technicalities. Section 4 presents our model based on cryptographic puzzles and the application of a distance-bounding protocol used in wireless sensor network. Finally, we draw the main conclusions in Sect.5.

2   Definitions

In this paper we use a general model for RFID systems, similar to the definitions introduced in [4]. An RFID system has of a set of tags *T*, and a reader *R*. Each tag is identified by an identifier ID. The memory of the tags contains a tag state S. The tag's ID may or may not be saved in S, which may change during the lifetime of the tag. Tags can be spied: the adversary has the capability to disclose secrets from the tags which are chosen. The reader *R* has one or more transceivers and a central database. The reader's task is to identify legitimate tags and refuse all other unknown communication. The reader has a database of every tag, its ID and a matching secret *K*.

Definition 1 (RFID Scheme[4]). An RFID scheme is composed by:
– a setup scheme **SetupReader**(1^s) which generates a private/public key pair (K_S, K_P) for the reader depending on a security parameters. The key K_S is to be stored in the reader backend. The key K_P is publicly released. The paper assumes that is implicitly specified in K_P so that there is no need to mention s any longer.
-a polynomial-time algorithm **SetupTag** K_P (ID) which returns (K, S): the tag specific secret K and the initial state S of the tag. The pair (ID, K) is to be stored in the reader backend when the tag is legitimate.
-a polynomial-time interactive protocol between a reader and a tag in which the reader ends with a tape **Output**.

Definition 2 (WSNs Scheme [15]). A WSNs scheme is composed by:
Wireless sensor network has applications in environment, disaster prevention, healthcare, home automation, intelligent transportation, precision agriculture, etc. The sensors are used to collect and transmit information about their surrounding environment. The node collects the information from a group of sensors and facilitates communication with a control center. The software helps the system in collecting and processing of large volumes of data.

RFID relates to the technique of transmitting the identification of an object in the form of a unique serial number using radio waves. The basic components of RFID technology are the tags, readers and host computer. RFID reader reads information on the tag and passes it to the host computer for analysis. RFID software helps in collection and processing the data. WSN and RFID are complementary because they were originally designed with different objectives (RFID for identification while WSN for sensing). For these reasons integrations of WSN and RFID provides a significant improvement on monitoring. This provides the RFID to work in multi-hop to extend applications to operate in a wider area.

Definition 3 (Integration RFID with WSN Scheme [16]). Integration RFID with WSN is composed by:

We are witnessing an increasing trend towards integration of RFID and wireless sensor networks technologies. Integration of sensor networks to the global database about physical objects introduces a staggering amount of new application opportunities, as well as demanding challenges in security and privacy. Convergence of sensing and identification technologies, together with deployment of a global IT and communication systems, can enable us to gain impressive awareness about the state of the real world. This kind of awareness, including identification of physical objects and their context, can drastically change the way we interact with our environment. Logistics, telemedicine, environmental monitoring, home applications and control, security and surveillance, industrial applications like process industry automation and agricultural applications are examples of potential applications of real-world aware systems. Therefore, a particular care has to be taken in order to provide appropriate security and privacy control mechanisms.

Wireless Sensor networks (WSNs) are highly distributed networks of small, lightweight wireless nodes. Each node consists of three subsystems: the sensor subsystem which senses the environment, the processing subsystem which performs local computations and the communication subsystem. Users are able to read tags from distance 100-200m that is well beyond normal range of readers. Integration of RFID and WSN can provide RFID to work in multi hop to extend application of RFID to operate in a wider area. The integrated WSN node consists of an RFID reader, an RF transceiver, and micro-controller that coordinate different components in the node. Integrated tags with WSN can communicate with other tags and form a multiple loop network. Each integrated node transmits not only its unique ID number but also details of its sensed data to all other nodes. The integrated tag listens to the RFID reader radio of neighboring nodes.

3   Distance-Bounding Protocols

As a main hypothesis, we assume that legitimate readers are generally in close proximity and that dishonest readers are the most often distant. There are many scenarios in which this assumption defend. Nevertheless, it may happen in other situations that a dishonest reader is as close as it wants to the tags. If we remind the example of a Panda again, an honest reader is close the tag in the Panda's collar, and an attacker equipped with an RFID reader could be outside or at the hedge of the protection field of Panda, which means far away from the tag attached to the Panda.

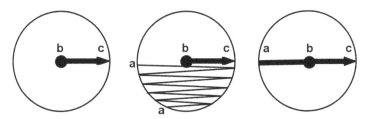

Fig. 1. The tag could deduce the distance to the reader

To the best of our knowledge, if a tag of Panda's collar has a function of its distance which infers an upper bound from a reader, the reader is closer to the tag, information of a tag may be discovered, in our scheme, the tag could deduce the distance to the reader as Fig.1.

In Fig.1, we surpose b is our tagged objective, c is a honest reader and a is a dishonet of adversary. If we combine the use of distance checking and cryptographic puzzle and thus the time/computation associated with its solution depending on distance measures. For example,when an honest reader c is in the field of circle, it is easy for c to get private information from b if the distance is right and they also need to confirm the cryptographic puzzle of tag $b.a$ is a dishonest reader which does not know the right distance between the tag and reader, so it has to spend tine to search the objective b in all the area of circle.

The only remaining question is how tags can estimate their distance to readers. A direct approach is to measure the time challenges and responses in a rapid bit exchange. As low-cost tags do not possess an on-chip clock, a capacitor's discharge time can be enough for a rough estimate of the round trip time (distance). The round-trip time taken between tag and reader are then calculated. The tag is assumed to be valid if the distance between tag and reader, as calculated from the round-trip times, is within a reasonable range with respect to the speed of light. Mafia fraud attacks occur while the honest tag and reader are unaware of the process. Terrorist fraud attack, on the other hand, occurs when a dishonest tag colludes with an adversary, without sharing its secret information, to trick a reader of its physical proximity [5].

The problem involved with securing reader communications with a secure backend database will not be considered; instead, about the central database, in April of 2011 a paper titled A Secure distance-based RFID identification protocol with an off-line back-end database [2] was published, the authors Pedro Peris-Lopez et al proposed a secure RFID identification scheme without the need of an online back-end database that is based on a proof-of-work and a distance checking. We will also discuss the viewpoint of database's transferring in an RFID system with WSNs in section 4.

In the protocol [2], there are two parameters defined: a certain degree of inaccuracy (e_i) regarding distance (d_i) does not represent a major security risk. The tag can distinguish between honest readers and rogue reader accurately, which is our main objective, if:

$$\frac{d_2 \pm e_2}{d_1 \pm e_1} \gg 1 \tag{1}$$

where $d_1(d_2)$ is the distance to honest (rogue) readers and $e_1(e_2)$ is the error in each distance measurement.

The goal of the protocol [2] is to preserve the private information of a large number of tags providing the untraced-ability property as well. An adversary may compromise the privacy of a specific tag—after a huge computational work—but she would fail when a large population of tags is her target.

Considering the current electromagnetic compatibility (EMC) regulations, the operating range of low cost labels is limited to a few meters. It is assumed that the labels within reading range have a means of revealing their presence, but not their data, when interrogated by a reader. It is assumed that the labels will reply with a non-identifying signal to an interrogation by using a randomly generated number [13].It is also assumed that the previously mentioned class of labels implement a 'kill' command that will physically render the label unreadable perhaps by setting off a fuse or disconnecting the antenna [14], as we mentioned that in Section 2 "The reader's task is to identify legitimate tags and refuse all other unknown communication. The reader has a database o f every tag, its ID and a matching secret *K*.", thus the reader is able verify that tags must indeed pose 'acknowledged' or 'secured' the secret K and arbitrate that therefore is the legitimate tag (see Fig.2).

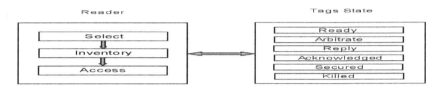

Fig. 2. Reader/Tag operations and Tags state

4   Our Authorization Protocol Model Based on WSNs

The privacy of RFID tags has been a hot issue recently [6,7,8]. Unfortunately, privacy features have initially been close to security authentication protocol model and therefore there is a lot of work to be done in the context of RFID applications as follows. Our RFID systems (Fig.3.) connect with Database Management through Internet, and our server1 and server2 will work based on WSNs. We can define one application scenario about monitoring wildlife conservation. Secure Positioning of a tagged Panda will be used by combining RFID and WSNs. Some of these applications are used much more in industry and academia then others. In addition, WSN nodes can be independent or attached to objects/people. The example of integration at the application level is provided as follows Fig.3:

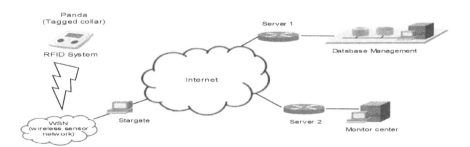

Fig. 3. Authorization Protocol Model Based on WSN

There were many attempts to obtain authentication protocols for RFID tags by means of symmetric-key primitives [9,10,11]. Engberg et al. [12] proposed a zero-knowledge authentication protocol for RFID tags which employs symmetric operations such as *XOR* and cryptographic has functions. Let us introduce some notation according to Fig.4. We denote X as the base point, and a and $x(aX)$ are the tag's *public-key* and *private-key* pair, where $x(aX)$ devotes the point derived by the point multiplication operation on the Elliptic Curve group. r and $u(rU)$ are a sever's *public-key* and *private-key* pair. A tag's public-key is also called a verifier. One should note, although the name suggests that is can be publicly known, that the public-key of tag should be kept secret in the sever1 which may transfer all the information to Datebase Management. Server2 will get database from wireless sensor network and Monitor Center will deduce if the key of RFID systems is disclosed. Revealing this key causes tracking attacks.

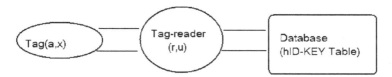

Fig. 4. The Key table scheme

The *hID-KEY* table scheme is shown in Fig. 4. In the scheme, a tag generates a random number a, Tag $a \in \{0, 1\}$ and $x \in \{0, 1\}$, transfers a to the Tag and transfers x to the server. Then Tag receives a, calculates $r=(aX) \oplus v$, $v \in \{0, 1$ Prob$[v=1]=u\}$, $u \in (0, 1/2)$, transfers r and hID to Tag—Reader, hID is Hash value of the Tag's code. After receiving $u(r, hID)$, the server calculates a tag's ID-verifier $aX(=x)$, which is used to check whether the corresponding tag is registered in the servers.

5   Conclusions

We define a new model of monitoring wildlife conservation for secure positioning in networked RFID systems, and introduce a novel identification protocol based on distance-bounding protocols. We twist the above model and protocol combining them with Wireless Sensor Networks. Nevertheless, in this paper the correctness and security property is not discussed further (as defined in Section 2). We have tried through a new approach to extend the limits of classical distance bounding protocols. The further analysis must be followed by developments of RFID tag technologies. We believe that this new model combining protocol with Wireless Sensor Networks is a first step and we will continue our research in this way. We are sure that future research works about PUFs and WISPs will develop a good enough security mechanism for the expected RFID applications.

Acknowledgments. This work was supported in part by (a) the National Science Foundation of China (Grant No. 60903157) and (b) the Fundamental Research Funds for the Central Universities of China (No. ZYGX2011J066).

References

1. Hermans, J., Pashalidis, A., Vercauteren, F., Preneel, B.: A New RFID Privacy Model. In: Atluri, V., Diaz, C. (eds.) ESORICS 2011. LNCS, vol. 6879, pp. 568–587. Springer, Heidelberg (2011), http://www.avoine.net/rfid/index.php

2. Pedro, P.-L., et al.: A Secure distance-based RFID identification protocol with an off-line back-end database (This article is published with open access at Springerlink.com, 2011) (2011)

3. Fishkin, K., Roy, S.: Enhancing RFID privacy via antenna energy analysis. Technical Report IRS-TR-03-012, ECRYPT (2003)

4. Vaudenay, S.: On Privacy Models for RFID. In: Kurosawa, K. (ed.) ASIACRYPT 2007. LNCS, vol. 4833, pp. 68–87. Springer, Heidelberg (2007)

5. Yu-Ju, T., Piramuthu, S.: RFID Distance bounding protocols. In: Proceedings of the First International EURASIP Workshop on RFID Technology (2007)

6. Phillips, T., Karygiannis, T., Kuhn, R.: Security Standards for the RFID market. Security & Privacy 3(6), 85–89 (2005)

7. Razaq, A., Luk, W., Shum, K., Cheng, L., Yung, K.: Second-Generation RFID. Security & Privacy 6(4), 21–27 (2008)

8. Siekermann, S., Evdokimov, S.: Critical RFID Privacy-Enhancing Technologies. IEEE Security and Privacy 7(2), 56–62 (2009)

9. Berbain, C., Billet, O., Etrog, J., Gilbert, H.: An efficient forward private RFID protocol. In: Proceedings of 16th ACM Conference on Computer and Communications Security (CCS 2009), pp. 43–53. ACM (2009)

10. Feldhofer, M.: An Authentication Protocol in a Security Layer for RFID Smart Tags. In: IEEE Mediterranean Electrotechnical Conference-IEEE MELECON 2004 (2004)

11. Feldhofer, M., Dominikus, S., Wolkerstorfer, J.: Strong Authentication for RFID Systems Using the AES Algorithm. In: Joye, M., Quisquater, J.-J. (eds.) CHES 2004. LNCS, vol. 3156, pp. 357–370. Springer, Heidelberg (2004)

12. Engberg, S., Harning, M., Jensen, C.: Zero-knowledge Device Authentication: Privacy & Security Enhanced RFID preserving Business Value and Consumer Convenience. In: Proceedings of Second Annual Conference on Privacy, Security and Trust (PST 2004), pp. 89–101 (2004)

13. Ranasinghe, D.C., Engels, D.W., Cole, P.H.: Security and Privacy: Modest Proposals for Low-Cost RFID Systems (2004), http://citeseer.ist.psu.edu/viewdoc/summary?doi=10.1.1.58.9559

14. Weis, S.A., Sarma, S.E., Rivest, R.L., Engels, D.W.: Security and Privacy Aspects of Low-Cost Radio Frequency Identification Systems. In: Hutter, D., Müller, G., Stephan, W., Ullmann, M. (eds.) Security in Pervasive Computing. LNCS, vol. 2802, pp. 201–212. Springer, Heidelberg (2004)

15. Jain, P.C., Vijaygopalan, K.P.: RFID and Wireless Sensor Networks. In: Proceedings of ASCNT 2010, CDAC, Noida, India, pp. 1–11 (2010)

16. 1st ACM Workshop on Convergence of RFID and Wireless Sensor Networks and their Applications, http://www.lifl.fr/POPS/SenseID2007/

17. Ruuska, P., et al.: Roadmap for Communication Technologies. Services and Business Models 2010, 2015 and Beyond (Tekes Review 275/2010, Finland), p. 15 (2010)

18. Edward Suh, G., Devadas, S.: Physical Unclonable Functions for Device Authentication and Secret Key Generation. In: 44th ACM/IEEE Design Automation Conference, DAC 2007 (2007)

19. Montefiore, A., Parry, D., Philpott, A.: A Radio Frequency Identification (RFID)-based wireless sensor device for drug compliance measurement, http://www.hinz.org.nz/uploads/file/2010conference/P23_Montefiore.pdf

Parallelization Research of Characteristic Set Algorithm

Suping Wu, Jiamei Liu,
Xinbo Yao, and Fang Du

School of Mathematics and Computer Science
Ningxia University
Yinchuan, China
wusup@263.net

Abstract. This paper gives three methods of characteristic set parallel implementation by using of multi-threaded on MAPLE :parallelization of the polynosimial pseudo-remainders, parallelization of characteristic series and parallel computation for these two parts.The timing statistics on a set of test problems is given,the results have demonstrated significant gains.The encountered problems of these three methods are discussed.

Keywords: characteristic set, parallel comptation, multi-threaded.

1   Introduction

Wu's method supplies an integrated theory and efficient method for solving non-linear algebraic equations, computing characteristic set is the core of Wu's method, but its computation complexity is very high. Some achievement has been made in the research of characteristic set parallelization , Ajwa I. et al. [1,2] implement a specific package of parallelizing the computation of characteristic set in the environment of PVM and SACLIB; Wang D. M. [3, 4] researched on the parallelism of computing characteristic set in Maple system using distributed workstation connected by a local network; Wu Y. W. et al. [5,6,7,8] implemented the parallelization of computing characteristic set based on MPI and ELIMINO, besides they also designed a distributed computing environment for the parallelization of Wu's method by combining different techniques including ELIMINO, MPI and Globus Toolkits 3, which get a preferable speedup ratio of about 2. Wu [9] has made more beneficial exploration based on distributed Maple system.

For how to make full use of multicore resources and improve the computational efficiency of the characteristics set, This paper tries to parallelize the computation of characteristic series on Maple on the platform of multicore computer, and gives three parallelization methods, The experimental results show the higher speedup of these three methods.

M. Zhao and J. Sha (Eds.): ICCIP 2012, Part I, CCIS 288, pp. 277–284, 2012.
© Springer-Verlag Berlin Heidelberg 2012

2   The Theorems and Sequential Algorithm

2.1   Main Theorems [10,11]

Definition 1 (Characteristic set). A polynomial equation system PS={P1(x), P2(x),..., Pm(x)} is given, here, Pi(x1, x2,..., xn)∈K[x1, x2,..., xn],i=1, 2, ..., m. Ascending set

$$CS=\{C1(x), C2(x),..., Cr(x)\},$$

here Ci(x1, x2,..., xi)∈K[x1, x2,..., xi], i=1, 2, ..., r, is called the characteristic set of PS, if it satisfy the following two conditions:

   (1) the pseudo remainder of each polynomial Pi in PS with respect to CS is zero, i.e.

$$Rem(P_i / CS) = 0, \; i = 1, \; 2, \; ..., \; m.$$

(2) the polynomial equation system PS and ascending set CS satisfy

$$Zero(PS) \subset Zero(CS).$$

Theorem 1 (Well Ordering Principle). Given a finite, non-empty set PS of non-zero polynomials, PS={P1, P2, ..., Pm}, Pi∈K[X], i=1, 2, ..., m, there certainly exists a mechanized algorithm, with which after limited steps of computation a basic set of PS, denoted by BS, can be computed, which satisfies that the pseudo remainder of each polynomial in PS with respect to BS is zero. If this BS is non-contradictory, then it is the characteristic set of PS, denoted by CS.

Theorem 2 (Zero Set Structure Theorem). Given the characteristic series CS, CS={C1, C2, ..., Cr}, of polynomial set PS, PS={P1, P2, ..., Pm}. The initial of Ci is Ii, i=1, 2, ..., r. The zero set of PS, denoted by Zero(PS) has this structure:

$$Zero(PS) = Zero(CS / I) \bigcup \bigcup_{i=1}^{r} Zero(PS, I_i), I = \prod_{i=1}^{r} I_i.$$

Theorem 3 (Zero Set Decomposition Theorem). Given the polynomial sets PS, PS={P1, P2, ..., Pm}, whose zero set can be decomposed into a set, union of a series of characteristic sets' zero sets:

$$Zero(PS) = \bigcup_j Zero(CS_j / I_j),$$

The set of index j in this equation is finite, Ij represents the product of all the initials in CSj.

2.2   Sequential Algorithm[12]

The process of computing polynomial equations characteristic set series includes : calculating basic set, pseudo division of polynomials, factorization, factorizating and computing characteristic set   series. the process of computing characteristic set   is the process of repeat   computing modulo, According to Wsolve packages of Dr. Wang Dingkang,   the Sequential Algorithm is given as follows[12],

```
input: PS (polynomial equation system)
output: CS (characteristic series)
findCS ( )
{PS0:= PS
RS   := PS0
while( RS !=Φ)
{PS0:= PS0 U RS
BS := basic set of PS0
 RS := rem( (PS0-BS) / BS )-{0}
}
CS := BS
return CS
}


input: PS (polynomial equation system)
output: CSS (characteristic series)
findCSS(PS)
{PS0:= PS
CS1 := characteristic  series of PS0
 I:= init(CS1 )
 I:= I-{constant}
while( i in I)
{CSS :=  CS1UfindCSS(PS U {i})
}
return CSS
}
```

3   Parallel Algorithm

The parallel algorithm is to parallelize computing pseudo remainder of polynomial equation system and computing characteristic set series. There are three ways to test the parallel speedup, these three ways are to parallelize computing pseudo remainder of polynomial equation system, to parallelize computing characteristic set series , to parallelize computing pseudo remainder of polynomial equation system and computing characteristic set series concurrently. The approach is to divide the input data into several even parts, whose number is equal to the computing cores', then data blocks are allocated to the threads.

Maple creates a pool of threads, where the number of threads is equal to the value of kernelopts (numcpus). By default this is the number of processors available on the computer. Each thread can execute one task at a time. As tasks are created they are stored in Task Queue. When a thread completes a task, it takes another task from Task Queue. Task Queue, storing tasks, contains a double ended queue for each thread. By default a thread will always execute the task that is at the head of its queue. Further, new tasks are added to the current thread's queue. If a thread finds that its queue is empty, it will try to steal a task from another thread's queue. When stealing a task, the task is removed from the tail of the queue[13].

When programming with multithreading, in order to get a good scalability it is so vital for us to consider how to divide the workload seriously to achieve a state of load balancing and the full use of computing capabilities. One approach to solve this problem is to create a large number of small tasks. In this way even if one task requires more time to run, the other cores can run many other tasks while one core is running the long task. One limitation is that creating tasks requires much more resources and overhead.

In parallel programming the parallel granularity has to be suitable to achieve a good state of load balancing. Here two tactics are used: granularity control and recursive interlaced bisection.

(1) Granularity control mainly contributes to divide the input data evenly. Hereon we design a granularity control formula:

$$granularity := ceil\left(\frac{scale(inputdata)}{k \cdot numcpu}\right).$$

Function note: granularity, upper limit of granularity for each task; inputdata, input; numcpu, the number of cores in CPU; k, control parameter; scale(), function to compute the input scale; ceil(), top integral function.

After analyzing the input scale and the number of computing cores, the function can regulate through control parameter k to achieve a good scalability. With this function, the input scale is divided into k×numcpu parts evenly.

(2) In order to ensure the workload in each part divided by the upper fornula is as even as possible, the recursive interlaced bisection method is imported. This tactic could ease the load imbalancing problem resulting from the different workload between evenly divided parts. Recursive bisection based on divide and conquer [11] can be put like this: split the given domain on one-dimensional direction; then split in the two subdomains recursively till each sub domain meets the demand of granularity. The interlaced bisection can be described in this way: suppose there is a given task, task=[task1, task2, ..., task2n], after disposition with interlaced bisection method the two child-tasks should be like this, childtask1=[task1, task3, ..., task2n-1], childtask2=[task2, task4, ...,task2n]. The combining method of these two ways is the so called recursive interlaced bisection strategy, which we need.

The method 1 is first determining the set conditions; then Starting command to assign threads, calling RemTask computing pseudo-remainders; then calling SetUnion collecting and mergeing remainder of each thread return, the main steps are as follows:

```
RemTask (ps, as, ord, T)
rset := {}; ps1 := {}
if grain < nops(ps) and ((1/2)*nops(ord) < nops(ps) or
    (1/2)*nops(ord)< nops(as))
then for j by 2 to nops(ps)
```

```
ps1 := union (ps1, {ps[j]})
ps2 := minus (ps, ps1)
Threads:-Task:-Continue(SetUnion, Task = [RemTask,
ps1, as, ord, T] ,Task = [RemTask, ps2, as, ord, T])
else for i in ps do rs := Premas(i, as, ord, T);
if op(rs) <> 0 and Class(op(rs), ord) = 0
then Threads[Task][Return]({1})
else rset := union (rset, rs)
Remset (ps, as, ord, T)
rset := {}; pset := minus ({op(ps)}, {op(as)})
grain := ceil(nops(pset)/numcpu)
if pset <> {} then
rset := Threads:-Task:-Start(RemTask, pset, as, ord, T)
rset := minus (rset, {0})
```

The method 2 is first according to the number of cores to set start thread command condition to run Threads:-Task:-Start (CSSTask, pset, ord, nonzero, asc), then according to start thread command condition to determine whether allocation thread command Threads:-Task:-Continue() is run, As to meet the condition, calling CSSTask to parallel computing characteristic series, then calling Set Union to collecte and merge computing results.

```
CSSTask(ps,ord,nzero,T)
cset:={};ps1:={}
if (nops(ps)>grain) then
  for j from 1 by 2 to nops(ps) do
            ps1:=ps1 union {ps[j]}
   ps2:=ps minus ps1
    Threads:-Task:-Continue(SetUnion,Task=[
    CSSTask,ps1,ord,nzero,T],
    Task=[CSSTask, ps2,ord,nzero,T ])
else
   for i in ps do
  cset:=cset union Css(i,ord,nzero,T);
CSS (ps, ord1, nzero, T)
if nargs < 2 then
  ord := [op(indets(ps))]
else
  ord := [op(ord1)]
if nargs < 3 then
  nonzero := {} else nonzero := realfac({op(nzero)},
ord)
if nargs < 4 then
  asc := 'std_asc' else
  asc := T
```

```
pset := Nrs(ps, ord, nonzero)
  N := nops(pset)
  grain := ceil((1/25)*nops(pset)/numcpu)
  cset := Threads:-Task:-Start(CSSTask, pset, ord,
nonzero, asc)
  result := []
  for i in cset do
  if Degenerate(nonzero, i, order) <> 1 then
result := [op(result), i]
```

4   Experimental Result and Analysis

4.1   Experimental Result

Platform: (1)Celeron(R)CPU2.8GHz processor,512M memory;
          (2)Intel(R)Core(TM)2Duo dual-coreprocessor,1Gmemory;
          (3) Intel (R) Core (TM) i7 quad-core processor, 4G memory.
Software environment: Windows XP, Maple 14

Table 1. Single-core and Dual-core Experimental Results

Example	Serial time	Method 1(s)	Method1speedup	Method 2(s)	Method2 Speedup	Method3 (s)	Method 3 Speedup
1	0.236	0.203	1.163	0.108	2.185	0.140	2.269
2	11.765	5.586	2.106	3.524	3.334	4.118	2.857
3	19.541	14.805	1.320	5.975	3.270	6.240	3.132
4	31.964	14.742	2.168	9.432	3.889	9.813	3.257
5	95.505	52.946	1.804	30.904	3.090	33.041	2.890
6	107.510	64.946	1.655	35.958	2.990	39.750	2.705
7	282.174	199.570	1.414	96.752	2.916	111.245	2.536

Table 2. Single-core and quad-core Experimental Results

Example	Serial time	Method 1(s)	Method1 Speedup	Method 2(s)	Method2 Speedup	Method3 (s)	Method 3 Speedup
1	0.236	0.094	2.511	0.062	3.806	0.061	3.806
2	11.765	7, 812	1.506	2.672	4.403	2.875	4.092
3	19.541	6.829	2.861	1.798	10.868	2.423	8.065
4	31.964	8.797	3.634	3.438	9.297	3.625	8.818
5	95.505	36.468	2.619	11.500	8.305	10.626	8.988
6	107.510	42.484	2.530	13.421	8.011	14.813	7.258
7	282.174	131.266	2.150	54.577	5.170	74.828	3.771

4.2   Experimental Analysis

According to the experimental results shown in the table, we can get the following analysis results:

(1) The computing efficiencies of the parallelization method 1,2,3 for all the given problems are obviously much higher than that of serial method and get a better speedup.

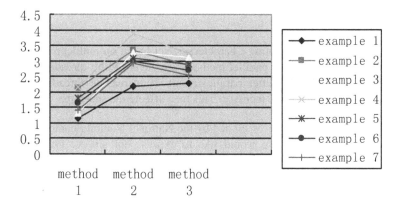

Fig. 1. Speedup compare single-core to dual-core

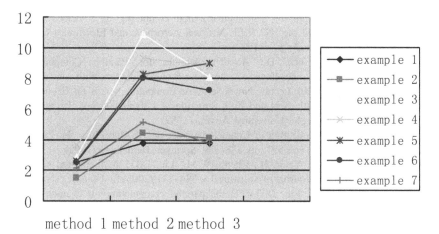

Fig. 2. Speedup compare single-core to quad-core

(2) Compare method 1 to method 2,the speedup of method 2 is better than method 1.This is because parallel computing characteristic series is coarse-grained parallel ,but polynomial equation set parallel computing modulo is fine-grained parallel. Another reason may be related with the examples.

(3) Compare method 3 to method 1 and 2, the speedup of method 3 is not better than method 1 and 2. This is because two part parallelization concurrently will increase the cost of the thread, if problem size is not big enough, thread switching overhead larger proportion, which resulted in relatively low speed.

(4) As the problem size increases, the speedup under both platforms are gradually tend to go smoothly. This is because as the problem size increases, the processor core number remains constant, the parallel overhead is the same .According to the speedup formula, Speedup will tend to a certain value, and for specific questions, because of the absolute load balancing can not be achieved ,then cause some fluctuations.

5   Conclusion

Multi-threaded parallel computing Characteristic set based on multicore environment is feasible, In this paper three parallel methods are gaven, Multi-threaded parallelism with coarse-grain may get better parallel result, If increasing thread number, the thread switching overhead will increase, This may affecte the speedup.

Acknowledgments. This paper is funded by the National Natural Science Foundation of China (No. 60963004). We would like to express our sincere gratitude to the National Natural Science Foundation for the financial support. And many thanks to all those people who supported us.

References

1. Ajwa, I., Wang, P.: Applying parallel/distributed computing to advanced algebraic computations. In: Proc. of the1997 IEEE National Aerospace and Electronics Conf., pp. 156–164. IEEE Press, Washington (1997)
2. Ajwa, I., Wang, P., Lin, D.: Another Attempt for Parallel Computation of Characteristicsets. In: Proceedings of the Fourth Asian Symposium on Computer Mathematics (ASCM 2000). Lecture Notes Series on Computing, vol. 8, pp. 63–66 (2000)
3. Wang, D.M.: Characteristic Sets and Zero Structure of Polynomial Sets. Lecture Notes, RISC-LINZ, Johannes Kepler University, Austria (1989)
4. Wang, D.: On the Parallelization of Characteristic-set-Based Algorithms. In: Zima, H.P. (ed.) ACPC 1991. LNCS, vol. 591, pp. 338–349. Springer, Heidelberg (1992)
5. Wu, Y.W., Yang, G.W., Yang, H., Zheng, W.M., Lin, D.D.: A distributed computing model for Wu's method. Journal of Software 16, 384–391 (2005) (in Chinese)
6. Wu, Y.W., Yang, G.W., Lin, D.D.: On the parallel computation for characteristic set method. Chinese Journal of Electronics 18(3), 383–388 (2004)
7. Lin, D.D., Liu, J., Liu, Z.J.: Mathematical research software: ELIMINO. In: Li, Z.B. (ed.) Proc. of the ACM 1998, pp. 107–114. Lanzhou University Press, Lanzhou (1998)
8. Yang, H., Liu, Z., Lin, D.: Development of an object-oriented number system. Mathematics Mechanization Research 18, 212–219 (2000)
9. Wu, S.P.: Research on parallelization of the related characteristic set method based on distributed Maple system. Modern Computer, 14–16 (October 2009) (in Chinese)
10. Shi, H.: Introduction to mathematics mechanization Changsha. Hunan Education Press (1998) (in Chinese)
11. Wu, W.T.: Review and prospects of mathematics mechanization. System Science and Mathematics 28(8) (2008) (in Chinese)
12. Wang, D.: A Maple Package for Solving System of Polynomial Equations. Mathematics-Mechanization Research Preprints, 10 (1993)
13. http://www.maplesoft.com/support/help

Application of Neural Network in the Process Modeling of WEDM

Changtao Cai

Sch.of Mechanical Eng. and Automation, Xihua Univ
Chengdu 610039, China
cct0622@mail.xhu.edu.cn

Abstract. It is difficult to build a strict mathematical model for WEDM due to the complication of the machining process and the nonlinear relation between process parameters and process targets. The neural network is suited to the modeling of complex system, because it has the functions of self-organized, self-learning and associative memory, and properties of distributed parallel type and high robustness. Therefore, this paper attempts to use the RBF neural network for the process modeling of WEDM.

Keywords: WEDM, RBF Neural Network, Process Modeling.

1 Introduction

Owning to the process mechanism of WEDM that is a highly nonlinear system is very complex, and the randomness phenomenon of the processing of WEDM influenced by chance is very serious, therefore, it is difficult to build a strict mathematical model. Especially, the influences of special phenomenon such as unstable arc processing make it more difficult to do it.

Based on the system analysis of processing regularity, it is very important to build the mathematical model of WEDM with the computer analysis results. The thesis will establish an artificial neural network model of WEDM based on lots of process experiment analysis, and use it to research the relationship between performance parameters of performance voltage, amplifiers tube number, pulse width, pulse interval and performance goal of process time, surface roughness. Thus, the regularity of processing technology can be summarized, the mathematical model will be build, processing optimization and the parameters optimization, results optimization of machining process also will be improved.

2 Characteristics and Engineering Application of ANN

As a new modeling tool, ANN with self-learning, self-organizing and strong fault tolerance ability is a large-scale distributed parallel information processing system composed by interactive neurons, and it has strong nonlinear modeling ability, can simulate the complex relationship between input and output that make up the

M. Zhao and J. Sha (Eds.): ICCIP 2012, Part I, CCIS 288, pp. 285–293, 2012.

insufficient of traditional model analysis, which can well satisfy the modeling requirement of various mechanical engineering fields [1].

The given model is not necessary to ANN, it can automatically extracted regularity from a large amount of data, get the through the associative memory and law generalization ability to acquire data, and have strong fault tolerance to the sample data. According to the basic theory of the ANN, any function can be simulated by a three layers of network structure. Given an appropriate network structure, the network model can be established after ensuring the network weights of layers. Then, other sample data can through the re-learning function to make network adapt the new sample data and avoid establishing a new model [2,3]. Therefore, it is very suitable for solving complex nonlinear problems.

WEDM is a complicated MIMO system, it is difficult to describe the relationship between performance parameters and performance goal, therefore, ANN can be used to solve the tacit knowledge which is difficult to express by language. The information processing ability of ANN contains data storage and computing, computing often means the conversion process of dynamic system state, and the computing of ANN signifies the conversion of state. For a given inputs, the end of computing is the state of network transition into a stable state, the output is the computing results of ANN [4].

3   RBF Neural Network Structure and Working Principle

In the application of ANN, BP networks maybe the most popular. Most engineering problems can be solved by BP network or its deformation form. BP algorithm embodies the essence parts of ANN. Generally, the BP algorithm possesses high precision, but BP network needs revise all the weights and threshold in the training process, which can be called globe approximation neural network. The learning speed of this network is very slowly, and easily falls into the local minimum value, therefore, its application is restricted in some real-time occasions. By contrast, RBF neural network is a local approximation network, it needs revise small amount of weights and threshold to each sample data, therefore, the training speed of RBF neural network is very fast and overcome the weakness of BP algorithm.

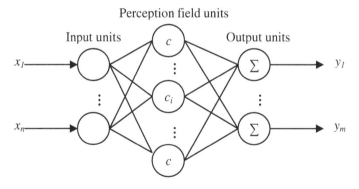

Fig. 1. The structure of RBF neural network

The RBF neural network has a very strong biological background. In the human brain cortex areas, local regulation and overlapping perception field is the characteristics of the responses of human brain. Based on the characteristics of perception field, Moody and Darken presents a neural network structure, namely the RBF neural network [5,6]. RBF neural network is a kind of feed-forward neural network, which is three layers structure. The network structure of RBF neural network is shown in figure1.

The structure of RBF neural network shown in figure 1 is an *n-h-m* layout neural network structure, namely the RBF neural network has n inputs, h hidden nodes, m outputs. Input layer nodes transfer inputs signal to hidden layer, hidden nodes is composed by radial effect function such as Gaussian function and output layer nodes usually is simple linear function. The base function of hidden layer nodes responds to input signal in local. That is to say, when input signal approach the central area of base function, hidden layer nodes will produce larger output. Therefore, the network has local approximation ability. Thus, RBF neural network also can be called local perception field network.

Radial basic function (RBF) are radial symmetry, the most popular is Gaussian function:

$$R_i(x) = \exp\left[-\frac{\|x - c_i\|^2}{2\sigma_i^2}\right], i = 1,2,...,h \qquad (1)$$

In formula, x is dimension n input vector; c_i is the center of ist basic function, it has the same dimension as x; σ_i is the ist perception variable, it decide the width of basic function around the center; h is the number of perception unit. $\|x-c_i\|$ is the bound norm of $x-c_i$, it indicate the space of x and c_i; $R_i(x)$ has the only maximum in the place of ci, As $\|x-ci\|$ increases, Ri(x) quickly attenuation to zero. For a given input $x\in R_n$, only a fraction that near to x can be activated.

Figure 1 show the input layer realize the nonlinear mapping from x to $R_i(x)$, output layer realize the linear mapping from $R_i(x)$ to y_k, namely:

$$y_k = \sum_{i=1}^{h} w_{ik} R_i(x), k = 1,2,...,m \qquad (2)$$

In formula, m is the number of output nodes, BP or OLS algorithm can be used to revise the connection weights. Due to the $R_i(x)$ is Gaussian function, for arbitrary x are $R_i(x)>0$ then lose the advantages of local adjusting relevance weights; In fact, when x far from c_i, $R_i(x)$ has very small, can be treated as 0. Therefore, when $R_i(x)$ is greater than some numerical (such as 0.05), the weight of wij can be revised. Last, RBF neural network also have the advantage of short training time and quick convergence speed, at the same time, the approximate handling can overcome the lack of compact of RBF neural network[7,8].

4   Build RBF Neural Network Model Based on Orthogonal Experiment Data

It is difficult to build an effective mathematical model to describe the process rule between performance parameters and performance goal, and ANN has advantage in solving the nonlinear problem, therefore, ANN can be used to the process modeling of WEDM. Compared with BP neural network, RBF neural network is not easily fall into local extreme value and learning fast, more stable. Therefore, this thesis will adopt RBF neural network to the processing model of WEDM.

4.1   Gain the Sample Data

When ANN is used to build the process modeling of WEDM, it needs to get a certain amount of sample data to train the ANN. The sample data can be gained through orthogonal experiment. The orthogonal experiment is performing in DK7725C reciprocating WEDM; a 0.18mm in diameter molybdenum wire is applied to be processing electrode;   machining area is 3×10mm2; apply positive polarity machining: work piece meet positive, processing electrode meet negative; working fluid is ordinary DX-1 emulsion electrolyte.

The levels of electric parameters are as follows:

Processing voltage (U/V): 60, 80, 90, 100, 110
Amplifiers tube number(N/num.): 2, 3, 4, 5, 6
Pulse width (T_{on}/μs): 4, 8, 16, 24, 32
Pulse interval (T_{off}/μs): 5, 6, 7, 8, 9

The results of experiment: processing time is evaluated by the finish time of work piece; surface roughness is evaluated by the surface finish after finishing operation.

Table 1 shows the sample data gained through orthogonal experiment.

4.2   Sample Data Normalization

Because of the sample data vectors different from each other and the data level of sample data also different from each other, the input of sample data will be normalized in order to calculate and prevent partial neurons assume super saturation state.

The neurons of RBF neural network often adopt interval-valued as the normalization function. The output of interval-valued normalization function is 0~1 or -1~1. It is common that the weights adjusted are to total error in the network training. If no normalization, the absolute error of large numerical outputs is large and the absolute error of small numerical outputs is small. After normalization, the neurons can be prevented from saturating because of the absolute value of inputs is too large, and the weights can enter into the flat area of error curve. The interval-valued normalization function can be expressed as follow:

$$\overline{x}_i = \frac{x_i - x_{min}}{x_{max} - x_{min}} \tag{3}$$

x_i is the input data or output data, xmin is the minimum of the range of data varies. x_{max} is the maximum of the range of data varies.

After normalization, the performance goal of the sample data in table 1 can be turned to the results shown in table 2.

Table 1. Sample data

Number	Processing Voltage	Amplifiers Tube Number	Pulse Width	Pulse Interval	Mean Processing Time	Mean Surface Roughness
1	60	2	4	5	84.51	1.78
2	60	3	8	6	43.42	1.95
3	60	4	16	7	22.14	2.70
4	60	5	24	8	17.95	3.14
5	60	6	32	9	15.36	3.91
6	80	2	8	7	35.13	1.28
7	80	3	16	8	20.76	2.46
8	80	4	24	9	13.08	3.08
9	80	5	32	5	7.44	3.51
10	80	6	4	6	5.11	3.88
11	90	2	16	9	34.44	2.41
12	90	3	24	5	13.18	3.21
13	90	4	32	6	8.21	3.40
14	90	5	4	7	6.27	3.61
15	90	6	8	8	5.46	3.76
16	100	2	24	6	23.30	2.84
17	100	3	32	7	14.58	3.13
18	100	4	4	8	8.26	3.62
19	100	5	8	9	7.06	3.85
20	100	6	16	5	4.11	4.45
21	110	2	32	8	23.48	2.15
22	110	3	4	9	12.14	2.27
23	110	4	8	5	5.47	3.34
24	110	5	16	6	4.37	4.28
25	110	6	24	7	4.31	4.36

4.3   The Training of ANN Based on Sample Data

The RBF neural network can be used in performance parameters prediction of WEDM after training. The establishing and training of RBF neural network can be practiced by MATLAB. MATLAB develop a neural network toolbox as internal module. The neural network toolbox offers a variety of learning algorithm and hundreds of related function [9,10]. The functions used in this thesis are as follow:

(1) The creation function of RBF neural network
The newrbe function is used in creating the RBF neural network, the calling procedure of it is as follow: net=newrbe

$$[net,tr]=newrbe(P,T,SPREAD)$$

The net is the new RBF neural network; tr is the training records, P is the matrix composed by input vector, T is the matrix of objective vector, SPREAD is the spread constant of RBF, it's default value is 1.0, after experimental verification, this thesis selects SPREAD=1.2.

Table 2. Normalized sample data

Number	Mean Processing Time Normalized	Mean Surface Roughness Normalized
1	1.0000	0.1595
2	0.4890	0.2130
3	0.2242	0.4470
4	0.1721	0.5855
5	0.1399	0.8300
6	0.3858	0.0000
7	0.2070	0.3725
8	0.1116	0.5666
9	0.0413	0.7030
10	0.0124	0.8185
11	0.3773	0.3578
12	0.1128	0.6086
13	0.0509	0.6674
14	0.0268	0.7345
15	0.0168	0.7828
16	0.2386	0.4921
17	0.1302	0.5834
18	0.0516	0.7366
19	0.0367	0.8111
20	0.0000	1.0000
21	0.2408	0.2739
22	0.0999	0.3137
23	0.0168	0.6485
24	0.0032	0.9444
25	0.0025	0.9696

(2) The simulation function of RBF neural network

$$a=sim(net,P)$$

P is the testing samples, net is the network model after training, a is the results of prediction. sim is the simulation function of neural network.

According to the sample data in table 1, the creating and training procedure of RBF neural network are as follow:

p=[60 2 4 5;60 3 8 6;60 4 16 7;60 5 24 8;60 6 32 9;80 2 8 7;80 3 16 8;80 4 24 9;80 5 32 5;80 6 4 6;90 2 16 9;90 3 24 5;90 4 32 6;90 5 4 7;90 6 8 8;100 2 24 6;100 3 32 7;100 4 4 8;100 5 8 9;100 6 16 5;110 2 32 8;110 3 4 9;110 4 8 5;110 5 16 6;110 6 24 7]';

t=[84.51 1.78;43.42 1.95;22.14 2.70;17.95 3.14;15.36 3.91;35.13 1.28;20.76 2.46;13.08 3.08;7.44 3.51;5.11 3.88;34.44 2.41;13.18 3.21;8.21 3.40;6.27 3.61;5.46 3.76;23.30 2.84;14.58 3.13;8.26 3.62;7.06 3.85;4.11 4.45;23.48 2.15;12.14 2.27;5.47 3.34;4.37 4.28;4.31 4.36]';

P=p;

for i=1:2

T(i,:)=(t(i,:)-min(t(i,:)))/(max(t(i,:))-min(t(i,:)));   //normalized output variables
end
net=newrbe(P,T,1.2);

5   Use Neural Network Module of MATLAB for the Process Modeling

In order to use neural network module of MATLB for the process modeling, it needs to input "nntool" command in the command line of MATLAB to call the neural network module.

The steps of using ANN for the process modeling of WEDM are as follow:

(1) Select the sample data of table 1 as the input data and the normalized sample data in table 2 as the output data, then, inputting the data into the MATLB in sequence. The results are described in Figure 2 and Figure 3.

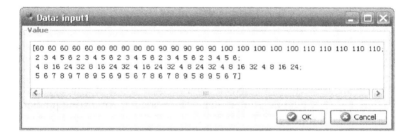

Fig. 2. The inputs of ANN

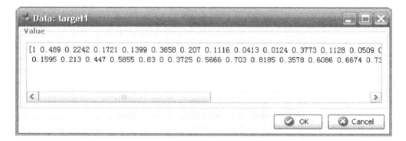

Fig. 3. The actual outputs of ANN

(2) Build the RBF neural network. Opening the ANN settings window, Network Type is Radial basis (exact fit), Input data is input1, Target data is target1, spread constant is 1.2.

(3) Because of the input data and output data are directly trained in the generation of RBF neural network, it needs no training after network setting as BP neural network and can directly view the training result. The predicted outputs after training are shown in figure 5. It can conclude that the difference between actual

outputs in Figure 3 and predicted outputs in Figure 5 are very small. Therefore, the neural network module can be used to the performance goal prediction, and it also lays the foundation for the optimized selection of performance parameters.

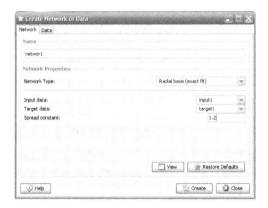

Fig. 4. ANN settings

6   Simulation Test of the ANN Module

In order to validate the accuracy of ANN module, another 5 sets of data are tested. Input the 5 data into the ANN module as input data. The results of comparing predicted data with actual data are as follow:

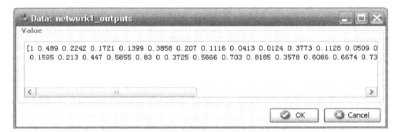

Fig. 5. The predicted outputs after training

Fig. 6. Validation data   **Fig. 7.** Prediction data   **Fig. 8.** Actual outputs

Comparison predicted output in figure 7 and actual output in figure 8. The maximum predicted error is 9.11% and the minimum predicted error is 1.52%. It is demonstrated that the ANN module can well reflect the processing regularity of WEDM.

The main reasons of the existing error are as follow: (1) The number of sample data is too small leads to the error existing in ANN is too large. (2)The influence factors of WEDM are great; this thesis only selects four performance parameters and ignores the interactions with each other, and cause the ANN no perfection. (3)Because of the processing mechanism of WEDM is not too clear, ANN module is just approximate description to the actual working state. It is surely confirm that the accuracy of ANN module will improve along with the clear of processing mechanism.

7   Summary

This thesis adopts orthogonal data as the sample data based on the research of processing mechanism, and uses RBF neural network to the process modeling for the performance goal prediction. At last, 5 sets of simulated data are inputted into the ANN module for validation. After validation, the ANN module has good prediction accuracy, and analyzes the reasons of existing errors.

Acknowledgment. The paper is funded by Key Subject Construction Project of Sichuan Province (No.SZD0409-08-0).

References

1. Haykin, S.: Neural Networks and Learning Machines. China Machine Press (2009)
2. McClary, D.W., Syrotiuk, V.R., Lecuire, V.: Adaptive audio streaming in mobile and hoc networks using neural networks. Ad Hoc Networks 6(4), 524–538 (2008)
3. Fukushima, K.: Neural network model for completing occluded contours 23(4), 528–540 (2010)
4. Ho, K.H., Newman, S.T., Rahimifard, S., Allen, R.D.: State of the art in wire electrical discharge machining. International Journal of Machine Tools & Manufactur (44), 1247–1259 (2004)
5. Moody, J., Darken, C.: Learning with localized receptive fields. In: Touretzky, D., Hinton, G., Sejnowski, T. (eds.) Proc. 1988 Connectionist Model Summer School. Camegie Mellon University, Morgan Kaufmann Publishers (1988)
6. Moody, J., Darken, C.: Fast learning in networks of locally-turned processing units. Neural Compulation (1989)
7. Hagan, M.T.: Neural Network Design. China Machine Press (2002)
8. Dua, D., Li, K., Fei, M.: A fast multi-output RBF neural network construction method. Neurocomputing 73, 2196–2202 (2010)
9. Strik, D.P.B.T.B., Domnanovich, A.M., Zani, L., et al.: Prediction of trace compounds in biogas from anaerobic digestion using the MATLAB Neural Network Toolbox. Environmental Modeling & Software 20, 803–810 (2005)
10. Seth, A.K.: A MATLAB toolbox for Granger causal connectivity analysis. Journal of Neuroscience Methods 186(2), 262–273 (2010)

Image Restoration Based on an AdaBoost Algorithm

Nian Cai [1], Feng Jin [1], Qing Pan [1], Shao-qiu Xu [1], and Fangzhen Li[2]

[1] School of Information Engineering, Guangdong University of Technology,
Guangzhou 510006, China
`{cainian,jinfeng,panqing,xushaoqiu}@gdut.edu.cn`
[2] Shandong Provincial Key Laboratory of Digital Media Technology,
Shandong University of Finance and Economics, Ji'nan 250014, China
`fzli1976@gmail.com`

Abstract. A novel image restoration method is developed based an AdaBoost algorithm. A sliding-window method is employed to extract image features and to obtain the input and output of BP neural network. An AdaBoost algorithm is established for image restoration, in which BP neural network is considered as a weak learner. Experimental results indicate that the proposed method is superior to tradition BP neural network in the field of image restoration and can be applied to restore turbulence-degraded images.

Keywords: image restoration, AdaBoost, BP neural network, sliding-window.

1 Introduction

Image restoration is most important in the fields of image processing. Traditional filtering methods, such as Winner filter, restore the images by means of degradation models which are constructed based on a prior knowledge. Actually a prior knowledge is often difficult to be obtained. Thus image restoration without distinct degraded models is a difficult and widely studied problem in image processing and computer vision[1]. Iterative blind deconvolution (IBD) is a popular approach to estimate the point spread function and the original clear image [2-5]. However it might cause ill-posed problem and is deficient in solving the problem of function approximation [6].

Artificial neural network has the advantages of self-adaptive, self-organization, self-learning, high-speed parallelism calculation, and great robustness. And neural networks are widely employed for image restoration[6]. Up to date, the most widely used neural network models for image restoration tasks are the Hopfield and the feed-forward neural networks [7]. The Hopfield network is used to formulate image restoration as a nonlinear optimization problem, but its computation burden is heavy. Wang and Cai et al proposed a method for blind image restoration using a three-layer multilayer perceptron [7].

AdaBoost is superior to tradition neural networks on learning abilities and applied in many fields of image processing, especially image recognition. In this paper, we propose a novel method for blind image restoration using an AdaBoost algorithm. A

M. Zhao and J. Sha (Eds.): ICCIP 2012, Part I, CCIS 288, pp. 294–301, 2012.

sliding-window technique is applied to obtain the features of the blurred image for dimension reduction. A BP neural network is applied to realize the obscure functional mapping from the degraded image space to the original image space. Then an AdaBoost model is constructed using BP neural networks as weak learners for blind image restoration. And the proposed method is applied to restore turbulence-degraded images.

2   Sliding-Window Technique

The grey levels of the neighborhood around one pixel have some paramount effects on its change when blur occurs. That is to say, pixels with the same grey level in an image will probably have different values when blurring, if there are different grey levels in their neighborhood. Therefore, a 3*3 sliding-window method is applied to obtain the input vector the BP network, which utilizes the region information. Each pixel in the blurred image has a vector P_k and T_k is the k desired output vector (shown in Fig.1 and Fig.2).

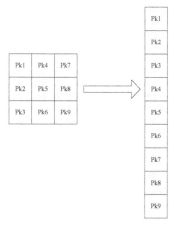

Fig. 1. 3*3 window and input vector

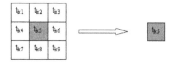

Fig. 2. output vector

Given input-output pattern (P_k, T_k) as training samples, $P_k=(P_{k1}, P_{k2}, ..., P_{kM})^T$ is the k input vector, in which M is the input dimension, and $T_k=(t_{k1}, t_{k2}, ..., t_{kN})^T$ is the corresponding output vector, in which N is the output dimension. The actual network output vector is $O_k=(O_{k1}, O_{k2}, ..., O_{kN})^T$.

Instead of considering all the elements in an image as integrity, the proposed algorithm classifies the training samples into two categories: one is the smoothing region of an image and the other is the region where edges are located. The reason of this separation is that the blurring process has more effects on the part with a larger gradient, compared to the smoothing part. Therefore, we add the edge constraints when we extract the training samples. First we implement edge detection using Sobel operator, then implement network training for the edge region and the smoothing region, respectively.

3   Image Restoration Using an AdaBoost Regression Algorithm

AdaBoost.RT, a regression algorithm proposed by Solomatine and Shrestha, employs the threshold to divide the regression problem into correct prediction and wrong prediction, then considers the regression problem as the two-class classification problem[8]. AdaBoost.RT solves some intrinsic problems existing in other AdaBoost regression algorithms. It uses absolute relative error (ARE) threshold to divide the training set into two classes (correct prediction and wrong prediction). It does not stop processing when error rate is low than 0.5. It applies mean method instead of median method to obtain outputs.

The AdaBoost.RT algorithm includes four fundamental steps.

(1) input
    1) m training samples$(x_1, y_1), \ldots, (x_m, y_m), y \in R$
    2) the algorithm of weak learners
    3) the iteration number T
    4) the threshold $\phi(0<\phi<1)$
(2) initialize
    1) the number of weak learners or initial iteration is 1
    2) each weight distribution $D_t(i)=1/m$
    3) error rate $\varepsilon_t=0$
(3) iterate until $t \leq T$
    1) call weak learners and give weights distribution of training samples.
    2) establish a regression model $f_t(x) \to y$
    3) calculate the ARE of each training sample in the weak learner with Eq. (1)

$$ARE_t(i) = \left| (f_t(x_i) - y_i)/y_i \right| \tag{1}$$

    4) calculate error rate of $f_t(x)$

$$\varepsilon_t = \sum_{i:ARE_t(i)>\phi} D_t(i) \tag{2}$$

    5) let $\beta_t = \varepsilon_t^n$

6) update weight distribution $D_t(i)$

$$D_{t+1}(i) = \frac{D_t(i)}{Z_t} \times \begin{cases} \beta_t, ARE_t(i) \le \phi \\ 1, otherwise \end{cases} \tag{3}$$

here Z_t is normalization factor.

7) let t=t+1

(4) output final hypothesis

$$f_{fin}(x) = \sum_t \left(\log \frac{1}{\beta_t} \right) f_t(x) \Big/ \sum_t \left(\log \frac{1}{\beta_t} \right) \tag{4}$$

In this paper, we choose BP neural network as weak learners. For image restoration, Eq. (1) should be changed as following

$$ARE_t(i) = \frac{1}{n} \sum_{k=1}^{n} \left| \frac{f_t(P_k) - T_k}{T_k} \right| \tag{5}$$

Please note that, if your email address is given in your paper, it will also be included in the meta data of the online version.

4   Results and Discussions

In order to increase training speed, Lena image is divided into 16 regions and we select 8 regions as the training set. Fig.3 shows the examples of 8 regions of original Lena Image. In this paper, the iteration number is 6.

Fig. 3. Examples of selected regions of Lena image

4.1   Gaussian-Blurred Image Restoration and Motion-Blurred Image Restoration

We chose the Gaussian-blurred image ($\sigma=3$) and motion-blurred image (the displacement was 15 and the angle is 11) to validate the proposed method (Fig. 4). Fig.5 and Fig.6 are the restoration results of Gaussian-blurred image and motion-blurred image with the present BP network at each iteration correspondingly. Fig. 7 and Fig.8 are their restoration results with AdaBoost.RT.

Fig. 4. (a) Gaussian-blurred image; (b) motion-blurred image

Fig. 5. Gaussian-blurred image restoration with BP network. (a) 1st iteration; (b) 2nd iteration; (c) 3rd iteration; (d) 4th iteration; (e) 5th iteration; (f) 6th iteration.

Fig. 6. Motion-blurred image restoration with BP network. (a) 1st iteration; (b) 2nd iteration; (c) 3rd iteration; (d) 4th iteration; (e) 5th iteration; (f) 6th iteration.

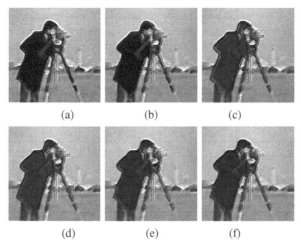

(a)   (b)   (c)

(d)   (e)   (f)

Fig. 7. Gaussian-blurred image restoration with AdaBoost.RT. (a) 1st iteration; (b) 2nd iteration; (c) 3rd iteration; (d) 4th iteration; (e) 5th iteration; (f) 6th iteration.

(a)   (b)   (c)

(d)   (e)   (f)

Fig. 8. Motion-blurred image restoration with AdaBoost.RT. (a) 1st iteration; (b) 2nd iteration; (c) 3rd iteration; (d) 4th iteration; (e) 5th iteration; (f) 6th iteration.

Shown in Figs.5-8, obviously the restoration performance of BP network is poor, while that of the AdaBoost algorithm is excellent, especially more weak learners are involved.

Normalized mean square error (NMSE) and peak signal noise ratio (PSNR) were employed to evaluate the restoration performance objectively.

Table 1. Objective restoration performance of Gaussian-blurred image with BP network

Iteration Number	1st	2nd	3rd	4th	5th	6th
NMSE	4.38	2.90	1.92	2.29	2.89	2.48
PSNR	14.26	16.05	17.86	17.09	16.07	16.74

Table 2. Objective restoration performance of Gaussian-blurred image with AdaBoost.RT

Iteration Number	1st	2nd	3rd	4th	5th	6th
NMSE	4.38	2.62	1.89	1.68	1.36	1.34
PSNR	14.26	16.50	17.91	18.41	19.34	19.41

Table 3. Objective restoration performance of motion-blurred image with BP network

Iteration Number	1st	2nd	3rd	4th	5th	6th
NMSE	5.21	5.47	5.88	2.66	2.63	3.72
PSNR	11.93	11.71	11.40	14.85	14.89	13.39

Table 4. Objective restoration performance of motion-blurred image with AdaBoost.RT

Iteration Number	1st	2nd	3rd	4th	5th	6th
NMSE	5.21	3.90	3.60	2.54	2.29	2.08
PSNR	11.93	13.18	13.53	15.04	15.49	15.92

Shown in Tables.1-4, the restoration performance of BP network is poor, while AdaBoost.RT has an excellent performance by organizing these BP network. Furthermore, the more iterations are, the more excellent performance is obtained. At 6th iteration, the restoration performance of AdaBoost.RT is superior to the BP network at any iteration. All above indicate that the AdaBoost algorithm greatly improves the restoration ability of weak learners.

4.2   Turbulence-Degraded Image Restoration

Simulated experiments above illuminate that it is feasible to apply AdaBoost.RT to restore blurred images. In this section, we applied the proposed method to turbulence-degrade image restoration. Fig.9 shows an image sequence of the wind-tunnel point target. We selected eight frames as the training set and one frame as the validation set. Shown in Fig.9(c), the proposed method can excellently restore the wind-tunnel point target.

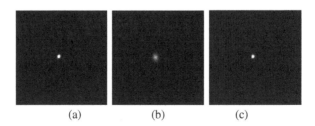

(a)   (b)   (c)

Fig. 9. Wind-tunnel image of the point target. (a) original clear image; (b) blurred image; (c) restored image.

Acknowledgments. This work was supported by the National Natural Science Foundation of China (Grant No. 61001179) and the Natural Science Foundation of Guangdong Province, China (Grant No. 07301038, 9451009001002667).

References

1. Gonzalez, R.C., Woods, R.E.: Digital Image Processing, 2nd edn. Publishing House of Electronics Industry, Beijing (2002)
2. Kundur, D., Hatzinakos, D.: Blind image deconvolution. IEEE Signal Processing Magazine 13, 43–64 (1996)
3. Moshe, B.E., Shree, K.N.: Motion-based motion deblurring. IEEE Trans. Pattern Analysis and Machine Intelligence 26(6), 689–698 (2004)
4. Hong, H., Zhang, T.: Investigation of Restoration Algorithm for Degraded Images Caused by Aero-optics Effects Using Multi-resolution Blind Deconvolution. Chinese Journal of Computers 27(7), 952–963 (2004)
5. Huang, J., Shen, M.: Blind deconvolution of atmospheric turbulence-degraded images based on total variation. Optical Technique, 525–527 (2008)
6. Shen, H., Li, S., Mao, J., Xin, J.: Digital Image Restoration Techniques: A Review. Journal of Image and Graphics 14(9), 1764–1775 (2009)
7. Wang, H., Cai, N., Li, M., Yang, J.: A Local-Information-Based Blind Image Restoration Algorithm Using a MLP. In: Beliczynski, B., Dzielinski, A., Iwanowski, M., Ribeiro, B. (eds.) ICANNGA 2007, Part II. LNCS, vol. 4432, pp. 582–589. Springer, Heidelberg (2007)
8. Solomatine, D.P., Shrestha, D.L.: AdaBoost.RT: a Boosting Algorithm for Regression Problems. In: Proc. of the International Joint Conference on Neural Networks, Budapest, Hungary, pp. 1163–1168 (2004)

Robust Fault-Tolerant Controller Design of Uncertain Discrete-Time System with Double Time-Delay

Xiaohua Zhang[1], Keyong Shao[1], Jialiang Liu[2], and Yongjing Ma[1]

[1] Northeast Petroleum university, School of Electrical and Information Engineering,
163318 Daqing, China
zxh327424@163.com
[2] Tianjin Research Institute of Construction Machinery,
Information Technology Research Institute, 300409 Tianjin, China
pai-zhang@163.com

Abstract. This paper aiming at a class of system in state and control input all have time-delay of parameters uncertain discrete-time of the system robust fault-tolerant control problem, based on Lyapunov theory and linear matrix inequality(LMI) get system when exists actuator fault, applied no memory state feedback controller and with memory state feedback controller, all can get the sufficient conditions which make the closed-loop fault system is stable, and the uncertainty of the closed-loop system that all meet the conditions is asymptotically stable. Simulation results show the effectiveness of the method.

Keywords: Double time-delay, Uncertain, Discrete-time system, Robust fault-tolerant, Actuator fault.

1   Introduction

In the practical control system, the reason for the transmission time-delay and the insensitivity of measurement, etc, the system will produce time-delay. And as the component aging, nonlinear, and modeling error and other cases, uncertainty exists in the system inevitably. In recent years, time-delay uncertain systems have been widely research[1-3], but most literature are continuous time-delay uncertain system as the research object[4,5], about discrete time-delay uncertain system robust fault-tolerant control research is still very rare. Literature[6] study the robust satisfaction fault-tolerant control of uncertain linear discrete-time system, not account of the system with time delays. Literature[7] only consider system contains the time-delay of state, not put the time-delay of control input into account. This paper makes a study of the system in state and control input all have time-delay of parameters uncertain discrete-time of the system, when there are actuator failures, by using two kinds of state feedback control methods, make the closed-loop control system reach asymptotic stable state.

M. Zhao and J. Sha (Eds.): ICCIP 2012, Part I, CCIS 288, pp. 302–309, 2012.

2 Problem Statement

Considering the state and control input all have time-delay and parameter uncertainty of the discrete-time system:

$$x(k+1) = (A_1 + \Delta A_1(k))x(k) + (A_2 + \Delta A_2(k))x(k-\tau_1) + (B_1 + \Delta B_1(k))u(k) + (B_2 + \Delta B_2(k))u(k-\tau_2) \tag{1}$$

Where: $x(k) \in R^n$ is the state vector, $u(k) \in R^m$ is the control-input vector, A_1, A_2, B_1, B_2 are known constant matrices with appropriate dimensions, $\tau_1 > 0$, $\tau_2 > 0$ are time-delay constant, $\Delta A_1(k), \Delta A_2(k), \Delta B_1(k), \Delta B_2(k)$ are parameter uncertainties for the system, and assume that is the norm bounded, meet the generalized matching conditions:

$$\left[\Delta A_1(k) \; \Delta A_2(k) \; \Delta B_1(k) \; \Delta B_2(k) \right] = DH(k)\left[E_1 \; E_2 \; E_3 \; E_4 \right] \tag{2}$$

Where: D, E_1, E_2, E_3, E_4 are constant matrices with appropriate dimensions. $H(k)$ said the real value of unknown time-varying continuous matrix function, and the elements are Lebegue measurable, and norm bounded meet the following relationship:

$$H^T(k)H(k) \leq I$$

System for initial conditions is:

$$x(k) = 0 \quad k < 0, x(0) = x_0$$

Assume that $(A_i, B_i), i, j = 1, 2$ can control. In the case of actuator fault, according to no memory state feedback controller and with memory state feedback controller discussed robust fault-tolerant control problem of the system, respectively.

3 Main Results

Lemma 1[8]. For any vector $x, y \in R^n$ and matrix $P \in R^{n \times m}$ and positive real number α, if P is positive definite, then we have:

$$x^T Py + y^T Px \leq \alpha x^T Px + \alpha^{-1} y^T Py$$

Lemma 2[9]. Set A, D, E and H are real matrices with appropriate dimensions, and have $H^T(k)H(k) \leq I$, For any symmetric positive definite matrices $P > 0$ and scalar $\varepsilon > 0$, if have $P^{-1} - \varepsilon DD^T > 0$, then

$$(A + DH(k)E)^T P(A + DH(k)E) \leq A^T \left(P^{-1} - \varepsilon DD^T \right)^{-1} A + \varepsilon^{-1} E^T E$$

3.1 Introducing No Memory State Feedback Controller

Adopting no memory state feedback controller:

$$u(k) = G_1 x(k) \tag{3}$$

Where G_1 is constant matrix with appropriate dimension, then the closed-loop system is:

$$x(k+1)=\left[\left(A_1+\Delta A_1(k)\right)+\left(B_1+\Delta B_1(k)\right)G_1\right]x(k)+\left(A_2+\Delta A_2(k)\right)x(k-\tau_1)+$$
$$\left(B_2+\Delta B_2(k)\right)G_1x(k-\tau_2) \tag{4}$$

Actuator fault is the most frequent failure in control systems. In this paper, we study the actuator failures situation.

In equation (4) between matrix B and matrix G_1 introduced the switch array L, actuator failures have the following form:

$$L=diag\left(l_1,\ l_2\ ;\cdots,\ l_n\right)$$

$$l_i=\begin{cases}0\text{ , the i-th actuator failure}\\0<l_i<1\text{, the i-th actuator partial failure}\\1\text{ , the i-th actuator normal}\end{cases}\quad(i=1,2,\cdots,n)$$

The practical closed-loop system with actuator fault is represented as the following:

$$x(k+1)=\left[\left(A_1+\Delta A_1(k)\right)+\left(B_1+\Delta B_1(k)\right)LG_1\right]x(k)+\left(A_2+\Delta A_2(k)\right)x(k-\tau_1)+$$
$$\left(B_2+\Delta B_2(k)\right)LG_1x(k-\tau_2) \tag{5}$$

For the case of actuator failure, the fault-tolerant controller design goal is to find the no memory state feedback controller (3) so that the closed-loop fault system (5) for all possible $L\in\Psi$ remain asymptotically stable, Ψ is the set of all possible faults of actuator faults switch matrix L.

Theorem 1. If the uncertain discrete-time with double time-delay system (1) for any matrix of the actuator faults $L\in\Psi$ and the positive constant α_1、 α_2、 α_3、 ε_1、 ε_2、 ε_3, if there exist symmetric positive matrix $P>0$, satisfy the following linear matrix inequality(LMI):

$$\begin{bmatrix}-X&W\\W^T&-M\end{bmatrix}<0 \tag{6}$$

Where:

$$W=\left[\sqrt{1+\alpha_1+\alpha_2}\left(A_1X+B_1LY_1\right)^T\ \sqrt{1+\alpha_1+\alpha_2}\left(E_1X+E_3LY_1\right)^T\ \sqrt{1+\alpha_1^{-1}+\alpha_3}\left(A_2X\right)^T\right.$$
$$\left.\sqrt{1+\alpha_1^{-1}+\alpha_3}\left(E_2X\right)^T\ \sqrt{1+\alpha_1^{-1}+\alpha_3^{-1}}\left(B_2LY_1\right)^T\ \sqrt{1+\alpha_1^{-1}+\alpha_3^{-1}}\left(E_4LY_1\right)^T\right]$$
$$M=diag\left(X-\varepsilon_1DD^T\ ,\ \varepsilon_1I,X-\varepsilon_2DD^T,\varepsilon_2I,X-\varepsilon_3DD^T,\varepsilon_3I\right)$$

Then, when actuator failure the closed-loop system (5) still asymptotically stable, and the state feedback gain matrix is: $G_1=Y_1X^{-1}$

Proof: For any matrix of the actuator faults $L\in\Psi$ we select the Lyapunov function for the closed-loop system (5) is:

$$V(k)=x^T(k)Px(k)+\sum_{i=1}^{\tau_1}x^T(k-i)Q_1x(k-i)+\sum_{i=1}^{\tau_2}x^T(k-i)Q_2x(k-i) \tag{7}$$

Two continuous time of Lyapunov function for minus is:

$$
\begin{aligned}
V(k+1)-V(k) &= x^T(k+1)Px(k+1)-x^T(k)Px(k)+x^T(k)Q_1x(k)-x^T(k-\tau_1)Q_1 \\
&\quad x(k-\tau_1)+x^T(k)Q_2x(k)-x^T(k-\tau_2)Q_2x(k-\tau_2) \\
&= \left\{x^T(k)\left[(A_1+\Delta A_1(k))+(B_1+\Delta B_1(k))LG_1\right]^T+x^T(k-\tau_1)\right. \\
&\quad (A_2+\Delta A_2(k))^T+x^T(k-\tau_2)\left[(B_2+\Delta B_2(k))LG_1\right]^T\right\}P\left\{\left[(A_1+\Delta A_1(k))\right.\right. \\
&\quad +(B_1+\Delta B_1(k))LG_1\right]x(k)+(A_2+\Delta A_2(k))x(k-\tau_1)+(B_2+\Delta B_2(k)) \\
&\quad \left. LG_1x(k-\tau_2)\right\}-x^T(k)Px(k)+x^T(k)Q_1x(k)-x^T(k-\tau_1)Q_1x(k-\tau_1) \\
&\quad +x^T(k)Q_2x(k)-x^T(k-\tau_2)Q_2x(k-\tau_2)
\end{aligned}
\tag{8}
$$

By Lemma 1 can be obtained:

$$
\begin{aligned}
&x^T(k)\left[(A_1+\Delta A_1(k))+(B_1+\Delta B_1(k))LG_1\right]^T P(A_2+\Delta A_2(k))x(k-\tau_1)+ \\
&x^T(k-\tau_1)(A_2+\Delta A_2(k))^T P\left[(A_1+\Delta A_1(k))+(B_1+\Delta B_1(k))LG_1\right]x(k) \\
&\le \alpha_1 x^T(k)\left[(A_1+\Delta A_1(k))+(B_1+\Delta B_1(k))LG_1\right]^T P\left[(A_1+\Delta A_1(k))+(B_1+\Delta B_1(k))LG_1\right]x(k) \\
&+\alpha_1^{-1}x^T(k-\tau_1)(A_2+\Delta A_2(k))^T P(A_2+\Delta A_2(k))x(k-\tau_1)
\end{aligned}
\tag{9}
$$

$$
\begin{aligned}
&x^T(k)\left[(A_1+\Delta A_1(k))+(B_1+\Delta B_1(k))LG_1\right]^T P(B_2+\Delta B_2(k))LG_1x(k-\tau_2)+ \\
&x^T(k-\tau_2)\left[(B_2+\Delta B_2(k))LG_1\right]^T P\left[(A_1+\Delta A_1(k))+(B_1+\Delta B_1(k))LG_1\right]x(k) \\
&\le \alpha_2 x^T(k)\left[(A_1+\Delta A_1(k))+(B_1+\Delta B_1(k))LG_1\right]^T P\left[(A_1+\Delta A_1(k))+(B_1+\Delta B_1(k))LG_1\right] \\
&x(k)+\alpha_2^{-1}x^T(k-\tau_2)\left[(B_2+\Delta B_2(k))LG_1\right]^T P(B_2+\Delta B_2(k))LG_1x(k-\tau_2)
\end{aligned}
\tag{10}
$$

$$
\begin{aligned}
&x^T(k-\tau_1)(A_2+\Delta A_2(k))^T P(B_2+\Delta B_2(k))LG_1x(k-\tau_2)+ \\
&x^T(k-\tau_2)\left[(B_2+\Delta B_2(k))LG_1\right]^T P(A_2+\Delta A_2(k))x(k-\tau_1) \\
&\le \alpha_3 x^T(k-\tau_1)(A_2+\Delta A_2(k))^T P(A_2+\Delta A_2(k))x(k-\tau_1)+ \\
&\alpha_3^{-1}x^T(k-\tau_2)\left[(B_2+\Delta B_2(k))LG_1\right]^T P(B_2+\Delta B_2(k))LG_1x(k-\tau_2)
\end{aligned}
\tag{11}
$$

By Lemma 2 and equation (2) can be obtained:

$$
\begin{aligned}
&\left[(A_1+\Delta A_1(k))+(B_1+\Delta B_1(k))LG_1\right]^T P\left[(A_1+\Delta A_1(k))+(B_1+\Delta B_1(k))LG_1\right] \\
&=\left[(A_1+B_1LG_1)+DH(k)(E_1+E_3LG_1)\right]^T P\left[(A_1+B_1LG_1)+DH(k)(E_1+E_3LG_1)\right]^T \\
&\le (A_1+B_1LG_1)^T\left(P^{-1}-\varepsilon_1 DD^T\right)^{-1}(A_1+B_1LG_1)+\varepsilon_1^{-1}(E_1+E_3LG_1)^T(E_1+E_3LG_1)
\end{aligned}
\tag{12}
$$

$$
\begin{aligned}
&(A_2+\Delta A_2(k))^T P(A_2+\Delta A_2(k))=(A_2+DH(k)E_2)^T P(A_2+DH(k)E_2) \\
&\le A_2^T\left(P^{-1}-\varepsilon_2 DD^T\right)^{-1}A_2+\varepsilon_2^{-1}E_2^T E_2
\end{aligned}
\tag{13}
$$

$$
\begin{aligned}
&\left[(B_2+\Delta B_2(k))LG_1\right]^T P(B_2+\Delta B_2(k))LG_1=\left[B_2LG_1+DH(k)E_4LG_1\right]^T P\left[B_2LG_1+DH(k)E_4LG_1\right] \\
&\le (B_2LG_1)^T\left(P^{-1}-\varepsilon_3 DD^T\right)^{-1}(B_2LG_1)+\varepsilon_3^{-1}(E_4LG_1)^T(E_4LG_1)
\end{aligned}
\tag{14}
$$

The formula (9) - (14) into equation (8) can be obtained:

$$
V(k+1) - V(k) \le x^T(k) \left\{ (1 + \alpha_1 + \alpha_2) \left[(A_1 + B_1 LG_1)^T (P^{-1} - \varepsilon_1 DD^T)^{-1} (A_1 + B_1 LG_1) + \right. \right.
$$
$$
\left. \varepsilon_1^{-1} (E_1 + E_3 LG_1)^T (E_1 + E_3 LG_1) \right] - P + Q_1 + Q_2 \right\} x(k) + x^T(k - \tau_1)
$$
$$
\left\{ (1 + \alpha_1^{-1} + \alpha_3) \left[A_2^T (P^{-1} - \varepsilon_2 DD^T)^{-1} A_2 + \varepsilon_2^{-1} E_2^T E_2 \right] - Q_1 \right\} x(k - \tau_1) +
$$
$$
x^T(k - \tau_2) \left\{ (1 + \alpha_2^{-1} + \alpha_3^{-1}) \left[(B_2 LG_1)^T (P^{-1} - \varepsilon_3 DD^T)^{-1} (B_2 LG_1) + \right. \right.
$$
$$
\left. \varepsilon_3^{-1} (E_4 LG_1)^T (E_4 LG_1) \right] - Q_2 \right\} x(k - \tau_2)
$$

Take $Q_1 = (1 + \alpha_1^{-1} + \alpha_3) \left[A_2^T (P^{-1} - \varepsilon_2 DD^T)^{-1} A_2 + \varepsilon_2^{-1} E_2^T E_2 \right]$

$\quad Q_2 = (1 + \alpha_2^{-1} + \alpha_3^{-1}) \left[(B_2 LG_1)^T (P^{-1} - \varepsilon_3 DD^T)^{-1} (B_2 LG_1) + \varepsilon_3^{-1} (E_4 LG_1)^T (E_4 LG_1) \right]$

Seen by the Lyapunov stability theory, if

$$
(1 + \alpha_1 + \alpha_2) \left[(A_1 + B_1 LG_1)^T (P^{-1} - \varepsilon_1 DD^T)^{-1} (A_1 + B_1 LG_1) + \varepsilon_1^{-1} (E_1 + E_3 LG_1)^T (E_1 + E_3 LG_1) \right] +
$$
$$
(1 + \alpha_1^{-1} + \alpha_3) \left[A_2^T (P^{-1} - \varepsilon_2 DD^T)^{-1} A_2 + \varepsilon_2^{-1} E_2^T E_2 \right] + (1 + \alpha_2^{-1} + \alpha_3^{-1}) \left[(B_2 LG_1)^T (P^{-1} - \varepsilon_3 DD^T)^{-1} \right. \quad (15)
$$
$$
\left. (B_2 LG_1) + \varepsilon_3^{-1} (E_4 LG_1)^T (E_4 LG_1) \right] - P < 0
$$

Then the closed-loop system formula (5) is asymptotically stable.

To equation (15) left and right by the same P^{-1}, and make $P^{-1} = X$, $G_1 X = Y_1$

$$
W = \left[\sqrt{1 + \alpha_1 + \alpha_2} (A_1 X + B_1 LY_1)^T \quad \sqrt{1 + \alpha_1 + \alpha_2} (E_1 X + E_3 LY_1)^T \quad \sqrt{1 + \alpha_1^{-1} + \alpha_3} (A_2 X)^T \right.
$$
$$
\left. \sqrt{1 + \alpha_1^{-1} + \alpha_3} (E_2 X)^T \quad \sqrt{1 + \alpha_1^{-1} + \alpha_3^{-1}} (B_2 LY_1)^T \quad \sqrt{1 + \alpha_1^{-1} + \alpha_3^{-1}} (E_4 LY_1)^T \right]
$$

$$
M = diag \left(X - \varepsilon_1 DD^T, \; \varepsilon_1 I, X - \varepsilon_2 DD^T, \varepsilon_2 I, X - \varepsilon_3 DD^T, \varepsilon_3 I \right)
$$

Can be obtained by the Schur complement[10] formula (15) is equivalent to formula(6), the proof of Theorem.

3.2   Introducing Memory State Feedback Controller

Adopting memory state feedback controller:

$$
u(k) = G_1 x(k) + G_2 x(k - \tau) \tag{16}
$$

The practical closed-loop system with actuator fault is represented as the following:

$$
x(k+1) = \left[(A_1 + \Delta A_1(k)) + (B_1 + \Delta B_1(k)) LG_1 \right] x(k) + (A_2 + \Delta A_2(k)) x(k - \tau_1) + (B_2 + \Delta B_2(k)) \tag{17}
$$
$$
LG_1 x(k - \tau_2) + (B_1 + \Delta B_1(k)) LG_2 x(k - \tau) + (B_2 + \Delta B_2(k)) LG_2 x(k - \tau_2 - \tau)
$$

For the case of actuator failure, the fault-tolerant controller design goal is to find the memory state feedback controller (16) so that the closed-loop fault system (17) for all possible $L \in \Psi$ remain asymptotically stable.

Theorem 2. If the uncertain discrete-time with double time-delay system (1) for any matrix of the actuator faults $L \in \Psi$ and the positive constant $\alpha_1, \alpha_2, \alpha_3, \alpha_4, \alpha_5, \alpha_6,$ $\alpha_7, \alpha_8, \alpha_9, \alpha_{10}, \varepsilon_1, \varepsilon_2, \varepsilon_3, \varepsilon_4, \varepsilon_5$, if there exist symmetric positive matrix $P > 0$, satisfy the following linear matrix inequality (LMI):

$$\begin{bmatrix} -X & W \\ W^T & -M \end{bmatrix} < 0 \tag{18}$$

Where:

$$W = \left[\sqrt{1 + \alpha_1 + \alpha_2 + \alpha_3 + \alpha_4} \left(A_1 X + B_1 LY_1 \right)^T \quad \sqrt{1 + \alpha_1 + \alpha_2 + \alpha_3 + \alpha_4} \left(E_1 X + E_3 LY_1 \right)^T \right.$$

$$\sqrt{1 + \alpha_1^{-1} + \alpha_5 + \alpha_6 + \alpha_7} \left(A_2 X \right)^T \quad \sqrt{1 + \alpha_1^{-1} + \alpha_5 + \alpha_6 + \alpha_7} \left(E_2 X \right)^T$$

$$\sqrt{1 + \alpha_1^{-1} + \alpha_5^{-1} + \alpha_8 + \alpha_9} \left(B_2 LY_1 \right)^T \quad \sqrt{1 + \alpha_1^{-1} + \alpha_5^{-1} + \alpha_8 + \alpha_9} \left(E_4 LY_1 \right)^T$$

$$\sqrt{1 + \alpha_3^{-1} + \alpha_6^{-1} + \alpha_8^{-1} + \alpha_{10}} \left(B_1 LY_2 \right)^T \quad \sqrt{1 + \alpha_3^{-1} + \alpha_6^{-1} + \alpha_8^{-1} + \alpha_{10}} \left(E_1 LY_2 \right)^T$$

$$\left. \sqrt{1 + \alpha_4^{-1} + \alpha_7^{-1} + \alpha_9^{-1} + \alpha_{10}^{-1}} \left(B_2 LY_2 \right)^T \quad \sqrt{1 + \alpha_4^{-1} + \alpha_7^{-1} + \alpha_9^{-1} + \alpha_{10}^{-1}} \left(E_4 LY_2 \right)^T \right]$$

$$M = diag \left(X - \varepsilon_1 DD^T, \ \varepsilon_1 I, X - \varepsilon_2 DD^T, \varepsilon_2 I, X - \varepsilon_3 DD^T, \varepsilon_3 I, X - \varepsilon_4 DD^T, \varepsilon_4 I, X - \varepsilon_5 DD^T, \varepsilon_5 I \right)$$

Then, when actuator failure the closed-loop system (17) still asymptotically stable, and the state feedback gain matrix is: $G_1 = Y_1 X^{-1}$, $G_2 = Y_2 X^{-1}$

See the proof process of Theorem 1.

4   Simulation Example

Consider uncertain discrete-time with double time-delay system (1) with the parameters:

$$A_1 = \begin{bmatrix} -0.3 & -0.5 \\ 0.6 & -0.8 \end{bmatrix}, \ A_2 = \begin{bmatrix} 0.1 & 0.2 \\ 0.2 & 0.1 \end{bmatrix}, \ B_1 = \begin{bmatrix} 0.7 & 0.3 \\ 0.5 & 0.6 \end{bmatrix}, \ B_2 = \begin{bmatrix} 0.1 & 0.2 \\ 0.3 & 0.2 \end{bmatrix}, \ D = \begin{bmatrix} 0.1 & 0 \\ 0 & 0.1 \end{bmatrix}, \ E_1 = \begin{bmatrix} 0.1 & 0 \\ 0 & 0.1 \end{bmatrix},$$

$$E_2 = \begin{bmatrix} 0.2 & 0 \\ 0 & 0.2 \end{bmatrix}, \ E_3 = \begin{bmatrix} 0.1 & 0.2 \\ 0.2 & 0.1 \end{bmatrix}, \ E_4 = \begin{bmatrix} 0.1 & 0.2 \\ 0.2 & 0.1 \end{bmatrix}$$

Take into account the case of actuator failures, matrix $L_0 = diag(1,1)$ express actuator is normally, matrix $L_1 = diag(0,1)$ and $L_2 = diag(1,0)$ express the actuator 1 and 2 occur completely ineffective fault, respectively.

4.1   Introducing No Memory State Feedback Controller

The introduction of no memory state feedback controller (3), according to this paper theorem 1, use of MATLAB LMI Toolbox can be obtained formula (6) for the solution:

$$P = \begin{bmatrix} 1.9840 & 0.3344 \\ 0.3344 & 1.4228 \end{bmatrix} > 0, \ G_1 = \begin{bmatrix} -0.1098 & -0.4671 \\ 0.3119 & 1.3268 \end{bmatrix},$$

So the no memory for state feedback controller is:

$$u(k) = \begin{bmatrix} -0.1098 & -0.4671 \\ 0.3119 & 1.3268 \end{bmatrix} x(k)$$

Take $\tau_1 = 0.1s, \tau_2 = 0.5s$, $H(k) = diag\left(\sin(0.1k), \sin(0.1k)\right)$ system for initial conditions is $x(0) = \left[-5;6\right]^T$. For actuators in L_0, L_1, L_2 case, the zero-input state response curve of the state $x_1(t)$, $x_2(t)$ respectively as shown in Figure 1, Figure 2.

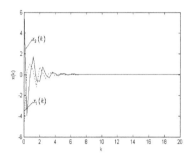
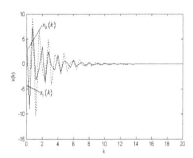

Fig. 1. System zero- input response when actuator 1 failure

Fig. 2. System zero-input response when actuator 2 failure

4.2   Introducing Memory State Feedback Controller

The introduction of memory state feedback controller(16), according to this paper theorem 2, use of MATLAB LMI Toolbox can be obtained formula(18) for the solution:

$$P = \begin{bmatrix} 18.7665 & 2.3758 \\ 2.3758 & 11.2850 \end{bmatrix} > 0, \; G_1 = \begin{bmatrix} -0.0734 & -0.3485 \\ 0.2813 & 1.3363 \end{bmatrix}, \; G_2 = \begin{bmatrix} -0.0025 & 0.6735 \\ 0.0655 & 0.0796 \end{bmatrix}$$

So the memory for state feedback controller is:

$$u(k) = \begin{bmatrix} -0.0734 & -0.3485 \\ 0.2813 & 1.3363 \end{bmatrix} x(k) + \begin{bmatrix} -0.0025 & 0.6735 \\ 0.0655 & 0.0796 \end{bmatrix} x(k-\tau)$$

Take $\tau_1 = 0.1s, \tau_2 = 0.5s, \tau = 0.3s$, $H(k) = diag\left(\sin(0.1k), \sin(0.1k)\right)$, system for initial conditions is $x(0) = \left[-3;3\right]^T$. To actuators in L_0, L_1, L_2 case, the zero-input state response curve of the state $x_1(t)$, $x_2(t)$ respectively as shown in Figure 3, Figure 4.

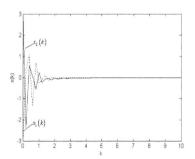
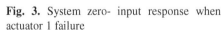
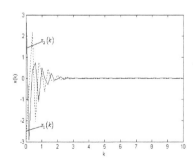

Fig. 3. System zero- input response when actuator 1 failure

Fig. 4. System zero-input response when actuator 2 failure

Through the above comparisons can be concluded that introduced into the memory state feedback controller than no memory state feedback controller with good control effect, although the two methods finally make the system achieve asymptotic stability of the state, but when introduced the memory state feedback controller into the system can relatively early to achieve steady state, and unstable parts of the concussion reduced significantly.

5   Conclusions

Time-delay and uncertainty exist is a lead to instability and system performance becomes poor, the main reason of the system analysis become more complicated. This paper, based on the Lyapunov stability theory, using the lincar matrix inequality (LMI), and in state and control input all have time-delay of uncertain discrete-time system, when actuator happen general fault, were applied no memory state feedback controller and a state feedback controller is memory, can make the system to achieve stable state, and further proof have memory state feedback controller control effect is better than no memory state feedback controller. The simulation results show the effectiveness of the method.

References

1. Fridman, E., Shaked, U.: An improved stabilization method for linear time-delay systems. IEEE Transactions on Automatic Control 47(11), 1931–1937 (2002)
2. Ge, J.H., Frank, P.M., Lin, C.F.: Robust H_∞ state feedback control for linear systems with state delay and parameter uncertainty. Automatica 32(8), 1183–1185 (1996)
3. Sun, J., Li, J., Wang, Z.: Robust fault-tolerant control of uncertain time-delay systems. Control Theory & Application 15(2), 267–271 (1998) (in Chinese)
4. Yang, J., Wu, F., Shi, Z.: Parameter uncertainty systems with time-delay robust fault-tolerant controller design. Control Theory & Application 17(3), 442–444 (2000) (in Chinese)
5. Liu, P., Zhou, D.: Uncertain time-delay linear system robust fault-tolerant control study. Control Theory &Application 20(1), 78–81 (2003) (in Chinese)
6. Zhang, D., Wang, Z., Hu, S.: Robust satisfactory fault-tolerant control of uncertain linear discrete-time systems: an LMI approach. International Journal of Systems Science 38(2), 151–165 (2007)
7. Xiang, Z., Wang, R.: Robust stabilization of discrete-time switched non-linear systems with time delay under asynchronous switching. Transactions of the Institute of Measurement and Control 33(5), 591–609 (2011)
8. Liu, Z., Chen, Z., Li, R.: With nonlinear parameter disturbance of delay control system robust stability. Xian Mining of Journals 19(2), 165–168 (1999) (in Chinese)
9. Li, X., De Souza, C.E.: Criteria for robust stabilization of uncertain linear systems with time-varying state delays. In: Proc. of IEAC 13th Triennial World Congress, San Francisco, USA, pp. 137–142 (1996)
10. Li, Y.: Robust control-the linear matrix inequality (lmi) processing method. Qinghua University Press, Beijing (2002) (in Chinese)

Research on Emotion Modeling
Based on Three-Dimension Emotional Space

Haishan Chen, Huailin Dong[*], and Bochao Hu

Software School of Xiamen University, Xiamen 361005, China
{hschen,hldong}@xmu.edu.cn

Abstract. Combined with the particle system and active field, this paper establishes an artificial emotion model on the basis of the three-dimension emotional space and OCC model. The model converts the external stimuli into the active field in the space, and the potential energy generated by the active field has the combined impact on the particles' state of motion. The states of motion in the particle system represent the model's emotional state. In addition, the model outputs a time-varying multi-dimensional vector, and the vector values in all dimensions describe the activation level of the corresponding emotion.

Keywords: Emotional Space, Particle System, Active Field, OCC Model.

1   Introduction

The idealistic goal of the emotional modeling is to make computers "emotional". According to cognitive psychology, human emotion has the following main characteristics: (1) Attenuation of emotional responses. After an emotional response has continued for some time, it will decay to a level below perception. (2) Non-linearity. However frequently an emotion is activated, the system will always reach the status of saturation. (3) Time constancy. Human emotions can be tested in a completely independent manner within a sustained period of time. To sum up, the human emotional system is a nonlinear dynamics response system determined by many factors [1].

This paper applies the particle system, a nonlinear system, to the modeling of human emotional system. With the active field concept from physics, the model converts the external stimuli into multiple active fields in the emotional space, and the potential energy generated by the active field has the combined impact on the particles' state of motion. The states of motion in the particle system represent the model's emotional state. In addition, the model outputs a time-varying multi-dimensional vector, and the vector values in all dimensions describe the activation level of the corresponding emotion, so as to show that the intelligent entities involve complex emotional changes of various emotions.

---

[*] Corresponding author.

M. Zhao and J. Sha (Eds.): ICCIP 2012, Part I, CCIS 288, pp. 310–319, 2012.

2   Model Design

2.1   Definition of Emotional Space

Breazeal C. and Scassellati B.'s emotional space constitutes the three dimensions: Arousal, Valence and Stance [2, 3], as shown in Fig. 1. Each emotion in human emotional space can be described by the vector consisting of these three dimensions.

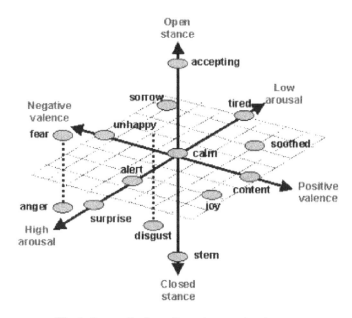

Fig. 1. Breazeal's three-dimension emotional space

Fourteen points in the emotional space

$$s_i, (\, i = 1, 2, \ldots, 14, s_i \in \mathbf{R}^3\,)$$

Corresponding the 14 sentiments in human emotions. And fourteen spheres with s_i as the central point represent the activation regions of all these 14 emotions, denoted by

$$B_i = \{x \mid \|x - s_i\| \leq r_i, x \in \mathbf{R}^3, r_i \in \mathbf{R}\,)$$

In which, x represents a point in the three-dimension emotional space, the sphere radius r_i represents the intelligent entity's preference for the emotion i. The higher the value of r_i, the more likely the particle fall into the region Bi. The greater the number of particles that fall into the region Bi, the higher activation level of the emotion i and the more likely the intelligent entity is experiencing this emotion. Therefore, any emotion of an intelligent entity can be represented by a 14 dimensions vector $R(r_1, r_2, \ldots, r_{14})$, so as to determine the preferences of emotional responses.

2.2   Definition of Space Particle

N_p moving particles are added into the emotional space, and these particles do Brownian motions in the free status, as shown in Fig. 2. The particle positions are updated according to the following formula:

$$\overrightarrow{P_{t+1}}=\overrightarrow{P_t}+v\cdot\overrightarrow{e_i}$$

In which, v represents the preset particle velocity, $\overrightarrow{P_t}$ represents the space position of the particle at the moment of t, $\overrightarrow{e_i},(i=1,2,...26)$ represents 26 discrete unit vectors separated evenly by all the normal vectors of the sphere surface, and the particle positions are updated by choosing one of they randomly each time.

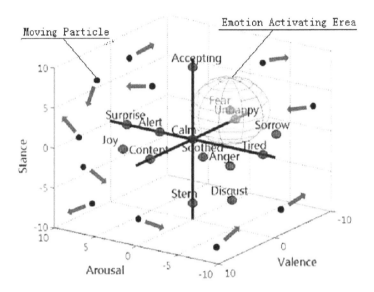

Fig. 2. Brownian motion of the free status particles in the emotional space

2.3   The External Stimuli's Influence in Particle Motion

The examples of the model's external stimuli can be greeting the emotional intelligence body, giving it a toy or arousing their own sense of hunger. The specific emotional stimulus is defined as an active field emerging in the emotional space. The strength of external stimuli determines that of the active field. The potential energy of any point in the space is proportional to the intensity of the active field, and inversely proportional to the distance from the point to the field source. There may be more than one active field in the space.

Potential energy generated by the active field affects the selection of particles' moving direction. The higher the active field's intensity, the closer the field source is from the particle, the greater the probability of the particle moving in several directions where the field source locates. After the birth of the active field, its intensity will continue to decay over time, as shown in Fig. 3. Based on different types and causes of the external stimuli, different decay functions apply as follows,

$$y(t) = \begin{cases} c, t < a, \\ \dfrac{c(b-t)}{b-a}, a \le t \le b. \\ 0, t > b \end{cases} \tag{1}$$

$$y(t) = \begin{cases} c, t < a, \\ c\left(\dfrac{b-t}{b-a}\right)^k, a \le t \le b \\ 0, t > b \end{cases} \tag{2}$$

$$y(t) = \begin{cases} c, t \le a, \\ \dfrac{c}{1 + \alpha(x-a)^\beta}, t > a \\ (\alpha > 0, \beta > 0) \end{cases} \tag{3}$$

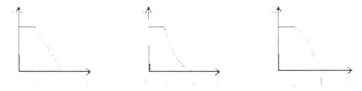

Fig. 3. Image of decay function of (1), (2) and (3)

In all these three decay functions, the y axis indicates the strength of the active field, and the x axis indicates the time duration of the active field. In x axis, the time period from 0 to a marks the stability phase of the active field strength, and the attenuation function is a horizontal line with y-intersect of c; the time period from a to b marks the recession phase of the active field strength, during which (1) is a steadily declining straight line; (2) is a slowly declining curve, and the parameter k determine the rate of curve decline; (3) is a rapidly declining curve, and the coefficients α and β determine the rate of curve decline. For active fields arising from a number of unexpected events, the attenuation function is (3), while for other active fields corresponding to some relatively gentler events, we can choose (1) or (2) as the attenuation function.

When there is only one active field existing in the emotional space, the potential energy and its direction $\vec{e}_u$ at any point $u(x, y, z)$ in the space are described as follows,

$$\varphi(u) = \frac{\mu \cdot y(t)}{|\vec{E} - \vec{u}|^2}$$

$$\vec{e}_u = \frac{\vec{E} - \vec{u}}{|\vec{E} - \vec{u}|}$$

In which, $\vec{E}$ and $\vec{u}$ respectively represent the vectors from the origin point to the field source and $y(t)$ is the attenuation function of E, u is the impact factor.

When there is more than one active field in the emotional space, the potential energy at any point in the space is determined by the superposition of multiple active fields' potential energy. Assume that there exists an active field in the space,

$$E_i, (i = 1, 2 ... N_E)$$

In which, N_p represents the number of active fields. The potential energy φ and direction $\vec{e}_u$ of any point u in the space as follows,

$$\varphi(u) = \sum_{i=1}^{N_E} \frac{(\overrightarrow{E_i} - \vec{u}) \cdot \mu_i \cdot y_i(t)}{|\overrightarrow{E_i} - \vec{u}|^3}$$

$$\vec{e}_u = \sum_{i=1}^{N_E} \frac{\overrightarrow{E_i} - \vec{u}}{|\overrightarrow{E_i} - \vec{u}|}$$

By means of vector calculation, the equipotent lines of emotional space can thus be acquired from the conversion of multiple active fields into a single active field, as shown in Fig. 4.

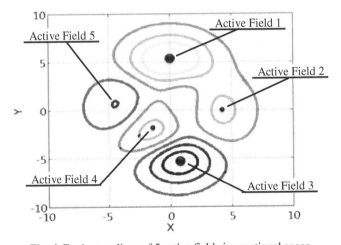

Fig. 4. Equipotent lines of 5 active fields in emotional space

To enhance the randomness of the system, the set is defined as follows,

$$S = \{\vec{e_j} \mid \arccos \frac{(\overrightarrow{E} - \vec{u}) \cdot \vec{e_j}}{2|\overrightarrow{E} - \vec{u}| \cdot |\vec{e_j}|} \le \theta, (i = 1, 2 .. 26)\}$$

Here θ is 45°, representing the range of influence of the active field E. The larger θ is, the more likely the particle p in point u chooses to move in direction $\vec{e_i}$ adjacent to $|\overrightarrow{E} - \vec{u}|$ at the next moment.

Ns represents the number of elements in set S, for $\forall \vec{e_i} \in S$, the probability of particle p moving in the direction $\vec{e_i}$ at the next moment is

$$P(\vec{e_i}) = \frac{\varphi(u)}{N_S \cdot \varphi(u) + (26 - N_S)}$$

For $\forall \vec{e_j} \notin S$, the probability of particle P moving in the direction $\vec{e_j}$ at the next moment is

$$P(\vec{e_j}) = \frac{1}{N_S \cdot \varphi(u) + (26 - N_S)}$$

Based on the probability formula of $P(\vec{e_i})$ and $P(\vec{e_j})$, the particle's random moving direction $\vec{e}$ at the next moment is $\overrightarrow{P_{t+1}} = \overrightarrow{P_t} + v \cdot \vec{e}$, and the particle's space coordinates are thus updated.

2.4   Corresponding Relationship between External Stimuli and the Position in Field Source

Various external stimuli in the emotional space correspond to the different location emerging in the active field. With the OCC emotion model, all the external stimuli can be divided into three categories –"object", "Incident" and "Conduct". Assume that the emotional space is a cube with length, width and height of 20, and the cube center is set as the original point of coordinates. Corresponding to the 14 emotion points in the emotional space, the emergence regions of all three categories of field source are shown in Table 1.

Table 1. Emergence regions of three categories of field sources in the space

	Feature	Arousal	Valence	Stance
Object	Strange	4<x<8	-2<y<2	-2<z<2
	Familiar	4<x<8	-4<y<-8	-4<z<-8
	Dangerous	4<x<8	-4<y<-8	-4<z<-8
	Like	-2<x<2	4<y<8	-2<z<2
	Not Like	-4<x<-8	-4<y<-8	-4<z<-8
Event	Expectant	-2<x<2	4<y<8	-2<z<2
	Not Expectant	-5<x<-1	-4<y<-8	-2<z<2
	Beneficial	-5<x<-1	-2<y<2	-2<z<2
	Not Beneficial	1<x<5	-4<y<-8	1<z<5
	Lethal	4<x<8	-4<y<-8	-4<z<-8
	Expected	4<x<8	-2<y<2	-2<z<2
Action	Success	-2<x<2	4<y<8	-2<z<2
	Praised	-2<x<2	4<y<8	-2<z<2
	Criticized	-4<x<-8	-4<y<-8	-2<z<2
	Hated	-4<x<-8	-4<y<-8	-4<z<-8
	Intimate	-4<x<-8	-4<y<-8	-4<z<-8
	Good Behavior	-2<x<2	4<y<8	-2<z<2

2.5   Definition of Output Vector

At every certain time interval, the model calculates the number of particles separately falling into 14 types of emotional activation region. The more particles in an emotional area, the higher the level of emotional activation is (see Fig. 5). Therefore, the emotional changes of the emotion intelligent entity over time can be represented by a group of time-variant 14-dimensional vectors. If the vector values over some dimensions exceed a given threshold, the entity is judged to have these types of emotions at this moment.

Assume that St is the current emotional state of the intelligent entity, and Qi is the activation level of the emotion i in St, therefore

$$s_t \mapsto Q_i(s_t) = \frac{n_{B_i}}{N_p}, \ (i = 1, 2 \ldots 14)$$

In which, n_{Bi} is the number of active particles within the emotion activation region Bi, and Np is the number of all particles in the emotional space, therefore the intelligent entities emotional state represented by the model at moment t can be described as

$$S_t(Q_1(s_t), Q_2(s_t), \ldots Q_{14}(s_t)),$$

As per specific need, a number of dimensions can be selected from the fourteen-dimension output vector, and marked as the changes of the emotional system faced with external stimuli.

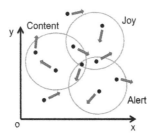

Fig. 5. Particles fall into different emotional activation regions

3   Simulation Experiment

Applying a cube with length, width and height of 20 as the simulated emotional space, the experiment sets the cube center to be the original point of coordinates, and a three-dimensional Cartesian coordinate system is thus established. There are 14 emotional activation areas in the space, with a common Bi radius of 5, the number of particles is 100, at the speed of 1, and the following experiment is conducted with the abovementioned conditions.

3.1   Operation and Output of the Model with No External Stimulation

In the absence of external stimuli, the particles do Brownian motion. Within the time periods from 0 to 100, all the emotional activation curves experience slight oscillations, with no significant ups and downs (see Fig. 6). This is similar to the real human emotional reactions.

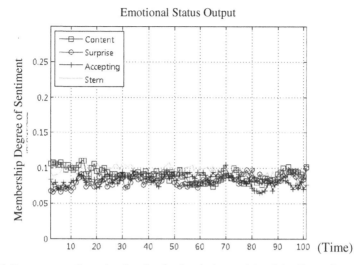

Fig. 6. Four curves of emotional activation levels for particles doing Brownian motion

3.2   Operation and Output of the Model for a Single Active Field

According to the classification of external stimuli to OCC model, an active field with the attenuation function of (1) in the emotional space (7, 1, 1). The model can describe the scenario in which the intelligent entity notices a strange object nearby (such as a pig), as shown in Fig. 7.

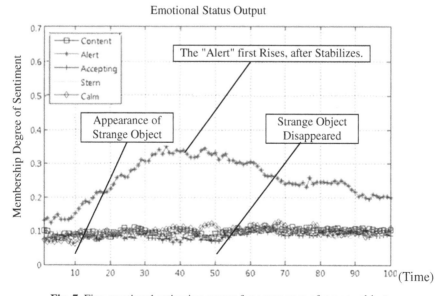

Fig. 7. Five emotional activation curves for emergence of strange objects

Experiments show that when the emotional intelligent entity encounters a strange object, the "Alert" emotional activation curve first rises at a relatively rapid rate, and then gradually declines till the ultimate convergence with other emotional activation curves. This is similar to the real human emotional reactions.

3.3   Operation and Output of the Model for Multiple Active Fields

When t=10, an active field is established with the attenuation function (1) in the space (1, 6, 4), describing the scenario in which the intelligent entity encounters a lovely object (such as a dog). When t = 30 an active field is established with the attenuation function (2) in the space (8, -1, 0, during which the active field's intensity is not 0, which shows that the intelligent entity suddenly discovers dangerous objects (such as a snake), as shown in Fig. 8.

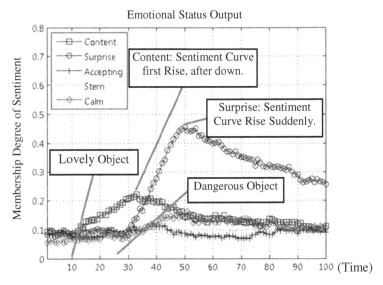

Fig. 8. Five emotional activation curves for the emergence of dogs and then snakes

Experiments show that:

When t=10, the emotional intelligent entity encounters a lovely object, and the "Satisfied" emotional activation curve rises at a uniform rate.

When t=30, the emotional intelligence entity notices a dangerous object, and the "Panic" emotional activation curve rises sharply and the other curves experience slight oscillation. Afterwards the "Panic" emotional activation curve gradually declines until the ultimate convergence with the other curves. The simulation model experiment results are similar to human emotional reactions.

4   Conclusions

Compared with the China's research results in the field of artificial emotional modeling in recent years, the model in this paper has the following characteristics: (1)

Faced with the same external stimuli, the model may experience changes among different emotional states, thus reflecting the local randomness under the overall uncertainty. (2) Due to the non-linear nature of the particle system itself, the system will reach a certain degree of saturation in emotional activation and will not infinitely rise no matter how strong an external stimulation is. (3) The model can not only reflect the combined effects of emotional changes from multiple external factors, but also reflect the effect of the background emotions on the current emotional changes. (4) The model outputs a set of multi-dimensional vector with up to 14 types of emotional activation levels, reflecting the model's emotional state of mixed emotions.

On the other hand, the model's shortcomings are: (1) Coordinates corresponding to the field sources in the space lack adequate theoretical support, and the coefficients of attenuation functions in the experiment require manual correction. (2) The establishment of the emotional model depends on the development and cooperation of psychology, anatomy and other related disciplines. (3) The field of artificial emotion modeling lacks common evaluation criteria; therefore, it is difficult to carry out comparative research of this model and other models.

Research shows that human's intrinsic emotional motivation is usually divided into two parts -- physiological instinct and cognitive reasoning. This model mainly simulates the physiological instinct of emotional responses. Future research can be done with the combination of the cognitive process of emotions, such as the emotional experience of an unfamiliar environment, etc.

Acknowledgments. The work was Supported by the Leading Academic Discipline Program, "Project 211 (the 3rd phase)" of Xiamen University.

References

1. Zhou, C.: Summary of Heart and Brain Computing, pp. 158–167. Tsinghua University Press, Beijing (2003)
2. Breazeal, C., Scassellati, B.: How to build robot that make friends and influence people. In: International Conference on Intelligent Robots and Systems, IROS 1999, pp. 858–863 (1999)
3. Breazeal, C., Scassellati, B.: Infant-like social interactions between a robot and a human caretaker. Adaptive Behavior 8(1), 49–74 (2000)
4. Ortony, A., Clore, G., Collins, A.: The cognitive structure of emotions. Cambridge University Press, Cambridge (1988)
5. Ortony, A., Robert, T., Paolo, P.: On making believable emotional agents believable. Emotions in Humans and Artifacts. MIT Press, Cambridge (2003)
6. Fang, Y., Chen, Z., Yuan, Z.: Emotion Modeling Based on Artificial Intelligence. Information and Control 35(6), 673–678 (2006) (in Chinese)
7. Zhao, J., Wang, Z., Wang, C.: Research on Emotion Modeling and Emotional Virtual Human. Computer Engineering 33(1), 212–215 (2007) (in Chinese)

Web Applications Based on Ajax Technology and Its Framework

Yuanyuan Liao, Zhenyu Zhang, and Yanqing Yang

Institute of Information Science and Engineering, Xinjiang University,
Shenglistr. 14, 830046, Urumqi, Xinjiang, China

Abstract. Ajax technology, as a kind of Web applications, has become a hot research in recent years. This article introduces the Ajax technology and advantages first of all, and then focuses on the several framework of Ajax. Finally, discusses and gives a simple example of a Web application by using Ajax technologies.

Keywords: Web application, Ajax, jQuery.

With the deepening of Web applications, it is required for the building site have become more sophisticated, emphasizing the site's security, stability, high interactivity, flexibility and so on.

Traditional web application process is as follows: the user fill out a form, and then sends a request to the web server when submitting the form, server receives and processes the form, and then returns a new page.

It wastes a lot of bandwidth, because most the HTML code of two pages is often the same. Because each application requires time depends on the server's response time. This leads to the response of user interface is much slower than the native application.

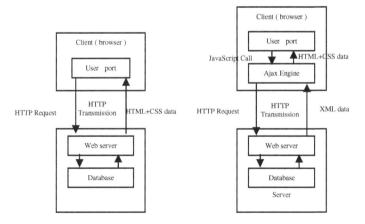

Fig. 1. Contrast traditional Web application model and Ajax model

M. Zhao and J. Sha (Eds.): ICCIP 2012, Part I, CCIS 288, pp. 320–326, 2012.
© Springer-Verlag Berlin Heidelberg 2012

The Ajax technology brings a whole new experience, greatly improved the shortcomings of traditional Web development model, and enhanced and improved service performance. Ajax as the middle layer between client and server, based on the actual situation to interact with the server, update the page without having to reload all the content is only partial update which can achieve the desired results, thereby greatly reducing the interaction time and the amount of data download, and avoiding data redundancy.

1   Ajax Technology Overview and Advantages

In February 2005, JesseJamesGarrett proposed "Ajax" the first time in his article, "Ajax: A new Approach to Web Application". This article describes, the mix use of JavaScript, XHTML/CSS, DOM, XMLHTTP Request, etc. will become a new trend of Web development. Ajax is an abbreviation of asynchronous JavaScript and XML, it refers to a web development technology of creating interactive web applications. [1]

Jesse James Garrett defined Ajax as Ajax is not a technology. In fact, it's a new powerful way to combination of several booming technology which play their respective roles by a common cooperate. [2]

Ajax includes:

(1) XHTML and CSS standard information representation;
(2) Operation DOM (Document Object Model) by using JavaScript for dynamic display and interaction;
(3) The use of XML and XSLT for data interchanges and related operations;
(4) Asynchronous data exchange with the Web server by using the XMLHTTP request object;
(5) Using JavaScript to bind everything together.

We can see through the introduction of Ajax technology, Ajax technology has the following advantages: [3]

(1) Reduce the burden on the server. AJAX engine bear part of the original work undertaken by the server when it is running on the client, thus reducing the server load of large number of users.
(2) Has a partial page refresh function. AJAX techniques can communicate between the page and the server without refreshing the entire page, thus reducing the user wait time.
(3) With asynchronous communication. AJAX techniques have a more rapid response capability, without interrupting the user's operation, thus resulting in a more fluid user experience.
(4) AJAX technology doesn't need to download plug-ins or applets.
(5) With asynchronous data transfer. AJAX technology allows asynchronous data transfer, so data and page show the separation.

2   Ajax Framework

2.1   ASP.NET AJAX

Ajax.NET is to support a variety of ways to access the server NET-free libraries through JavaScript. Its main features are as follows:

(1) Can access the Session and Application in JavaScript;
(2) Cache query results;
(3) Without modifying the source code, allow for the Ajax.NET to add and modify methods and properties;
(4) Can return the data tables, data views, arrays and collections.

In some cases, it is the Contact Volume Editor that checks all the pdfs. In such cases, the authors are not involved in the checking phase.

2.2   Dojo

Dojo is an excellent in all aspects of JavaScript toolbox, including JavaScript own language extensions and a more complete page Component library. Its main features are as follows:

(1) Support a wide range of deployment, and download all the packages at a time;
(2) A rich component library of prefabricated window;
(3) Drag and drop support and general support for animation;
(4) B/S news and other mechanisms to support an XHR support;
(5) Provide frame support of creating self-definition JavaScript window components;
(6) Support bookmarks and URL manipulation of browser;
(7) Database is very comprehensive through long time development, which provides a complete lightweight window components and browser/server message map.

The disadvantage is that files are large, and the first download is slow. In addition, Dojo class library is not so easy to use.

2.3   DWR

DWR[4] is an open source class library, to help developers to construct a website include Ajax technology. JavaScript to use it remotely form the client calls the server-side Java methods to carry out the transaction operations. Main features are:

(1) Can be effective eliminate all Ajax request-response cycled from the application code. Client code can be adjusted Ajax requests to call the Java object, without dealing directly with the XHR object code or server response, even without writing Server;
(2) Can be used with any Web framework such as Struts, Tapestry, etc.

\

2.4   Google AjaxSLT

Google AjaxSLT (established in June 2005) is a JavaScript framework. It is used to perform the AjaxsLT conversion and xPath query. Its main features are as follows;

(1) Founded on the basis of the work of Google Maps (heep://maps.google.com)
(2) Open source, supported by the famous Google Company.

2.5   jQuery

JQuery is the most watched Ajax framework created by JohnResig in early 2006, it is based on Prototype, and to simplify and improve the function of JavaScript syntax. [5] jQuery a bit like an upgraded version of Prototype , allows designers to change the original writing JavaScript method and it has a strong function of the access page elements, whether the file node, CSS or Xpath selection of sub-expressions can be used "$()" to access functions quickly, and give it more functionality.

In addition, its chainable methods can string handling functions together, so that the code more concise. JQuery also offers a number of dynamic effects, compared to other frameworks, this part look lively.

JQuery's strengths and weaknesses are actually on the same thing. On the one hand, it simplifies the syntax of JavaScript, the code easier to write, on the other hand, beginners need to speed more time to understand.

In addition, there are some more popular frameworks. For example: Prototype, Qooxdoo, Flash, JavaScript and so on.

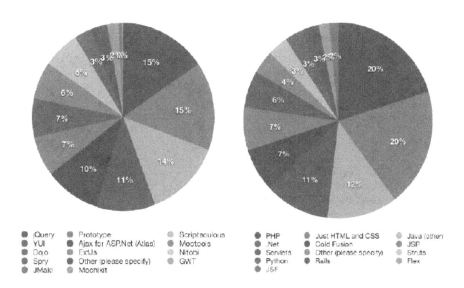

Fig. 2. Usage of popular Ajax framework in 2008(left)and Ajax development platform in 2008(right) [6]

3   Using jQuery and Ajax to Develop Web Application

(1) JQuery is a very useful JavaScript library, without distinction the browser is one of the advantages. Different browsers with AJAX support is not the same, it is usually in the realization of AJAX, the need for different browsers to judge, and then perform the corresponding operations. The jQuery framework help designers reduce the burden without considering the browser, simply use the jQuery function can be achieved.[7] jQuery support browsers, including IE 6.0+, FF1.5+, Safari2.0+, Opear9.0+ and so on.

(2) Code concise, easy to understand the semantics, learning fast, document rich. jQuery is developed against JavaScript' shortcoming which leads to code duplication and reduced readability, while jQuery is a powerful package through a function to simplify the code, with the result that writing code become simplified.

(3) Visit the original site, after three-tier architecture, from the browser to the WEB server, and then to the database, as designed from the three levels, namely the page display, back-end logic and database design. These three areas coupling is very close, if there is a new demand, may be modified the whole site, which will bring great difficulties to maintain the website.

It will be greatly improved if Web site design use the jQuery framework, which can be layered four-level, page design, logic design front, the business logic design and database design, each level is relatively independent.

(4) JQuery support for CSS1-CSS3, and basic xPath. Styles for different versions of the jQuery library support are a major feature, and the resolution achieved by xPath support for XML.

4   Code Example

There is a simple example of Ajax to achieve login.

```
<script               src              ="./js/jquery.js"
type="text/javascript"></script>
<script type = "text/javascript">
$(document).ready(function(){
$("#button_login").mousedown(function(){
login();
});
});
function login(){
Var username = $("#username").val();
Var password = $("#password").val();
$.ajax({
type:"post",
url:"login.php",
dataType:'json',
data:'username='+userame+'&password='+password,
success : function(json){
//alert(json.username+'\n'+json.password);/
$('#result').html("name:"+json.username+"<br/>password
:"+json.password);
}
```

```
    });
    //$.post()way:
    $('#test_post').mousedown(function(){
    $.post(
    'login.php'
    {
    username:$('#username').val(),
    password:$('#password').val()
    },
    function(data)
    {
    var myjson=";
    eval('myjson='+data+';');
    $('#result').html("name1:"+myjson.username
+"<br/>password1:"+ myjson.password);
    }
    );
    });
    //$.get()way:
    $('#test_get').mousedown(function()
    {
    $.get(
    'login.php',
    {
    username:$('#username').val(),
    password:$('#password').val()
    },
    function(data)
    {
    var myjson=";
    eval("myjson="+data+";");
    $('#result').html("name2:"+myjson.username+"<br/>passw
ord2:"+myjson.password);
    }
    );
    });
    }
    </script>
    <body>
    <div  id="result"  style="background:orange;border:1px
solid red;width:300px;height:200px;"></div>">
    <form id="formtest" action="" method="post">
    <p><span>Enter      name:</span><input      type="text"
name="username" id="username" /></p>
    <p><span> Enter  password:</span><input  type="text"
name="password" id="password" /></p>
    </form>
    <button id="button_login">ajax Submit</button>
    <button id="test_post">post Submit </button>
    <button id="test_get">get Submit </button>
```

5   Conclusion

AJAX technology has been gradually swept the web design industry, the new WEB application developers to use almost all the technology and peopleWe will this new generation of WEB pages labeled WEB 2. 0 of theTag. JQuery framework can be very convenient and efficient development of a website,WEB design from the original and three into four, between themRelatively independent, web design clear structure, post-maintenance easier.

References

1. Dino, E., Luo, X.: The discussion JavaScript library-Dojo, jQuery and Prototype comparison. Programmer (8), 105–107 (2008)
2. Ullman, C., Dykes, L., (Xu, L., trans.): Ajax started the classic, vol. (8), pp. 23–27. Tsinghua University Press, Beijing (2008)
3. Yang, G., Zhang, S.: Web application architecture design based on Ajax. Modern Electronic Technology (15), 33–36 (2006)
4. Li, G.: Collection of Ajax based JZEE. Electronic Industry Press, Beijing (2007)
5. Wang, B.-P.: JavaScript framework for rethinking. Programmers (11), 24 (2008)
6. Louxue: The Study and Application of Enterprise WEB Development Technique Based on Ajax (Master thesis). Dalian Jiaotong University, 23 (2009)
7. Liu, W.: Develop WEB application based on Ajax technology and its framework. China Science and Technology Information (1), 69–70 (2009)

Improved Trusted Storage Key Authorization Management Scheme Based on Timestamp

Guang-hui Zhai[1], Juan Li[2], and Cheng Song[3]

[1] School of Computer Science and Technology, Xuchang University,
Xuchang, Henan, 461000, China
xczgh@163.com
[2] School of Computer Science and Technology, Xuchang University,
Xuchang, Henan, 461000, China
zimulj@163.com
[3] College of Computing Science and Technology,
Henan Polytechnic University, Jiaozuo, Henan
songcheng@hpu.edu.cn

Abstract. One of the important functionalities in trusted computing platform is secure storage. Although the technologies about secure storage in trusted computing platform become more sophisticated, and the applications are increasingly popular, the key authorization management mechanism still needs further improvement. Aiming at the key synchronization problem of the key authorization data update in the existing schemes, we propose a timestamp-based trusted storage key management scheme. The proposed scheme can effectively solve the key synchronization problem and disadvantages in the existing schemes, so the trust and security of the trusted storage is further enhanced.

Keywords: Key Synchronization, Trusted Storage, Authorization Dat.

1 Introduction

Along with the network spreading over every corner, the internet and local area network (LAN) is an important part of our lives, but some network security issues are sadly emerged. To overcome the shortcomings and deficiencies in the traditional information security measures to ensure network security, trusted computing technologies have been proposed and widely studies. Over the last decade, in both enterprise and economic field, trusted computing [1] is always a hot topic in the field of information security, which has achieved encouraging results. Especially, the secure storage technology of trusted computing platform has been widely recognized and used.

There are three core functionalities in trusted computing platform. They are secure storage, identity attestation and platform integrity measurement, storage and reporting. The secure storage is a relatively more perfect and mature than the other two functionalities. Confidentiality which is tied to key management is the core

M. Zhao and J. Sha (Eds.): ICCIP 2012, Part I, CCIS 288, pp. 327–333, 2012.

technology of secure storage, so secure storage technology of trusted computing platform comes down to key management technology. Although there have been some improvements in the existing key management schemes about secure storage in trusted computing platform, some of which ignore the key synchronization problem of the key authorization data update and some are infeasible in the implementation. To solve the key synchronization problem and enhance the trust and security of the trusted storage, we propose a timestamp-based trusted storage key management scheme, the basic idea of which is to add timestamp for every key and issue the certificate for every timestamp.

The rest of this paper is organized as follows: In section 2 we introduce the secure storage mechanism for trusted computing platform. Section 3 introduces the existing schemes and analysis their advantages and disadvantages. Section 4 describes the timestamp-based trusted storage key management mechanism which we present. We discuss the security and feasibility of the improved scheme in section 5. Finally future work and conclusions are presented in Section 6.

2   Secure Storage Mechanism for Trusted Computing Platform

2.1   Trusted Computing Platform

The trusted computing Platform Alliance (TCPA) was formed in October 1999 by Compaq, HP, IBM, Intel and Microsoft. In 2003, TCPA was renamed Trusted Computing Group (TCG). Different from the traditional security technology, the trusted computing technology defend all kinds of attacks from a terminal through combining software and hardware. The idea of trusted computing technology is to turn a computing platform into a trusted one, and then improve the security of the terminal system through embedding a secure chip (usually called Trusted Platform Module, TPM) to hardware platform and . TPM is a core technology of TCG. The major components of TPM are shown in Fig.1[2]. In every TPM there are at least 4 concurrent monotonic counters which provide an ever-incremental value. The Value in the counters will not reset when the platform powers off or restarts. Actually TPM is chip which has the functions of crypto operation and storage. The specification about TPM is decided by TCG.

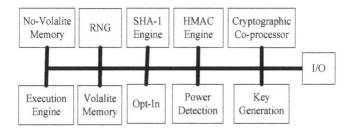

Fig. 1. TPM Component Architecture

A computing platform which contains TPM and matched software (Trusted Software Stack, TSS) [5] is called a Trusted Computing Platform (TCP). They co-realize the functionalities for computing platform, such as secure storage, crypto operation, identity attestation, and platform integrity measurement, storage and reporting. TCP's goal is to ensure the whole platform trust, and then ensure the entire internet trust through establishing root of trust, and then building a chain of trust [6]. For example, in computer platform, BIOS trusts the root of trust(Core Root of Trusted for Measurement, CRTM), then Operating System(OS) trusts BIOS and then the upper application trusts the OS, finally, the whole system is trusted.

2.2   Secure Storage Mechanism for Trusted Computing Platform

In TPM1.1 and TPM1.2 specification [2] the storage hierarchy of key management mechanism is illustrated in fig.2. Because all aspects of consideration, all key are stored out of TPM except for Storage Root Key (SRK) and Endorsement Key (EK). EK is a 2048 bit RSA-based public private key pair which is created randomly on chip at manufacture. SRK is a 2048 bit RSA-based public private key pair which is created whenever a new owner is established. SRK is located at the top level of the hierarchy and is never exported from TPM. The external storage is addressed by using key hierarchy which is described in the Fig2. All objects in the mass-storage device are directly or indirectly protected by the SRK. Whenever a protected object is exported from TPM, its private part (AuthData and PrivKey in the curve shown in Fig.2) is encrypted using the public key of the parent object. These storage keys are used to protect other Keys or data. So these storage keys form the nodes of the protected storage object hierarchy while the protected data and signing keys always are leaves.

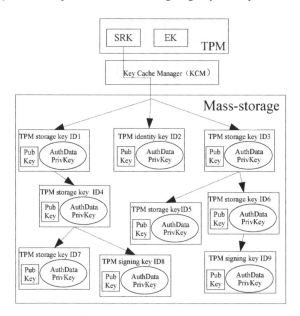

Fig. 2. Protected storage object hierarchy

There is a key management system (Key Cache Management, KCM) between the external storage space and TPM, which is a part of TSS. In the external storage space, every node is a TPM key object (TPM identity key, TPM storage key or TPM sign key). They have all the same data structure that includes the TPM key flag ID, the corresponding public key and the ciphertext block (AuthData and PrivKey) etc. The AuthData is the shared secret between TPM and the owner of the object. In the trusted platform, if a user wants to use an external TPM key object, the object must be loaded into TPM and decrypted by its parent key object beforehand. There is also a core area before using the key. The user must input the matched share secret, or else the user is refused. That is to say, the AuthData is the Access Rights for users to use the corresponding key object.

3   The Existing Schemes and Problems

According to the introduction about TCG key management system in Secure Storage Mechanism for Trusted Computing Platform, we can obviously know that the privacy key and the corresponding authorization data is secret stored in key object node as a whole. Whether the privacy key will be authorized to use depends entirely on whether the external provided value matching the AuthData. Under the circumstance, there is a key synchronization problem. If the owner of a key object is ware of the AuthData insecure and wants to update the AuthData, the corresponding original key node should have been passed into disuse. However, if an attacker can obtain the original key nodes and know the AuthData, he can be authorized to use the key as before. So there is a potential security problem in the TCG key management system.

In Zhang Xing [7] etc. find the key synchronization problem in the TCG key management system. To solve the problem, they presented a new AuthData management scheme. Although the scheme overcomes the key synchronization problem and improves the TCG scheme in a sense, some new problems emerge. In this scheme, firstly, the AuthData list is encrypted with SRK, which is not fit because SRK is based on RSA public key cryptosystem and the efficiency is relatively low. What's more, with the number of key object adding, the list length of AuthData will also increase. Secondly, when a user wants to add a TPM key object or updating a TPM key AuthData, the list of AuthData must be decrypted, reconstructed and re-encrypted in TPM. Thirdly, the big list is also not fit to encryption and decryption in TPM because there is not enough space.

4   Timestamp-Based Trusted Storage Key Management Mechanism

4.1   Key Management Scheme Based on Timestamp

In order to effectively solve the key synchronization problem in TCP key management mechanism and some new problems in [7], we propose a timestamp-based trusted storage key management scheme. The main idea is that a data item (timestamp) is added in the ciphertext block of every TPM key node in the external storage space, and at the same time the system creates a corresponding timestamp certificate for every timestamp.To manage the timestamp certificates systematically, we extend the existing KCM system through adding a timestamp certificate management module. Improved key storage hierarchy is shown in fig.3.

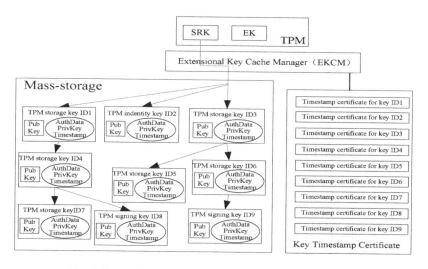

Fig. 3. Protected storage object hierarchy based on timestamp

When a user creates a new TPM key object, the EKCM not only performs all actions as before but also call the command TPM_ReadCounter and obtain the value in monotonic counter. The value acts as the data item (timestamp). Then, the TPM creates a certificate for the timestamp which is signed with TPM Attestation Identity Key (AIK) and then forward the certificate to timestamp certificate management module. When a user wants to update an AuthData for a key object, the user first inputs new AuthData instead of old one, and then the timestamp certificate management module obtains the new value in monotonic counter instead of the old one in the ciphertext block. Then the TPM creates a certificate for the timestamp as before and forward it to the timestamp certificate management module. Finally, the timestamp certificate management module replaces the old certificate for the timestamp with the new one.

4.2   Key Authorization Flows

The trusted key authorization flows based on timestamp are shown in Fig.4.

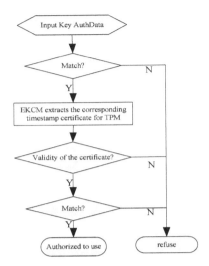

Fig. 4. Trusted key authorization flows based on timestamp

Detailed steps are as follows:

Step1: the user inputs the corresponding key AuthData to TPM.

Step2: after TPM receives the inputted key AuthData, it judges whether the inputted AuthData matches the AuthData in the ciphertext block of the key object node or not. If they are matched, the system executes step3; else, jumps to step6.

Step3: the timestamp certificate management module extracts the corresponding key timestamp certificate according to key identity ID from the list of key Timestamp certificate and forwards it to TPM.

Step4: after TPM receives the corresponding key timestamp certificate, it verifies the validity of the certificate. If it is valid, the system executes step5; else, jumps to step6.

Step5: the user is authorized to use the key object.

Step6: the user is refused to use the key object.

5   Discussion

5.1   Security

When a user wants to use a key object, he first the input the corresponding key AuthData, then the TCP not only attests the inputted AuthData but also verifies whether the key timestamp in the ciphertext block is the latest through the corresponding key timestamp certificate in the list. In our scheme, even if an attacker owns a discarded key object and knows the corresponding key AuthData, he will not be able to be authored to use the key object. The reason is that the old timestamp certificate is discarded and the timestamp certificate management module can't be able to find the matched timestamp certification in the list of key timestamp certificate. Obviously, in our scheme, there is not the key synchronization problem that is mentioned above.

5.2   Feasibility

Our scheme is absolutely feasible in two aspects of hardware and software. Firstly, we don't need to change the hardware (TPM chip) to make it match the scheme because the existing commands can meet the scheme needs completely. Secondly, though the existing TCG Software Stack (TSS) specification vision 1.2[5] doesn't support our scheme, yet slight modification to TSS specification can solve this problem. We simply extend the existing KCM and add a timestamp certificate management module which specially manages the timestamp certificates.

6   Conclusion and Further Work

In this paper we first describe the secure storage mechanism for trusted computing platform and then analysis the existing schemes and problems. Aimed at the problems of the existing schemes, a timestamp-based trusted storage key management scheme is proposed. Our scheme can effectively solve the key synchronization problem and disadvantages in the existing schemes, so the trust and security of the trusted storage is further enhanced. In hardware, we needn't modify the upcoming publishing TPM specification because the existing interfaces of TPM can meet the needs. In software, slight modification to TSS specification can meet the requirements of our scheme. We conclude that our scheme is secure and feasible in theory.

In the future, we plan to establish the platform, extend the KCM, debug and implement our scheme in lab.

References

1. TCG: TCG Specification Architecture Overview. TCG Specification Version 1.2, The Trusted Computing Group (TCG), Portland, Oregon, USA (April 2003)
2. TCG: TPM Main, Part 1: Design Principles. TCG Specification Version 1.2 Revision94, The Trusted Computing Group (TCG), Portland, Oregon, USA (March 2006)
3. TCG: TPM Main, Part 2: TPM Data Structures. TCG Specification Version 1.2 Revision 94, The Trusted Computing Group (TCG), Portland, Oregon, USA (March 2006)
4. TCG: TPM Main, Part 3: Commands. TCG Specification Version 1.2 Revision 94, The Trusted Computing Group (TCG), Portland, Oregon, USA (March 2006)
5. Trusted Computing Group, TCG Software Stack (TSS) Specification, Version 1.2 (January 6, 2006)
6. Boris, B., Liqun, C., Siani, P., David, P., Graeme, P.: Trusted Computing Platforms: TCPA Technology in Context. Prentice-Hall (2003)
7. Zhang, X., Zhang, X., Liu, Y., Shen, C.: A New AuthData Management Scheme. Journal of Wuhan University (Natural Science Edition) 53(5), 518–522 (2007)

Corn Leaf Diseases Diagnostic Techniques Based on Image Recognition

Juan-hua Zhu, Ang Wu[*], and Peng Li

College of Mechanical and Electrical Engineering,
Henan Agricultural University, Zhengzhou 450002, P.R. China
cwuang@163.com

Abstract. Corn leaf diseases are automatically recognized by digital image processing techniques and pattern recognition method. The method is separated into three steps. First, the gray-scale images are gotten from color images which were caught by numeral camera, which is enhanced by histogram equalization method, and the unwanted noise is removed from the image. Secondly, the disease spots were segmented from leaves based on the iterative threshold method and morphological methods. Finally, the shape characteristic parameters of disease spots, such as area, perimeter, rectangularity, circularity and shape complexity, are extracted, which are used to identify and diagnose diseases. The results show that the corn leaf diseases of the 30 images could be well diagnosed with a diagnostic rate of 80%.

Keywords: Corn Leaf, Spots, Diseases Diagnostic, Image Recognition, Feature Extraction.

1 Introduction

Corn is an important food, feed and crops in China. However, in recent years, corn disease increased year by year. In order to ensure a reasonable application of pesticides, agricultural producers must obtain accurate disease information. Therefore, automatic identification system disease corn needs to be established. This study provides an important theoretical basis and technology application in protecting the corn security intelligently, automated monitoring, variable spraying and remote identification of corn diseases.

More and more domestic and foreign experts and scholars have applied computer image processing technology in agriculture [1]. But these studies are few on the diagnosis of crop diseases, and the recognition technology studies for corn diseases are even fewer [2].

2 Image Pre-processing and Segmentation of Corn Diseases

In the process of image generation, transmission or conversion, many factors will result in the image degraded [3]. In order to segment and recognize single disease image accurately, the image re-processing is needed. For different input images, there

---

[*] Corresponding author.

M. Zhao and J. Sha (Eds.): ICCIP 2012, Part I, CCIS 288, pp. 334–341, 2012.
© Springer-Verlag Berlin Heidelberg 2012

are a variety of types pretreatment methods, such as image enhancement and image denoising [4].

In corn diseases recognization system, the acquisition image is often affected by external environment, it is not necessarily well suited to extract and identify corn diseases. So before recognition, the corn diseases image must first be enhanced and denoised to highlight the area of corn diseases.

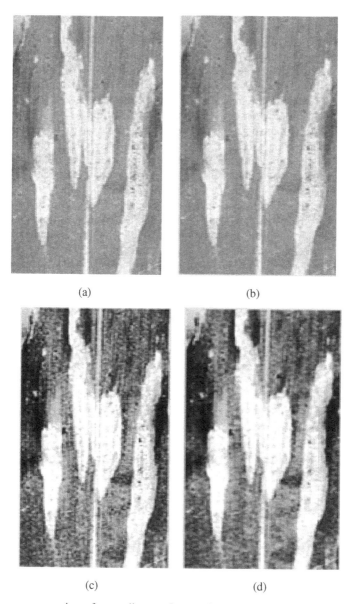

(a)   (b)

(c)   (d)

Fig. 1. The pre-processing of corn diseases Image. (a) original color image; (b) gray-scale image; (c) Equalization image; (d) de-noising image.

2.1   Corn Diseases Image Pre-processing

The corn leafs were collected in the field of Henan Province. In order to better identify the disease part, it was cut out by photoshop software. All the corn diseases images captured were color, which contained a large number of information. In order to improve recognition speed, the color images were converted to grayscale images before processing. In this paper, the pretreatment effect was explained by the example of corn leaf blight image. The color image and the gray-scale images transformed are shown in Figure 1 (a) and (b).

In the corn diseases grayscale image, contrast is the difference in brightness between light and dark. The objects are chiseled in high-contrast corn diseases images. On the contrary, the objects contours are blurred in low-contrast images. If an image is too dark because of light imaging or underexposed, the whole image is too dim, and if the light is too bright or overexposed, the image is too bright. All these reasons will result in low image contrast. This is known as gray excessive concentration.

From the figure 1 (b), the histogram shows the gray-scale distribution ranges from 60 to 240, which is grayscale excessive concentration, so this image should be processed by enhancement method. The main methods of gray-scale image enhancement have gray-scale transformation method. Histogram equalization method can automatically enhance the image and improve the image quality. In this paper, this method was adopted to enhance the corn diseases image and simulated by MATLAB.

The treatment effect is shown in Figure 1 (c). After equalization transform, the distribution of the image pixels is more uniform, and the contrast is enhanced.

In figure 1 (c), the enhanced image contains noise, which is denoised by neighborhood average method. The result is shown in figure 1 (d). It can be seen that the fuzzy texture in the original image becomes more clear, and the whole corn diseases image noise has been optimized.

2.2   The Segmentation of Corn Diseases Image

The denoised image is still grayscale image. In order to better identify, it needs to be split into binary image. Because corn diseases have many types, and the disease onset time and severity are all different, it is difficult to segment the diseases image. By comparison, the iterative threshold segmentation method is adopted. The effect is not very satisfactory by using only a way to split, so in this paper, the binary image after segmentation is optimized by the morphological methods [5].

2.2.1   The Iterative Threshold Segmentation Method

$$u_1 = \frac{\sum_{i=0}^{T_i} i n_i}{\sum_{i=0}^{T_i} n_i} \quad , u_2 = \frac{\sum_{i=T_i}^{L-1} i n_i}{\sum_{i=T_i}^{L-1} n_i} \tag{1}$$

The iterative threshold algorithm is as follows:

(1) Choose an initial threshold value T1 (usually take the middle value).

(2) The image is divided into two parts (G1 and G2) according to the threshold value T1., Calculate respectively the average gray value µ1 and µ2 of G1 and G2.
ni: the number of pixels with the gray-level value i.

(3) Calculate the new threshold value T2 = (µ1 + µ2) / 2.

(4) If | T2-T1 | ≤ T0 (T0 for the pre-specified small positive number), that is, the two adjacent thresholds are close in iterative process, the iteration will be terminated. Otherwise, when T1 = T2, repeat the step of (2) and (3). Finally, the value T2 is the desired threshold.

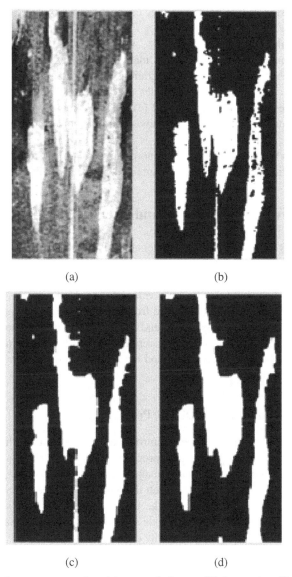

(a)   (b)

(c)   (d)

Fig. 2. gray-scale image segmentation. (a) grayscale image; (b) the results of iterative threshold segmentation algorithm; (c) closing operation; (d) opening operation.

Figure 2 shows the segmentation results of the exserohilum turcicum of corn leaf gray-scale image. Figure 2 (b) is the split turcicum binary image by iterative threshold algorithm.

It can be seen from figure 2 (b), the leaf lesions and healthy parts are separated basically in the binary image created by iterative thresholding segmentation. However, there is little noise in the image, the lesion parts have a small hole inside, and there are some errors split (the edge is not continuous). These can be processed by the opening operation and closing operation of morphological operations for the purpose of denoising, filling holes and edge connections.

2.2.2   Morphological Processing

Opening and closing operations are the main methods of morphology, which are formed by the erosion and dilation operations [6]. By circular structure element closing operation in figure 2 (b), the holes are filled and the disconnected edge is connected. The result is shown in figure 2 (c). Then by linear structural element open computing in figure 2 (c), the noise is removed, and the corresponding result is shown in figure 2 (d).

It can be seen from the figure, after morphological processing, the image noise, holes and discontinuous edge are almost removed.

3   Image Feature Extraction and Recognition

The purpose of corn diseases image segmentation is to extract disease image features of and to determine the classification. In many pattern recognition problems, the shape features are often very important. It describes the geometric properties of the target area, and is irrespective of the gray value of the region.

Therefore, the corn lesion is segmented from the binary image before extracting the shape characteristics of the target area, and the area boundary is shown through the chain code. Then the segment table is converted from the chain code table. Finally the characteristics, such as perimeter, area and etc., are derived according to chain code table and segment table.

3.1   The Chain Code of Corn Disease Profile

In the sixties of last century, Freeman introduced the concept of chain code in the research of image processing. In image processing, the chain code is widely used in the portrayal of the border region and image coding. In the contour tracking, it can represent the position relationship between the adjacent boundary points, can control the order of the neighbor detection in the tracking process, and also can track the direction by the chain code. The chain code can be divided into 4-connectivity and 8-connectivity chain code. The 8-connectivity chain code is adopted.

In the binary image, corn leaf lesion geometry generally presents irregular shape graph, where the lesion shape constitutes a closed curve. Figure 3 shows the extraction process and the chain code representation of the lesion boundary contour.

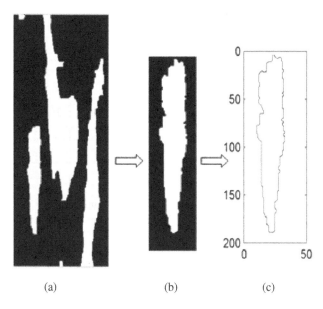

(a)   (b)   (c)

Fig. 3. The chain code of corn leaf lesion. (a)binary image, (b) amplification of lesion site, (c) chain code is that the edge of the lesion.

As the chain code table can not directly distinguish the inside and outside of the region, the pixel within the region can not be processed. To achieve the various parameters calculation of the internal pixel gray value, it needs to the convert chain code table into the segments table. After converting, the characteristic parameters of the lesion can be calculated.

3.2   The Feature Extraction and Recognition of Corn Disease Image

By comparison, there is significant difference between disease area and normal area of corn leaves, which mainly shows in the following aspects: size, color, shape, and etc.. Therefore, the morphological parameters of corn diseases parts, including area, perimeter, rectangularity, circularity, shape complexity, and others, can be seen as the characteristics identifying the disease types.

In this paper, the morphological parameters of corn disease image are calculated by the chain code table and segment table. It needs contour tracking before operation, and then calculating the characteristic values of area, perimeter and shape parameters .

In experiments, 20 standard samples of lesion images were selected to extract the features. Finally, the lesion characteristics are captured by average. Table 1 shows the characteristics parameters of corn leaf diseases image obtained by contour tracking using the chain code.

Table 1. The characteristics parameters of corn leaf diseases image

Disease Category	Area S (pixels)	Perimeter P (pixels)	Circularity C	Rectang ularity R	shape complexity E
blight	2914	413.92	0.21373	0.68484	58.796
round spot	11	9.6569	0.9823	0.8975	8.4777
curvularia leaf spot	205	101.36	0.25077	0.91111	50.112
gray leaf spot	474	110.87	0.48457	0.86182	25.933
small leaf spot	1012	201.5	0.19081	0.50343	55.678

These characteristic parameters are used to identify and diagnose diseases. Table 2 shows the actual number of samples pests and the number of diseases found by identifying.

Table 2. The disease results identified

disease category	The actual number of diseases in samples	the number of diseases found by identifying
blight	20	18
round spot	20	19
curvularia leaf spot	20	16
gray leaf spot	20	17
small leaf spot	20	23

It can be seen from the table, although there is a certain error, most lesions were correctly identified. There are mainly two reasons for the occurrence of the error. The first and foremost reason for the error is that it can not guarantee that the angle, light and distance are exactly the same when taking pictures. Thus, the lesion area and perimeter of different images represent the shortcomings of poor comparability. On the other hand, the difference between different types of lesion is relatively small, and it can not be distinguished with a few simple features. It becomes a focus to study how to extract the large differences between the different characteristics of the lesion in the next step.

4   Conclusion

The automatic recognition technology of corn diseases by digital image processing techniques and pattern recognition methods can identify most corn diseases. It can improve the efficiency of image recognition by converting a color image to a grayscale, and then converting it to a binary image. The morphological method can well improve the image segmentation effectiveness which has been segmented by the iterative thresholding method. The morphological parameters of corn diseases parts, including area, perimeter, rectangularity, circularity, shape complexity, and others, can be calculated according to the chain code table and segment table. It can well recognize variety of corn diseases images with a recognition rate of 80%.

Acknowledgment. This study was financed by scientific research tackling key subject of Henan Province (No. 102102210156, No. 112102110113) and Natural Science Basic Research Subject of Henan Province Education Department (No. 2011B210024).

References

1. Tapas, K., Nathan, S., Angela, Y.: An Efficient k-Means Clustering Algorithm: Analysis and Implementation. IEEE Transactions on Pattern Analysis and Machine Intelligence 24, 4739–4746 (2002)
2. Leuven, K.U.: Automatic detection of 'yellow rust' in wheat using reflectance measurements and neural networks. Computers and Electronics in Agriculture 44, 173–188 (2004)
3. Hojjatoleslami, S.A., Kiltler, J.: Region Growing: A New Approach. IEEE Transactions on Image Processing, 1079–1084 (1998)
4. Fan, J.P., David, K.Y.: Automatic Image Segmentation By Integrating Color-Edge Extraction And Seaded Region Growing. IEEE on Image Processing 10, 1454–1466 (2001)
5. Wu, J., Poehlman, S., Michael, D.N., Markad, V.K.: Texture feature based automated seeded region growing in abdominal MRI segmentation. Biomedical Science and Engineering 2, 1–8 (2009)
6. Mat-Isa, N.A., Mashor, M.Y., Othman, N.H.: Seeded Region Growing Features Extraction Algodthm; Its Potential Use in Improving Screening for Cervical Cancer. International Journal of The Computer, the Interact and Management 13, 61–70 (2005)

Application of Matrix VB in the Test Data Prcessing of Chemiluminescence Analyzer

Ang Wu and Juan-hua Zhu[*]

College of Mechanical and Electrical Engineering, Henan Agricultural University,
Zhengzhou 450002, P.R. China
cwuang@163.com

Abstract. When VB is used to develop the visualization software of chemiluminescence detection system, it needs to process complex data computing and dynamic graphics rendering. Matrix VB function can effectively be integrated into VB. In this paper, the test data of chemiluminescence analyzer is processed by the two ways of VB built-in function and called matrix VB in VB, and the programming effects of the two methods are compared through experiments. Experiments show that it is easier to write the program code by calling matrix VB in VB and the graphics drawn is more reasonable and beautiful. It can effectively solve the problems of complex regression equations fitting and regression curves display to combine the calculation functions of Matrix VB with the graphical interface of VB.

Keywords: Matrix VB, VB, chemiluminescence, data processing.

1   Introduction

In order to facilitate the operation and get better experimental results, the testing equipments developed for industry and agriculture require automation and visualization testing systems. In this study the chemiluminescence analyzer needs real-time and visual display the data collected by the way of graphics for the purpose of observing the test object state. This requires to develop a beautiful and feature-rich test software in PC. VB has unique advantages in user interface design and rapid development, so it is often selected as the development tool of visualization test software. In this article VB is used as the development tool. However VB provides only basic mathematical functions, it is difficult to satisfy the development of fully functional large-scale computing systems. If the special functions math library is written by the basic function library of VB, it not only requires the user has a better understanding of the algorithm, but also can not guarantee the correctness of each function because of the lack of error handling mechanism during the design process[1-2].

Matlab is a powerful mathematical tool and has unique advantages in numerical analysis, scientific computing, algorithm development, modeling and simulation, however its user interface design is not as convenient as VB. Based on the

---

[*] Corresponding author.

M. Zhao and J. Sha (Eds.): ICCIP 2012, Part I, CCIS 288, pp. 342–349, 2012.

characteristics of VB and Matlab, they are used to develop software together. If the math library of Matlab is called by VB, the development cycle can be shortened and the applications from VB and Matlab software can be developed. Matrix VB, as a Matlab function library, can be called easily in VB. The programming method of calling Matrix VB in VB can greatly reduce the difficulty, and draw graphics more easily[3-5]. In this paper, by the test data prcessing of chemiluminescence analyzer, the programming effects of the two methods are compared. The results show that the programming has more advantages by calling Matrix VB in VB in the detection field of complex data operations and display real-time curve.

2   Matrix VB Introduction

Matrix VB is a matrix mathematical functions COM (Commponet Object Model) library for Visual Basic developed by the Mathworks. It provides more than 600 MATLAB functions, which can be mainly divided into 8 categories: matrix operations, operator overloading, graphics, image processing, optimization, operations, polynomials, signal processing, stochastic and statistical analysis and control system. The matrix operations can be carried out by these functions in the Visual Basic environment. In signal processing, numerical computation and graphics display, the use of Matrix VB not only can enhance the functionality of VB programming, but also can reduce the programming complexity, facilitate the engineering debug and improve system reliability.

3   The Data Processing Method of Chemiluminescence Analyzer

Chemiluminescence analyzer detects solution concentration by the chemiluminescence method. Chemiluminescence is a method to determine the material content according to the total luminous intensity generated by chemical reactions. Chemiluminescence analysis method has the advantages of high sensitivity, wide linear range and accuracy. Chemiluminescence analyzer not only can detect the heavy metal residues in vegetables and fruits, but also can detect a number of indexs in water samples.

3.1   Measurement Principle

The solution concentration can be calculated according to the known concentration and the solution luminescence. The process is divided into the following steps. First, the corresponding luminescence value of the standard solution is measured. Usually it includes 3 ~5 groups test data in different concentrations and 1~10 parallel luminescence value in each group. Q-test is used to process the parallel data. The data that deviate from the mean value far in a set is rejected. The average of the remaining data in parallel is as the luminescence value of this concentration. The regression equation of Y = a0 + a1X, fitted by least-squares, expresses the corresponding relationship between the solution concentration and luminescence value. If there is a blank solution luminescence, you need calculate sample concentration after subtracting the corresponding value of the blank solution. Assuming that the luminescence values of sample, blank and standard solution are respectively S_{sa}、S_b、S_{st}, sample concentration is set to C_{sa}, and ample solution be diluted n fold. then the sample concentration conversion formula is:

$$C_{sa} = (S_{sa} - S_b) \div (S_{st} - S_b) \times C_{sa} \times n \qquad (1)$$

3.2   Least-Squares Regression Equation

As there is a linear relationship, $Y = a_0 + a_1 X_1 + \cdots + a_n X_n$, between the solution concentration and luminescence values, which is fitted according to a known solution concentration. In this paper, the regression equation is fitted by the least-squares.

The linear regression equation of $Y = a_0 + a_1 X$ is fitted according to these discrete set of values. The coefficients a_0 and a_1 are calculated by following equation:

$$
\begin{cases}
a_0 = \dfrac{\sum\limits_{i=1}^{n} y_i - a_1 \sum\limits_{i=1}^{n} x_i}{n} \\[4mm]
a_1 = \dfrac{n\sum\limits_{i=1}^{n} x_i y_i - \sum\limits_{i=1}^{n} x_i \sum\limits_{i=1}^{n} y_i}{n\sum\limits_{i=1}^{n} x_i^2 - (\sum\limits_{i=1}^{n} x_i)^2}
\end{cases}
\qquad (2)
$$

x_i is the concentration value of the standard sample, and y_i is the luminescence value of it.

The correlation coefficient r tests the curve fitting results. The closer it is to 1, the better the fitting results. The correlation coefficient can be calculated with the following formula.

$$r = \frac{\sum XY - \dfrac{\sum X \sum Y}{N}}{\sqrt{\left(\sum X^2 - \dfrac{(\sum X)^2}{N} \times \sum Y^2 - \dfrac{(\sum Y)^2}{N}\right)}} \qquad (3)$$

Because of the huge amount of data, it is very difficult to calculate the coefficient a0, a1, and r by VB built-in function programming. And due to the magnitude difference in the number of levels, to display the regression curve has to resize the coordinate scale based on the test value, which increases the programming difficulty. In this paper, this part is implemented by the two ways of VB built-in function and called matrix VB in VB, and the pros and cons of both methods are compared.

4   The Curve Fitting of Built-In VB Functions and Matrix VB

4.1   The Curve Fitting of VB Built-In Functions

Since there is not the function of solving regression equation coefficients in VB, when the curve is fitted with built-in VB functions, it first need calculate gradually the mean and variance of x and y according to equation (1), and then find the coefficients a0 and a1. Similarly, the correlation coefficient r of the curve fitting is also calculated the gradual based on equation (2). When it shows curves and related information, the setting of coordinates, scale, etc. is realized by programming according to the test data.

The main code of calculating a0, a1 and r is provided below. The X, Y values were:

X: 0.03, 0.09, 0.15, 0.21, 0.3,   Y: 1.02E4, 2.18E6, 7.18E6, 1.19E7, 1.60E7, 2.31E7。

(1) Calculate the regression equation and correlation coefficient r

```
'''''''''' The main code of regression equation '''''''
Public Function curve-fitting ()
.........
' Read the values of concentration and luminescence,
' the concentration value stores in X (i, 0),
' the luminescence value stores in Y (i, 0)
 ReDim u(5, geshu)
    For i = 1 To geshu
        u(1, i) = X(i - 1, 0)          '
        u(2, i) = Y(i - 1, 0)
        u(3, i) = u(1, i) * u(2, i)
        u(4, i) = u(1, i) ^ 2
        u(5, i) = u(2, i) ^ 2
        u(1, 0) = u(1, 0) + u(1, i)
        u(2, 0) = u(2, 0) + u(2, i)
        u(3, 0) = u(3, 0) + u(3, i)
        u(4, 0) = u(4, 0) + u(4, i)
        u(5, 0) = u(5, 0) + u(5, i)
    Next i
    u(1, 0) = u(1, 0) / geshu
    u(2, 0) = u(2, 0) / geshu
a0 = u(2, 0) - a * u(1, 0)
a1= (u(3, 0) - geshu * u(1, 0) * u(2, 0)) / (u(4, 0) -
geshu * u(1, 0) ^ 2)
    If a0 >= 0 Then
        v = "Y = " & a1 & "X" & " + " & a0 'Regression
curve: Y=a1X+a0
        Else: v = "Y = " & a1 & "X" & a0
```

```
     End If
   '''''calculate the correlation coefficient r '''''
fenzi = (u(3, 0) - geshu * u(2, 0) * u(1, 0)) 'molecular
'The square of the denominator
   fenmu = Sqr((u(4, 0) - u(1, 0) ^ 2 * geshu) * (u(5,
0) - u(2, 0) ^ 2 * geshu))
   If fenmu <> 0 Then
     r = fenzi / fenmu
   Else: r = 0
   End If
End Function
```

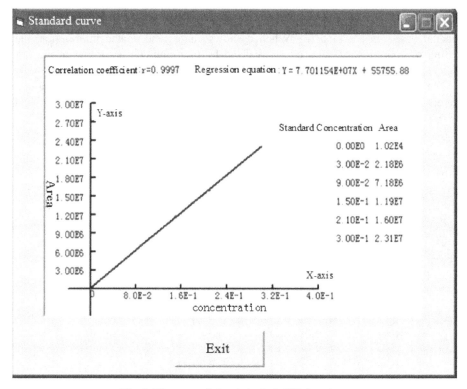

Fig. 1. The curve fitting in built-in VB functions

(2) The regression curve display the regression curve is displayed as follows.

1)Draw axes;
2)select coordinate scale according to the concentration and luminescence values
3)draw the regression curve and trace point.
4) display the concentration value and area value in the upper right corner.
5) show the regression curve and correlation coefficient

The regression curve fitted by VB 6.0 function is shown in figure 1. The figure shows the fitted regression curve, five discrete points and related information.

It can be seen from the figure that the selected maximum coordinate of horizontal axis is 4.0E-1, and the selected maximum coordinates of longitudinal axis is 3.00E7. The coordinate scale selection is reasonable, but the programming is complex. Because the discrete points are the same width as the regression curve, when the discrete points locate on or near the curve, they can't be distinguished.

4.2   The Curve Fitting in Matrix VB

MATLAB also has a large number of matrix functions, including curve fitting function and rich graphics functions (two-dimensional graphics, three-dimensional graphics, custom graphics, color capabilities, imaging, user interface dialogue, Handle Graphics functions, etc.). They can fit the curve and display the results real timely and visually.

The code of the curve fitting and display part using Matrix VB is as follows:

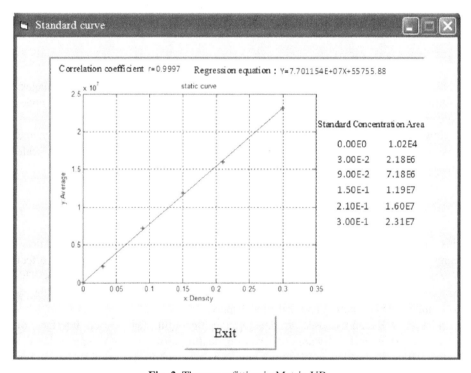

Fig. 2. The curve fitting in Matrix VB

```
.........
'Read the concentration value of X and luminescence value
Y
.........
  ' calculate the regression equation coefficients p
  p = polyfit(X, Y, 1)
```

```
a1 = p.r1(1)
a0= p.r1(2)
yfit = polyval(p, X)            ' yfit : regression curve
'show regression curve in picture1
ax = vbaxes(project 1.frmStatic.Picture1.hWnd)
' draw points and regression curve
Call Plot(X, Y, "r*", X, yfit, "b-")
xlabel ("x:Density ")
ylabel ("y:Average")
Title ("static curve")
r=corrcoef(Y, yfit)..............'r: correlation coefficient
```

The regression curve fitted with Matrix VB is shows shown in Figure 2. The figure shows the same information in Figure 1. It can be seen from the figure that the coordinates scale generated automatically is very reasonable and the discrete points and the curve were distinguished very clearly. The programming is simple, easy to implement.

4.3   Experiment Results

As can be seen from the above, VB library approach has the following disadvantages: starting from the most basic computing, computational complexity, lengthy code, more error-prone and discrete point display not clear.

However the Matrix VB method is easy to implement curve fitting and display, and it is simple to write the program code. Its graphics Display and coordinate scale adjusts automatically with the measurement values.

5   Conclusion

This paper discusses the method of using Matrix VB and least squares to fit and draw regression curve in the field of chemiluminescence detection. The programming effect of VB function library and Matrix VB methods is compared through examples. The experiments show that the Matrix VB method is superior to the method of VB library in complex data computing and real-time display.

In short, VB can be used to develop the Beautiful, feature-rich interface of detection system test software, however in dealing with complex data using the Matrix VB method called in VB, it not only can draw and display graphics easily, but also can shorten the length of the code and improve the efficiency of programming. More importantly, the system does not rely on the MATLAB environment to run.

Acknowledgements. This study was financed by scientific research tackling key subject of Henan Province (No. 102102210156, No. 112102110113) and Natural Science Basic Research Subject of Henan Province Education Department (No. 2011B210024).

References

1. Hu, Z.W., Deng, T.U., Yu, Z.L., Chen, L.Y.: The Integration between VB Applications and MATLAB. Computer Engineering and Applications 39, 104–106 (2003)
2. Kang, J.L., Wu, Z.Q.: Methods of data fitting and graph drawing in Visual Basic. Computers and Applied Chemistry 26, 763–766 (2009)
3. Eimeligoda, T., Henkel, H.: The spacing calculator software-A Visual Basic program to calculate spatial properties of linealnents. Computers and Geosciences 32, 542–553 (2006)
4. Chell, C., Ramaswamy, H.: Visual Basics computer simulation package for thermal process calculations. Chemical Engineering and Processing 46, 603–613 (2007)
5. Posavec, K., Bacani, A., Nakic, Z.: A Visual Basic spread-sheet macro for recession curve analysis. Ground Water 44, 764–767 (2006)

Research on Quantitative Recognition for Composite Plate Bonding Flaw Based on Feature Weighting SVM

Ze Zhang, Xiu-fei Wang, Hai-tao Wang, and Yong-xin Liu

College of Electronic Information and Engineering, Inner Mongolia University
Inner Mongolia, China
{Zhangzeimu,wanghaitaozy}@163.com, wangxiufeifreefly@yahoo.cn,
Y. X. Liu@126.com

Abstract. In consideration of the problem that different features have different contributions to recognition results in pattern recognition for composite plates bonding flaws, this paper proposes feature weighting SVM algorithm based on information gain. The algorithm firstly calculates the contributions of all features to recognition results by means of information gain, then weights kernel function in recognition and decision making via the results combining with Support Vector Machines in order to emphasize the roles of important features in the process of recognition and eliminate or alleviate the influence of wake-relevant and irrelevant features on recognition results. Both theory analysis and experience show that this algorithm can be used to recognize bonding flaw of composite plate accurately and quantitatively.

Keywords: Quantitative Recognition, Information Gain, Feature Weighting, SVM.

1 Introduction

Bonding flaws in interface of composite plates threat significantly the stability and security of aerospace equipment, so it is urgent for people to find bonding flaws of composite materials and recognize them accurately. Many researches on ultrasonic testing do exist, but most of them are focused on qualitative recognition and evaluation, research on quantitative recognition is still in primitive stage. Quantitative recognition is detecting degree of de-bonding; it is a new and meaningful researching field. Ref [1] employs neural network and combines with time-frequency analysis to identify bonding flaws of composite plates. In consideration of the fuzziness of features in ultrasonic echo, Ref [2] and Ref [3] combine inferential capability of fuzzy theory with self-learning ability of neural network, resolving those plausible and fuzzy problems existing in bonding flaws testing to some extent. All the researches above are founded on the basis of recognition method and importance of sample, but the influence of feature importance on recognition results is not taken into consideration. These researches assume that the contribution of feature of each dimension in unclassified samples to

M. Zhao and J. Sha (Eds.): ICCIP 2012, Part I, CCIS 288, pp. 350–358, 2012.

classification is even, without considering the face that influence of each feature is different from each other. Moreover, there are some problems of over-learning and poor-generalization when artificial neural network is used to identify a small sample event [4]. However, in quantitative recognition for bonding flaws, contribution of feature to recognition results is different from each other.

In view of the analysis above, this paper proposes a method named feature weighting support vector machine (FWSVM) based on information gain. FWSVM firstly estimates the importance degree of each feature on classification using information gain and sets the corresponding weight according to this importance degree, imposing bigger weights on strong-relevant features than those on weak-relevant ones, then weights kernel function in process of quantitative recognition and decision making by means of the obtained results combining with Support Vector Machines in order to emphasize the roles of important features in quantitative recognition and eliminate or alleviate the influence of wake-relevant and irrelevant features on recognition results.

2   Support Vector Machine

Support Vector Machine (SVM) is not only a new kind of learning algorithm based on Statistical Learning Theory (STL) but also a new technique of data-mining used in classification and regression. According to information of the limited samples, SVM finds the optimal compromise between complexity of model and capacity of learning in order to obtain better generalization.

In terms of the classification which is linearly separable, assume training set is Equation (1),

$$\{(x_1, y_1), \cdots, (x_l, y_l)\}, x_i \in R^n, y_i \in \{1, -1\}, i = 1, \cdots, l \tag{1}$$

SVM selects the optimal hyper-plane according to the maximal distance. Normalize the equation of classifying line $(w \bullet x_i) + b = 0$ and then make the linearly-separable sample set (Equation (1)) satisfy Equation (2).

$$y_i[(w \cdot x_i) + b] \geq 1, i = 1, \cdots, l \tag{2}$$

So it is equivalent to solving the quadratic programming problem shown as follow Equation (3),

$$\min_{w,b} \quad \frac{1}{2} \|w\|^2 \tag{3}$$
$$s.t. \quad y_i[(w \cdot x_i) + b] \geq 1, i = 1, \cdots, l$$

Equation (3) has the only one minimum and its dual problem (Equation (4)) can be solved by means of Lagrange multiplier.

$$\min_{\alpha} \frac{1}{2} \sum_{i=1}^{l} \sum_{j=1}^{l} y_i y_j a_i a_j (x_i, x_j) - \sum_{j=1}^{l} \alpha_j$$

$$s.t. \quad \sum_{i=1}^{l} y_i \alpha_i = 0 \tag{4}$$

$$\alpha_i \geq 0, i = 1, \cdots, l$$

Equation (4) is a problem of quadratic function constrained by inequality. According to the optimal condition-Karush-Kühn-Tucker (KKT) condition, this optimization problem must satisfy Equation (5).

$$\alpha_i (y_i ((w \cdot x_i) + b) - 1) = 0, i = 1, \cdots, l. \tag{5}$$

The optimal decision function (Equation (6)) can be obtained via the dual problem (Equation (4))

$$f(x) = \text{sgn}(\sum_{i=1}^{l} \alpha_i y_i (x \cdot x_i) + b) \tag{6}$$

In terms of the classification which is non-linearly separable, data should firstly be mapped into a high-dimensional feature space by non-linear mapping, and then linear division is carried out in the high-dimensional space. In order to avoid complicated calculations in the high-dimensional space, inner product calculations ($\Phi(x) \cdot \Phi(x')$) in high-dimensional space is replaced by kernel function $K(x, x')$. In addition, slack variable is introduced to solve this problem that some samples may not be classified correctly by hyper-plane. And then dual problem is transformed into Equation (7).

$$\min_{\alpha} \frac{1}{2} \sum_{i=1}^{l} \sum_{j=1}^{l} y_i y_j a_i a_j K(x_i, x_j) - \sum_{j=1}^{l} \alpha_j$$

$$s.t. \quad \sum_{i=1}^{l} y_i \alpha_i = 0 \tag{7}$$

$$0 \leq \alpha_i \leq C, i = 1, \cdots, l$$

The optimal decision function (Equation (8)) is available after solving this dual problem.

$$f(x) = \text{sgn}(\sum_{i=1}^{l} \alpha_i y_i K(x \cdot x_i) + b) \tag{8}$$

Where, $b = y_j - \sum y_i \alpha_i K(x_i, x_j)$. Discrimination function (8) is called Support Vector Machine.

3   Feature Weighting

In quantitative recognition for composite plates bonding flaws, the accuracy of recognition results for each feature is different from each other. Furthermore, it can be found that correlation degree between each characteristic and category is different from each other when using contingency table to analyze each feature. This is to say, various characteristics have different contributions to recognition results. Those uncorrelated features should be excluded by means of feature selection.

Feature weighting is to impose a specific weight on each intensive feature according to some criterion. Methods of feature weighting can be divided into two categories: strategies for features are independent and those for features are interrelated. The former, which affect independently categorical properties, include information gain, gain ratio, symmetric uncertainty, χ^2 verification and Gini indicator. The latter, which have dependently effect that occurs in the context of other features, contain Relief-F algorithm et al.

3.1   Information Gain

Suppose that there is a problem of K categories and the feature A has m different values. Let C_i ($i=1, 2,..., K$) and a_i ($i=1, 2,..., m$) represent respectively categories and feature values; N_{ij} is the number of the samples belonging to C_i and having value of a_j; $n_{j.}$ is the number of the samples belonging to C_i; $n_{.j}$ is the number of the samples having value of a_j; $n_{..}$ is the number of the whole samples.

$$n_{i.} = \sum_{j=1}^{m} n_{ij}; n_{.j} = \sum_{i=1}^{k} n_{ij}; n_{..} = \sum_{i=1}^{k}\sum_{j=1}^{m} n_{ij} = N \tag{9}$$

Define the following probability shown as Equation (10).

$$p_{ij} = \frac{n_{ij}}{n_{..}}; p_{i.} = \frac{n_{i.}}{n_{..}}; p_{.j} = \frac{n_{.j}}{n_{..}} \tag{10}$$

If target property have l different values, entropy of samples set S with respect to the l status is shown as Equation (11).

$$Entropy(S) = \sum_{i=1}^{l} -p_i \log_2 p_i \tag{11}$$

Where, P_i is the percentage of category i accounting for S. Entropy describes the purity of a random sample set and is a kind of measure standard widely used in information theory. It can be used to define information contained in categories and features; the weighted sum of the information (all values of feature A corresponding to K categories) is defined as Equation (12).

$$H_c = -\sum_{i=1}^{k} p_{i.} \log_2 p_{i.}; H_A = -\sum_{i=1}^{m} p_{.j} \log_2 p_{.j}; H_{C/A} = -\sum_{j=1}^{m} p_{.j} \sum_{i=1}^{k} p_{ij} \log_2 p_{ij} \qquad (12)$$

Now, use these expressions to measure the importance of features based on information gain. Information gain of A is defined as Equation (13):

$$H_{IG} = (H_C - H_{C/A}) / H_A \qquad (13)$$

H_C shows entropy of sample set S with respect to K categories, $H_{C/A}$ shows the weighted sum of the entropy. Information gain is the standard of measuring ability of classification. Information gain of feature A indicates the reduction of expected entropy because of being aware of the value of feature A. In other words, because of the given value of feature A, the information of objective function will be obtained. The bigger the value of information gain is, the more important the feature is, and the bigger the weighted value is.

Three features referred in this paper include energy torque of three different frequency bands; these three features are represented to be A_1, A_2 and A_3, respectively.

$$H_{IGA1} = (H_C - H_{C/A1}) / H_{A1}; H_{IGA2} = (H_C - H_{C/A2}) / H_{A1}; H_{IGA3} = (H_C - H_{C/A3}) / H_{A3} \qquad (14)$$

Vector $H_{IG}= [H_{IGA1}, H_{IGA2}, H_{IGA3}]$ describes weighted value of these three features, where, H_{IGA1}, H_{IGA2} and H_{IGA3} represent the gain value of A_1, A_2 and A_3, respectively.

3.2   Construction of Feature Weighting SVM

Quantitative recognition for composite plates bonding flaws can be viewed as a classifying problem which is linear-separable. So kernel function must be introduced. Support Vector Machine based on feature weighting kernel function is called feature weighting Support Vector Machine.

Concept of feature weighting kernel function is shown as follows:

Definition 1. Define K is kernel function of $X \times X$ ($X \in R^d$), P is a d-order linear transformation matrix of the definite space, and d is dimension of input space. Feature weighting kernel function K_P is defined as Equation (15).

$$K_p(x_i, x_j) = K(Px_i, Px_j) \qquad (15)$$

Linear transformation matrix P is also called feature weighting matrix, then the following feature weighting kernel function is obtained.

1. Feature weighting Polynomial kernel function:

$$K_p(x_i, x_j) = (Px_i, Px_j + 1)^d = (x_i^T PP^T x_j + 1)^d, d = 1, 2, \cdots \qquad (16)$$

2. Feature weighting Gaussian kernel function:

$$K_P(x_i, x_j) = \exp(-\frac{\left\| Px_i - Px_j \right\|^2}{\sigma^2}) = \exp(-\frac{1}{\sigma^2}((x_i - x_j)^T PP^T (x_i - x_j))) \qquad (17)$$

3. Feature weighting Sigmoid kernel function:

$$K_P(x_i, x_j) = \tanh(b(Px_i \cdot Px_j) + c) = \tanh(b(x_i^T PP^T x_j) + c), b > 0, c > 0 \qquad (18)$$

Feature weighting kernel function is replaced with kernel function $K(x_i, x_j)$ in dual problem (7), then resolve the new dual problem and the optimal decision function Equation (19) is obtained.

$$f(x) = \text{sgn}(\sum_{i=1}^{l} \alpha_i y_i K(Px \cdot Px_i) + b) \qquad (19)$$

Where, $b = y_j - \sum y_i \alpha_i K(Px_i, Px_j)$ and the Lagrange multiplier α_j corresponding to the point (x_j, y_j) satisfies $0 < \alpha_j < C$.

4   Experiment of Quantitative Recognition

Each echo signal of de-bonding level collected by ultrasonic testing system was decomposed by wavelet pack, then energy-torque of three frequency bands are selected as features to recognize interface bonding flaws of composite plates. Take four de-bonding levels (0%, 40%, 60% and 80%) for examples, select random 59 samples and separate those into two parts, the first 29 samples are viewed as training samples and others as samples to be recognized. Bonding flaws testing is seemed as a classification containing 29 training samples and adopts M-SVM classification of DTSVM. Kernel function is selected to be Gaussian kernel function. Training samples are normalized which are shown in Table 1 (partial data is listed here).

Table 1. Training samples

A_1	0.2873	0.2919	0.0469	0.2465	0.7191	0.8559
A_2	0.7959	0.7771	0.5193	0.9258	0.2957	0.0000
A_3	0.5866	0.5923	0.0614	0.0494	0.6280	0.3306
De-bonding Level	0%	0%	40%	40%	60%	60%

Discrete original data with the step of 0.1 and contingency tables of the 3 features are obtained, which are shown as Table 2, Table 3 and Table 4, respectively. From these 3 contingency tables, it is found that the importance degree of A_1 is high. Use information gain to calculate the weight value of each feature and weight value vector. We will get $\beta = (H_{IGA1}, H_{IGA2}, H_{IGA3})^T = (0.4, 0.3, 0.3)^T$.

From Fig. 1 and Fig. 2, we can see that the relative distance is larger after feature weighting, and generalization ability of SVM is enhanced.

Define punishment parameter C=Inf, Table 5 shows the comparative experimental results under parameters of different kernel functions. It is found that average test accuracy of FWSVM is higher than that of SVM and the total number of support vectors is less. The reason is that FWSVM uses feature weighting to alleviate the influence of feature whose correlation is weak so that generalization capability of the algorithm is improved.

Table 2. Contingency table of feature A_1

Value \ Level	[0.0,0.1]	[0.1,0.2]	[0.2,0.3]	...	[0.7,0.8]	[0.8,0.9]	[0.9,1.0]
0%	0	0	2	...	0	0	0
40%	0	0	0	...	4	0	2
60%	0	0	0	...	0	0	0
80%	5	5	0	...	0	0	0

Table 3. Contingency table of feature A_2

Value \ Level	[0.0,0.1]	[0.1,0.2]	[0.2,0.3]	...	[0.7,0.8]	[0.8,0.9]	[0.9,1.0]
0%	2	1	1	...	0	0	0
40%	0	0	0	...	1	4	1
60%	6	2	0	...	0	0	0
80%	0	0	0	...	6	1	3

Table 4. Contingency table of feature A_3

Value \ Level	[0.0,0.1]	[0.1,0.2]	[0.2,0.3]	...	[0.7,0.8]	[0.8,0.9]	[0.9,1.0]
0%	0	0	0	...	2	1	1
40%	3	0	3	...	0	0	0
60%	0	0	0	...	0	0	0
80%	0	0	0	...	0	0	0

Table 5. Experimental results under different parameters

	SVM		FWSVM	
Kernel parameter P	Test accuracy	Total number of support vector	Test accuracy	Total number of support vector
0.1	100%	50	100%	28
1	95%	8	100%	9
10	90%	12	95%	8
50	95%	43	95%	19
100	95%	59	95%	37

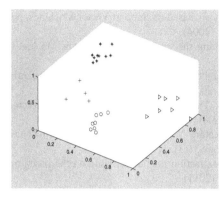

Fig. 1. Original training samples

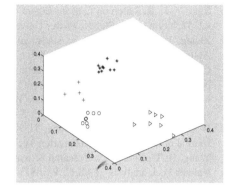

Fig. 2. Weighted training samples

5   Conclusion

This paper proposes a recognition algorithm called feature weighting SVM (FWSVM) based on current achievement in pattern recognition for bonding flaws in composite plates and discusses the construction and properties of non-linear feature weighting kernel function. The relative distance between two samples at different de-bonding level is enlarged by means of feature weighting; the contribution of strong-relevant features to recognition is enhanced, but it is alleviated for-relevant ones. Both theoretical analysis and experience show that this algorithm improves the generalization of classification obviously and it can be used to recognize bonding flaws of composite plates accurately and quantitatively.

Acknowledgements. This work is supported by National Natural Science Foundation of China under Grant No. 60862004.

References

1. Zhao, Y.-G., Zhang, Z.: Study of ultrasonic detection for bonding flaws of thin plate based on time-frequency analysis and artificial neural network, pp. 27–33. Inner Mongolia University (2008)
2. Xu, Y.-H., Zhang, Z.: Study on the fuzzy neural network pattern recognition method for ultrasonic detection on bonding detect of thin composite materials, pp. 26–36. Inner Mongolia University (2009)
3. Wang, Z.-J., Zhou, R.-J.: Application of improved FCM clustering algorithm in felting quality ultrasonic detection of composite material. In: Proceedings of the 29th Chinese Control Conference, pp. 2953–2956 (2010)
4. Zhu, L.-Y., Cao, C.-X.: The recognition of flaws based on Support Vector Machine. Journal of ChongQing University 25(6), 42–45 (2002)
5. Du, S.-X., Wu, T.-J.: Support vector machines for pattern recognition. Journal of ZheJiang University 37(5), 521–526 (2003)

6. Zhai, Y.-J.: Research on fault intelligent diagnosis based on Support Vector Machines, pp. 42–57. North China Electric Power University (2004)
7. Zhang, X.-G.: Introduction to statistical learning theory and Support Vector Machines. Automatica Sinica 26(1), 33–41 (2000)
8. Chen, Z.-Z., Li, L., Yao, Z.-G.: Feature weighting KNN based on SVM. Scientiarum Naturalium Universitatis Sunyatseni 44(1), 17–20 (2005)
9. Lin, Y.-M., Lu, Z.-Y., Zhao, S., Zhu, W.-D.: The study of feature weighting for vector space model. Journal of Information 3, 5–7 (2008)
10. Wang, T.-H., Tian, S.-F., Huang, H.-K.: Feature Weighted Support Vector Machine. Journal of Electronics & Information Technology 31(3), 514–517 (2009)
11. Wang, H.-T., Zhang, Z.: Research of feature extraction for flaw ultrasonic echo based on wavelet Pack analysis. ICMLC, V2-68–V2-72 (2011)
12. Trafalis, T.B., Oladunni, O., Papavassiliou, D.V.: Two-Phase Flow Regime Identification with a Multi-classification on Support Vector Machine (SVM) Model. Ind. Eng. Chem. Res. 44, 4414–4426 (2005)

General Local Routing on Complex Networks

Dan Wang and Zhen Li

Key Laboratory of Manufacturing Industrial Integrated Automation, Shenyang University,
110044 Shenyang, China
wangdan0307@126.com, lizhen414@yeah.net

Abstract. Motivated by the problem of traffic congestion in large communication networks, three kinds of general local routing strategies are proposed respectively based on local topological, dynamic information and the estimated waiting time for enhancing the efficiency of traffic delivery on scale-free networks. The three strategies are governed separately by a single parameter. Simulations show that the maximal network capacity corresponds to an optimal controlled parameter. Moreover, a simulation is performed in a model of scale-free network with different clustering coefficient, and the results revealed that the more clustered network, the less efficient the packet delivery process.

Keywords: routing strategy, scale-free network, traffic.

1 Introduction

Nowadays we increasingly depend on large networks, such as communication, transportation, the Internet, and power systems. Thus, ensuring free traffic flow on these networks is of significant importance in modern society. To this end, a suite of protocols for the dissemination of information from a given source to thousands of users has been developed in the last several years [1-6]. However, both the physical network and the numbers of users are growing continuously. The scalability of current protocols and their performance for larger system sizes and heavier loads on the network are critical issues to be addressed in order to guarantee networks' functioning in the near future. From this perspective, one of the fundamental problems we face nowadays is to find optimal strategies for packet delivery between a given sending node and its destination host.

The ultimate goal of studying these large communication networks is to control the increasing traffic congestion and improve the efficiency of information transportation. It has been recently shown that the real architecture of communication networks determines many of their properties in front of dynamical processes such as the resilience to random failures and attacks and the spreading of virus and rumors [7–11]. The latter has been achieved in recent years by unraveling the complex patterns of interconnections that characterize seemingly diverse systems. It turns out that most real networks can be described by growing models in which the number of nodes forming the network increases with time and that the probability that a given node has k connections to other nodes follows a power law. Therefore, the above analysis

M. Zhao and J. Sha (Eds.): ICCIP 2012, Part I, CCIS 288, pp. 359–367, 2012.

shows that it is necessary to develop better routing strategies [12-17] or structure the real network architecture [18].

Recent works have proposed some models to mimic the traffic routing on complex networks. In these models, information packets are forwarded following the random walking [19], the shortest path [20], the traffic awareness routing strategy [13-15] the local information [16], the efficient path information [17]. In this paper, we study the influence of the local static information, dynamic information and the estimated waiting time of the scale-free network on the efficiency of traffic delivery processes. The efficiency of the packet-delivery process is defined in two ways: one is the critical value R_c of an order parameter H which is zero in the uncongested phase and different of zero when congestion is present.

2   Scale-Free Networks with Tunable Clustering

In order to discuss how the local topological properties influence the efficiency of a given routing protocol, we use the network studied in Ref. [21]. In this model, an additional step-Triangle formation is added to the Barabási-Albert (BA) algorithm [1].This network shows the same global properties, such as degree distribution and the average shortest path of the BA network. However, the clustering coefficient differs from the original BA network.

We construct the scale-free networks with tunable clustering coefficient as follows [21]:

(i)   Initial condition: Start the network with m_0 vertices and no edges.

(ii) Growth: One vertex v with m edges is added at every time step.

(iii) Preferential attachment (PA) with probability $1-p$: Attaching each edge of v to an existing vertex with the probability proportional to its degree. Each edge of v is then attached to an existing vertex with the probability proportional to its degree, i.e., the probability for a vertex w to be attached to v is $\Pi_w = k_w / \sum_v k_v$.

(iv) Triangle formation (TF) with probability p : If an edge between v and w was added in the previous PA step, then add one more edge from v to a randomly chosen neighbor of w. If all neighbors of w were already connected to v, do a PA step instead.

It should be noted that, when $p = 0$, this model recovers the original BA model.

3   Dynamical Process and Local Routing Strategies

In this section, we model the traffic of packets on the given network. Motivated by the previous local routing models, the system evolves in parallel according to the following rules:

Step 1-Add New Packets: Packets are added with a given rate R (number of packets per time step) at randomly selected nodes and each packet is given a random destination.

Step 2-Navigate Packets: Each node performs a local search among its neighbors. If a packet's destination is found within the searched area of node l, i.e., the immediate neighbors of l, the packet will be delivered from l directly to its target and then removed from the system. Otherwise, its will be delivered to a neighboring node i with preferential probability according to Routing I, Routing II or Routing III.

$$\text{Routing I} : \Pi_{l \to i} = \frac{k_i^{\alpha}}{\sum\limits_{j \in g(i)} k_j^{\alpha}}, \tag{1}$$

$$\text{Routing II} : \Pi_{l \to i} = \frac{(q_i + 1)^{\beta}}{\sum\limits_{j \in g(i)} (q_j + 1)^{\beta}}, \tag{2}$$

$$\text{Routing III} : \Pi_{l \to i} = \frac{k_i^{\gamma} e^{-t_i}}{\sum\limits_{j \in g(i)} k_j^{\gamma} e^{-t_j}}, \tag{3}$$

where the sum runs over the immediate neighbors of the node l. k_i is the degree of node i and q_i is the number of packets in the queue of i. α, β, γ are introduced tunable parameter. $t_i = q_i / c_i$ is the estimated waiting time at node i. k_i and q_i are the so-called local and dynamic information, respectively. Adding 1 to q_i is to guarantee the nodes without packets have a probability to receive packets.

Step 3-Deliver Packets: We treat all nodes as both hosts and routers for generating and delivering packets and assume that each node can deliver at most c_i packets corresponding to the capacity of packet delivery of the node per step towards their destinations. Once a packet is generated, it is placed at the end of the node queue, which contains the undelivered packets created at current time steps or transmitted from the other nodes. The queue length of each node is assumed to be unlimited. During the evolution of the system, the FIFO (first-in first-out) rule is applied. Once a packet arrives at its destination, it will be removed from the system.

In order to characterize the phase transition, we introduce the order parameter:

$$H(R) = \lim_{t \to \infty} \frac{W(t + \tau) - W(t)}{\tau R}, \tag{4}$$

where $W(t)$ is the total number of packets in the network at time t, and τ is the observation time. The order parameter represents the ratio between the outflow and the inflow of packets during a time window τ. In the free flow state, due to the balance of created and removed packets, the load does not depend on time, which brings a steady state. Thus, when time tends to be unlimited, H is around zero. Otherwise, when $R > R_c$, the number of packets $W(t)$ in the network is increased with time and will lead to traffic congestion. Hence, the quantities of packets within the system will be a function of time, which makes H constant more than zero.

A sudden increment of H from zero to nonzero characterizes the onset of the phase transition from the free flow state to congestion, and the network capacity can be measured by the maximal generating rate R_c at the phase transition point. H equals 1 when the congestion is maximal (no packet reaches its destination) and 0 when an equilibrium is established, i.e., in the stationary state.

4   Simulations and Discussions

As an appropriate measure of the efficiency of the packet-delivery process, we monitor the number $W(t)$ of packets that have not reached their destinations at each time step t. Fig. 1 shows the obtained results for distinct values of R and α by adopting routing strategy I in the scale-free networks with tunable clustering coefficient. It can be seen that, when the packet creation rate is low (i.e., $R = 30$), the total number of packets $W(t)$ is at a steady state. In this case, the system is able to balance the in-flow of packets with the flow of packets that reach their destinations. As we can see below, when the packet creation rate is large (i.e., $R = 60$), $W(t)$ turns to be a linear function of t. There is a critical value R_c beyond which a congested phase shows up.

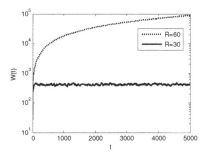

Fig. 1. The total number of packets $W(t)$ as a function of time steps with different packet creation rate R corresponding to $\alpha = 0$

As mentioned above, the efficiency of the system is reflected by the network capacity. We first investigate the order parameter α as a function of the generating rate R for different model parameter in high scale-free network with size $N = 100$, $m = m_0 = 3$. As shown in Fig. 2, the order parameter H versus generating rate R with different value of parameter α is reported. One can see that, for different α, H is approximately zero when R is small; it suddenly increases when R is larger than the critical point R_c. It is easy to find that the capacity of the system is not the same for different parameter. As we can see from Fig. 3, when choosing $c_i = k_i$ and $\alpha = 0.3$, the system's capacity can be enhanced maximally in the case of adopting local topological information (Routing I). However, these points from our experiments seem different from that of [16] in which the result shows that the optimal R_c corresponds to $\alpha = 0$ with $c_i = k_i$. This is due to the fact that network size is $N = 100$ in this paper while $N = 1000$ is explored in [16]. This means network size has an important effect on the optimal parameter's value of the routing strategy.

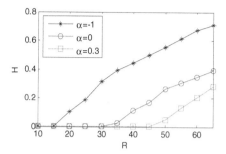

Fig. 2. The order parameter H versus R with different values of parameter α

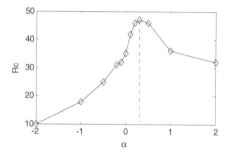

Fig. 3. The critical R_c versus α with network size $N = 100$

Now, we study the effect of the dynamic information on network capacity. Here we use original BA model ($p = 0$) with $m = m_0 = 3$ and network size $N = 100$ fixed for simulation. Figure 4 shows that in the Routing II, the network capacity is considerably enhanced by controlling β. As we can see from Fig. 4, when $\beta = -3$, the critical value is maximal and $R_c = 50$. Moreover, we can find that the capacity of the network with $\beta < 0$ is larger than that with $\beta > 0$.

Then we discuss the effect of cluster property on traffic delivery in scale-free networks with varied clustering coefficients by adopting the routing strategy with local topological information (Routing I). We find that the optimal α is increased in the more clustered network as shown in Fig. 5, which means the Routing I with larger parameter α offers packets more chance to be delivered to the destination through the neighbors of the jamming nodes that are usually the most connected ones, when the network becomes more clustered. Figure 6 shows that the value of the critical traffic R_c with the optimal parameter α_c is gradually decreased as the clustering coefficient becomes large. For the scale-free network with high clustering coefficient,

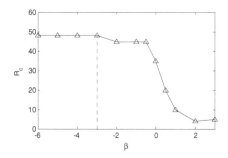

Fig. 4. The critical R_c versus β with network size $N = 100$

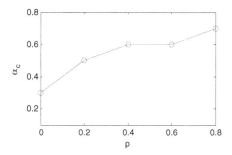

Fig. 5. The optimal value α_c in scale-free networks with different clustering coefficients

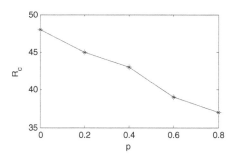

Fig. 6. The value of the critical traffic R_c with the optimal parameter α_c scale-free networks with different clustering coefficients

the neighbors of the jamming node are very likely to be jammed too, thus the packets will also get trapped in the neighbors, leading to less enhancement of the network capacity and less efficiency of the routing algorithm compared to the scale-free network with small clustering coefficient.

From Fig. 7, we find in range of $\alpha = 1$, the system's capacity can be enhanced maximally by adopting the routing strategy with waiting time (Routing III). Next, we study the simulations of packets distribution $P(n)$ versus n for different γ, where n represents the number of packets and $P(n)$ is the probability that a given node has n packets. As Fig. 8 shows, when $\gamma = -5, -10, -20$ and $R = 40$, packets length approximately displays a power law in the jamming state, which represents the highly heterogenous traffic on each node. While $\gamma = -1, 1, 10$ and $R = 20$ in Fig. 9, the packets distribution follows the Poisson distribution in the free flow state, which indicates the homogenous traffic on each node. Combining Figs. 8 and 9, we can conclude that the capacity of the system with packets distribution follows the Poisson distribution is smaller than that with packets distribution displays the power law, considering the capacity of each node is proportional to the degree.

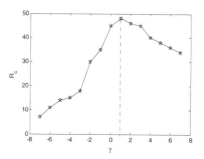

Fig. 7. The critical R_c versus α in the case of node capacity proportional to its degree $c_i = k_i$ with network size $N = 100$

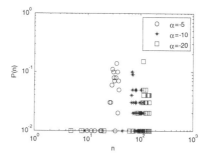

Fig. 8. The distribution of packet in the jamming state $R = 40$

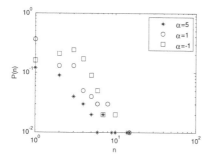

Fig. 9. The distribution of packet in the free flow state $R = 20$

5   Conclusion

We discuss respectively the effects of static and dynamic information on network capacity for scale-free networks. We find, in both routing strategies, that there is an optimal value of tunable parameter, below which the network traffic is free but above which traffic congestion occurs. Specially in scale-free with tunable clustering, the maximal network capacity decreases as the clustering coefficient increases, while the optimal value of tunable parameter is gradually enhanced as the clustering coefficient becomes larger. We find that there exists an optimal tuning parameter α, β, γ which makes the routing policy the most efficient.

References

1. Barabási, A.L., Albert, R.: Emergence of scaling in random neteorks. Science 286, 509–512 (1999)
2. de Menezes, M.A., Barabási, A.L.: Separating Internal and external dynamics of complex systems. Physical Review Letter 93, 068701 (2004)
3. Ling, X., Hu, M.B., Jiang, R., Wang, R.L., Cao, X.B., Wu, Q.S.: Pheromone routing protocol on a scale-free network. Physical Review E 80, 066110 (2009)
4. Sanders, D.P.: Exact encounter times for many random walkers on regular and complex networks. Physical Review E 80, 036119 (2009)
5. Wu, J.J., Sun, H.J., Gao, Z.Y.: Dynamic urban traffic flow behavior on scale-free networks. Physica A-Statistical Mechanics and Its Applications 387, 653–660 (2008)
6. Naganuma, Y., Igarashi, A.: A packet routing strategy using neural networks on scale-free networks. Physica A-Statistical Mechanics and Its Applications 389, 623–628 (2010)
7. Cohen, R., Erez, K., Ben-Avraham, D., Havlin, S.: Resilience of the Internet to random breakdowns. Physical Review Letter 85, 4626–4628 (2000)
8. Callaway, D.S., Newman, M.E.J., Strogatz, S.H., Watts, D.J.: Network robustness and fragility: percolation on random graphs. Physical Review Letter 85, 5468–5471 (2000)
9. Moreno, Y., Pastor-Satorras, R., Vespignani, A.: Epidemic outbreaks in complex heterogeneous networks. European Physical Journal B 26, 521–529 (2002)
10. Vázquez, A., Moreno, Y.: Resilience to damage of graphs with degree correlations. Physical Review E 67, 015101(R) (2003)
11. Newman, M.E.J.: Spread of epidemic disease on networks. Physical Review E 66, 016128 (2002)
12. Tadić, B., Thurner, S., Rodgers, G.J.: Traffic on complex networks: Towards understanding global statistical properties from microscopic density fluctuations. Physical Review E 69, 036102 (2004)
13. Echenique, P., Gómez-Gardeñes, J., Moreno, Y.: Improved routing strategies for Internet traffic delivery. Physical Review E 70, 056105 (2004)
14. Chen, Z.Y., Wang, X.F.: Effects of network structure and routing strategy on network capacity. Physical Review E 73, 036107 (2006)
15. Wang, D., Jing, Y.W., Zhang, S.Y.: Traffic dynamics based on a traffic awareness routing strategy on scale-free networks. Physica A-Statistical Mechanics and Its Applications 387, 3001–3007 (2008)

16. Wang, W.X., Wang, B.H., Yin, C.Y., Xie, Y.B., Zhou, T.: Traffic dynamics based on local routing protocol on a scale-free network. Physical Review E 73, 026111 (2006)
17. Yan, G., Zhou, T., Hu, B., Fu, Z.-Q., Wang, B.-H.: Efficient routing on complex networks. Physical Review E 73, 046108 (2006)
18. Singh, B.K., Gupte, N.: Congestion and decongestion in a communication network. Physical Review E 71, 055103(R) (2005)
19. Noh, J.D., Rieger, H.: Random walks on complex networks. Physical Review Letter 92, 118701 (2004)
20. Park, K., Lai, Y.C., Zhao, L.: Jamming in complex gradient networks. Physical Review E 71, 065105(R) (2005)
21. Holme, P., Kim, B.J.: Growing scale-free networks with tunable clustering. Physical Review E 65, 026107 (2002)

Propagation Model of Reputation in P2P Networks

Hua Sun[1], Li Li[2], Wenzhong Yang[2], and Yurong Qian[1]

[1] School of Software, Xinjiang University,
Xinjiang, Urumqi 830046, China
[2] School of Information Science and Engineering, Xinjiang University,
Xinjiang, Urumqi 830046, China
{xj_sh,ywz_xy}@163.com, {li_lixj,qyr}@xju.edu.cn

Abstract. Reputation represents a collective measure of trustworthiness, which are referrals or ratings from other peers in P2P networks. Before transaction, the peers always use aggregated ratings to derive reputations each other to decide whether or not to have a transaction, so reputation ratings will transmit in the networks before transaction. In this paper, we mainly analyze the propagation process of reputation ratings in P2P networks. When querying reputation, the querying peer will transmit the messages to the networks, and other peers will respond them. The number of querying will vary with time for the dynamic network environments, and the numbers of peers who respond the messages are also vary with time. The purpose of this paper is to analyze the factors that influence propagation of reputation. Through the propagation model, we give an answer about how the reputation messages transmit in the networks and what about the relationship of these factors.

Keywords: Reputation, propagation, connection rate, response rate, Peer-to-Peer networks.

1 Introduction

More and more transactions have occurred upon the platform of P2P networks, which is a loose environment with different technologies on it. So the transactions are not uniformly well intentioned for kinds of reasons. As a consequence, the topic of trust and reputation in open networks, like P2P network, is receiving considerable attention in the academic community and the Internet industry. Although evaluation of trust and reputation isn't an easy thing, before transactions, the peers always derive measures of trustworthiness of opposing peers, and this can help them to decide whether or not to have a transaction with the object peer in the future. They assumed that this can provide protection against viruses, worms, and any other threats that peers can be exposed to through the networks.

Many sites have set up simple reputation systems [1, 2] for users, especially for the buyers, to help them by providing reputation information. These reputation systems need the buyers and the sellers to evaluate each other after every transaction. For example, in eBay's reputation feedback forum, users can evaluate the opposing parties

M. Zhao and J. Sha (Eds.): ICCIP 2012, Part I, CCIS 288, pp. 368–377, 2012.

through the forum using 1, 0 and -1 to express satisfaction, neutrality and dissatisfaction about the partners' behavior. The evaluation system is simple and rough, and most of the users don't like to leave negation evaluation or give nothing to the evaluation system. From the data in [3], in eBay, buyers provide ratings about sellers 51.7% of the time, and sellers provide ratings about buyers 60.6% of the time. Of all ratings provided, less than 1% is negative, less than 0.5% is neutral and about 99% is positive. These may make the reputation information lose the authenticity in some degree, but it affects eBay deeply. These reputation information seems enough for the users to evaluate reputation of the potential partners.

Although transaction experiences can make assessments and decisions directly, little quantity of transaction history may be insufficient to evaluate the reputation of the potential partners. In normal, peers will obtain reputation information from the other peers [4], and when evaluating, using different factors to show their weightiness, and personal history experience typically carries more weight than second hand reputation referrals. For example, the P2Prep system [5] proposed the protocol and algorithm for sharing reputation information with peers in a peer-to-peer network, and literature [6] gives a detail introduction about the methods of obtaining the reputation information.

Information transmission is a natural phenomenon in the network. Such as content generation and delivery in dynamic network [7], the model of the epidemic infection [8] and the gossip of the social network [9]. Bin Wu et al. designed a model to analyze the process of the data transmitting in the networks [10]. If knowing nothing about the object entity, the author employs the blind search, such as ransom walk, flooding and all kinks of their varieties to find the distribution of the content. They send the messages to as many peers as possible. No matter what methods adopted, they will be restricted under certain conditions, such as response time.

Also, there are some existing self-storage P2P reputation systems in the literatures, like RCert [11], R-Chain [12], PRIDE [13] and [14], the self-storage of reputation values needn't the query all over the network. The process of query is simple. But most of reputation systems don't save reputation information in local [15]. Our work is focused on the distributed P2P network with reputation information stored in the third party and need query multi peers to obtain the information.

In the open and distributed P2P networks, peers will freely join to or leave the network at any time, and the number of the peers is varying, so is the number of response peers. That is to say, when some peer query the reputation of the object peer at different time, the messages will transmit in different routes and the querying peer may get different response information coming from different peers. We build a model of propagation of reputation to analyze this process in P2P networks and name the model as PMR(Propagation Model of Reputation). Through the model, we draw a conclusion and find the number of the query is influenced by connection rate and response rate. Although this model is carried out in distributed environments, it also adapts to the part distributed network and alike ones.

2   Propagation Model of Reputation

2.1   Design Principle

When a peer (query peer) queries reputation of the other peer (peer O), he will broadcast the query messages to the neighbors. The peers who have the transaction experience with peer O will respond the messages with the reputation information [16]. Whether will all the peers who having transaction experience with peer O receive the message? And does it need all of them receive the message? If not, and how many is enough? We will give a deep introduction below. We give some design principles at first.

Firstly, the research area is in the distributed network. Connection rate of the network is dynamic, and the peers are freely to join to or leave the network at any time without any limit in the model.

Secondly, the number of the response peers is shift. Because the peers who have transaction experience with the queried peer may be off line. And the peers may be out of the boundary of the transmission or unwilling to respond. It will be other reasons brought by the network and man-made and so on.

Thirdly, although the query is responded, the peer will query again in the next time. The reason is that the information may be outdated or the peer wants to query again to get the new information.

2.2   The Process of Propagation

Before transaction, the peers need query reputation information from other peers. A typical propagation process of query messages in P2P networks is divided into four steps. The peer (say peer X) will query other peers to obtain reputation information of the object peer. Firstly, peer X sends out the query messages, such as Gnutella [17], the message will be transmitted to the neighbors like flooding. The messages must be restricted otherwise the increasing messages will make the network paralysis. In Gnutella, when the messages passing over a peer, TTL(Time-To-Live) or Tops reduces one. After it gets to zero, the messages stop to transmit. Secondly, the peers who receive the query messages will respond it if they have the queried information, otherwise they will transmit the messages to the neighbors again before TTL gets to zero. Thirdly, the peer X will give the confirmation messages to the response peers, and the last step, the response peers will transmit the reputation information to peer X.

2.3   Description of the Notation

We can use graph to describe the relationship of the peers. All the peers in the network can be seen as a connection graph (name as graph G1). The propagation of reputation composes a directed graph (name as a logic graph G2). If ignore the direction of the edges in G2, then $G1 \supseteq G2$.

Before transaction, the peers will query reputation of the potential opposing party to be sure of its trustworthiness. Use a directional edge from peer V_i to peer V_j to show peer V_i query reputation of object peer towards V_j, show as Fig. 1. After peer V_j

receives the message, he has two choices: one is to send the message again if without the queried information, and the other is to respond the query using corresponding information. If the number of the peers is N in the network, then we can get a digraph G(V, E(t)), where V is a set of the peers, and |V|=N; E(t)is a set of the edges, where t is the parameter about time, and this means the connection is varying with the time.

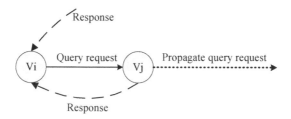

Fig. 1. Query request and response

If peer V_i and peer V_j have had a transaction, they have a direct trust relationship. Peer V_i can infer reputation of peer V_j according to their history experience; otherwise peer V_i need query reputation of peer V_j towards other peers. At the same time, peer V_i may receive some requests from other peers. But at time t, one peer can only send one query request to other peers to query reputation value of the object peer, and may receive many query requests. We can use degree of the graph to describe the relationship of the request, and in-degree and out-degree respectively denote queried by other peers and querying other peers. At time t, one peer can send one request at most, but he may receive requests from other peers in the network, and the range is between 0 to N-1. Therefore, in-degree of the peer is more than or equal to zero, and N-1 at most. Out-degree is zero or one. Because the number of peers is N, at time t, the number of directional edges is N-1 at most. For the convenient, we give some notations below:

P: Probability of query, it is varying in different environments;

C(t): Connection rate of the network at time t;

Q(t): The number of peers who query reputation of the peers at time t;

R(t): The ratio of the number of response to total number of query, namely response rate at time t;

Q(t)R(t): The number of peers who respond the query at time t;

N-Q(t): The number of peers without requesting query at time t.

2.4   Modeling

Suppose that peer V_i will have a query at time t, at the same time, it may be queried by other N-1 peers. The number of neighbor peers is C(t)(N-1), and the radio of peers who don't send request is $(1-\frac{Q(t)}{N})$, then $C(t)(N-1)(1-\frac{Q(t)}{N})$ is the number of peers who connect to peer V_i and may send request at time t. For the probability of query is P, the increment number of query requests towards V_i is $\Delta PC(t)(N-1)(1-\dfrac{Q(t)}{N})$, The

total number of query requests is Q(t), so the increment number of peers is

$\Delta PC(t)(N-1)(1-\dfrac{Q(t)}{N})Q(t)$. Because response rate is R(t), the decrease number of

peers is R(t)Q(t).

From above, we can get a differential equation:

$$\frac{dQ(t)}{dt} = PC(t)(N-1)(1-\frac{Q(t)}{N})Q(t) - R(t)Q(t) \tag{1}$$

If N is big enough, $N-1 \approx N$, so adjust Equation 1 as:

$$\frac{dQ(t)}{dt} = PNC(t)Q(t) - R(t)Q(t) - PC(t)Q^2(t) \tag{2}$$

So Equation 2 is the Propagation Model of Reputation (PMR, Propagation Model of Reputation). When t=0, set Q(t)=Q_0, then:

$$Q(t) = \frac{e^{\int_0^t (PNC(s)-R(s))ds}}{\dfrac{1}{Q_0} + \displaystyle\int_0^t PC(s)e^{\int_0^s (PNC(x)-R(x))dx} ds} \tag{3}$$

2.5   Discussion

From Equation 3, we know that the number of query is effected by connection rate C(t) and response rate R(t), and they are both varying with time t. Through analyzing relationship of two factors: C(t) and R(t), we can get the number of query, and this work has been done in our former work [18]. Following, we will discuss them according to some other circumstances.

Sometime, connection rate is stabilization relatively. For example, in the large distributed network, although the node churn is evidence, the number of the online peers is steady from the point of statistics for the reason that the number of the peers is tremendous large. And connection rate is also stable. For example, in some period, like working hours, connection rate is higher than other time. And the connection of daytime is higher than night.

The number of query is varying in different environments. We can use the Equation 3 to analyze the relationship of three factors: the number of query, the probability of query and the number of response peers. Suppose the number of response peers is increasing in a period time, while connection rate and probability of query may be low and high respectively. According to their relation, we can get four circumstances as follows, and we use fixed number to discus and analyze the trend line for convenience.

Low Connection Rate and Low Probability of Query
In this situation, connection rate and probability of query are both low. In this simulation, we set C(t)=0.3, P=0.2, and N=1000 to analyze the relationship of them,

and also can choice other number to simulate. Take them into Equation 3 and plot it. The relationship can be shown as Fig. 2. Where x-axes represent time t, and y-axes represents the number of reputation query.

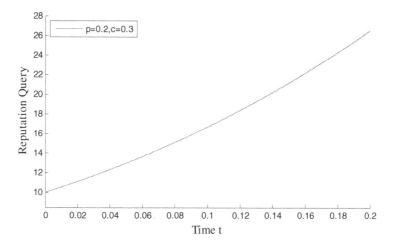

Fig. 2. Situation 1: Low connect rate and low probability of query

In this period, the number of query is small, and not more than 30. The increasing amount is subtle a few, and the curve is smoothness. Because connection rate of the network is poor, and the probability of query is low. These means the number of online peers is small, and correspondingly, the number of peers who need query reputation is also small, and both of these lead to a little of query.

Low Connection Rate and High Probability of Query
In this situation, connection rate of the network is low and probability of query is high. Take C(t)=0.3 and P=0.7 into Equation 3, we can get a cure shown as Fig. 3.

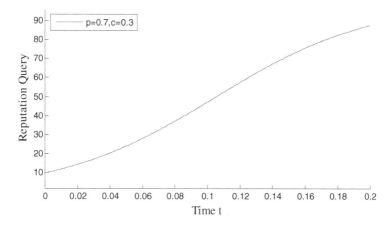

Fig. 3. Situation 2: Low connect rate and high probability of query

Fig. 3 shows an interesting thing. If probability of query is high, although connection rate is relative low, the total number of query will also be big comparing to situation 1, and it's almost three times more than situation 1. The peers will query reputation information no matter what the connection is.

High Connection Rate and Low Probability of Query
In this situation, connection rate is high and probability of query is low, suppose C(t)=0.8 and P=0.2, and Fig. 4 shows the relationship between the number of query and time.

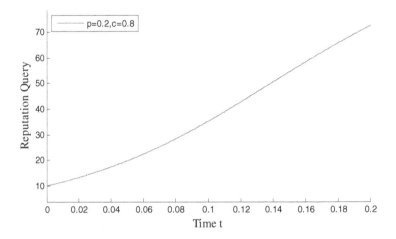

Fig. 4. Situation 3: High connect rate and low probability of query

If the network is built with good connection, although the peers with low probability to query reputation, the number of query is relative high. We make a comparison to situation 2. If response rate is same, high probability of query will produce more query, and this is apparent phenomena. If connection rate is normal, the query will increase.

High Connection Rate and High Probability of Query
If connection rate and probability of query are both very high, such as C(t)=0.8 and P=0.7. In this situation, the relationship between the number of query and time can be shown as Fig. 5.

If connection rate and probability of query are both high, the number of query will increase sharply in a short period and retain in a higher level. From the figure, the number of query is almost the same as the number of the peers in the network. That is to say, almost the whole peers are all querying.

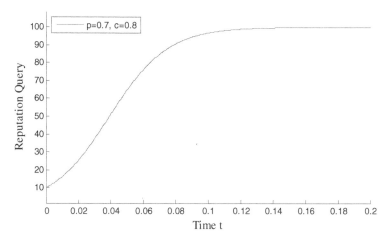

Fig. 5. Situation 1: high connect rate and high probability of query

2.6   Analysis

From the data shown above, the number of query is affected by connection rate of network and probability of query. This can give us some instructions when building the network. If most of peers want to have transaction, and they need reputation of possible transaction partners, this is to say, the probability of query is very high, the higher connection rate and response rate will promote the network to transmit the messages, and the querying peer will get more reputation information of the queried peer. But the connection rate isn't the most important factor, like situation 2, connection rate may be poor, but the number of query is very large for the reasons that the response rate is high. So we need some encouragement and punishment mechanisms to encourage peers to transmit message and respond query. And this will do well to every peer.

3   Conclusion and Future Works

From above, we know that the number of query will increase continuously with the increment of response rate in a period time. Although the network connection is necessary for transmission of message, the network needn't keep higher connection rate for this. High connection rate will lead to quick query result, and low connection rate will get response with some period of time. Just as eBay, although the web site can't offer the whole response data from every transaction people, it seems enough for people to estimate the reputation of the corresponding party.

To the best of our knowledge, our proposal model is the first contribution in the distributed P2P reputation network in which transmission of reputation information influenced by some factors discussed above. Most traditional models of trust and reputation focus on methods of computing reputation score in P2P networks, seldom consider or analyze the factors that influence of propagation of reputation. This work focuses on the research of propagation model of reputation in P2P networks, takes reputation of the peers as subjects, and describes a propagation model. Our work gets the solution equations through analyzing the propagation of reputation of each peer. We also analyze the influence of factors on the propagation model.

The propagation of reputation information has a tendency of diversification for the reason that the network are becoming more and more complex, we just analyze some factors and measure the propagation model using some values. How to choose parameters to reflect the actual behavior of peers in real world P2P networks, and dynamic interaction of these factors also need our further research.

References

1. Jøsang, A.: Trust and Reputation Systems. In: Aldini, A., Gorrieri, R. (eds.) FOSAD 2007. LNCS, vol. 4677, pp. 209–245. Springer, Heidelberg (2007)
2. Hoffman, K., Zage, D., Nita-Rotaru, C.: A survey of attack and defense techniques for reputation systems. ACM Comput. Surv. 42, 1–31 (2009)
3. Jøsang, A., Ismail, R., Boyd, C.: A survey of trust and reputation systems for online service provision. Dec. Supp. Syst. 43, 618–644 (2007)
4. Victora, P., Cornelis, C., Cock, M.D., da Silva, P.P.: Gradual trust and distrust in recommender systems. Fuzzy Sets and Systems 160, 1367–1382 (2009)
5. Cornelli, F., Damiani, E., Vimercati, S.D.C.: Choosing reputable servents in a p2p network. In: Lassner, D. (ed.) Proceedings of the 11th International World Wide Web Conference, pp. 376–386. ACM Press, New York (2002)
6. Morzy, M.: New Algorithms for Mining the Reputation of Participants of Online Auctions. Algorithmica 52, 95–112 (2008)
7. Ravi, J., Yu, Z., Shi, W.: A survey on dynamic Web content generation and delivery techniques. Journal of Network and Computer Applications 32, 943–960 (2009)
8. Risson, J., Moors, T.: Survey of research towards robust peer-to-peer networks:Search methods. Computer Networks 50, 3485–3521 (2006)
9. Han, L., Liu, H., Asiedu, B.K.: Analytic Model for Network Viruses. In: Wang, L., Chen, K., S. Ong, Y. (eds.) ICNC 2005, Part III. LNCS, vol. 3612, pp. 903–910. Springer, Heidelberg (2005)
10. Wu, B., Kshemkalyani, A.D.: Modeling message propagation in random graph networks. Comput. Commun. 31, 4138–4148 (2008)
11. Ooi, B.C., Liau, C.Y., Tan, K.-L.: Managing Trust in Peer-to-Peer Systems Using Reputation-Based Techniques. In: Dong, G., Tang, C., Wang, W. (eds.) WAIM 2003. LNCS, vol. 2762, pp. 2–12. Springer, Heidelberg (2003)
12. Liu, L., Zhang, S., Ryu, K.D., Dasgupta, P.: R-chain: A self-maintained reputation management system in P2P networks. In: Bader, D.A., Khokhar, A.A. (eds.) 17th International Conference on Parallel and Distributed Computing Systems, San Francisco, CA, pp. 131–136 (2004)
13. Dewan, P., Dasgupta, P.: Pride: Peer-to-Peer reputation infrastructure for decentralized environments. In: Proceedings of the 13th International World Wide Web Conference on Alternate Track Papers & Posters, pp. 480–481. ACM, New york (2004)
14. Hao, L., Lu, S., Tang, J., Yang, S.: An Efficient and Robust Self-Storage P2P Reputation System. Int. J. Distrib. Sens. Netw. 5, 81–88 (2009)

15. Hua, S., Hui-qun, Y., Nianhua, Y.: Local Storage of Reputation without the Third Parties to Validate Integrity in Peer-to-Peer Environments. Acta Electronica Sinica 39, 104–109 (2011)
16. Wang, Y., Lin, K.-J., Wong, D.S., Varadharajan, V.: Trust management towards service-oriented applications. In: SOCA, pp. 129–146. Springer, London (2009)
17. The Gnutella Protocol Specifications, http://www.clip2.com
18. Sun, H., Yu, H.: A Propagation Model of Reputation Query Request. In: 2010 the 2nd IEEE International Conference on Information Management and Engineering, Chengdu, China, vol. 1, pp. 539–543. IEEE (2010)

Complex System Collapse Control Based on Complex Networks

Song Wang[1,2] and Ying Wang[1]

[1] The Engineering Institute, Air Force Engineering University, Xi'an, Shaanxi 710038, China
[2] Engineering University of Armed Police Force of China, Xi'an, Shaanxi 710086, China
onesoon@163.com

Abstract. STCCM(System Theory Cognize-Constraint Model) is a new accident analysis and prevent technique based on systems theory, which is first introduced in this paper. After distilled the evaluation parameter of node importance, designed an improved complex system node importance evaluation arithmetic. Finally, introduced the conception of constraint entropy, constructed the constraint entropy measurement model. Research result can provide reference for complex system safety accident prevent and control.

Keywords: complex system, STCCM, constraint entropy, collapse control.

1 Introduction

In system theory, under the established external environment, system structure determines the system function. Therefore, the safety of complex system depends on stability of systems structure and system boundary. Safety is the whole emergent property of complex system, which caused by system-components' dangerous failure or dysfunctional interaction between system-elements [1]. For the complex systems countless nodes, and complex association between nodes, complex network should be used to describe the system structure, and analyze the brittleness structure collapse process of complex system.

2 System Theory Cognize-Constraint Model(STCCM)

Safety accident models play a critical role in accident investigation and analysis. With the increased complexity of complex systems, the traditional accident models for mechanical system or electrical-mechanical system which underlying chain of events have serious limitations when used for complex, socio-technical systems. Previously, Leveson proposed a new accident model (STAMP) based on system theory. In STAMP, the basic concept is not an event but a constraint [2,3]. This model treats the safety as the system emergent property, and considers the safety as a control problem. Though it is used in many fields, and gained effective influence, but it does not offer the essence of accident causation. Therefore, the systematic and dynamic accident

M. Zhao and J. Sha (Eds.): ICCIP 2012, Part I, CCIS 288, pp. 378–385, 2012.

models should be offered for complex system accident investigation and analysis. This paper a system theory cognize-constraint model(STCCM) is proposed.

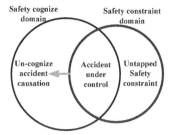

Fig. 1. Relationship between safety cognize and safety constraint

Figure 1 shows the relationship between safety cognize and safety constraint, intersection of safety cognize domain and safety constraint domain is the current complex system accident domain which is under human control. And human need to dig into unknown incidents mechanism and lots of constraint approaches should be applied. However, what we need to do is to maximize safety constraint domain to mostly coincide with safety cognize domain, which need to strengthen the safety cognitive ability, as while as implement effective safety constraints.

From system theory cognize-constraint model(STCCM) in Figure 2, safety cognize includes safety original cognize and safety emergent cognize. Safety original cognize formed in accident knowledge and can be used to guide safety constraint design. Safety emergent cognize formed when outside disturb and impact happened, and need the control unit to perceive the hazard and inflict the effective emergent constraint, knowledge formed in emergent situation can augment the original cognize.

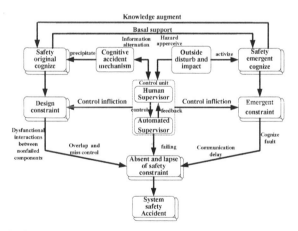

Fig. 2. The system theory cognize-constraint model(STCCM)

The control unit contains human supervisor and automated supervisor, both inflict control to safety constraint. Absent and lapse of safety constraint which is the direct result of system safety accident may caused from dysfunctional interactions between non-failed components, overlap and miss control, cognize fault, communication delay, or the failure of the control unit, so put more attention to those factors and effectively avoid safety accident.

3   Safety Cognize—Find Key Nodes for Complex System

STCCM shows that the collapse control of complex systems has to strengthen the safety cognitive ability and hazards constraint capacity. Abstract the complex system by complex networks which composed of nodes and edges, the complex system topology structure model can be gained, which as shown in Figure 3.

Definition 1. Complex system topology structure. Assume node set $V=\{v_1,v_2,\ldots,v_n\}$ as set of complex system components, among which i=1,2,...,n is the number of components; edge set $E=\{e_{ij},i,j=1,2,\ldots,n;i\neq j\}$ represent the set of association between the complex system components, then G=(V,E) is the complex system topology structure.

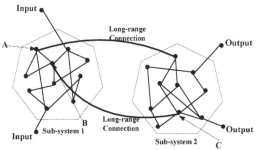

Fig. 3. Complex system topology structure model

Figure 3 shows only two subsystems of complex system, due to complex system countless number of components, and complex relations between components, which makes it difficult to accurately mathematical descript its structure, particularly functional structure, and, therefore, difficult to achieve effective control. In fact, the complex network owns a large number of nodes and complex topology structure, the traditional means of control are no longer applicable. Fundamental reason is that, in the actual complex network systems, we can not control all of the nodes to achieve a particular goal. In most cases, we want to control as little as possible nodes to achieve a specific goal, which is so-called implicated control.

Since the complex system safety accident causation STCCM holds that avoid accidents should improve the safety cognitive ability, and set an effective safety constraints, so key nodes' implicated control can save limited control resources and gain excellent control effect.

3.1   Extract Key Nodes Evaluation Parameters

The existing key nodes evaluation parameters include node degree, clustering coefficient of nodes, node betweenness. And the common evaluation model contain node removal method, node contraction method etc. These parameters and models generally used for the assessment of the Internet, transportation networks, or other widely distributed network which with a strong practical range, but as for complex network which abstract from real complex system, some parameters will no longer be applicable. Such as the node removal method which remove the nodes to measure the network performance degradation then determine the node importance, In fact, the absence of any node in real complex systems may lead to structural collapse. Therefore, for the complex networks abstracted from real complex system, other key nodes evaluation parameters should be extracted.

Definition 2. Node Degree. The degree (or connectivity) of a node is the number of edges incident with the node. Assume the node i and node j(j≠i) use the edge e_{ij} to connect, when between node I and node j(j≠i) exist edge, take $e_{ij}=1$, then $e_{ij}=0$.The degree of node i can be described as

$$k_i = \sum_{j=1, j\neq i}^{n} e_{ij} \tag{1}$$

Where n is the total numbers of complex system components. The higher node degree means that more edges connect to the node, this component has more association with other components, so it is a important node. In Figure 3, node A and node C has a higher degree. In aircraft systems, engine system provide work energy for many components, then create many relationship with others, whose node degree is higher.

The reason why small-world network has a unique geometric properties, because in the course of its construction, the introduction of a very small amount of long-range connection   Long-range connection links the subsystem which contains large number of components, promote system structure become more closely, and thus emergence new system features. In Figure 3, between subsystem 1 and subsystem 2 exist long-range connections.

Definition 3. End Node of Long-range Connection. Within different subsystems exist long-range connection nodes. Long-range connection is the key factor which cause the collapse rapid spread in complex system.

Definition 4. The Peripheral Node. Node that directly exchange material, energy, information with the outside world is called the peripheral node. Such as in aircraft systems, body structure, communication systems, which are peripheral nodes interact with the outside world. In Figure 3 is the system input and output nodes are the peripheral nodes. Complex systems must continue to dissipate outside matter, energy and information to maintain stability. The collapse of peripheral node led to this exchange termination, thus contributing to the increase of entropy within the system, which led to the collapse.

Definition 5. Node Betweenness. The communication of two non-adjacent nodes, say s and t, depends on the nodes belonging to the paths connecting s and t. Consequently, a measure of the relevance of a given node can be obtained by counting the number of geodesics going through it, and defining the so-called node betweenness. Together with the degree and the closeness of a node(defined as the inverse of the average distance from all other nodes), the betweenness is one of the standard measures of node centrality[4].

Node betweenness is defined as proportion of shortest edge of the road through i divided by the all shortest edge of the road in complex network. With $g_{st,i}$ as the shortest edge of the road through i between node s and node t, n_{st} represent all shortest edge of the road in complex network. between node s and node t, then the node betweenness of node i can be described as

$$C(i) = \frac{2\sum\limits_{s<t} g_{st,i}/n_{st}}{n(n-1)} \tag{2}$$

Where, $C(i)$ stand for the node betweenness. Node Betweenness can measure the importance of node, which means more shortest edge pass the node, more important the node is. In reality, in complex systems, shortest edge is an abstract of strong association.

Definition 6. Node Load. Weighted sum the node degree and node betweenness can gain node load, assume L_i is the node load of node i, then

$$L_i = \alpha k_i + \beta C(i) = \alpha \sum_{j=1, j\neq i}^{n} e_{ij} + 2\beta \frac{\sum\limits_{s<t} g_{st,i}/n_{st}}{n(n-1)} \tag{3}$$

$$\alpha + \beta = 1 \tag{4}$$

Where, α is the weight of node-degree in node load, and β is the weight of node-betweenness in node load.

Assume I_i is the significant degree of node i, then

$$I_i = L_i + \eta k_i + \delta k_i \tag{5}$$

Where, ηk_i stands for value increments when node is the end node of long-range connections, η is the correction factor, if the node is not the end node of long-range connections, take $\eta = 0$; δk_i stands for value increments when node is the peripheral nodes, and δ is the correction factor, if the node is not the peripheral nodes, take $\delta = 0$.

Equation (5) offered the node significant degree calculation model, which not only considers the association between nodes(degree), node location in the network (node betweenness), but also considers the reality of complex systems in a small world effects (long-range connections) and dissipative structures (peripheral node).

Therefore, Relative to the node contraction method and node delete method which relying on the Internet or other large network, this method is more suitable for real complex systems significant degree calculation.

3.2   Node Significant Degree Evaluation Algorithm

In order to find the key node in complex system, design the node significant degree evaluation algorithm as flollows:

① construct network topology structure map $G = (V, E)$ for complex systems;

② calculate the node degree k and node betweenness C;

③ determine the weight of node degree α and node betweenness weight β, calculate node load L;

④ determine whether the node is the end nodes of a long-range connection, and determine the correction factor η, and calculate ηk;

⑤ judge whether the node is the peripheral node, and determine the correction factor δ, and calculate δk;

⑥ calculate node significant degree I.

4   Safety Constraint—Provide Constraint Entropy for Key Nodes

4.1   Constraint Entropy

As for the closed complex system, according to the second theorem of classical thermodynamics, irreversible processes will cause the system transform from order state to disorder state, namely into the direction of increasing entropy. And for the open complex system, its entropy changes can be divided into two parts: one is within the system caused by the irreversible process of entropy $d_i H$, $d_i H \geq 0$; the other part is the system of energy and material exchange with the outside world caused by entropy $d_e H$, $d_e H$ may greater than zero, or may also be less than zero. Proven, in an area far from equilibrium, the evolution of complex systems does not follow a variational principle, the change in entropy of the entire system should be

$$dH = \alpha d_i H + \beta d_e H \qquad (6)$$

$d_i H$ multiplied by the factor α, means that due to the outside world into the role of the entropy of the system elements, so that the incremental change in entropy within the system after the correction value; $d_i H$ multiplied by the factor β, means that the outside world into the role of the entropy by the system after the last internal entropy. The collapse of the external environment by changing the boundaries of the stability of the system, thereby affecting the order of the system-element arrangement, resulting in entropy increase, prompting the collapse of the internal structure of the system, giving rise to safety incidents, so that the safety incidents' root cause is due to the internal structure of the system collapse, and this place has its inevitable collapse.

As the key node in a complex system may lead to the collapse of the system paralyzed, requiring a high degree of importance to focus on monitoring nodes performance, while nodes in the safety testing, repair, maintenance, etc. should also be given priority. Especially in the node by the attack, emergency measures must be taken by the resources available to learn from the outside world to suppress the entropy inside the node, the node to prevent breaking the threshold of collapse.

Definition 7. Constraint Entropy. Defined the inhibition of outside negative entropy which used to control the node collapse as constraint entropy. The introduction of outside limited constraint entropy to safety-critical node, or significant node is the effective way for avoiding complex system safety accidents.

Constraint entropy is binding in the node inherent design flaws of safety constraint, or safety margin is less than the premise, in the operation of complex systems used in the way of safety constraints. The introduction of entropy bound to be modest, on the one hand an important node in the collapse of the need to suppress the same time not restrict the trend of self-organization within the system, which is the prerequisite for the development system.

4.2   Constraint Entropy Measurement Model

Since the constraint entropy is introduced to control complex system significant node collapse, and must introduce an appropriate degree of entropy, then how to measure the constraint entropy? This part will build a constraint entropy measurement model.

Assume one of the significant node in complex system is a safety-critical node, the collapse of the node may cause the whole system collapse. When system is running, monitor the node important parameters $j = 1, 2, ..., m$, this m parameters value during normal operation is $r_j, j = 1, 2, ..., m$, allowing the volatility interval $[r_j^-, r_j^+]$. The value for the real-time monitoring is r_j' , if $r_j^- \leq r_j' \leq r_j^+$, at this time the node is operating normally, and when $r_j' < r_j^-$ or $r_j' > r_j^+$, the entropy will increase within the node, then the entropy of the internal node is

$$d_i H = |H_1| + |H_2| \tag{7}$$

$$H_1 = -\sum_{j=1}^{m} \frac{|r_j' - r_j^-|}{r_j'} \ln \sum_{j=1}^{m} \frac{|r_j' - r_j^-|}{r_j'} \tag{8}$$

$$H_2 = -\sum_{j=1}^{m} \frac{|r_j' - r_j^+|}{r_j'} \ln \sum_{j=1}^{m} \frac{|r_j' - r_j^+|}{r_j'} \tag{9}$$

To achieve the entropy balance, to maintain structural stability of the system, therefore $dH \leq 0$, assume $d'_e H$ is the needed constraints entropy from the outside world, because it is an negative entropy which used to control node collapse, so $d'_e H < 0$, then

$$\alpha d_i H - \beta \left| d'_e H \right| \leq 0 \tag{10}$$

$$\left| d'_e H \right| \geq \frac{\alpha d_i H}{\beta} = \frac{\alpha (\left| H_1 \right| + \left| H_2 \right|)}{\beta} \tag{11}$$

Where, $\alpha(\left| H_1 \right| + \left| H_2 \right|)/\beta$ is the minimum entropy constraint which should be pulled in from outside world.

5   Conclusion

This paper proposed a new safety accident model, which named STCCM(System Theory Cognize-Constraint Model). Then, offered the key nodes evaluation parameters and node significant degree evaluation algorithm. Finally, constraint entropy measurement model was gave. The result can provide reference for complex system safety accident prevent and control.

Acknowledgments. This work was supported by national natural scientific fund of china(Grant No. 71171199).

References

1. Leveson, N.G.: Applying systems thinking to analyze and learn from events. Safety Science (49), 55–64 (2011)
2. Leveson, N.G.: Safety as a system property. Communications of the ACM 38(11), 146 (1995)
3. Leveson, N.G.: A new accident model for engineering safer systems. Safety Science 42(4), 237–270 (2004)
4. Boccalettia, S., Latora, V., Moreno, Y., et al.: Complex networks: Structure and dynamics. Physics Reports (424), 175–308 (2006)
5. Reason, J.: Human Error. Cambridge University Press, Cambridge (1990)
6. Leveson, N.G.: Software Challenges in Achieving Space Safety. Journal of the British Interplanetary Society (JBIS) 62 (2009)
7. Wang, S., Wang, Y.: Causation Analysis of Complex System Safety Accident Based on Brittle Structure Collapse Theory. Procedia Engineering 15, 365–369 (2011)

Improved Genetic Algorithm Optimizing PID Parameters for Electro-hydraulic Servo System

Ze Wu, Wu Wang, and Zhengmin Bai

School of Electrical and Information Engineering, Xuchang University, Xuchang, China
jhwlz@tom.com

Abstract. Electro-hydraulic servo system was widely used in industrial application for its good performance, but the dynamic behavior is highly nonlinear, structure uncertainty, and very difficult to control by conventional method. PID control was applied into this system control and the parameters were tuned by improved genetic algorithm. The operation steps of GA was proposed and improved GA which can improve the convergence properties of standard GA was presented with the crossover probability and mutation probability adaptively changed with fitness value and evolution epochs, the total process of improved GA for PID parameters tuning was programmed. The mathematical models of Electro-hydraulic servo system was analyzed and taken as control object, the simulation was taken with standard GA PID control and improved GA PID control, the high performance and control characteristic of this improved control strategy was successfully demonstrated.

Keywords: PID parameters tuning, genetic algorithm, electro-hydraulic servo system, simulation.

1   Introduction

Electro-hydraulic servo system integrates with the characteristics of electrics and hydraulic pressure aspects which were widely used in various areas of industrial applications because of their high power-to-weight ratio, high stiffness, and high payload capability, and at the same time, achieve fast responses and high degree of both accuracy and performance. However, the dynamic behavior of these systems is highly nonlinear due to phenomena such as nonlinear servo valve flow pressure characteristics, variations in trapped fluid volumes and associated stiffness, which, in turn, cause difficulties in the control of such systems, also the system with the characteristics of parameter and structure uncertainty, time-variant, and uncertain load disturbance in most cases. These characteristics make it very difficult to realize high accuracy control for it by conventional methods and some new control techniques used to compensate the nonlinear behavior of hydraulic systems include adaptive control, sliding mode control and feedback linearization [1].

The PID controller is the most frequently used control element in the industrial world due to their simple structure and robust performance under a wide range of

M. Zhao and J. Sha (Eds.): ICCIP 2012, Part I, CCIS 288, pp. 386–393, 2012.

operating conditions. It is implemented in industrial single loop controllers, distributed control systems, and programmable logic controllers. The drawback is that the parameters of the PID controller are partially tuned by trial and error process, which makes it less intelligent. The normal tuning method in many applications is carried out using the classical tuning rules proposed by Ziegler-Nichols, which in general, does not yield optimal or near-optimal behavior in many industrial plants and just cannot be counted as a feasible solution [2]. However, the performance of a PID controller fully depends on the tuning of its parameters. It has been a problem to tune properly these parameters because many industrial plants are often burdened with problems such as high order, time delays, and nonlinearities. To overcome this problem, some intelligent computation techniques such as genetic algorithm may provide a solution for it.

Genetic algorithms are considered wide range numerical optimization methods which use the natural processes of evolution and genetic recombination. The genetic algorithm focuses on all the individuals in one population, and uses random techniques to search efficiently for a coded parameter space. Selection, crossover and mutation are the basic operators in genetic algorithm; parameter coding, the setting of initial population, the design of fitness function, the selection of genetic operations and control parameters consist of the critical part of genetic algorithm [3]. As a global optimization search algorithm of high efficiency, the genetic algorithm has distinctive advantage in solving the difficult problems. Study shows that searching excellently in the standard genetic algorithm selection operator will be weakening with the increasing of evolutionary optimization iterations gradually. There are many phenomenons which are in the practical application most far from the overall advantages of the standard genetic algorithm. An improved genetic algorithm was proposed in this paper to optimizing the parameters of PID controller and applied this control to electro-hydraulic servo system.

2   PID Tuning with Improved GA

2.1   Genetic Algorithm

GA was first presented by John Holland in the early 1970s, is becoming an important tool for optimization problems, GA is a stochastic search algorithm based on the mechanisms of natural selection and heredity, where stronger individuals are likely to be the winners in a competing environment. The main feature of the algorithm is that it approaches the near-global optimum by evolving chromosomes without the necessity of gradient evaluations. With such a characteristic, the GA is capable of jumping out of local optimum and achieving the global optimum. GA is the operation that continuously selects crossovers and mutates the initial population, which enables the population to evolve along the direction of the set goal. During the progress of searching, the direction is guided by a fitness function, so GA is efficient and covers a large range of search. The flow chart of the GA is depicted in Fig.1.

GA including following steps:

Step1: Encoding, encoding the solution parameters as genes, when code with binary, the chromosomes will be longer, here the real number encoding was taken to decrease coding length and also enhance precision.

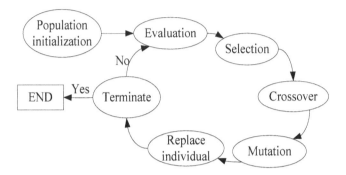

Fig. 1. The Flowchart of Genetic Algorithm

Step2: Generate initial population. Set the size of chromosomes and randomly generate an initial population. It is beneficial if some knowledge is known about the distribution of potential optimal solution.

Step3: The evaluation of fitness. Each chromosome is decoded as network parameter. Input the training samples and calculate the fitness of each individual according to RBF neural networks structure and parameters.

Step4: Selection. Selection operation is a process of generating new population through choosing and reproducing better individual from the old generation. The roulette wheel selection method was used.

Step5: Crossover. Crossover operation imitates the gene recombination of generative reproduction in nature, randomly select two parent individuals from the mating pool, and single-point stochastic crossover was used.

Step6: Mutation. Mutation operation imitates trans generation in natural biological evolution, it can change the structure and physical character of chromosome.

2.2   Improved Genetic Algorithm

However, it is known that the main shortcoming of GA is premature, which occurs due to loss of the population diversity. Study shows that the with crossover and mutation operation, the crossover probability and mutation probability can influence the algorithm, the function of searching excellently in the standard genetic algorithm selection operator will be weaken with the increasing of evolutionary optimization iterations gradually. It is seeking a standstill excellent work, and at this time, it is similar to many individuals and even to repeat. To this end, it is believed that the initial change is the new range of initial changes. Returning the standard genetic algorithm gives rise to accelerate the formation of operation. The range of outstanding individuals will be gradually reduced, with the most advantages from the getting closer and closer, until individual value of the optimal criterion function is less than a stetted value or the accelerating frequency is achieved in the process of algorithm. Then end up the entitle algorithm.

In order to avoid this problem and improve the convergence properties of SGA, the improved GA was proposed based on SGA, the crossover probability and mutation probability was adaptively changed with fitness value and evolution epochs, the improved algorithm was given as:

$$
p_c = \begin{cases} p_{c1}, & f' < f_{avg} \\ p_{c1} - \dfrac{(p_{c1} - p_{c2})(f' - f_{avg})}{f_{max} - f_{avg}}, & f' \geq f_{avg} \end{cases} \tag{1}
$$

$$
p_m = \begin{cases} p_{m1}, & f < f_{avg} \\ p_{m1} - \dfrac{(p_{m1} - p_{m2})(f_{max} - f)}{f_{max} - f_{avg}}, & f \geq f_{avg} \end{cases} \tag{2}
$$

f_{max} was the maximum fitness of the population, f_{avg} was the average fitness, f' was the bigger fitness in two crossover individual and f was the fitness of mutation individual.

2.3   PID Controller Tuning

Here, the PID parameters tuning with improved genetic algorithm, the steps was [4]:

Step 1: Encoding, the real number encoding was taken to decrease coding length and also enhance precision, the encoding for chromosome was defined as:

$$
E^G = [k_p^G \quad k_i^G \quad k_d^G] \tag{3}
$$

k_p, k_i, k_d was the proportional, integral and differential coefficient respectively, G was the individual label.

Step 2: Generate initial population. Randomly generate an initial population with N character string. The population was generated based on encoding mode, and here the initial population was given as:

$$
POP_{PID} = \begin{bmatrix} E^1 \\ E^2 \\ \vdots \\ E^N \end{bmatrix} = \begin{bmatrix} k_p^1 & k_i^1 & k_d^1 \\ k_p^2 & k_i^2 & k_d^2 \\ \vdots & \vdots & \vdots \\ k_p^N & k_i^N & k_d^N \end{bmatrix} \tag{4}
$$

Step 3: Computing fitness. The fitness function was selected as $F_{\text{FITNESS}} = \dfrac{1}{F}$, F was objective function which was given as:

$$F = \int_0^\infty |e(t)| + 0.002u^2(t) + 2|y(t) - y(t-1)| \tag{5}$$

Step 4: Selection. Selection operation is a process of generating new population through choosing and reproducing better individual from the old generation. The elitist selection and roulette wheel selection method was used.

Step 5: Crossover. Arithmetic crossover was used, and the crossover probability was selected with adaptive algorithm which as (1), here the probability with value $p_{c1} = 0.95$, $p_{c2} = 0.65$.

Step 6: Mutation. Mutation operation change the chromosome randomly with mutation probability as (2), here the value was selected with $p_{m1} = 0.09$, $p_{m2} = 0.0015$.

Step 7: Convergence judgment. If the convergence object reached, the optimal character string can get for parameters, otherwise, step into step3 for repeat.

Step8: decode. Decode the optimal character string into PID parameters.

3   Mathematical Models of Electro-hydraulic Servo System

3.1   The Structure of Electro-hydraulic Servo System

Electro-hydraulic servo control system was a typical hydraulic controls system, the structure of electro-hydraulic servo system with PID controller as shown in Fig.2. In this control system, the controlled plant composed of a hydraulic power supply, an electro-hydraulic servo valve, a cylinder, a piston etc, also the signal feedback with displacement detector, servo amplifier was applied for signal amplify and power match and the main controller is PID controller [5].

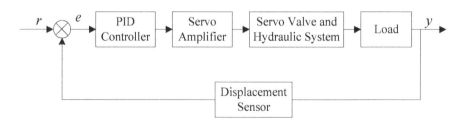

Fig. 2. The Structure of electro-hydraulic control system

3.2   Mathematical Models of Electro-hydraulic Servo Valve

Electro-hydraulic servo valve was composed of electro-mechanic transformer, hydraulic valve and feedback control mechanism, here we assume: Q_{sv0} was flow of servo valve without load; I_c was input current; K_{sv} was static flow-gain coefficient ; K_c was flow pressure coefficient; P_L was the load pressure; when take current as input and output flow as output, if viscous damping and elasticity of load are ignored, the linear equation can be given as [6]:

$$Q_L = Q_{sv0} - K_c P_L \qquad (6) \qquad Q_{sv0} = K_{sv} I_c \qquad (7)$$

Assume the nature frequency as ω_{sv}, the damping ratio was ξ_{sv}, when hydraulic system with $\omega_H \leq 50\text{Hz}$, the dynamic equation of hydraulic servo valve can be expressed as (8); When hydraulic system with $\omega_H > 50\text{Hz}$, the dynamic equation of hydraulic servo valve can be expressed as (9):

$$Q_{sv0} = \frac{K_{sv}}{\dfrac{s}{\omega_{sv}} + 1} I_c \qquad (8) \qquad Q_{sv0} = \frac{K_{sv}}{\dfrac{s^2}{\omega_{sv}^2} + 2\xi_{sv}\dfrac{s}{\omega_{sv}} + 1} I_c \qquad (9)$$

Assume C_{tp} was total leakage coefficient; A_p was the piston ram area; β_e was effective bulk modulus of oil; V_t was total volume of the servo valve; m_t was the mass of the piston; B was viscous damping coefficient; k was elastic stiffness; F_L was resistant force that the rock specimen acts on the piston; X_p was piston displacement, the continuity equation and the force balance equation of the cylinder can be obtained as:

$$Q_L = A_p s X_p + C_{tp} P_L + \frac{V_t}{4\beta_e} s P_L \qquad (10)$$

$$F_p = A_p P_L = m_t s^2 + B s X_p + k X_p + F_L \qquad (11)$$

Another link of control system can be described as proportion operator, assume the gain of power amplifier as K_p, displacement sensor with gain K_s ,the actual displacement measured with sensor was y and the control output U, then the model can be described as:

$$I_c = K_p U \qquad (12) \qquad Y = K_s X_p \qquad (13)$$

4   Simulations and Conclusions

4.1   Simulation with GA Optimizing PID Control

Actual electro-hydraulic control system was a complicated higher order nonlinear system, in order to verify the control characteristic of RBF-SMC controller, here the simplified mathematical models was adopted with the parameters of electro-hydraulic system was selected as $K_s = 100$, $K_p = 0.001$, $K_{sv} = 8.33 \times 10^{-3}$, $\xi_h = 0.25$, $\omega_h = 49$ for simulation [7], simulated with GA and improved GA respectively, the function J changing curve simulated with GA as shown in Fig.3, also the system was simulated with improved GA, the function changing curve as shown in Fig.4, the comparison of step response curve as shown in Fig.5 [8].

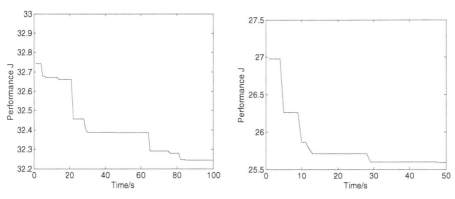

Fig. 3. Performance of J changing with GA

Fig. 4. Performance of J changing with improved GA

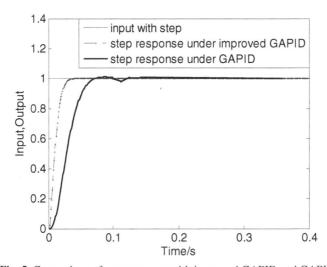

Fig. 5. Comparison of step response with improved GAPID and GAPID

4.2   Conclusions

Electro-hydraulic servo control system were widely used in various areas of industrial applications because of their high performance, this paper constructed electro-hydraulic servo control system and taken it as research object, the structure and mathematical models was electro-hydraulic serve control system was created. PID control was widely used, but the performance of a PID controller fully depends on the tuning of its parameters, so, PID parameters tuning with GA was presented in this paper, the standard GA and improved GA for PID parameters tuning was analyzed in this paper and at last taken this strategy into electro-hydraulic servo control system, with simulation, we can see that normal GA algorithm can not realize good control characteristic, the improved GA can easily realized parameters tuning for PID control with perfect control characteristics.

Acknowledgments. It is a project supported by natural science research in office of education, HeNan Province. With the Grant NO: (2011B470005) and Grant NO: (12A470007).

References

1. Cominos, P., Munro, N.: PID Controllers: Recent Tuning Methods and Design to Specification. IEEE Proceedings Control Theory and Applications 149, 46–53 (2002)
2. Meng, X.Z., Song, B.Y.: Fast Genetic Algorithm Used for PID Parameter Optimization. In: IEEE Proceedings of International Conference on Automation and Logistics, pp. 2144–2148. IEEE Press, New York (2007)
3. Gaing, Z.L.: A Particle Swarm Optimization Approach for Optimum Design of PID Controller in AVR System. IEEE Transactions On Energy Conversion 19(2), 384–391 (2004)
4. Howell, M.N., Best, M.C.: On-Line PID Tuning for Engine Idle-Speed Control Using Continuous Action Reinforcement Learning Automata. Control Engineering Practice 8, 147–154 (2000)
5. Zhang, Y.-W., Gui, W.-H.: Compensation for secondary uncertainty in electro-hydraulic servo system by gain adaptive sliding mode variable structure control. J. Cent. South Univ. Technol. (15), 256–263 (2008)
6. Leung, F.H.F., Lam, H.K., Ling, S.H., Tam, P.K.S.: Tuning of the structure and parameters of a neural network using an improved genetic algorithm. IEEE Transactions on Neural Networks 14(1), 79–88 (2003)
7. Liu, J.K.: Advanced PID Control and MATLAB Simulation. Publishing House of Electronics Industry, Beijing (2003)
8. Krishnakumar, K., Goldberg, D.E.: Control System Optimization Using Genetic Algorithms. J. Guidance, Control, Dyn., 735–740 (1994)

An LED Driver Using Joint Frequency-Pulse Width Modulation Scheme

Chen Guanghua, Wu Changqian, Wang Anqi, and Zeng Weimin

School of Mechatronics Engineering and Automation,
Shanghai University, Shanghai 200072, China
chghua@shu.edu.cn

Abstract. In order to provide LCD backlighting with multiple strings of LEDs, an LED driver using the joint frequency-pulse width modulation scheme is proposed in the paper. A PWM signal is generated by the Pulse Width Modulation (PWM) module in MCU chip, which is used to drive a DC-DC boost converter for LED power. The voltage and current of the boost circuit, along with all the channels current of LED, are measured by the Analog Digital Converter (ADC) module in MCU chip, which are used to adjust the voltage of the boost circuit and supply comprehensive protection for the LED driver. To minimize the step size of the output voltage, the joint frequency-pulse width modulation scheme is proposed to regulate the output voltage of the boost circuit to an ideal value in the range of error, which increases the efficiency of the power. To reduce the crossover power dissipation of the MOSFET switch, the MOSFET driver is designed to charge or discharge the gate with big drive current capability, which can reduce the time of MOSFET to be turned on and off efficiently. The measurement results show that the LED driver is extremely efficient and steady, the maximum step size of the output voltage is less than 0.3V, and the conversion efficiency of the DC-DC converter is up to 94%. Thus the LED driver not only meets the demand of the parameter of LED, but also has high cost performance.

Keywords: LED Driver, DC-DC, joint frequency-pulse width modulation, MOSFET Driver.

1   Introduction

In recent years, Liquid Crystal Display (LCD) flat panel display has become the leading role in monitor or TV applications. Since LCD is non-emissive display devices, LCD Backlight Units (BLU) play a very important role. Due to various advantages such as mercury-free, lower power consumption, wider color gamut, and better dimming capability, Light Emitting Diode (LED) is used as an alternative to the Cold Cathode Fluorescent Lamp (CCFL) for LCD BLU. It is evident that the trend today is to replace CCFL into LED as the LCD BLU, Which is now one of the hotspot of LED industry growth and study [1-8].

Dozens of even hundreds of high-brightness LEDs are usually adopted to provide sufficient luminance for medium or large sized LCD. It is necessary for the LED

M. Zhao and J. Sha (Eds.): ICCIP 2012, Part I, CCIS 288, pp. 394–402, 2012.

driver to provide higher driving voltage, greater driving current, stricter heat dissipation and more flexible control. There are several methods of LED drivers. A straightforward approach is to employ a current regulator for a multi-string LEDs group. The current regulator can be of linear or switch-mode type. The approach employing linear regulators is simple, cheap and free of EMI, but suffers from poor operating efficiency because of the voltage drop across the linear regulator. This drawback of the linear current regulator LED driver can be overcome by employing a more efficient switch-mode current regulator to drive the multi-string LEDs group. Although this approach offers a higher operating efficiency compared with its linear counterpart, it can not supply comprehensive protection for the LED driver when an LED is in short circuit or in open circuit. To compensate for these shortcomings, some advanced driver ICs have been launched, they can drive dozens of LEDs and supply comprehensive protection for the LED driver. But these driver ICs are expensive [1, 9].

Using the joint frequency-pulse width modulation scheme, an LED driver based on MCU is proposed in the paper. The joint frequency-pulse width modulation scheme is proposed to regulate the output voltage, which improves the efficiency of the power. The MOSFET driver is designed to charge or discharge the gate with big drive current capability, which can reduce the time of MOSFET to be turned on and off efficiently and enhanced the system performance-to-price ratio. The paper is organized as follows. In section 2, we begin with a brief introduction of the principle of proposed LED driver based on MCU. In section 3, the joint frequency-pulse width modulation scheme is proposed. In section 4, The MOSFET driver is designed. Measurement results are presented in section 5. The last section concludes the paper.

2   Proposed LED Driver Based on MCU

PIC16F1937 is used as the main control MCU in the proposed LED driver using the joint frequency-pulse width modulation scheme. Making full use of peripherals in the chip, the LED driver is integrated with external MOSFETs, transistors, inductors, resistors, capacitors, and controllable constant current sources. The proposed LED driver can not only drive dozens of LEDs and supply comprehensive protection for the LED driver, but also change the number of LEDs driven flexibly. The proposed LED driver shown in Fig. 1 consists of the main control MCU, the MOSFET driver, the DC-DC boost converter and the controllable constant current sources. The input voltage is measured by the Analog Digital Converter (ADC) module in MCU chip after the chip operates, and then the system control parameters are loaded from the on-chip memory. A PWM signal is generated by the Pulse Width Modulation (PWM) module in MCU chip, and amplified by the MOSFET driver, which is used to drive a DC-DC boost converter for LED power. During the startup and normal work of the DC-DC boost converter, the voltage and current of the boost circuit, along with all the channels current of LED, are measured by ADC, which are used to adjust the voltage of the boost circuit and provide over-current protection for the DC-DC boost converter, and provide short circuit and open circuit protection for all LED channels.

PWM dimming for all the LED string is implemented by the Timer module. SPI or I2C is a serial interface useful for communicating with other peripheral or microcontroller devices. The following will focus on the joint frequency-pulse width modulation scheme and the MOSFET driver.

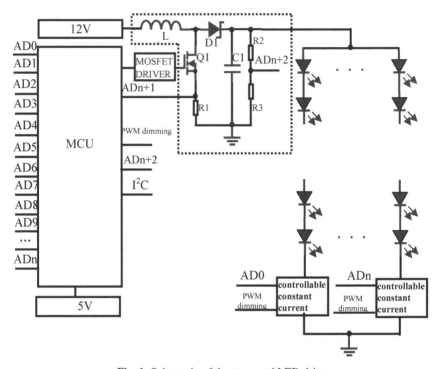

Fig. 1. Schematic of the proposed LED driver

3   Joint Frequency-Pulse Width Modulation Scheme

PWM control technology with its easy and flexible has become widely used for power electronics control mode. In the PIC16F1937 PWM mode, the PWM module produces up to a 10-bit resolution PWM output signal on the CCPx pin. According to the formulas of the PIC16F1937 PWM signal[10], the period, pulse width, duty cycle ratio and output voltage of the DC-DC boost converter can be expressed explicitly as following when the chip crystal oscillator operating frequency is 32MHz, the prescaler is 1: 1.

$$\text{PWM } Period = (PR2_X + 1) \times 4 \times T_{OSC} \times (TMR_X \text{ Prescale Value}) \tag{1}$$

$$\text{PWM Width} = B_{10} \times T_{OSC} \times (TMR_X \text{ Pr escale Value}) \tag{2}$$

$$Dute \text{ cycle Ratio} = \frac{B_{10}}{(PR2_X + 1) \times 4} \tag{3}$$

$$V_{OUT} = \frac{(PR2_X + 1) \times 4 \times V_{IN}}{(PR2_X + 1) \times 4 - B_{10}} \tag{4}$$

where $PR2_X$ is the value of the period register, T_{OSC} is the chip clock cycle, B_{10} is a 10-bit value to multiple registers: CCPRxL register and CCPxCON register, which specifies the PWM duty cycle ratio. $PR2_X$ specifies the period, also specifies available duty cycle ratio. Equation (3) shows that the PWM duty cycle ratio is only related to B_{10} and $PR2_X$, and it has nothing to do with the chip clock cycle. Therefore, $(PR2_X+1)\times4$ denotes the period, and B_{10} denotes the pulse width in the following. The operating frequency of the DC-DC boost converter is 500KHz when $PR2_X$ is equal to 15, and the input voltage is 12V. According to equation (4), the pulse width and corresponding output voltage is given in table 1 in the vicinity of 30V.

Table 1. Part of the pulse width and corresponding output voltage when the operating frequency of the DC-DC boost converter is 500KHz

pulse width	34	35	36	37	38	39	40
output voltage	25.6	26.48	27.43	28.44	29.54	30.72	32.

Table 1 shows that the output voltage is a series of discrete values because the pulse width is discrete. Equation (4) indicates that the output voltage and the pulse width are in reverse proportion. The output voltage and the pulse width are not on the same scale change, but with increasing the pulse width, the difference of the output voltage value increases.

The typical LED forward voltage drop is approximately 3.4V in the paper. LED is 12-series and 8-parallel (the structure can be changed flexibly according to the actual application). Then the typical voltage drop of LED strings is 27.2V. The controllable constant current source requires voltage about 1V. Therefore the typical output voltage of the DC-DC boost converter is 28.2V. The output voltage must reserve approximately the 2V redundancy for the LED individual difference or power fluctuation. Finally the output voltage range is 26.2-30.2V. Table 1 shows that the output voltage is a series of discrete values. In order to meet the drive voltage of a group of LEDs, according to the ADC measurement results, MCU will adjust the output voltage to a higher value than the drive voltage LED required. For an example, the drive voltage of a group of LED is 28.5V, but the converter is unable to output 28.5V, MCU will adjust the output voltage to 29.54V to meet the drive voltage LED required. Unnecessary 1V will drop in the controllable constant current source, and generate heat. In this way, not only there is a waste of energy, but also producing heat reduces the reliability of the system.

From Equation (4), one can see that the output voltage of the DC-DC boost converter is not only related to B_{10}, but $PR2_X$. Different $PR2_X$ is set to change the frequency of the DC-DC boost converter. The pulse width and corresponding output voltage is given in table 2 when the frequency of the DC-DC boost converter is 421.052KHz, and the input voltage is 12V too.

Table 2. Part of the pulse width and corresponding output voltage when the operating frequency of the DC-DC boost converter is 421.052KHz

pulse width	41	42	43	44	45	46	47
output voltage	26.06	26.82	27.64	28.5	29.42	30.4	31.45

Table 3. Part of the pulse width and corresponding output voltage when the joint frequency-pulse width modulation scheme is used

frequency (KHz)	444.44	470.588	500	533.33	...	444.44	400.000	470.588
PR2$_X$	17	16	15	14	...	17	19	16
period	72	68	64	60	...	72	80	68
pulse width	39	36	35	33	...	43	48	43
output voltage	26.18	26.32	26.48	26.67	...	29.79	30.00	30.22

Table 2 shows that the output voltage meets the requirement of the LED driver when the pulse width is 44.

Based on the above, the joint frequency-pulse width modulation scheme is proposed to regulate the output voltage of the DC-DC boost converter to an ideal value in the range of error, which improves the efficiency of the power, reduces producing heat, and increase the reliability of the system. The steps of the method are as follows.

The first step, within the frequency range set, the pulse width and corresponding target output voltage of the different pulse width are listed in the table as shown in tables 1, 2.

The second step, the required voltage and its corresponding parameters are ordered by the output voltage from small to large, as shown in table 3. Maybe the output voltage is the same in a pulse width of the different frequency, the parameters of smaller frequency is selected. Measurement results show that the period is long, and the precision is high when the frequency is low. Table 3 shows that the step size of the output voltage is much smaller than the original only adjusting pulse width after using the joint frequency-pulse width modulation scheme, while the pulse width is still discrete. Most of the output voltage step size is minimized to about 0.1V, and the maximum step size is less than 0.3V in the paper.

The third step, the values of PR2$_X$ and pulse width are saved in the table of the program. During MCU running, according to the measurement results of the voltage and current of the DC-DC boost converter, along with all the channels current of LED, MCU adjusts dynamically the frequency and the pulse width. As a result, the output voltage is regulated to an ideal value in the range of error, and the efficiency of the power is increased.

4   MOSFET Driver

MOSFET is the voltage controlled component. Theoretically, as long as an appropriate voltage is powered to the gate and maintained, MOSFET is turned on. But in fact, in order to speed up the MOSFET switching, it is necessary to charge or discharge the grid capacitance with big drive current, typically 1 - 2 A [11]. Some famous semiconductor design companies such as Microchip have launched the MOSFET driver chip [12]. These chips can effectively reduce the switching times, decrease the switching cross loss, and improve the power conversion efficiency. But these driver chips are more expensive, which is detrimental to lower manufacturing costs for the entire system.

The MOSFET driver composed of transistors is a very high performance-to-price ratio. The MOSFET driver circuit is shown in Fig.2. The transistor T1 can increase the speed of the MOSFET turn-off, and the transistor T2 can shorten the time of the MOSFET turn-on [11]. But the transistor T1 and T2 are working in linear amplification, which can not achieve the best MOSFET performance, the power conversion efficiency can be further improved still.

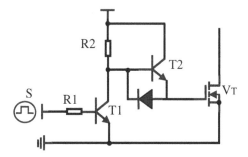

Fig. 2. Circuit diagram of the MOSFET driver composed of transistors

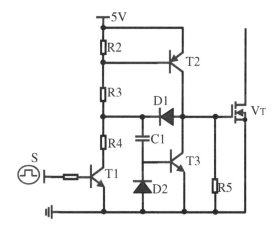

Fig. 3. Circuit diagram of the proposed MOSFET driver

To reduce the time of the MOSFET switching and improve the power conversion efficiency, the MOSFET driver shown in fig.3 is designed to charge or discharge the gate with big drive current capability. The transistor T2 is quickly into the saturated area, which can accelerate the MOSFET turn-on. The transistor T3 can rapidly extract the current from the MOSFET grid capacitance, which can shorten the time of the MOSFET turn-off. As a result, the proposed MOSFET driver can decrease the switching cross loss, and improve the power conversion efficiency. At the same time, the proposed MOSFET driver is composed of transistors, which lowers manufacturing costs for the entire system.

5   Measurement Results

After completing the LED driver using the joint frequency-pulse width modulation scheme, the whole system is measured. Measurement results show that the measured output voltage of the DC-DC boost converter is a little larger than the theoretical calculations results about 0.2V. Furthermore, the measured output voltage is more larger than the theoretical calculations results when the frequency is more higher, and the period is more shorter. But most of the output voltage step size is still about 0.1V, the maximum step size is less than 0.3V. The system operates steadily, and keeps sensitive to the power changes. Therefore the proposed LED driver meets the demand of the parameter of LED. The efficiency of the DC-DC boost converter is up to 94%, and the LED consumption power to input power ratio is more than 85%. Fig. 4 and 5 show the two photos at the nominal current and LED PWM dimming operating. The power parameters shown in the photos prove the dimming module to work correctly from the perspective of power, and the precision of PWM dimming is confirmed.

Fig. 4. Photo at the nominal current (20mA)

Fig. 5. Photo at the PWM dimming operation (50% duty cycle ratio)

6   Conclusions

Using the joint frequency-pulse width modulation scheme, An LED driver based on MCU is proposed in the paper. A PWM signal is generated by PWM in MCU chip, which is used to drive a DC-DC boost converter for LED power. The voltage and current of the boost circuit, along with all the channels current of LED, are measured by ADC module in MCU chip, which are used to adjust the voltage of the boost circuit and supply comprehensive protection for the LED driver. To minimize the step size of the output voltage, the joint frequency-pulse width modulation scheme is proposed to regulate the output voltage of the boost circuit to an ideal value in the range of error, which increases the efficiency of the power. To reduce the crossover power dissipation of the MOSFET switch, the MOSFET driver is designed to charge or discharge the gate with big drive current capability, which can reduce the time of MOSFET to be turned on and off efficiently, and lower manufacturing costs for the entire system. The measurement results show that the LED driver is extremely efficient and steady, the maximum step size of the output voltage is less than 0.3V, and the conversion efficiency of the DC-DC boost converter is up to 94%. Thus the LED driver not only meets the demand of the parameter of LED, but also has high cost performance.

Acknowledgments. The research is supported by Development Special Fund of Shanghai Software and Integrated Circuit Industry and Postgraduate Innovation Fund of Shanghai University.

References

1. Cho, S.H., Lee, S.H., Hong, S.S., et al.: High-Accuracy and Cost-Effective Current-Balanced Multichannel LED Backlight Driver using Single-Transformer. In: 8th International Conference on Power Electronics - ECCE Asia, May 30-June 3, pp. 520–527 (2011)
2. Hsieh, C.Y., Chen, K.H.: Boost DC-DC Converter with Fast Reference Tracking (FRT) and Charge-Recycling (CR) Techniques for High-Efficiency and Low-Cost LED Driver. IEEE Journal of Solid-State Circuits 44(9), 2568–2579 (2009)
3. Lo, Y.K., Wu, K.H., Pai, K.J., et al.: Design and Implementation of RGB LED Drivers for LCD Backlight Modules. IEEE Transactions on Industrial Electronics 56(12), 4862–4871 (2009)
4. Liou, W.R., Lin, C.Y., Chen, T.H., et al.: Multi-channel Constant Current LED Driver with Temperature and Voltage Compensation. In: 2010 International Conference on Communications, Circuits and Systems (ICCCAS), July 28-30, pp. 527–531 (2010)
5. Hsieh, Y.T., Liu, B.D., Wu, J.F., et al.: A High Current Accuracy Boost White LED Driver Based on Offset Calibration Technique. IEEE Transactions on Circuits and Systems—II: Express Briefs 58(4), 244–248 (2011)
6. Wu, C., Hui, S.Y.R.: A Dimmable Light-Emitting Diode (LED) Driver With Mag-Amp Postregulators for Multistring Applications. IEEE Transations on Power Electronics 26(6), 1714–1722 (2011)

7. Wang, K.F.: Design and research of High-power LED driver power supply based on Optimized PID algorithm. In: 2010 International Conference on Computer, Mechatronics, Control and Electronic Engineering (CMCE), vol. 3, pp. 372–375 (2010)

8. Zhang, J.M., Xu, L.H., Qian, Z.M.: A Precise Passive Current Balancing Method for Multioutput LED Drivers. IEEE Transations on Power Electronics 26(8), 2149–2159 (2011)

9. MAX16809/MAX16810 Integrated 16-Channel LED Drivers with Switch-Mode Boost and SEPIC Controller, http://www.maxim-ic.com/

10. PIC16F193X/LF193X Data Sheet, http://www.microchip.com

11. Sanjaya, M.: Swithing Power Supply Design & Optimization. The McGraw-Hill Companies, Inc. (2006)

12. TC4426/27/28 System Design Practice, http://www.microchip.com

Robust H-Infinity Control for a Class of Discrete-Time Nonlinear Uncertain Singular Systems with Time Delays Both in State Equation and Output Equation

Jiqing Qiu, Zirui Xing, Xiuyun Suo, Tao Su, Mohan Yang, Wei Rong,
Yi Li, and Long Zhao

School of Science Hebei University of Science and Technology
Shijiazhuang 050018, China
qiujiqing@263.net, xing-zirui@163.com

Abstract. In this paper, we discuss the problem of robust H-infinity control for a class of discrete-time nonlinear uncertain singular systems with time delay. A new delay-dependent bounded real lemma for singular systems with interval time delays is derived and expressed in terms of LMI. Based on the result, considering the nonlinear disturbance link to uncertain discrete-time singular systems with time delay effects, we come up with the design idea of robust H-infinity controller based on the Lyapunov stability theory. Using Lyapunov stability theory and linear matrix inequality (LMI) methods, we give a robust H-infinity controller design example of such nonlinear uncertain discrete-time singular systems with time delay both in state equation and output equation. Under the condition that nonlinear uncertain functions satisfy Lipschitz condition, we get a sufficient condition of such nonlinear uncertain singular discrete-time delay systems which are asymptotically stable and satisfy the robust H-infinity performance. Finally, a numerical example is given to show the applicability of the proposed method.

Keywords: Singular discrete-time delay systems, Nonlinear, Uncertain, Linear matrix inequality (LMI), Robust H-infinity control.

1   Introduction

The research of singular system dated from the 1970 s, it widely exists in many practical system models, such as electric power system, energy system, aerospace engineering, chemical reaction process, economic system and social system and biological systems, etc. So a great number of results based on the theory of state-space systems have been generalized to singular systems [1]. Control theory for linear discrete singular systems has achieved substantive achievements [2-7]. However, in engineering practice, a lot of systems have uncertain and nonlinear features. And it is not easy to control and make models, so many scholars began the researches in linear uncertain discrete-time singular systems with time delay [8-11]. Robust H-infinity control problem for linear uncertain discrete-time singular systems with time delay was discussed in [9-11]. Stability and

M. Zhao and J. Sha (Eds.): ICCIP 2012, Part I, CCIS 288, pp. 403–414, 2012.

H-infinity control problem for linear uncertain discrete-time singular systems with time-varying delay was considered in [12-15]. A new delay-dependent bounded real lemma for singular systems with interval time delays is derived and expressed in terms of LMI in [17]. Stability and robust control problem for nonlinear discrete-time singular systems was investigated in [19-20]. Stability analysis problem for discrete-time singular systems with nonlinear perturbation was studied in [19]. It has not involved the time delay and the uncertainty of the coefficient matrix; Robust H-infinity control and H-infinity guaranteed cost control problem for discrete-time singular systems with nonlinear perturbation was studied in [20]. This uncertainty is a function of time and state, and meets the conditions of Lipschitz, but it still does not involve the uncertainty of the coefficient matrix.

In this paper, the linear uncertain discrete-time singular systems are extended to the nonlinear uncertain discrete-time singular systems with time delay. A new delay-dependent bounded real lemma for discrete-time singular systems with interval time delays is derived and expressed in terms of LMI. Based on the result, considering the uncertainty and time delays both in state equation and output equation, we give asufficient conditions of the nonlinear uncertain discrete-time singular systems with time delay with nonlinear disturbance vector function which is asymptotically stable and satisfies the robust H-infinity performance criteria. This can guarantee the stability of the closed-loop system, and meet the robust H-infinity performance criteria.

2   Problem Formulation

Consider the following discrete-time nonlinear uncertain singular systems with time delays described as:

$$Ex(k+1) = (A + \Delta A)x(k) + (A_1 + \Delta A_1)x(k-h) + f_1(k, x(k)) + f_2(k, x(k-d)) + (B_1 + \Delta B_1)\omega(k) + B_2 u(k)$$
$$z(k) = (C + \Delta C)x(k) + (C_1 + \Delta C_1)x(k-h) + (D_1 + \Delta D_1)\omega(k) + D_2 u(k)$$
$$x(k) = \varphi(k), k = -\tau, -\tau+1, ..., 0$$

$$(1)$$

where $x(k) \in R^n$ is the state vector; $\omega(k) \in R^p$ is the disturbance input vector; $u(k) \in R^m$ is the control input vector which belongs to $L_2[0, +\infty)$; $z(k) \in R^q$ is the control output vector; $\varphi(k)$ is a known initial sequence; $E, A, A_1, B_1, B_2, C, C_1, D_1, D_2$ are known real constant matrices of appropriate dimensions, where the matrix $E \in R^{n \times n}$ may be singular, and is assumed that rank $(E) = r \le n$; h, d are positive integer time-delay constants, and τ is a known constant satisfying $\tau = \max[h, d]$; $f_1(k, x(k)), f_2(k, x(k-d)) \in R^n$ are vector functions of n dimensions; $\Delta A, \Delta A_1, \Delta B_1, \Delta C, \Delta C_1, \Delta D_1$ are unknown matrices representing the parameter uncertainties of the system, which are assumed to be of the following form:

$$\begin{bmatrix} \Delta A & \Delta A_1 & \Delta B_1 \\ \Delta C & \Delta C_1 & \Delta D_1 \end{bmatrix} = \begin{bmatrix} X_1 \\ X_2 \end{bmatrix} \Delta(k) \begin{bmatrix} Y_1 & Y_2 & Y_3 \end{bmatrix} \qquad (2)$$

where X_1, X_2, Y_1, Y_2, Y_3 are known real constant matrices of appropriate dimensions, $\Delta(k)$ is the time-varying matrix with Lebesgue-measurable elements and satisfies the following form:

$$\Delta^T(k)\Delta(k) \le I .\tag{3}$$

The parameter uncertainties $\Delta A, \Delta A_1, \Delta B_1, \Delta C, \Delta C_1, \Delta D_1$ are said to be admissible if both type (2) and (3) hold.

$f_1(k, x(k)), f_2(k, x(k-d)) \in R^n$ are vector-valued time-varying and state-dependent nonlinear perturbations with

$$f_1(k, 0) = 0, f_2(k, 0) = 0 \text{ for all } k \ge 0, k \in Z.\tag{4}$$

and satisfy the following Lipschitz conditions

$$\begin{aligned}&\left\| f_1(k, x(k)) - f_1(k, \tilde{x}(k)) \right\| \le \left\| F_1(x(k) - \tilde{x}(k)) \right\|,\\&\left\| f_2(k, x(k-d)) - f_2(k, \tilde{x}(k-d)) \right\| \le \left\| F_2(x(k-d) - \tilde{x}(k-d)) \right\|.\end{aligned}\tag{5}$$

$$\forall x(k), \tilde{x}(k), x(k-d), \tilde{x}(k-d) \in R^n .$$

where F_1, F_2 are known real constant matrices of appropriate dimensions, $\left\| x \right\|$ is the Euclidean norm of the vector x .

By type (4) and (5), it follows that

$$\begin{aligned}&\left\| f_1(k, x(k)) \right\| \le \left\| F_1 x(k) \right\|,\\&\left\| f_2(k, x(k-d)) \right\| \le \left\| F_2 x(k-d) \right\|.\end{aligned}\tag{6}$$

For system (1), we design a memoryless state feedback controller

$$u(k) = Kx(k)\tag{7}$$

to make the closed-loop system

$$\begin{aligned}Ex(k+1) &= (A + \Delta A + B_2 K)x(k) + (A_1 + \Delta A_1)x(k-h) + f_1(k, x(k)) + f_2(k, x(k-d)) + (B_1 + \Delta B_1)\omega(k)\\z(k) &= (C + \Delta C + D_2 K)x(k) + (C_1 + \Delta C_1)x(k-h) + (D_1 + \Delta D_1)\omega(k)\\x(k) &= \varphi(k), k = -\tau, -\tau+1, \ldots, 0\end{aligned}$$

$$\tag{8}$$

The purpose of this paper is designing a memoryless robust H_∞ state feedback controller (7) for the system (1) such that the closed-loop system is asymptotically stable, and the H_∞ performance index satisfies $J = \sum_{k=0}^{\infty} [z^T(k)z(k) - \gamma^2 \omega^T(k)\omega(k)] < 0$ for all time delays and uncertainties, $\gamma > 0$ is given.

Before concluding this section, we recall some lemmas which will be used in the sections.

Lemma 1 [13]. *For given the matrices Ω, A, B with appropriate dimensions and Ω with symmetric, we have the matrix inequality $\Omega + A^T CB + B^T C^T A < 0$ for any*

C satisfying $C^T C \leq I$, if and only if there exists a scalar $\varepsilon > 0$ such that $\Omega + \varepsilon^{-1} A^T A + \varepsilon B^T B < 0$.

For simplicity, we introduce the matrix $\Gamma \in R^{n \times (n-r)}$ satisfying $E^T \Gamma = 0$ and rank $(\Gamma) = n - r$. $x(k), x(k-h), x(k-d), f_1(k, x(k)), f_2(k, x(k-d))$ were recorded as x, x_h, x_d, f_1, f_2 .

3   New Delay-Dependent Bounded Real Lemma

In this section, we present the new bounded real lemma for the following discrete-time nominal unforced singular systems with time delays:

$$Ex(k+1) = Ax(k) + A_1 x(k-h) + f_1(k, x(k)) + f_2(k, x(k-d)) + B_1 \omega(k)$$
$$z(k) = Cx(k) + C_1 x(k-h) + D_1 \omega(k) \tag{9}$$

In the following, we introduce two vectors:

$$\xi(k) = \begin{bmatrix} x^T & x_h^T & x_d^T & f_1^T & f_2^T & \omega^T(k) \end{bmatrix}^T,$$
$$y(k) = x(k+1) - x(k) \tag{10}$$

then

$$Ex(k+1) = \begin{bmatrix} A & A_1 & 0 & I & I & B_1 \end{bmatrix} \xi(k) \equiv \Omega_1 \xi(k),$$
$$Ey(k) = \begin{bmatrix} A-E & A_1 & 0 & I & I & B_1 \end{bmatrix} \xi(k) \equiv \Omega_2 \xi(k). \tag{11}$$

The following lemma gives the relationship between the vectors $\xi(k)$ and $Ey(k)$, which will play an important role in the new delay-dependent bounded real lemma.

Lemma 2. *For any constat matrices* $G_1, G_2, G_3, G_4, G_5, G_6, H$ *and positive definite matrices* Q_1, Q_2 *with proper dimensions and time delays, we have*

$$-\sum_{l=k-h}^{k-1} y^T(l) E^T Q_1 Ey(l) - \sum_{l=k-d}^{k-1} y^T(l) E^T Q_2 Ey(l) \leq \xi^T(k)(\Phi_1 + \Phi_2 + h N_1^T Q_1^{-1} N_1 + d N_2^T Q_2^{-1} N_2) \xi(k) \tag{12}$$

where

$$\Phi_1 = \begin{pmatrix} G_1^T E + E^T G_1 & -G_1^T E + E^T G_2 & 0 & 0 & 0 & E^T H \\ * & -G_2^T E - E^T G_2 & 0 & 0 & 0 & -E^T H \\ * & * & 0 & 0 & 0 & 0 \\ * & * & * & 0 & 0 & 0 \\ * & * & * & * & 0 & 0 \\ * & * & * & * & * & 0 \end{pmatrix}, \Phi_2 = \begin{pmatrix} G_3^T E + E^T G_3 & 0 & -G_3^T E & E^T G_4 & E^T G_5 & E^T H \\ * & 0 & 0 & 0 & 0 & 0 \\ * & * & 0 & -E^T G_4 & -E^T G_5 & -E^T H \\ * & * & * & 0 & 0 & 0 \\ * & * & * & * & 0 & 0 \\ * & * & * & * & * & 0 \end{pmatrix},$$

$$N_1 = [G_1 \ G_2 \ 0 \ 0 \ 0 \ H], N_2 = [G_3 \ 0 \ 0 \ G_4 \ G_5 \ H], \tag{13}$$

part $(*)$ *can be available by symmetry.*

Proof. Similar to Lemma 3 of the paper [13].

Based on Lemma 2., a new delay-dependent bounded real lemma is derived.

4   Main Results

In this section, we will first consider the discrete-time delayed nominal unforced singular system (9).

Theorem 1. *For given scalar $\gamma > 0$, the system (9) is asymptotically stable and satisfies the robust H_∞ performance criteria if there exist symmetric positive definite matrices P, Q_1, Q_2, Q_3, Q_4 and matrices $M, G_1, G_2, G_3, G_4, G_5, G_6, H$ such that the following LMI holds*

$$
\Theta = \begin{pmatrix}
\Theta_{11} & \Theta_{12} & \Theta_{13} & \Theta_{14} & \Theta_{15} & \Theta_{16} & A^T P & \Theta_{18} & \Theta_{19} & E^T & F_1^T & hG_1^T & dG_3^T & C^T \\
* & \Theta_{22} & 0 & 0 & 0 & \Theta_{26} & A_1^T P & hA_1^T Q_1 & dA_1^T Q_2 & 0 & 0 & hG_2^T & 0 & C_1^T \\
* & * & \Theta_{33} & \Theta_{34} & \Theta_{35} & \Theta_{36} & 0 & 0 & 0 & 0 & 0 & 0 & 0 & 0 \\
* & * & * & -I & 0 & 0 & P & hQ_1 & dQ_2 & 0 & 0 & 0 & dG_4^T & 0 \\
* & * & * & * & -I & 0 & P & hQ_1 & dQ_2 & 0 & 0 & 0 & dG_5^T & 0 \\
* & * & * & * & * & -\gamma^2 I & B_1^T P & hB_1^T Q_1 & dB_1^T Q_2 & 0 & 0 & hH^T & dH^T & D_1^T \\
* & * & * & * & * & * & -P & 0 & 0 & 0 & 0 & 0 & 0 & 0 \\
* & * & * & * & * & * & * & -hQ_1 & 0 & 0 & 0 & 0 & 0 & 0 \\
* & * & * & * & * & * & * & * & -dQ_2 & 0 & 0 & 0 & 0 & 0 \\
* & * & * & * & * & * & * & * & * & -P & 0 & 0 & 0 & 0 \\
* & * & * & * & * & * & * & * & * & * & -I & 0 & 0 & 0 \\
* & * & * & * & * & * & * & * & * & * & * & -hQ_1 & 0 & 0 \\
* & * & * & * & * & * & * & * & * & * & * & * & -dQ_2 & 0 \\
* & * & * & * & * & * & * & * & * & * & * & * & * & -I
\end{pmatrix} < 0
$$

$$\tag{14}$$

where

$$\Theta_{11} = A^T \Gamma M^T + M \Gamma^T A + G_1^T E + E^T G_1 + G_3^T E + E^T G_3 + hQ_3 + dQ_4,$$

$$\Theta_{12} = M \Gamma^T A_1 - G_1^T E + E^T G_2, \Theta_{13} = -G_3^T E, \Theta_{14} = M \Gamma^T + E^T G_4, \Theta_{15} = M \Gamma^T + E^T G_5,$$

$$\Theta_{16} = M \Gamma^T B_1 + 2E^T H, \Theta_{22} = -G_2^T E - E^T G_2 - Q_3, \Theta_{26} = -E^T H, \Theta_{33} = -Q_4 + F_2^T F_2,$$

$$\Theta_{34} = -E^T G_4, \Theta_{35} = -E^T G_5, \Theta_{36} = -E^T H, \Theta_{18} = h(A-E)^T Q_1, \Theta_{19} = d(A-E)^T Q_2.$$

part $(*)$ can be available by symmetry.

Proof. To get the expected result, we define a Lyapunov function as follows:

$$V(k) = V_1(k) + V_2(k) + V_3(k) + V_4(k) + V_5(k) + V_6(k) + V_7(k) \tag{15}$$

where

$$V_1(k) = x^T E^T P E x, V_2(k) = \sum_{i=-h+1}^{0} \sum_{l=k-1+i}^{k-1} y^T(l) E^T Q_1 E y(l),$$

$$V_3(k) = \sum_{i=-d+1}^{0} \sum_{l=k-1+i}^{k-1} y^T(l) E^T Q_2 E y(l), V_4(k) = \sum_{l=k-h}^{k-1} x^T(l) Q_3 x(l),$$

$$V_5(k) = \sum_{l=k-d}^{k-1} x^T(l) Q_4 x(l), V_6(k) = \sum_{i=0}^{k-1} [F_1 x(i)]^T [F_1 x(i)] - \sum_{i=0}^{k-1} f_1^T(i) f_1(i),$$

$$V_7(k) = \sum_{i=0}^{k-1} [F_2 x(i-d)]^T [F_2 x(i-d)] - \sum_{i=0}^{k-1} f_2^T(i) f_2(i).$$

Using the forward differences $\Delta V(k) = V(k+1) - V(k)$ along the trajectory of the system(9) , we can be obtained as follows:

$$\Delta V_1(k) = x^T(k+1)E^T PEx(k+1) - x^T(k)E^T PEx(k) = \xi^T(k)\Omega_1^T P\Omega_1\xi(k) - \xi^T(k)\Omega_3\xi(k),$$

$$\Delta V_2(k) = h\xi^T(k)\Omega_2^T Q_1\Omega_2\xi(k) - \sum_{l=k-h}^{k-1} y^T(l)E^T Q_1 Ey(l),$$

$$\Delta V_3(k) = d\xi^T(k)\Omega_2^T Q_2\Omega_2\xi(k) - \sum_{l=k-d}^{k-1} y^T(l)E^T Q_2 Ey(l)$$

$$\Delta V_4(k) = hx^T(k)Q_3 x(k) - x^T(k-h)Q_3 x(k-h) = \xi^T(k)\Omega_4\xi(k),$$

$$\Delta V_5(k) = dx^T(k)Q_4 x(k) - x^T(k-d)Q_4 x(k-d) = \xi^T(k)\Omega_5\xi(k),$$

$$\Delta V_6(k) = [F_1 x(k)]^T [F_1 x(k)] - f_1^T(k)f_1(k) - [F_1 x(0)]^T [F_1 x(0)] + f_1^T(0)f_1(0)$$
$$\leq [F_1 x(k)]^T [F_1 x(k)] - f_1^T(k)f_1(k) = \xi^T(k)\Omega_6\xi(k),$$

$$\Delta V_7(k) = [F_2 x(k-d)]^T [F_1 x(k-d)] - f_2^T(k)f_2(k) - [F_2 x(0-d)]^T [F_2 x(0-d)] + f_2^T(0)f_2(0)$$
$$\leq [F_2 x(k-d)]^T [F_2 x(k-d)] - f_2^T(k)f_2(k) = \xi^T(k)\Omega_7\xi(k),$$

where

$$\Omega_3 = \begin{pmatrix} E^T PE & 0 & 0 & 0 & 0 & 0 \\ * & 0 & 0 & 0 & 0 & 0 \\ * & * & 0 & 0 & 0 & 0 \\ * & * & * & 0 & 0 & 0 \\ * & * & * & * & 0 & 0 \\ * & * & * & * & * & 0 \end{pmatrix}, \Omega_4 = \begin{pmatrix} hQ_3 & 0 & 0 & 0 & 0 & 0 \\ * & -Q_3 & 0 & 0 & 0 & 0 \\ * & * & 0 & 0 & 0 & 0 \\ * & * & * & 0 & 0 & 0 \\ * & * & * & * & 0 & 0 \\ * & * & * & * & * & 0 \end{pmatrix}, \Omega_5 = \begin{pmatrix} dQ_4 & 0 & 0 & 0 & 0 & 0 \\ * & 0 & 0 & 0 & 0 & 0 \\ * & * & -Q_4 & 0 & 0 & 0 \\ * & * & * & 0 & 0 & 0 \\ * & * & * & * & 0 & 0 \\ * & * & * & * & * & 0 \end{pmatrix},$$

$$\Omega_6 = \begin{pmatrix} F_1^T F_1 & 0 & 0 & 0 & 0 & 0 \\ * & 0 & 0 & 0 & 0 & 0 \\ * & * & 0 & 0 & 0 & 0 \\ * & * & * & -I & 0 & 0 \\ * & * & * & * & 0 & 0 \\ * & * & * & * & * & 0 \end{pmatrix}, \Omega_7 = \begin{pmatrix} 0 & 0 & 0 & 0 & 0 & 0 \\ * & 0 & 0 & 0 & 0 & 0 \\ * & * & F_2^T F_2 & 0 & 0 & 0 \\ * & * & * & 0 & 0 & 0 \\ * & * & * & * & -I & 0 \\ * & * & * & * & * & 0 \end{pmatrix}.$$

According to Lemma 2., we have

$$\Delta V(k) \leq \xi^T(k)(\Omega_1^T P\Omega_1 - \Omega_3 + h\Omega_2^T Q_1\Omega_2 + d\Omega_2^T Q_2\Omega_2 + \Phi_1 + \Phi_2$$
$$+ hN_1^T Q_1^{-1}N_1 + dN_2^T Q_2^{-1}N_2 + \Omega_4 + \Omega_5 + \Omega_6 + \Omega_7)\xi(k) < 0, \tag{16}$$

Noticing that $E^T\Gamma = 0$, we can deduce

$$2x^T(k+1)E^T\Gamma M^T x(k) = \xi^T(k)\Omega_8\xi(k) = 0, \tag{17}$$

where

$$\Omega_8 = \begin{pmatrix} A^T\Gamma M^T + M\Gamma^T A & M\Gamma^T A_1 & 0 & M\Gamma^T & M\Gamma^T & M\Gamma^T B_1 \\ * & 0 & 0 & 0 & 0 & 0 \\ * & * & 0 & 0 & 0 & 0 \\ * & * & * & 0 & 0 & 0 \\ * & * & * & * & 0 & 0 \\ * & * & * & * & * & 0 \end{pmatrix}.$$

We first consider that the system (9) with $\omega(k) = 0$ is asymptotically stable. In fact, type (14) implies

$$\Theta' = \begin{pmatrix} \Theta_{11} & \Theta_{12} & \Theta_{13} & \Theta_{14} & \Theta_{15} & A^T P & \Theta_{18} & \Theta_{19} & E^T & F_1^T & hG_1^T & dG_3^T \\ * & \Theta_{22} & 0 & 0 & 0 & A_1^T P & hA_1^T Q_1 & dA_1^T Q_2 & 0 & 0 & hG_2^T & 0 \\ * & * & \Theta_{33} & \Theta_{34} & \Theta_{35} & 0 & 0 & 0 & 0 & 0 & 0 & 0 \\ * & * & * & -I & 0 & P & hQ_1 & dQ_2 & 0 & 0 & 0 & dG_4^T \\ * & * & * & * & -I & P & hQ_1 & dQ_2 & 0 & 0 & 0 & dG_5^T \\ * & * & * & * & * & -P & 0 & 0 & 0 & 0 & 0 & 0 \\ * & * & * & * & * & * & -hQ_1 & 0 & 0 & 0 & 0 & 0 \\ * & * & * & * & * & * & * & -dQ_2 & 0 & 0 & 0 & 0 \\ * & * & * & * & * & * & * & * & -P & 0 & 0 & 0 \\ * & * & * & * & * & * & * & * & * & -I & 0 & 0 \\ * & * & * & * & * & * & * & * & * & * & -hQ_1 & 0 \\ * & * & * & * & * & * & * & * & * & * & * & -dQ_2 \end{pmatrix} < 0$$

(18)

According to Schur Complement Lemma and type(17), it is easy to know that type (18) is equivalent to type (16) and (17). So, we have $\Delta V(k) < 0$. Therefore, the system (9) is asymptotically stable.

By type (16) and (17), it follows that $(\omega(k) \neq 0)$

$$J = \sum_{k=0}^{\infty} [z^T(k)z(k) - \gamma^2 \omega^T(k)\omega(k)]$$

$$\leq \sum_{k=0}^{\infty} [z^T(k)z(k) - \gamma^2 \omega^T(k)\omega(k) + V(\infty) - V(0)]$$

$$= \sum_{k=0}^{\infty} \{[Cx + C_1 x_h + D_1 \omega(k)]^T [(Cx + C_1 x_h + D_1 \omega(k)] - \gamma^2 \omega^T(k)\omega(k) + V(\infty) - V(0)\}$$

$$= \sum_{k=0}^{\infty} \{[Cx + C_1 x_h + D_1 \omega(k)]^T [(Cx + C_1 x_h + D_1 \omega(k)] - \gamma^2 \omega^T(k)\omega(k) + \Delta V(k)\}$$

$$= \sum_{k=0}^{\infty} \xi^T(k)\Theta\xi(k) < 0.$$

This completes the proof.
Then, we have a corollary.

Corollary 1. *For given scalar $\gamma > 0$, the system (9) is asymptotically stable and satisfies the robust H_∞ performance criteria if there exist symmetric positive definite matrices P, Q_1, Q_2, Q_3, Q_4 and matrices $M, G_1, G_2, G_3, G_4, G_5, G_6, H$ such that the following LMI holds*

$$
\Theta^{"} = \begin{pmatrix}
\Theta_{11} & \Theta_{12} & \Theta_{13} & \Theta_{14} & \Theta_{15} & \Theta_{16} & C^T & 0 & E^T & F_1^T & hG_1^T & dG_3^T \\
* & \Theta_{22} & 0 & 0 & 0 & \Theta_{26} & C_1^T & 0 & 0 & 0 & hG_2^T & 0 \\
* & * & -Q_4 & \Theta_{34} & \Theta_{35} & \Theta_{36} & 0 & F_2^T & 0 & 0 & 0 & 0 \\
* & * & * & -I & 0 & 0 & 0 & 0 & 0 & 0 & 0 & dG_4^T \\
* & * & * & * & -I & 0 & 0 & 0 & 0 & 0 & 0 & dG_5^T \\
* & * & * & * & * & -\gamma^2 I & D_1^T & 0 & 0 & 0 & hH^T & dH^T \\
* & * & * & * & * & * & -I & 0 & 0 & 0 & 0 & 0 \\
* & * & * & * & * & * & * & -I & 0 & 0 & 0 & 0 \\
* & * & * & * & * & * & * & * & -P & 0 & 0 & 0 \\
* & * & * & * & * & * & * & * & * & -I & 0 & 0 \\
* & * & * & * & * & * & * & * & * & * & -hQ_1 & 0 \\
* & * & * & * & * & * & * & * & * & * & * & -dQ_2
\end{pmatrix} < 0
$$
(19)

part (*) *can be available by symmetry.*

Based on Theorem 1. and Corollary 1., we get a sufficient condition for the existence of robust H_∞ state feedback controller (7).

Theorem 2. *Considering the discrete-time delays nonlinear uncertain singular system (1), for given scalars $\gamma, \alpha_1, \alpha_2 > 0$ and all allowed uncertainty, the closed-loop system (8) is asymptotically stable and satisfies the robust H_∞ performance criteria if there exist symmetric positive definite matrices P, Q_1, Q_2, Q_3, Q_4 and matrices $M, G_1, G_2, G_3, G_4, G_5, G_6, H$ and positive scalars $\mathcal{E}$, such that the following LMI holds*

$$
\Xi = \begin{pmatrix} \Xi_1 & \Xi_2 \\ * & \Xi_3 \end{pmatrix} < 0
$$
(20)

where

$$
\Xi_1 = \begin{pmatrix}
\Xi_{11} & \Xi_{12} & \Xi_{13} & \Xi_{14} & \Xi_{15} & \Xi_{16} & \Xi_{17} & 0 & E^T & F_1^T & hG_1^T & dG_3^T \\
* & \Xi_{22} & 0 & 0 & 0 & \Xi_{26} & C_1^T & 0 & 0 & 0 & hG_2^T & 0 \\
* & * & -Q_4 & \Xi_{34} & \Xi_{35} & \Xi_{36} & 0 & F_2^T & 0 & 0 & 0 & 0 \\
* & * & * & -I & 0 & 0 & 0 & 0 & 0 & 0 & 0 & dG_4^T \\
* & * & * & * & -I & 0 & 0 & 0 & 0 & 0 & 0 & dG_5^T \\
* & * & * & * & * & \Xi_{66} & D_1^T & 0 & 0 & 0 & 0 & 0 \\
* & * & * & * & * & * & -I & 0 & 0 & 0 & 0 & 0 \\
* & * & * & * & * & * & * & -I & 0 & 0 & 0 & 0 \\
* & * & * & * & * & * & * & * & -P & 0 & 0 & 0 \\
* & * & * & * & * & * & * & * & * & -I & 0 & 0 \\
* & * & * & * & * & * & * & * & * & * & -hQ_1 & 0 \\
* & * & * & * & * & * & * & * & * & * & * & -dQ_2
\end{pmatrix} < 0
$$

$$\Xi_2 = \begin{pmatrix} M\Gamma^T X_1 & M\Gamma^T X_1 & 0 & 0 & 0 & M\Gamma^T X_1 Y_1^T & \varepsilon_1 M\Gamma^T B_2 & M\Gamma^T B_2 \\ 0 & 0 & 0 & 0 & 0 & 0 & Y_2^T & 0 & 0 \\ 0 & 0 & 0 & 0 & 0 & 0 & 0 & 0 & 0 \\ 0 & 0 & 0 & 0 & 0 & 0 & 0 & 0 & 0 \\ 0 & 0 & 0 & 0 & 0 & 0 & Y_3^T & 0 & 0 \\ 0 & 0 & 0 & 0 & 0 & 0 & 0 & 0 & 0 \\ 0 & 0 & 0 & 0 & 0 & 0 & 0 & 0 & 0 \\ 0 & 0 & 0 & 0 & 0 & 0 & 0 & 0 & 0 \\ 0 & 0 & 0 & 0 & 0 & 0 & 0 & 0 & 0 \\ 0 & 0 & 0 & 0 & 0 & 0 & 0 & 0 & 0 \\ 0 & 0 & 0 & 0 & 0 & 0 & 0 & 0 & 0 \end{pmatrix},$$

$\Xi_{11} = A^T \Gamma M^T + M\Gamma^T A + G_1^T E + E^T G_1 + G_3^T E + E^T G_3 + hQ_3 + dQ_4 + \varepsilon Y_1^T Y_1,$

$\Xi_{12} = M\Gamma^T A_1 - G_1^T E + E^T G_2, \Xi_{13} = -G_3^T E, \Xi_{14} = M\Gamma^T + E^T G_4, \Xi_{15} = M\Gamma^T + E^T G_5,$

$\Xi_{16} = M\Gamma^T B_1 + 2E^T H, \Xi_{22} = -G_2^T E - E^T G_2 - Q_3 + \varepsilon Y_2^T Y_2, \Xi_{26} = -E^T H,$

$\Xi_{34} = -E^T G_4, \Xi_{35} = -E^T G_5, \Xi_{36} = -E^T H, \Xi_{66} = -\gamma^2 I + \varepsilon Y_3^T Y_3, \Xi_{17} = (C + D_2 K)^T,$

$\Xi_3 = Diag\{-\varepsilon I, -\varepsilon I, -\varepsilon I, -\varepsilon I, -\varepsilon I, -\varepsilon I, -\varepsilon I, -\varepsilon_1 I, -\varepsilon_1 \gamma^2 I\},$

then the robust H_∞ state feedback controller is constructed by

$$u(k) = Kx(k), \quad K = -\gamma^{-1} B_2^T \Gamma M^T.$$

Proof. At first, using $A + B_2 K$ and $C + D_2 K$ to replace A and C, respectively, we can get the following inequality:

$$\Theta^* = \begin{pmatrix} \Theta_{11}^* & \Theta_{12} & \Theta_{13} & \Theta_{14} & \Theta_{15} & \Theta_{16} & (C + D_2 K)^T & 0 & E^T & F_1^T & hG_1^T & dG_3^T \\ * & \Theta_{22} & 0 & 0 & 0 & \Theta_{26} & C_1^T & 0 & 0 & 0 & hG_2^T & 0 \\ * & * & -Q_4 & \Theta_{34} & \Theta_{35} & \Theta_{36} & 0 & F_2^T & 0 & 0 & 0 & 0 \\ * & * & * & -I & 0 & 0 & 0 & 0 & 0 & 0 & 0 & dG_4^T \\ * & * & * & * & -I & 0 & 0 & 0 & 0 & 0 & 0 & dG_5^T \\ * & * & * & * & * & -\gamma^2 I & D_1^T & 0 & 0 & 0 & hH^T & dH^T \\ * & * & * & * & * & * & -I & 0 & 0 & 0 & 0 & 0 \\ * & * & * & * & * & * & * & -I & 0 & 0 & 0 & 0 \\ * & * & * & * & * & * & * & * & -P & 0 & 0 & 0 \\ * & * & * & * & * & * & * & * & * & -I & 0 & 0 \\ * & * & * & * & * & * & * & * & * & * & -hQ_1 & 0 \\ * & * & * & * & * & * & * & * & * & * & * & -dQ_2 \end{pmatrix} < 0$$

where

$\Theta_{11}^* = A^T \Gamma M^T + M\Gamma^T A + G_1^T E + E^T G_1 + G_3^T E + E^T G_3 + hQ_3 + dQ_4 + \varepsilon Y_1^T Y_1 + \varepsilon_1 M\Gamma^T B_2 B_2^T \Gamma M^T + \varepsilon_1^{-1} K^T K,$

Then, using $A + \Delta A, A_1 + \Delta A_1, B_1 + \Delta B_1, C + \Delta C, C_1 + \Delta C_1$ and $D_1 + \Delta D_1$ to replace A, A_1, B_1, C, C_1 and D_1, respectively, where

$\Delta A = X_1\Delta(t)Y_1, \Delta A_1 = X_1\Delta(t)Y_2, \Delta B_1 = X_1\Delta(t)Y_3, \Delta C = X_2\Delta(t)Y_1, \Delta C_1 = X_2\Delta(t)Y_2, \Delta D_1 = X_2\Delta(t)Y_3,$
we can get the following inequality:

$$\Theta^* + \Pi^T\Delta\Psi + \Psi^T\Delta^T\Pi < 0 \tag{21}$$

where

$$\Psi = \begin{pmatrix} Y_1 & 0 & 0 & 0 & 0 & 0 & 0 & 0 & 0 & 0 & 0 & 0 \\ 0 & Y_2 & 0 & 0 & 0 & 0 & 0 & 0 & 0 & 0 & 0 & 0 \\ 0 & 0 & 0 & 0 & 0 & 0 & 0 & 0 & 0 & 0 & 0 & 0 \\ 0 & 0 & 0 & 0 & 0 & 0 & 0 & 0 & 0 & 0 & 0 & 0 \\ 0 & 0 & 0 & 0 & 0 & 0 & 0 & 0 & 0 & 0 & 0 & 0 \\ 0 & 0 & 0 & 0 & 0 & Y_3 & 0 & 0 & 0 & 0 & 0 & 0 \\ 0 & 0 & 0 & 0 & 0 & 0 & X_2^T & 0 & 0 & 0 & 0 & 0 \end{pmatrix},$$

$\Delta = Daig\{\Delta(k), \Delta(k), \Delta(k), \Delta(k), \Delta(k), \Delta(k), \Delta^T(k)\},$

$$\Pi^T = \begin{pmatrix} M\Gamma^T X_1 & M\Gamma^T X_1 & 0 & 0 & 0 & M\Gamma^T X_1 Y_1^T \\ 0 & 0 & 0 & 0 & 0 & 0 & Y_2^T \\ 0 & 0 & 0 & 0 & 0 & 0 & 0 \\ 0 & 0 & 0 & 0 & 0 & 0 & 0 \\ 0 & 0 & 0 & 0 & 0 & 0 & 0 \\ 0 & 0 & 0 & 0 & 0 & 0 & Y_3^T \\ 0 & 0 & 0 & 0 & 0 & 0 & 0 \\ 0 & 0 & 0 & 0 & 0 & 0 & 0 \\ 0 & 0 & 0 & 0 & 0 & 0 & 0 \\ 0 & 0 & 0 & 0 & 0 & 0 & 0 \\ 0 & 0 & 0 & 0 & 0 & 0 & 0 \\ 0 & 0 & 0 & 0 & 0 & 0 & 0 \end{pmatrix},$$

According to Lemma 1., it is easy to know that (20) holds, if and only if:

$$\Theta + \varepsilon^{-1}\Pi^T\Pi + \varepsilon\Psi^T\Psi < 0 \tag{22}$$

According to Schur Complement Lemma and $K = -\gamma^{-1}B_2^T\Gamma M^T$, it is easy to know that Type (22) is equivalent to type (20). This completes the proof.

5   Numerical Example

Consider the discrete-time nonlinear uncertain singular systems with time delay both in state equation and output equation with parameters as follows:

$$E = \begin{bmatrix} 1 & 0 \\ 0 & 0 \end{bmatrix}, A = \begin{bmatrix} 3 & 6 \\ 5 & 8 \end{bmatrix}, A_1 = \begin{bmatrix} 0.1 & 0.2 \\ 0.4 & 0.1 \end{bmatrix}, B_1 = \begin{bmatrix} 0.1 \\ 1 \end{bmatrix}, B_2 = \begin{bmatrix} 0.2 \\ 0.1 \end{bmatrix}, \Gamma = \begin{bmatrix} 0 & 0 \\ 0 & 1 \end{bmatrix},$$

$$C = \begin{bmatrix} 0.1 & 0 \\ 0 & 1 \end{bmatrix}, C_1 = \begin{bmatrix} 0 & 0.1 \\ 0.1 & 0 \end{bmatrix}, D_1 = \begin{bmatrix} 0.1 \\ 0.1 \end{bmatrix}, D_2 = \begin{bmatrix} 0.1 \\ 0.1 \end{bmatrix}, F_1 = \begin{bmatrix} 1 & 0 \\ 0 & 1 \end{bmatrix}, F_2 = \begin{bmatrix} 1 & 0 \\ 0 & 1 \end{bmatrix},$$

$$X_1 = \begin{bmatrix} 0.02 \\ 0.01 \end{bmatrix}, X_2 = \begin{bmatrix} 0.01 \\ 0.02 \end{bmatrix}, Y_1 = \begin{bmatrix} 0.01 & 0.1 \end{bmatrix}, Y_2 = \begin{bmatrix} 0.01 & 0.03 \end{bmatrix}, Y_3 = 0.01,$$

$$f_1 = \begin{bmatrix} \sin x_1(k) \\ \sin x_2(k) \end{bmatrix}, f_2 = \begin{bmatrix} \sin x_1(k-4) \\ \sin x_2(k-4) \end{bmatrix}, \Delta(k) = \sin(k), k \in [-4,0],$$

$$\varepsilon = 0.1, \varepsilon_1 = 0.2, \gamma = 1, h = d = 4.$$

Then, using Matlab LMI Control Toolbox to solve LMI (20), we obtain a solution as follows:

$$P = \begin{bmatrix} 1.4919 & -0.0887 \\ -0.0887 & 1.2134 \end{bmatrix}, Q_1 = \begin{bmatrix} 0.3385 & -0.0064 \\ -0.0064 & 0.3349 \end{bmatrix}, Q_2 = \begin{bmatrix} 0.3366 & -0.0064 \\ -0.0064 & 0.3349 \end{bmatrix},$$

$$Q_3 = \begin{bmatrix} -2.2723 & 0.1472 \\ 0.1472 & -2.0414 \end{bmatrix}, Q_4 = \begin{bmatrix} 1.6845 & 0.0900 \\ 0.0900 & 1.7754 \end{bmatrix}, M = \begin{bmatrix} 0 & -0.0476 \\ 0 & -0.1264 \end{bmatrix},$$

$$G_1 = \begin{bmatrix} -0.0102 & 0.0053 \\ 0.0000 & 0.0000 \end{bmatrix}, G_2 = \begin{bmatrix} -0.0444 & 0.0077 \\ 0.0002 & 0.0000 \end{bmatrix}, G_3 = \begin{bmatrix} -0.0067 & 0.0031 \\ 0.0000 & 0.0000 \end{bmatrix},$$

$$G_4 = \begin{bmatrix} 0 & 0.0026 \\ 0 & 0.0000 \end{bmatrix}, G_5 = \begin{bmatrix} 0 & -0.2522 \\ 0 & 0.0000 \end{bmatrix}, H = \begin{bmatrix} 0.0144 \\ 0 \end{bmatrix}.$$

Thus, by Theorem 2., we know that the robust H_∞ control problem is solvable and a desired state feedback controller is given by

$$u(t) = \begin{bmatrix} 0.0048 & 0.0126 \end{bmatrix} x(t).$$

The simulation results show the effectiveness and flexibility of the proposed method.

6   Conclusions

This paper studies the robust H-infinity controller design methods of a class of nonlinear uncertain discrete-time singular systems with time delay both in state equation and output equation. A new delay-dependent bounded real lemma for discrete-time singular systems with time delays has been derived. On the basis of the result, by using Lyapunov stability theory and linear matrix inequality (LMI) method, we present the sufficient conditions in which robust H-infinity controller exists. We present a parameters notation of the controller when these conditions have a feasible solution. Then, by using Matlab LMI Control Toolbox, we obtain a solution. Finally, a numerical example has been provided to demonstrate the applicability of the proposed approach.

Acknowledgments. This work is partially supported by the National Natural Science Foundation of China (60874003).

References

1. Dai, L.: Singular Control Systems. Springer, Berlin (1989)
2. Ibrir, S.: Regularization and robust control of uncertain singular discrete-time linear systems. IMA Journal of Mathematical Control and Information 24, 71–80 (2007)

3. Ma, S.P., Cheng, Z.L.: An lmi approach to robust stabilization for uncertain discrete-time singular systems. In: Proceedings of the 41st IEEE CDC, Las Vegas, Nevada, USA, pp. 1090–1095 (2002)

4. Shuping, M.A., Zhang, C., Liu, X.: Robust stability and H-infinity control for uncertain discrete-time Markovian jump singular systems. Journal of Control Theory and Applications 6, 133–140 (2008)

5. Ji, X., Su, H., Chu, J.: Robust state feedback H∞ control for uncertain linear discrete singular system. IET Control Theory Appl. 1, 196–200 (2007)

6. Xu, S., Lam, J.: Robust stability and stabilization of discrete singular systems: an equivalent characterization. IEEE Trans. Automat. Control. 49, 568–574 (2004)

7. Xu, S., Song, B., Lu, J., Lam, J.: Robust stability of uncertain discrete-time singular fuzzy systems. Fuzzy Sets and Systems 158, 2306–2316 (2007)

8. Shi, P., Lin, Z., Shi, Y.: Robust Output Feedback Control for Discrete Time-Delay Uncertain Systems. Control and Intelligent Systems 34, 57–63 (2006)

9. Xu, S., Lam, J., Yang, C.: Robust H∞ control for discrete singular systems with state delay and parameter uncertainty. Dynamics Continuous Discrete Impul. Systems. 11, 497–506 (2002)

10. Ma, S., Zhang, C., Cheng, Z.: Delay-dependent robust H∞ control for uncertain discrete-time singular systems with time-delays. Journal of Computational and Applied Mathematics 217, 194–211 (2008)

11. Xu, S., Chen, T.: Robust H∞ control for uncertain discrete-time systems with time-varying delays via exponential output feedback controllers. Systems Control Lett. 51, 171–183 (2004)

12. Du, Z., Zhang, Q., Liu, L.: New delay-dependent robust stability of discrete singular systems with time-varying delays. Asian Journal of Control 13, 136–147 (2011)

13. Kim, J.H.: Delay-dependent robustH∞ control for discrete-time uncertain singular systems with interval time-varying delays instate and control input. Journal of the Franklin Institute 347, 1704–1722 (2010)

14. Zhou, W., Lu, H., Duan, C., Li, M.: Delay-dependent robust control for singular discrete-time Markovian jump systems with time-varying delay. International Journal of Robust and Nonlinear Control 20, 1112–1128 (2010)

15. Wang, H., Xue, A., Lu, R., Chen, Y.: Delay-dependent robust H∞ control for uncertain discrete singular time varying delay systems based on a finite sum inequality. In: Proceedings of the Chinese Control Conference, pp. 595–599 (2007)

16. Zhang, X.M., Han, Q.L.: Delay-dependent robust H∞ filtering for uncertain discrete-time systems with time-varying delay based on a finite sum inequality. IEEE Trans. Circuits Syst. II. 53, 1466–1470 (2006)

17. Zhang, G., Xia, Y., Shi, P.: New bounded real lemma for discrete-time singular systems. Automatica 44, 886–890 (2008)

18. Kim, J.H.: Delay-dependent robust filtering for uncertain discrete-time singular systems with interval time-varying delay. Automatica 46, 591–597 (2010)

19. Park, K.S., Lim, J.T.: Stability Analysis of Nonstandard Nonlinear Singularly Perturbed Discrete Systems. IEEE Transactions on Circuits and Systems II: Express Briefs 58, 309–313 (2011)

20. Wo, S.L., Shi, G., Zou, Y.: Robust H-infinity control for discrete-time singular systems with time-delay and nonlinear perturbation 31, 916–921 (2009)

Multi-objective Self-Adaptive Differential Evolution with Dividing Operator and Elitist Archive

Yuelin Gao[*], Yingzhen Chen, and Qiaoyong Jiang

Institute of Information and System Science, Beifang University of Nationalities,
Yinchuan Ningxia, 750021, China
gaoyuelin@263.net

Abstract. A multi-objective self-adaptive differential evolution algorithm with dividing operator and elitist archive is proposed for solving the multi-objective optimization problems. In every generation, the population is divided into two parts randomly and one of the parts will be done by the dividing operator which will enhance the diversity of the population and avoid falling into the local optimal. The numerical experiments implement in four groups: the first group compare the MSDEDE algorithm with five other evolution algorithms; the second group compare the MSDEDE algorithm with NSGA-II, SPEA2 and MOPSO, the simulation results show the effectiveness of the proposed algorithm; the third group compare it with three other DE algorithms, the results show the effectiveness of the proposed self-adaptive method; the fourth group compare it with the multi-objective self-adaptive differential evolution without the dividing operator on five benchmark problems, the results show the proposed dividing operator can improve the convergence speed.

Keywords: multi-objective optimization, differential evolution, dividing operator, elitist archive, self-adaptive.

1 Introduction

Multi-objective optimization problem is prevalent in scientific research and engineering practice. The solution of the multi-objective optimization problem is a Pareto optimal solution set. However, the single-objective methods often only get one solution rather than the solution set. The evolutionary algorithm is a kind of stochastic method that simulates the natural evolutionary process. It has opened up a new method for solving the multi-objective optimization problem. The researchers have pointed out that the multi-optimization problem is a field in which evolutionary algorithm can do better than other search methods. Multi-objective evolutionary algorithm has become one of the research hot points in the evolutionary computation. In recent years, researchers have proposed lots of multi-objective evolutionary algorithms, such as vector evaluated genetic algorithms [1], a niched Pareto genetic algorithm (NPGA) [2], non-dominated sorting genetic algorithms (NSGA) [3] and the improved NSGA algorithm: NSGA-II[4], the strength Pareto evolutionary algorithms (SPEA)[5]and the improved algorithm SPEA-2[6],

---

[*] Corresponding author.

M. Zhao and J. Sha (Eds.): ICCIP 2012, Part I, CCIS 288, pp. 415–429, 2012.

the Pareto archived evolutionary strategy(PAES)[7], an improved multi-objective particle swarm optimizer for multi-objective problems (PDJI-MOPSO)[8]and so on.

Differential evolution (DE) algorithm [9], which is introduced by Storn and Price in recent years, uses real component to synthesize parameter vector. It has aroused a lot of researchers' attention. The mutation operator in DE has the fine-turning capability and few control variables in the evolution process. In recent years, some scholars attempt to use DE algorithm to solve multi-objective optimization problems, and have achieved some fruits. Such as Pareto-based multi-objective differential evolution (Xue F) [10]; adaptive differential evolution algorithm for multi-objective optimization problems (Weiyi Qian) [11].There are also other differential evolutions for solving multi-objective optimization problems [12-14].

However, similar to GA, PSO and other intelligent algorithms, DE also has the disadvantage of falling into local optima frequently. In order to enhance the explore ability and avoid trapping into local optima, this article combines the jump improved operation from reference [8], and proposes a multi-objective self-adaptive differential evolution with dividing operator and elitist archive (MSDEDE).

2   Basic Concept of MOP

The multi-objective optimization problem can be mathematically described as [15]

$$
\begin{cases}
\min \quad f(x) = [f_1(x), f_2(x), \cdots, f_m(x)] \\
\text{s.t.} \quad x = (x_1, x_2, \cdots, x_n) \in X \subseteq R^n \\
\quad X = \{(x_1, x_2, \cdots, x_n) \mid l_i \leq x_i \leq u_i\} \\
\quad l = (l_1, l_2, \cdots, l_n), u = (u_1, u_2, \cdots, u_n)
\end{cases}
\tag{1}
$$

where x is called decision vector, $f(x)$ is the objective vector, X is the decision space, l and u are the lower bound and upper bound respectively.

There are several basic concepts which are often used in multi-objective optimization [16]:

(1) Pareto dominate: A decision vector x^0 is said to dominate a decision vector x^1 (also written as $x^0 \succ x^1$) if and only if

$$
\forall i \in \{1, \cdots, m\} : f_i(x^0) \leq f_i(x^1)
$$

$$
\wedge \; \exists j \in \{1, \cdots, m\} : f_j(x^0) < f_j(x^1)
$$

(2) Pareto optimal solution: A decision vector x^0 is said to be non-dominated, if and only if there is no decision vector x^1 which dominates x^0, formally:

$$
\neg \exists x^1 : x^1 \succ x^0
$$

(3) Pareto optimal set: The Pareto optimal set P_S is defined as $P_S = \{x^0 \mid \neg \exists x^1 \succ x^0\}$ also called non-dominated optimal set.

(4) Pareto optimal front: The Pareto front P_F is defined as

$$
P_F = \{f(x) = (f_1(x), f_2(x), \cdots, f_m(x)) \mid x \in P_S\}
$$

3   Basic Concept of Differential Evolution Algorithm

Differential evolution algorithm is a simple and effective evolutionary algorithm. Its main steps include mutation, crossover and selection which are described briefly in the following.

(1) Mutation operation

The mutation's element is the vector in parent generation. Each differential vector is generated by two different individuals $x_{r_1}^G, x_{r_2}^G$ from the parent generation. The differential vector is defined as $D_{1,2} = x_{r_1}^G - x_{r_2}^G$. The mutation operation is defined as:

$$\hat{x}_i^G = x_i^G + F \times (x_{r1}^G - x_{r2}^G) \tag{2}$$

where, $\hat{x}_i^G$ is the mutated individual, x_i^G is the parent individual, $x_{r1}^G, x_{r2}^G, x_i^G$ are three different individuals. F is called mutation constant, which presents the degree of the differential vector influence the next generation individual. The value of F has an important influence on the performance of the algorithm. If the value of F is too large, the convergence of the algorithm becomes slow. Conversely, the diversity of the population reduces, and then the algorithm traps into local optimum easily. So the value of F is usually between 0 and 2.

(2) Crossover operator

A trial vector is generated by the individual $\hat{x}_i^G$ and x_i^t, through the following scheme:

$$x_{ji} = \begin{cases} \hat{x}_{ji}^G, & rand() \leq CR; \\ x_{ji}^G, & otherwise. \end{cases} \tag{3}$$

where, $rand(\ )$ is a random number within $[0,1]$, $j \in \{1, 2, \cdots, m\}$, m is the dimension of the decision vector, CR is a crossover constant. The value of CR is larger, the contribution of $\hat{x}_i^G$ to x_i is greater, the speed of the evolution is faster, the algorithm falls into local optima easier. It shows that, the population diversity maintain and the algorithm convergence speed improve are contradictory. The value of CR is usually between 0 and 1.

4   Key Technology of MSDEDE Algorithm

4.1   The Selection Operator of MSDEDE Algorithm

In multi-objective optimization problems, the quality of the individual can be judged by the dominant relation and the density. The selection operator in MSDEDE algorithm is inspired from reference [4], which adopts the non-dominated grading strategy and the crowding distance method. The selection steps of the MODEDE algorithm are as follows:

1. The test individual and the parent individual compete with each other, if one individual Pareto dominate the other, the non-dominated one accede to the new population; if the two individuals do not dominate each other, both are kept in the new population.
2. The new population is rearranged by the non-dominated sorting strategy. First, we find all non-dominated solutions in the population, and take their rating for 1. Then we find all non-dominated solutions in the rest of the population, and take their rating for 2. The process is repeated, until all individuals in the population have a corresponding rate.
3. The new population is sorted descending by the crowding distance, then select N individuals as the next generation evolutionary population.

4.2   Dividing Operator

The existing methods focus on how to transform the evolutionary algorithm from single-objective optimization to multi-objective optimization, but ignore the important operator - the recombination operators. So the algorithm falls into the local Pareto optimal solution set easily and slows down the convergence. Licheng Jiao, etc. design a Pareto crossover operator and three co-operators include co-operator, the annexation operator and dividing operator, which can maintain the population diversity and speed up the convergence [17]. The dividing operator is described in the following.

The population $P_t = (x_1, x_2, \cdots, x_M)$ was divided into two sub-populations $P_{t+1}^a = (z_1^a, z_2^a, \cdots, z_{M/2}^a)$ and $P_{t+1}^b = (z_1^b, z_2^b, \cdots, z_{M/2}^b)$ randomly. Mutation operation is executed on the individuals in one of the population such as P_{t+1}^a:

$$z_i^a = \begin{cases} z_i^a, & U(0,1) \le 1/n; \\ z_i^a + G(0,1/t), & otherwise. \end{cases} \tag{4}$$

where, $i = 1, 2, \cdots, n$, $U(0,1)$ is a random number within $[0,1]$, $G(0,1/t)$ present the Gaussian distribution that the random number generator, t is the evolution iteration. Inspired by this, we propose a new dividing operator.

Differential evolution algorithm has a strong depth of search capability, but lacks breadth of search capability, so falls into local Pareto optimal solution set easily. In order to overcome this phenomenon, reference [8] proposes an improved jump out operator which can enhance the ability to explore the unknown searching spaces and avoid falling into local optimal prematurely. The new dividing operator are described in the following briefly.

$$O_{c1} = c_1 + \alpha_1 (c_1 - c_2) \tag{5}$$

$$O_{c1} = c_1 + \alpha_1 (c_1 - c_2) \tag{6}$$

where, c_1, c_2 are two different random individuals in the Pareto optimal solution set, α_1, α_2 are random numbers between 0 and 1. This article incorporates the improved jump out operator with the dividing operator to get a new dividing operator, which is described in the following:

$$z_i^a = \begin{cases} z_i^a, & U(0,1) \le \min(0.1, 1/n); \\ z_i^a + (c_1 + \alpha_1(c_1 - c_2)), & otherwise. \end{cases} \tag{7}$$

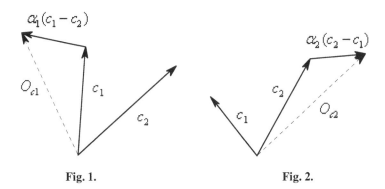

Fig. 1.   Fig. 2.

There are two differences in (4) and (7). One is that $U(0,1) \le 1/n$ instead of $U(0,1) \le \min(0.1, 1/n)$. The (7) considers the case that the decision variables equal 1, because the (4) makes no sense to this case. Another one is the employ of $(c_1 + \alpha_1(c_1 - c_2))$ or $(c_2 + \alpha_2(c_2 - c_1))$ instead of $G(0, 1/t)$. Besides, the improved jump out operator is different from the one in reference [8]. The improved jump out operator is operated on the optimal solution set in reference [8], but on the evolutionary population here. This is to say c_1, c_2 are two different random individuals in sub-populations P_{t+1}^a or P_{t+1}^b. The advantages of this are on one hand, the population diversity is increased, and the choice of the evolution populations is expanded, so premature convergence is avoided. On the other hand, more Pareto optimal solutions may be obtained.

4.3   Description of MDEM Algorithm

Step 1: Set the algorithm's parameters D, NP, F, CR and so on.

Step 2: Generate initial population P_0 uniformity in the decision space.

Step 3: The non-dominated solutions in population P enter the Pareto optimal solution set.

Step 4: Implement the mutation and crossover operations, and then obtain the trial individual. The new solution replaces the objective individual if it dominates the objective individual; if the objective individual dominates the new solution, keep the objective individual; if the two individuals do not dominate each other, both are kept in the population. This gives a complex population P1 whose bound is N to 2N.

Step 5: Operate dividing operator on new population P1according to 4.2, and obtain the temporary population P2.

Step 6: Implement elitism on the population $P_1 \cup P_2$ according to 4.2.

Step 7: Select the evolutionary population of the next generation from $P_1 \cup P_2$ according to 4.1.

Step 8: If the maximum iteration is reached, stop and output Pareto optimal solution set, otherwise return Step4.

5   Experimental Results

5.1   Quality Indicators

The quality evaluation of the solutions in multi-objective optimization problems is mainly concerned in the distance between the obtained non-dominated solutions set and the Pareto optimal set, and in the diversity of the obtained non-dominated solutions set. Here adopt the generational distance [18] (Van Veldhuizen and Lamont, 1998) to measure the distance between the obtained non-dominated solutions set and the Pareto optimal set, and the extend indicator [19] (Zhou et al. 2006) to evaluation the diversity of the solutions. The generational distance is defined as

$$GD = \frac{(\sum_{i=1}^{n} d_i^P)^{\frac{1}{P}}}{n} \tag{8}$$

where n is the number of vectors in the set of non-dominated solutions found so far, and d_i is the Euclidean distance (measured in objective space) between each of these solutions and the nearest member of the Pareto optimal set, p is a positive integer, usually p=1or p=2. The smaller value of GD, the better extent to approximate the Pareto optimal solution set. It is clear that $GD = 0$ indicates that all the generated elements are in the Pareto front.

The extend indicator is proposed by Deb, and is modified as

$$\Delta = \frac{d_f + d_l + \sum_{i=1}^{n-1} | d_i - \overline{d} |}{d_f + d_l + (n-1)\overline{d}} \tag{9}$$

where, the parameter d_i is the Euclidean distance between neighboring solutions in the obtained non-dominated solutions set and $\overline{d}$ is the mean of all d_i: The parameters d_f and dl are the Euclidean distances between the extreme solutions and the boundary solutions of the obtained non-dominated set. A value of zero for this metric indicates all members of the Pareto optimal set are equidistantly spaced. When the non-dominated solutions found so far are complete distribute evenly on the balance surface, that

$d_f = 0, d_l = 0$ and $d_i = \bar{d}$, so $\Delta = 0$. The indicate Δ reflect the distribution and the diversity of the non-dominated solutions. However, the above indicator works only for bi-objective problems and can not be used directly to evaluate for problems of more than two objectives. Based on the metric proposed in Zhou et al. (2006) and Durillo et al. (2006), the indicator is extended to the problems of more than two objectives by computing the distance from a given point to its nearest neighbor. The indicator is modified as

$$\Delta = \frac{\sum_{i=1}^{m} d(E_i, \Omega) + \sum_{x \in \Omega} | d(X, \Omega) - \bar{d} |}{\sum_{i=1}^{m} d(E_i, \Omega) + (|\Omega| - m)\bar{d}} \tag{10}$$

where Ω is a set of solutions, $E_i (i = 1, 2, ..., m)$ are m extreme solutions in the set of Pareto optimal solutions, m is the number of objectives and

$$d(X, \Omega) = \min_{Y \in \Omega, Y \neq X} \| F(X) - F(Y) \|$$

$$\bar{d} = \frac{1}{|\Omega|} \sum_{x \in \Omega} d(X, \Omega).$$

5.2   Parameter Settings and Results Analysis

In order to know how competitive the MSDEDE algorithm is, it is compared with five other multi-objective evolutionary algorithms. Five benchmark functions are chosen to test the performance of the algorithm, which are commonly used in multi-objective evolutionary algorithm test. In order to evaluate the convergence and diversity degree, formulas (8) and (9) were used, where p=1 in (8). The MSDEDE parameters were set as: population size 100, Pareto optimal archive size 100. The algorithms run 30 times independently. The control parameter is $F = 0.1 + 0.5 * rand(0, 1)$, where $rand(0, 1)$ is generated within 0 and 1 randomly. The crossover constant is $CR = p_r$, where p_r is based on the simulated annealing-line [20] and described as

$$\begin{cases} p_r^0 = p_r^{max} \\ p_r^{G+1} = p_r^{min} + \beta(p_r^G - p_r^{min}) \end{cases},$$

where p_r^{min}, p_r^{max} is the upper and lower limits of the scale factor, $0 \leq \beta \leq 1$ is the annealing factor, $p_r^{min} = 0.2$, $p_r^{max} = 0.9$, $\beta = 0.95$. In order to compare the effectiveness of the MSDEDE algorithm with the other algorithms, table 1-5 show the convergence and the diversity indicators and their variance of six algorithms with the population size 100 and the iteration 250. The dates of the other five algorithms are from the reference [21].

Table 1. Test results of ZDT1

Algorithm	Convergence ± metric	Diversity ± metric
NSGA-II(binary-coded)	0.000894 ± 0.000000	0.463292 ± 0.041622
SPEA	0.001799 ± 0.000001	0.784525 ± 0.004440
PAES	0.082085 ± 0.008679	1.229794 ± 0.000742
PDEA	N/A	0.298567 ± 0.000742
MODE	0.005800 ± 0.000000	N/A
MSDEDE	0.001015 ± 0.000000	0.249762 ± 0.000379

Table 2. Test results of ZDT2

Algorithm	Convergence ± metric	Diversity ± metric
NSGA-II(binary-coded)	0.000824 ± 0.000000	0.435112 ± 0.024607
SPEA	0.001339 ± 0.000000	0.755184 ± 0.004521
PAES	0.126276 ± 0.036877	1.165942 ± 0.007682
PDEA	N/A	0.317958 ± 0.001389
MODE	0.005500 ± 0.000000	N/A
MSDEDE	0.000754 ± 0.000000	0.259935 ± 0.000417

Table 3. Test results of ZDT3

Algorithm	Convergence ± metric	Diversity ± metric
NSGA-II(binary-coded)	0.043411 ± 0.000042	0.575606 ± 0.005078
SPEA	0.047517 ± 0.000047	0.672938 ± 0.003587
PAES	0.023872 ± 0.000010	0.789920 ± 0.001653
PDEA	N/A	0.623812 ± 0.000225
MODE	0.021560 ± 0.000000	N/A
MSDEDE	0.004579 ± 0.000000	0.506214 ± 0.000278

Table 4. Test results of ZDT4

Algorithm	Convergence ± metric	Diversity ± metric
NSGA-II(binary-coded)	3.227636 ± 7.307630	0.479475 ± 0.009841
SPEA	7.340299 ± 6.572516	0.798463 ± 0.014616
PAES	0.854816 ± 0.527238	0.870458 ± 0.101399
PDEA	N/A	0.840852 ± 0.035741
MODE	0.638950 ± 0.500200	N/A
MSDEDE	0.204720 ± 0.016153	0.436322 ± 0.008906

Table 1 and table 2 show that the convergence indicator of the MDEM algorithm is better than the other five algorithms, except the NSGA-II (binary-coded) in ZDT1. The diversity indicator of the MSDEDE algorithm is better than the other five algorithms.

Table 5. Test results of ZDT6

Algorithm	Convergence ± metric	Diversity ± metric
NSGA-II(binary-coded)	7.806798 ± 0.001667	0.644477 ± 0.035042
SPEA	0.221138 ± 0.000449	0.849389 ± 0.002713
PAES	0.085469 ± 0.006664	1.153052 ± 0.003916
PDEA	N/A	0.473074 ± 0.009923
MODE	0.026230 ± 0.000861	N/A
MSDEDE	0.000819 ± 0.000000	0.245382 ± 0.001381

Table 6. Comparison results of four algorithms based on the convergence indicator

Algorithm	NSGA-II	SPEA2	MOPSO	MSDEDE
SCH	2.1572E-3	2.1232E-3	2.9285E-2	9.3130E-4
	2.0999E-4	2.1130E-4	1.5566E-2	3.3882E-5
KUR	2.8974E-3	1.8573E-3	2.1416E-2	1.4347E-3
	2.3637E-4	1.0731E-4	7.4183E-3	1.4778E-4
FON	2.5656E-3	1.8573E-3	2.1416E-2	1.1790E-3
	2.0082E-4	1.0731E-4	7.4183E-3	1.8527E-5
ZDT1	1.3437E-3	3.8175E-3	1.8564E-1	2.3223E-4
	1.4078E-4	4.9142E-3	7.7429E-2	1.2660E-5
ZDT2	9.8112E-4	8.6104E-3	5.2428E-1	9.1867E-5
	6.4138E-4	2.5973E-3	2.9699E-1	4.9857E-6
ZDT3	2.4783E-3	9.7165E-3	4.3418E-1	6.2109E-4
	1.2746E-4	5.2305E-3	6.4880E-2	1.9861E-5
ZDT4	5.1635E-2	9.2512E-1	-	1.8991E-2
	1.3281E-3	4.2821E-1	-	1.5948E-2
ZDT6	7.5818E-2	1.9309E-2	5.2135E-2	1.2373E-4
	6.0797E-3	1.3994E-3	2.4963E-2	8.7098E-6
DTLZ1	2.7102E-2	9.0259E-2	2.1374E-1	2.4414E-2
	6.6459E-2	7.6880E-1	1.5577E-1	1.1027E-2
DTLZ2	1.1089E-1	2.8136E-2	9.1269E-2	3.2998E-4
	1.0559E-1	1.2532E-2	2.6896E-2	1.6512E-5

To further test the performance of MSDEDE algorithm, it is compared with the other three multi-objective evolutionary algorithms, among which two are based on genetic algorithm: NSGA-II and SPEA2, another one is based on PSO: MOPSO [22]. Ten benchmark functions are chosen to test the performance of the algorithms, which are commonly used in multi-objective evolutionary algorithm test. In order to evaluate the convergence and diversity degree, formulas (8) and (9) were used, where p=2 in (8). For bi-objective problems, parameters are the same with the above. For the problems of more than two objectives, parameters are the same with the above except that the iteration is 500. The parameters were set as: population size 100, archive size 100, maximum number of generation 250 for bi-objective problems and 500 for the problems of more than two objectives. The four algorithms MSDEDE、NSGA-II、SPEA2 and MOPSO run 30 times independently. The average convergence indicator, standard deviation and the average spread indicator, the standard deviation are summarized in Table 6 and Table 7 respectively. If the algorithm can not converge, '−'is used. The dates of the other three algorithms are from the reference [15]. The figures 3 to 12 express the parent fronts of MSDEDE and Pareto optimal fronts.

Table 7. Comparison results of four algorithms based on the spread indicator

Algorithm	NSGA-II	SPEA2	MOPSO	MSDEDE
SCH	0.29228	0.27503	0.72572	0.24541
	2.1339E-2	2.5711E-2	1.3476E-1	1.9189E-2
KUR	0.434041	0.28611	0.37595	0.26328
	1.8178E-2	1.1474E-2	1.6664E-2	3.3552E-2
FON	0.37672	0.17661	0.64970	0.16270
	2.5222E-2	1.1100E-1	3.1212E-1	1.2866E-2
ZDT1	0.50429	0.29644	0.293805	0.20745
	3.9251E-2	1.0850E-1	1.6956E-2	2.6556E-2
ZDT2	0.48775	0.50517	0.28803	0.20785
	2.7686E-2	1.8356E-1	1.7580E-2	2.5520E-2
ZDT3	0.59025	0.50310	0.61780	0.28947
	3.0439E-2	9.7283E-2	3.5019E-2	2.5049E-2
ZDT4	0.37524	0.72766	0.32355	0.33676
	2.4448E-2	5.1517E-1	3.2953E-2	1.1906E-1
ZDT6	0.48611	0.24861	1.12326	0.23291
	3.6054E-2	4.9667E-2	1.7311E-1	4.1655E-2
DTLZ1	0.91867	0.30236	0.70809	0.415952
	6.6108E-2	2.4919E-1	7.8854E-2	5.4991E-2
DTLZ2	0.83092	0.24673	0.93628	0.40634
	6.8427E-2	3.5181E-2	3.1684E-1	3.1496E-2

From table 6 to table 7, we can conclude that the convergence indicator of the MDEM algorithm is better than the other three algorithms. The diversity indicator of the MSDEDE algorithm is better than the other three algorithms in functions SCH, KUR, FON, ZDT1, ZDT2, ZDT3 and ZDT6. The diversity indicator is weaker than the MOPSO in ZDT4, but better than the other two algorithms; and is weaker than the SPEA2 in DTLZ1 , DTLZ2, but better than the other two algorithms. Figures 3 to 11 express the parent fronts of the MSDEDE and the Pareto optimal fronts.

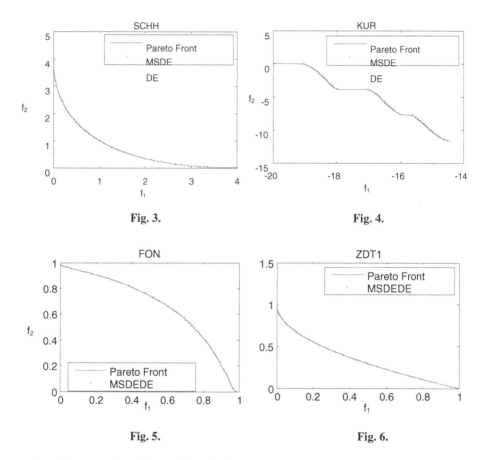

Fig. 3.   Fig. 4.

Fig. 5.   Fig. 6.

In order to test the effect of the adaptive parameter, the MSDEDE is compared with the other three multi-objective differential evolution algorithms: MODE (case1) [23], MODE (case2) [24], MODE (case3) [25]. The parameters of the self-adaptive DE are set as:

Case1: $F = 0.5$, $CR = 0.9$;
Case2: $F = 0.5$, $CR = 0.5$;
Case3: $F = 0.2$, $CR = 0.2$.

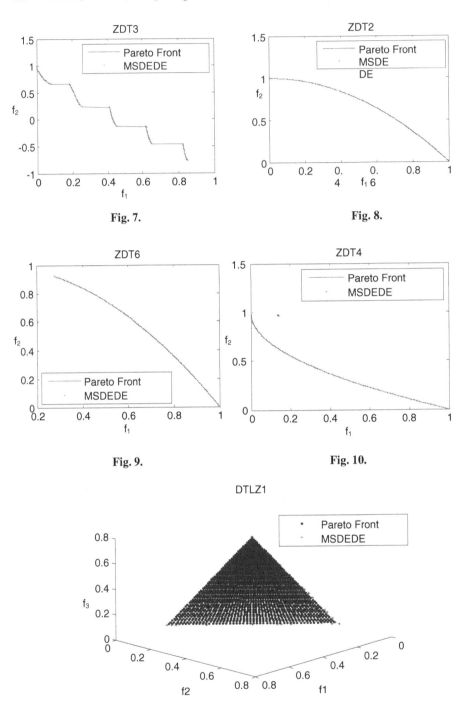

Fig. 7.

Fig. 8.

Fig. 9.

Fig. 10.

Fig. 11.

Table 8 shows the convergence indicator and its variance of the four algorithms with the population size 100 and the iteration 250, which runs 30 times independently. Formulas (8) is used to calculate the convergence degree, where p=2. The dates of the other three algorithms are from the reference [24].

Table 8. Comparison results of four algorithms based on the convergence indicator

Algorithm	MODE(case1)	MODE(case2)	MODE(case3)	MSDEDE
ZDT1	1.8769E-2	3.4757E-3	1.3185E-3	2.3223E-4
	2.9535E-3	2.2958E-4	1.1279E-3	1.2660E-5
ZDT2	2.2017E-2	3.1473E-3	1.1279E-3	9.1867E-5
	3.0029E-3	1.9666E-4	1.7158E-4	4.9857E-6
ZDT3	1.8247E-2	2.7552E-3	2.3201E-3	6.2109E-4
	2.6679E-3	1.5224E-4	1.6899E-4	1.9861E-5
ZDT4	-	-	3.0532E-3	1.8991E-2
	-	-	7.7427E-4	1.5948E-2
ZDT6	3.7450E-2	8.0092E-3	1.8974E-3	1.2373E-4
	2.9730E-2	6.2214E-3	8.1660E-4	8.7098E-6

The table 8 shows that the convergence indicator of the MSDEDE algorithm is better than the other three algorithms in ZDT1, ZDT2, ZDT3 and ZDT6. The diversity is weaker than the MODE (case3) in ZDT4, but better than the other two algorithms. The results show that the self-adaptive strategy is effectively.

In order to test the effect of the dividing operator, the MSDEDE algorithm is compared with the multi-objective adaptive differential evolution algorithm without dividing operator (MSDEE). Figs 12 to 15 are the convergence comparison map of the two algorithms on the five ZDT test functions. Clearly, the dividing operator speeds up the convergence rate.

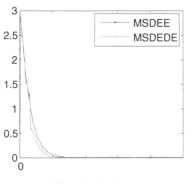

Fig. 12. ZDT1

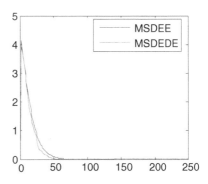

Fig. 13. ZDT2

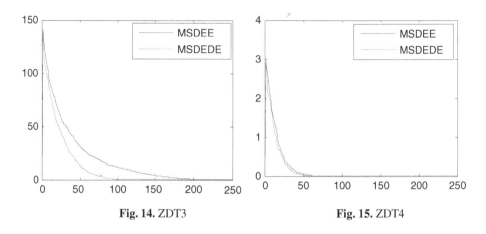

Fig. 14. ZDT3   **Fig. 15.** ZDT4

6   Conclusion

This paper proposes the MSDEDE algorithm for solving multi-objective optimization problems. The dividing operator is implemented on the evolution population in each generation, in order to expand the population space, avoid falling into the Pareto local optimal and accelerate the convergence. Elitist strategy maintains the diversity of the population. Besides, the self-adaptive method, not only obtains the good results, but also avoids the unnecessary computational. The results show that the MSDEDE algorithm nor only increases the diversity and convergence of the solutions, but also accelerates the convergence.

Acknowledgments. The work is supported by the Foundations of National Natural Science China under Grant No.60962006 and No. 11161001.

References

1. Schaffer, J.D.: Multiple objective optimization with vector evaluated genetic algorithms. In: Proceedings of the 1st International Conference on Genetic Algorithms, pp. 93–100. Lawrence Erlbaum (1985)
2. Horn, J., Nafpliotis, N., Goldberg, D.E.: A niched Pareto genetic algorithm for multi-objective optimization. In: Proceedings of the 1st IEEE Conference on Evolutionary Computation, Piscataw, vol. 1, pp. 82–87 (1994)
3. Srinivas, N., Deb, K.: Multi-objective function optimization using non-dominated sorting genetic algorithms. Evolutionary Computation 2(3), 221–248 (1994)
4. Deb, K., Pratap, A., Agarwal, S., Meyarivan, T.: A fast and elitist multi-objective genetic algorithm: NSGA-II. IEEE Transactions on Evolutionary Computation 6(2), 182–197 (2002)
5. Zitzler, E., Thiele, L.: Multi-objective evolutionary algorithms: a comparative case study and the strength Pareto approach. IEEE Transactions on Evolutionary Computation 3(4), 257–271 (1999)
6. Zitzler, E., Thiele, L.: SPEA2: improving the strength Pareto evolutionary algorithm for multi-objective optimization. Research Report (May 2001)

7. Knowles, J., Corne, D.: The Pareto archived evolutionary strategy: A new baseline algorithm for multi-objective optimization. In: Proceedings of the Conference on Evolutionary Computation, pp. 98–105. IEEE Press, Piscataway (1999)
8. Tsai, S.-J., Sun, T.-Y., Liu, C.-C., et al.: An improved multi-objective particle swarm optimizer for multi-objective problems. Expert Systems with Applications 2(18), 1–15 (2010)
9. Storn, R., Price, K.: Differential evolution – a simple and efficient adaptive scheme for local optimization over continuous spaces. Journal of Global Optimization 11(4), 341–359 (1997)
10. Xue, F., Sanderson, A.C., Graves, R.J.: Pareto-based multi-objective differential evolution. In: Proceedings of the 2003 Congress on Evolutionary Computation, Canberra, pp. 862–869 (2003)
11. Qian, W., Li, A.: Adaptive differential evolution algorithm for multi-objective optimization problems. Applied Mathematics and Computation, 431–440 (2008)
12. Madavan, N.K.: Multi-objective optimization using a Pareto differential evolution approach. In: Proceedings of the IEEE International Conference on Evolutionary Computation, New Jerssey, pp. 1145–1150 (2002)
13. Robič, T., Filipič, B.: DEMO: Differential Evolution for Multiobjective Optimization. In: Coello Coello, C.A., Hernández Aguirre, A., Zitzler, E. (eds.) EMO 2005. LNCS, vol. 3410, pp. 520–533. Springer, Heidelberg (2005)
14. Wang, Y.-N., Wu, L.-H., Yuan, X.-F.: Multi-objective self-adaptive differential evolution with elitist archive and crowding entropy-based diversity measure. Soft Compute., 193–209 (2010)
15. Deb, K.: Multi-Objective Optimization Using Evolutionary Algorithm. John Wiley&Sons, Chichester (2001)
16. Gong, M., Jiao, L., Yang, D.: Research on evolution multi-objective optimization algorithms. Journal of Software 20(2), 271–289 (2009)
17. Jiao, L., Liu, J., Zhong, W.: Co-evolutionary computation and multi-agent system, pp. 148–151. Science Press, Beijing (2007)
18. Van Veldhuizen, D.A., Lamont, G.B.: Evolutionary Computation and Convergence to a Pareto Front. In: Koza, J.R. (ed.) Late Breaking Papers at the genetic Programming 1998 Conference, pp. 221–228. Stanford University, California (1998)
19. Zhou, A., Jin, Y., Zhang, Q., et al.: Combing model-based and generics-based offspring generation for multi-objective optimization using a convergence criterion. In: 2006 Congress on Evolutionary Computation, pp. 3234–3241 (2006)
20. Wang, X., Cheng, Y.: Machine learning theory, methods and applications, pp. 118–119. Science Press, Beijing (2009)
21. Qian, W., Li, A.: Adaptive differential evolution algorithm for multi-objective optimization problems. Applied Mathematics and Computation, 431–440 (2008)
22. Coello, C.A., Pulido, G.T., Lechuga, M.S.: Handling multiple objectives with particle swarm optimization. IEEE Trans. Evol. Comput. 8(3), 256–279 (2004)
23. Qin, A.K., Suganthan, P.N.: Self-adaptive differential evolution algorithm for numerical optimization. In: Proceedings of the IEEE Congress on Evolutionary Computation, Edinburgh, Scotland, vol. (2), pp. 1785–1791 (2005)
24. Alfredo, G., Luis, V., Coello, C.C., et al.: A new proposed for multi-objective optimization using differential evolution and rough sets theory. In: Proceedings of the 8th Annual Conference on Genetic and Evolutionary Computation, Seattle, Washington, pp. 675–682 (2006)
25. Kukkonen, S., Lampinen, J.: GDE3: the third evolution step of generalized evolution. In: Proceedings of the IEEE congress on Evolutionary Computation, Edinburgh, pp. 443–450 (2005)

Research about Immune Ant Colony Optimization in Emergency Logistics Transportation Route Choice

Li-yi Zhang[1], Teng Fei[1], Xiaoqin Zhang[1], Yanqin Li[2], and Jun Yi[1]

[1] Information Engineering College, Tianjin University of Commerce, Tianjin, China
[2] College of Disaster Prevention Equipment,
Institute of Disaster Prevention Science and Technology, Beijing, China
{zhangliyi,feiteng,zhangxiaoqin}@tjcu.edu.cn

Abstract. Emergency logistics transportation route choice is the key problem to emergency logistics. Choosing routes scientifically and reasonably can save life and property timely and maximally to reach the maximum effect of emergency relief. This article builds up mathematical model which owns timeliness of emergency logistics to reach the goal that the delivery time is shortest, and solves this model by Immune Ant Colony Optimization (IACO). Computer simulation indicates that IACO has more effective timeliness to this model, and can find the path saves more time.

Keywords: Immune Ant Colony Optimization, path choice, emergency logistics.

1 Introduction

After the SARS in 2003, the research about emergency logistics gains much attention and lasts now with many disasters happened. In order to deal with serious natural disasters, public health emergency, public security incident, military conflict and other emergency, emergency logistics makes emergency security for materials, personnel, funds and other demand. Emergency logistics transportation route choice is the key problem to emergency logistics. Choosing routes scientifically and reasonably can save life and property timely and maximally to reach the maximum effect of emergency relief. This article builds up mathematical model which owns timeliness of emergency logistics to reach the goal that the delivery time is shortest, and solves this model by Immune Art Colony Optimization (IACA). Computer simulation indicates that IACA has more effective timeliness to this model, and can find the path saves more time.

2 Emergency Logistics Transportation Route Choice Model

After disasters, the real situation is complex. In order to facilitate the model's establishment, suppose there is only one Disaster Relief Distribution Centers (DRDC), and its location is known. The load and average speed of haulage vehicles is

M. Zhao and J. Sha (Eds.): ICCIP 2012, Part I, CCIS 288, pp. 430–437, 2012.

known. Because emergency haulage vehicles are deployed to the DRDC as a whole, all vehicles start from the DRDC. After the distribution mission, cars will not return to the DRDC. The materials can be mixed. The materials needed by each point is no more than the maximum load of vehicles. he affected point's position and quantity demanded are known, and demand of each point can be satisfied by one car and only once distribution. After disasters, the emergency vehicles' velocity might be reduced because of the probable damage of some parts of the pathways. Therefor, Infogo Coefficient is brought in to indicate the damaged condition of pathways. The larger the Infogo coefficient is, the worse the pathways' condition and the longer the distribution time are. Since the urgency, requiring the goods, of each affected point is different, using shortage degree to discribe the situation: the worse the shortage, the faster running, delivery time is shorter. Due to the influence of disasters, emergency vehicles must arrive the affected point before the demanding time, otherwise, the road will become impassable and discarded because of the objective cause.

Based on the assumptions above, establish the mathematical model to shorten the distribution time for the best.

$$\min T = \sum_{k=1}^{m} T_k \tag{1}$$

S.T.

$$T_k = \sum_{i=0}^{l} \sum_{j=0}^{l} t_{ij} x_{ijk} \tag{2}$$

$$t_{ij} = \frac{d_{ij}}{v} \times \varphi_{ij} \times \mu_i \tag{3}$$

$$\sum_{i=0}^{l} g_i y_{ki} \leq q \quad k \in [1, m'] \tag{4}$$

$$\sum_{k=1}^{m'} y_{ki} = 1 \quad i \in [0, l], k \in [1, m'] \tag{5}$$

$$\sum_{i=0}^{l} \sum_{k=1}^{m'} x_{ijk} = 1 \quad j \in [0, l], k \in [1, m'] \tag{6}$$

$$\sum_{j=0}^{l} \sum_{k=1}^{m'} x_{ijk} = 1 \quad i \in [0, l], k \in [1, m'] \tag{7}$$

$$\sum_{i=0}^{l} x_{ijk} = y_{kj} \quad i \in [0, l], k \in [1, m'] \tag{8}$$

$$\sum_{j=0}^{l} x_{ijk} = y_{ki} \quad i \in [0, l], k \in [1, m'] \tag{9}$$

$$t_{ik} < t_{ei} \tag{10}$$

Where, l is the number of the affected points; m' is the number of the vehicles; d_{ij} is the distance between point i and point j; T_k is the driving time of car k; t_{ij} is the time that vehicles driving from affected point i to point j; g_i is the quantity demanded of point i; q is the maximum load for vehicles; k is number of vehicles; v is the driving velocity of vehicles; φ_{ij} is the situation of roads; μ_i is the material shortage coefficient; t_{ik} is the time that the car k arrives at point i; t_{ei} is the dead time of the distribution time for the affected points.

The DRDC will be numbered as 0, and affected points will be numbered from 1 to l. Define variable x_{ijk} and y_{ki} as:

$$y_{ki} = \begin{cases} 1 \ \text{point i is seviced by vehicle k} \\ 0 \ \text{,other} \end{cases} \tag{11}$$

$$x_{ijk} = \begin{cases} 1 \ , \ \text{vehicle k travel from i to j} \\ 0 \ , \ \text{other} \end{cases} \tag{12}$$

Formula (1) is target function of the model, which aims to shorten the time for the best. Formula (2) indicates the driving time of car k. Formula (3) indicates the time that vehicles pass by affected points i, j, in which the degree of shortage and traffic situation for each affected points is also considered. Formula (4) indicates that for each car, the total weight of the goods does not exceed the maximum weight of the vehicle itself in the transit. Formulas (5), (6) and (7) guarantee that only one car passes by each affected point. Formula (8) indicates the mission of the j demand point is accomplished by car k transferring from point i. Formula (9) indicates the mission of the i demand point is accomplished by car k transferring from point j. Formula (10) indicates the time demand of goods arriving at affected points.

3   The Solving Model of Immune Ant Colony Optimization

Step 1. Enter target functions as formula (1). Enter constraint conditions as formulas (2) ~ (10). Treat target functions and constraint conditions as antigens.

Step 2. Utilize natural coding method to code the antibodies creating initial antibodies. Random generate a whole arrangement of l affected points, $(i = 1,2,...a_1 - 1, a_1,...,b_1 - 1, b_1,...l)$. If $\sum_{i=1}^{a_1-1} g_i y_{ki} \leq q$ and $\sum_{i=1}^{a_1} g_i y_{ki} > q$, then move a_1 to l back one place. Insert 0 into a_1. If $\sum_{i=a_1}^{b_1-1} g_i y_{ki} \leq q$ and $\sum_{i=a_1}^{b_1} g_i y_{ki} > q$, then move b_1 to l back one place. Insert 0 into b_1. Continue like this until insert m' 0 into corresponding place. This forms initial antibodies.

$$\left(0, i_1 y_{11}, i_2 y_{12}, \cdots, i_{a_1-1} y_{1, a_1-1}, 0, i_{a_1} y_{2, a_1}, i_{a_1+1} y_{2, a_1+1}, \cdots, \right.$$
$$\left. i_{b_1-1} y_{2, b_1-1}, 0, \cdots, 0, i_r y_{m'r}, \cdots, i_l y_{m'l} \right)$$

Haulage vehicle 1 (serial number 0) starts from DRDC and goes through affected point 1 to affected point $a_1 - 1$ as Transit Route 1. Haulage vehicle 2 (serial number 0) starts from DRDC and goes through affected point $a_1 - 1$ to affected point $b_1 - 1$ as transit route 2. So on, m' vehicles form m' transit routes.

Step 3. Calculate the affinity A_s between Antibody s and antigen based on formula (13).

$$A_s = 1/T(s) \tag{13}$$

Where, $T(s)$ is the haulage time of antibody s.

Step 4. Calculate the affinity $B_{s,t}$ between Antibody s and Antibody t based on formula (14).

$$B_{s,t} = 1/|T(s) - T(t)| \tag{14}$$

Where, $T(s)$ is the haulage time of antibody t.

Step 5. Selecting, crossing and mutating to produce new antibodies. Generate a better feasible haulage pathes. Selecting is to use the method combine with best individual copy and roulette to copy the superior individuals to next generation directly or using roulette [3] to choose.Crossing is to select superior individuals from current population as Father generation to breed next generation. Mutating is to use reversal variation[2].

Step 6. Produce initial value of pheromone $\tau_{ij}(0)$ based on formula (15).

$$\tau_{ij}(0) = \begin{cases} \tau_0 & if \ (i, j) \ get \ feaseble \ solution \ by \ step5 \\ 0 & others \end{cases} \tag{15}$$

Step 7. Regarding NC=0 (NC is iteration), load_bus=0(load_bus is the load of vehicles), proceed parameters initialization.

Step 8. Put m ants at the DRDC, which $m = \sum_{i=1}^{n} b_i(t)$ is the sum of the ants, $b_i(t)$ indicates the sum of the ants in city i at time t.

Step 9. Calculate the transition probability of ant k based on formula (16).

$$P_{ij}^k = \begin{cases} \dfrac{[\tau_{ij}(t)]^\alpha \cdot [\eta_{ij}(t)]^\beta}{\sum\limits_{s \in allowed_k} [\tau_{is}(t)]^\alpha \cdot [\eta_{is}(t)]^\beta} & j \in allowed_k \\ 0 & other \end{cases} \tag{16}$$

Where, $allowed_k = (1, 2, ..n) - tabu_k$ indicates the set of cities that ant k can choose at present; $tabu_k \ (k = 1, 2, \cdots, m)$ indicates that the list of ant k's taboo, in which record the cities that ant k has passed by, illustrating the memo ability of artificial ants; $\eta_{ij}(t)$ is inspiration function that indicates the expectation of the transference from city i to city j, usually $\eta_{ij}(t) = 1/d_{ij}$; α is the importance of residual information in the pathway ij; β is the importance of the inspirational information.

Step 10. Based on the transition probability, chooses and moves the ants to the next city j, and adds j to $tabu_k$ at the same time. Check whether the vehicles' load is larger than the maximum load. If so, return to DRDC.

Step 11. Check whether $tabu_k$ is full. If not, return to Step9. Otherwise, go on Step12.

Step 12. Calculate the target function. Record the best solution currently. Update the pheromone based on formula (17).

$$\tau_{ij}(t+1) = (1-\rho)\tau_{ij}(t) + \Delta\tau_{ij}(t) \qquad (17)$$

Where ρ is the volatile factor of global pheromone, of which the value is [0,1) [3] usually, determining the volatile speed of pheromone. $\Delta\tau_{ij}(t)$ is the pheromone's increment of this circling in the pathway ij.

$$\Delta\tau_{ij}(t) = \sum_{k=1}^{m} \Delta\tau_{ij}^{k}(t) \qquad (18)$$

Assume at the initial moment, $\Delta\tau_{ij}(0) = 0$, $\Delta\tau_{ij}^{k}(t)$ indicates the pheromone that ant k releasing in the pathway ij during the circling. The value is based on the performance of ants. The shorter the pathway, the more the pheromone is released.

$$\Delta\tau_{ij}^{k}(t) = \begin{cases} Q/L_k & \text{section } k \text{ of ants pass edge } ij \text{ in the course of this tour} \\ 0 & else \end{cases} \qquad (19)$$

Step 13. If $NC < NC_{max}$, then $NC = NC + 1$, empty $tabu_k$, and go back to Step8. If $NC = NC_{max}$, end.

4   Simulation

The coordinate of the DRDC is known as (500, 150). The disaster relief materials should be distributed to 20 affected points by 3 vehicles from the DRDC. Table1 indicates the coordinate data of each affected point, quantity demanded, terminate time, and discharge time and shortage of each affected point. The maximum load of each vehicle is 450t. The velocity of cars is $45km/h$. Document [7] provides traffic coefficient of the pathway between every affected point. Document [8] provides the basis of the values of the parameters α, β, ρ. According to the results of many experiments, the operation result is the best when $\alpha = 1$, $\beta = 5$, $\rho = 0.6$. The distances between each affected point and between the DRDC and each point can be calculated by the distance formula, as follow:

$$d_{ij} = \sqrt{(x_i - x_j)^2 + (y_i - y_j)^2} \qquad (20)$$

Table 1. Experimental Data

NO.	coordinate	Requirements(t)	End time(h)	unloading time(h)	Shortage degree(h)
1	(700,264)	30	15	0.1	0.99
2	(166,295)	90	30	0.2	0.98
3	(378,332)	90	35	0.5	0.65
4	(398,112)	60	25	0.4	0.76
5	(214,276)	70	40	0.3	0.97
6	(386,198)	70	20	0.5	0.85
7	(496,368)	90	30	0.2	0.67
8	(583,240)	90	10	0.4	0.83
9	(175,118)	40	40	0.1	0.94
10	(544,242)	70	10	0.3	0.92
11	(318,138)	60	40	0.5	0.86
12	(414,218)	20	25	0.4	0.87
13	(482,297)	40	30	0.1	0.90
14	(281,226)	60	35	0.3	0.73
15	(127,576)	100	25	0.2	0.69
16	(814,198)	50	20	0.2	0.88
17	(690,300)	80	15	0.3	0.95
18	(72,540)	60	25	0.1	0.78
19	(705,518)	80	35	0.4	0.87
20	(364,652)	90	30	0.3	0.93

The path of the IACO is showed in the Figure 1. The distribution scheme of haulage vehicles is as table 2.

Table 2. IACO distribution scheme

Number of vehicles	Running routes(0 is DRDC)
vehicle1	0—10—8—7—13—12—6—4
vehicle2	0—1—17—16—19—3—14—11
vehicle3	0—20—15—18—2—5—9

The path of the Basic Ant Colony Algorithm is showed in the Figure 2. The distribution scheme of haulage vehicles is as table 3.

Table 3. Basic Ant Colony Algorithm distribution scheme

Number of vehicles	Running routes(0 is DRDC)
vehicle1	0—10—8—17—1—16—7—13
vehicle2	0—4—6—12—9—2—5—3
vehicle3	0—11—14—15—18—20—19

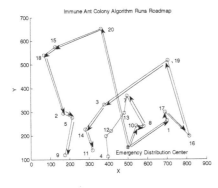
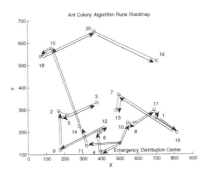

Fig. 1. IACO operating map   **Fig. 2.** Basic ant colony algorithm operating map

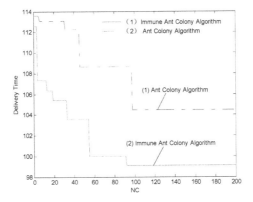

Fig. 3. The optimal solution optimal curve

Figure 3 indicates a optimal solution optimal curve under the same situation between the Immune and Basic Ant Colony Algorithm. Through the contrast, the time of immune ant colony algorithm distribution is shorter, and efficiency is higher. It is because IACO brings "immune" into Basic Ant Colony Algorithm, enhancing the global search capability of Basic Ant Colony Algorithm and improving the solution quality of emergency logistics transportation route choice.

5   Conclusion

IACO, which is a new method to solve the problem about emergency logistics transportation route choice, have both advantages of IA and CA. First, IACO obtains pheromone distribution from IA. Then, use BACA to optimize. Simulation results indicate that this algorithm is better than Basic Ant Colony Algorithm in both optimization ability and convergence speeding. For the establishment of the model, although this article has contained some real situation, numerous actual conditions are not considered in it. In the future, the establishment of the model to solve the emergency logistics path optimization problems should be further perfected and fulfilled.

Acknowledgment. This work is supported by Funding Issues of Soft Science Research Projects in Shanxi Province (2010041077-3).The Central University of Basic Scientific Research Foundation of China under Grant (ZY20120210).

References

1. Kuang, X., Wang, T., Liao, R.: Emergency logistics decision-making of path optimization Grey. Chinese Water 10(12), 85–86 (2010)
2. Wang, A.: Optimization Strategy based on artificial immune algorithm. Daqing Petroleum Institute (2005)
3. Lian, X.: Study of Logistics and distribution path optimization based on Combination of ant colony and immune algorithm. Ji Lin University (2007)
4. Yan, W.: Study of Logistics and distribution path optimization based on Immune Algorithm. Chang An University (2005)
5. Lang, M., Hu, S.: Study of Logistics and distribution path optimization based on Hybrid genetic algorithm. China Management Science 10(5), 51–56 (2002)
6. Liu, L.: Research of Improved Ant Colony Optimization Algorithm. Southwest Jiaotong University (2005)
7. Fei, T.: Research of ACO in the medical devices logistics distribution routing optimization. Taiyuan University of Technology (2010)
8. Ye, Z., Zheng, Z.: Study on the parameters $\alpha\ \beta\ \rho$ in Ant colony algorithm——An example to TSP. Wuhan University (Information Science) 29(7), 597–601 (2004)

Application of Improved ACO in the Selection of Emergence Logistics Distribution Routing

Teng Fei[1], Li-yi Zhang[1,*], Yanqin Li[2],Cheng Zhu[1], Xiaopei Liu[1], and Hongwei Ren[1]

[1] Information Engineering College, Tianjin University of Commerce, Tianjin, China
[2] College of Disaster Prevention Equipment,
Institute of Disaster Prevention Science and Technology, Beijing, China
{zhangliyi,feiteng,zhucheng,liuxiaopei}@tjcu.edu.cn

Abstract. Combined characteristic of emergency logistic, established dual-target delivery model in the principle for "distribution efficiency first, both economy" and solved the model with Fish-Swarm Ant colony algorithm. The algorithm initially explores the logistics and distribution in emergency routing application.

Keywords: emergency logistics, routing selection, Fish-Swarm Ant Colony Optimization (FSACO).

1 Introduction

Natural disasters as earthquake occurred frequently in the recent years. Arriving in time of post-disaster rescue workers, rescuing and rapid transferring of property, transporting and releasing of relief supplies make a significant contribution to saving rescue time and reducing loss of life and property. [1] Specially, because of increasing demand for a variety of relief materials after disaster, mobilization of relevant materials is urgently needed from all parts of the country to earthquake-stricken area. In the process, the problem of selection of emergence logistics distribution routing is the key to ensure that this work can be carried out quickly, efficiently and smoothly.

This article is combined characteristic of emergency logistic, established dual-target delivery model in the principle for "distribution efficiency first, both economy" and solved the model with Fish-Swarm Ant Colony Optimization. The algorithm initially explores the logistics and distribution in emergency routing application.

2 Modeling

2.1 Analysis

First, mobilization of relevant materials for emergency rescue from all parts of the country will be served to relief supplies collection center(RSCC). Second, emergency

---

* Corresponding author.

M. Zhao and J. Sha (Eds.): ICCIP 2012, Part I, CCIS 288, pp. 438–445, 2012.
© Springer-Verlag Berlin Heidelberg 2012

relief supplies will be delivered to relief supplies distribution centers(RSDC) by road, rail, aviation and other modes of transport from relief supplies collection center(RSCC).Third, materials used in the rescue will be sent to victims assistance center(relief materials reserve center, RMRC) from relief supplies distribution centers(RSDC). Finally, supplies will be distributed to disaster-affected from relief materials reserve center(RMRC).For all emergency relief supplies distribution process, not only multiple conversions in transport modes but also distribution network in multiple levels are all exist, situation is more complicated, therefore, single-level distribution network will be considered in the model, that is to say, emergency relief supplies are distributed from relief supplies relief materials reserve center(RMRC) to affected points ,and only considered one mode of transportation is highway.

Emergence logistics has characteristics of sudden, unpredictability, uncertainty, imbalance and weak economy, and because of this, high efficiency for distribution was a prime target for the model's establishment, all the same, to consider economy of distribution is also important. Therefore, the model established is a multi-objective optimization model. The basic idea about the multi-objective optimization problem is a evaluation function that converts a multi-objective to a numerical targets, Hence, the linear weighted method is generally adopted.

2.2   Modeling

In order to facilitate the model's establishment, the assumptions has been taken:

(1) Consider only a single RMRC that location is known, all delivery cars start from RMRC. Because, emergence logistics has characteristics of sudden and unpredictability, transport of relief supplies are non-routine activities by government after disaster, the cars RMRC demanded is usually temporarily requisitioned from social groups or individuals by government, as a result, the cars should not be back when the distribution task is completed.(2) Distribution material can be mixed, and material what each affected point need does not exceed the maximum load of the car.(3) Location and demand of each affected point are known, requirements of each affected point is distributed by only one vehicle.(4) Type of the car is single, load of the vehicle is known.(5) Car services for each affected point, only the case of loading without unloading on the way.(6) Average speed of cars is known and definite, traveling distance is proportionate to running time of vehicles.(7) After disaster, some of the roads are destroyed, thereby increasing the traffic of other well-sections and leading to traffic jams. Therefore, changes in traffic flow are described by traffic factor. The greater the traffic factor is, the worse the road conditions, the slower the vehicle speed and the longer the time are.(8) Short degree for materials of each affected point is different. As the subjective factor, the shorter the materials are, the faster the car speed and the less the time is.(9) Due to the impact of disasters, emergency transport cars must arrive before time that relief supplies demand points required, otherwise, the road which is impassable is abandoned, because of objective reasons.

Establish the mathematical model based on the assumptions above.

$$\min W = (W_1, W_2) = aW_1 + bW_2 \tag{1}$$

$$W_1 = \sum_{k=1}^{m'} T_k + \sum_{i=0}^{L} T_{kx} \tag{2}$$

$$W_2 = c_0 m' + \sum_{i=0}^{L} \sum_{j=0}^{L} \sum_{k=1}^{m'} c d_{ij} x_{ijk} \tag{3}$$

$$T_k = \sum_{i=0}^{L} \sum_{j=0}^{L} t_{ij} x_{ijk} \tag{4}$$

$$t_{ij} = \frac{d_{ij}}{v} \times \varphi_{ij} \times \mu_i \tag{5}$$

$$\sum_{i=0}^{L} g_i y_{ki} \le q \quad k \in [1, m'] \tag{6}$$

$$\sum_{k=1}^{m'} y_{ki} = 1 \quad i \in [0, L], k \in [1, m'] \tag{7}$$

$$\sum_{i=0}^{L} \sum_{k=1}^{m'} x_{ijk} = 1 \quad j \in [0, L], k \in [1, m'] \tag{8}$$

$$\sum_{j=0}^{L} \sum_{k=1}^{m'} x_{ijk} = 1 \quad i \in [0, L], k \in [1, m'] \tag{9}$$

$$\sum_{i=0}^{L} x_{ijk} = y_{kj} \quad i \in [0, L], k \in [1, m'] \tag{10}$$

$$\sum_{j=0}^{L} x_{ijk} = y_{ki} \quad i \in [0, L], k \in [1, m'] \tag{11}$$

$$t_{ik} < t_{ei} \tag{12}$$

Where, a, b is the weight of objective function coefficients ; L is the number of the affected points; m' is the number of the vehicles; d_{ij} is the distance between point i and point j ; T_k is the driving time of car k ; T_{kx} is unloading time of car k at point i ; t_{ij} is the time that vehicles driving from affected point i to point j ; g_i is the quantity demanded of point i ; q is the maximum load for vehicles; k is number of vehicles; v is the driving velocity of vehicles; φ_{ij} is the situation of roads; μ_i is the material shortage coefficient; t_{ik} is the time that the car k arrives at point i ; t_{ei} is the dead time of the distribution time for the affected points; c_0 is the unit cost of the cars; c is the unit cost of vehicle distance.

The RMRC will be numbered as 0, and affected points will be numbered from 1 to L . Define variable x_{ijk} and y_{ki} as:

$$y_{ki} = \begin{cases} 1 \text{ ,point i is seviced by vehicle } k \\ 0 \text{ ,other} \end{cases} \tag{13}$$

$$x_{ijk} = \begin{cases} 1 \text{ , vehicle k travel from i to j} \\ 0 \text{ , other} \end{cases} \tag{14}$$

Formula (1)is target function, the value of objective evaluation function is lower, it indicates that paths select better. Formula (2)is time target function. Formula (3)is economy target function ,include tow parts: one is the fixed costs of the cars, the other is transportation costs. Formula (4) indicates the driving time of car k . Formula (5) indicates the time that vehicles pass by affected points i, j , in which the degree of shortage and traffic situation for each affected points is also considered. Formula (6) indicates that for each car, the total weight of the goods does not exceed the maximum weight of the vehicle itself in the transit. Formulas (7), (8) and (9) guarantee that only one car passes by each affected point. Formula (10) indicates the mission of the j demand point is accomplished by car k transferring from point i .

Formula (11) indicates the mission of the i demand point is accomplished by car k transferring from point j . Formula (12) indicates the time demand of goods arriving at affected points.

Earthquake relief period is divided into quick stage, sudden stage and urgent stage. Quick stage means 24 hours after earthquake, main task is to save lives. Sudden stage means 2-3 days after earthquake, main task is wounded. Urgent stage means 4-10 days after the earthquake, main task is to placement the victims' life. In view of different periods of the earthquake relief, the weight coefficient a,b 's value of objective evaluation function is different also. relief supplies of quick stage are scarce, therefore, only the time problem consider, while ignoring the economic factors, let $a = 1, b = 0$; The demand for relief supplies is still relatively large for sudden stage, therefore, to consider the time problem is first, to consider the economic factors is second, let $a > b$; the urgent stage aims at to reduce the distribution costs as possible at the same time of considering the time problem, let $b > a$.

3   Fish-Swarm Ant Colony Optimization Solution Model

3.1   Ant Colony Algorithm(ACO)

Suppose that there are n cities. The distance between every two cities i, j is d_{ij} ($i, j = 1,2,\cdots,n$). $b_i(t)$ is the number of ants at city i at time t . $m = \sum_{i=1}^{n} b_i(t)$ is total number of the ants. $\tau_{ij}(t)$ is pheromone amount at time t on the branch ij .Information intensity on each branch is equal when $t = 0$. $\Delta\tau_{ij}(t) = 0$.

As time goes on, new pheromone will add in and old pheromone will volatilize. Suppose ρ is the volatile coefficient of pheromone which shows the speed of pheromone's volatilization. When all the ants have travelled overland, the pheromone on each path is

$$\tau_{ij}(t+1) = (1-\rho)\tau_{ij}(t) + \Delta\tau_{ij}(t) \tag{15}$$

$$\Delta\tau_{ij}(t) = \sum_{k=1}^{m} \Delta\tau_{ij}^{k}(t) \tag{16}$$

$\Delta\tau_{ij}(t)$ is incremental pheromone on path ij during traveling. At the beginning, $\Delta\tau_{ij}(0) = 0$. $\Delta\tau_{ij}^{k}(t)$ is the pheromone that ant k release on the path ij during traveling, which is determined by ants' performance. The shorter the path is, the more pheromone is released.

$$\Delta\tau_{ij}^{k}(t) = \begin{cases} Q/L_k & \text{section k of ants pass edge ij in the course of this tour} \\ 0 & else \end{cases} \tag{17}$$

Where, Q is constant, L_k is the length of the circuit which is formed by ant k in this traveling. The transition probability p_{ij}^{k}, about ant k traveling from city i to city j is:

$$P_{ij}^{k} = \begin{cases} \dfrac{[\tau_{ij}(t)]^{\alpha} \cdot [\eta_{ij}(t)]^{\beta}}{\sum\limits_{s \in allowed_k} [\tau_{is}(t)]^{\alpha} \cdot [\eta_{is}(t)]^{\beta}} & j \in allowed_k \\ 0 & other \end{cases} \tag{18}$$

Where, $allowed_k = (1,2,...,n) - tabu_k$ is the cities that ant k can choose currently. $tabu_k$ $(k = 1,2,\cdots,m)$ is the taboo list of ant k, recording the cities that ant k has traveled through, to indicate ants' memorability. $\eta_{ij}(t)$ is prior knowledge visibility. In the TSP study, is the elicitation information deliver from one city to another, and in general $\eta_{ij}(t) = 1/d_{ij}$, α is the importance of residual information on path ij. β is the importance of elicitation information.

3.2   Fish-Swarm Ant Colony Optimization Solution Model

Step 1 regarding NC=0 (NC is iteration), load_bus=0(load_bus is the load of vehicles), $\tau_{ij} = 0$, proceed parameters initialization.

Step2 put m ants at the RMRC.

Step3 calculate the transition probability of ant k based on formula (18). Choose and move to the next city j, and add j to $tabu_k$ at the same time.

Step4 calculate the crowding factor h_{ij}, if crowded, go on step 5, if not, return step 3.

$$h_{ij}(t) = 1 - \tau_{ij}(t) / \sum_{i \neq j} \tau_{ij} \tag{19}$$

$$\delta(t) = \gamma e^{-zt} \tag{20}$$

Where, $\delta(t)$ is congestion threshold, γ is extremely near level, b is threshold variation coefficient.

Suppose, the ant finds a path based on the transition probability p_{ij}^k , and $h_{ij}(t) > \delta(t)$, it is said that the path is not crowded, then choose this path. Otherwise, it will re-select the other path according to he transition probability p_{ij}^k .

Step5 check whether the vehicle load reaches maximum load. If so, vehicle return to RMRC.

Step6 check whether the arrival time t_i of distribution vehicle is less than the distribution dead time of affected point. If not, return to Step3. Otherwisego on Step 7;

Step7 check whether $tabu_k$ is full. If not, return to Step3. Otherwise, go on Step8;

Step8 calculate target function, and update pheromone based on formula (16)

Step9 If $NC < NC_{max}$, then $NC = NC + 1$, empty $tabu_k$, and go back to Step2. If $NC = NC_{max}$, end.

4   Simulation

Suppose that disaster relief work has entered a sudden stage, let $a = 0.8, b = 0.2$, the coordinate of RMRC is(62, 142), RMRC allocates deliver materials to 12 affected points. Diagram 1 indicates the coordinate data of each affected point, quantity demanded, terminate time, and discharge time and shortage of each affected point. The load weight of per car is 55 tons, and the average speed of each car is $40km/h$. Document [5] provides traffic coefficient of the pathway between every affected point. Let $c_0 = 0$, $c = 1$ .Document[6] provides the basis of the values of the parameters α, β, ρ .According to the results of many times experiments, when $\alpha = 1, \beta = 5, \rho = 0.6$, the operation result is the best. The distances between each affected point and between the RMRC and each affected point can be calculated by the distance formula (21).

$$d_{ij} = \sqrt{(x_i - x_j)^2 + (y_i - y_j)^2} \qquad (21)$$

Fig.1 is an optimal solution to route based on ACO. The routing is: RMRC- affected point 9- affected point 1- affected point 4;RMRC- affected point 7- affected point 6-affected point 3;RMRC- affected point 5- affected point 8;RMRC- affected point 12-affected point 11- affected point 2- affected point 10.

Fig.2 is an optimal solution to route based on FSACO. The routing is :RMRC-affected point 9- affected point 1;RMRC- affected point 4- affected point 3- affected point 10- affected point 2;RMRC- affected point 7- affected point 8;RMRC- affected point 5- affected point 6- affected point 11- affected point 12.

Fig.3 is an optimal solution to optimization curve about ACO and FSACO in the same conditions. Because of the crowding factor is used in the ACO, it is easy to find the path to reduce the distribution time as soon as possible in the saluting problems of emergency logistics distribution based on FSACO.

Table 1. Experimental Data

NO.	coordinate	Requirements	unloading time	Shortage degree	End time
1	(34,110)	15	0.1	0.99	3.5
2	(42,38)	18	0.2	0.98	7.5
3	(46,98)	20	0.5	0.65	5.5
4	(50,122)	8	0.4	0.76	2.0
5	(94,152)	15	0.3	0.97	5.0
6	(96,62)	10	0.5	0.85	8.0
7	(90,104)	25	0.2	0.67	2.5
8	(100,108)	30	0.4	0.83	4.5
9	(40,164)	17	0.1	0.94	1.8
10	(24,50)	6	0.3	0.92	7.8
11	(102,38)	2	0.5	0.86	6.5
12	(138,80)	24	0.4	0.87	8.5

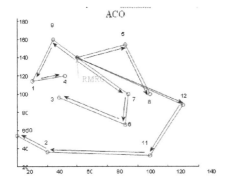

Fig. 1. FSACO operating map

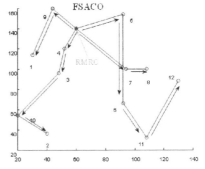

Fig. 2. ACO operating map

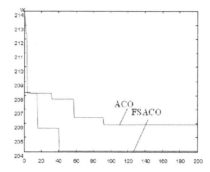

Fig. 3. The optimal solution optimal curve

5   Conclusion

Since the introduction of congestion factor of FSACO, the global search ability of ants is increased. Compared with the ACO, Convergence speed of FSACO has been improved. It is able to achieve the high quality solutions in the problems of emergency logistics distribution. FSACO has opened up a new Solution for searching the best routing.

Acknowledgment. This work is supported by Funding Issues of Soft Science Research Projects in Shanxi Province (2010041077-3). The Central University of Basic Scientific Research Foundation of China under Grant(ZY20120210).

References

1. Fiedrich, F., Gehbauer, F., Rickers, U.: Optimized Resource Allocation for Emergency Response After Earthquake. Disasters Safety Science 35(1), 41–57 (2000)
2. Dorigo, M.: Ant colony system: A cooperative learning approach to the traveling salesman problem. IEEE Transactions on Evolutionary Computation 1(1), 53–66 (1997)
3. Gao, J.: Staging of earthquake emergency period. Disaster Science 19(1), 11–15 (2004)
4. Gong, Y.: Emergency relief supplies vehicles optimal path selection and implementation of research. Wuhan University of Technology (2004)
5. Fei, T.: Research of ACO in the medical devices logistics distribution routing optimization. Taiyuan University of technology (2010)
6. Ye, Z., Zheng, Z.: Study on the parameters $\alpha\ \beta\ \rho$ in Ant colony algorithm——An example to TSP. Wuhan University (Information Science) 29(7), 597–601 (2004)

A New Adaptive Algorithm for Digital Predistortion Using GNGD with Momentum Factor

Zhibin Zeng and Dian Xie

Engineering Research Center of Digital Audio and Video,
Ministry of Education
Communication University of China
Beijing, China
zhbzeng@cuc.edu.cn

Abstract. Adaptive algorithm plays an important role in digital predistortion for the linearization of power amplifiers. In this paper, a new approach which use GNGD adapative algorithm with momentum factor is presented. As an improved NLMS adaptive algorithm, the GNGD, if combined with momentum factor, can not only eliminate the stochastic perturbation which exits inherently in NLMS algorithm, but also bear a faster convergence and a lower misadustment.

Keywords: power amplifier, digital predistortion, NLMS, GNGD, momentum factor.

1 Introduction

It is well known that today's communication systems are characterized by broad bandwidth signals which generally exhibit high peak to average power ratio (PAPR). One problem with high PAPR is that their performance is strongly dependent on the linearity of the transmission. Power amplifier (PA) is one of the main components during transmission, which will always introduce nonlinear products such as out-of-band emissions and in-band distortions, more or less, and consequently degrading communication quality.

The inherent nonlinearity of power amplifier makes it difficult to satisfy the linear requirements of broad communication system with high PAPR. An optimum solution to this problem is deploying linearization techniques to minimize the power amplifier's out-of-band and in-band distortion products. Techniques for achieving this include the feed-forward method, negative feedback, postdistortion and prdistortion. Today, digital predistortion (DPD) has become the predominant technique for power amplifier's linearization due to its strong stability, high effectiveness and simple implementation [1]. On the other hand, to adapt to the varying nonlinear characteristics of power amplifiers, adaptive algorithm such as NLMS and RLS, is indispensable and plays the core role in digital predistortion system. However, both NLMS and its improved algorithm GNGD have the disadvantage of stochastic perturbation when updating weight values [2]. A so-called movement factor (MF) is proposed in this paper to overcome this problem. Combing GNGD algorithm with MF will eliminate stochastic perturbation and get better linearization [3].

M. Zhao and J. Sha (Eds.): ICCIP 2012, Part I, CCIS 288, pp. 446–453, 2012.

Power amplifier which can be modeled by a complex series is another important part in digital predistortion system. The Volterra series is the most frequently used complex series to model power amplifiers. For the sake of simplicity, Volterra series is often deployed in its simplified form such as memory polynomial.

2   Adaptive Algorithm

2.1   DPD Overview

Techniques for achieving linearization to minimize the power amplifier's out-of-band emission and in-band distortion include the feed-forward method, negative feedback, postdistortion and prdistortion. Digital predistortion, in which the kernel adaptive algorithm is performed, is a promising method among these linearization techniques. Power amplifier's nonlinear characteristics can be described by amplitude modulation to amplitude modulation conversion (AM/AM) and amplitude modulation to phase modulation conversion (AM/PM). The digital predistortion is in responsible for generating inverse AM/AM and AM/PM curves to cancel the AM/AM and AM/PM nonlinear characteristics of power amplifier. In other words, the predistortion curves and the distortion curves are complementary to achieve linear amplification.

2.2   Predistorter Architecture

The architectures of DPD system are divided into two types. One is the direct learning architecture, which must identify nonlinear characteristics of PA and then find the inverse characteristics of PA, which is of high computational complexity. Another type is the indirect learning architecture [4], which doesn't need to finding inverse nonlinear characteristics of PA. As a consequence, the indirect learning architecture is more attractive in the adaptive algorithm.

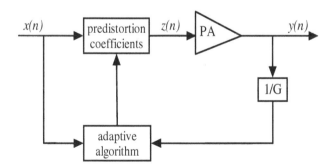

Fig. 1. Indirect learning architecture block diagram

The block diagram of indirect learning is demonstrated in Fig. 2. It can be seen that adaptive algorithm update the predistortion coefficients through comparing the difference between the input and output samplings until the difference equal or approximate to zero [5].

2.3   Adaptive Algorithm

The NLMS algorithm is relatively simple to implement. For this reason, it has been widely used in many adaptive applications. Equations of NLMS algorithm are given by as below:

$w = [w_0,...,w_{N-1}]^T$: Tap-weight vector

$x(n) = [x(n), x(n-1),..., x(n-N+1)]^T$: Input vector

$y(n) = w^T x(n)$: Output vector

$e(n) = d(n) - y(n)$: Error signal

$w(n+1) = w(n) + 2\dfrac{\mu}{\|x(n)\|_2^2} e^*(n)x(n)$: Tap-weight updating

One of limitations on NLMS algorithm is its weak antijamming ability to gradient noise during value estimation. To solve this problem, a adjustment factor ε is added to $\|x(n)\|_2^2$, and consequently, the recursion expression of tap-weight updating is given by:

$$w(n+1) = w(n) + 2\frac{\mu}{\|x(n)\|_2^2 + \varepsilon} e^*(n)x(n) \ (\varepsilon > 0) \tag{1}$$

GNGD is an improve algorithm based on NLMS algorithm. Although NLMS algorithm has a faster convergence and a smaller steady-state misadjustment, it is sensitive to initial parameters, and should be improved to maintain stability in finding predistortion coefficients. And therefore, adaptive adjustment coefficient ε is introduced.

First, define minimum cost function as

$$E(k) = |e(k)|^2 \tag{2}$$

Adaptive adjustment coefficient ε is given by

$$\varepsilon(k+1) = \varepsilon(k) - \rho \nabla_{\varepsilon(k-1)} E(k) \tag{3}$$

Using Equation (2) and (3), $\nabla_{\varepsilon(k-1)} E(k)$ can be derived as follows

$$\frac{\partial E(k)}{\partial \varepsilon(k-1)} = \frac{\text{Re}[e(k)e^*(k-1)x^T(k-1)x^*(k)]}{(\|x(k-1)\|_2^2 + \varepsilon(k-1))^2} \tag{4}$$

Then the tap-weight up-data equations are given as

$$w(n+1) = w(n) + \eta(n)x(n)e^*(n),$$

$$\eta(n) = \frac{\mu}{\|x(k)\|_2^2 + \varepsilon(k)},$$

$$\varepsilon(k) = \varepsilon(k-1) - p\mu \frac{\text{Re}[e(k)e^*(k-1)x(k-1)x^*(k)]}{(\|x(k-1)\|_2^2 + \varepsilon(k-1))^2} \tag{5}$$

where p denotes a constant for correction, μ is step size, and ε is adjustment factor with the initial value of 0.1.

The merit of the GNGD algorithm lies in that it can compensate for the study speed, exhibiting high robustness at the same time. The stochastic disturbance, however, is evitable when weight is updated. Combing GNGD with MF is a simple and effective solution to this problem.

Weight updating equation is expressed as

$$w(n+1) = w(n) + \eta(n)x(n)e^*(n) + \lambda \Delta w(k-1) \tag{6}$$

In this equation, $\Delta w(k-1)$ $(\Delta w(k-1) = w(k) - w(k-1))$ is the momentum, λ $(0 < \lambda < 1)$ is the momentum adjustment factor. During the beginning of the weight adjustment, $\Delta w(k-1)$ is relatively big, and the convergence is rapid. Combing GNGD with MS can enhance the stability of convergence of adaptive algorithm.

And the GNGD+MF method is given as the following steps:

a) Initialize predistortion coefficients.
b) Get the input of the power amplifier $z(n)$ and its output $y(n)$;.
c) Using GNGD+MF algorithm calculating predistortion coefficients
d) If the system not meets the linearization requirements,   i.e. $e(n)$ is not equal to or approximates to zero, then jump to step2. If not, then the GNGD+MF algorithm is complete.

3   Simulation and Analysis

The original signals are generated by a 16-QAM and OFDM multi-carrier modulation with bandwidth of 8MHz. We use the memory polynomials as the PA model and 16-QAM signal as the input vector to perform Matlab simulation using the joint adaptive algorithm:

In terms of choice of PA model for simulation, two aspects should be taken into consideration. One is the memory effect. In general, any PA has memory effect, i.e., the current output of PA depends not only on the current input, but also on the previous input. The more signal bandwidth, the stronger the memory effect, and vice verse [6]. The other is the complexity of the PA model. As mentioned above, Volterra series provides an excellent approximation to the practical power amplifier, but is too complicated for implementation. The memory polynomial, as the simplified Volterra series, can provide a similar PA modeling performance meanwhile maintaining a significant lower complexity in comparison to Volterra series. For these two reasons, memory polynomial is adopted as the PA model for the simulation.

Simulations are carried out on error curve using the NLMS algorithm, the GNGD algorithm and GNGD+MS algorithm.

3.1   Error Curve Performance

Error curve plot is most direct-viewing to observe the erroneous value and the convergence speed.

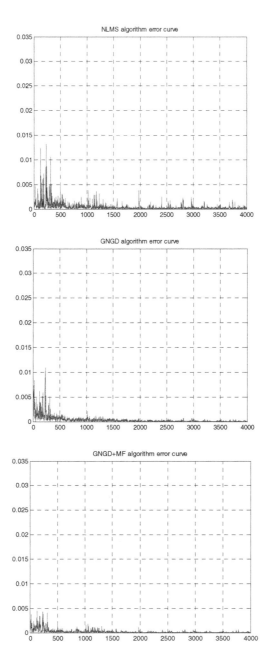

Fig. 2. Error curves comparision with NLMS, GNGD and GNGD+MF

As seen in Fig. 2, GNGD+MF exhibts better error and convergence performance to its other two counterparts. Furthermore, the stochastic perturbation is suppressed to a great degree.

3.2   AM-AM and AM-PM Performance

AM-AM and AM-PM performance with joint algorithm DPD is shown in Fig. 3 and Fig. 4.

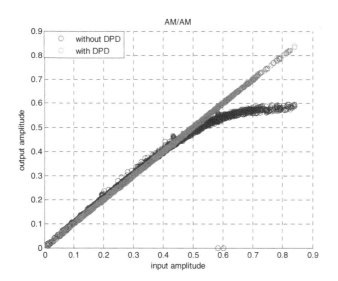

Fig. 3. AM-AM curve with GNGD+MF in DPD

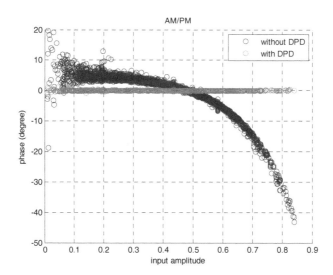

Fig. 4. AM-PM curve with GNGD+MF in DPD

As displayed in Fig. 3 and Fig. 4, GNGD+MF bears an excellent AM/AM and AM/PM preditortion performance for DPD.

3.3   Constellation Performance

The Fig.s shown below are constellation with and without the adaptive algorithm in DPD. Simulation results show that constellation dispersion is significantly improved by using GNGD+MF algorithm.

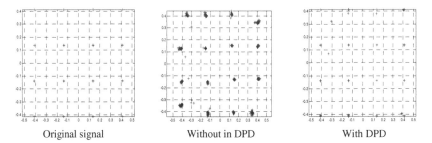

Original signal   Without in DPD   With DPD

Fig. 5. Constellation with and without GNGD+MF DPD

3.4   PSD Performance

It is clear from the Fig. 6 that some 40 dB improvement in PSD is achieved with the GNGD+MF algorithm in DPD.

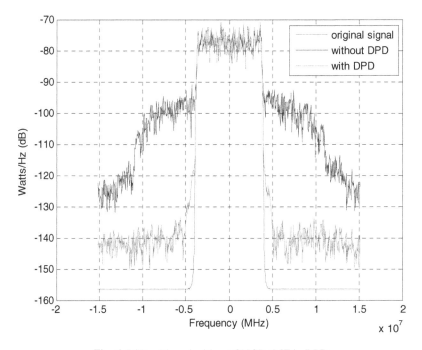

Fig. 6. PSD with and without GNGD+MF in DPD

4 Conclusion

In this paper, a new approach which use GNGD adapative algorithm with momentum factor is presented. As an improved NLMS adaptive algorithm, the GNGD, if infused with MF, will not only eliminate the stochastic perturbation which appears inherently in NLMS algorithm, but also exhibits a more rapid convergence and a lower misadustment. Simulations show that GNGD+MF algorithm contributes about 40dB of PSD improvement for memory polynomial model, and at the same time, the AM-AM and constellation performance are also significantly improved, hence obtaining desirable linearization performances.

Acknowledgment. Sponsor by Important National Science and Technology Specific Projects (2010ZX03005-001).M.

References

1. Vuolevi, J.H.K., Rahkonen, T., Manninen, J.P.A.: Measurement technique for characterizing memory effects in RF power amplifiers. IEEE Trans. On Microwave Theory Tech. 49(8), 1383–1388 (2001)
2. Proakis, J.G., Manolakis, D.G.: Digital Signal Processing, Principles, Algorithm, and Applications, 4th edn. (July 2007) ISBN: 978-7-121-04042-9
3. Rupp, M.: The behavior of LMS and NLMS algorithm in the presence of spherically invariant processes. IEEE Transaction on Signal Processing 41(3), 1149–1160 (1993)
4. Mandic, D.P., Obradovic, D., Kuh, K.: A robust general normalized gradient descent algorithm. In: IEEE/SP 13th Workshop on Statistical Signal Processing, Paris, pp. 133–136 (2005)
5. Ai, B., Zhong, Z.D., Zhu, G., et al.: A Novel Scheme for Power Amplifier Predistortion Based on Indirect Leaning Architecture. Wireless Personal Communications 46(4), 523–530 (2008)
6. Bosch, W., Gatti, G.: Measurement and Simulation of Memory Effects in Predistortion Linearizers. IEEE Trans. Microwave Theory Tech. 37(12), 1885–1890 (1989)

An Improved Feed-Forward Neural Network Blind Equalization Algorithm Based on Construction Function

Yunshan Sun[1,2], Li-yi Zhang[1,2,*], Yanqin Li[3], Jin Zhang[4], and Youpin Chen[1]

[1] College of Information Engineering, Tianjin University of Commerce,
300134 Tianjin, China
[2] College of Electric Information Engineering, Tianjin University, 300072, Tianjin, China
[3] College of Disaster Prevention Equipment,
Institute of Disaster Prevention Science and Technology, 100106, Beijing, China
[4] Office of Equipment, First Hospital of Shanxi University of Medicine,
030024, Taiyuan, China
sunyunshan@tjcu.edu.cn

Abstract. In QAM communication system, CMA without phase information was only utilized to module statistical property of signals. In the phase deviation channel, great phase error was brought out. Simultaneously, it affected the convergence rate. A restraint function utilizing the amplitude of the signal was constructed in this article. The function must approach zero when the amplitude was chosen. The cost function was converted into a restraint function. The restraint stem includes the information of module property and phase characteristic. A new neural network blind equalization based on construction function was realized. Computer simulation indicates that the algorithm overcomes QAM signal phase deviation, speeds up the convergence rate, and reduces bit error ratio.

Keywords: blind equalization, feed-forward neural network, constant module algorithm, construction function.

1   Introduction

In order to eliminate the inter-symbol interference in the communications system, equalization technology need be adopted in the receiving port. Blind equalization utilizes the prior information of transmitted signals to equalize the channel character without referring to a training sequence. In the actual project, any system more or less includes non-linear ingredient, it needs to solve the nonlinear system equalization problem. Neural network has good approximation ability and handling ability, it can approach nonlinear function with any random precision[1,2]. In blind equalization, people utilize the characteristic structure of neural network to construct neural network blind equalization algorithm model. Because blind equalization based on neural network has many merits such as fast convergence rate, low bit error ratio and so on, it has become the researching hot spot of blind equalization technology.

---

* Corresponding author.

M. Zhao and J. Sha (Eds.): ICCIP 2012, Part I, CCIS 288, pp. 454–461, 2012.

Because the form of CMA blind equalization algorithm is simple, it was widespread applied. But CMA algorithm does not contain the phase information of signals, and it has only used the signal module statistical property. In the phase deviation channel, the large phase error was brought out, simultaneously affected the convergence rate. This article constructed a restraint CMA cost function, weights and parameters of neural network were obtained by LMS algorithm, and a new blind equalization was realized. It speeds up the convergence rate, overcomes the phase deviation and reduces bit error ratio.

2   Principle of Neural Network Blind Equalization Algorithm

Diagram of neural network blind equalization algorithm is shown in the Fig.1[3].

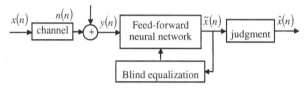

Fig. 1. Diagram of Feed-forward Neural Network Blind Equalization Algorithm

In the neural network blind equalization algorithm, neural network selects three-layer feed-forward neural network, as shown in Fig.2. Feed-forward neural network only contains the front output. Neural network was connected by the weight between each neuron. $w_{ij}(n)$ is the weight between the input layer and hidden layer, i describes the input neuron($i = 0,1,\cdots, m$); $w_j(n)$ is the weight between the hidden layer and the output layer, j describes the hidden neuron($j = 0,1,\cdots, k$). Supposing the input of the input layer is $\mathbf{Y}(n) = [y(n), y(n-1),\cdots, y(n-m)]^T$, the input of the hidden is $u_j(n)$, the output is $I_j(n)$, the output of the output layer is $v(n)$, the output of network is $\tilde{x}(n)$. State equations of feed-forward neural network were represented as [4].

$$u_j(n) = \sum_{i=0}^{m} w_{ij}(n)y(n-i) \tag{1}$$

$$I_j(n) = f[u_j(n)] \tag{2}$$

$$v(n) = \sum_{j=0}^{k} w_j(n)I_j(n) \tag{3}$$

$$\tilde{x}(n) = f[v(n)] \tag{4}$$

Where, $f(\cdot)$ is the transfer function between the hidden layer, the output layer and the input layer.

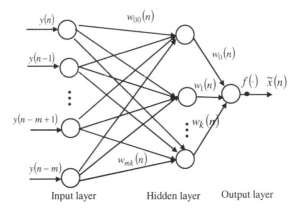

Fig. 2. Diagram of feed-forward neural network with a hidden layer

3   Plural Number System Feed-Forward Neural Network Blind Equalization Algorithm

In the plural number system blind equalization algorithm, weight iterative formula is composed by the real component and the imaginary component.

$$\mathbf{W}(n+1) = \mathbf{W}(n) + \mu \frac{\partial J(n)}{\partial \mathbf{W}(n)} \tag{5}$$

$$\mathbf{W}(n) = \mathbf{W_R}(n) + j\mathbf{W_I}(n) \tag{6}$$

Cost function is

$$J(n) = \frac{1}{2}\left[\left|\tilde{x}(n)\right|^2 - R_2\right]^2 \tag{7}$$

Neural network signal can be shown in the complex form

$$\frac{\partial J(n)}{\partial \mathbf{W}(n)} = 2\left[\left|\tilde{x}(n)\right|^2 - R_2\right]\left|\tilde{x}(n)\right|\left[\frac{\partial\left|\tilde{x}(n)\right|}{\partial \mathbf{W_R}(n)} + j\frac{\partial\left|\tilde{x}(n)\right|}{\partial \mathbf{W_I}(n)}\right] \tag{8}$$

$$y(n-i) = y_R(n-i) + jy_I(n-i) \tag{9}$$

$$w_{ij}(n) = w_{ij,R}(n) + jw_{ij,I}(n) \tag{10}$$

$$\begin{aligned} u_j(n) &= \sum_i w_{ij}(n)y(n-i) \\ &= \sum_i \left[w_{ij,R}(n)y_R(n-i) - w_{ij,I}(n)y_I(n-i)\right] + j\sum_i\left[w_{ij,R}(n)y_I(n-i) + w_{ij,I}(n)y_R(n-i)\right] \end{aligned} \tag{11}$$

$$I_j(n) = f\left[u_{j,R}(n)\right] + jf\left[u_{j,I}(n)\right] \tag{12}$$

$$w_j(n) = w_{j,R}(n) + jw_{j,I}(n) \tag{13}$$

$$
\begin{aligned}
v(n) &= \sum_j w_j(n) I_j(n) \\
&= \sum_j \left[w_{j,R}(n) I_{j,R}(n) - w_{j,I}(n) I_{j,I}(n) \right] + j \sum_j \left[w_{j,R}(n) I_{j,I}(n) + w_{j,I}(n) I_{j,R}(n) \right]
\end{aligned} \tag{14}
$$

$$\tilde{x}(n) = f\left[v_R(n) \right] + jf\left[v_I(n) \right] \tag{15}$$

Because three-layer plural number system forward feed neural network has the hidden layer and the output layer, its weight iterative formula is different.

(1) Weight iterative formula of the output layer
$w_j(n)$ is the weight between the output layer and hidden layer of feed-forward neural network, then

$$
\begin{aligned}
\frac{\partial |\tilde{x}(n)|}{\partial w_{j,R}(n)} &= \frac{1}{2|\tilde{x}(n)|} \frac{\partial \left[\tilde{x}(n) \tilde{x}^*(n) \right]}{\partial w_{j,R}(n)} \\
&= \frac{1}{2|\tilde{x}(n)|} \frac{\partial \left\{ f^2\left[v_R(n) \right] + f^2\left[v_I(n) \right] \right\}}{\partial w_{j,R}(n)} \\
&= \frac{1}{|\tilde{x}(n)|} f\left[v_R(n) \right] f'\left[v_R(n) \right] I_{j,R}(n) + \frac{1}{|\tilde{x}(n)|} f\left[v_I(n) \right] f'\left[v_I(n) \right] I_{j,I}(n)
\end{aligned} \tag{16}
$$

$$
\begin{aligned}
\frac{\partial |\tilde{x}(n)|}{\partial w_{j,I}(n)} &= \frac{1}{2|\tilde{x}(n)|} \frac{\partial \left[\tilde{x}(n) \tilde{x}^*(n) \right]}{\partial w_{j,I}(n)} \\
&= \frac{1}{2|\tilde{x}(n)|} \frac{\partial \left\{ f^2\left[v_R(n) \right] + f^2\left[v_I(n) \right] \right\}}{\partial w_{j,I}(n)} \\
&= \frac{-1}{|\tilde{x}(n)|} f\left[v_R(n) \right] f'\left[v_R(n) \right] I_{j,I}(n) + \frac{1}{|\tilde{x}(n)|} f\left[v_I(n) \right] f'\left[v_I(n) \right] I_{j,R}(n)
\end{aligned} \tag{17}
$$

Equation (16) and (17) were deduced,

$$
\begin{aligned}
\frac{\partial |\tilde{x}(n)|}{\partial w_{j,R}(n)} + j \frac{\partial |\tilde{x}(n)|}{\partial w_{j,I}(n)} &= \frac{1}{|\tilde{x}(n)|} \left\{ f\left[v_R(n) \right] f'\left[v_R(n) \right] I_{j,R}(n) + f\left[v_I(n) \right] f'\left[v_I(n) \right] I_{j,I}(n) \right\} \\
&\quad + j \frac{1}{|\tilde{x}(n)|} \left\{ f\left[v_I(n) \right] f'\left[v_I(n) \right] I_{j,R}(n) - f\left[v_R(n) \right] f'\left[v_R(n) \right] I_{j,I}(n) \right\} \\
&= \frac{1}{|\tilde{x}(n)|} \left\{ f\left[v_R(n) \right] f'\left[v_R(n) \right] + jf\left[v_I(n) \right] f'\left[v_I(n) \right] \right\} I_j^*(n)
\end{aligned} \tag{18}
$$

The weight iterative formula of the output layer can be obtained

$$w_j(n+1) = w_j(n) - 2\mu k(n) I_j^*(n) \tag{19}$$

Where, $k(n) = \left| |\tilde{x}(n)|^2 - R_2 \right| \{f[v_R(n)]f'[v_R(n)] + jf[v_I(n)]f'[v_I(n)]\}$.

(2) Weight iterative formula of the hidden layer
$w_{ij}(n)$ is the weight between the input layer and the hidden layer of feed-forward neural network, then

$$w_{ij}(n+1) = w_{ij}(n) - 2\mu k_j(n) y^*(n-i) \tag{20}$$

Where,

$$k_j(n) = 2\left[|\tilde{x}(n)|^2 - R_2\right]f'[u_{j,R}(n)] \times Re\{f[v_R(n)]f'[v_R(n)] + jf[v_I(n)]f'[v_I(n)]]w_j^*(n)\}$$
$$+ j2\left[|\tilde{x}(n)|^2 - R_2\right]f'[u_{j,I}(n)] \times Im\{f[v_R(n)]f'[v_R(n)] + jf[v_I(n)]f'[v_I(n)]]w_j^*(n)\} \tag{21}$$

4   Restraint Plural Number System Feed-Forward Neural Network Blind Equalization Algorithm

Establishing a construct function using QAM own characteristic, it was utilized to restrain constant module cost function. A new forward feed neural network blind equalization algorithm based on construct function was obtained. Take 16QAM modulation signal for example, the receiving signal was decomposed into the real part and the imaginary part, and then the tap coefficient of the equalizer will be adjusted by restraint cost function. Speaking of the single-channel signal, the sending signal only has four data -3,-1,1,3, according with these four data, establish a function $\phi(x)$, then

$$\phi(x) = 0 \qquad x \in \{-3,-1,1,3\} \tag{22}$$

The goal to construct the cost function enables the equalization output signal to satisfy equation (22). Because equation (22) contains the definite information of signal, it makes the equalizer better overcome ISI. MSE will become much smaller when the equalizer restrain. The cost function of new algorithm is as follows:

$$J(n) = \frac{1}{2}\left[|\tilde{x}(n)|^2 - R_2\right]^2 + E\left[\phi(\tilde{x}_R(n))^2\right] + E\left[\phi(\tilde{x}_I(n))^2\right] \tag{23}$$

Where, $\tilde{x}_R(n)$, $\tilde{x}_I(n)$ separately represents the real component and the imaginary component of the equalization signal $\tilde{x}(n)$.

In order to obtain the weight coefficient iterative formula by LMS algorithm, $\phi(x)$ must be determined. Many functions can satisfy equation (22), therefore,

$\phi(x) = A\cos\left(\dfrac{\pi}{2}x\right)$ (A represents the amplitude of cosine function), equation (18), (20) can be deduced:

$$w_{ij}(n+1) = w_{ij,R}(n) - \frac{\partial|\tilde{x}(n)|}{\partial w_{ij,R}(n)} \times \left\{ 4\mu|\tilde{x}(n)|^3 - 4\mu|\tilde{x}(n)|R_{2,R} - \frac{\mu\pi A^2}{2}\sin[\pi(\tilde{x}_R(n))] \right\}$$

$$+ w_{ij,I}(n) - \frac{\partial|\tilde{x}(n)|}{\partial w_{ij,I}(n)} \times \left\{ 4\mu|\tilde{x}(n)|^3 - 4\mu|\tilde{x}(n)|R_{2,I} - \frac{\mu\pi A^2}{2}\sin[\pi(\tilde{x}_I(n))] \right\} \tag{24}$$

$$w_{j}(n+1) = w_{j,R}(n) - \frac{\partial|\tilde{x}(n)|}{\partial w_{j,R}(n)} \times \left\{ 4\mu|\tilde{x}(n)|^3 - 4\mu|\tilde{x}(n)|R_{2,R} - \frac{\mu\pi A^2}{2}\sin[\pi(\tilde{x}_R(n))] \right\}$$

$$+ w_{j,I}(n) - \frac{\partial|\tilde{x}(n)|}{\partial w_{j,I}(n)} \times \left\{ 4\mu|\tilde{x}(n)|^3 - 4\mu|\tilde{x}(n)|R_{2,I} - \frac{\mu\pi A^2}{2}\sin[\pi(\tilde{x}_I(n))] \right\} \tag{25}$$

By the characteristic of cosine function, A not only represents the amplitude of $\phi(x)$ function, but also contains the rate of change of $\phi(x)$ function in $\{-3,-1,1,3\}$. The larger A is, the larger the rate of change is, and the larger the difference of function is. But when A is too large to guarantee the convergence of the algorithm. The new blind equalization algorithm can be realized by equation (24) and (25).

5   Experimental Simulation

Simulation condition: the signal transmitting port adopts Glay code mapping independent distribute 16QAM signal; the channel adopts plural impulse response wireless digital communication channel $H(z) = (0.0410 + j0.0109) + (0.0495 + j0.0123)z^{-1}$ [5]; the finite equalizer coefficient tap N=31; signal-to-noise ratio is 30dB; the value of L is 0.00002.

Fig.3 shows MSE convergence comparison curve of 16QAM in the wireless digital communication channel. The iterative step-size is $\mu = 0.0002$. Fig.4 is a curve of bit error ratio after 10000 times iterations. Fig.3 shows that the new algorithm speeds up convergence rate, and reduces the stable state remainder error and bit error ratio.

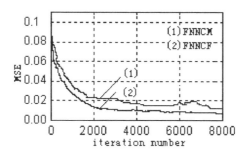

Fig. 3. Convergence rate curve

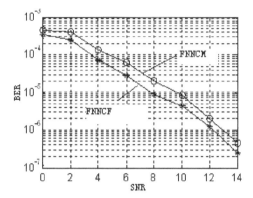

Fig. 4. BER curve

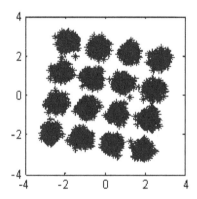

Fig. 5. Signal convergence constellation of CMA

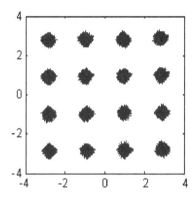

Fig. 6. Signal convergence constellation of construction function

Fig.5 is constellation of CMA after 10000 times iterations. Fig.6 is constellation of CF algorithm 10000 times iterations when A is 4. As was known in the chart, constellation of new blind equalization algorithm is more centralized and clearer than constellation of CMA neural network algorithm. And new blind equalization algorithm overcomes the phase deviation of QAM signal.

6   Conclusion

Neural network is a novel optimized method. It possesses many characteristics such as self-study, adaptation, good tolerance-fault, large-scale parallel processing, highly robustness and so on. It is widespread applied in the non-linear dynamic question system. Neural network theory and blind equalization technology are combined to overcome inter-symbol interference. It has become a development tendency. It possesses some merits such as fast convergence rate, small bit error ratio etc. This article analyzed the traditional constant module algorithm, and defined a construct function. Compared with CMA blind equalization, simulation indicates that the new algorithm overcomes phase ambiguity of QAM signal and improves the convergence rate.

Acknowledgements. This work was supported by Tianjin College Science and Technology Development Foundation of China under Grant (No.20110709) and Shanxi Nature Science Fund project (No. 2011011015-3).

References

1. Zhang, J., Xiao, X.X.: Chaotic signal source design and synchronization based on neural networks. Journal of Electronics and Information Technology 24(1), 37–44 (2002)
2. Kobayashi, M.: Exceptional Reducibility of Complex-Valued Neural Networks. IEEE Transaction on Neural Network 21(7), 1060–1072 (2010)
3. Lu, R.: The study on the neural network blind equalization Algorithm, Taiyuan: Master's degree Thesis of Taiyuan University of Technology (2003)
4. Sun, Y., Zhang, L., Zhang, J., et al.: Feed-forward Neural Network Medical CT Image Blind Equalization Algorithm based on Zigzag Transform. Journal of Computational Information Systems 7(16), 5683–5689 (2011)
5. You, C., Hong, D.: Nonlinear blind equalization schemes using complex-valued multilayer feed forward neural networks. IEEE Transaction on Signal Processing 6, 1442–1455 (1998)

The Design of a Hybrid Time-Share Drive Electric Vehicle on a High Mobility Vechile

Yan Sun[1,2,*], Shishun Zhu[1], Shiliang Yan[1], Sujun Luo[3], and Peng Ye[4]

[1] Military Transportation University Department of Automobile Engineering, Tianjin, China
[2] 66417 troops , xuanhua, China
[3] Military Transportation University Department of Military logistics, Tianjin, China
[4] Military Transportation University Department of Scientific Research
sunyan021001@yahoo.cn

Abstract. A kind of hybrid electric tactical vehicle structure scheme was proposed here, and its characteristics was expounded. In the investigation, the power and the torque requirements for the powertrain were calculated, and parameters for powertrain components were designed preliminarily. After that, the hybrid electric tactical vehicle was modeled in MATLAB/ Simulink. The simulation results show that the parameter design of each powertrain component is reasonable, and the vehicle can achieve predetermined performance goals. The results supplied the foundation for the next step vehicle development.

Keywords: hybrid electric vehicle, time-share drive, structure design, power – train, simulation.

1 Introduction

Hybrid technology has obvious advantages in military vehicles and now research institutions of many countries are refitting and studying new military vehicles development. Military vehicle hybrid system is based on electric power as auxiliary power to improve vehicle dynamics, concealment and fuel economy to reduce engine noise and emissions,and to reduce engine wear. Through matching engines, motive battery, generators and motor for the best, Hybrid military vehicle can improve the mobility of a vehicle, response speed, accelerating performance ,climbing ability. Hybrid military vehicle can not only reduces the noise and reduce heat characteristics and improve its protective performance through the pure electric mode, but also can provide plenty of power equipment for the other car weapon system by using hybrid carriage platform system integration ability. Hybrid military vehicle can improve the efficiency of energy utilization, and effectively reduce logistics supply, increase mobile weapons platform combat radius, and can clean emissions, reduce the pollution of the environment.

---

[*] Corresponding author.

M. Zhao and J. Sha (Eds.): ICCIP 2012, Part I, CCIS 288, pp. 462–468, 2012.

2   The Use Features of Military Vehicles

Military tactical vehicles is the army mobile platform, security transportation platform and weapon equipment safeguard platform. It is the important component of army armament system. The tactical and technical index of military vehicles is put forward by army and its study and manufacture have special organization. Military vehicles are required to have high maneuverability and through performance, so that it can get through various roads.

Usually, in order to adapt to the need of the battlefield, the design and manufacture of military tactical vehicles are set in the worst off-road conditions. The driving ability is designed to pass through the country road, rough crossing the rugged mountain hills, rain muddy soil fantastic path. For that reason the power and dynamic of military vehicles is maximized which is designed. But in the time of peace, military vehicles used usually in highway driving conditions and other good conditions, its power demand is far below design power and only partly powering can meet the requirements.The design drive ability is superfluous.

To adapt to the battlefield requirements, various countries emphasize maneuvering performance and environmental adaptability of military vehicles in researching vehicles. Through using the advanced structure and technology, the mobility and military survival ability further are improved. In this paper, a high mobility vechile highly maneuverable is reformed hybrid time-share drive vehicle to adapt to the environment demand of the military.

3   Hybrid Time-Share Drive Structure Design

The design methods of hybrid tactics vehicle basically have two kinds. They are special design and manufacture of the new vehicle and modified.Because manufacturing cost of special design is high and the design time cycle is long,this method is not suitable for research. As far as test and small batch production is concerned, modification is a kind of economic and feasible method. For the research project of the modular hybrid vehicles time-share driving tactics vehicles, we will study hybrid modified research in the basic model with high motor and light vehicle chassis equipped now. Through modular design research to the 4 x 4 driving suvs power system, the vechile can choose different driving options by application environment and driving conditions. Usually, the vehicle chooses single axis 4 x 2 drive. But in wartime or special military vehicles realize all 4 x 4 wheel drive by using the utilization of the modular standard interface hybrid assembly components (including generator system, motor system and battery pack) on the vehicle to upgrade the vechile. This model can not only meet the driver points at low load of small power demand, but also meet the performance requirements of military vehicles in bad use under the environment to effectively improve the dynamic performance of the military. The technology solutions of the high motor sport utility vehicle modular hybrid time-share drive that is studied in this paper is shown in figure 1 below.

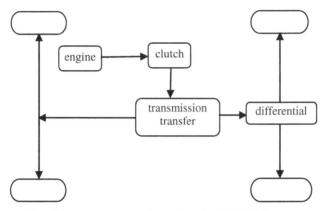

Fig. 1. The power transmission sketch of 4×4 driving suv

As shown in figure 1, the power transmission line of a high mobility vechile (4 x 4 driving suvs) high motor sport utility vehicle chassis basic models is as follows:

(a) Engine passes power to thansfer through the clutch after startup;
(b) Thansfer passes part of power forward to the front axle to driver front wheel rotation and passes other part of power to rear axle differential at the same time.

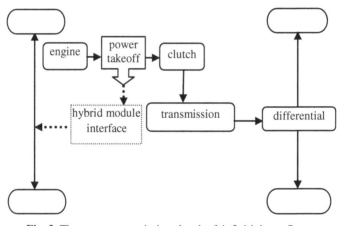

Fig. 2. The power transmission sketch of 4×2 driving refit suv

As shown in figure 2, the power transmission line of the modified vehicle used in the peacetime 4 x 2 driven model the is as follows:

(a) The power takeoff is fit between the engine and the clutch and hybrid assembly components (including generators, motors and battery pack) are designed modules possessing standard interface;
(b) The motor is added on the front axle, but the front wheel is in the state with the move in the work mode due to no hybrid modules.
(c) The engine passes power to to the transmission through the power takeoff and the clutch power transfer, the transmission transfer power backwards to rear axle.

As shown in figure 3, the power transmission line of the modified vehicle used in wartime 4 x 4 driven model is as follows:

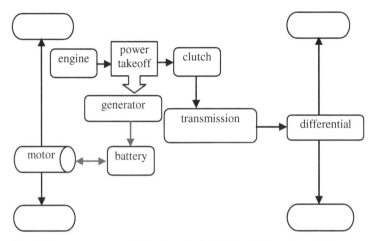

Fig. 3. The power transmission sketch of 4×4 hybrid time-share driving suv

(a) The vehicle is upgraded by Using hybrid assembly components with standard interface modular to realize the hybrid fore-wheels drive vehicle;
(b) After the engine will transfer power to the transmission, the transmission pass power to rear axle;
(c) The power takeoff will psss part of power to the generator,then the generator are ready to charge the battery;
(d) The battery supply power to front wheel drive and motor driver turn, in this time the hybrid power modules are single axis electric driven parallel-series type.

4   Power Flow Control Strategy

4.1   Drive Power Flow

The actual running condition of vehicles is relatively complex. For convenience of analysis, in this paper the running mode will be simplified to four typical working conditions as shown in figure 1 below. And typical working conditions can be divided into two categories: steady-state condition p_i transient condition p_j. Therefore, according to the vehicle dynamics, the vehicle driving drive demand for power is following:

$$p_r = \begin{cases} p_i & \text{steady-state condition} \\ p_j & \text{transient condition} \end{cases} \tag{1}$$

In Eq. (1),P_r is drive power demand, P_i is steady-state power demand and P_j is transient power demand, kW.

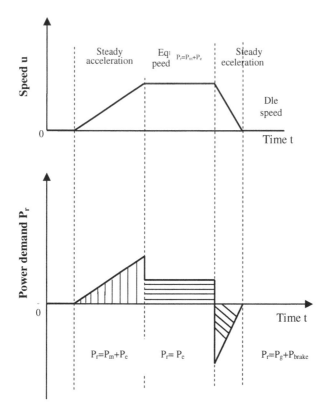

Fig. 4. Drive power allocation of typical working conditions

4.2   Control Strategy

In the process of the vehicle running, the vehicle controller distributes energy in the engine, the battery and motor on the basis of energy management strategy formulated. This paper established corresponding power flow control strategy for engine, motor and battery power for the management and basic idea is:

(1) Automobile driving demand power Pr is divided into steady-state power and transient power, respectively provided by the engine and electric motor;

(2) In the steady-state condition, the power of engines Pe provide demand power of vehicle steady-state operation. To improve fuel economy of the whole vehicle , the engine power output is optimized and engine is controled in optimization working point.In this time the difference of the engine output power Popt and the driving demand power Pr is generator power Pg;

(3) In the Accelerating condition, when the speed is below set value ua, driving demand power Pr is provided completely by motor; When the speed is higher than ua, motor works in a rated output state, power output is Pm, the difference of Pr and Pm is Pm transient conditions of engine power demand;

(4) The battery power must meet operation needs of the motor and the generator. The battery energy meets the state (SOC) keep in a range of requirements.

5   Vehicle Performance Simulation

5.1   The Simulation Parameters

Table 1. Hybrid time-driven vehicle simulition parameter

Parameter name	Parameter values
load quality	1750kg
front axle load	2000 kg
rear axle load	3000 kg
No-load total	3250 kg
length	7495mm
wide	2470mm
hight	2412 mm
axle distance	3300mm
wheel track front	1802mm
wheel track rear	1806mm

Table 2. The motor parameters

name	parameters	Value
	Rating power	20kw
	maximum power	30kw
motor	rating revolution	750 r/min
	maximum revolution	3000 r/min
	rating torque	150N.m
	maximum torque	200N.m

Table 3. Battery parameters

assembly	parameters	Value
	type	lithium battery
battery	voltage	320v
	capability	55A.h
	energy	12.5kw.h

5.2   The Simulation Analysis

By ADVISOR2002 application software and the development control strategy, a high mobility vechile hybrid suvs power performance and the simulation of economic behavior are completed.the results satisfy the design index such as table 4.

Table 4. Performance parameters of a high mobility vechile hybrid time-share drive vehicle

Performance parameters	hybrid driving mode
fuel consume	9.8 L. $(100km)^{-1}$
Maximum speed	112 $km.h^{-1}$
maximum climbing capability	61%
accelerate time (0-80km/h)	21.8s
accelerate time (60-90 km/h)	16.4s

6   Conclusion

This paper puts forward parameters matching method of double-axis parallel hybrid vehicle power system considering running condition, control strategy and and vehicle dynamic performance. This method guidance completed mengshi hybrid time-share drive tactics vehicle design.In MATLAB/Simulink environment, using ADVISOR simulation software mode of auxiliary control strategy simulation model is established based on batteries work and the simulation results show that the matching parameters of dynamic assembly parts can satisfy the requirements of vehicle performance. This mothod provide the basis for product development.

Acknowledgment. This project is supplied by post-doctoral fund (20100481484).

References

1. Montazeri-Gh, M., Poursamad, A., Ghalichi, B.: Application of genetic algorithm for optimization of control strategy in parallel hybrid electric vehicles. Journal of the Franklin Institute 343, 420–435 (2006)
2. Langari, R., Won, J.-S.: A Driving Situation Awareness-Based Energy Management Strategy for Parallel Hybrid Vehicles. SAE PAPER 2003-01-2311
3. Salmasi, F.R.: Control Strategies for Hybrid Electric Vehicles: Evolution, Classification, Comparison, and Future Trends. IEEE Transactions on Vehicular Technology 56(5), Part 1, 2393–2404 (2007)
4. Miller, J.M.: Propulsion Systems for Hybrid Vehicles. IEEE Power and Energy Series (2004)
5. Salmasi, F.R.: Designing control strategies for hybrid electric vehicles. Tutorial Presentation in EuroPes 2005, Benalmadena, Spain, June 15-17 (2005)

Performance Evaluation of HAPS-CDMA Cells with Different Positions

Zhaoqun Qi, Li Fangzhou, Xiaojun Jing, and Siqing You

Beijing University of Posts and Telecommunications
P.O. BOX 151, No.10 Xi Tu Cheng Road
Beijing, P.R. China, 100876
{Qizhaoqun,ysq6228}@gmail.com, lfzasx@live.cn,
jxiaojun@bupt.edu.cn

Abstract. High Altitude Platform Stations' (HAPS) performance can be affected by cells' position. In this paper, a novel HAPS-CDMA system model with different positions is presented. And the impacts of the model are examined. From numerical results it is observed that the effect of positions on HAPS-CDMA system can't be neglected. The farther the cell is away from the platform, the larger of 3db radius and the smaller capacity it has, the greater power loss the users of the cell need.

Keywords: HAPS, CDMA, beam forming, power loss, system capacity, interference factor.

1 Introduction

The HAPS-CDMA system has many significant advantages compared with the traditional satellite communication system and terrestrial cellular mobile communication system, such as the lower cost of deployment, the larger system capacity, the larger area of coverage , the faster speed of distribution network ,and the more suitable for areas with less population density and emergency situations. It is widely considered as the third generation mobile communication (3G) systems complement and extend [1][2].

[1] proposes a general method of analyzing the HAPS-CDMA downlink system capacity, the result shows that the capacity of HAPS-CDMA is 1.2-1.67times of the capacity of the terrestrial CDMA system. [2] presents the methods of embedded beam to solve the problem of the hot spot area which needs a large system capacity; [3] considered the system capacity changes and solutions of the quasi-static state HAPS platform. Study of the above only analyzes the central cell, which is located just below the HAPS platform. In fact, the HAPS-CDMA covers a wide range of area, for example, the one at 22km altitude, it can cover a circular area which maximum diameter is 1056km .Considering the block of the topography, the minimum communication elevation angle should be about 5° in order to ensure the communication quality and other requirements, so a single HAP can cover a circular area diameter of 420km[3]. Therefore, it can not just simply make the analysis of the central cell.

This paper calculates the 3dB radius of the cells with different positions, and analyzes the power losses of the users in different cells. Finally, this paper evaluates the

M. Zhao and J. Sha (Eds.): ICCIP 2012, Part I, CCIS 288, pp. 469–477, 2012.

cell uplink system capacity of the HAPS-CDMA at different locations. As the simulation results show, the farther the cell away from the platform, the larger of 3db radius and the smaller capacity it has, the greater power loss the users of the cell need.

The rest of this paper is organized as follows: Sec. 2 illustrates the platform system model which operates in stratosphere, and illustrates how to calculate the central cell system capacity. Sec. 3. analyzes 3dB radius of the cells at different positions, and the power losses of the users in different cells. The other cells' system uplink capacity formula and results are presented in Sec. 4. Finally, conclusions are given in Sec. 5.

2   HAPS-CDMA System Model and The Central Cell System Capacity Analyse

2.1   System Model of the Central Cell

CDMA base stations are located at HAPS platform, which use array antennas with beam forming to cover the terrestrial cells, the main beam center arms at the cells' center, and the gain of the antenna conforms to the ITU recommendations [4], and is modeled in dB , where θ is the angle away from the main beam.

$$G(\theta) = \begin{cases} -3\,(\dfrac{\theta}{1.57})^2 & 0^\circ \le \theta \le 4.53^\circ \\ -25 & 4.53^\circ < \theta \le 5.87^\circ \\ 21.15 - 60\log(\theta) & 5.87^\circ < \theta \le 37^\circ \\ -73 & 37^\circ < \theta \le 90^\circ \end{cases} \quad (1)$$

Central reference cell B_0 is located just below the HAPS away from the platform 21km. Other cells B_j means the jth ring cell around the central cell B_0 by the cellular structure with radius R_j and area S_j . We assume users are uniformly distributed on the service area[6], the use density is ρ , The relationship between the location of cell users illustrated in Fig.1.

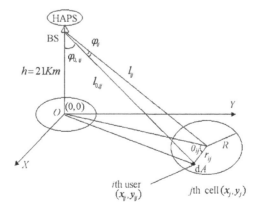

Fig. 1. Geometrical relationship of HAPS'users

As Fig.1, the coordinate of the center of the central cell is $(0,0)$,and (x_j, y_j) is the other cells' coordinate, where $\varphi_{0,ij}$ and φ_{ij} is the angle between mobile user i and the base station, and r_{ij} is the distance from user i to the center of the jth cell which provides the serve for it. $l_{0,ij}$ and l_{ij} represent the distance between mobile users i and the central cell or the jth cell respectively, $l_{0,ij} \approx l_{ij}$. dA is the integral of the per unit area, θ_{ij} is the angle of the user and the line which connects the center of the central cell and the center of the j area.

2.2   System Capacity

HAPS-CDMA in the stationary state served by an ideal power control, the power base station received from the users is P, then the transmit power is,

$$P_{sent} = P \cdot G(\varphi_{ij})^{-1} \cdot pl^{-1} \tag{2}$$

Where $G(\varphi_{ij})$ is the antenna gain which is expressed in decimal, pl is the path loss [3].

Assuming the voice activation factor is α, the central cell system capacity is[1,5]:

$$M = \frac{1}{\alpha(1+f)} \left[\frac{W/R_b}{E_b/I_0} - \frac{\sigma_n^2}{P} \right] + 1 \tag{3}$$

E_b is the bit energy, I_0 is the total interference power, R_b is the bit rate, W is the system bandwidth, σ_n^2 is the Gaussian white noise power, f is the interference factor,

$$f = \frac{I_{inter}}{I_{intra}} = \sum_{j \in T, j \neq 0} \int_A \frac{G(\varphi_{0,ij})}{G(\varphi_{ij})} \frac{1}{S_0} dA$$

$$= \sum_{j \in T, j \neq 0} \int_0^{2\pi} \int_0^R \frac{G(\varphi_{0,ij})}{G(\varphi_{ij})} \frac{1}{\pi R_0^2} r_{ij} dr_{ij} d\theta_{ij} \tag{4}$$

T means cell coverage size, I_{intra} is interference from the users inside the cell, I_{inter} is the interference from other adjacent cell users.

$$I_{intra} = \alpha(M-1)P \tag{5}$$

So HAPS-CDMA uplink capacity is limited by the same cell and other adjacent cell users' interference.

3   3dB Radius and Power Loss

According to ITU recommendations [4], if the maximum gain G_m in the main lobe is 34.8dBi, and the 3 dB beam width $(2y_b)$ is estimated by,

$$y_b = \sqrt{\frac{7\,442}{10^{0.1G_m}}} = 1.57° \tag{6}$$

The vertical profile of the HAPS-CDMA multi-beam coverage is Fig 2.

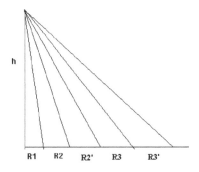

Fig. 2. The vertical profile of the HAPS-CDMA multi-beam coverage

R_j is the 3dB radius, which is near the platform, of the jth ring cell. And R_j' is the 3dB radius, which is far away from the platform, of the jth ring cell.

Define

$$\Delta R_n = R_n' - R_n \tag{7}$$

So

$$tg1.57° = R_1 / h \tag{8}$$

$$tg[1.57° \times (2n-2)] = \{h \times tg[1.57° \times (2n-3)] + R_n\} / h \tag{9}$$

$$tg[1.57° \times (2n-1)] = \{h \times tg[1.57° \times (2n-2)] + R_n'\} / h \tag{10}$$

Table 1. 3dB Radius of the Cells in Different Rings

Ring No.	1	2	3	4	5	6	7	8	9	10
R_n (m)	575	576	580	588	600	616	636	662	693	730
R_n' (m)	575	578	584	594	608	626	648	676	711	752
ΔR_n	0	2	4	6	8	10	12	14	18	18

From the Table1 we know the farther away from the platform, the larger 3dB radius the cell has. For example, the 3dB radius of the 10th ring cell is 730m, which is about 1.3 times of the central cell' s, while the 5th ring cells' only is 1.04 times. At the same time, the ΔR_n is larger too, which means the cell is out of shape more.

Assuming the sent and receive antenna gain is 1, the path loss of the HAPS-CDMA system will be

$$PL(dB) = -32.4 - 20\log f(MHz) - 20\log l(km)$$ (11)

Here f=1950MHz is the system carrier frequency.

So we can get Table2 the path loss of cells in different rings.

Table 2. The Path Loss of Cells in Different Rings

No	1	2	3	4	5	6	7	8	9	10
pl_n	-124.67	-124.67	-124.73	-124.81	-124.91	-125.05	-125.21	-125.4	-125.62	-125.88
pl_n'	-124.67	-124.73	-124.81	-124.91	-125.05	-125.21	-125.4	-125.62	-125.88	-126.17

pl_n is the path loss, which is near the platform, of the jth ring cell boundary. And pl_n' is the 3dB radius, which is far away from the platform, of the jth ring cell boundary.

Assuming the total power of every mobile terminal is the same, according to equation (2), we can get the normalization battery duration, show as Fig.3.

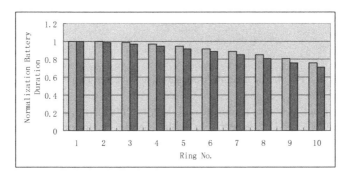

Fig. 3. The normalization battery duration of the jthe ring cell

From the Table2 we know the farther away from the platform, the larger path loss is and bigger sent power is needed, so the shorter battery duration is. For example, the path loss of the 10th ring cell is 125.88dB, which is larger 1.5dB than the central cell' s, so its battery duration is only about   0.7 times of the central cell's.

4   Other Cells Uplink System Capacity Analysis

4.1   System Model of the Nth Ring Cell

[4] shows that the intercell interference mainly from the first ring cell around the service cell, the interference from other cells in this area can be ignored. At the same time, considering the symmetry of the cells' distribution, the cell which is the same far away from the platform has the same system capacity. Therefore, we only need evaluate one cell each ring. Considering the antenna gain and path loss, and in order to simplify the calculation, we assume all of the cells' radiuses are R.

Assuming the central cell is the first ring cell, main interference cells of the ring Nth cell are: one N-1th ring cell, two Nth ring cell, three N+1th ring cell. In order to simplify the analysis, the cell has a honeycomb structure, as shown in Fig.4 below.

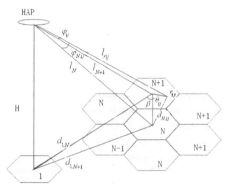

Fig. 4. The main interference cells of the Nth ring cell

The Nth ring cell becomes reference cell, 1 represents the first ring cell, which is the central cell; N,N+1,N-1 , respectively, Nth, N+1th, N-1th ring cell, $d_{1,N}$, $d_{1,N+1}$ express the distance between the central cell and Nth,N+1the ring cell, and $d_{N,ij}$ means the distance of the central cell to the user; l_N , l_{N+1} , l_{rij} , respectively, express the distance of the platform to Nth, N+1th ring cell and the distance to the user; β express the angle of the line which connects the center of the central cell and the center of the Nth ring cell, and the line which connects the center of the central cell and the center of the N+1th ring cell. θ_{ij} , φ_{ij} and $\varphi_{N,ij}$ have the similar meaning as Fig.1.

The interference suffered by the Nth ring cell is

$$I_{intra}(N) = 3I(N+1,N) + 2I(N,N) + I(N-1,N) \tag{12}$$

$I(a,b)$ expresses the bth ring reference cell's interference from the ath ring cell.

So, the Nth ring's interference factor f_N is

$$f_N = 3f_{N+1,N} + 2f_{N,N} + f_{N-1,N} \tag{13}$$

$f_{a,b}$ expresses the bth ring cell's interference from the ath ring cell,

$$f_{N+1,N} = \int_0^{2\pi}\int_0^R \frac{G(\varphi_{N,ij})}{G(\varphi_{ij})} \frac{1}{\pi R^2} r_{ij} dr_{ij} d\theta_{ij} \tag{14}$$

Put the interference factor of equation (14) into equation (3), and we can get the uplink system capacity of the Nth ring reference cell.

4.2   Simulation Parameters

The main simulation parameters are showed in the following Table3[7].

Table 3. Simulation parameters

Parameter	Value
Cell Radius R(km)	1
Carrier Frequency f_c (Hz)	1950
Voice Activity Factor α	0.6
Spreading Gain W / R_b	256
E_b / I_0 (dB)	5
P / σ_n^2 (dB)	-1

4.3   System Capacity of the Nth Ring Reference Cell

From the equation (3), the Nth ring cell's uplink system capacity is mainly determined by the intercell interference factor. As the result of Fig.5, the central cell, which is located just below the platform, the intercell interference factor is 0.3863, while the 10th ring cell's 0.6436, which is 1.67 times of the former. So the total interference, including inter cell and intra cell interference, suffered by the 10th ring cell is 1.18 times of the central cell.

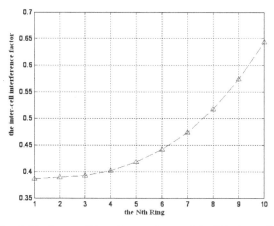

Fig. 5. The inter-cell interference factor of the Nth ring cell

So we can work out the system capacity of the Nth ring cell by putting the results into equation (3), as showed by Fig.6 below.

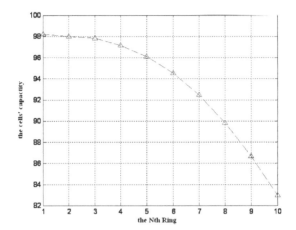

Fig. 6. The capacity of the Nth ring cell

From Fig 6, we get that the cell system capacity decrease from 98 people of the central cell, to 83 people of the 10th ring cell, a decrease of 15.4%. If the platform continues to increase its coverage, system capacity of the edge of the district's will deteriorate further. Therefore, the problem affects system performance seriously.

5   Conclusion

CDMA system is uplink interference limited system[6], this paper analyzes the uplink system capacity changes of the different locations. From numerical results, it is observed that the effect of positions on HAPS-CDMA system can't be neglected. The farther the cell is away from the platform, the larger of 3db radius and the smaller capacity it has, the and greater power loss the users of the cell need.

References

1. Foo, Y.C., Lim, W.L., Tatazoli, R.: Forward link power control for high altitude platform station W-CDMA system. In: Proc. IEEE VTC 2001, vol. 2, pp. 7–11 (Fall 2001)
2. Cheng, Y.-B., Jin, R.-H., et al.: An Embedded Multibeam Configuration for CDMA Communication Systems on HAPS. Journal of Electronics and Information Technology 28(8), 1395–1399 (2006) (in Chinese)
3. Guan, M.X.: Research on Resource Management and Capacity Estimation Method for HAPS. HIT, Harbin (2008) (in Chinese)

4. Huang, J.-J., Wang, W.-T., et al.: Interference Reduction for Terrestrial Cellular CDMA Systems via High Altitude Platform Station. In: Proc. IEEE VTC 2007, pp. 1350–1354 (Spring 2007)
5. Huang, J.-J., Wang, W.-T., et al.: Capacity Enhancement for Integrated HAPS-Terrestrial CDMA System. In: IEEE VTC 2006, pp. 2597–2601 (Spring 2006)
6. Huang, J.-J., Wang, W.-T., et al.: Intersystem Interference Reduction for Overlaid HAPS-Terrestrial CDMA System. IEICE Trans. on Commun. E91-B(1), 334–338 (2008)
7. Tsai, Y.-C., Ferng, H.-W., Huang, J.-J.: Design and Performance Modeling of Resource Allocation Strategies for GPRS. Journal of Chinese Institute of Engineers 31(3), 385–401 (2008)

Boiler Combustion Process Modeling and Sensitivity Analysis

Xuguang Wang and Jie Su

School of Control and Computer Engineering, North China Electric Power University,
619 YongHua North Street, Baoding, China
wang_xuguang@163.com

Abstract. In order to overcome the noise caused influence on the result of neutral network training, the paper introduces the RANSAC algorithm into the neutral network training and puts forward a RANSAC-BP neutral network training algorithm. In this algorithm a t-distribution based confidence interval is constructed to replace the distance threshold, which overcomes the weakness that the threshold selection in the neutral network training has to rely on experience; the algorithm culls noisy data during neutral network training and then re-train the neutral network with noise free data, thus making the neutral network training algorithm less sensitive to data noises. This algorithm has been validated by a simulation experiment. At the phase of model analysis, taking the optimal working conditions as the reference points, the paper takes the partial differential of the function (the relation between inputs and outputs, trained through RANSCK-BP) as the transfer function, which portrays how the small changes in the input parameters influence the output parameters. This provides a method to analyze the sensitivity of the combustion optimization model.

Keywords: Combustion optimization, RANSAC-BP, Sensitivity Analysis, Transfer Function.

1 Introduction

In China at the current stage, the thermal power generation is the major approach for energy acquisition. In the overall thermal power generation cost, the fuel generally accounts for over 70%, thus to improve the efficiency of the boiler combustion system is of great significance to decreasing the operation cost of the electric power system. The coal-dominant energy structure results in serious air pollution in China, which costs high economic as well as environment cost. Therefore, the high efficiency and low emission combustion of coal-fired boiler has become the objective of the boiler combustion optimization research, which could effectively increase the operation efficiency, decrease the power generation cost, reduce the emission of pollutants, and monitor the safe operation of the boiler [1], thus attracting more and more attention.

The boiler combustion optimization techniques include three categories [2]. The first category detects on line the important parameters of the boiler combustion, and

M. Zhao and J. Sha (Eds.): ICCIP 2012, Part I, CCIS 288, pp. 478–489, 2012.

then directs the operators to regulate the combustion, which takes the domestic predominance at present [3,4]. The second category is a kind of boiler operation monitoring and control system based on DCS, which adopts advanced control logic, control algorithm or artificial intelligence technology [5] to realize the boiler combustion optimization. This category has been developing rapidly with the gradual maturity of the advanced control and artificial intelligence technology and its successful application in industry [6]. The third category optimizes the boiler combustion through improving the combustion equipment, such as combustor, heating surface, etc. The three categories mentioned above have their respective advantages in practice, however, the second one doesn't need to transform the boiler equipment, instead it takes full advantage of the boiler operating data, takes DCS control as the basis, applies the advanced modeling, optimization and control techniques, and directly increases the operating efficiency of the boiler and decreases the NOx emission. For its advantages of small investment, low risk, and obvious effect [7,8], it has become the most preferred combustion optimization technique. Neutral network is usually used for boiler combustion modeling. However, in the working conditions used for neutral network training normally exist noises which will seriously affect the training results. Thus it is necessary to find an approach to cull noises before training neutral network.

Inspired by the RANSAC algorithm and combing the BP network training algorithm, the paper proposes the RANSAC-BP neutral network training algorithm, which overcomes the influence caused by noises on the result of neutral network training. The algorithm has been validated by a simulation experiment. Besides, taking the optimal working conditions as the reference points, the paper creates a total differential form for the relation between inputs and outputs of combustion model, forms a function to describe the input and output parameters of the combustion model, and then takes the function's partial differential as the transfer function to portray how the small changes in the input parameters influence the output parameters, which provides a method to analyze the sensitivity of the combustion optimization model.

2   Robust Training of BP Network

The power generation in a thermal power plant is a process where firstly the pulverized coal is burnt to turn chemical energy to thermal energy, and then through steam doing work, the thermal energy is turned to electric energy finally. At the boiler combustion stage, the measured values of all the parameters at certain moment are called a working condition, which can be represented as $d = [X, Y]^T$. Hereinto, $X = [X_{var}, X_{con}]$ denotes the combustion parameters besides the output parameters, which could be grouped into the improvable parameters X_{var} (e.g. the primary air quantity, the secondary air quantity, combustion angle, etc.) and the un-improvable parameters X_{con} , (e.g. pulverized coal composition, etc.). Y refers to the output parameters of boiler combustion, e.g. combustion efficiency, emission load of NOx, exhaust smoke temperature, etc.

To model the boiler combustion process is to determine the relation between X and Y. This is a complicated multivariable coupling nonlinear problem. Based on experience, we should take a BP network with at least two hidden layers as the learning machine to obtain the relation between X and Y after training. This paper takes the network model with two hidden layers. Generally, the outputs of the neutral network are the boiler combustion efficiency and the NOx discharge. Multiple experiments showed that the relation between X and Y is better expressed by two neutral networks with multi inputs and single output than one neutral network with multi inputs and binary outputs. Thus this paper will separately train two neutral networks with multi inputs and single output as Figure 1 demonstrates.

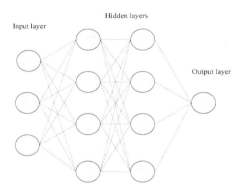

Fig. 1. A neutral network with two hidden layers

Although steady data can be obtained through the steady data judgment criterion, there inevitably exist noises or even gross errors in the steady data due to measuring equipment precision, human operation and other factors. If the neutral network is trained with data containing noises, the training result will not be satisfying. Thus it is necessary to find a method to cull the data noises before training.

2.1   RANSAC-BP Algorithm

RANSAC[9] algorithm is a robust estimation algorithm. Its core idea is selecting appropriate data subset to train the model, and use the obtained model to judge whether the data in the data set satisfy the given conditions. All the data satisfying the given conditions form a consensus set corresponding to the model. In the end the model is recalculated with the consensus set satisfying certain conditions to obtain the final model.

Based on the RANSAC algorithm, we put forward the RANSAC-BP algorithm as follows:

① Let $ite = 0$. Randomly select a subset of the steady data set $D_{sel}^{ite} \subset D$, train BP network $f(\cdot)$, $ite = ite + 1$; $D_{con}^{ite} = \phi$;

② For all $d \in D$, calculate the confidence interval $CI_\alpha(X, D_{sel}^{ite})$ of $f(\cdot)$ determined by d and D_{sel}^{ite}. If $Y \in CI_\alpha(X, D_{sel}^{ite})$, then $d \in D_{con}^{ite}$;

③ If $\left|D_{con}^{ite}\right| \geq T_{num}$, then go to ③ ; if $ite \geq T_{ite}$, then go to ④ ; otherwise go back to ①;

④ Take all the steady data in D_{con}^{ite} for training to obtain BP network $f(\cdot)$;

⑤ Let $D_{\max} = \arg\max\left\{\left|D_{con}^{ite}\right|\right\}$, take all the steady data in $D_{\max}$ for training to obtain BP network $f(\cdot)$.

2.2   Algorithm Specification

In the algorithm, ite is the iteration number of the algorithm; $f(\cdot)$ refers to the BP network obtained through training, and D_{con}^{ite} is the consensus set to which the ite time's iteration corresponds. α is the remarkable level, and $CI_{\alpha}(X, D_{sel}^{ite})$ is the confidence interval of $100(1-\alpha)\%$ of $f(\cdot)$. According to [10], $CI_{\alpha}(X, D_{sel}^{ite})$ can be represented in the form below

$$f(X, \theta_0) \pm t_{N-q}(1-\frac{\alpha}{2})s\sqrt{Z^T(\mathbf{Z}^T\mathbf{Z})^{-1}Z} .$$ (1)

Hereinto, θ_0 is the parameter vector to determine the neutral network $f(\cdot)$; N is the number of data in D_{sel}^{ite} , i.e. $N = \left|D_{sel}^{ite}\right|$; q is the dimension of θ_0 , i.e. $\theta_0 \in R^q$; t_{N-q} refers to the t distribution with the freedom degree of $N-q$.

If Ψ indicates the actual output column vector of neutral network, then the expected output column vector $\hat{\Psi}$ can be expressed as

$$\hat{\Psi} = [f(X_1, \theta_0), f(X_1, \theta_0), ..., f(X_N, \theta_0)]^T , \quad d_k = [X_k, Y_k]^T \in D_{sel}^{ite} , \quad k = 1...N .$$ (2)

Thus in formula (1)

$$s = \frac{(\Psi - \hat{\Psi})^T(\Psi - \hat{\Psi})}{N - q} .$$ (3)

Column vector

$$Z = \frac{\partial f(X, \theta)}{\partial \theta}\bigg|_{\theta=\theta_0} .$$ (4)

Matrix

$$\mathbf{Z} = [Z_1, Z_2, ..., Z_N]^T .$$ (5)

In Formula (5)

$$Z_k = \frac{\partial f(X_k, \theta)}{\partial \theta}\bigg|_{\theta=\theta_0} , \quad d_k = [X_k, Y_k]^T \in D_{sel}^{ite} , \quad k = 1...N .$$ (6)

In general the threshold T_{num} can be selected according to experience, but $T_{num} > q$ must be satisfied; when the estimated value of the sample probability is given,

T_{ite} can be obtained adaptively[9], in general conditions it also can be obtained according to experience.

The reason we use the form of confidence interval described in Formula (1) instead of the fixed threshold to evaluate the training result of neutral network is that when remarkable level is given, the confidence interval is self-adaptive and determined by the network input, which is more significant. Meanwhile, one point worthy notice is that in step ② of RANSAC-BP algorithm, working condition $d \in D_{con}^{ite}$ is on condition that when remarkable level α is given, the actual outputs to which the two neutral networks with multi-input and single output correspond should fall within the respective confidence intervals to which X responds.

3   Sensitivity Analysis

Let the combustion efficiency BP network be $f_\eta(\cdot)$, and the NOx discharge BP network be $f_{NO_x}(\cdot)$, then the mathematical model of the combustion optimization can be expressed as follows

$$\begin{cases} \max & ay_\eta - by_{NO_x} \\ s.t. & y_\eta = f_\eta(X_{var}, X_{con}) \\ & y_{NO_x} = f_{NO_x}(X_{var}, X_{con}) \\ & X_{var}^{\min} \le X_{var} \le X_{var}^{\max} \end{cases}$$ (7)

In the formula above, y_η and y_{NO_x} refer to the combustion efficiency and the NOx discharge respectively; a and b are weighting coefficients of y_η and y_{NO_x} respectively, and $a + b = 1$, $ab \ge 0$. When $b = 0$, the model only focuses on the combustion efficiency; when $a = 0$, the model only pays attention to the NOx discharge minimization, without regard to the combustion efficiency. Thus, the different combination of a and b can be used for different optimization purposes. $[X_{var}^{\min}, X_{var}^{\max}]$ refers to the value range of variable inputs.

What Formula (7) describes is a multivariable nonlinear coupling optimization problem, which can be solved by the genetic algorithm with global optimum capability.

Suppose the optimal solution obtained is $\hat{X}_{var}$, then around $\hat{X}_{var}$ the total differential formula exists as follows

$$dy_\eta = \frac{\partial f_\eta}{\partial x_1} dx_1 + \frac{\partial f_\eta}{\partial x_2} dx_2 + \cdots + \frac{\partial f_\eta}{\partial x_r} dx_r,$$

$$dy_{NO_x} = \frac{\partial f_{NO_x}}{\partial x_1} dx_1 + \frac{\partial f_{NO_x}}{\partial x_2} dx_2 + \cdots + \frac{\partial f_{NO_x}}{\partial x_r} dx_r.$$ (8)

Now take the first function of (8) as an example to explain the meaning of the total differential formulas.

When the transfer coefficient $\dfrac{\partial f_\eta}{\partial x_j}, j = 1,2,\ldots r$ is known, we can see to what extent the small changes in the variable parameters influence the combustion efficiency. For example, the small change of x_1 brings the influence $\dfrac{\partial f_\eta}{\partial x_1}\Delta x_1$ on the efficiency, i.e. the transfer coefficient of the variable parameters is its corresponding weight. Meanwhile, the transfer coefficient can reflect which variable parameters or variable parameter combinations should be adjusted to achieve the small change in efficiency with minimal cost.

The transfer coefficient could be obtained in the way below:

For example, to calculate the transfer coefficient $\dfrac{\partial f_\eta}{\partial x_1}$ of x_1, we only need to let x_1 make small perturbation, the perturbation size is Δx_1, and the other parameters stay the same. For $f_\eta(\cdot)$ is a determined functional relation already, then

$$\Delta y_\eta = f_\eta\left(\widehat{X}_{var} + \delta, X_{com}\right) - f_\eta\left(\widehat{X}_{var}, X_{com}\right) = \frac{\partial f_\eta}{\partial x_1}\Delta x . \tag{9}$$

Hereinto, $_r\delta = \left[\Delta x_1, \underbrace{0, \cdots, 0}_{r-1}\right]$, thus

$$\frac{\partial f_\eta}{\partial x_1} = \frac{f_\eta\left(\widehat{X}_{var} + \delta, X_{com}\right) - f_\eta\left(\widehat{X}_{var}, X_{com}\right)}{\Delta x_1} . \tag{10}$$

Suppose the coupling relation of variable parameters is negligible, the variance of y_η can be represented as

$$\sigma_{y_\eta}^2 = (\frac{\partial f_\eta}{\partial x_1})^2\sigma_{x_1}^2 + (\frac{\partial f_\eta}{\partial x_2})^2\sigma_{x_2}^2 + \cdots + (\frac{\partial f_\eta}{\partial x_r})^2\sigma_{x_r}^2 . \tag{11}$$

Here $\sigma_{x_i}^2$ refers to the variance of x_i.

Formula (12) means if the variance of variable parameters is known, through the transfer coefficient of variable parameters we can know to what extent the variable parameters influence the combustion efficiency stability, which therefore can provide referential information for adjusting combustion efficiency.

4   Simulation Experiments

4.1   RANSAC-BP

In order to test the validity of the RANSAC-BP algorithm, this section designs a simulation experiment.

Table 1. Training data

Index of sampling point	x	y without noises	y added with noises
1	1	0.333333	0.333333
2	1.05	0.350855	0.635683
3	1.1	0.370178	0.370178
4	1.15	0.391454	0.391454
5	1.2	0.414855	3.081775
6	1.25	0.440571	0.588775
7	1.3	0.468819	0.468819
8	1.35	0.499838	0.499838
9	1.4	0.533898	0.294777
10	1.45	0.571298	0.571298
11	1.5	0.612372	0.612372
12	1.55	0.657496	0.657496
13	1.6	0.707084	-1.37379
14	1.65	0.761601	0.761601
15	1.7	0.821565	1.557592
16	1.75	0.887555	0.887555
17	1.8	0.960217	0.960217
18	1.85	1.040271	1.040271
19	1.9	1.128523	-2.21193
20	1.95	1.225875	1.225875
21	2	1.333333	1.333333
22	2.05	1.452025	1.452025
23	2.1	1.583213	3.369024
24	2.15	1.728309	1.728309
25	2.2	1.888899	1.888899
26	2.25	2.066757	6.125662
27	2.3	2.263877	2.263877
28	2.35	2.482494	0.753055
29	2.4	2.725121	4.870112
30	2.45	2.994578	6.129582
31	2.5	3.294039	3.294039
32	2.55	3.627072	-0.35725
33	2.6	3.997693	3.997693
34	2.65	4.410424	0.808013
35	2.7	4.870358	4.870358
36	2.75	5.383239	5.383239
37	2.8	5.955541	7.38341
38	2.85	6.594572	6.594572
39	2.9	7.308579	7.308579
40	2.95	8.106879	8.106879
41	3	9	9

Take the simple neutral network with single input and single output as example, then the functional relation to be trained is a simple function $y = x^x/3$. To takes samples at a interval of 0.05 between 1-3, then 41 input points can be obtained, as demonstrated in Table 1 (Lines 2 and 6). If there is no noise, according to the function $y = x^x/3$, the ideal outputs are showed in Lines 3 and 7. Now we randomly select 15 ideal output data from Line 3 and 7, add Gaussian noise with standard deviation 2.5, the stained data is shown in Lines 4 and 8.

If there are noises, we use the original BP algorithm to train the neutral network, i.e. using the data x (Lines 2 and 6 in Table 1) and y added with noises (Lines 4 and 8 in Table 1) to training the network, then we get the results shown in Figure 2.

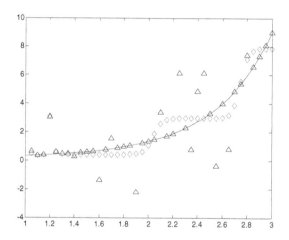

Fig. 2. Neutral network trained by BP

In Figure 2, the blue curve represents function $y = x^x/3$, the black triangles refer to locations of the data with noises, and the red diamonds indicate the expected outputs of the neutral network. Obviously, when noises exist, there is big deviation between the expected outputs and the actual data, which illustrates that the noise has great influence on the result of the neutral network training. Thus, it is necessary to find a way to cull the noisy data first and then train the neutral network.

With the same noisy data, we use the RANSAC-BP algorithm to train the neutral network and show the training result in Figure 3. Here the blue curve represents the function $y = x^x/3$, the black triangles (overlapped with red diamond) refer to locations of the data without noise, the red diamonds indicate the expected outputs of the neutral network, and the green "*" mark the locations of the identified noisy data. As the RANSAC-BP algorithm culled the noises first and then trained the network with data without noises, the noise-free data agree well with the expected data of the neutral network.

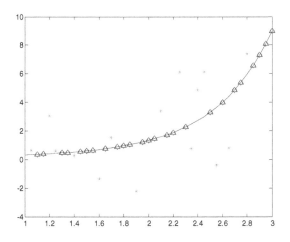

Fig. 3. Neutral network trained by RANSAC-BP

4.2   Sensitivity Analysis of Combustion Model

In this section we sample data from a simulator which simulates a unit in a real power plant. We sample a working condition every 5 minutes. Seven conditions are shown in Table 2.

In Formula (7), let $a = b = 0.5$, though combustion optimization the optimal working conditions are obtained in Table 3 (column 2).

Formulas (10-11) are used to calculate and get the transfer function listed in Lines 3 and 4 in Table 3. We take $\Delta x_i = x_i/100$ to specifically calculate the transfer function.

As the total differential's reference points are taken as the optimal working conditions, thus when we make slight perturbation Δx_i to a certain input parameter x_i , the NOx discharge will increase or the combustion efficiency will decrease. From Table 3 we can see that for the transfer function of the NOx-focused input parameters, the NOx discharge is most sensitive to oxygen content and most insensitive to pulverized coal feeder revolving speed. And for the transfer function of the combustion efficiency focused input parameters, the combustion efficiency is also most sensitive to oxygen content and most insensitive to pulverized coal feeder revolving speed.

Table 2. Steady working conditions

Working condition	1	2	3	4	5	6	7
Oxygen content (%)	4.705	6.395	3.79	5.09	4.99	5.16	4.225
Secondary air speed A (m/s)	30.9	34.8	29.7	30.8	30.7	29.5	30.7
Secondary air speed B (m/s)	29.5	31.9	28.5	29.3	29.7	30.4	28.7
Secondary air speed C (m/s)	32.3	35.9	30.8	32.3	32.8	33.3	31.5
Secondary air speed D (m/s)	30.2	33.3	28.8	30.3	30.6	30	29.5
Secondary air speed E (m/s)	31.2	35.2	30	31.2	32	33.8	30.7
Primary air speed A (m/s)	27.7	28.3	28.8	28.2	28.6	28.6	28.4
Primary air speed B (m/s)	28.6	28.8	29	29.4	29.5	28.6	27.3
Primary air speed C (m/s)	28.2	28.3	28.4	28.8	28.6	28.7	28.7
Primary air speed D (m/s)	28.5	28.5	27.8	28.9	28.6	28.9	28.6
Pulverized coal feeder revolving speed A (rpm)	337	334	330	378	327	341	321
Pulverized coal feeder revolving speed B (rpm)	342	456	342	345	351	359	389
Pulverized coal feeder revolving speed C (rpm)	391	389	397	388	393	396	399
Pulverized coal feeder revolving speed D (rpm)	396	377	395	399	386	401	336
NOx emission (mg/Nm2)	888	960	791	809	797	781	723
Boiler efficiency (%)	92.29	91.56	92.07	91.96	91.07	91.67	92.02

Table 3. Optimal working conditions and transfer function

Working condition	Optimal working condition	NOx	η
Oxygen content (%)	2.36	150.7415	-0.3258
Secondary air speed A (m/s)	29.8	75.29362416	-0.141412599
Secondary air speed B (m/s)	31.9	70.3369906	-0.132095959
Secondary air speed C (m/s)	32.5	69.03846154	-0.129738006
Secondary air speed D (m/s)	28.8	77.90798611	-0.14635083
Secondary air speed E (m/s)	35.1	63.92450142	-0.120130267
Primary air speed A (m/s)	27.4	81.88868613	-0.153895518
Primary air speed B (m/s)	27.2	81.88868613	-0.153891317
Primary air speed C (m/s)	28.8	78.4527972	-0.147257671
Primary air speed D (m/s)	28.2	77.90798611	-0.146413753
Pulverized coal feeder revolving speed A (rpm)	376	5.967420213	-0.011214026
Pulverized coal feeder revolving speed B (rpm)	450	4.899017467	-0.009200473
Pulverized coal feeder revolving speed C (rpm)	494	4.569755601	-0.008587623
Pulverized coal feeder revolving speed D (rpm)	305	7.405115512	-0.01391551
NOx emission (mg/Nm2)	581		
Boiler efficiency (%)	92.21		

5   Conclusion

Inspired by the RANSAC algorithm and combing the BP network training algorithm, the paper proposes the RANSAC-BP neutral network training algorithm. In this algorithm a t-distribution based confidence interval is constructed to replace the distance threshold, which overcomes the weakness that the threshold selection in the neutral network training has to rely on experience. The algorithm culls noisy data during neutral network training and then re-trains the neutral network with noise free data, thus making the neutral network training algorithm less sensitive to data noises. Besides, taking the optimal working conditions as the reference points, the algorithm creates a total differential form for the relation between inputs and outputs of combustion model, forms a function to describe the input and output parameters of the combustion model, and then takes the function's partial differential as the transfer function to portray how the small changes in the input parameters influence the output parameters, which provides a method to analyze the sensitivity of the combustion optimization model.

The paper only studies the transfer function with single input parameter, i.e. the influence of single input parameter on output. For the influence from combination of multi parameters, it needs further study. Besides, to find the optimal working condition is the ultimate objective of the combustion optimization. The traditional practice is to use the genetic algorithm or other optimization algorithms to realize the optimization, but between different components of working condition always exist complicated coupling relations, which are left out of consideration when genetic algorithm is used in sample variance. Thus, how to measure the coupling degree between working condition components and how to apply the coupling relation in generic algorithm sample variance will also be the further research direction.

References

1. Wang, P., Li, L., Chen, Q., et al.: Optimal algorithm research on high efficiency and low emission combustion of coal-fired boiler. Power Engineering 24(4), 4 (2004)
2. Zhou, J., Fan, Z., Si, F., et al.: A review about the development of boiler combustion optimization technology. Boiler Technology 39(5), 5 (2008)
3. Li, Z.: Visual method of flame's development and application. Institute of Engineering Thermophysics, Cas (2006)
4. Hill, S.C., Douglas Smoot, L.: Modeling of nitrogen oxides formation and destruction in combustion systems. Progress in Energy and Combustion Science 26 (2000)
5. Daqi, G., Yi, W.: An optimization method for the topological structures of feed-forward multi-layer neural networks. Pattern Recognition (31), 1337–1342 (1998)
6. Wang, P., Li, L., Chen, Q., et al.: Research on applications of artificial intelligence to combustion optimization in a coal-fired boiler. Proceedings of Chinese Society for Electrical Engineering 24(4), 5 (2004)
7. Schnell, U., Kaess, M., Brodbek, H.: Experimental and numerical investigation of NOx formation and its basic interdependencies on pulverized coal flame characteristics. Combustion Science and Technology (1993)
8. Lwendt, J.O.: Mechanisms governing the formation and destruction of NOx and other Nitrogenous species in Low NOx coal combustion systems. Combustion Science and Technology (1995)
9. Fisher, M.A., Bolles, R.C.: Random sample consensus: a paradigm for model fitting with application to image analysis and automated cartography. Communications of the ACM 24(6), 381–395 (1981)
10. Rivals, I., Personnaz, L.: Construction of confidence intervals for neural networks based on least squares estimation. Neural Networks 13, 463–484 (2000)

Study on Expert Systems Based Fault Diagnosis of Communication Equipment

Chen Bin and Li Juan

College of Electronic Engineering, Naval Univ.of Engineering
Wuhan, China

Abstract. To satisfy requirement of communication equipment maintenance, our study is developed. Focusing on the fault diagnosis technology based on expert systems, rule based knowledge base had been designed. Reasoning machine had also construct with forward and blend inference strategies. Further, rational knowledge base maintenance had been applied. Basing on these approaches, fault of equipment and/or units can be located accurately. Furthermore, speed and accuracy of fault diagnosis for communication equipment can be ensured.

Keywords: Expert System, Fault Diagnosis, Reasoning, Knowledge.

1   Introduction

Many communication equipments have characters of high integration, small volume and large power. The field maintenance of this kind of equipment in real time is very difficult. Because of complex control, mixing of digital signals and analog signals, and misinformation of BITE, it is hard to locate, segregate and eliminate fault. To satisfy requirement of accuracy and rapid fault diagnosis, our study is developed for reliable and uninterrupted communication.

Intelligent fault diagnose with Expert Systems, doesn't depend on mathematical model, but scheme out a set of intelligent computer programs according to practical experiences and huge fault information to resolve problems of fault diagnosis in complex system [1]. When system is gone wrong, realm experts will receive some facts from senses and measures, and then. They'll fast determine causations and positions of fault depending on their deep understanding of system structure and fault histories. Expert Systems method of Fault Diagnosis is especially efficient for complex electronic equipments such as Communication Equipments.

2   Principles of Expert Systems Based Fault Diagnosis

Expert system is commonly compose of knowledge base, reasoning machine, integrated database, explained machine, knowledge access, and man - machine interface, as shown in figure 1. Capacity of expert system comes from its own specialist

M. Zhao and J. Sha (Eds.): ICCIP 2012, Part I, CCIS 288, pp. 490–497, 2012.

knowledge. It provides application mechanism by method of knowledge representing and reasoning. The design of expert systems based fault diagnosis is achieved focusing on knowledge base and reasoning machine.

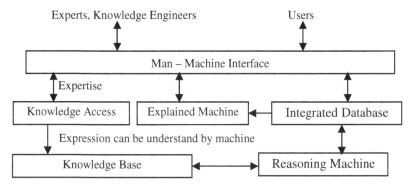

Fig. 1. Architecture of Expert System

2.1 Knowledge Representation

Knowledge representation expresses realm knowledge obtained by using artificial intelligence language, and store in the computer with appropriate manner [2]. Two ways are always applied for knowledge representing which are Predicate Logic and Production Rule. Knowledge representation adopting Production Rule, is convenient for modification, deletion and extension of the knowledge base, thereby functions of knowledge base maintenance and self-study are enhanced. So, Production Rule is selected in our study.

As a process method, Production Rule presents certain working process for the special problem. Expert knowledge with Production Rule is usually presented as the following form.

IF Condition THEN Result

Further, an example is shown to explain knowledge representation with Production Rule.

During normally working of a certain type of communication equipment, SWR is not more than2. But SWR is cannot read from any measurement directly. We should calculate SWR with parameters of load input power and reflection power. When the equipment is running with p0 as normal emission power, we can obtain the following conclusions according measured Value of reflection power, representing by Pr.

$Pr \leq 50W$	excellent working environment
$50W < Pr \leq 111W$	normal working environment
$111W < Pr \leq 250W$	early warning environment
$Pr > 250W$	malfunction environment

This knowledge can be express as follows.

$def(P,Ps):IF\{(Pr \in P) \wedge (Pr \leq 50W)\}$

THEN   "the equipment is running well."

def(P,Ps):IF{(Pr∈P)∧(50W<Pr≤111W)}
  THEN   "the equipment is running normally."
def(P,Ps):IF{(Pr∈P)∧(111W<Pr≤250W)}
              Beep
  THEN   "the equipment has excessive SWR"
def(P,Ps):IF{(Pr∈P)∧(Pr>250W)}
              Beep, Beep
  THEN   "the equipment cannot run because of excessive SWR."

In these rules, def is used to indicate fault code. P presents the measured value of reflected power while Ps is the standard value of reflected power. Beep is shown as alarm signal.

From the above expression we can see, each item of production rules includes two parts, which the first term represents the condition and the latter is conclusion. During the fault detection and diagnosis, starting from the initial facts, pattern matching techniques is used to find the right production. If the match is successful, this production is active to export new facts. And so on, until the fault results are come.

2.2   Expert Reasoning

Reasoning is a kind thought process to come to a judgment from given condition basing on a certain strategy. With relative knowledge selecting from knowledge base the expert, reasoning drew the inferences from symptoms provide by user, until find the fault.

Rule-Based Reasoning (RBR) is used as a way of expert reasoning in our study. With RBR, when a rule is executed, it equals to reasoning done once, and knowledge gained will be closer to the final goal.

In RBR approach, there are three commonly used strategies [3]: forward reasoning, backward reasoning and mixed reasoning. Forward reasoning, the main strategy in our study, has the advantage of intuitive, allowing users to take the initiative to provide useful factual information. It is propitious to solve the problems of design, prediction, monitoring, diagnosis, and so on. But when the facts are not fully known, it is possible that none of knowledge in point is picked, which make the reasoning cannot be gone on. In this case, mixed reasoning is in effect program.

By the use of forward reasoning, first matching of facts and knowledge will be done. Then when the known conditions can not fully match the knowledge, backward reasoning is processed on the assumption of the collusion might derive by the foreword conditions. Asking the user relative new evidence is allowed to make the reasoning proceed. And at last, we can obtain the result of failure diagnosis.

2.3   Machine Learning

Knowledge access, also known as machine learning, is a major area of artificial intelligence research [4]. Usually learning is defined as a knowledge acquisition process for specific objective. Its internal behavior is to acquire knowledge, gain experience and found orderliness. It is a process from ignorance to knowledge, to increase knowledge. The external performance is to improve performance, adapt to the environment, and achieve the system's self-improvement.

Learning is a complex intelligence activities, the highest level of machine learning is summarized. It requires the system to constantly sum up the practical work, summarize the successful experiences and failures, and adjust and modify the knowledge by the using of knowledge base to enrich and improve the system knowledge.

3   Diagnosis Method Analysis

Function of Expert system is to complete diagnosis of abnormalities or failure automatically according to measurement information and knowledge of computerized diagnostics. Thus, a diagnostic problem can be described as a four-tuple form.

$$P= (M, F, K, OBS)$$

In this formula, M is a collection of system observable symptoms, F is a collection of system failure, and K is the mapping between symptoms and failures (i.e. diagnostic knowledge, $K{\subset}M{\times}F$). OBS is symptoms currently observed. For different systems, K, the diagnostic knowledge, depends on structure and behavior of the target system.

For many communication equipments we researched, the relation of components is clear. Roles of subsystems have some of the causal and logical contacts, and we also can measure the behavior of subsystems. So the diagnostic knowledge can be described by using knowledge of the system structure and function. The more common diagnosis methods are based causal network model [5] and system structure and function model [6].

Fault Diagnosis of Communication Equipment always involves two levels, of diagnostic equipment (machine) diagnoses and module (board) diagnoses. Faulty module can be found by Machine fault diagnosis. We can replace the fault module at once to make the equipment get right. Furthermore, special component will be located by the other level diagnosis, board diagnoses. Thus, replacing the fault component can restore the fault module. Thereby, process of fault diagnosis is finished. According to two different levels of diagnosis, diagnostic methods based on causal network model and system structure and function model can be used respectively.

3.1   Diagnostic Methods of Causal Network Model

If system monitored can be disassembled, generally causal relations among measurements are existent. Then, the diagnosis knowledge can be presented with fault propagation model. Fault propagation model is a causal network diagram. For a complete fault propagation model, fault diagnosis can be completed by searching the path of fault propagation.

The degenerative causal network, tree structure is always applied to represent causal knowledge. For fault diagnosis of communication equipment, fault tree is used to describe causal relationship between fault and measurements directly. Knowledge is generally derived from the system analysis, which makes it low cost and rapid prototyping. Figure 2 is a fault tree for the actuator output malfunction.

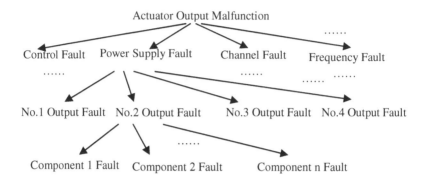

Fig. 2. Example of Fault Tree

3.2   Diagnostic Methods of System Structure and Function Model

System fault propagation model abstracts from the system behavior model, which obviously depends on structure and component characteristics of the system. So the system structure and function model provide a more general description for system fault propagation. As the behavior of the circuit components is simple, full description of system behavior can be obtained easily through the system structure. Using diagnostic methods of system structure and function model problem for diagnosing can be described as the following.

$$P= (SD, \ COMPONENTS, \ ORS)$$

SD is defined as the system structure; COMPONTS is used as a set of system components, and ORS is performance values of system behaviors.

Characters of system abnormity can be calculated forward, while the key of diagnosis is to calculate the cause of the malfunction backward. Procedure of Fault Diagnosis contains two steps: conflicts set generation and candidate verification. A set of conflicts is corresponding to measurements one time or a type of symptom. It means that at least there has one element in the conflicts set wrong which lead to abnormal measurements or the certain symptom. a candidate set Means that current system performance can be explained with anomalies of all elements in the set.

4   Design of Expert System

Expert system based fault diagnosis project is designed for both the equipment fault diagnosis and panel fault diagnosis. The knowledge stored in the database is used to the fault location after implementation of a series of necessary operations following the phenomenon of fault.

4.1   Design of Knowledge Base

Knowledge Base of Expert Systems based Fault Diagnosis of Communication is designed according to function dividing. For each module, it is needed to gather the following information from the experts: (1) fault phenomena due to one or more fault modes of the module; (2) For each fault mode, input from other modules; (3) For each failure mode, all possible solutions.

After getting domain knowledge, it is need to store in appropriate form. Database, such as SQL Server 2005 database we used, is the form to present the knowledge base of Expert System, and it is also the object of maintenance part operating. Relevant data table in expert system knowledge contains: modules table, units (panels) table, components table, nodes table, nodes relationship table, fault tables, rules tables, and so on.

4.2   Design of Reasoning Machine

Reasoning machine is a set of programs to control the running of the system. Applying knowledge in Diagnosis knowledge base, reasoning and Diagnosing is progressed by some problem-solving strategies according to facts of fault phenomena, and ultimately Diagnosis result is given.

During Fault Diagnosis of Communication Equipment, first selecting the module which is suspected fault, reasoning machine will transfer rules/facts datum included in this function module to the dynamic database. Further selecting unit which is suspected fault, it will give all possible problems, and provide a reference diagnostic process.

Reasoning machine makes inference according to the actual situation of the fault. It should examine whether the input is right first. If the input is wrong, reasoning machine will guide user to correct. Otherwise, then the inference engine for reasoning based on these symptoms. Inference engine first to check the unit's input is correct, if not correct, the inference engine to guide the user to correct input; reasoning machine will list all possible fault modes and the corresponding solutions. Dynamic database (DDB) records the user's input, intermediate results of reasoning machine and the final diagnosis result. Detail process of reasoning is shown as follow.

(1) After observed information and/or measured values are received, reasoning machine certificates fault phenomena by function faultfind() according rules.
(2) Reasoning machine outputs possible fault queue by function possiblelefault(), and corresponding solution queue by function possiblesolution().
(3) Reasoning machine gets element from possible fault queue to make an assumption in turn. If the queue is empty, there has no result for Fault Diagnosis. Function check() is called to validate assumption. If the assumption is accepted, the assumption and datum of verification is stored in DDB and the relative solution is called. Then（ⅰ）further reasoning is gone on starting from (1) while the leaf (end of reasoning) is not reached, or（ⅱ）reasoning is end when it is the leaf. If the assumption is rejected, more effort will be done by repeat this step.

4.3   Maintenance of Knowledge Base

Knowledge Base is used to store the expertise of experts, which contains many "facts" and "rules" [7]. "Facts" will be continuously changed during system running, while the "rules" can be used to generate new facts and obtain assumption basing on the facts. According to the actual needs, Maintenance of Knowledge base is to complete the management of knowledge base with querying, adding, deleting, and modifying of knowledge base. Performances of expert system are closely related to scale and quality of Knowledge Base. So, Knowledge base must be maintained in order to make the knowledge to continuously improve.

5   Realization of Fault Diagnosis

Fault diagnosis of communication equipment is implemented through continuous human-computer interaction. The following steps are processed for fault diagnosis.

The first step, according to system requirements, the operator input observed parameters such as the RF output, reflected power and other values. Then the system begins the diagnostic process. Whether there is a fault phenomenon is determined with the parameters table. If failure is existed, matching with the content of rules table is done. All of the possible failure module will be listed to prompt the user for selection.

The second step, the operator chooses fault assumption empirically or randomly. Following user choice, the system then prompts the user to measure the values of relative nodes according to the fault table and node table. If the measured value is normal, foregoing assumption is refused, and this measured module is deleted from possible modules set. The next assumption is suggested to make and then this step is repeated. Otherwise, we should analysis and judge in development. We should know whether and which of other modules can influence the measurement values following node relationship table. So, we need to measure parameters of the related nodes according to system's cue. If the values are not normal, foregoing assumption is refused, and this measured module is deleted while module where the related nodes locate is added. Then this step is repeated. If the values are normal, foregoing assumption is accepted, and we can conclude that fault is occur in this module. Then according to the rule type, whether it is the terminal rule is determined. If it's the terminal rule, fault diagnosis is successful and over, otherwise goes to the next step.

The third step, after determining the fault module, fault will be located in a certain unit of the module further, with using a similar approach with the second step. If necessary, the next step, unit test is processed.

The fourth step, removing the failed unit and inserting into the system unit testing interface, the system measure related parameters automatically. Using the same reasoning strategies in the second step, it is continued to narrow the scope of possible reasons for failure, until reaching the end. The fault will be located to a component, or all assumptions are rejected.

During diagnostic process, after each step of diagnosis, the system prompts the users all possible failure to provide them hypothesis testing, and record the user behaviors. After all the diagnosis, the system gives the user the reasons for failure, failure solutions, and displays the entire fault diagnosis for users review.

6   Conclusion

Focusing on the practical needs of communication equipment maintenance, our study has designed and realized real-time fault diagnosis system with taking expert system-based fault diagnosis technology as the core. After researching of expert system fault diagnosis theory, design of rule-based knowledge for the communication equipment is completed, reasoning machine with forward add mixed reasoning strategy is constructed as well. Knowledge base maintenance is realized to make machine learning feasible and effective. Thus, fault location for the machine or the unit can be processed accurately.

The relative testing and application experiments of fault diagnosis system discussed in this paper has completed. The results indicate that the desired performance requirements are achieved and speed and accuracy of fault diagnosis for communication equipment can be ensured.

References

1. Wang, X.: Study on Intelligent Fault Diagnosis Based on Neural Network and Expert System. Southeast University, Nanjing (2005)
2. Robert, B., Susan, S.: Collection, Storage and application of human knowledge in expert system development. Expert Systems 11, 346–355 (2007)
3. Palade, V.: Cosmin Danut Bocaniala: Computational Intelligence in Fault Diagnosis. Springer, Berlin (2005)
4. Ricardo, B.V., Orallo, H.: Knowledge acquisition through machine learning: Minimising expert's effort. In: Proceedings-ICMLA 2005, Fourth International Conference on Machine Learnng and Applications, Los Angeles US, pp. 49–54 (2005)
5. Wei, Z.: The Multiple Fault Diagnosis Technique of an Avionic System based on Causal Network, Northwestern Polytechnical University, Xi'an (2007)
6. Liming, Z., Dantong, O.: Diagnostic Methods Based on Model of Fault Behavior. Computer Integrated Manufacturing Systems 9, 183–187 (2008)
7. Huang, W., Yang, J.: Maintenance of Knowledge Base in Expert System. Computer Era 1, 42–43 (2005)

On Traffic Pricing Model Based on Incentive Stackelberg Strategies for Communication Networks

Dan Wang and Zhen Li

Key Laboratory of Manufacturing Industrial Integrated Automation, Shenyang University,
110044 Shenyang, China
wangdan0307@126.com, lizhen414@yeah.net

Abstract. This paper deal with a kind of traffic pricing control problems of communication networks. The incentive Stackelberg strategy concept in the game theory was introduced to the network traffic model that comprises subsidiary systems of users and network. A linear incentive strategy, a nonlinear incentive strategy and a self-reported traffic modle with linear incentive strategy were proposed to the traffic problem. Some numerical examples and simulations were given to illustrate the proposed method.

Keywords: Rate control, Incentive Stackelberg strategy, Game theory.

1   Introduction

We focus on the system model of charging, routing and flow control, where the system comprises both users with utility functions and a network with capacity constraints. Kelly [1] showed that the optimization of the system may be decomposed into subsidiary optimization problems, one for each user and one for the network , by using price per unit flow as a Lagrange multiplier that mediates between the subsidiary problems . Low and Varaiya [2] and Murphy et al [3] described how such results may be used as the basis for distributed pricing algorithms, and MacKie-Mason and Varian [4] described a "smart market" based on a per-packet charge when the network is congested. As mentioned in Kelly's work [1], price per unit flow is the mediating variable. The system optimum can be achieved when users' choice of charges and the network's choice of allocated rates are in equilibrium.

By using the incentive Stackelberg strategy concept, we try to find a new way to deal with such a kind of routing control problems. In a game theoretic model [5], [6], there are at least two players who control their own inputs to make the state of the system to reach their own outcomes from the system, respectively. Therefore, the game theory [7] provides a systematic framework to treat the dynamic behavior of noncooperative networks. Two major concepts in game theory, Nash and Stackelberg equilibria, have been applied to the study of noncooperative networks[8]-[15]. In these references, the game theoretic models are all based on the classical noncooperate strategy concepts .

M. Zhao and J. Sha (Eds.): ICCIP 2012, Part I, CCIS 288, pp. 498–505, 2012.

In this paper, we consider the traffic rate control problem by means of the incentive Stackelberg strategy, which was introduced into the game theory by Ho et al [12]. The incentive strategy proposed here consists of two parts, one of them being the regular price, and the other being punishment price which varies on the variance of traffic rate linearly or functionally.

2   System Model

Consier a network with a set J of resources, and let C_j be the finite capacity of resource j, for $j \in J$. A set S of users use the network with rates $p = (p_1, p_2, ..., p_S)$. For each user s, the utility maximization is as follows.

$$\max \ U_s(p_s) - \lambda_s p_s, \qquad p_s \geq 0, \tag{1}$$

where $U_s(p_s)$ is the utility function of user s, and it is an increasing, strictly concave and continuously differentiable function of p_s over the range $p_s \geq 0$. λ_s is a price charged to user s per unit flow.

If the network receives a revenue λ_s per unit flow from user s, then the revenue optimization problem for the network is as follows.

$$\max \ \sum_{s=1}^{S} \lambda_s p_s ,$$

subject to $\qquad\qquad Hy = p, Ay \leq C, \quad p, y \geq 0, \tag{2}$

where H and A are the $0-1$ matrixes, y is the flow pattern.

From Kelly's work [1], there exists a price vector $\lambda = (\lambda_1, \lambda_2, ..., \lambda_s)$ such that the vector $p = (p_1, p_2, ..., p_S)$, formed from the unique solution p_s to (1) for each $s \in S$, solves (2).

The problem (2) is just opposite to the problem (1), because there are the same parts $\lambda_s p_s$ in their formulations with the opposite symbols. Therefore, they are non-cooperate in general.

Here, we introduce the Stackelberg strategy in game theory to the model [13]-[15]. The network should be the leader in the game, and the users should be the followers who act at the Nash equilibrium among them. Note that both of the users and network are allowed to freely vary the flow p_s, $s = 1, 2, ..., S$. So if the leader wants users to be at the rates which are arranged by the network, the leader must have the leadership in the game which is indicated in the following Stackelberg strategy:

$$\xi_s(p_s) = \lambda_s + q_s(p_s) - q_s(p_s^a), \tag{3}$$

where $\xi_s(p_s)$ is incentive strategy function, $q_s(p_s)$ is any function of p_s to be determined, p_s^a is a desired point arranged by the network.

3 Incentive Strategy

3.1 Linear Incentive Strategy

In this section, we restructure Stackelberg strategy as follows:

$$\xi_s(p_s) = \lambda_s + q_s(p_s) - q_s(p_s^a),$$ (4)

Take $q_s(p_s)$ as a linear function

$$q_s(p_s) = kp_s,$$ (5)

where q_s is some kind of punishment price. It will be determined by the leader.

Take the linear function (4) as the Stackelberg incentive strategy to force users to act at the point p_s^a. According to Basar's work [5] the Stackelberg incentive strategy should subject to as follows:

$$\xi_s(p_s^a) = \lambda_s,$$ (6)

and

$$\arg\max \ [U_s(p_s) - \lambda_s p_s - q_s(p_s)p_s] = p_s^a.$$ (7)

When $p_s \geq \hat{p}_s$, let $q_s(p_s) = kp_s$, and replacing λ_s in (1) by ξ_α with linear structure , the problem (1) becomes:

$$\max \ U_s(p_s) - \lambda_s p_s - k(p_s - p_s^a)p_s$$ (8)
$$\text{over} \ p_s \geq 0.$$

To get k, calculate the derivative of (8) with respect to p_s, and let it be zero. Then let p_s take the value at p_s^a, we can get

$$k = \frac{U_s'(p_s^a) - \lambda}{p_s^a - \hat{p}_s}.$$ (9)

Therefore, the strategy (4) should be

$$\xi(p_s) = \lambda + \frac{U_s'(p_s^a) - \lambda}{p_s^a - \hat{p}_s}(p_s - p_s^a).$$ (10)

It is obvious that (6) is held from the structure of (10), and (7) means that the following inequality should hold

$$U_s(p_s^a) - \lambda_s p_s^a \geq U_s(p_s) - \lambda_s p_s - k(p_s - p_s^a)p_s$$ (11)

Now, denote by p_s^u the optimal rate of user s which maximizes the problem (1). Then, we can get

$$U_s'(p_s^u) - \lambda_s = 0,$$ (12)

and

$$U_s'(p_s^u) - \lambda_s > 0 \quad \text{if} \quad p_s < p_s^u, \tag{13}$$

$$U_s'(p_s^u) - \lambda_s < 0 \quad \text{if} \quad p_s > p_s^u. \tag{14}$$

If the optimal rates of users coincide with the arranged rates of the network, i.e. $p_s^u = p_s^a$, then preferred rate of user s is just p_s^a. Therefore,

$$U_s(p_s^a) - \lambda_s p_s^a = U_s(p_s^u) - \lambda_s p_s^u > U_s(p_s) - \lambda_s p_s. \tag{15}$$

So (7) is satisfied in the case of $p_s^u = p_s^a$.

If $p_s^u \neq p_s^a$, we have two cases to discuss.

(i) $p_s^u > p_s^a$: Denote by $W_s(p_s)$ the entire utility function of user s in (8). Substituting (9) into $W_s(p_s)$, we get

$$W_s(p_s) = U_s(p_s) - \lambda_s p_s - \frac{U_s'(p_s^a) - \lambda_s}{p_s^a}(p_s - p_s^a)p_s. \tag{16}$$

Calculating the first and second derivatives of (16) with respect to p_s, we can get

$$W_s'(p_s) = U_s'(p_s) - U_s'(p_s^a), \tag{17}$$

$$W_s''(p_s) = U_s''(p_s). \tag{18}$$

Then let p_s take the value at p_s^a in (17), we can get

$$W_s'(p_s^a) = U_s'(p_s^a) - U_s'(p_s^a) = 0.$$

Because $U_s(p_s)$ is the increasing, strictly concave and continuously differentiable function, it is obvious that (18) is held. So we can come to the conclusion that $W_s(p_s^a) > W_s(p_s)$. That is, (7) holds.

(ii) $p_s^u < p_s^a$: It is evident that $p_s^u = C$, At most, $p_s^a = C$. So there cannot be $p_s^u < p_s^a$.

3.2   Non-linear Incentive Strategy

In this section, we deal with such a non- linear function as

$$q_s(p_s) = \begin{cases} kp_s & \text{if } p_s < p_s^a \\ kp_s^a e^{\phi(p_s - p_s^a)} & \text{if } p_s \geq p_s^a \end{cases}, \tag{19}$$

where $\phi > 0$.

If $p_s < p_s^a$, it is equivalent to linear incentive strategy. Therefore (4) becomes $\xi_s(p_s^a) = \lambda_s$. It is just the first condition (6).

If $p_s \geq p_s^a$, to meet the second condition, substitute (4) into (1) with the structure described in (19). The problem becomes

$$\max \ W_s(p_s), \tag{20}$$

where $p_s \geq 0, W_s(p_s) = U_s(p_s) - \lambda_s p_s - q_s(p_s)p_s$.

We can get $W_s(p_s) = U_s(p_s) - \lambda_s p_s - kp_s^a e^{\mu(p_s - p_s^a)} p_s$, $W_s(p_s^a) = U_s(p_s^a) - \lambda_s p_s^a$.

We have $U_s(p_s) - \lambda_s p_s < U_s(p_s^a) - \lambda_s p_s^a$ for $e^{\mu(p_s - p_s^a)} > 1$, It is shown that $W_s(p_s) < W_s(p_s^a)$, which indicates the satisfaction of the second condition for incentive strategy.

3.3   Self-reported Traffic Modle with Linear Incentive Strategy

Construct a network traffic price model with incentive strategy as follows:

$$B_s = \beta \hat{p}_s + \begin{cases} \alpha(p_s - \hat{p}_s) & \text{if } p_s \geq \hat{p}_s \\ \gamma(p_s - \hat{p}_s) & \text{if } p_s < \hat{p}_s \end{cases}, \tag{21}$$

where B_s is network traffic total price, $\hat{p}_s$ is user self-reported traffic, p_s is user actual used traffic. Assumption that $\alpha > \beta > \gamma > 0$, is traffic unit.

If the user self-reported traffic is larger than the user actual used traffic, i.e. $p_s > \hat{p}_s$, the part of excess $p_s - \hat{p}_s$ will be punished by larger traffic unit α. If the user self-reported traffic is less than the user actual used traffic, i.e. $p_s < \hat{p}_s$, the part of leavings $\hat{p}_s - p_s$ will be deducted by minor traffic unit γ. Thus it can be seen, when the user self-reported traffic is equal to the use actual used traffic, users profit the most.

For most users seek to maximize profits, the self-reported traffic will return as accurately as possible, so that is conducive to the allocation of network resources, thereby effectively realizing the optimization of the whole network performance.

In this section, we restructure Stackelberg strategy as follows:

$$\xi_\alpha(p_s) = \lambda_\alpha + q_s(p_s) - q_s(p_s^a), \tag{22}$$

$$\xi_\gamma(p_s) = \lambda_\gamma + q_s(p_s) - q_s(p_s^a). \tag{23}$$

Take $q_s(p_s)$ as a linear function

$$q_s(p_s) = kp_s, \tag{24}$$

where q_s is some kind of punishment price. It will be determined by the leader.

Take the linear function (22) and (23) as the Stackelberg incentive strategy to force users to act at the point p_s^a. According to Basar's work [9] the Stackelberg incentive strategy should subject to (6) and (7). When $p_s \geq \hat{p}_s$, let $q_s(p_s) = k_\alpha p_s$; when $p_s < \hat{p}_s$, let $q_s(p_s) = k_\gamma p_s$, similarly we can see:

$$k_\gamma = \frac{U_s'(p_s^a) - \lambda_\gamma}{p_s^a - \hat{p}_s},\tag{25}$$

$$\xi_\gamma(p_s) = \lambda_\gamma + \frac{U_s'(p_s^a) - \lambda_\gamma}{p_s^a - \hat{p}_s}(p_s - p_s^a).\tag{26}$$

According to the constraints of (3), i.e. $\alpha > \beta > \gamma > 0$, we can get

$$\xi_\alpha(p_s) = \lambda_\alpha + \frac{U_s'(p_s^a) - \lambda_\alpha}{p_s^a - \hat{p}_s}(p_s - p_s^a) > \beta,\tag{27}$$

$$\xi_\gamma(p_s) = \lambda_\gamma + \frac{U_s'(p_s^a) - \lambda_\gamma}{p_s^a - \hat{p}_s}(p_s - p_s^a) < \beta.\tag{28}$$

When $p_s = \hat{p}_s$, $\xi_\alpha(p_s)$ obtains a minimum, $\xi_\gamma(p_s)$ obtains a maximum.

4   Numerical Examples and Simulations

We take the example from Kelly's work [1]. Take $U_s(p_s) = \mu \log p_s$, and let finite capacity is $C = 14$. If $\mu = 5$ and $\lambda_s = 0.5$, we can get

$$W_s(p_s) = 5\lg p_s - 0.5 p_s - k(p_s - p_s^a)p_s$$

Fig. 1 gives out the result in the contour curves, where $\mu = 5$ and $\lambda_s = 0.5$. The folding curve is the non-linear incentive strategy $\xi_s(p_s)$. According to (19), we have

$$\xi_s(p_s) = \begin{cases} \dfrac{1}{2} + \dfrac{1}{18} p_s & \text{if } p_s < 6 \\ \dfrac{1}{2} + \dfrac{1}{3} e^{\phi(p_s - 6)} & \text{if } p_s \geq 6 \end{cases}$$

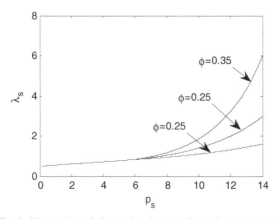

Fig. 1. Illustration of simulation for non-linear incentive strategy

Fig. 2 gives out the curves of subsection linear incentive strategy, where $k_\alpha = 0.05$, $k_\gamma = 0.1$, respectively. When $p_s \geq \hat{p}_s$, we can see that the unit price of the use is linear increasing at rates $k_\alpha = 0.05$. While $p_s < \hat{p}_s$, that is the user use the network capacity fail to come up to the self-reported capacity, the unit price of the unused part $(p_s - \hat{p}_s)$ is $\xi_\gamma(p_s)$, where $\xi_\gamma(p_s)$ is linear decreasing at rates $k_\gamma = 0.1$.

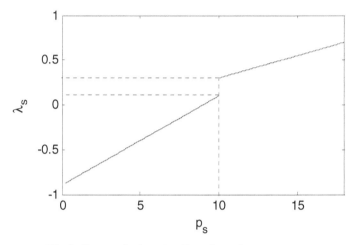

Fig. 2. Curves of subsection linear incentive strategy

From Fig.3, we can see that the expense of the use is linear increasing function in the general strategy, while the expense of the use is concave function in the incentive strategy. It can also be seen in Fig. 3 that the expense of the use is minimal at $p_s = \hat{p}_s$.

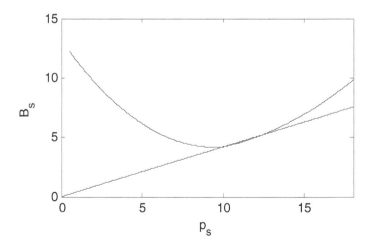

Fig. 3. Price illustration of simulation with incentive strategy

5   Conclusion

In this paper, we discussed the traffic rate control problem by introducing the concepts of game theory. The network models based on traffic are considered and the valid linear and non- linear incentive Stackelberg strategies are proposed. In the user's own reporting network traffic model, the part of excess or leavings will be appropriate punished according to the linear incentive Stackelberg strategy. In the long term, network resource can be saved and uses' demand can be satisfied. It is useful way that the network traffic control problem is dealt with by using the game theory. However, much challenging work is waiting for us to cope with, such as the studies on practicality and technicality.

References

1. Kelly, F.: Charging and rate control for elastic traffic. European Transactions on Telecommunications 8(1), 33–37 (1997)
2. Low, S.H., Varaiya, P.P.: A new approach to service provisioning in ATM networks. IEEE Transactions on Networking 1, 547–553 (1993)
3. Murphy, J., Murphy, L., Posner, E.C.: Distributed pricing for embedded ATM network. In: Labetoulle, J., Roberts, J.W. (eds.) The Fundamental Role of Teletraffic in the Evolution of Telecommunications Networks, pp. 1053–1063. Elsevier, Amsterdam (1994)
4. MacKie-Mason, J.K., Varian, H.R.: Pricing the Internet. In: Keller, J., Kahin, B. (eds.) Public Access to the Internet. Prenticee Hall, Englewood Cliffs (1994)
5. Jing, Y.W., Chen, B., Dimirovski, M., Sohraby, K.: On Leader-Follower Model of Traffic Rate Control for Networks. Control Theory and Applications 18(6), 817–822 (2001)
6. Basar, T., Olsder, G.J.: Dynamic noncooperative game theory, pp. 7–201. SIAM, Philadelphia (1998)
7. Fudenberg, D., Tirole, J.: Game Theory, pp. 17–25. MIT Press, Cambridge (1992)
8. Myerson, R.B.: Game theory: analysis of conflict, pp. 97–101. Harvard University Press, Cambridge (1991)
9. Bertsekas, D., Gallager, R.: Data networks, pp. 86–88. Prentice-Hall, Englewood Cliffs (1992)
10. Economides, A.A., Silvester, J.A.: Priority load sharing: An approach using Stackelberg games. In: Proceedings of the 28th Annual Allerton Conference on Communications, Control, and Computing, Baltimore, MD (1990)
11. Korilis, Y.A., Lazar, A.A., Orda, A.: The role of the manager in a noncooperative network. In: Proceeedings of the IEEE INFOCOM 1996, San Francisco, CA (1996)
12. Orda, A., Rom, R., Shimkin, N.: Competitive routing in multiuser communication networks. IEEE/ACM Transactions on Networking 1(10), 510–521 (1993)
13. Zhang, L., Tian, H., Wang, C.R.: Stackelberg-based dynamic incentive pricing algorithm in heterogeneous ubiquitous network. Science in China Series F: Information Sciences 52(12), 2445–2449 (2009)
14. Ho, Y.C., Luh, P.B., Olsder, G.J.: A control-theoretic view on incentive. Automatica 18(2), 167–179 (1982)

Identification of Early Moldy Rice
Samples by PCA and PNN

Lili Wu, Chao Yuan, Aiying Lin, and Baozhou Zheng

College of Sciences, Henan Agricultural University,
95 Wenhua Road, Zhengzhou, 450002, P.R. China

Abstract. A method of identifying early moldy rice by principal component analysis (PCA) and probabilistic neural network (PNN) was presented in this paper. In the experiment, eight gas sensors were chosen to compose the electronic nose's array, which was used to gather early different level mildew data of rice samples. These gathered data were reduced dimensions by PCA and then were passed through PNN to identify their categories. The rate of identification was 91.67%. Compared with the method of PNN only used, the identification method of PCA and PNN has higher recognition accuracy and less classification time. Thus the experimental results of this paper showed that the method of PCA and PNN in classifying early different degrees moldy rice was effective.

Keywords: Principal component analysis, Probabilistic neural networks, Electronic nose, Early rice mildew.

1   Introduction

Food security is an important issue that has attracted worldwide attention, cereal grains are the world's largest reserves of food. Fungal growth on cereal grains not only decreases their nutritional value but also constitutes health hazards, probably, because of the production of toxic metabolites [1]. Grain mildew occurred when the microbes decomposed organics in cereal grains, and early mildew was the stage when microbes began to make metabolic activities in a favorable environment. At this stage food grains might show minor changes in color, odor, humidity and temperature, meanwhile the value of fatty acid and acidity, the total amount of mold and fungi would all increase. If diagnosis and treatment made in time, it could prevent the metabolic activities of grains to reach the mildew stage.

Mildew may occur in some parts of the grains, and the odor is the most likely to feel. Many research results show that bacteria and fungi are likely to be volatile, and much of them can be smelled. The main components of the odor are the hydroxyl, aldehyde and sulfide compounds, etc. Thus the early moldy grains can be detected by an electronic nose. The electronic nose dose not give any specific information about the compounds of the odor nor about their identity. However, with the aid of appropriate mathematical techniques [2-4], like artificial neural networks (ANN) or statistical methods, the electronic nose could recognize the odor pattern from a particular sample and help in distinguishing it from other samples.

M. Zhao and J. Sha (Eds.): ICCIP 2012, Part I, CCIS 288, pp. 506–514, 2012.

From the perspective of pattern recognition, a method of identifying early moldy grains by principal component analysis (PCA) and probabilistic neural network (PNN) was proposed in this paper. The rice samples and their different levels of early mildew data were collected by the electronic nose system, and these gathered data could be classified by the method. So we can eliminate subjective effects and get high accuracy to identify early different degrees of mildew rice samples.

2   Experimental

2.1   Rice Samples

The aim of this study was to detect early different degrees of mildew rice samples, and the rice samples were Yuanyang Rice (Growth in Yuanyang, Henan Province, China). The 250g rice samples were divided into 5 groups (50g for each group), which were placed into 5 biochemical incubators with different storage conditions. The normal rice samples stored at 10°C and RH 15-20%, and the samples that would take place early mildew stored at temperature 25°C and RH50-55% for 6,10,13,15 days. At this time, these 5 group samples had no significant difference in appearance, and a little diversity in odor.

2.2   The Electronic Nose System

The general scheme of the electronic nose system used in this work was presented in Fig. 1. The system was composed of a gas injection device, a gas sensor array, a data acquisition device and a computer analysis software. We had chosen the sensory array that composed of eight TGS tin oxide-based gas sensors,   which were arranged in an optimized test chamber[5-7]. The eight sensors were TGS813, TGS821, TGS822, TGS825 , TGS826 , TGS842 , TGS2201 and TGS2610, which had different responses to sulfide, hydrocarbons, nitrogen compounds, ethanol, etc. In the experiment nitrogen was used as a carrier gas, which delivered an atmosphere from the 'head-space' of the rice samples to sensors.

2.3   The Electronic Nose Data Preprocessing

In order to eliminate external interference and produce the consistent data for the pattern recognition process, the collected original data were smoothed and filtered, then normalized by the following equation:

$$X_j^* = (X_j - X_j^{\min j})\big/(X_j^{\max j} - X_j^{\min j}) \tag{1}$$

Where, X_j is the transient response value of the sensor j at a given instant, $X_j^{\max j}$ and $X_j^{\min j}$ are the maximum and minimum sensor response values in a complete cycle, and X_j^* is the normalized response value of the sensor j. The transient output value of each sensor is between 0 and 1 by normalizing, thus all measured values are in the same order of magnitude, which provides the appropriate training data for neural network. Fig. 2 shows the response curves of eight sensors to normal rice samples. These curves are composed of the discrete sampling data that transformed by A/D converter and then normalized.

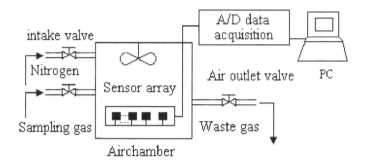

Fig. 1. Diagram of electronic nose system

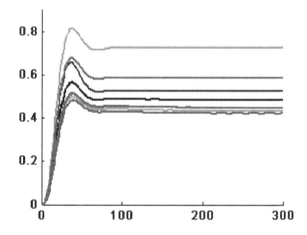

Fig. 2. Response curves of sensor array to normal rice samples

3   Results and Discussion

3.1   Overview

The method of classifying early moldy rice samples with different degrees consists of two main parts: PCA and PNN. In the experiment there have 5 categories need to be distinguished, which are normal rice samples, 6 days, 10 days, 13 days and 15 days moldy rice samples. The data of each category that collected by the sensor array is 8 dimension, and we can get the resulting data of each class is 8×200 dimension by keeping the first 200 sampling points. So the PCA algorithm will be used to reduce the dimension firstly before classification.

3.2   Data Processed by Principal Component Analysis

3.2.1   The Principle of PCA

PCA is a popular modeling technique used to extract information from process data by relating its variables [8]. It is widely used in many applications, such as data compression and regression, image processing, pattern recognition and time series prediction. PCA is based on the assumption that most information about classes is contained in the directions along which the variations are the largest. The most common derivation of PCA is in terms of a standardized linear projection, which maximizes the variance in the projected space [9]. It transforms the process variables by rotating their axes of representation to capture the variation of the original variables in a lower dimension space. The new axes of rotation are represented by the projection directions or principal component loadings. This transformation can equivalently be obtained by minimizing the sum of square errors in all estimated variables [8].

Assume that there is a n-dimensional random vector $\mathbf{x} = (x_1, x_2, \cdots, x_n)^T$, vector $\mathbf{y}$ can be obtained by the orthogonal transformation of orthonormal matrix $\mathbf{A}$, that is

$$\mathbf{y} = \mathbf{A}^T \mathbf{x} \tag{2}$$

The correlation matrix of $\mathbf{y}$ is given by

$$\mathbf{R}_y = E(\mathbf{y}\mathbf{y}^T) = E(\mathbf{A}^T \mathbf{x}\mathbf{x}\mathbf{A}^T) = \mathbf{A}^T \mathbf{R}_x \mathbf{A} \tag{3}$$

Where $\mathbf{R}_x$ is the correlation matrix of $\mathbf{x}$, and it is symmetric. Matrix $\mathbf{A}$ is selected by the equation (4):

$$\mathbf{R}_x \mathbf{a}_i = \lambda_i \mathbf{a}_i \tag{4}$$

Here, λ_i is the ith largest eigenvalue of $\mathbf{R}_x$, that is $\lambda_1 \geq \lambda_2 \geq \cdots \geq \lambda_n$; and $\mathbf{a}_i$ is the orthogonal, normalized eigenvectors of λ_i; and $\mathbf{R}_y$ is a diagonal matrix, it can be obtained by:

$$\mathbf{R}_y = \mathbf{A}^T \mathbf{R}_x \mathbf{A} = diag(\lambda_1, \lambda_2, \cdots, \lambda_n) \tag{5}$$

If $\mathbf{R}_y$ is a positive definite matrix, its eigenvalues are positive.

Equation (6) can be obtained by equation (2):

$$\mathbf{x} = (\mathbf{A}^T)^{-1}\mathbf{y} = \mathbf{A}\mathbf{y}$$

$$= (\mathbf{a}_1, \mathbf{a}_2, \cdots, \mathbf{a}_n) \begin{bmatrix} y_1 \\ y_2 \\ \vdots \\ y_n \end{bmatrix} = \sum_{i=1}^{n} y_i a_i \tag{6}$$

We choose the m leading items of $\mathbf{a}_i$ to estimate $\mathbf{x}$ according to the minimum mean-square error criteria, and the estimated value $\hat{\mathbf{x}}$ is:

$$\hat{\mathbf{x}} = \sum_{i=1}^{n} y_i a_i \qquad (1 \le m \le n) \tag{7}$$

The mean-square error of the estimated value is:

$$\varepsilon^2(m) = E(\|\mathbf{x} - \hat{\mathbf{x}}\|^2) = E\left(\left\|\sum_{i=m+1}^{n} y_i a_i\right\|^2\right)$$

$$= \sum_{i=m+1}^{n} E(y_i^2) = \sum_{i=m+1}^{n} \mathbf{a}_i^T E(\mathbf{xx}^T)\mathbf{a}_i \tag{8}$$

$$= \sum_{i=m+1}^{n} \lambda_i$$

In order to get the minimum error, the matrix $\mathbf{A}$ must be composed by the eigenvectors corresponding to the m leading eigenvalues[10].

3.2.2   Reducing the Data Dimension by PCA

The data collected by the electronic nose system was 8 dimension, and the first 200 sampling data were chosen, thus the 8×200 dimension data were obtained. Now the five categories were normal rice samples, 6 days, 10 days, 13 days and 15 days moldy rice samples. Then the PCA algorithm was used to reduce the dimension of each category respectively, and the first two contribution rate of principal components was shown in Table 1. Obviously the average contribution rate of the first principal component for each type was above 99.4%, thus the 8 dimension data was compressed to 1 dimension, and the original 8 dimension data was replaced by the first principal component for subsequent classification.

Table 1. The contribution rate of the first two principal components by PCA processing

Moldy rice level	Contribution rate of the first principal component(%)	Contribution rate of the second principal component (%)
Normal	99.676	0.29673
6 days	99.759	0.20761
10 days	99.431	0.47697
13 days	99.992	0.00721
15 days	99.989	0.00985

3.3   Training the Probabilistic Neural Network by the Dimension Reduced Data

3.3.1   Probabilistic Neural Network

Probabilistic neural network (PNN) is proposed by D. F. Specht [11] on the basis of radial basis function (RBF) neural network, and its main idea is based on Bayesian decision theory. Because the Bayesian classifier based on minimum error probability has the best classification performance. PNN uses Parzen window which has Gaussian kernel to estimate the posterior probability of the sample and to achieve Bayesian classifier. It has the merits of simple structure and fast training, so it is commonly used to solve pattern classification [12-14].

PNN has a radial basis network layer and a competitive network layer, as it shown in Fig. 3. It is a two hidden layer structure network. In the Fig. 3, R is the dimension of the input sample vector, Q is the dimension of the input target vector, and K is the category number of input sample. Target vector is passed to the first layer of RBF neurons by the input layer, and the number of the hidden layer neurons is Q.

The distance $\|dist\|$ between the input objective vectors and the input sample vectors is calculated by the layer of radial primary. The nonlinear mapping is achieved by the Gaussian kernel:

$$p_j^k(x) = \exp(-\|x - \omega\|^2 / 2\sigma^2) \tag{9}$$

Where k is the number of categories, $k = 1, 2, \cdots, K$; j is the number of training samples, $j = 1, 2, \cdots R$; ω is the weight vector. Choose the different variance, and the different classifier can be got. For example: if the variance $\sigma = \infty$, then the classifier is linear; if the variance $\sigma = 0$, then the classifier is close to the nearest neighbor classification.

3.3.2   Training the PNN

Back Propagation (BP) network is widely used in pattern recognition algorithm of the electronic nose, but it has low generalization capacity when the number of samples is small. Compared with BP network, the PNN has fast learning speed, good convergence, and flexible designing. Thus PNN is used in this paper to classify the signal collected by the electronic nose. In the process of designing the PNN, the distribution density of the radial basis function *SPREAD* could affect the classification performance greatly, so it is necessary to determine the value of *SPREAD* before

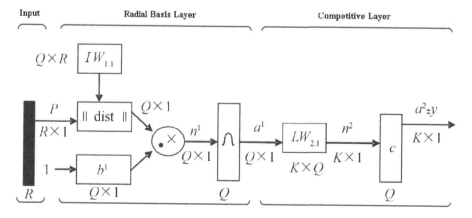

Fig. 3. Structure of PNN

classification. Table 2 showed the different value of *SPREAD* corresponds to its recognition rate when the PNN was used to classify the training sample set (normal rice samples). In the experiment, the training sample set was the data reduced dimension by PCA, among them 50 samples were selected randomly as training samples and 24 samples for test. The recognition rate was the best when the value of *SPREAD* was in the range of 0.003~0.005, so the value of *SPREAD* was chosen 0.004 for the test samples classification.

Table 2. The PNN recognition rate of training samples under the different value of *SPREAD*

Type of samples Spread	1 Recognition rate (%)	2 Recognition rate (%)	3 Recognition rate (%)	4 Recognition rate (%)	5 Recognition rate (%)	Overall Recognition rate (%)
0.001	96.00	96.00	100.00	96.00	100.00	97.60
0.002	96.00	100.00	100.00	96.00	100.00	98.40
0.003	100.00	100.00	100.00	100.00	100.00	100.00
0.004	100.00	100.00	100.00	100.00	100.00	100.00
0.005	100.00	100.00	100.00	100.00	100.00	100.00
0.006	100.00	100.00	100.00	96.00.	100.00	99.20
0.007	96.00	96.00	100.00	96.00	100.00	97.60
0.008	94.00	96.00	100.00	96.00	100.00	97.20
0.009	92.00	96.00	100.00	96.00	96.00	96.00
0.01	92.00	96.00	100.00	94.00	96.00	95.60

3.3.3   Classification of Rice Samples by PCA and PNN

The 5 categories data that processed by PCA were selected 50 samples of each type as the study samples to train the PNN network, and the classification results were shown in Table 3. Table 3 also showed the results of PNN only used, PCA not used.

Table 3. Classification of training samples

Level of moldy rice samples	PNN only (training samples) Correct	 Error	Recognition rate (%)	PCA and PNN (training samples) Correct	 Error	Recognition rate (%)
Normal	49	1	98.00	50	0	100.00
6 days	50	0	100.00	50	0	100.00
10 days	49	1	98.00	50	0	100.00
13 days	48	2	96.00	49	1	98.00
15 days	48	2	96.00	49	1	98.00

Then the 5 categories data were selected 24 test samples of each type as input vectors for the trained PNN network, and the classification results were shown in Table 4. Table 4 also showed the results of PNN only used, PCA not used.

Table 5 showed the influence to the PNN network performance whether the PCA algorithm used or not. From these tables, it was obvious that the identification method of PCA and PNN has higher recognition accuracy and less classification time than the PNN only used. This was because the characteristics of early mildew rice were very similar between the samples, so the data of 5 categories were very close to each other.

When these data were processed by PCA, the confusing data that easily led to fuzzy classification were just abandoned.

Table 4. Classification of test samples

Level of moldy rice samples	PNN only (test samples) Correct	Error	Recognition rate (%)	PCA and PNN (test samples) Correct	Error	Recognition rate (%)
Normal	22	2	91.67	23	1	95.83
6 days	21	3	87.50	22	2	91.67
10 days	22	2	91.67	23	1	95.83
13 days	20	4	83.88	21	3	87.50
15 days	20	4	83.88	21	3	87.50

Table 5. The influence to the PNN network performance whether the PCA algorithm used or not

The PNN network performance	PNN (training samples)	PCA and PNN (training samples)	PNN (test samples)	PCA and PNN (test samples)
Overall recognition rate (%)	97.6	99.2	87.50	91.67
Convergence time (s)	0.5340	0.1888	0.2574	0.0782

4   Conclusion

The data of early different degrees moldy rice samples were collected and pre-treatmented by the electronic nose system in this paper. The data were reduced dimensions by PCA and then identified by PNN network. Because of its weight is the probability distribution of the sample, the PNN has short training time and good classification performance. The PNN recognition rate is 99.2% for 50 training samples, and the accurate identification rate is 91.67% for 24 test samples of the 5 categories. Compared with the method of PNN only used, the identification method of PCA and PNN has higher recognition accuracy and less classification time. Then the next research work is how to optimize the PNN and integrate other information of the sensor array to improve the recognition rate.

Acknowledgments. The authors acknowledge the financial support of the Scientific and technological project of Zhengzhou City (083SGYG24123-2). Meanwhile the authors are grateful to the College of Food Science and Biotechnology in Zhejiang Gongshang University for experiment aid.

References

1. Paolesse, R., Alimelli, A., Martinelli, E., et al.: Detection of fungal contamination of cereal grain samples by an electronic nose. Sensors and Actuators B 119, 425–430 (2006)
2. Balasubramanian, S., Panigrahi, S., Kottapalli, B., et al.: Evaluation of an artificial olfactory system for grain quality discrimination. LWT 40, 1815–1825 (2007)
3. Brudzewski, K., Osowski, S., Wolinska, K., Ulaczyk, J.: Smell similarity on the basis of gas sensor array measurements. Sensors and Actuators B 129, 643–651 (2008)
4. Presicce, D.S., Forleo, A., Taurino, A.M., et al.: Response evaluation of an E-nose towards contaminated wheat by *Fusarium poae* fungi. Sensors and Actuators B 118, 433–438 (2006)
5. Falasconi, M., Gobbi, E., Pardo, M., et al.: Detection of toxigenic strains of Fusarium verticillioides in corn by electronic olfactory system. Sensors and Actuators B 108, 250–257 (2005)
6. Zheng, X.-Z., Lan, Y.-B., Zhu, J.-M., et al.: Rapid identification of rice samples using an electronic nose. Journal of Bionic Engineering 6(3), 290–297 (2009)
7. Peris, M., Escuder-Gilabert, L.: A 21st century technique for food control: Electronic noses. Analytica Chimica Acta 638(1), 1–15 (2009)
8. Goel, P.K., Shen, X.: Bayesian principal component analysis
9. Wang, X., Paliwal, K.K.: Feature extraction and dimensionality reduction algorithms and their applications in vowel recognition. Pattern Recognition. The Journal of The Pattern Recognition Society 36, 2429–2439 (2003)
10. Shlens, J.: A Tutorial on Principal Component Analysis (2005)
11. Specht, D.F.: Probabilistic neural networks for classification mapping or associative memory. In: IEEE International Conference on Neural Networks, vol. 1, pp. 525–532 (1988)
12. Specht, D.F.: Probabilistic neural networks. Int. J. Neural Networks 3, 109–118 (1990)
13. Miguez, R., Georgiopoulos, M., Kaylani, A.: G-PNN: A genetically engineered probabilistic neural network. Nonlinear Analysis: Theory, Methods & Applications 73(6), 1783–1791 (2010)
14. Berthold, M.R., Diamond, J.: Constructive training of probabilistic neural networks. Neurocomputing 19(1-3), 167–183 (1998)

Multi-model Based Channel Estimation for Doubly Selective Wireless Fading Channels

Zhi Kun Song, Rui Zhe Yang, Li Zhang, Peng Bo Si, and Yan Hua Zhang

College of Electronic Information and Control Engineering,
Beijing University of Technology, Beijing 100124, China
songzhikun05@163.com,
{yangruizhe,sipengbo,zhangyh}@bjut.edu.cn, zn8681@vip.sina.com

Abstract. In the wireless communication system, the traditional single model channel estimation method cannot tack the complex variability of the doubly selective channels. To solve this problem, in this paper, a multi-model channel estimation scheme is proposed. Based on basis expansion models (BEMs) of different kernel functions, the multiple models set for the doubly selective channel estimation is established, each of which is combined with the sub-block data tracking adaptive filtering estimator, and the optimal output is obtained by switching to the estimator having the minimum estimated error. The simulation results indicate that the proposed multi-model channel estimation algorithm can effectively track the complex variability of the channels and perform well in NMSE.

Keywords: Doubly selective channels, Multi-model, Kalman, Sub-block tracking.

1 Introduction

In the wireless communication system, due to the multipath propagation of radio waves and the Doppler frequency shift produced by relative movement between sender and receiver, the wireless channels are characterized by frequency-selectivity and time-selectivity [2] [3] [5] [10], making the signal suffer from a more complex fading. Consequently, in order to correctly demodulate the signal at the receiving end, the knowledge of channel state information (CSI) must be acquired, that is, the accurate channel estimation is required.

Recently, the basis expansion models which contain a basic function, time-varying coefficients and Doppler parameters are used to describe the values of time-varying multiple channels. Because BEM effectively describes the feature of the time- and frequency-selective, it has been widely used in doubly selective channel estimation molding. Depending on the different basic functions, widely used models contain the complex exponential BEM (CE-BEM) [2], the polynomial BEM (P-BEM) [5], discrete prolate spheroidal BEM (DPS-BEM) [6] and the discrete Karhuen-Loève BEM (K-L-BEM) [11]. In [6], the author points out that each model is not always optimal in the whole circumstances. The K-L-BEM is optimal in terms of mean square error, but is sensitive to statistical channel mismatches, the CE-BEM is independent of channel statistics, but induces a large modeling error, whereas the

M. Zhao and J. Sha (Eds.): ICCIP 2012, Part I, CCIS 288, pp. 515–525, 2012.
© Springer-Verlag Berlin Heidelberg 2012

P-BEM modeling performance is rather sensitive to the Doppler spread, so it provides a better fit for low, than for high Doppler spreads.

As the above shows that, for the complex wireless communication channel, based on single channel model the channel estimation cannot have robust result with high performance. Therefore, we introduce the multi-model control theory to the channel estimation [1]. In this paper, for the double selective channel, we propose a multi-model channel estimation scheme, which establish different adaptive estimators based on different basis expansion models and have the optimal estimation output through switching between these estimators. The simulation indicates that the proposed multi-model channel estimation algorithm performances well with effectively tracking the channel variety.

2   System Model

2.1   Time- and Frequency-Selective Channel Model

Assume $\tau_{\max}$ and $f_{\max}$ as the maximal delay-spread and Doppler-spread respectively for time- and frequency-selective channel, satisfying $2\tau_{\max}f_{\max} < 1$ [2]. Let $h(t;\tau)$ denote the time-varying impulse response between the transmitted symbol at time $(t-\tau)$ and the received symbol at time t. We will take the sampling period at the receiver equal to the symbol period T_s, and in the digital communication system, replace τ with $l = \lfloor \tau/T_s \rfloor$. From the transmit symbols $u(i)$, $i = \lfloor t/T_s \rfloor$, we choose N symbols to form a data block $\boldsymbol{u}_k$, where k denotes the data block index and n denotes the position of symbols in the block. Considering the wireless channel to be the Rayleigh fading channel varying slowly in one data block, our discrete-time baseband equivalent channel model described by the basis expansion model, is written as:

$$h_k(n;l) = \begin{cases} \sum_{q=0}^{Q} h_{k,q}(l)f_q(n), & l \in [0,L] \\ 0 & \text{others} \end{cases} \tag{1}$$

where $h_{k,q}(l)$ represents the qth coefficient of the lth tap at block time k, $f_q(n)$ is called the basic function or BEM kernel function at time n, $L = \lfloor \tau_{\max}/T_s \rfloor$ is the number of the paths and $Q \geq \lceil 2f_{\max}MNT_s \rceil$ is with different values in different BEM. Thus, in the kth data block, we can replace $h_k(n;l)$ having $N \times (L+1)$ unknown parameters with $h_{k,q}(l)$ having $(Q+1) \times (L+1)$ unknown parameters, which significantly simplifies the channel estimation. As the characteristics of Rayleigh channel, the BEM coefficients $h_{k,q}(l)$ are zero-mean complex Gaussian random variables with variance $\delta_{q,l}^2$.

2.2   Transmitted and Received Signals

In this paper, we use the pilot symbol assisted method (PSAM) in the channel estimation, the system model is shown in Fig. 1.

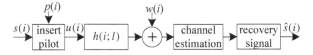

Fig. 1. Equivalent model with baseband discrete-time system

In PSAM, periodic insertion of training symbols during the transmission has been optimized based on several criteria within general class of doubly selective channels.

We describe the transmitted sequence $u(i)$ in the form of $\boldsymbol{u}_k$, each of which consists of two parts. One is the information symbols $s(i)$ and another is the pilot symbols $p(i)$ known by both the transmitter and receiver, in the shape of the classic ZP (zero padding) sequence, $\boldsymbol{p}_g = \left[\boldsymbol{0}_L^T, 1, \boldsymbol{0}_L^T\right]^T$, $g = 0, \cdots, G-1$. We insert G of $\boldsymbol{p}_g$ in each data block, which is depend on the channel environment. When the channel is better, G can be appropriately reduced to improve data transmission efficiency; otherwise, G is require being larger. The data block can be expressed as:

$$\boldsymbol{u}_k = \left[\boldsymbol{s}_0^T, \boldsymbol{p}_0^T, \boldsymbol{s}_1^T, \boldsymbol{p}_1^T, \cdots, \boldsymbol{s}_{G-1}^T, \boldsymbol{p}_{G-1}^T\right]^T \tag{2}$$

where $N = N_s + N_p$, N_s and N_p are the total number of information s_g and the pilot sequence $\boldsymbol{p}_g$, respectively.

Because of the multi-path effects, when the symbols $u(i)$ are transmitted through the channel $h(i;l)$, the received symbol $y(i)$ is:

$$y(i) = \sum_{l=0}^{L} h(i;l)u(i-l) + w(i) \tag{3}$$

where $w(i)$ is additive white Gaussian noise (AWGN) with mean zero and variance δ_w^2. Correspondingly, the received blocks $\boldsymbol{y}_k$ can be expressed as:

$$\boldsymbol{y}_k = \boldsymbol{H}_k \boldsymbol{u}_k + \boldsymbol{w}_k \tag{4}$$

$$\boldsymbol{H}_k = \sum_{q=0}^{Q} \boldsymbol{F}_q \boldsymbol{H}_{k,q} \tag{5}$$

where $\boldsymbol{w}_k \in \mathbb{C}_{N \times 1}$ is AWGN vector with mean zero and variance δ_w^2, and $\boldsymbol{H}_k$ is a lower triangular matrix with $\left[\boldsymbol{H}_k\right]_{n,m} = h_k(n; n-m)$, $\boldsymbol{H}_{k,q}$ is a Toeplitz matrix with first column $\left[h_{k,q}(0), \cdots h_{k,q}(L), 0, \cdots 0\right]^T$ and $\boldsymbol{F}_q = diag\left[f_q(0), f_q(1), \cdots, f_q(N-1)\right]$.

Note that the inner block interference (IBI) in the current block has been eliminated by the ZP training sequence.

3   Multi-model Channel Estimation

The unknown channel state information (CSI) is estimated at receiver relying on the known training sequences in PSAM, the essence of which is similar to the system parameters estimation in the control theory.

In the control theory, when the system parameters of the charged object are time-invariant or changing slowly, the conventional adaptive control method is usually adopted [8] [9]. When the environment is relatively complex or the system parameters are more active transition, the conventional adaptive control fails whereas the multi-model method stands out. In the wireless communications, the channel parameters vary fiercely due to the mobile station velocity and the uncertain environment, therefore, we introduce the theory of multi-model method into the wireless channel estimation, to effectively track the dramatic changes of the parameters.

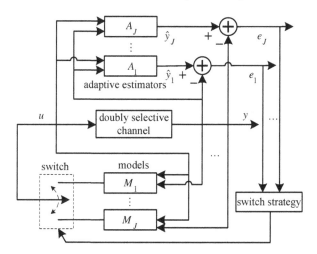

Fig. 2. The diagram of multi-model channel estimator

Based on the theory of multi-model and the estimation methods of doubly selective channel, we establish the multi-model channel estimator, shown in Fig. 2, which includes channel estimation models, adaptive estimators and the switcher [9]. Each adaptive estimator runs using different channel estimation models and the switcher selects the optimal results between the models-estimators according to the designed switch indicator.

We give the model set $\Omega = \left\{ M_j \mid j = 1, 2, \cdots, J \right\}$ and the corresponding adaptive filter estimator set $\Gamma = \left\{ A_j \mid j = 1, 2, \cdots, J \right\}$. For simplification, here, the model set consists of CE-BEM and the P-BEM, and the adaptive filter estimator of each model adopts the sub-block tracking Kalman algorithm [3].

3.1   Multi-model Channel Set

a) CE-BEM

For the CE-BEM, $f_q(n) = e^{j\omega_q n}$, $\omega_q = 2\pi(q - Q/2)/MN$, if M is an integer greater than 1, it is called over-sampling CE-BEM. The simulation followed uses $M = 2$ over-sampling CE-BEM. Thus, the equation (1) can be rewritten as:

$$h_k(n;l) = \begin{cases} \sum_{q=0}^{Q} h_{k,q}(l) e^{j\omega_q n}, & l \in [0, L] \\ 0, & \text{others} \end{cases} \tag{6}$$

where $Q \geq \lceil 2 f_{max} MNT_s \rceil$. In general with $Q \geq 4$, the CE-BEM can track the changes of the channel [7]. In the simulation, if f_{max} satisfies $Q \geq 4$, we take $Q = \lceil 2 f_{max} MNT_s \rceil$, otherwise, take $Q=4$.

b) P-BEM

For the P-BEM, based on the Taylor theory, we use the Taylor expansion at $n = n_0$ with n_0 at the midpoint of the data block [5], $f_q(n) = (n - n_0)^q$. Thus, the equation (1) can be transformed to:

$$h_k(n;l) = \begin{cases} \sum_{q=0}^{Q} h_{k,q}(l)(n - n_0)^q, & l \in [0, L] \\ 0, & \text{others} \end{cases} \tag{7}$$

where $h_{k,q}(l) = \dfrac{1}{q!} \left[\dfrac{d^q h_k(n;l)}{dn^q} \right]_{n=n_0}$ is the parameters to be estimated. For the P-BEM, with $Q \leq 5$ it is enough to track changes of the channel [6]. In the simulation, the value of Q is 4.

c) Multiple Models Set

According to the aforementioned expansion of the CE-BEM and P-BEM, we have the multi-model set, $\Omega = \{M_1, M_2\}$, $M_j = \left(f_{k,q}^j(n), h_{k,q}^j(l), Q_j \right)$, $j = 1, 2$, where $f_{k,q}^1(n)$ and $f_{k,q}^2(n)$ correspond to the basic functions $e^{j\omega_q n}$ and $(n - n_0)^q$, respectively. $h_{k,q}^1(l)$ and $h_{k,q}^2(l)$ are the model coefficients to be estimated. Q_j is the parameter that reflects the Doppler shift, and different models correspond to the different Q_j as mentioned above.

3.2   Adaptive Filtering Estimators

We adopt the adaptive Kalman filter, and analyze the measurement equation, the state equation and the adaptive algorithm as follow, based on the system model.

a) Measurement Equation of Kalman

Among the received signal, $y_p(i)$ is the ones only related to the pilot sequence $p(i)$. By (4), the corresponding signals y_k^p in data block y_k can be expressed as:

$$y_k^p = H_k^p \mathbf{p} + w_k^p \tag{8}$$

where H_k^p and w_k^p are sub-matrixes of H_k and w_k corresponding to the pilot $\mathbf{p}$ respectively. There are $(Q+1) \times (L+1)$ unknown parameters $h_{k,q}(l)$ in (8), which requires inserting at least $(Q+1)$ pilots in a data block as each pilot $\mathbf{p}_g$ affords $(L+1)$ unknown parameters. That is, $G \geq Q+1$. Combined with (5), we rewrite (8) as:

$$y_k^p = \begin{bmatrix} y_{k,0}^p \\ \vdots \\ y_{k,G-1}^p \end{bmatrix} = \begin{bmatrix} H_{k,0}^p \mathbf{p}_0 \\ \vdots \\ H_{k,G-1}^p \mathbf{p}_{G-1} \end{bmatrix} + w_k^p = \sum_{q=0}^{Q} \begin{bmatrix} F_{q,0}^p H_{k,q,0}^p \mathbf{p}_0 \\ \vdots \\ F_{q,G-1}^p H_{k,q,G-1}^p \mathbf{p}_{G-1} \end{bmatrix} + w_k^p \tag{9}$$

where $H_{k,g}^p = \sum_{q=0}^{Q} F_{q,g}^p H_{k,q,g}^p$, $H_{k,q,g}^p$ and $F_{q,g}^p$ are sub-matrixes of $H_{k,q}$ and F_q corresponding to the pilot $\mathbf{p}$ respectively. Due to the commutativity that the product of a Toeplitz matrix and a vector, we have $H_{k,q,g}^p \mathbf{p}_g = \mathbf{P}_g h_{k,q}$, where $\mathbf{P}_g$ is a $(L+1) \times (L+1)$ Toeplitz matrix,

$$\mathbf{P}_g = \begin{bmatrix} p_L & \cdots & p_0 \\ \vdots & \ddots & \vdots \\ p_{2L} & \cdots & p_L \end{bmatrix} \tag{10}$$

where p_l denotes the lth entry of pilot $\mathbf{p}_g$, and the vector $h_{k,q}$ is

$$h_{k,q} = \begin{bmatrix} h_{k,q}(0), \cdots h_{k,q}(L) \end{bmatrix}^T \tag{11}$$

Hence, (9) can be further written as:

$$y_k^p = \boldsymbol{\Phi}^p \mathbf{h}_k + w_k^p \tag{12}$$

where $\boldsymbol{\Phi}^p = \begin{bmatrix} F_{0,0}^p \mathbf{P}_0 & \cdots & F_{Q,0}^p \mathbf{P}_0 \\ \vdots & \ddots & \vdots \\ F_{0,G}^p \mathbf{P}_G & \cdots & F_{Q,G}^p \mathbf{P}_G \end{bmatrix}$, $\mathbf{h}_k = \begin{bmatrix} h_{k,0}^T, \cdots, h_{k,q}^T, \cdots, h_{k,Q}^T \end{bmatrix}^T$.

b) State Equation of Kalman

The channel coefficients h_k of each block follow an AR model and we set the state equation of Kalman as a simple first-order AR model given by

$$h_k = \alpha h_{k-1} + v_k \tag{15}$$

where the AR model coefficients α can be obtained from (1) (15) and Yule-Walker equations [3]. Note that we require the knowledge of $R_h(\tau)$ to calculate α.

However, $R_h(\tau)$ is typically unavailable, we can arbitrarily pick a value of α such that $\alpha \approx 1$ but $\alpha < 1$. v_k is AWGN with mean zero and variance δ_v^2.

c) Adaptive Algorithm

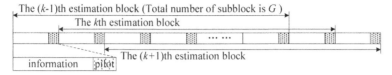

Fig. 3. The relationship diagram of the two between previous and current estimation block

Consider (12) and (15) as the measurement and the state equations of the Kalman adaptive algorithm, respectively. The construction of block h_k, h_{k-1} in (15) is shown in Fig. 3. Using Kalman adaptive algorithm to track the coefficient vector h_k for each sub-block, steps are as follows:

1) Initialization
$$\hat{h}_{-1|-1} = \mathbf{0}_{N \times 1}, \quad R^h_{-1|-1} = \delta_v^2 \mathbf{I}_N$$

2) Kalman recursion, the index of sub-block is $k = 0, 1, 2 \cdots$
Update $\hat{h}$ and R^h
$$\hat{h}_{k|k-1} = \alpha \hat{h}_{k-1|k-1}, \quad R^h_{k|k-1} = \alpha^2 R^h_{k|k-1} + \delta_v^2 \mathbf{I}_N$$
Kalman gain
$$\mathbf{K}_k = R^h_{k|k-1}(\boldsymbol{\Phi}^{\mathrm{P}})^H \times (\boldsymbol{\Phi}^{\mathrm{P}} R^h_{k|k-1}(\boldsymbol{\Phi}^{\mathrm{P}})^H + \delta_w^2 \mathbf{I}_{L+1})^{-1}$$

3) Measurement update
$$\hat{h}_{k|k} = \hat{h}_{k|k-1} + \mathbf{K}_k(y^{\mathrm{p}}_k - \boldsymbol{\Phi}^{\mathrm{p}}\hat{h}_{k|k-1}), \quad R^h_{k|k} = R^h_{k|k-1} - \mathbf{K}_k\boldsymbol{\Phi}^{\mathrm{P}} R^h_{k|k-1}$$

where the vector $\hat{h}_{k|k}$ is the estimation of h_k using the observation y^{p}_k. R^h_k is the error covariance matrix of h_k.

Base on (1) and $\hat{h}_{k|k}$, we can generate the whole sub-block channel value,

$$h(n;l) = \mathcal{F}_n \hat{\mathbf{h}}^{(l)}_{k|k} \tag{16}$$

where $\mathcal{F}_n = \left[f_0(n), f_1(n), \cdots, f_Q(n)\right]$ and $\hat{\mathbf{h}}^{(l)}_{k|k}$ is the sub-matrixes of $\hat{h}_{k|k}$, $\hat{\mathbf{h}}^{(l)}_{k|k} = \left[h_{k,0}(l), h_{k,1}(l), \cdots, h_{k,Q}(l)\right]^T$.

d) Adaptive Filter Estimator Set
Based on a) -c) in the part 3.2, we can establish the adaptive filter estimator set, $\boldsymbol{\Gamma} = \{A_1, A_2\}$, $A_j = (y^{\mathrm{p}}_k, \boldsymbol{\Phi}^{\mathrm{p}}_j, \hat{h}^j)$, $j = 1, 2$, where, y^{p}_k is the received symbols of the transmitted pilot. $\boldsymbol{\Phi}^{\mathrm{p}}_1$ and $\boldsymbol{\Phi}^{\mathrm{p}}_2$ are matrixes of the basic function of CE-BEM and P-BEM, generated by $f^1_{k,q}(n)$ and $f^2_{k,q}(n)$ in the channel multi-model set,

respectively. Channel model parameters vector $\hat{h}_k^1$ and $\hat{h}_k^2$ are obtained by estimation using each model.

3.3   Model Switching Strategy

To track the uncertain channel changes more accurately, it is particularly important when we switch the channel model. During the channel estimation, the determination of switching only relies on the pilot, thus, we define the error between the real received and the estimated of Kalman as e_k^j :

$$e_k^j = E_k(M_j, A_j) = y_k^p - \hat{y}_k^{p,j} = y_k^p - \boldsymbol{\Phi}^p \hat{h}_{k|k-1}^j \tag{17}$$

During the iteration k of the Kalman algorithm, each model in $\boldsymbol{\Omega} = \{M_j \,|\, j = 1, 2, \cdots, J\}$ has its own pilot estimation error e_k^j, and in the estimation sub-block, model j^* is selected as the optimal estimation model:

$$j_k^* = \arg \min_j \operatorname{sum}(|e_k^j|) \tag{18}$$

Then we can generate the optimal channel parameters with model j_k^* by (16), and for the unselected models, to reduce their estimation error in the next sub-block, we have to update the channel parameters using the optimal output based on (1).

3.4   Scheme Flow

The system scheme flow of multi-model channel estimation is shown in Fig. 4.

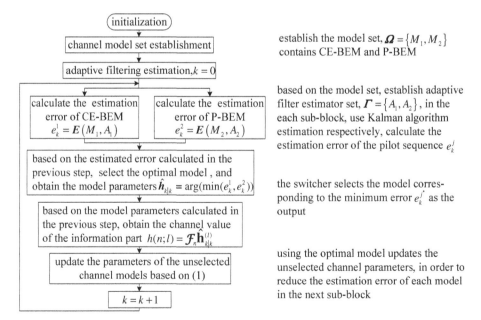

Fig. 4. The flow figure of the scheme in this paper

4   Simulation Results and Analysis

In this section, we test the performance of the proposed algorithm by simulations. The channel model is the time- and frequency-selective Rayleigh model [4], with multipath $L = 2$, carrier frequency $f_c = 2\text{GHz}$ and sampling interval $T_s = 25\mu s$. We consider the data block size $N = 200$ and the sub-block size 20 with $G = 10$ of pilot sequence per block. Here, the total length of data in the simulation is 4×10^4. The two models in the multi-model set are over-sampling CE-BEM with $M = 2$ and $Q \geq 4$ and P-BEM with $Q = 5$. The performance is evaluated by the normalized mean-square error (NMSE) [3], defined as:

$$NMSE = \frac{\sum_{n=1}^{N} \sum_{l=0}^{L} \left| \hat{h}(n;l) - h(n;l) \right|^2}{\sum_{n=1}^{N} \sum_{l=0}^{L} \left| h(n;l) \right|^2} \tag{19}$$

4.1   Constant Velocity

In this section, we consider the mobile station velocity as 40, 60, 120, 140km/h, and the range of signal to noise ratio as [0, 30]dB. The simulation results shown in Fig. 5, 6, 7 and 8:

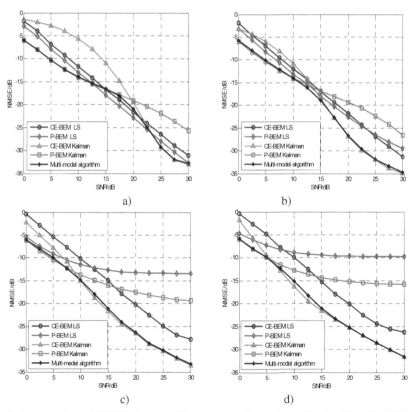

Fig. 5. Comparison of NMSE for the different case of velocity: 40km/h, 60 km/h, 120 km/h and 140 km/h respectively

As is shown in Fig.5., in the case of 40km/h, due to the slow channel variation, the performances of CE-BEM Kalman and P-BEM Kalman are better or worse than CE-BEM LS and P-BEM LS in different SNR range. However, the proposed multi-model algorithm performs closely or better than LS algorithms in the most range of SNR, through the switching among the models. As the velocity increases, in the case of 60km/h, 120km/h and 140km/h, the LS algorithm gradually deteriorates, whereas the Kalman adaptive algorithm shows the advantage in performance. The algorithms based on the single model such as CE-BEM Kalman and the P-BEM Kalman show their advantages at the high SNR and at the low SNR, respectively, whereas, the proposed multi-model algorithm achieves the better performance output in the entire range of SNR.

4.2   Changed Velocity

In this section, the mobile station's velocity is not constant but variant. We consider the relationship between transmission data and mobile station's velocities as follows: for $0 \le i \le 7999$, the velocity is 80km/h; for $8000 \le i \le 15999$, the velocity is 82.5km/h; for $16000 \le i \le 23999$, the velocity is 85km/h; for $24000 \le i \le 31999$, the velocity is 87.5km/h; and for $32000 \le i \le 39999$, the velocity is 90km/h, which corresponds to the scenario that the mobile station's acceleration is $3.6m/s^2$. Simulation result is shown in Fig. 6:

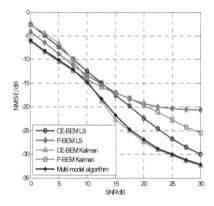

Fig. 6. Comparation of NMSE in the case of velocity varying within 80-90 km/h

Fig. 6 shows that the multi-model algorithm is still able to effectively switch between the models, between the SNR of 10-25dB, it is better than the CE-BEM LS with about 5dB NMSE lower. We can therefore conclude that the multi-model algorithm is superior to others in velocity change scenario.

5   Conclusion

In this paper, to deal with the weakness of the single-model based channel estimation in the time- frequency-selective channel, we proposed a multi-model channel estimation scheme. The simulation indicates that the proposed multi-model approach can switch between the models and estimated output along with the environmental changes, showing the superior performance to the single model channel estimation.

Acknowledgments. This work is supported by National Natural Science Foundation of China under Grant Nos. 61072088, 61101113, and Doctoral Research Foundation of Beijing University of Technology.

References

1. Zuocheng, Z., Yanhua, Z.: Channel Estimation Based on Multiple-Model Adaptive Technique. High Technology Letters 19(12), 1233–1237 (2009)
2. Xiaoli, M., Georgios, B.G., Shuichi, O.: Optimal Training for Block Transmissions over Doubly Selective Wireless Fading Channels. IEEE Transactions on Signal Processing 51(5), 1351–1366 (2003)
3. Jitendra, K.T., Shuangchi, H., Hyosung, K.: Doubly Selective Channel Estimation Using Exponential Basis Models and Subblock Tracking. IEEE Transactions on Signal Processing 58(3), 1275–1289 (2010)
4. Yahong, R.Z., Chengshan, X.: Simulation Models with Correct Statistical Properties for Rayleigh Fading Channels. IEEE Transactions on Communications 51(6), 920–928 (1999)
5. Deva, K.B., Brian, D.H.: Frequency-Selective Fading Channel Estimation with a Polynomial Time-Varying Channel Model. IEEE Transactions on Communications 47(6), 862–873 (1999)
6. Hussein, H., Laurent, R.: Joint Data QR-Detection and Kalman Estimation for OFDM Time-Varying Rayleigh Channel Complex Gains. IEEE Transactions on Communications 58(1), 170–178 (2010)
7. Shaowei, J., Hong, X., Wu, X.: Channel Estimation of MIMIO Time- Frequency-selective Channels Based on Data-dependent Superimposed Training. Applied Science and Technology 37(4), 43–46 (2010)
8. Lingji, C., Narendra, K.S.: Nonlinear Adaptive Control using Neural Networks and Multiple Models. Automatica 37(8), 1245–1255 (2001)
9. Wei, W., Xiaoli, L.: Multi-model Adaptive Control. Science Press, Beijing (2001)
10. Yingnan, L., Wei, J., Shubo, R., Qinglin, L.: Least Square Estimation of Doubly Selective Wireless Fading Channels. Journal of Electronics and Information Technology 30(9), 2185–2188 (2008)
11. Teo, K.A.D., Shuichi, O.: Optimal MMSE Finite Parameter Model for Doubly-Selective Channels. In: IEEE Global Telecommunications Conference, vol. 6, pp. 3503–3507 (2005)

Analysis of Nonlinear EEG Time Series Based on Local Support Vectors Machine Model

Lisha Sun, Kaixu Lin, Yugui Xu, and Congtao Xu

College of Engineering, Shantou University, Guangdong 515063, China
lssun@stu.edu.cn

Abstract. The modeling of Electroencephalography (EEG) signals is an important issue in clinical diagnosis of brain functional diseases. The proposed method using support vectors machine (SVM) with the structure risk minimization provides us an effective way of learning machine and modeling. The problem of solving the quadratic programming becomes a bottle-neck of training the SVM due to the long time of SVM training. In this paper, a local-SVM algorithm is proposed for modeling EEG time series. The local model is developed for improving the prediction of EEG signals. Furthermore, the presented model is used to detect the epilepsy from EEG signals in which dynamical characteristics are difference between normal and epilepsy EEG signals. Several experimental results were given to show that the training of the local-SVM provides a good behavior. Finally, the local SVM approach significantly improves the prediction and detection precision.

Keywords: EEG signal, Support Vector Machine, Prediction, Local model.

1 Introduction

The EEG signals are very complicated nonlinear signals and serve as windows for us to understand the cerebral activities because these signals are the synthetical reflection of the electricity activities of cerebral tissue and brain function status. EEG plays a more and more important role for analyzing the brain mechanism and the clinical manifestations of brain diseases with the development of computer and signal processing technology. For instance, the analysis of cerebral diseases attack help to better understand the pathophysiological and pharmacological basis. The most significant example is epilepsy detection and prediction in clinical applications [1]. In the domain of nonlinear dynamics, the Lyapunov exponent of EEG signal varies when the epilepsy comes and changes. At that time, the orderliness of signal is stronger and the chaos become weaker. If the EEG signals can be predicted, high-risk operation can be avoided when cerebral diseases happen to the patient [2].

Many research results have shown that EEG signal has the characteristics of chaos [1]. However, EEG signal also indicates as a nonlinear spatiotemporal chaotic sequence. According to the Takens's embedded theorem [3], we can reconstruct phase space as long as we choose the appropriate parameters of time delay and embedding

M. Zhao and J. Sha (Eds.): ICCIP 2012, Part I, CCIS 288, pp. 526–533, 2012.

dimension. Recently, support vector machine (SVM), proposed by Vapnik [4] according to statistical theory, become an effctive method and is widely used in classification and regression [5, 6]. SVM applies the structure risk minimization instead of the empirical risk minimization, which avoids the method selection and over learning problems and solves the problems of non-linear, dimensionality curse and local minimum efficiently. However, in practice, Training global SVM will meet great obstacles when the number of the training samples is large. To solve this problem, combining with some other optimization algorithms, we present a new method based on the idea of local method, namely the local SVM model This new method inherits characters of local method which has the advantage of small samples, simplicity and high precision [7]. Combined with these characters, an accurate high-speed prediction method is expected to predict the EEG signals.

Moreover, to verify the effectiveness of the proposed model and make use of this new model, we use this method to build an epilepsy detector. The instantaneous detection or prediction of the occurrence of epilepsy in the background of normal EEG signal is a challenge task for bio-signal processing, which can help us to observe and diagnose the state of the brain function.

This paper is organized as follows. In section 2, the ε-SVM for the prediction of chaotic signal was introduced. In the section 3, a local method was proposed to improve the training speed of SVM in prediction. In section 4, the proposed method was applied to the Logistic chaotic sequence and real EEG signal. Conclusion was given in section 5.

2   Sequence Prediction with SVM

It is assumed that the finite measured data samples $(\mathbf{x}_1, y_1), \cdots, (\mathbf{x}_l, y_l) \in (\mathbf{X} \times R)$ were obtained from a sample set $P(\mathbf{x}, y)(\mathbf{x} \in R^m, y \in R)$. The regression of support vector machine is to find a real function $f(\mathbf{x}) = \mathbf{w} \cdot \phi(\mathbf{x}_i) + b$ to fit these samples that make the risk function $R[f] = \int c(\mathbf{x}, y, f) dP(\mathbf{x}, y)$ minimum. The error between the observed y and prediction $f(\mathbf{x})$ could be measured by a so called ε insensitive loss function described by equation (1):

$$\left| y_i - f(\mathbf{x}_i, \mathbf{x}) \right|_\varepsilon = \max \left\{ 0, \left| y_i - f(\mathbf{x}_i, \mathbf{x}) \right| - \varepsilon \right\} \tag{1}$$

In other words, it may allow some errors. In most cases, the probability density $P(\mathbf{x}, y)$ is not known. It can't make the risk function minimum directly. Therefore the minimum problem of the following equation (2) is proposed to substitute the risk function.

$$E(\mathbf{w}) = \frac{1}{2}(\mathbf{w} \cdot \mathbf{w}) + C \frac{1}{l} \sum_{i=1}^{l} \left| y_i - f(\mathbf{x}_i, \mathbf{x}) \right|_\varepsilon \tag{2}$$

Where $\left| y_i - f(\mathbf{x}_i, \mathbf{x}) \right|_\varepsilon = \max \left\{ 0, \left| y_i - f(\mathbf{x}_i, \mathbf{x}) \right| - \varepsilon \right\}$ is the ε insensitive loss function. The first term of right equation (2) represents the complexity of $f(\mathbf{x})$, the second term represents the loss. C represents the compromise relationship between complexity and loss. It equivalents to

$$
\begin{cases}
\min_{w,\xi_i,\xi_i^*,b} \dfrac{1}{2}(\mathbf{w}\cdot\mathbf{w})+C\dfrac{1}{l}\sum_{i=1}^{l}(\xi_i+\xi_i^*) \\
s.t. \quad \left(\mathbf{w}\cdot\phi(\mathbf{x}_i)+b\right)-y_i \le \varepsilon+\xi_i \\
\qquad y_i-\left(w\cdot\phi(\mathbf{x}_i)+b\right)\le \varepsilon+\xi_i^* \\
\qquad \xi_i,\xi_i^* \ge 0
\end{cases}
\tag{3}
$$

It can yield the dual optimization problem:

$$
\begin{cases}
\max_{\alpha,a^*} \sum_{i=1}^{l}\left[\alpha_i^*(y_i-\varepsilon)-\alpha_i(y_i+\varepsilon)\right] \\
\qquad -\dfrac{1}{2}\sum_{i=1}^{l}\sum_{j=1}^{l}(\alpha_i-\alpha_i^*)(\alpha_j-\alpha_j^*)K(\mathbf{x}_i,\mathbf{x}_j) \\
s.t. \quad \sum_{i=1}^{l}(\alpha_i-\alpha_i^*)=0 \ \ 0\le\alpha_i,\alpha_i^* \le C/l, i=1\cdots l
\end{cases}
\tag{4}
$$

Where $K(\mathbf{x}_i,\mathbf{x}_j)=\phi(\mathbf{x}_i)\phi(\mathbf{x}_j)$ is kernel. The linear kernels $K(x,y)=xy$, polynomial kernels $K(x,y)=(xy+1)^d$ and RBF kernels $K(x,y)=\exp(-\|x-y\|_2^2/\sigma^2)$ are commonly used. From equ.(4), we can get the optimal solutions of α_i and α_i^*, denoted by $\overline{\boldsymbol{\alpha}}=[\overline{\alpha}_1,\overline{\alpha}_1^*,\overline{\alpha}_2,\overline{\alpha}_2^*,\cdots,\overline{\alpha}_l,\overline{\alpha}_l^*]^T$. Then the dynamic system model can be obtained by solving the dual optimization problem. For the input vector $\mathbf{x}$, the prediction can be deduced from:

$$
f(\mathbf{x})=\mathbf{w}\cdot\phi(\mathbf{x})+\overline{b}=\sum_{i-1}^{l}(\overline{\alpha}_i-\overline{\alpha}_i^*)K(\mathbf{x}_i,\mathbf{x})+\overline{b}
\tag{5}
$$

Where $\overline{b}$ can be gotten by equ.(6) or (7). If $\overline{\alpha}_j$ is chosen, then

$$
\overline{b}=y_j-\sum_{i=1}^{l}(\overline{\alpha}_i^*-\overline{\alpha}_i)K(\mathbf{x}_i,\mathbf{x}_j)+\varepsilon \quad \overline{\alpha}_j \in (0,C/l)
\tag{6}
$$

If $\overline{\alpha}_k^*$ is chosen, then

$$
\overline{b}=y_k-\sum_{i=1}^{l}(\overline{\alpha}_i^*-\overline{\alpha}_i)K(\mathbf{x}_i,\mathbf{x}_k)-\varepsilon \quad \overline{\alpha}_k^* \in (0,C/l)
\tag{7}
$$

3   Local ε-SVM

When the samples become large, training the SVM has become the bottle-neck of SVM application. Colin Campbell made an overview of existing training algorithms [8]. In that overview he mainly introduced the SVM light decomposition algorithms

[9], sequential minimal optimization (SMO) algorithms proposed by Platt [10], the nearest neighbor algorithms proposed by Kerrthi [11] and the least squares support vector machine algorithms proposed by J. A. K. Suykens [12]. These algorithms aimed to improve the SVM training speed in the application of classification or regression.

The advantage of SMO is that there is no need to store the kernels matrix as well as use quadratic programming package. Combining with the local method, this paper proposes a local ε-SVM. In the prediction process, the local method selects the vectors which are close to the target vector. Meanwhile, it uses these vectors to train the SVM by SMO algorithm. This increases the training speed because of the little samples. The following part introduces using the local ε-SVM for one-step prediction in chaotic signal.

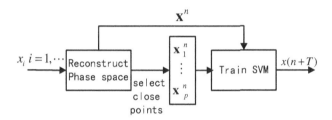

Fig. 1. Local SVM for prediction

1. For a chaotic sequence $x(t)$, select embedding dimension m and delay time τ, reconstruct phase space according to the Takens's embedding theorem. For the final vector $\mathbf{X}(N)$ which is used as the input target vector to predict the next point of the sequence, compute the distance between the target vector and preformed N-1 vectors as (8)

$$d(i) = \|\mathbf{X}(i) - \mathbf{X}(N)\|, i = 1, 2, ...N - 1 \tag{8}$$

2. Select p distances that are most close to the vector $\mathbf{X}(N)$, then select p vectors and value D_r corresponding to the p distances.

$$\mathbf{X}_r^n = [x(t_r), x(t_r + \tau), \cdots x(t_r + (m-1)\tau)]^T, \quad r = 1, 2, \cdots p \tag{9}$$

$$D_r = x(t_r + T), \quad r = 1, 2, \cdots p \tag{10}$$

For one-step prediction, $T = t_r + m\tau$.

3. $\mathbf{X}_r^n, r = 1 \cdots p$ are taken as the input vectors of the SVM and D_r, $r = 1, 2, \cdots p$ is taken as the output values gained from training of the SVM.
4. $\mathbf{X}(N)$ is used as an input vectors, then the prediction value $x(n+T)$ can be obtained.
5. Iterate step 1-4 till obtaining all prediction values.

4   Simulations and Application

4.1   Local ε-SVM Prediction for Logistic Sequence

To verify the prediction performance, a 1000 point Logistic signal was generated from equation (11) for modeling and predicting.

$$x(n+1) = ax(n)(1-x(n)) \tag{11}$$

Initial value was 0.8 and a=4. Setting m=3 and τ=1 to reconstruct the phase space. The first 800 points were used for training the SVM, and the following 200 points were used for testing. The hidden center of BP neural network and RBF neural network were both set to 10 and the training precision was 0.005. The parameters were set as C=1000 and ε=0.01 in training the ε-SVM. The close points was selected as p=20. The mean square error (MSE) was used here to evaluate the prediction performance.

Table 1 lists the prediction MSE of four learning machines. It's obvious that the MSE of SVM is less than the neural network. It shows that the SVM performs better than the neural network. Applying the SMO algorithm in the LIBSVM toolbox, the times for training global ε-SVM was 24.13 seconds. While for local ε-SVM, training 20 close samples only needed 0.0062 second, the total times for predicting 200 points include the time used in sorting and searching the close points is 11.97 seconds. Therefore we can conclude that local ε-SVM has not only smaller prediction MSE but also fast prediction speed. Figure 2 shows the result of prediction for logistic sequence.

Table 1. MSE of four learning machine

	BP	RBF	Global ε-SVM	Local -SVM
MSE	3.0882 e-4	3.1979 e-4	3.6377 e-5	3.0000 e-5
Time(s)	-	-	24.13	11.97

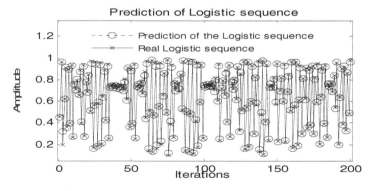

Fig. 2. Prediction of logistic sequence based on local SVM

4.2   Local ε-SVM for Real EEG Prediction

To evaluate the performance of the proposed method, EEG signal, taken from Mental Health Center in Shantou University, is analyzed. In this section a segment of these real spontaneous EEG signal with 1000 data points was selected for the purpose. The first 800 points were used for training the SVM and the following 200 points were used for testing. The embedding dimension was selected as $m=5$ and delay time as $\tau=1$. The training parameters C=1000 and $\tau=0.01$ were set in both global ε-SVM and local ε-SVM. Close points was selected as $p=25$.

Table 2 lists the training MSE of two SVM and its iterations times using SMO in the LIBSVM toolbox. Figure 3 shows the prediction result of global and local SVM. The local SVM improves the prediction precision. In addition, because of the reducing number of the training samples in local method, the training time at every prediction is cut down. Although it's necessary to train the SVM in every prediction process over again, it can still reduce the total training times. It shows that the time reduces almost 50 times from the table 2.

Table 2. Prediction MSE and Training Iteration Times

Method	Global ε-SVM	Local ε-SVM
MSE	3.1084 e-3	2.2000 e-3
Time(s)	583.1	12.42

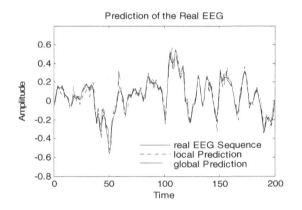

Fig. 3. The real EEG data and its prediction

4.3   Epilepsy Detection Based on Local ε-SVM

According to the dynamical characteristics difference between normal EEG signals and epilepsy signals, a new epilepsy detecting method based on local ε-SVM model is proposed in this paper. The detection framework is in Fig.4, which can be introduced as follows:

(1) Both normal EEG signal and epilepsy signal are recorded through international 10-20 system with $c(t)$ and $s(t)$ for their representation.

(2) Train the local ε-SVM model with normal EEG signals data $c(t)$, and then take the trained model as predictor.

(3) Insert some epilepsy segments into the normal EEG signal to form mixed signal $x(t)$. And take such a mixed signal as local ε-SVM model's input.

(4) Predict the mixed signals with local ε-SVM model. And compare the prediction error with threshold η. If the error is less than η, we think the input signal is H_0, namely: $x(t) = c(t)$. If not, the input signal is H_1, namely: $x(t) = s(t)$.

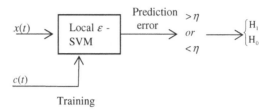

Fig. 4. The epilepsy detection framework based on local ε-SVM

1200 points EEG data were selected for testing. Here, the first 1000 points are normal EEG signals and the last 200 points are the epilepsy signals. The first 800 points are used for training model and the last 400 points are for detection experiment. The detecting error result based on local ε-SVM model is shown in Fig.5. We can see from the figure that the detection error is obviously bigger at the last 200 points than the first 200 points. There are mainly two reasons for this: 1. local ε-SVM model which is trained based on normal EEG signal can exactly describe the characteristics and evolvement of chaotic dynamical of EEG, so the detection error will be small in the non-epilepsy region 2. The chaotic dynamic characteristics have obvious difference between epilepsy and normal EEG signal. Therefore, detection error will be bigger at epilepsy region and the model we proposed is the effective model for epilepsy detecting.

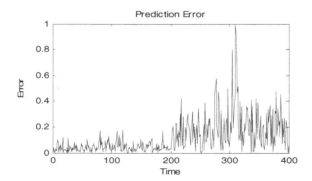

Fig. 5. The prediction error in normal and epileptic EEG, the first 200 points are normal EEG prediction error, and the last 200 points are epileptic EEG prediction error

5   Conclusion

This paper provides a new method for investigating the problem of prediction of EEG signals using SVM method. A local SVM procedure was developed to deal with the problem of training global SVM when it comes to a large of training samples. A local SVM model based on the local procedures was proposed and combined with the existing training algorithms, such as SMO, to predict EEG signals. Several simulation results indicated that the presented local SVM model can not only significantly increase the training speed but also effectively reduced the prediction MSE. The rsults proof that the proposed algorithm provides an effective way for detecting epilepsy waveforms.

Acknowledgement. This paper was supported by the projects of Natural Science Foundation of China (61072037), and Natural Science Foundation ôf Guangdong (10151503101000011).

References

1. Lasemidis, L.D., Sackellares, J.C.: Chaos Theory and Eilepsy. The Neuroscientist 2, 118–126 (1996)
2. Lin, X.B., Qiu, T.S.: EEG Signal Analysis and Processing based on Prediction of Epileptic Seizures and Research Progress. Biomedical Engineering Foreign Medical Sciences 27, 9–12 (2004) (in Chinese)
3. Takens, F.: Dynamical Systems and Turbulence. Spring, Berlin (1981)
4. Vapink, V.P.: The Nature of Statistical Learning Theory. Springer, NewYork (1995)
5. Smola, A.J., Scholkopf, B.: A Tutorial on Support Vector Regression. Statistics and Computing 14, 199–222 (1998)
6. Burges, C.J.C.: A Tutorial on Support Vector Machines for Pattern Recognition. Data Mining and Knowledge Discovery 2(2), 121–167 (1998)
7. Zhang, J.S., Dang, J.J., Li, H.C.: Spatiotemporal Chaos Sequence Prediction using Local Support Vector Machine. Acra Physica Sinca 56, 67–77 (2007) (in Chinese)
8. Colin, C.: Algorithmic Approaches to Training Support Vector Machines: A Survey. In: Proceedings of ESANN 2000, pp. 27–36. D-Facto Publications, Belgium (2000)
9. Joachims, T.: Making large Scale SVM Learning Practical. Advances in Kernel Methods: Upport Vector Machines. MIT Press, Cambridge (1998)
10. Platt, J.C.: Fast Training of Support Vector Machines using Sequential Minimal Optimization. Advances in Kernel Methods: Support Vector Learning, pp. 185–208. MIT Press, Cambridge (1999)
11. Keerthi, S., Shevade, S., Bhattcharyya, C., et al.: Improvements to Platt's SMO Algorithm for SVM Classifier Design. Neural Computation 13(3), 637–649 (2001)
12. Suykens, J.A.K., Vandewalle, J.: Least Squares Support Vector Machine Classifiers. Neural Processing Letters 9, 293–300 (1999)

Research of Design and Application about Mobile Learning System Suiting Specialty Practice Link

Haojun Li[1] and Xiaoping Xu[2]

[1] College of Information Engineering, Zhejiang University of Technology,
Hangzhou, ZheJiang, China
zgdlhj@zjut.edu.cn
[2] Binjiang Middle School, Ruian, ZheJiang Province, China
xxp_602@126.com

Abstract. The application research of mobile learning is promoted by rapidly development of intelligent mobile terminal and wireless communication technology. It is that learners use the handheld devices to learn at any given time or place becomes possible. This article analyzes the existing application fields of mobile learning, and puts the mobile learning models to specialty practice link which suits clothing sales practice link of clothing specialty in secondary vocational school. It firstly presents some existing handheld device-based mobile learning systems, then analyzes the design and implement procedures of mobile learning system suiting clothing sales in detail, and lastly conducts experiments in practice link of clothing sales of clothing in secondary vocational school. The result of experiments indicates that the system is not only good for the learners to study the knowledge about clothing sales, but also has a remarkable improvement in learning efficiency relative to the traditional learning.

Keywords: mobile learning, system design, learning style, practice link.

1   Introduction

With the rapid development of wireless communication technology and mobile technology, a large number of network connect-based and high value-added information products make networks and computing technology application popular in people's work, study and every aspect of daily life. Mobile and wireless communication technology make it possible to study at any time or place, and that provide a learning style which contacts digital learning resources with actual scene resources [1]. Learners can study in actual learning scene with adaptive learning content, and capture resources anytime, anywhere [2]. This will change the existing man-machine interaction models of learning activity gradually.

The application of mobile and wireless technology in learning areas puts forward to the development of mobile learning (M-learning), which makes the use of mobile learning more and more widespread and becomes the important research content in current education technology [3]. According to Molenet, mobile learning can be

M. Zhao and J. Sha (Eds.): ICCIP 2012, Part I, CCIS 288, pp. 534–542, 2012.

broadly defined as the exploitation of ubiquitous handheld technologies, together with wireless and mobile phone networks, to facilitate, support, enhance and extend the reach of teaching and learning.

The unceasing development of information technology is changing the learning model from traditional and formal learning to informal learning about E-learning,M-learning, and Ubiquitous Learning.In these novelty learning models, M-learning's mobility procedure and individuation contents behave more efficient and flexible than traditional learning style on overcoming the restrict of time and space; with the increasing of the cost performance of handheld device and the diversification of Internet Access, M-learning will stand for the next generation learning model which is based on the future information technology, which will bring the brand-new strategies, practices, instruments, and resources, in order to realize the ubiquitous and individuation lifelong learning goals at last[4].

Clothing sales is the significant practice link in clothing of secondary vocational school. In internship, students need to grasp various kinds of knowledge, like garment material, workmanship, brand concept, color matching and sales skill, which is related to the actual scene of practice. For this, we require clothing sales M-learning system related to the actual working situation urgently, and we can provide the students knowledge and information when they needed. In addition, students can make use of the handheld device by themselves to study and satisfy their need.

2   Related Research Work

Wireless communication, the core of mobile computing technology, is the direct reason to drive the study and application of M-learning. M-learning means that learners can study under the variable and not pre-establish situation, or use mobile technology to study effectively [5]. This learning model can mix mobile computing technology and digital learning, individual learning and study anywhere at any time. Learners can use handheld devices to realize one-to-one communication between equipments and themselves; and these devices can also control and filter the learning information and interaction contents, make good use of the learners' spare time. M-learning has portability, society interactivity, situation perceptibility, connectivity and individuality, which is making thorough in the theoretical study of it, research and develop more application systems and variable application areas [6].

Now M-learning application area covers elementary and secondary school, university, distance education, mass education, vocational training. For example, there are many projects about mobile learning, which are Noah "Palmtop Thinking English","Peasants M-learning and information service platform "in Gansu,"Mobile - phone School" in Zengcheng area of Guangdong,China Mobile "Nongxintong", "Mobile School" of University of Shanghai television,"Mobile Education" project of University of California-Berkeley,Singapore "MobiSKoolz project","Learning system of tourists' navigation" in Taiwan museum, "Nature course outdoor-assisted learning system" in Taiwan primary school,"Pocket-WI" Project of Vienna University of

Technology Campus-Mobil" project of Germany University, "MOBILearn" action launched by some countries in Europe , "Africa country M-learning research and practice project" of Plymouth hektoria university in South-Africa and so on [7][8]. These application projects give full play to M-learning' dominant position, combine individual learning requirement with situation perception learning, provide the individual communication patterns between learners and learning contents under the actual situation, promote M-learning theories application vastly, widen its application areas, and enhance the practice influence of it.

High-efficiency learning used to grow out of actual situation, M-learning can be used in the actual learning situation, which makes the learners connect theories to the actual situation better. Therefore, this article studys the existing M-learning application system and puts M-learning pattern into the practice link of clothing in secondary vocational school. It provides a novel handheld device-based clothing sales learning system, analyses and realizes the design process and every function of this system in particular. We use the student interns, clothing in secondary vocational school from Wenzhou in Zhejiang province, as experimental subject, perform an experiment about the learning system mentioned in this article, and at last we can discuss this experiment result from degree of satisfaction and learning efficiency.

3   The System Design of Clothing Sales Mobile Learning

According to the documents which are stated about the research contents of individual English-words M-learning [9][10], this article combines with the practice ability requirements of clothing sales of clothing in secondary vocational school, analyzes the clothing sales learning system design sustained by handheld devices from learning target planning, learning object analyzing, design philosophy analyzing, system architecture planning, and systemic function planning.

3.1   Learning Target Planning

Learning Target is the specific and visible performance after having studying. In terms of situation cognition and relative learning theories, we should respect the students' learning autonomy of clothing sales of clothing in secondary vocational school, pay attention to the existing theoretical knowledge of them. We hold that the setting of learning target must be connected to the task of them students, and then we can do our best to create an actual mobile learning environment for clothing sales personnel.

The target of this system is to help the salesmen master the related knowledge and contents, know well about clothing brand, garment martial, clothing display skills, language expression of clothing sales and color matching. Beyond that, learners can use Internet communication mode to get the newest fashion and how to exchange the mind with customers.

3.2   Learning Object Analyzing

This article makes a depth exploration about learning objects' characteristics to satisfy the learners' need. The characteristics refer to intelligence factor and nonintellectual factor, the first one is that the objects have related knowledge and skills to their upcoming study, including related cognition and attitude of learning contents; the other one means that apart from all other outside intelligence psychological factors, such as: motivation, interests, emotions, will, character, outlook on life, world outlook and so on. Before we try to understand the objects' various characteristics, we should consider the stable of the learners, the similar reasons and also the diversity. Similarity characteristic research can provide theoretical direction for socialization learning contents design, yet diversity research can help design individual learning contents.

The system asks these objects for 18 years old, which are the interns of clothing sales of clothing in secondary vocational school, for that, they are much different with professional clothing salesmen from psychology and physiology. Because of the professional salesmen have richer working and social experience; they have upper ability to comprehensive the objective things; but the interns can't compare with professionals on cognitive sophistication, they are only good at accepting new knowledge and remembering contents. So interns have stronger learning interest and knowledge seeking.

We discuss learning system of clothing sales based on handheld device in this article, and we should also consider the operant skills about hangdheld device in mobile learning environment, mobile learning resources adaptability, and individual character of learners.

3.3   Design Philosophy Analyzing

Mobile learning system design is different from traditional network learning system design; it expresses the goodness of M-learning system, and achieves these goals, such as: practicability of learning contents,miniaturization of learning resources, controllability of learning plans, individuation of learning patterns, and interaction of processes[11]. There are four principles on designing this system:

1. Practical applicability oflearning contents: The learning information should be closely related to clothing sales, and the expression of learning contents should be brief; at the same time, handheld devices can help learners study the related knowledge easily and update information from Internet conveniently.
2. Miniaturization of learning resources: Learners can be disturbed from outside inevitable when they are studying. So we should disassemble learning resources into various miniaturization information to the learners, for this, the learners may master the independent knowledge in a short time and get a better learning effect.
3. Rationality of architecture: System architecture should be well-designed and reasonable-planned, this will be the most important part for the whole system's sustainable development. This system use modularization to help learners to select the contents which is adapted to themselves.

3.4   System Architecture Planning

The normative system architecture can make sure the system operation and expand its function. In this case, there are application software based on handheld mobile device and management software based on server in this system architecture about clothing sales mobile learning. System administrator collects, settles and gathers variable learning resource according to the practice ability need of clothing sales in secondary vocational school, administrator publishes these resources into resource database and case database. The management software based on server will choose adaptive learning contents by the learners asking and learning ability and display in the learners' handheld devices at last. Learners should send their learning results and suggestions to system administrator after learning some times, while the administrator can adjust information to make M-learning a benign cycle-learning-process. Figure 1 provides an overview of system architecture about clothing sales mobile learning.

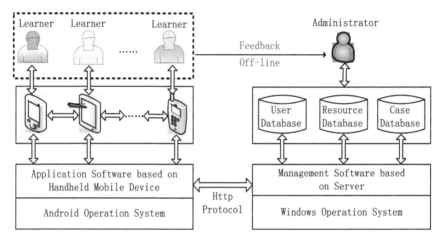

Fig. 1. System Architecture about Clothing Sales Mobile Learning

3.5   System Functional Planning

According to the design and analysis contents above, the functions of handheld device-based clothing sales learning system can be divided into learners' functions on the application software based on mobile device and administrator' functions on the management software based on server. Learners' functions all move on handheld mobile devices, which could provide fashion cloth information, garment material knowledge,etiquette of clothing sales,language expression of sales, clothing display skills,cloth color matching, sales cases sharing and online intercommunion between learners; thus administer' functions move on the Application Server, provide learners management, resources management and application data analysis and so on. The administrator' functions can help the system administrator preserve this system function, be familiars with the actual learning group, maintain all kinds of learning resources, and analyze the dates about resources frequency. The whole system functional design is illustrated on figure 2.

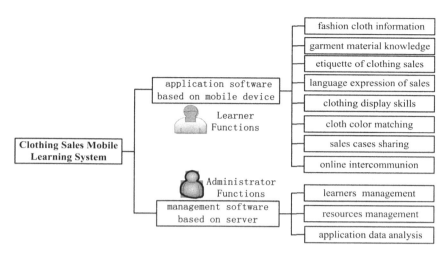

Fig. 2. System Function about Clothing Sales Mobile Learning

4   Implementation of Clothing Sales M-learning System

In accordance with the system design contents in the third part of this article, this system has accomplished Application Server functions managed by administer and the handheld device functions used by learners. SQL Server 2000 is regarded as the system database in clothing sales M-learning system. For remote management, Application Server develops with Web and JSP, and realizes learners management, resources management, and application data analysis under integrated development environment of MyEclipse. The handheld device in this system is Smart Phone with Android 2.1 above; we achieve fashion cloth information, garment material knowledge, etiquette of clothing sales, language expression of sales, clothing display skills, cloth color matching, sales cases sharing and online intercommunion by using Java language in MyEclipse environment.

5   Analysis of Experiment Result

To analyses learners' satisfaction and learning efficiency of handheld devices-based clothing sales learning system, our experiment chooses the current graduation students of a secondary vocational school in Wenzhou city of ZheJiang province. There are 33 clothing sales interns (6 boys and 27 girls) working in 8 clothing sales internship positions for 6 weeks. 33 interns were randomly divided into Experimental group (E group) and Control group (C group): E group (4 boys; 15 interns) uses our M-learning system, thus C group (18 interns) adopts traditional learning style. In order to reduce the influence of the difference between E group and C group, teachers will receive training before internship.

5.1   Analysis of Experiment Result about System Satisfaction

We design the questionnaire which includes the service conditions about handheld devices, convenience of system operation, attitude of system using, and the view of learners in order to analyses the learners' satisfaction about clothing sales M-learning system according to reference [12]. 15 interns in E group will be invited to finish the questionnaire after 6 weeks internship. The result of questionnaire survey about system satisfaction is given in Table 1.

Table 1. The result of questionnaire survey about system satisfaction

Question	Amount of learner	Percentage
Using handheld devices daily	14	93.3%
Learning by handheld device before	0	00.0%
System using satisfaction	12	80.0%
Willing to learn by M-learning system	13	86.7%
System operation convenience	11	73.3%
Learning resource deprivation	10	66.7%
Online interactive function weakly	9	60.0%

We can get a conclusion from Table 1 that almost all the interns have used intelligent handheld devices, but never study with them. There are 80% interns feel satisfied with the system; more than 85% think it is useful for learning; 86.7% interns like to exercise with this system. All these results mean that students are interested in M-learning. Besides, 73.3% learners consider the system operation is convenient and 66.7% hope it can provide more helpful learning resources.

5.2   Analysis of Experiment Result about Learning Efficiency

In order to analyze the learning efficiency of clothing sales M-learning system, some experienced teachers of secondary vocational school are invited to design the tests. The maximum score on these tests is 40, choice questions account for 20 and other 20 is completions. All 33 interns should be taken part in these tests, and the analysis about experiment data is performed using SPSS software. The result of data analysis is given in Table 2.

Table 2. The T-test with paired samples about Pre and Post practice score

	Interns	Learning style	Pre-test	Post-test	Correlation	P value
E group	15	Mobile learning	19.33	27.60	0.808	0.000
C group	18	Traditional learning	19.78	25.11	0.522	0.000

Notes: The Pre-test is defined as the average of the test results before the practice; the Post-test is defined as the average of the test results after the practice.

According to the information from Table 2, both E group and C group are all improved on clothing sales skills after practice. But the coefficient of E group is 0.808(C group is 0.522), which means using this system has more relativity performance than traditional learning method. From the result of paired sample T, students with M-learning exhibited an appreciated mark 8.27(C group is 5.33); and a significant difference is (P=0.039; <0.05) considering from learning methods. Then we found that higher marks are got by the students with clothing sales M-learning system.

Studying with handheld devices, E group proves the satisfaction and learning efficiency. A new study on handheld devices-based clothing sales M-learning helps learning at any time or place; learning resources which is provided from the system is suited for piece time, it is helpful for learners to grasp knowledge and get the related skills in a short time. Moreover, clothing sales learning system can make a big difference from traditional learning contents, which is more comprehensive and prompt.

6   Conclusion

In this paper, we have proposed handheld devices-based clothing sales learning system which can guide and sustain the learners to get related knowledge at any time or place, realize the individuation and normalization of learning process and space-time, and reflect the current M-learning design concept. It is believed that mobile learning could be a essential factor in involving young adults in learning,where   more traditional methods have failed [13].Nevertheless, this article is only a new attempt on M-learning in clothing sales, a depth research should be hold on development and manufacture of fragments' learning resources,communication interaction of among users,result feedbacks. To make the best use of M-learning, system executors need to design the learning resources well and pay a close attention to learning process performance except for positive participation of learners.

Acknowledgment. The work reported in this paper was supported in part by a grant from the Science and Technology Department project of Zhejiang Province (No. 2010C33147).

References

1. Sharples, M.: The design of personal mobile technologies for lifelong learning. Computers & Education 34(3-4), 177–193 (2000)
2. Liu, T.Y.: A context-aware ubiquitous learning environment for language listening and speaking. Journal of Computer Assisted Learning 25(6), 515–527 (2009)
3. Martin, S., et al.: New Technology Trends in Education: Seven Years of Forecasts And Convergence. Computers & Education 57(3), 1893–1906 (2011)
4. McConatha, D., Praul, M., Lynch, M.J.: Mobile learning in higher education: An empirical assessment of a new educational tool. Turkish Online Journal of Educational Technology 7(3), 15–21 (2008)

5. Huang, R., Salomaa, J.: Mobile Learning: theory·current situation·trend. Science Press, Beijing (2008)
6. Sharples, M., Arnedillo-Sánchez, I., et al.: Mobile Learning Small Devices, Big Issues. In: Technology-Enhanced Learning, pp. 233–249. Springer, Netherlands (2009)
7. Frohberg, D., Gothe, C., Schwabe, G.: Mobile Learning projects - a critical analysis of the state of the art. Journal of Computer Assisted Learning 25(4), 307–331 (2009)
8. Fu, J., Yang, X.: Browsing theory research and practise about mobile learing in China for ten years. China Educational Technology (7), 36–41 (2009)
9. Chen, C.M., Chung, C.J.: Personalized mobile English vocabulary learning system based on item response theory and learning memory cycle. Computers & Education 51(2), 624–645 (2008)
10. Huang, Y.M., Chiu, P.S., et al.: The design and implementation of a meaningful learning-based evaluation method for ubiquitous learning. Computers & Education 57(4), 2291–2302 (2011)
11. Nordin, N., Embi, M.A., et al.: Mobile Learning Framework for Lifelong Learning. Procedia - Social and Behavioral Sciences 7, 130–138 (2010)
12. Chen, C.-M., Hsieh, Y.-L., Hsu, S.-H.: Mining learner profile utilizing association rule for web-based learning diagnosis. Expert Systems with Applications 33(1), 6–22 (2007)
13. Hashemi, M., Azizinezhad, M., et al.: What is Mobile Learning? Challenges and Capabilities. Procedia - Social and Behavioral Sciences 30, 2477–2481 (2011)

A Real-Time Task Scheduling Strategy Supporting Compensatory Task

Jiali Xia, Zhonghua Cao*, Wenting Zhu, and Wenle Wang

Jiangxi University of Finance and Economics
Nanchang, China
chonghuac@gmail.com

Abstract. Based on the real-time system model that supports compensatory tasks, this paper proposed a method to evaluate the urgency to the tasks. Also, we discussed three possible situations that will influence the urgency of the task. And hence, based on above analysis, we discussed the occasion to schedule the compensatory tasks when the main tasks abort. Finally, the experimental results show that the proposed strategy of scheduling real-time tasks can effectively reduce the ratio of missing deadline.

Keywords: Real-time task, Compensatory task, Urgency, Workload, Scheduling Strategy.

1   Introduction

In the recent years, the real-time system was widely applied in a number of such diverse environments as space or airborne platform management system, industrial control system, flexible manufacturing system and wireless sensor network. In the system, the real-time tasks are normally divided into hard task, soft task and firm task, A real-time system is usually used to schedule the real-time tasks with time constraints under restricted workload, and one of the important goals of the scheduling algorithm is to make sure that all of the hard tasks can be accomplished within their deadline limits and as less soft and firm tasks as possible miss their deadlines.

In order to improve the adaptivity of the real-time system, Nag and Bestavros[1,2] thought that a real-time task contained two parts: the main task and the compensatory task. If a main task is start, but it cannot accomplish its work, then the related compensatory task should be execute to eliminate the inconsistency that caused by the main task. Moreover, the compensatory task should be executed with time limits. Usually, the compensatory task is executed immediately as soon as the main task is aborted. Therefore, a pessimistic strategy is schedule the main task binding its compensatory task, and the compensatory task can commit only after the main task abort[3].however, it will increase the system burden to pre-execute a compensatory

---

* Corresponding author.

M. Zhao and J. Sha (Eds.): ICCIP 2012, Part I, CCIS 288, pp. 543–551, 2012.
© Springer-Verlag Berlin Heidelberg 2012

task as the main task executing. In order to improve the performance of the real-time system, it is sensible to choose an appropriate occasion to schedule the compensatory task.

In this paper, we analysis the relationship between executive urgencies of the tasks and the workload of the real-time system, and propose a strategy to schedule the compensatory task based on the relative workload of the main task. Based on the real-time scheduling algorithms of EDF(Earliest Deadline First)[4] and LSF(Least Slack First)[5], we study the performance of our strategy by experiments. In the experiments, we preset a threshold, $\mu(\mu > 1.0)$, of the workload of the real-time system. If the relative workload of a task is greater than μ, we start the compensatory tasks according to the proposed strategies. The experimental results show that our method can efficiently schedule the compensatory tasks as their main tasks abort, and the rate of missing the tasks' deadline can be reduced.

2   Analysis on Scheduling Strategy

2.1   Real-Time Task Model

Support $T = T_1, T_2, ..., T_n$ is the set of tasks in the real-time system, for any a task T_i, if it is a hard task, then it is comprise of the main task T_{im} and the compensatory task T_{ic}; else it only contains the main task T_{im}. T_{im} and T_{ic} are the sub-tasks of T_i, and there is no conflict between the sub-tasks. Thus the tasks in the system can be described as $T = \{T_i \mid T_i =< T_{im}, T_{ic} >, 0 < i < n\}$.

For any a task T_i, it is comprised by the following attributes:

- D_{im} and D_{ic}, denote the deadline of T_{im} and T_{ic}.
- A_{im} and A_{ic}, denote the arrival time of T_{im} and T_{ic}.
- c_{im} and c_{ic}, denote the estimated execution time of T_{im} and T_{ic}.
- τ_{im} and τ_{ic}, denote the executed time of T_{im} and T_{ic}.

At the moments of t_0, the tasks in the real-time system can be divided into the following three status:

-Running task, which has obtained the CPU.
-Ready task, which is already in the scheduling queue but waits the CPU.
-Waiting task, this is not in the scheduling queue although it has arrived.

2.2   Urgency Analysis

When there are many tasks which are ready to execute, a task T_i might be more urgency if the valid time, $D_i - t_0$, for the task is much closer to its rest execution time $c_i - \tau_i$. Under this situation, if no other tasks are compete the system resources with T_i, T_i will theoretically be sure to commit even though $D_i - t_0$ equals $c_i - \tau_i$. However, if the workload of the system is high, T_i might be abort by other higher priorities tasks although $D_i - t_0$ is long. Therefore, not only the time attributes of a task but also the workload of the system can affect the scheduling of the task. In order to evaluate the affection of workload on the concrete real-time tasks, we define the relative execution urgency of a real-time task, and discuss the relationship between the chance to execute compensatory task and it.

Suppose the set of ready tasks in the system is denoted by $TR = \{T_1, T_2, .., T_n\}$. For a task T_i with deadline being D_i, the set of the tasks whose deadlines are less than D_i is denoted by $TKR_{<j} = \{Tk_i \mid Tk_i \in TKR \wedge D_i \le D_j \wedge Tk_i \ne Tk_j\}$.

Definition 1. *At the moment of* t_0, *the total time that is necessary to execute the tasks including* D_i *and* $TR_{<i}$ *during the period from* t_0 *to* D_i *can be calculated by* $(\sum_{T_j \in TR_{<i}} (c_j - \tau_j)) + (c_i - \tau_i)$. *The urgency of* T_i *is defined as the following formula:*

$$LU(T_i, t_0) = \frac{(\sum_{T_j \in TR_{<i}} (c_j - \tau_j)) + (c_i - \tau_i)}{D_i - t_0} \tag{1}$$

Where $D_i - t_0$ *denotes the available time in the system.*

2.3   Urgency Analysis with Overload

Theorem 1. *At the moment* t_0, *if there is* $LU_{T_i} > 1$, *then* LU_{T_i} *will increase as* T_i *waits more time.*

Proof. Suppose the urgency of T_i is $LU(T_i, t_0) = \frac{(\sum_{T_j \in TR_{<i}} (c_j - \tau_j)) + (c_i - \tau_i)}{D_i - t_0}$ at the moment t_0, and T_i have waited x time units to the moment $t_0 + x (t_0 + x < D_i)$. Next we will discuss the relationship between LU_{T_i} and x by considering the following two situations:

- Firstly, we suppose no new task arrives during the period from t_0 to $t_0 + x (t_0 + x < D_i)$, and during the x time units, $y (0 \le y \le x)$ time units are spent to execute the tasks in TR_{T_i}. Obviously, at the moment $t_0 + x$, the urgency of T_i, $LU(T_i, t_0 + x) = \frac{(\sum_{T_j \in TR_{<i}} (c_j - \tau_j)) + (c_i - \tau_i) - y}{D_i - t_0 - x}$.

Let $a = D_i - t_0$, $b = \sum_{T_j \in TR_{<i}} (c_j - \tau_j) + (c_i - \tau_i)$, and $f(x) = \frac{b - y}{a - x}$.

Distinctly, there are $a > x > 0, b > y > 0$. Therefore $f(x) = \dfrac{b-y}{a-x} > 0$, and

$f'(x) = \dfrac{b-y}{(a-x)^2} > 0$. And then $f(x)$ is an increasing function on x, that is

also to say that the urgency of T_i, LU, will increase with x increasing.

- Secondly, suppose some new tasks whose deadlines are less than D_i will be

added in the ready task queue. As a result the value of $\sum\limits_{T_j \in TR_{<i}} c_j - \tau_j$ will increase.

Based on the analysis in the first situation, no matter how many time are spent to execute the tasks in TR_{T_i}, the urgency of T_i will increase as x increases.

According to the analysis of above two situations, we can conclude that LU_{T_i} will

increase as the waiting time of T_i increases.

Obviously, not all the tasks whose deadlines are less than D_i can successfully execute before their deadlines if the urgency of T_i, LU_{T_i}, is greater than 1. In other words, some tasks must abort, and higher the LU is, more possible a task is to abort. If $LU(T_i)$ is greater than a given threshold $\mu\,(\mu > 1)$, the system can choose to abort the main task, $T_{\min}$, in $TR_{<i}$ with the lowest priority. If $T_{\min}$ has started to executed, the Compensatory task of $T_{\min}$ should be added into the scheduling queue at the same time.

2.4   Urgency Analysis with Underload

Theorem 2. *At the moment t_0, if the urgency of T_i, $LU_{T_i} \leq 1$, and no new task is added in the scheduling queue during the following $x(0 < x < D_i - t_0 - (c_i - T_i))$ time units, moreover the x time units are spent to execute the tasks in $TR_{<i}$, then the urgency of T_i is reduced as x increases.*

Proof. At the moment t_0, there is $LU(T_i, t_0) = \dfrac{(\sum\limits_{T_j \in TR_{<i}} (c_j - \tau_j)) + (c_i - \tau_i)}{D_i - t_0} \leq 1$.

Because no new task arrives in the following $x(0 < x < D_i - t_0 - (c_i - T_i))$ time units, and all the x time units are spent to execute the tasks in TR_{T_i}, so the urgency of

T_i at the moment $t_0 + x$ will be $LU(T_i, t_0 + x) = \dfrac{(\sum\limits_{T_j \in TR_{<i}} (c_j - \tau_j)) + (c_i - \tau_i) - x}{D_i - t_0 - x}$.

Let $a = D_i - t_0$, $b = \sum\limits_{T_j \in TR_{<i}} (c_j - \tau_j) + (c_i - \tau_i)$, and there is $. b < a$ because

$LU(T_i) < 1$.

Let $f(x) = \dfrac{b-x}{a-x} > 0$, it is easy to prove that $f(x)$ is a decreasing function as x increases. Therefore, the proposition given in Theorem 2 is proven.

According to the Theorem 2, the system has enough time to accomplish all the tasks in TR_{T_i} if the urgency of T_i, LU_{T_i}, is less than 1, and the LU_{T_i} will further reduced if the tasks in $TR_{\prec i}$ are continuously executed. Under such situation, it is not necessary to schedule the compensatory task of a main task in advance.

Theorem 3. *At the moment* t_0, *if the urgency of* T_i, $LU(T_i) \leq 1$, *and no new task is added in the scheduling queue during the following* $x(0 < x < D_i - t_0 - (c_i - T_i))$ *time units, and the x time units are spent to execute the tasks beyond* $TR_{\prec i}$, *then the urgency of* T_i *is increased as* x *increases.*

Proof. At the moment t_0, there is $LU(T_i, t_0) = \dfrac{(\sum\limits_{T_j \in TR_{\prec i}} (c_j - \tau_j)) + (c_i - \tau_i)}{D_i - t_0} \leq 1$.

Because no new task arrives in the following $x(0 < x < D_i - t_0 - (c_i - T_i))$ time units, and all the x time units are spent to execute the tasks beyond TR_{T_i}, so the

urgency of T_i at the moment $t_0 + x$ will be $LU(T_i, t_0 + x) = \dfrac{(\sum\limits_{T_j \in TR_{\prec i}} (c_j - \tau_j)) + (c_i - \tau_i)}{D_i - t_0 - x}$.

Let $a = D_i - t_0$, $b = \sum\limits_{T_j \in TR_{\prec i}} (c_j - \tau_j) + (c_i - \tau_i)$, and there is . $b < a$ because

$LU(T_i) < 1$.

Let $f(x) = \dfrac{b}{a - x} > 0$, it is easy to prove that $f(x)$ is a decreasing function as x increases. Therefore, the proposition given in Theorem 2 is proven.

3   Occasion Analysis for Scheduling Compensating Transaction

In the real-time system supporting compensatory tasks, for a main task containing a compensatory task, if it is abort without accomplish its execution, then it is essential to execute its compensatory task to eliminate the incomplete result caused by the main task, or else a disastrous error will be brought into the system. In order to make sure a compensatory task higher priorities than can start to executed. However, when a compensatory task joins into the schedule queue? In the following context, we will discuss this problem based on the analysis on the urgency of a task.

For any a task T_i, it is more possible to miss its deadline if the task is more urgent. If T_i is a main task, it should be early to schedule its compensatory task in order to keep the consistent of the real-time system. Moreover, if T_i is a compensatory task, it should be started to process as soon as possible. Because the estimate execution time, c_i, of T_i is the worst case execution time, and it is usually longer than the real execution time. Therefore, the real-time system allows that the system workload can be bigger than 1, but less than a given threshold $\mu(0 < \mu < 1)$ in order to ensure the successful execution ratio.

Suppose the set of the ready tasks is $TR = \{T_1, T_2, .., T_n\}$, and the tasks in TR are sorted in the ascending order on the tasks deadlines. For a task T_i with deadline D_i, $TR_{\prec i}$ is the set of the tasks whose deadlines are less than D_i, and $TR_{\prec i}$ is exact the tasks that are before T_i in TR. According to the urgency, $LU(T_i)$, of the T_i in TR, we can schedule the tasks based on the following two strategies.

- *If $LU(T_i) \leq \mu$, the CPU time is plenty to execute the tasks in $TR_{\prec i}$. In other words, the task can accomplish with high probability. According to the Theorem 2, it is unnecessary to start the compensatory task when a main task is executing.*
- *However, if $LU(T_i) > \mu$, then some of the tasks in $TR_{\prec i}$, will be abort due to they can not compete the system resources. According to the Theorem1, we can abort the task with lowest priorities. Suppose $T_{\min}$ is exact the task to be abort, and it has already started to execute. If there is a compensatory task $T_{\min c}$ for $T_{\min}$, then we must execute $T_{\min c}$ to keep the consistent of the system. However, if $LU(T_{\min c}) < 1$, then $T_{\min c}$ can be postponed to execute till $LU(T_{\min c}) = 1$ according to Theorem 3.*

According to the urgency analysis of the tasks, we present the following scheduling algorithm based on the execution urgency of the tasks and the workload.

Algorithm: SASCT: The scheduling algorithm supporting compensatory task

```
Input:  Pri(T_i): the priority of task T_i
        μ : the threshold of urgency
        TR_<i : the set of tasks whose deadlines are less
               than T_i's deadline
for T_i in TR_<i do
     calculate the urgency, LU(T_i) according to formula
1;
     while LU(T_i) > μ do
        Select the task, T_min , with the lowest priority
        from TR_<i;
        Abort T_min based on Theorem 1;
        if T_min has a compensatory task T_minc then
           calculate the urgency, LU(T_minc)
           if LU(T_minc) ≥ 1 then
              Schedule T_minc immediately;
           else
              Postpone to execute T_minc till LU(T_minc) ≥ 1
              according to Theroem 3;
```

```
            end
        end
    end
    Select the task with highest priority in TR_{<i} and
        schedule it;
end
```

4   Experiment

In this section, we report the results of our performance study. We first describe our experimental setup, and then present our results.

4.1   Experimental Setup

All of our experiments are performed on a PC with a Dual-Core 3.2GHz processor, 2GB of main memory, and running Windows XP. All program are written in Visual C++. The parameters in the experiments are set as follows.

- The worst execute time, c_i, of task T_i is calculated with the formula[6] $p_i = N * c_i / L$, in which, N denotes the number of the tasks in the system, L denotes the desired workload of the system.
- The relative deadline of an instance of a task equals the period of the task.
- The probability that a main task has a compensatory task is about to te 0.1.
- The worst execute time, c_{ci} of a compensatory task is randomly generated from 1 to 3.
- The deadline of a compensatory task is calculated with the formula $D_i + c_{ci} * \lceil L + 1 \rceil$, where D_i is the deadline of the main task.

In the simulation, two priorities of EDF[4] and LSF[5] are used in the SASCT algorithm, and we can have two scheduling algorithms EDF-SASCT and LSF-SASCT. We compare them with the EDF and LSF methods, and report the performance of the miss deadline ration, MDR.

4.2   Performance Results

Firstly, we study the performance of MDR on different μ. In the experiments, the number of the tasks is set to be N=20, the workload of the system is about 1.5, and the threshold μ is range from 1.0 to 2.0. The experimental results is shown in Figure 1.

Obviously, the performance of the EDF-SASCT and LSF-SASCT methods are much better than the EDF and LSF as the threshold μ is less than the workload of the system, L, of the system is above 1.0, some tasks will miss their deadline. If the threshold μ is less than L, some tasks with lower priorities will be aborted by the SASCT algorithm, which can ensure the deadlines of the tasks with higher priorities. However, if the value of μ is greater than the workload, the SASCT has no attribution to the system performance.

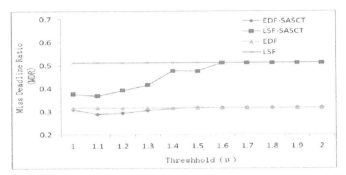

Fig. 1. The MDR of our method based on LSF and EDF on threshold μ

Secondly, we study the performance of MDR as the workload varies by six sets of experiments. In the experiments, the number of the tasks is 5, and the workload of the system ranges from 0.5 to 3.0. Under the situation with a given workload six possible values of the threshold μ are used, and we study the MDR of the system.

As shown in the Figure 2 and Figure 3, the MSRs is near 0 as the workload is less than 1, but they increase as the workload is added. Under the situations with same workload, the MDRs as $\mu < L$ is prior to those as $\mu > L$.

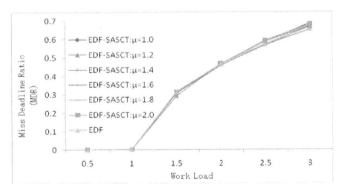

Fig. 2. The MDR of EDF with different thresholds μ

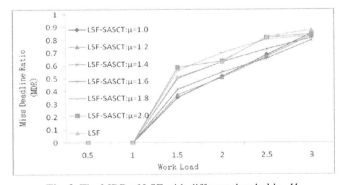

Fig. 3. The MDR of LSF with different thresholds μ

5   Conclusion

In this paper, we discuss the relative execute urgency of the real-time tasks in a real-time database system, and study the relationship between the urgency and waiting time of a task. Based on the analysis on the urgency and workload, we present the scheduling strategy supporting compensatory task. In the strategy, a threshold μ is used to make sure the successful execute ratio of the tasks. The experimental results showed that the scheduling strategy that supports compensatory task can reduce the missing deadline ration of the real time database system.

Acknowledgments. This work was partly supported by National Natural Science Foundation of China under Grant No.60763002, and the Natural Science Foundation of Jiangxi Province of China under Grant No. 2008GZS0021.

References

1. Nagy, S., Bestavros, A.: Admission control for soft-deadline transactions in ACCORD. In: Proceedings of the 3rd IEEE Real-Time Technology and Applications Symposium, Montreal, Canada, pp. 160–165 (1997)
2. Nagy, S., Bestavros, A.: Value-cognizant admission control for RTDB systems. In: Proceedings of the 17th IEEE Real-Time Systems Symposium, Washington D. C., USA, p. 230 (1996)
3. Xia, J.: IACM: An Admission Control Mechanism for Embedded Real-Time Database Systems. Chinese Journal of Computers 27(3), 295–301 (2004)
4. Haritsa, J.R., Livny, M., Carey, M.J.: Earliest deadline scheduling for real-time database systems. In: Proceedings of the12th IEEE Real-time Systems Symposium, pp. 232–243. IEEE Computer Society Press, Los Alamitos (1991)
5. Semghouni, S., Amanton, L., Sadeg, B., et al.: On new scheduling policy for the improvement of firm RTDBSs performances. Data & Knowledge Engineering 63(2), 414–432 (2007)
6. Buttazzo, G., Spuri, M., Sensini, F.: Value VS. deadline scheduling in overload conditions. In: Proc. of the 16th IEEE Real-Time Systems Symp., pp. 90–99. IEEE Computer Society Press, Los Alamitos (1995)

Intelligent Vehicle Monitoring System Based 3G

Wencang Zhao and Junxin Wang

College of Automation and Electronic Engineering,
Qingdao University of Science and Technology, Qingdao 266042, P.R. China

Abstract. This paper introduces the design of intelligent public transportation vehicle monitoring system on 3G network. A chip Hi3512 using ARM9 as its core is adopted as the system's control unit. The hardware and software design was introduced. The system through GPS module to collects the longitude, latitude, angle, velocity and other real-time information as well as voice files and configuration files stored in the SD card in order to achieve bus stop automatic function. At the same time, using 3G communication module to build a real-time video monitoring system to meet the needs of the intelligent bus, and has a good application prospect.

Keywords: 3G, Hi3512, Video monitoring, GPS.

1   Introduction

City public transportation is the main body of city passenger transport system, is the important infrastructure related to people's production and life,is beneficial to the people's livelihood, social welfare services. Bus travel is the main public transport. Commonly used automatic report station device is controlled by a manually semi automatic voice broadcast system[1,2,3], requires the driver to complete a variety of information broadcast. And bus in and out of the station is the most complex period of driving.This moment requires drivers concentrate on driving more carefully. The semi automatic broadcasting system have many problems,like the station broadcast is not accurate, exist hidden safety problems and etc[4,5]. The process of taking a bus may happen unpleasant things such as robbery, theft, bad bus service and so on. All of these things will give people great spirit hurt and property loss. In order to solve the problem, we will use automatic report station and add video monitoring[6,7] in the intelligent bus system. The video stream through the 3g module sent to the server real-time, it can be stored for a long time.

This paper adopts Hi3512 chip[8] as main control chip, through the serial port and GPS module for real-time communication, receiving bus location and direction data. When the bus get into a set range, the bus horn reporting station to remind passengers to prepare accordingly. At the same time, through the CCD camera to collect the video image data compression, then through 3G/Internet network transmission, completion of the bus network video monitoring task.

2   The Composition of the System

The intelligent public transportation vehicle monitoring system is mainly composed by the global positioning system, vehicle terminal, 3G/Internet network and monitoring

M. Zhao and J. Sha (Eds.): ICCIP 2012, Part I, CCIS 288, pp. 552–559, 2012.

center(Fig.1).Bus driving, vehicle terminal through the GPS module acquisition of GPS data automatic, and compared with the key information stored of the bus lines, then broadcast the bus station information automatic. At the same time the bus GPS positioning information, state information is sent to the monitoring center through 3G network, to realize the real-time monitoring of bus ,dispatching center can through the monitoring center get the monitoring data,and sent real-time dispatching informationto to the public transport vehicles,dispatching information can be displayed in the LCD screen.

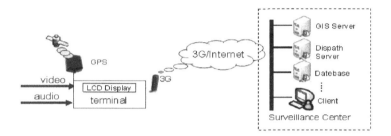

Fig. 1. Block diagram of the whole system

3   System Hardware Design

Hardware platform using the Hi3512 of multimedia chip as main control chip, the chip is a high performance communication media processor which based on a ARM9 processor core and video hardware acceleration engine, it has the advantages of high integration, programmable, support for H.264, MJPEG protocol and etc. The peripheral circuit mainly includes GPS module, 3G module, video and audio module, a network module, a storage module, power supply module, LCD display module and a reset module.The principle of the system shown in Fig. 2.

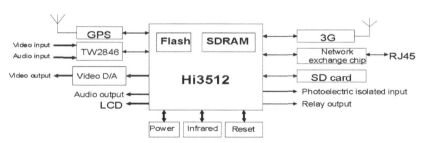

Fig. 2. The principle of the system

3.1   GPS Module

GPS module uses NEO-6M to accept the GPS satellite signal, and calculates the bus position. GPS module send positioning coordinate to the CPU via a serial port . CPU can also send settings commands to GPS module ,then control GPS module state and working. GPS module need special GPS antenna accept GPS satellite signal to the accurate positioning.

3.2   3G Module

3G communication module uses ZTE MC8630, support 1 x/EVDO Rev-A module terminal, voice, SMS, high speed data transmission, also support rate, download 3.1 Mbps, upload 1.8 Mbps. This module is the tie to vehicle terminal with backend server. Vehicle terminal build a wireless connection between the MC8630 and backstage communication server. When wireless connection channel established, vehicle terminal need to keep real-time 3G communications link. According to the monitoring scheduling system or other related application function needs to complete vehicle terminal and background system message interaction. Through the 3G network transmission video signal, to complete bus real-time monitoring and bus situation tracing, ensure transportation safety operation .

3.3   Video and Audio Module

The module use techwell TW2864 chip, which includes four high quality NTSC/PAL video decoder. It can convert analog composite video signal into a digital signal and take the signal input to the Hi3512. Hi3512 receives the video data, then H.264 video encoding after image processing. The TW2864 includes an audio codec, and the audio codec has a four audio ADC and an audio DAC. In order to playback received digital input, a built-in audio controller for recording / mixing to generates a digital output.

3.4   Network Module

RJ45 Ethernet module is used to realize the function of communication between chip inside and outside, which include two 10/100 Mbit/s Ethernet port, achieve non-blocking packet exchange between the two external port and CPU port .

3.5   LCD Display Module

LCD panel is the interactive window between bus driver and bus terminal.This paper choose 128 * 64 resolution screen, could display the command information which from center's dispatch in LCD screen in the way of text,and stored for future reference. LCD can also display speaker volume, GPS signals, text messaging information, the bus transit site information and the stops information, operation speed, the day of the operation mileage and other related informations.

3.6   Other Parts

The 12V power supply through the DC-DC conversion circuit output 5V. After the DC-DC circuit switching 5V converted to 3.3V, 1.8V and 1.2V chip for other use.The SDcard as the storage medium is more convenient. 32G storage space can be stored within a week of bus video data. All the reset source, first be choosed by CPLD reset logical, then CPLD reset logic output reset signal, each part of the system reset.

4   System Software Design

Linux system has the following advantages: 1 the open source code, has a rich software information; 2 the real-time performance of the system is high; 3 the system size, functions can be customized; 4.Support a large number of peripheral hardware equipment, drive rich; 5.support a variety of architectures. In this paper the software design is adopted on the embedded Linux operating system. the software of this system include video capture, video transmission,automatic report station and other modules.

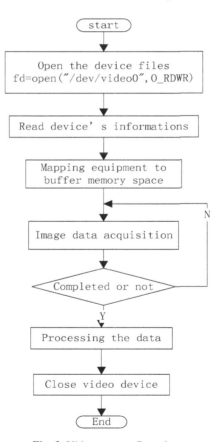

Fig. 3. Video capture flow chart

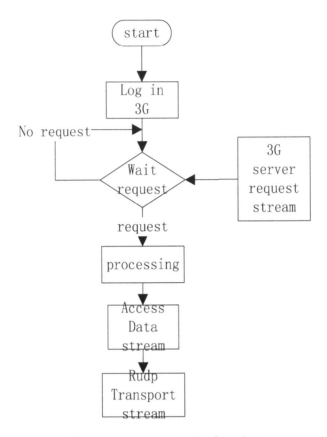

Fig. 4. 3G video transmission flow chart

4.1   Video Capture Module

Video Capture mainly uses the API interface,which is a uniform video equipment provided by a Linux system for video capture:video 4 linux (for short V4L).In V4L, video equipment was seen as a file. The camera in the system corresponding device file is /dev/video0. Using open function to open the equipment: fd =open("/dev/video0", O_RDWR). After opening the equipment, you can set this video equipment attribute and collecting method, etc. This paper uses ioctl function to manage the device I/O channels: ioctl(fd, int request ...).The first use VIDIOC_REQBUFS to obtain the cache and by calling the VIDIOC_QUERYBUF command to obtain the address of the cache.Then use the mmap function to convert the absolute address of the application, finally put this into the cache buffer queue.Circulating capture of video, and take the collection video to process.

4.2   Video Transmission Module

In the intelligent public transportation vehicle monitoring system,3G technology provides support for video monitoring of wireless transmission. The advantage of convenient, quick ,provides a high rate, high quality images for the transmission. The main processes of video transmission has shown in Figure 4. During transmission process, we use RUDP(Reliable User Datagram Protocol). As a reliable transport protocol, by using C++ to rdp portocol of Packaging. RUDP_RegInfoCallBack registered callback function can realize the dynamic data stream. Implementation: call the interface of NETDVR_Auto_BitRate

```
void DealInfo(struct RUDP_Info_Pkt_t *pInfoPkt, unsigned int
context)
{
NETDVR_Auto_BitRate(g_hdev, pInfoPkt);
}
```

In the RUDP transmission process, system will record the loss situation of the send packet. The packet loss situation back to the sender to control the increase or decrease the data stream. At the same time, the receiver registered callback function RUDP_RegLossCallBack will process the lost frames, to complete the RUDP packet decoding(Fig.5).

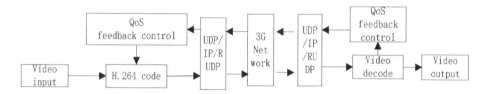

Fig. 5. Rudp video transmission block diagram

4.3   Automatic Report Station Module

The main work of automatic report station module is to realize GPS information receiving and processing. SD card is used to read and write. LCD screen is used to display.SD card has the advantages of large memory capacity, convenient use and low prices, we put the bus stop voice files, configuration files stored on SD cards, so we can later use and line upgrades working.

The automatic report station process generally is: through the GPS module receives the longitude and latitude information, compare with the station's latitude and longitude information where stored in the SD card, if consistent, sent MP3 file to the player for playing, while in the LCD screen to display the corresponding station number, station name and uplink & downlink information, so as to realize the automatic bus automatic report station functions. System flow chart shown in Fig. 6.

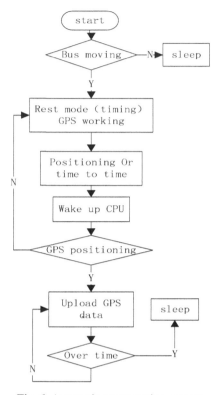

Fig. 6. Automatic report station process

5   The End

In this paper, we presents the overall design scheme of the vehicle monitoring system, also introduced the system hardware platform and the software design, put video monitoring and automatic report station system together, through the 3G wireless network ensures real-time data transmission of the intelligent public transportation vehicle monitoring system . With 3G network used more widely , the development of intelligent bus station systems were about to step a new phase,vehicle monitoring system will be more widely used in bus dispatching, real-time monitoring and other fields. It has a certain application prospect.

References

1. Wu, G., Zhang, X.: Design of locomotive supervisory system based on MiniARM9080. Application of Electronic Technique 35(6) (2009)
2. Zhu, C.: Design and Implementation of Network Camera Based on ARM. Chengdu University of Technology (June 2010)

3. Forouzan, B.A.: Data Communications and Networking. Tsinghua University Press, Beijing (2001)
4. Zhang, W., Zeng, L., Yao, N.: Vehicle terminal monitoring system based on GPS/GPRS. Computer Aided Engineering 17(4) (2008)
5. Chen, W., Li, B.: Study on GPS signal acquisition and processing based on ARM-linux platform. Microcomputer & Its Applications, 41–44 (2009)
6. Chen, B., Yang, B.: Design and Implementation of Wireless Video Monitoring on Vehicle. Journal of Changchun University of Science and Technology (Natural Science Edition), 128–130 (2011)
7. Cao, Y., Wu, Y., Zhao, Y., Wu, Y.: Design and implementation of video surveillance system based on Hi3511 chip. Computer Engineering and Design, 4592–4595 (2009)
8. HI3512 Linux Development environment user guide, Hisilicon Technology Company (2008)

Life Signal Noise Reduction on Wavelet Theory

Zhai Xiao-jun[1] and Jiang Chuan[2]

[1] Engineering University of CAPF, Xi'an, 710086, China
[2] Air Force Engineering University, Xi'an, 710038, China

Abstract. Wavelet method is used to de-noise life signal, and according to relevant theory,Through large amount of simulation experiments, contrast the results of using different wavelet to break down life signal, get a conclusion which is bior5.5 wavelet is the best wavelet, and according to the signal velocity and the frequency range of life signal, ascertain that wavelet is broken down 5 layer. And bior5.5 wavelet and fixed threshold method is selected to de-noise life signal. Finally, through experiments, simulate the effect of wavelet noise reduction, simulation results show that, wavelet method can effectively remove noise in life signal, meanwhile keep the details of life signal characteristics.

Keywords: Wavelet Noise Rduction, Life Signal, Simulation.

1   Introduction

In recent years, with the ultra-wideband radar detection technology development, advanced digital signal processing method is widely applied in the life signal detection processing field, such as Fourier analysis theory, narrowband digital filtering technology, independent component analysis technology, neural network technology, homomorphic filter technology, adaptive algorithm (LMS algorithm), and the wavelet analysis technology, These methods in life signal detection processing field which has received extensive attention has been thorough researched, And the application of wavelet theory in the life signal noise reduction, can do a better job in filtering the signals of life, which plays an important role in the further development of life detection technology.

2   The Basic Principle of Wavelet Noise Reduction

The wavelet de-noising is an important one in the field of wavelet application, comparing with Fourier transform de-noising, wavelet de-noising is more suitable for non-stationary signal, and it can remove the noise in the signal effectively, while retaining the original signal for more details.

Wavelet filtering method is mainly divided into Bayesian and non-Bayesian method, and non-Bayesian methods can be divided into three types: modulus maxima reconstruction filtering, spatial correlation filtering and wavelet threshold filtering. The modular maximum reconstruction filtering and spatial correlation filtering which need large amount of calculation, are not suitable for real-time applications, but generally used during later non-real-time signal processing. The wavelet threshold filtering

M. Zhao and J. Sha (Eds.): ICCIP 2012, Part I, CCIS 288, pp. 560–567, 2012.
© Springer-Verlag Berlin Heidelberg 2012

which need small amount calculation can filter well, and is suitable for low SNR signals. So we choose wavelet threshold de-noising algorithm for the life signal.

The wavelet transform has concentrating ability. Generally, during the wavelet transformation, the wavelet coefficient of useful signals is large, and the energy is concentrated; the wavelet coefficient of decomposed noise is small. According to the signal and noise in wavelet decomposition coefficients, we can suppress noise through the different decomposition level of wavelet coefficient threshold processing. The one which is larger than the threshold coefficient is saved, and the one which is smaller than the threshold coefficient is turn to zero.

3   The Selection of Wavelet Base

The coefficients of wavelet decomposition have great difference by using the different wavelet function for signal decomposition. So we must select the appropriate wavelet function to make the wavelet coefficient of useful decomposed signals is large and the coefficient of decomposed noise signal is small.

Common used wavelet basis have Harr, daubachies, coiflets, bi-orthgonal and so on. In order to select the suitable wavelet basis function, we experiment with the MATLAB simulation environment. The Harr wavelet is generally used for theoretical study, so we do not consider it. Put db5, sym5, coif2, boir5.5 four kinds of wavelet in to contrast. First construct two groups of signals: life signal $s(t)$ and Gauss white noise signal $n(t)$; then use four different wavelet basis decompose the the life signal and noise signal in 5 layers; finally compare with the energy of the wavelet coefficients. Results are as follows.

Table 1. Four wavelet analyzed signal contrast

wavelet basis	db5	sym5	coif2	bior5.5
Length of filter	10	10	12	9/11 *
Signal energy	6.870	7.007	6.863	6.343
noise energy	1.209	1.357	1.317	0.881
signal-to-noise ratio	5.682	5.163	5.210	7.199

* The length of decomposition low-pass and reconstruction high-pass filter are 9, and the length of decomposition high-pass and reconstruction low-pass filter is 11.

From the contrast in Table 1, the signal energy decomposed by sym5 wavelet is the biggest, but at the same time the decomposed noise energy is also the biggest, so the signal-to-noise ratio is not high; the db5 and coif2 wavelet decomposition results were similar, but the noise energy of db5 wavelet basis is small, so the signal-to-noise ratio is slightly higher than that of coif2 wavelet; the spline bi-orthogonal wavelet decomposition of bior5.5 signals derived from energy minimization, but its decomposition noise signal gains energy far less than other types of wavelet, so it received the highest signal-to-noise ratio.

4   Determination of Decomposition Level

The ultra-wide band through-wall detection radar signal sampling frequency is 100Hz.The Doppler signals produced by human breathing and heartbeat is in [0, 4] Hz. And Doppler signals produced by breathing frequency is the major part, concentrated on [0.1, 0.4] Hz.

If the the frequency band of the zeroth layer (signal) is L, then after the N layers wavelet decomposition, the low frequency band is in $[0, L/2^N]$, and the high frequency band is in $[L/2^N, L/2^{N-1}]$. The Doppler signals which are produced by Human breathing and heartbeat are concentrated within 2Hz. In order to remove the noise effectively, we need to decompose the signals lower than 2Hz into a separated low frequency sub-band, then quantize the threshold of the coefficient of the other high frequency sub-band wavelet in order to remove noise signal. Because low frequency component of the target signal frequency band is [0, 50 / 25] Hz, about [0, 1.56] Hz by 5 layers decomposition, and according to the signal sampling frequency ,the decomposition level is identified as the 5 layers.

5   The Selection of Threshold Function

There are two kinds of threshold function named hard threshold function and soft threshold function. The basic idea is to remove the small coefficient and shrink or keep the large coefficient. By hard threshold function, we compare wavelet coefficient absolute value with the threshold value, turn the absolute value which is less than or equal to the threshold into zero, and keep the one which is greater than the threshold ;by soft threshold function, we turn the absolute value which is less than the threshold into zero, and turn the one which is greater than the threshold into the D-value of coefficient and the threshold.

Expressions are as follows:

Hard threshold

$$\hat{\theta}_{j,i} = \begin{cases} 0, & |\omega_{j,i}| \leq t \\ \omega_{j,i}, & |\omega_{j,i}| > t \end{cases}$$

Soft threshold

$$\hat{\theta}_{j,i} = \begin{cases} 0, & |\omega_{j,i}| \leq t \\ \text{sgn}(\omega_{j,i})(|\omega_{j,i}| - t), & |\omega_{j,i}| > t \end{cases}$$

In which $\omega_{j,i}$ is the coefficients of wavelet decomposition, t is the threshold, $\hat{\theta}_{j,i}$ is wavelet coefficients after threshold processing, the sgn ( ) is function for symbols. If the wavelet coefficients distribute in [- 1, 1], the threshold is 0.4, and the results of using soft threshold and hard threshold processing as shown in figure 1.

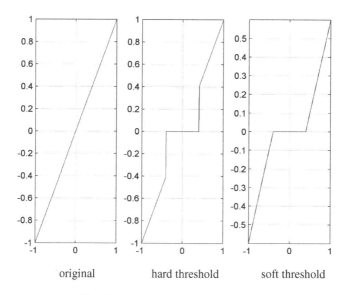

original   hard threshold   soft threshold

Fig. 1. Hard threshold and soft threshold

Experimental results show that, we obtain results from using the hard threshold to process signal are more rough than other ways, but we can obtain smoother signal from using soft threshold to process signal, and can more reserved the details of the signal components, so which is more suitable for more signal detail component. Because the life signal concentrates in the low frequency, which is harmonic signal of the breathing and heartbeat frequency, we need as much as possible to retain the details of the signal components, so we use the soft threshold method to process the detail component of wavelet coefficients. After wavelet decomposition, life signal frequency band is located on the fifth level approximation component sub-band, then use the soft threshold method to process 1-5 layer detail component of wavelet coefficients, finally make reconstruction to wavelet, receive the signals after noise reduction.

6   The Optimal Parameter Combination

In order to obtain the best noise reduction effect, we need to choose suitable wavelet and combination of threshold selection rule , and in order to compare the effect of reducing noise in the use of different wavelet bases and different combination of threshold rules, we define of mean square error

$$error = \sqrt{\frac{1}{N}\sum_{n}(f_d(n) - f(n))^2}$$

In which $f_d(n)$ is the de-noised signal, $f(n)$ does not add noise to the signal, N is signal.

Mean square *error* measures the degree of similarity of the de-noised signal and original signal. Error is smaller, which illustrates the de-noised signal more faithful to the original signal, which is means, *error* is better noise reduction effect. in order to select the best wavelet basis function and the combination of threshold principle, we select db5, sym5, coif2, bior5.5 as the wavelet basis function, rigrsure , heursure , sqtwolog and minimaxi as threshold selection rules, and combine and test the wavelet basis function and threshold principle. Signal noise intensity estimation uses the first layer of wavelet coefficients to make single estimation. On the base of the combination of wavelet and threshold selection principle, we get 16 kinds of method of the noise reduction, and after 1000 times of repeated experiments, the mean square error comparison is the table below:

Table 2. Different wavelet radix and threshold principle de-noise effect

	Db5	sym5	coif2	bior5.5
rir	0.091	0.090	0.092	0.085
heu	0.084	0.084	0.086	0.083
sqt	0.084	0.084	0.086	0.083
min	0.086	0.086	0.088	0.085

According to the table, horizontal direction to see, the noise reduction effect of using the way the heursure and the sqtwolog is better than the rigrsure and the minimaxi, and both noise reduction effect is the same, which is because when the SNR is small, the heursure selects the sqtwolog principle, but the computation complexity of the sqtwolog principle is much smaller than the heursure. Vertical direction to see, in different threshold rule, the de-noising effect of the bior5.5 wavelet is better than that of the other three kinds of wavelet. For the two points, to the life signal noise reduction, the best combination is bior5.5 wavelet and fixed threshold principle.

7   Experimental Simulation

In order to test the wavelet noise reduction effect, we make de-noising simulation experiment on the human body life signal. $s(t) = f(t) + \delta e(t)$ is simulation signal, in which $e(t)$ is subject to $N(0,1)$ Gauss white noise, δ is to adjust the signal to noise ratio of the noise weighting coefficient, and $f(t)$ is the simulation of human life signals.

$$f(t) = \cos\{2 * 2\pi / \lambda * [\Delta_1 \sin(2\pi f_1 t) + \Delta_2 \sin(2\pi f_2 t)] \}$$

Respiratory rate $f_1 = 0.23Hz$; Range: $\Delta_1 = 1cm$

Beat frequency $f_2 = 1.2Hz$; Range: $\Delta_2 = 0.1cm$

SNR $SNR = 3dB$

The original signal and added Gauss noise signals are as shown respectively in Figure 2 and figure 3. Firstly, we use bior5.5 wavelet signal to process wavelet decomposition, as shown in figure 4, secondly use the sqtwolog to process wavelet coefficients, the results in figure 5, at last reconstruct the wavelet coefficients, recovery the signal, as in figure 6.

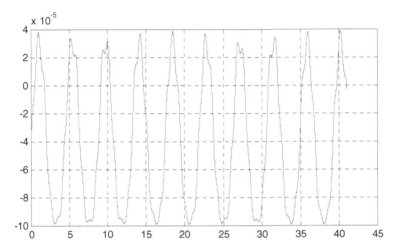

Fig. 2. Original life signal

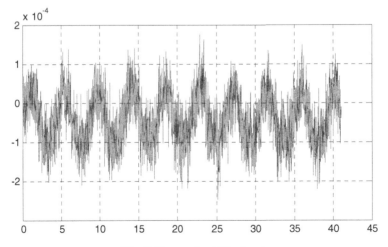

Fig. 3. Yawp mixed life signal

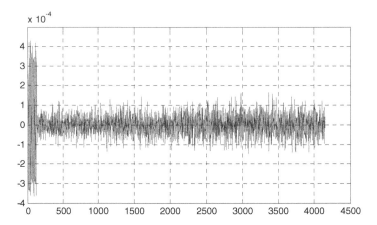

Fig. 4. Yawp mixed life signal wavelet analyze

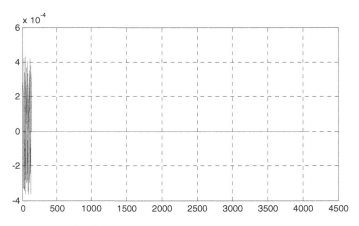

Fig. 5. Wavelet modulus disposed by threshold

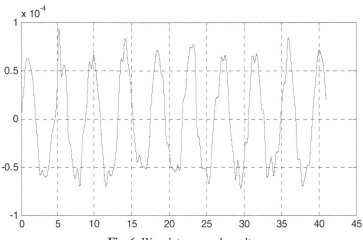

Fig. 6. Wavelet renewed results

We can reach the following conclusion from figure 4-6 wavelet threshold de-noising process:

(1) After the life signal which contains noise decomposed, noise component concentrates in the high-frequency part, the useful signal concentrates in the low frequency part, and the useful signal the amplitude of wavelet coefficient is greater than noise signal.
(2) By choosing appropriate threshold, we can suppress the noise component in the high frequency , and retain the useful signal components of low frequency.
(3) When wavelet coefficients disposed by the threshold are reconstructed, we can restore the original signal better, and achieve the purpose of removing noise.

8   Conclusion

As the increasingly serious situation of the fight against terrorism and emergency rescue, we have very urgent demand for the life detection radar. Life signal filtering technology is an important part of the life detection radar imaging technique, and according to the experimental results, using wavelet de-noising method can keep the original signal in detail, effectively remove the most of noise of life signal, which establish a solid foundation for the further development of the life detection through-wall radar.

References

1. Schalk, G., Kubanek, J., Miller, K.J., et al.: Decoding two- dimensional movement trajectories using electrocortico-graphic signals in humans. J. Neural. Eng. 4(3), 264–275 (2007)
2. Mallat, S.: Theory for multi-resolution signal decomposition:The wavelet representation. IEEE Transactions on Pattern Analysis and Machine Intelligence 11(7), 674–693 (1989)
3. Donoho, D.L.: De-noising by sofl-thresholding. IEEE Trans. on Inf. Theory 41(3), 613–627 (1995)
4. Berkner, K., Wells Jr., R.O.: Wavelet transforms and denoising algorithm. In: Conference Record of the Thirty-Second Asilomar Conference, Signal, System & Computers, pp. 1639–1643 (1998)
5. Pfurtscheller, G., Lopes da Silva, F.H.: Event-related EEG/MEG synchronization and desynchronization: basic principles. Clin. Neurophysiol. 110(11), 1842–1857 (1999)

An Execution Behavior Simulation Framework for Composite Web Service

Xizhe Zhang[1], Peibo Duan[1], Bin Fan[2], Ying Yin[1], and Bin Zhang[1]

[1] College of Information Science and Engineering, Northeastern University,
Shenyang 110819, China
[2] Department of Computer-Based Teaching, Shenyang Institute of Engineering,
Shenyang 110136, China
Zhangxizhe@ise.neu.edu.cn

Abstract. Web service is the major application of distributed computing at present. Dynamic composition and reconstruction of services are main value-added models of service application; however, there is still no useable data of service behavior, which makes it difficult to analysis behavioral characteristic and pattern of service. This paper proposes a simulation framework of service behavior oriented the behavior of service interaction, then research and test the related construction method. It firstly gives the definition of service behavior log and discusses the characteristic and evolution of execution behavior of service composition. And this paper gives the design of the simulation system of service execution behavior. The simulated experiment shows that the platform can provide the basis of data for related research with its effective simulation of large-scale log for dynamic web service interaction.

Keywords: web service, execution behavior, simulation.

1 Introduction

Service oriented computing [1], a new model for distributed computing, has become one of the most popular research at home and abroad. Academia and industry have obtained a lot of achievements through researching issues of the application of service computing such as service composition, service discovery and service selection .

The core concept of service computing is to build a collaborative software system with loose Coupling among interactive services based on SOA architecture, then implement an accrued business logic through service interaction[2]. A number of researchers pay attention for research of service computing from the view of the characteristic in service behavior. To reach the target of effective analysis and the management of business process, WSIM(Web service interaction mining)[3], proposed by Dustdar, obtains the knowledge of service application pattern by process mining and web usage mining. Zhang[4] has researched the description of web service behavior used for studying semantics and the service discovery based on functional semantics. Asbagh[5] gets frequent service interaction sequence by analyzing service log based on the algorithm of sequence mining. K Dong[6] and

M. Zhao and J. Sha (Eds.): ICCIP 2012, Part I, CCIS 288, pp. 568–574, 2012.

other people make Service clustering in order to achieve similarity retrieval based on related information of service parameter obtained from description documents of service.

From the jobs above, it is obvious to find out there is a problem that all of them ignore how to get service behavior and service log. It is particularly difficult to collect and abstract service log because currently there is no practical software system based on service combination. Aimed at solving current problem of the scarcity of service execution data, this paper starts form the following aspects: how to simulate the process that many web services dynamically combine and interactively complete different requirement under the WAN environment. The generated data of service implementation can be regard as the base of research for service data mining. This paper designed and implemented a simulation platform of web service log. The main function of the platform includes simulating the execution of multiple business processes in a period of time, invoking web services to execute business processes which usually described by BPEL language and recording the process in the form of log. This system also provides open interfaces with which users can import the BPEL document. At the same time, the system provides the function of setting parameter, allowing it to generate log records through the parameters set by users according to their requirements. It is convenient for users to extract data with log records saved in text files.

2   Related Concepts

The following are related concepts used in this section.

Definition 1. Web service s is a set composed by a group of operations which can be abstracted as a two-tuples $S = (n, p)$ where n is the name of the service and p is a set of service operations. Operation is the basic function entity of web service. It can be expressed as a two-tuples $p = (I, O)$ where I represents a set of input objects received by operation and O shows a set of output objects generated by operation.

Definition 2. Service execution log denoted by L(P), is the record of implementation process by business P. It records the executive information generated by all instances of actual implementation of operations in the business process P. $L(P) = \{l_1, l_2, ...l_n, ...\}$, l_i is called log entry which indicates the activity information generated by an operation instance in business process. It can be described as a five-tuples $l_i = \{(s_i, t_i, st_i, r_i, p_i) \mid s_i \in S\}$, where:

   s_i indicates the ID of executive service;
   t_i indicates the acquisition time of log entry;
   st_i indicates the execution status of service;
   r_i indicates the role of information in log records of service interaction;
   p_i indicates the parameters delivered in message;

Service execution log is a set of all logs generated from business execution in service space.

Definition 3. Service interaction: The connection of Services on the semantic concept of a business is called as interaction. The interaction between service s_i and s_j is recorded as $s_i \rightarrow s_j$.

Definition 4. Service interaction network: The interaction behavior of service operation is regard as service interaction network if it can be expressed as directed network. In a period of time, service interaction network recorded interaction between different services in service space. It is denoted by $G(S,E)$, where the set of nodes S is a set of services, and the set of edges E is the interaction between services whose direction indicates the timing between services.

   The diagram of service is a directed multi-graph because it is usually performed repeatedly. There is a concept of service community as following according to the systematization of the close relationship between interactive services.

Definition 5. Service community is an organic complex of multiple services with close interactive relationship. It generally complete a common business goal from business Angle, which performances a sub-graph of internal frequent interaction in the service interaction network.

3   The Simulation of Service Interaction Behavior

3.1   The Representation and Preprocessing of Service Data

The log records executive information of interaction among services. Due to the environment of services is a distributed system with loosely coupled, what makes the log lacked information of relative executive order and calling relationship is that service execution engine is just responsible for recording the executive record of interaction among services. Above all, we first preprocess the service log and refactor, calling relationship among services according to the temporal relation of log in order to establish service interaction network.

   The business process can be abstracted as graph. As there may be links between any two nodes caused by complicated graph structure, it can't express the relationship between elements with physical location of data elements in the area of storage, in other words, although graph doesn't have storage structure of sequence image, it can express the relationship between elements with the array of data type. The system in this paper adopts two-dimensional array to store adjacency matrix and stores information of data elements (vertexes) and their relationships (edges or arcs) with two arrays according to the operation of concrete graph and requirement.

   Business process shown in Figure 1 can be described by the BPEL language (Figure 2). its adjacency matrix is shown in Figure 3 which "1" indicates that there is relation between two nodes and"0"indicates opposite. We define two-dimensional array to store adjacency matrix: int bp[][]=new int[a][a]; (a is the number of nodes in business processes).

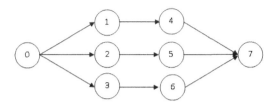

Fig. 1. Business process diagram

```
<?xml version="1.0" encoding="GB2312" ?>
<process id="5">
  <sequence>
    <flow>
         <sequence></sequence>
         <sequence></sequence>
         <sequence></sequence>
    </flow>
  </sequence>
</process>
```

Fig. 2. Business processes described with BPEL language

$$
\begin{bmatrix}
0 & 1 & 1 & 1 & 0 & 0 & 0 & 0 \\
0 & 0 & 0 & 0 & 1 & 0 & 0 & 0 \\
0 & 0 & 0 & 0 & 0 & 1 & 0 & 0 \\
0 & 0 & 0 & 0 & 0 & 0 & 1 & 0 \\
0 & 0 & 0 & 0 & 0 & 0 & 0 & 1 \\
0 & 0 & 0 & 0 & 0 & 0 & 0 & 1 \\
0 & 0 & 0 & 0 & 0 & 0 & 0 & 1 \\
0 & 0 & 0 & 0 & 0 & 0 & 0 & 0
\end{bmatrix}
$$

Fig. 3. Business process described by Adjacency matrix

3.2   The Method for Simulation of Service Behavior

This paper researches and accomplishes a platform which is able to simulate executive environment of web service in wide area network(WAN) and records web service logs. It recorded logs in service execution engine based on centralized structure of service execution engine, and, then spread them out to each web service. Figure 4 shows the generative process of logs. Figure (a) illustrates the process how to simulate service execution engine and generate records of logs in this paper. Figure (b) illustrates a generation method of single record of log.

Firstly, the system imports BPEL documents that describe the concrete business process and converts them to a two-dimensional array. Secondly, we define each business process as a thread and write a random method to set thread startup sequence of threads according to the generation frequency of logs and activate these threads by multi-threading mechanism. Finally, a random method is used to simulate executive time and parameters of each service, then we can get a record of log according to the properties simulated such as IDs of business process, web service, execution time, execution state and parameters.

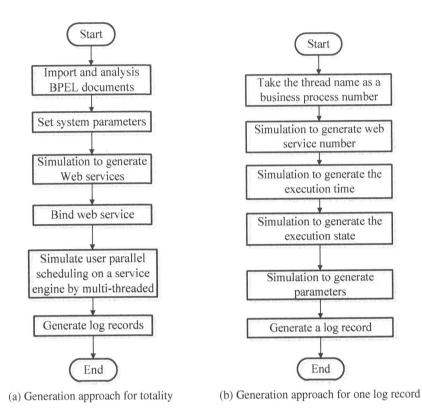

(a) Generation approach for totality   (b) Generation approach for one log record

Fig. 4. Flowchart of generation approach

4   Implementation of System

This section describes concrete implementation mechanism for simulation system of web service log. This system simulates the process of service implementation and change of network environment, and then generates web services log. Firstly, we generate network topology with generation tool of network topology in order to configure dynamic network flow model for network connection among nodes. Then we release service based on the actual service WSDL documents and design the composite process of some services based on the actual business process by manual method. At last we get the service log through service simulation. The class diagram of system is given in Figure 5.

Class Gui is responsible for offering a graphical user interface. It calls method m_Diary in class Gui, then starts the business process to generate log by simulation. Class Diary transfer input parameters in graphical user interface to the bottom program. Class Gui stores the parameters configured in the graphical interface into the database or removes from the database through operations of additions and deletions accomplished by method query and method execute in class odbcConn. Class Diary uses constructor in OperationFlow to activate the Parallel business process to simulate the generation of log records. Class OperationFlow is the central part of this paper which responsible for simulating the generation of log records.

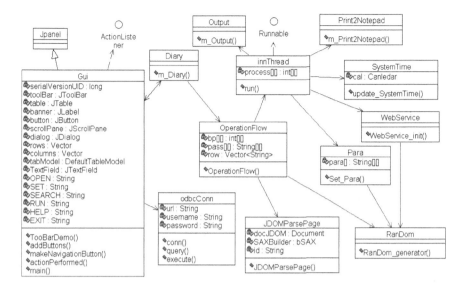

Fig. 5. The class diagram of system

When user configures parameters and clicks the execution button, system dynamically simulate the generation of log records. As shown in Figure 8. We set system time as start time of simulation. Each group of logs is divided into four states to record including Request、Request_tag、Response and Response_tag; State Request and state Response have the same parameter. If there is adjacency relationship between two nodes, the export parameters of previous node should be passed to the entry parameters of next node.

BP_ID	WS_ID	TIME	STATE	PARA
2	11	08-5-11 12:17:56	Request	2023
2	11	08-5-11 12:18:45	Request_tag	www
3	19	08-5-11 12:18:56	Request	militias
1	4	08-5-11 12:19:44	Request	rib
4	13	08-5-11 12:20:05	Request	2022
5	16	08-5-11 12:20:19	Request	2034
2	11	08-5-11 12:20:31	Response	2023
4	13	08-5-11 12:21:04	Request_tag	innocent
3	19	08-5-11 12:22:03	Request_tag	version1 0
2	11	08-5-11 12:22:06	Response_tag	ise
5	16	08-5-11 12:22:38	Request_tag	highlight
1	4	08-5-11 12:22:51	Request_tag	$
2	10	08-5-11 12:23:19	Request	ise
4	13	08-5-11 12:23:58	Response	2022
2	10	08-5-11 12:24:29	Request_tag	get
4	13	08-5-11 12:24:45	Response_tag	pandas
5	16	08-5-11 12:25:07	Response	2034
3	19	08-5-11 12:25:08	Response	militias
4	8	08-5-11 12:25:41	Request	<
1	4	08-5-11 12:25:47	Response	rib
3	19	08-5-11 12:25:59	Response_tag	to
2	10	08-5-11 12:26:08	Response	ise
5	16	08-5-11 12:26:58	Response_tag	like
4	8	08-5-11 12:27:43	Request_tag	Saturday
1	4	08-5-11 12:28:28	Response_tag	2020
5	2	08-5-11 12:29:19	Request	whose

Fig. 6. The log records generated by simulation system

5   Conclusion

Web service is not widely used currently. At the same time, there is no available service log set. In order to better support the web services it is necessary to design a platform which can simulate the execution environment for web service in wide area network factually. It is a centralized architecture based on service execution engine. The main function of platform is to simulate the execution of multiple business processes in a period of time by calling web service in order to execute business processes. At last these processes are recorded in the form of log. This paper introduces the research and implementation of the simulation system of web service log from aspects of analysis, design and implementation of system. The system can provide the basis of data for the research of service through its perfect simulation for the characteristics of web service.

Acknowledgment. This work is sponsored by the Natural Science Foundation of China under grant number 60903009, 61073062, 61100027, 61100028, and the Fundamental Research Funds for the Central Universities under grant number N090104001.

References

1. Huhns, M.N., Singh, M.P.: Service-oriented computing: Key concepts and principles. IEEE Internet Computing 6(1), 75–81 (2005)
2. Zheng, G., Bouguettaya, A.: A Web Service Mining Framework. In: IEEE International Conference on Web Services (ICWS 2007), pp. 1096–1103 (2007)
3. Dustdar, S., Gomboz, R., Baina, K.: Web Services Interaction Mining. Technical Report (2004)
4. Zhang, L.-J., Li, B., Chao, T., Chang, H.: Requirements Driven Dynamic Services Composition for Web Services and Grid Solutions. Journal of Grid Computing 2(2), 121–140 (2004)
5. Asbagh, M.J., Abolhassani, H.: Web service usage mining: mining for executable sequences. In: Proceedings of the 7th Conference on 7th WSEAS International Conference on Applied Computer Science, Venice, Italy, pp. 266–271
6. Dong, X., Halevy, A., Madhavan, J., Nemes, E., Zhang, J.: Similarity Search for Web Services. In: Proceedings of the 30th VLDB Conference, Toronto, Canada, pp. 372–383 (2004)

The Study on Data Mining for Customer Behavior Modeling in Electronic Commerce

Jun Ma

Department of Economics and Business Administration,
LuoYang Institute of Science and Technology,
Luo Yang, China
mj@lit.edu.cn

Abstract. The impact of Internet on consumer behavior and marketing practices is now a major and challenging area of research. Internet offers many choices of products, services and content. But the multitude of choices has altered the manner in which customers choose and buy products and services. The paper is to investigate how different dimensions of consumer perception and consumer attitude may affect behavior in electronic commerce environments using data mining. The aim is to define a conceptual modeling in order to establish the role played by reference groups and social information in the development of these variables.

Keywords: ad hoc networks, Energy consumptions, parameter configurations.

1   Introduction

Nowadays market is characterized by being global, products and services are almost identical and there is an abundance of suppliers. And because of the size and complexity of the markets, mass marketing is expensive (Figure 1) and the returns on investment are frequently questioned. Among the several new situations or possibilities raised by the emergence of Internet is rapid and more expansive communications in a virtual world without face-to-face interaction. Hypothetically, such an environment should facilitate the identification of needs or desires which stimulate consumers first, to search for products or services, and afterwards to purchase them. Indeed, this electronic environment is starting to modify the more traditional perceptions and attitudes that take place in traditional markets.

Instead of aiming all aspects evenly or offering the same attention offers to everyone, a firm can be selected only for those customers who meet certain profitability criteria based on their individual needs and buying patterns. It is useful to build a model to forecast the future value of the consumers based on their demographic characteristics, life-style, and previous behaviors. The information which are produced by the model will focus customers retention and recruitment programs on building and keeping the most profitable customer base. It is called customer behavior modeling (CBM) or customer profiling. A customer profile is a tool to help target marketers better understand the characteristics of their customer base.

M. Zhao and J. Sha (Eds.): ICCIP 2012, Part I, CCIS 288, pp. 575–582, 2012.
© Springer-Verlag Berlin Heidelberg 2012

The role of the customers in this competitive environment becomes ever more considerable since they pass on ideas, impressions or feelings on webs, concentrated in "customers' opinions" or on costumer forums. Furthermore, buyers are, to some extent, at the connector between retailers and consumers, and their presence is highly influential in maintaining the relationship between them. Thus, electronic transactions, while ostensibly economic in function, demands more and more acute and detailed perceptional knowledge, and finely honed social skills. Group influences, such as those associated with belonging to or identifying with a social class, culture or subculture, or reference groups, for instance family and other social groups have been more and more influential in electronic transactions. But the specific details regarding consumer perceptions, attitudes on line have only received little attention.

Fig. 1. Communication with customers, B2B & B2C

The long term analysis of customer's profiles is to convert this understanding into an automated interaction with their customers. For these reasons, it is necessary to use wide ranges of processes and IT tools. These tools have been used to collect data and simplify the process of extracting knowledge about the market and planning marketing campaign. Data mining tools have been used to distinguish meaningful data from the historical database, e.g. define the selection criteria of customer's mailing lists, or to determine if the market still has much potential, or local media and people's living habits of target customers. In brief, data mining tools are able to find human interpretable patterns that describe the data; they also can use some way to forecast unknown values of other variables in future.

In this paper it introduces the way how a data mining system work to describes data and forecast the future value of the variables in electronic commerce transactions.

2   Customer Segmentation and Customer Profiling

Customer relationship management (CRM) includes customer segmentation and customer profiling.

Customer segmentation is a term used to describe the process of dividing customers into homogeneous groups by the conventional attributes (habits, tastes etc.). Customer profiling is the data which describe the customers with their age, income, and lifestyles. It can be done by using a customer's behavior model and setting up its parameters. Customer profiling is the way to apply external data to identify potential customers. By using data available, they can be used to develop new customers or to remove existing bad customers. The aim is to predict behavior of customers based on the information we have on each customer. Profiling is performed after customer segmentation.

Having the two components, the administrator of market can decide which marketing actions to take to allocate scarce resources to segments in order to meet specific business objectives in electronic commerce transactions. (Figure 2).

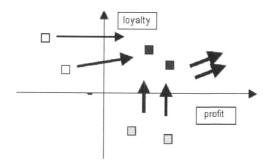

Fig. 2. Segmentation offers to a company a way to know about loyalty and profitability of their customers

2.1   Customer Segmentation

Segmentation is a way to have more targeted communication with the customers. The process of segmentation describes the characteristics of the customer groups (called segments or clusters) within the data. Segmenting means to devide a lot of data into segments according to their similar attributes. Customer segmentation is the preparation work to assort each customer according to the customer groups that have been defined.

Segmentation is very important to deal with today's dynamically fragmenting consumer marketplace. By using it, the marketers are more effective to management of resources and identify opportunities. But difficulties in making segmentation are :

It is very important of quantity, quality and relevance of data to develop meaningful segments. If the company has little customer data or too much data, it can lead a very complicated analysis. If the data is in poor texture (different formats, different source systems) then it is also hard to extract useful information. In addition, the result of the segmentation can be too complicated for the organization to use effectively. In particular, the use of too many segmentation variables can be confusing, resulting in segments which are unfit for management decision making. Alternatively, apparently effective variables may not be identifiable. Many questions are due to lack of enough customer database.

2.2   Customer Profiling

Customer profiling provides a basis for marketers to "communicate" with existing customers in order to offer them better services and retaining them. This is done by assembling collected information on the customer such as demographic and behavioral data. Customer profiling is also used to prospect new customers using external sources, such as demographic data purchased from various sources. This data is used to break the database into clusters of customers with shared purchasing traits.

Depending on the goal, one has to select what is the profile that will be relevant to the project. A simple customer profile is a file containing at the least his name, address, city, state, and zip code. And if one needs profiles for specific products, the file would contain product information and/or volume of money spent.

The customer features that can be used for profiling are:

- Geographic.
- Cultural and ethnic.
- Economic conditions, income and/or purchasing power.
- Age.
- Values, attitudes, beliefs.
- Life cycle.
- Knowledge and awareness.
- Lifestyle.

2.3   Data Collection and Preparation

There are many ways of collecting the data:

- In-house customer database. Names can come from direct mailers used in the past, frequent buyer programs, contest, warranty registrations, receipts and membership cards.
- External sources. There are software or databases that can discover lifestyle, demographic information by using for example only zip code. E.g. Suomi CD can find Finnish demographic data from Finnish zip code.
- Research survey either face-to-face, over the telephone, via a postal questionnaire or through Internet. There are two types of information from the data that should be collected : classification variables and descriptor variables.

2.3.1   Classification Variables

Classification variables are used to classify survey respondents into segments. These variables are demographic, geographic, psychographic or behavioral variables.

- Demographic variables-Age, gender, income, ethnicity, marital status, education, occupation, household size, length of residence, type of residence, etc.
- Geographic variables-City, state, zip code, census tract, county, region, metropolitan or rural location, population density, climate, etc.

- Psychographic variables-Attitudes, lifestyle, hobbies, risk aversion, personality traits, leadership traits, magazines read, television programs watched, etc.
- Behavioral variables-Brand loyalty, usage level, benefits sought, distribution channels used, reaction to marketing factors, etc.

2.3.2   Descriptor Variables

Descriptors are used to depict everyone and differentiate each group from the others. The variables in descriptor must be easily obtained or able to easily obtained that exist in or can be appended to customer files. In fact, most of the classification variables can be treated as variables. But, there are a small amount of those variables in descriptor can be useful from external data.

2.3.3   Data Preparation

Before the data can be introduced to a data mining tool, they need to be cleaned and prepared in a required format.

New fields can be generated through combinations, e.g. frequencies, cross-tabulations, averages and min/max values, relationships between different profiling variables etc. The number of variables can be reduced to a more manageable size while also removing correlations between each variable. Techniques used for this purpose are often referred to as factor analysis, correspondence analysis and conjoint analyses.

When there is a large amount of data, it is also useful to apply data reduction techniques. Dimension reduction means that one has to select relevant feature to a minimum set of attributes such that the resulting probability distribution of data classes is as close as possible to the original distribution given the values of all features. For this additional tools may be needed, e.g. clustering, decision trees or associations.

3   Model Building

Modeling is a major way to determine whom to confront in the electronic commerce transaction. Profiling techniques is very effective s to build the model, since they can divide a large number of mailing population into manageable segments. The information obtained from the model will be very useful by providing comparative information for a specific electronic commerce transaction. Modeling usually regards a test mail as a sample which is on behalf of the company's database. The model is then constructed by analyzing the response from that mailing, determining how each customer innovations variable affected the response. In order to build a customer's behavior model, we need to :

- Identify the variables for inclusion in the profile.
- Build the model which segments and profiles the different customers.
- Use the model to prognosis which customers are most likely to buy the product , respond to a selling offer from the database.
- Identify the most discriminating data variables

Data mining is a way to learn the variation which uses a database as source data. Historical data are used to train and get the model, and new data are used for prediction (Figure 3).

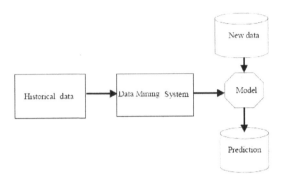

Fig. 3. The information gathered into the historical database about the customer would be used to build a model of customer behavior and could be used to predict which customers would be likely to respond to the new catalog

3.1   Data Sampling

The historical data are sampled into different datasets. These datasets should be distinct from each other. Random sampling is the most used sampling technique. If there is plenty of information, a little informaition limited to a small percentage of the whole database will still offer enough variability to build a good model. The datasets are:

- Training set is the data to build the model.
- Test set is used during the modeling phase by the model builder to evaluate the accuracy of a particular model.
- Validation set is often used by the data miner to evaluate the accuracy of the final model by comparing predictions from the model to known outcomes.
- Control set is used in some techniques while building the model to control over-training.

3.2   Training, Testing and Validating the Model

The first phases of building the model is training or learning process. It uses the information from the training set which is consisted of the result is known. The information or variable that contains the result, e.g. credit risk, is called the associated or result variable. The rest of the fields, e.g. income or marital status, are called the unattached variables.

If the information is not very precise, the inaccurate information may influent the process of building the predictive model and the model will make inaccurate forecasts to the evaluate that it has been affected by errors in the training data. This model is called overtrained (see Figure 4).

In case we obtain the model, we must evaluate it by an independent dataset which that has not been used to create the model.

Fig. 4. Example of over-training or over-fitting

3.3   Model Deployment

To deploy the model means that we has to identify the most accurate information - i.e. the variables which are most effective at predicting the customer's possibility of buying in electronic commerce transactions, or take-up a cross-selling offer or defect to the competitor. Deployment may require building computerized systems that capture the appropriate data and generate a prediction in real time so that a decision maker can apply the prediction. For example, a model can determine if a credit card transaction is likely to be fraudulent.

4   Conclusion

The research appears to be an important support in understanding consumers and their purchasing and consumption related behavior on Internet. This extends into what cognitive and behavioral process cause some consumers to perceive product and situations in different ways in on-line buying situations. Such an approach can only enhance the effective utilization of consumer characteristics at a theoretical and practical level in understanding consumer behavior related to electronic commerce. The key idea was that buyers on Internet operate with a keen sense of the relationship between their areas of experiences. Buyers build up a picture of markets through their encounters with them. Much of this interaction is implicit and depends upon the information acquisition process. Externally, buyers also build up a picture of market through the relationship between the websites stores and their customers.

References

1. Liu, Y., Liu, K., Li, M.: Passive Diagnosis for Wireless Ad hoc Networks. IEEE/ACM Transactions on Networking 18(4), 1132–1144 (2010)
2. Tigert, D.J., King, C.W., Ring, L.R.: Fashion involvement: a cross-cultural analysis. Advances in Consumer Research 17, 17–21 (2010)
3. Bloch, P.H.: Involvement beyond the purchase process: conceptual issues and empirical investigation. Advances in Consumer Research 9, 413–430 (2008)
4. Babin, B.J., Babin, L.: Seeking something different A model of schema typicality, consumer affect, purchase intentions and perceived shopping value. Journal of Business Research 54(2), 89–96 (2006)
5. Harrell, G.: Industrial product class involvement, confidence in beliefs and attitude intent relationships. In: Attitude Research Conference 8th Las Vegas 2009: Attitude Research Plays for High Stakes, pp. 133–147. American Marketing Association, Chicago (2009)
6. Falk, F.E., Miller, N.B.: A Primer for Soft Modeling. University of Akron Press (2007)

Trust Evaluation Model Based on User Trust Cloud and User Capability in E-Learning Service

Wenan Tan[1,2,*], Jingxian Li[1], Anqiong Tang[2], Tong Wang[2], and Xiaoming Hu[2]

[1] School of Compute Sci. and Tech., Nanjing University of Aeronautics and Astronautics,
Nanjing 210016, China
`twajsj@sohu.com, ljxsuccess@163.com`
[2] School of Computer and Information, Shanghai Second Polytechnic University,
Shanghai 201209, China
`{aqtang,twang,xmhu}@it.sspu.cn`

Abstract. E-Learning services have become one of important way of education. How to use simple and effective evaluation methods for user trust assessment is the key technical in E-Learning services. This paper presents an evaluation model based on user trust cloud and user capability (TC-UCEM) for trusted E-Learning services, in which user trust cloud approach is proposed to assess user subjective trust, as well as capability matrix method is introduced to assess user objective trust.

Keywords: E-learning, User trust cloud, Capability matrix, TC-UCEM.

1 Introduction

Nowadays E-learning services have been widely accepted as a kind of modern learning model. As it can provide people with a flexible and personalized way to learn, many innovative changes of learning applications have also been witnessed, and currently the research community has believed that an E-learning ecosystem is the next generation learning system [1, 2]. Trust management for E-learning service providers and E-learning service receiver has become important and necessary, which aim is to ensure the security of E-learning service. However, research on the trust assessment of E-learning is so little because online learning is just in developing stage. Therefore, in this paper, we make a bold exploration on trust relationship and propose the evaluation model based on user trust cloud and user capability in E-learning service.

In recent years, there are lots of classic trust evaluation models: the concept of swift trust and examines changes in faculty roles as professors go online [3], in which the author presents an exploratory qualitative study of whether the formation of swift trust in the first few weeks of an online course can help explain the success of online course. Blaze, *etal.,* provided a comprehensive approach for trust management based on a simple language for specifying trusted actions and trust relationships [4]. The

---

* Corresponding author.

M. Zhao and J. Sha (Eds.): ICCIP 2012, Part I, CCIS 288, pp. 583–590, 2012.

role-based trust management framework was presented to estimate users' trust level to afford corresponding permissions according to the roles [5]. Abdul-rahman, *etal.*, proposed a trust model based on the real word social prop properties of trust, which is outlined for supporting trust measurement in virtual communities based on experience, reputation and distributed recommendations [6,7]. Jøsang presented an algebra called subjective logics, which is used to assess trust values based on the triplet representation of trust [8]. Xiangyi, *etal.*, introduced a formalism method to represent subjective user-trust-cloud model for computation of subjective uncertainty like randomness and fuzziness of subjective trust relationship [9].

Building on their previous work and considering the impact of user capability change with different interactive actions, we exploit a trust evaluation model integrating user trust cloud and user capability in E-learning services (TC-UCEM), in which user trust cloud concerns user subjective trust as well as user capability is used for evaluating capability objective trust.

The remainder of this paper is structured as follows: Section 2 introduces the related works. Section 3 focuses on discussion of trust evaluation based on user trust cloud and capability matrix. In Section 4, we summarize the paper and discuss further research directions.

2   Related Works

The proposed trust evaluation model is base on subjective dimension and objective dimension. In this section, we introduce some of the related works. Firstly, we introduce the notion of trusted service. Following is to explain how to make trust decision, and lastly we introduce the concept of USER-TRUST CLOUD and BEHAVIOR CAPABILITY.

2.1   Trusted Service

A trusted service means that service is trusted. As we know, a service includes three parts: service provider, service resources, service consumer. Most of researchers study trust evaluation models from service resources and service provider without considering the trust of service consumer. However, the trust of service provider and service consumer may affect the quality of service and the smooth implementation of service. For E-learning services, the service consumer (learner) is the most important part in E-learning. If the learner is a malicious user, he will destroy the learning platform and threat information security. So, we import trust evaluation on user to ensure E-learning platform can provide trusted services.

2.2   Decision Making

E-learning is a typical application of Internet technology in the field of education, it is just a learning service for users based on internet, therefore it is important that service provider be able to identify service receivers with whom to provide and untrustworthy ones with whom to avoid providing. E-learning service contains three main kinds of roles: E-learning service platform, E-learning service provider, E-learning service receiver (learner or user), we can recognize the E-learning service users as trust objects or trust subjects, here we call E-learning service providers trust objects or objects, E-learning service users evaluated trust subjects or subjects. In order to accurately evaluate the total trust value of our subjects, we evaluate not only the trust value of user itself but also the trust value of user comprehensive capability. User trust in the proportion of the entire trust is based on the user's expected value. We allocate different trust weights to user itself trust on the basis of the proportion of user itself trust value.

2.3   The Notion of User Trust Cloud

The cloud model can be used to describe trust randomness and fuzziness [10]. Here we propose user trust cloud model based on cloud model, which can be used to evaluate the user subject trust accurately.

Definition 1: User Trust Cloud (UTC) is E-learning trust concept represented by cloud model and composed of many cloud drops. UTD= [0, 1] is the universal set of UTC, for any $e \in STS$ is a qualitative trust concept of user trust system (UTS), and any $x \in UTD$ is a implement of e. The certainty degree of x for e, i.e., $\mu(x) \in [0,1]$ is a random value with stabilization tendency

$$\mu : UTD \to [0,1] \quad x \in UTD \ x \to \mu(x)$$

Then the distribution of x on UTD is defined as UTC(x), and every x is called E-learning user trust cloud drop.

User trust cloud can be described by three numerical characters: Ex, En, He. Ex is the user expected value, which is calculated according to historic operational records. En is the dispersion of user historic value, which indicates stability of user study. He is a measure of the dispersion on the user cloud drops, which can also be considered as the entropy of En and is determined by the randomness and fuzziness of En.

2.4   The Notion of Behavior Capability

User capability evaluation is another important evaluation for users in E-learning. For service provider, user trust denotes that not only the user itself is trusted but also the user ability is trusted. So, we introduce a capability matrix based on interactive objects and interactive activities to describe the notion of behavior capability.

Definition 2: User: every E-learning participant is an independent user. User is the subject of learning activities in community. Related users may complete learning tasks by communicating with others. We suppose each user may communicate with n users. Let Y is the sample set of n users, i.e., Y=$\{Y_1, Y_2, \cdots, Y_n\}$.

Definition 3: Behavior Capability: element of user, can be understood as a description of user at a particular point. User has m dimensional capability attributions. User capability attributions are reflected through interactive actions with others. For example, object x has m dimensional capability attributions, sample set X can be described: $X = \{x_1, x_2, \cdots, x_m\}$.

Definition 4: User Weight and Behavior Capability Weight: different weights are allocated to different users according to frequent degree of user interactive activities, user weights set can be described as $\omega'_j = \{\omega'_1, \omega'_2, \cdots, \omega'_n\}$; different weights are assigned appropriately to capability attributions according to the importance of interaction capability in E-learning services, behavior capability attribution weights sample set can be expressed: $\omega = \{\omega_1, \omega_2, \cdots, \omega_m\}$.

In user capability evaluation model, each user can interact with different users on the basis of different action, for convenience, we suppose user X interact m kinds of actions with n users.

3   Trust Evaluation Model Based on User Trust Cloud and Behavior Capability Matrix

This section we build user evaluation based on user trust cloud and capability evaluation based on capability matrix separately, in which we propose reasonable user evaluation algorithm according to expected value combined with entropy and user capability algorithm according to behavior matrix multiplication.

3.1   User Trust Evaluation Based on User Trust Cloud

In order to evaluate user trust more accurately, allocating appropriate weight to user trust is of great significance in trust evaluation of E-learning, paper [11] presents the idea that trust weights are assigned to user trust and user capability randomly. This view is idealized without considering the complexity of user trust, this paper we make an improvement is that we allocate weight to user trust according to its expected value.

For convenience, we divide different trust levels based on the concept of qualitative and allocate different user trust weights according to different expected values. The detailed expression can be shown in the table 1.

Table 1. User Trust Level and User Trust Weight

Expected value of user trust(Ex)	Trust level (TL)	Trust weight (α)
Ex=0	Distrusted	0
$0 < \text{Ex} \leq 0.25$	Little Trusted	0.1
$0.25 < \text{Ex} \leq 0.5$	Generally Trusted	0.2
$0.5 < \text{Ex} \leq 0.75$	Extremely trusted	0.3
$0.75 < \text{Ex} \leq 1$	Complete Trusted	0.4
Ex=1	Ultimate Trusted	0.5

From the table we can see that, the user weight was allocated the highest value 0.5 when the people are ultimate trusted while the user weight was allocated the lowest value 0 when the people is not trusted. The table states that the higher the expected value is, the more trusted the user is.

On the basis of x_i, we compute three numerical values of the user trust cloud, the trust values of Ex, En and He are calculated as follows:

$$Ex = \sum_{i=1}^{n} p_i x_i \tag{1}$$

$$S^2 = \frac{1}{N-1} \sum_{i=1}^{n} p_i (x_i - Ex)^2 \tag{2}$$

$$En = \sqrt{\frac{\pi}{2}} \sum_{i=1}^{n} p_i (x_i - Ex) \tag{3}$$

$$He = \sqrt{\left| S^2 - En^2 \right|} \tag{4}$$

In the formula (1), x_i is the historic record which reflects the user operating status, we define $x_i = 0$ when user has malicious operations. And $\sum_{i=1}^{N} p_i |x_i - Ex|$ represents the first-order absolute central moment and S^2 is sample variance of x_i in the formula (2). In the formula (3), p_i represents action $i's$ impact factor for all n actions of done by user x.

User trust evaluation formula can be expressed as below:

$$E^{Ctr}(X) = (1 - En) Ex + \frac{1}{\sigma}(1 - He^2) \tag{5}$$

Where $E^{Ctr}(X)$ represents user x trust cloud evaluation while σ is trust Hyper-Entropy factor, it changes as expected value and Entropy change. From the formula (3), we can see that user trust evaluation value is bigger when the expected value is bigger and Entropy is smaller.

3.2   User Behavior Capability Evaluation

In this section, we discuss our evaluation algorithm for comprehensive capability evaluation. User x is an entity of E-learning role and has m dimensional capability, let user x has m cooperation activities with n users. The user interactive action matrix can be given below as expression (6):

$$X_{x \leftarrow Y_j} = \begin{bmatrix} y_{11} & y_{12} & \cdots & y_{1n} \\ y_{21} & y_{22} & \cdots & y_{2n} \\ & & \ddots & \\ y_{m1} & y_{m2} & \cdots & y_{mn} \end{bmatrix} \tag{6}$$

Where $x \leftarrow Y_j$ represents object x has interactive action with object Y_j, Y_j is the j-th object in n object set, while Y_{ij} represent that X interact the i-th capability attribution action with j-th object.

Weights are allocated to different actions. Each interactive action contributes different probability to different dimensional capability attribution according to categories of the interactive actions

For user X, user trust value is obtained through weight matrix multiplied by interactive action matrix. Firstly we let capability attribution weight matrix multiply interactive action matrix, m weights are assigned appropriately to capability attributions according to history records, and the formula can be given below.

$$E^{Atr}(X \leftarrow Y_i) = \begin{pmatrix} \omega_1 & \omega_2 & \cdots & \omega_m \end{pmatrix} \begin{bmatrix} y_{11} & y_{12} & \cdots & y_{1n} \\ y_{21} & y_{22} & \cdots & y_{2n} \\ & & \ddots & \\ y_{m1} & y_{m2} & \cdots & y_{mn} \end{bmatrix} \tag{7}$$

$$E^{Atr}(X \leftarrow Y_i) = \begin{pmatrix} Y_{11} & Y_{12} & \cdots & Y_{1n} \end{pmatrix} \tag{8}$$

Where $E^{Atr}(X \leftarrow Y_i)$ is one dimensional matrix of n user evaluation values according to m dimensional capability attributions. ω_i is the weight for i-th interactive action. The weight ω_i satisfies: $\sum_{i=1}^{m} \omega_i = 1$.

$$(\omega_j')^T = \begin{pmatrix} \omega_1' & \omega_2' & \cdots & \omega_n' \end{pmatrix}^T = \begin{pmatrix} \omega_1' \\ \omega_2' \\ \vdots \\ \omega_n' \end{pmatrix} \tag{9}$$

$$E^{Atr}(X) = E^{Atr}(X \leftarrow Y_i)(\omega')^T \tag{10}$$

Where $(\omega_j')^T$ is the inverted matrix of ω_j', the weighting of the same capability attribution can be different according to different users (interactive action objects), ω_j' is allocated to n users on the basis of frequency degree of user interactions.

$$E^{Atr}(X) = \omega_1' Y_{11} + \omega_2' Y_{12} + \cdots + \omega_n' Y_{1n} \tag{11}$$

$E^{Atr}(x)$ is the comprehensive user capability value which we consider m dimension capability attributions of x and n interactive objects which x contact with. The contribution we make to this algorithm is that we propose matrix multiplication to finish capability evaluation.

3.3   The Comprehensive Evaluation Model

Here, we propose comprehensive evaluation model based on user trust evaluation and user capability evaluation, which reflects the reliability of user in E-learning. The integrated evaluation can help service provider select appropriate service receivers. The comprehensive model can be expressed as follows:

$$LE(X) = \alpha E^{Ctr}(X) + (1-\alpha)E^{Atr}(X) \tag{12}$$

Where $LE(X)$ represents E-learning comprehensive evaluation value; $E^{Ctr}(X)$ is user trust value while $E^{Atr}(X)$ is user capability evaluation we have discussed above, α is the weight allocated to user trust based on the expected value of user.

TC-UCEM considers both subjective user trust and objective capability trust. The new ideas we put forward are that user trust cloud is proposed to assess user trust itself and capability matrix multiplications are presented to evaluate user capability, considering capability attribution and interactive objects. Appropriate weights are assigned to user trust and capability trust.

The integrated evaluation of user trust and capability trust avoid the fraudulence of trust measure and extremely overcoming the faults of single capability estimate, service receiver selection and cooperative task delegation implements reliably and flexibly, which is effective for reducing risk and improving risk in E-learning service implementation.

4   Conclusions and Perspectives

This paper proposes an evaluation model based on user trust cloud and user capability in E-learning service. User trust cloud is proposed to assess user subjective trust, which expresses the randomness and fuzziness of user trust. Capability matrix multiplications are put forward to calculate user behavior capability by considering capability objects and interactive attributions. In order to evaluate compressive trust, we allocate appropriate weight to user subjective trust according to user expected value, which is more reasonable than before. We need lots of history records to validate our approach. However, most web sites don't provide this data. But with development of service and Internet, especially with more attention put on E-learning services, we believe that the evaluation of reputation change will be a novel and effective approach to assist us in user trust decision-making. Furthermore there is still a need for significant research in this field, such as how to apply our model on other service platform, how to design and allocate behavior capability weights more precisely, how to extend the approach to other related fields and so on.

Acknowledgment. This paper was supported in part by the National Natural Science Foundation of China under Grant No. 60874120, and Innovation Program of Shanghai Municipal Education Commission under Grant No. 11ZZ188.

References

1. Uden, L., Wangsa, I.T., Damiani, E.: The Future of E-learning: E-learning ecosystem. In: Proceeding of the First IEEE International Conference on Digital Ecosystems and Technologies, Cairns, pp. 113–117 (2007)
2. Chang, V., Guetl, C.: E-learning Ecosystem (ELES)-A Holistic Approach for the Development of more Effective Learning Environment for Small-and-Medium Sized Enterprise. In: Proceeding of the First IEEE International Conference on Digital Ecosystems and Technologies, Cairns, pp. 420–425 (2007)
3. Iacono, C.S., Weisband, S.: Developing trust in virtual teams. In: Proceedings of the 30th Annual Hawaii International Conference on System Sciences, Wailea, pp. 412–420 (1997)
4. Blaze, M., Feigenbaum, J., Lacy, J.: Decentralized Trust Management. In: IEEE Conference on Security and Privacy, Oakland, pp. 164–173 (1996)
5. Ninghui, L., Mitchell, J.C., Winsborough, W.H.: Design of a Role-based Trust-management Framework. In: Proceedings of IEEE Symposium on Security and Privacy, pp. 114–130. IEEE Computer Society Press, Washington (2002)
6. Abdul-rahman, A., Hailes, S.: Supporting Trust in Virtual Communities. In: Proceedings of the 33rd Annual Hawaii International Conference on System Science, Hawaii (2000)
7. Abdul-rahman, A., Hailes, S.: A Distributed Trust Model. In: Proceedings of 1997 New Security Paradigms Workshop, pp. 48–60. ACM Press, Hawaii (1998)
8. Jøsang, A.: An Algebra for Assessing Trust in Certification Chains. In: Proceedings of the Network and Distributed Systems Security (NDSS 1999) Symposium. The Internet Society (1999)
9. Meng, X., Zhang, G., Liu, C., Kang, J., Li, H.: Research on Subjective Trust Management Model Based on Cloud Model. Journal of System Simulation 19(14), 3310–3317 (2007)
10. Li, D., Du, Y.: Artificial Intelligence with Uncertainty. Chapman & Hall/CRC Taylor & Francis Group (2008)
11. Tan, W., Wen, X., Jiang, C., et al.: An Evaluation Model Integrating User Trust and Capability for Selection of Cooperative Learning Partners. Chinese Journal of Electronics 21(CJE-1), 42–46 (2012)

Development and Implementation of Real-Time Wireless Monitor System Using COFDM for the Competition of Intelligent Vehicles in China

Xu Wang[1], Guangming Xiong[1], Yang Sun[1], Peng Liu[1],
Weilong Song[1], and Yang Xu[2]

[1] Intelligent Vehicle Research Center, Beijing Institute of Technology, Beijing, China
[2] Beijing Huanjia Telecom Technology Company, Beijing, China

Abstract. In order to make it convenience to see the real-time competition for all viewers, the remote real-time image transmission and display system were established in the third competition for intelligent vehicles in China. The existing wireless image transmission technologies were analyzed since it is the core technology among the system and COFDM was chosen to build a real-time image transmission system according to requirements. The test experiment was made in a campus environment to validate the designed system. Some improved methods were presented for the real application in the third competition. The result shows that the proposed system performed successfully.

Keywords: COFDM, real-time monitor system, wireless image transmission.

1   Introduction

The unmanned vehicle with the natural environment perception and intelligent behavior decision-making ability is an integrated test platform of key technology of "Cognitive Computing of Visual and Auditory Information", a Major Research Plan (MRP) of National Natural Science Funds Commission (NSFC) of China. The comprehensive test environment and test system can be used to scientifically evaluate the research achievements of unmanned ground vehicles. Therefore, the test and evaluation of the integrated test platform in an unknown environment has a very important meaning in the development of key technology of MRP [1].

The first Chinese unmanned vehicles competition - The 2009 Future Challenge: Intelligent Vehicles and Beyond (FC'09) was held in Xi'an, China [2]. The competition is the first third-party test and evaluation for unmanned vehicles in China, and it pushes unmanned vehicles go out from laboratories into application environments. In 16-18th, October, 2010, the Second Future Challenge: Intelligent Vehicles and Beyond (FC'10) was held in Xi'an [3].

DARPA held three challenges, which are Grand Challenge in 2004 and 2005, Urban Challenge in 2007. The Grand Challenge in 2005 was accomplished successfully through detailed planning and training and applying lessons learned from the 2004 event. Some infrastructure support for the event was unique to the program.

M. Zhao and J. Sha (Eds.): ICCIP 2012, Part I, CCIS 288, pp. 591–598, 2012.

The communications and tracking network necessary to ensure a safe event, for example, required the coordination of four hilltop tower sites spread over 500 square miles. Personnel were utilized for track operations; in control vehicles; as E-stop master transmitter operators, route closure monitors, remote video technicians, and in a 40-person operations center at the start/finish area [4].

In the last two "Future Challenge" in China, the real-time image monitor and display system were not built. In order to provide the data support for the evaluation, the confirmation of final results, and to make convenience to see the real-time competition for all participating teams and experts, the remote real-time image monitor and display system were established in the third "Future Challenge".

The core technology of the real-time wireless monitor system is wireless image transmission technology. The existing wireless image transmission technologies are introduced in the second section of this paper, and one of them will be chosen to build a real-time image transmission system according to requirements. Section 3 describes the test experiment in a campus environment using designed wireless image transmission system. Section 4 presents improved methods for the real application in the third competition followed by the conclusion in Section 5.

2   Wireless Image Transmission Technology

At present, there are the following methods to realize the wireless image transmission [5,6,7]:

(1) Satellite communication lines.
(2) GSM/GPRS, CDMA mobile communication technology.
(3) COFDM (Code Orthogonal Frequency Division Multiplexing) transmission
    technology.

2.1   Satellite Communication

It is a kind of the communication between two or more earth stations through transmission of radio waves by use of man-made earth satellite as a relay station. The advantages of the satellite communication mainly include large communication range ,small impact of land disasters and quick construction speed.

The major disadvantages are as followings. (1) Band above 10 GHz can be influenced by snow and rain; (2) Communication charges is high; (3) There is 0.6 seconds time delay during the communication.

2.2   CDMA Mobile Communication

CDMA (Code Division Multiple Access) is a kind of new wireless communication technology developed from the spread spectrum communication technology. The main advantages of CDMA include the following aspects. (1) Good Internet access, high Internet access speed, wide cover range of single base station;(2) Clear communication, not easy to break, strong secrecy, accurate display time;(3) Small launch power consumption, small radiation, high safety coefficient;(4) High spectrum efficiency, support various business;(5) Better Modulation mode.

The major disadvantages are as followings. (1) CDMA base stations are not enough, and the service network covers less; (2) Delay time is longer, and extensibility is poorer; (3) CDMA1x only can provide the highest Internet access rate of 153.6 kbps, the requirement of high-quality image transmission cannot be reached.

2.3   COFDM Technology

COFDM namely coded orthogonal frequency division multiplexing, is a kind of the most advanced modulation technology at present in the world. It can break through view limit, and it is a kind of technology making full use of radio spectrum resources. Therefore it has very good immunity to noise and interference.

The main technical advantages of COFDM are as follows. (1) It can realize the stable transmission of video with the high probabilities in the out-of-sight and blocked environments of city, mountain and building. (2) It is suitable for high-speed transmission, high bandwidth, high code stream, high-quality audio and video; (3) It has excellent anti-jamming performance and high utilization rate of frequency and channel.

2.4   Wireless Image Transmission System

The COFDM technology is chosen to construct a real-time transmission system in terms of the above analysis.

The system consists of transmitting and receiving parts. The transmitting terminal includes three parts: comprehensive baseband, transmitter and antenna. The comprehensive baseband is one of the key components, and it completes the collection, compression, coding and interlacing of image data, the collection and coding of state data, the framing output of transmitting data, and sending control of the output signal. The transmitter is responsible for the modulation, amplification and output of data. The antenna completes the radiation of microwave signal.

The receiver includes four parts: receiving antenna, receiver, signal processor and receiving processing module. The receiving antenna receives the microwave signals. The signal processor is responsible for the decoding of image data and state data, the framing of decoding data, synchronization, cache and output of data.

3   Test in a Campus Environment

In order to test the actual effect of COFDM technology, the test was carried out in the campus environment using the designed wireless image transmission system.

3.1   Test One

The transmitter antenna was installed on the roof of Toyota car. The transmitter was placed inside the Toyota car, respectively connecting to the power supply line, the video input line (connecting camera) and the transmitter antenna, as shown in Fig.1(a). The receiver's antenna was installed on the roof of the blue car shown in Fig.1(b). The antenna was raised to 12m through the lifting mechanism. The receiver was placed inside the blue car, respectively connecting to the power supply line, the video output line (connecting displayer) and the receiver's antenna, as shown in Fig.1(c).

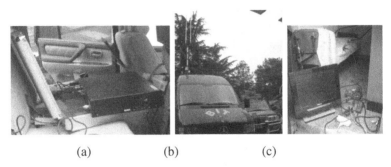

(a)   (b)   (c)

Fig. 1. Transmitter and receiver

The Toyota car with the transmitter and camera ran in the campus. The transmission effect of the wireless image transmission system was tested. The driving route and the actual effect are shown in Fig.2. The red means there's signal with the smooth image, and the blue means there isn't signal. The test shows that, in the blocked sections, sometimes the quality of the image became worse. In some areas, there is even no signal.

Fig. 2. Test route and result

3.2   Test Two

In order to further analyze the causes, test two was done in the campus environment.

The receiver was placed on the top of Central Teaching Building of Beijing Institute of Technology with the height of 70m. The transmitting terminal was still placed on the Toyota car. The video was send by the wireless image transmitter. It was received by the receiver to output to the network video server. Therefore, this video can be watched at any network point in the campus. The system structure is shown in Fig.3.

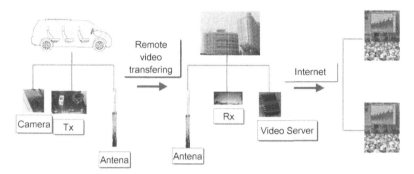

Fig. 3. System structure

Taking the Central Teaching Building as the center, within the south and north direction of 300m, the east direction of 800m, and the west direction of 1000m, the vehicle moved and the real-time image was transmitted to the receiver on the top of the building. The driving route and effect figure is shown in Fig.4. In the top left corner of Fig.4, there is a tall building, which is higher than Central Teaching Building. But the image is still clear and smooth behind the building. It can be seen that the wireless image transmission system can realize the stable transmission of image in the blocked environment.

Fig. 4. Wireless video image transmission test route and result

4   Experiments in the Real Environment

The third "Future Challenge" was held in Ordos,China [8]. The competition environment is shown in Fig.5 (the blue line) and the whole route is 10 km.

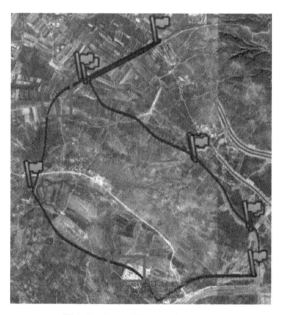

Fig. 5. Competition environment

In order to realize the transmission of wireless image in such large range, the relay was added. It was installed on the hilltop shown in Fig.6 (a). The relay is composed of receiver and transmitter shown in Fig.6 (b). The receiver is used to receive the car video of wireless transmission. The transmitter is used to wirelessly transfer the video to the specified terminal. Due to the direction of the terminal is known, the directional antenna is used shown in Fig.6 (c)

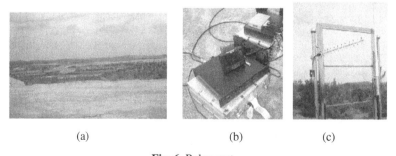

(a)   (b)   (c)

Fig. 6. Relay part

At the terminal, only the receiver and directional antenna need to be installed, as shown in Fig.7. The vehicle with the transmitter ran along the blue line shown in Fig.5. At the same time, the real-time video is observed at the terminal. The test result shows that the signal is good except in the red area shown is Fig.5.

Fig. 7. Receiver in the known terminal

To make signals more smooth in the red area shown in Fig.5, two directional antennas were installed at the relay station on the top of mountain shown in Fig.8 (a). Two upright antennas were used to receive the wireless images from two moving vehicles. In order to make the signals better and images smoother, two directional antennas were used and an augmenter was added for the receiver. The video from two cars is integrated on the one screen, shown in Fig.8 (b).

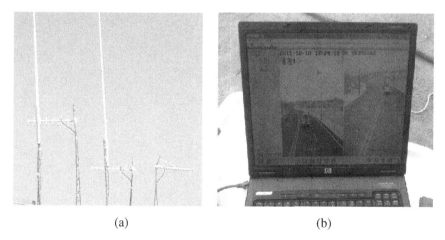

(a)   (b)

Fig. 8. Improvement and result

5   Conclusions

The proposed system continuously works for eight hours to transfer the video collected by two cars moving in the large environment to the terminal. The experiment shows that the system has the features of small time-delay, convenient operation, high image quality, and high receiving sensitivity.

Acknowledgements. This work was supported by the National Natural Science Foundation of China (Grant No. 90920304).

References

1. Li, X., Xiong, G., Sun, Y., et al.: Design on hierarchical testing system for unmanned ground vehicles. In: 2011 International Conference on Sustainable Construction Materials and Computer Engineering, ICSCMCE 2011 (2011)
2. http://ccvai.xjtu.edu.cn/news.do?method=getdetails&id=33
3. http://www.nsfc.gov.cn/Portal0/InfoModule_375/31231.htm
4. REPORT TO CONGRESS DARPA Prize Authority. Fiscal Year 2005 report in accordance with 10 U.S.C. § 2374a, Defense Advanced Research Projects Agency, Approved for Public Release, Distribution Unlimited (March 2006)
5. Hanzo, L., Cherriman, P.J., Streit, J.: Wireless Video Communications: Second to Third Generation System and Beyond. IEEE Press, New York (2001)
6. Zhang, Q., Zhu, W.-W., Zhang, Y.-Q.: Channel-Adaptive Resource Allocation for Scalable Video Transmission Over 3G Wireless Network. IEEE Trans. on CSVT 14(8), 1049–1063 (2004)
7. Zou, W.Y., Wu, Y.: COFDM: an overview. IEEE Transactions on Broadcasting 41(1), 1–8 (1995)
8. http://www.bit.edu.cn/xxgk/xysz/jxyclxy/70878.htm

The Design of Mathematical Evaluation Model about Data-Value in Hierarchical Storage of Digital Library

Li-zhen Shen

Libary, Wenzhou University, 325000 Wenzhou, Zhejiang, China
Wzu-slz@wzu.edu.cn

Abstract. This article describes the migration policies in a hierarchical storage model constraints of digital library based on information lifecycle management firstly, existing equipment and the data of digital library storage to be justly evaluated; Secondly, anglicized the type of data stored on the digital library in accordance with the resource types and properties of the storage data classification; Finally, proposed a mathematical model to evaluate data-value of storage, this value to determine migration strategies in a hierarchical storage system.

Keywords: data-value, hierarchical storage, the Information Lifecycle Management (ILM).

1 Introduction

Used hierarchical storage policies based on **the Information Lifecycle Management (ILM)** in the digital library storage, both can make rational utilization of storage hardware with limited resources, also meet the needs of long-term preservation of digital resources with high performance, on the basis, you can complete the unified management of digital library resources. The hierarchical storage strategy based on ILM is necessary in the digital library. How to develop an effective hierarchical storage strategy, firstly, comprehensive consideration of existing storage hardware, second is the data of digital library storage to be justly evaluated. Now hierarchical storage model for digital library mostly dominated by SAN architecture, separation line、 near-line and online storage-data depending on the existing hardware[1-7]. How to evaluate the store data, you should understand the properties of data, make adequate mathematical model refer to its lifecycle, in compliance with this mathematical model for evaluation of their data, and develop an effective hierarchical storage strategy.

2 Storage of Digital Library Information Classification

Digital Library storage resource types are diverse, from e-publications, dissertations, electronic journals to scientific data, and so on; each type of digital resources, their

M. Zhao and J. Sha (Eds.): ICCIP 2012, Part I, CCIS 288, pp. 599–606, 2012.

conservation methods and technologies are different. A large number of researchers and research projects are on this. It is worth noting is that each project in the solution is a type of resource.

2.1   From the Perspective of Resource Type Division

Web Resources

The web refers to the data on the Internet resources, including various kinds of publicly available digital resources; do not include published papers, online journals and online databases, and more. The web resources are abundant, variety, short life cycle, update speed. At present, more and more information in the form of Web publishing has become an important part of the digital resources of network resources. Domestic and foreign research has reached a certain consensus, that is, Web resources are an important part of national cultural assets, needed for long-term preservation in order to avoid loss of national cultural heritage.

E-publications

E-publications means of publication refers to the numeric code, will have the knowledge, thoughtful editing content of information stored in fixed physical form on magnetic, optical, electric and other media through electronic reading, display, playback device reads the use of mass media, include CD-ROM (CD-ROM, and DVD-ROM,), and once writes CD (CD-R, and DVD-R,), and may wipe wrote CD (CD-RW, and DVD-RW,), and floppy disks, and hard disk, and integrated circuit card,, As well as the press and publication administration recognized by the other media forms. For example, we use the large database: CNKI, Wanfang data, Journal of Chemical Research, CA, the small includes CD attached with books, audio and video tapes, disks, and the all is the electronic publications.

Examples of this are: Finland founded the save the Internet in Finland published electronic documentation project of EVA, Canada launched the electronic publication of the National Library project EPPP, United States, Ohio Historical Society, Ohio joint cooperation projects initiated by JERRI projects [8,9].

Scientific Data

The digitized data generated in scientific research are more and more, the generation and accumulation of huge amounts of data means that the increased intellectual wealth of the community, but also means that these valuable scientific records and documents of faces from technological obsolescence and deterioration caused by loss of carrier hazardous. Therefore, long-term preservation and sharing of scientific data is very seriously in States, related practices including the DISC、 SDS project of DDC, ERPANET/CODATA Forum, Netherlands ARNO items and more [10].

Multimedia Resources

The multimedia storage requirement is high, complex technologies. There have been many research projects around the world. Audio resources are related to the sound of digital resources.

DIAMM (Digital Image Archive of Medieval Music) project is a United Kingdom University of Oxford and Royal Holloway University cooperation projects. The DIAMM (Digital Image Archive of Medieval Music) project is a cooperation project of Oxford and Royal Holloway University [11]. The project of European middle ages polyphonic music is to establish a lasting music in e-archives-archives. The project also provides arts and humanities data service; also stressed that digital image persisted. The Video resources include film, video and other resources. Pres to Space is the EU funded project, whose goal is to establish framework for digital preservation of audio-visual information. This project established a save warehouse, providing easy management, low-cost, standardized processes, for institutions such as libraries or museums, and access technology framework of digital audiovisual assets [12].

The PRESTO project is a founding project of European Union information technology associations Union Information Society Technology (IST).The project research on issues related to the conservation and resource saving economy needs. Study on the resource type mainly for film, audio, and video. A participant of the project is several archives for public broadcasting and commercial research institutions in Europe. The purpose of the project is to evaluate status of audio and video data saved, establishing resource selection standards, research during the save process quality control, metadata management, third-party evaluation and testing methods. Variable vectors can be changes in the media resource. Founding fathers of variable media (Variable Media Initiative) launched by the Guggenheim Museum, encouraged the artist defines media-independent formats of their own works, provides how to convert other works for the new format of the Guide.

PANIC saving and archiving new media and interactive collection (Preservation and Archival New Media and Interactive Collections) project by the MAENAD (Multimedia Access across Enterprises, Networks And Domains), which includes case studies, Compare different multimedia Save method; Study on the life the best way to maintain digital objects; Determine the most optimal media formats, establishing guidelines and metadata schemas[13].

Other
Over several types of digital resources is the focus of research and practice in digital preservation.

Electronic degree thesis, artwork, and types of digital resources such as e-mail due to the features it has become a digital resource long-term preservation of research and practice in important content.

i. Electronic Degree thesis (ETD)
Traditionally, dissertations in paper form are saved in the library; very few exist in digital form. In recent years, many universities, research institutes have a dissertation digital and require students to submit an electronic version of a dissertation submitted at the same time as the corresponding, in this way, the electronic dissertations library is formed and formed from the papers upload, transmit to save, retrieve a complete set of system processes [14-15].

ii. Art

The Art has its own characteristics; you need to choose according to its characteristics of long-term preservation strategy. Save the policy in different carrier forms of art are

Table 1. Information data type table

	Category Of Digital Resource	Data Types Included In Resource	Applications Used To Create/Manage / Distribute Digital Resource	Notes
1	Data Sets	Alphanumeric Data	Wide range of data processing applications; bespoke software and application packages; managed in flat file; networked; hierarchical; relational and object oriented databases; presented via presentation graphics, modeling software, report writers etc	Survey data; results of experiments; transaction data; event data; administrative data; attribute data; bibliographic data
2	Structured Texts	Alphanumeric data; mark-up data; tags to other data types (raster and vector graphics)	Word processing; text editing; HTML editors; desktop/corporate publishing; LaTeX; SGML and application specific Document Type Definitions; XML;	Literary texts; formal documents; corporate publications; commercial publications; Web pages;
3	Office Documents	Alphanumeric data; mark-up data; raster and vector graphics;	Word processing; spreadsheets; document image processing; office suites; groupware; document management systems; relational databases;	Sets of digital documents; Digitized paper images; links/bundles created via office suites; groupware; HTML;
4	Design Data	Vector and raster graphics; alphanumeric data;	CAD; word processing; document image processing; relational databases; object oriented databases;	Product data; as built drawings; Models; plans;
5	Presentation Graphics	Vector/raster graphics; moving graphics alphanumeric data; full motion video; interleaved audio and video	Business graphics; clip art; creative graphics; presentation systems; Computer Based Training; multimedia	Business presentations; formal courseware; CBT packages;
6	Visual Images	Raster graphics; alphanumeric data	Image capture software; image processing and editing software; object oriented; relational and flat file databases	Fine art; picture libraries; photographic libraries; medical images; images of historic/manuscript documents;
7	Speech & Sound Recordings	Audio data; MIDI; metadata	Speech processing; audio recording and playback; symbolic music recording; relational and flat file databases	Music libraries; sound effects; radio broadcasts; sound recordings; media;
8	Video Recordings	Digital video; full screen, full motion video; interleaved audio and video; Metadata	Digital video frames stored as bitmaps; audio files; audio/video interleaved; compression systems; Relational & Flat File Databases	Media libraries; training centers; video clips games
9	Geographic/Mapping Data	Vector and raster graphics; Alphanumeric data	GIS systems; mapping software; relational & object oriented databases	Maps; co-ordinates; range of overlay data; links between data types;
10	Interactive Multimedia Publications	Interleaved audio and video data; moving graphics; vector and raster graphics; alphanumeric data;	Authoring software; editing software; access software;	Electronic publishing; educational and training material; marketing material; games etc

not the same, the appropriate choice of technologies, methods of special. Avert Gacde project saving strategy in study of carrier forms of art. Projects were made to the long-term preservation of the art research and practice, and have developed a set of saved digital art guidelines [16]. Besser, Howard at the International Conference on cultural heritage information held in 2001, General preservation method for electronic resources, particularities and challenges of electronic art and save electronic art practical methods such as put forward their views [17].

iii. E-mail

Email is a vital tool for scientific communication, email content often has value, at present, the type of theoretical study and practice of conservation is relatively small, but people have e-mail saved the cultural, legal, technical and other aspects of the research. Tested Digital Bewaring e-mail preservation project is on long-term preservation of e-mail of the corresponding solution which includes documents, legal, technical and practical issues. At the same time, the project compares the technologies such as migration, emulation method to save an e-mail message in the application.

2.2   From the Properties of Digital Information Storage Division

In the digital library in the information store, people face a variety of information types and data types [18] (Table 1), each with different encoding mechanisms, as well as the corresponding data format, the processing software or even hardware systems.

3   Information Utilization Value Evaluation Model

Digital library service aims to provide customers with a variety of digital resources to meet the information needs of users. Consider tiered storage management in the digital collection of resources utilization value, should primarily be used by the user from a resource point of view. Value assessment model presented involves the following indicators: frequency of use, time, file size, user categories.

Simple Usage: The main concern is the digital resource itself (does not include metadata, secondary information) access frequency, the calculation of frequency is: $f = \Delta N / \Delta t$ .Of which,ΔN is total number of times that the resource is accessed per unit of time, a unit of time is a migration cycle, it can be set through experience and adjustment.

Time: For a digital resource that you just created, its value has not been known, it should be kept at the online storage. You can set initial retention timeΔT, the resources within ΔT time of the new, not relocate to lower-level storage device. The resources is for the initial retention time, using a consistent formula to calculate its value. When calculating resource utilization, also taking into accounts the resource requirements of the access point in time. For more near next migration time points of access, its using value of contribution should more large, that is said, within a same judgment cycle, the access number of two different resources was equal, the binary digits of the access number is closer next migration time on the curve, The corresponding resources for systems, of using value should more large, should underlying retained in online storage device. For this reason, it is necessary to consider access points in time (Set i days visit last migration point in time T_i, its importance is logarithmic curve increases, the base is 2, then $N_i = N_i - 1 + \log_2 T_i$, of which Ni is the cumulative value, said that when the i times visit, Taking into account resource access time.

User Class: There are different types of users of digital libraries (such as university teachers, PhD students in undergraduate, master's, and so on), all types of users on the importance of the library (priority service) should be differentiated, to provide a more accurate evaluation of digital resources utilization value, you should also take into account the type of users who use the resources. Specific practices as digital library users into several classes, set a weight value for each type of user, certain types of user access to digital resources, visits should be multiplied by the weight after the frequency of utilization of computing resources.

File Size: Small heat resources and priority should be deposited in the online storage, so as to better increase the benefits of high performance storage devices. Taking into account the literature resources of digital library size as ranged from dozens of KB to hundreds of MB, its size on the system of shadow is not very large, so it should not be used to value is too large. Therefore, when considering file size effect on the value of this article, using the "additive" instead of "multiplication".

The above discussion, resource utilization value evaluation model is:

$$\text{Information value}: V_u = F_w + \frac{C}{S} = \frac{\sum_{i=1}^{n} W_{ij} \log_2 T_i}{\Delta t} + \frac{C}{S}$$

Among them, F_w consider the user type and access time weighting of resources utilization, S is the file size (in KB), C is the appropriate constant (determined according to practical experience), W_{ij} is the i times of visitor belongs to user type of weight values, T_i is the last transfer point in time when i visit days.

4   Information Utilization Value Evaluation Model

To achieve the above resource value calculation, need appropriate metadata records. Metadata resources involved are: Resource creation time T0, Resource size S, Resources weighted access accumulator N, Resource utilization value V_u. Of which, the worth of N reset 0 at the start of each migration cycle, after, when a resource is accessed at a time, depending on the value type a weight value which the user belongs and T_i, the result of $W_{ij} \log_2 T$ added to the accumulator.

When you need to perform data migrations, computing resource utilization value-V_u, then there is greater than the initial reservation of time Δt resources in accordance with the policy is assigned to perform the migration, and there is less than Δt resources does not perform the migration. After migration is complete, the N and V_u, is reset to 0, go to the next cycle of cumulative calculation.

5   Conclusion

This article is on a tiered storage model based on ILM of digital library and analysis on the characteristics of digital library resources, combined with the concept of information lifecycle management and tiered storage management, discussion on mathematical model of a data migration strategy to follow. On construction of digital library storage system has a certain value, on information life cycle management of exploration of the specific application of certain significance.

On digital library research is still at an early stage of information lifecycle management, theoretical and practical issues such as information life-cycle stages of constituencies, resource evaluation required further study and exploration. Mathematical model for further refinement of this article (such a model is more suitable for small file data migration, data migrations for large files will bring storage hardware systems and user access to a larger issue), and verified its feasibility and performance of the system; Resource utilization value evaluation model of parameters need to be determined by experiment and practice. These issues will be the next focus of the study.

References

1. Shen, L.-Z.: Research on hierarchical storage of digital library based on the information lifecycle management. In: 2010 2nd IEEE International Conference on Information Management and Engineering, ICIME 2010, vol. 3, pp. 64–66 (2010)
2. Liu, X., Li, Z., Huang, X., Song, Q.: Study of an integrated resource management system oriented to ferry companies. In: Proceedings of 2008 3rd International Conference on Intelligent System and Knowledge Engineering, ISKE 2008, pp. 619–624 (2008)
3. Cleveland, J., Loyall, J.P., Webb, J., Hanna, J., Clark, S.: VFILM: A value function driven approach to information lifecycle management. In: Proceedings of SPIE - The International Society for Optical Engineering, Defense Transformation and Net-Centric Systems 2011, vol. 8062 (2011)
4. Mitra, S., Winslett, M., Hsu, W.W.S.: Query-based partitioning of documents and indexes for information lifecycle management. In: Proceedings of the ACM SIGMOD International Conference on Management of Data, pp. 623–636 (2008)
5. Zhao, X., Li, Z., Zeng, L.: A Hierarchical storage strategy based on block-level data valuation. In: Proceedings - 4th International Conference on Networked Computing and Advanced Information Management, NCM 2008, vol. 1, pp. 36–41 (2008)

6. Yin, J.-W., Wang, B.-B., Chen, G., Dong, J.-X.S., Xitong, J.J.Z.: Development of distributed product data management system for group-scaled enterprises. Computer Integrated Manufacturing Systems, CIMS 11(5), 656–663 (2005)

7. Buzi, M., Sakkas, A.: Enabling unbounded imagery archives for the new millennium - And smart tools vital to the age of information overload. In: Proceedings of SPIE - The International Society for Optical Engineering, vol. 4169, pp. 416–421 (2001)

8. Digital Library Federation (DLF). The Andrew W. Mellon Foundation's e-Journal archives project (Regularly Updated), United States of America,
   `http://www.diglib.org/preserve/ejp.Htm`

9. Oskamp, Liesbeth Deposit of Digital Publications, Netherlands (July 16, 2003),
   `http://www.europeanlibrary.org/pdf/tel_d1.2v1.0.pdf`   Eumpean Library Report, 1ST-2001-25347

10. Amsterdam University Library. ARNO project (Academic Research in the Netherlands Online). Amsterdam University Library (UBA)(Regularly Updated), Netherlands,
    `http://www.uba.uva.nl/en/projects/amo/...`

11. Guggenheim Museum. Media Initiative,
    `http://www.guggenheim.org/varlablemedia/`

12. MAENAD PANIC (Preservation and Archival New Media and Interactive Collections) Project (2003), `http://metadata.net/newmedia/index.Html`,
    `http://presto.joanneum.ac.at/index.asp`

13. ADT, `http://adt.Gaul.edu.au/`

14. NDLTD, `http://www.ndltd.org/`

15. VT-ETD, `http://etd.vt.edu/backgmund/xxxi` Berkeley Art Museum and Pacific FiLn Axchive Archiving the Avant Garde: Documenting and Preserving Variable Media Art (2001),
    `http://www.Berkeley.edu/about-ampfa/avantgarde.html`

16. Mayfield, K.: A news articie providing an overview of the Archiving the Avant Garde project (July 23, 2002),
    `http://www.wired.com/news/culture/0,1284,5371,00.html`

17. Besser: Howard Longevity of Electronic Art (February 2001),
    `http://www.gseis.ucla.edu/~howard/Papers/`
    `elect-art-longevity.html`

18. Comparison of Methods Costs of Digital Preservation,
    `http://www.ukoln.ac.uk/services/elib/papers/`
    `tavistock/hendley/hendley.html`

Binary Exponential Backoff Based Congestion Control Mechanism in Multihop Wireless Networks

Lin Ma[1,2], Jun Zhang[1,2], and Kai Liu[1,2]

[1] School of Electronics and Information Engineering, Beihang University,
Beijing 100191, China
[2] National Key Laboratory of CNS/ATM, Beijing 100191, China
malin@ee.buaa.edu.cn, buaazhangjun@vip.sina.com,
liuk@buaa.edu.cn

Abstract. In multihop wireless networks, congestion mainly due to the medium contention in MAC layer, which is quite different from traditional wired networks. This paper presents a solution based on the binary exponential backoff algorithm, namely, MAC layer congestion control (MLCC) mechanism. As it is known, a node needs to generate a random backoff period each time when it failed to transmit a frame. Thus the more frequently one node generates the backoff period, the more seriously the network congests. In MLCC, we use this information as a metric for network congestion, thus a node can adaptively adjust its packet loss probability to alleviating MAC collisions and network congestion. Finally, this paper proposes a network throughput function and uses it to prove the validity of the novel congestion metric. Simulation results show that the MLCC algorithm effectively alleviate the network congestion, and significantly increase the network throughput.

Keywords: wireless networks, binary exponential backoff, congestion, throughput.

1   Introduction

Many studies have shown that the traditional TCP congestion control mechanism performs very poorly in wireless networks when using the IEEE 802.11 protocol [1-4]. In TCP, any packet loss is assumed as congestion, it works well in wired networks. But in wireless networks, packet loss is caused by a variety reasons, such as channel errors and MAC collisions. Therefore, the key idea is to research for the MAC layer congestion control algorithm, propose MAC layer congestion metric to adapt to the wireless environment.

The parameters for measuring local network congestion status largely depend on MAC layer and transport layer information, many studies have presented lots of algorithm to achieve this goal. LRED[5] used the number of packet retransmission times as the congestion metric, it performs good compatibility, but the packet retransmissions of the "starve" node are almost zero, LRED cannot help these nodes recovered from the congestion state. ARCD[6] used the MAC queue length to detect

M. Zhao and J. Sha (Eds.): ICCIP 2012, Part I, CCIS 288, pp. 607–614, 2012.
© Springer-Verlag Berlin Heidelberg 2012

the congestion of a given link, and it extended the MAC frame structure to piggyback the MAC congestion information to TCP sender. In [7], the ratio of retransmitted packets and successfully transmitted packets was used to indicate network congestion, the metric has higher accuracy than LRED. However, in wireless networks each packet retransmission will experience a longer period of time to take the channel, so this metric may easily outdated. Paper [8] uses the changes of MAC delay to estimate the MAC sending rate. With this knowledge, the nodes can adapt their contention window size in order to limit their sending rate.

In this paper, we mainly focus on the medium contention arising from node contending for the shared medium when the IEEE 802.11 DCF is used in the multihop wireless networks. A novel congestion control algorithm is proposed based on the binary exponential backoff algorithm, namely, MAC layer congestion control (MLCC). In MLCC, a novel MAC congestion metric called sensing failure ratio (p_{sfr}) is used to characterize the congestion status. The p_{sfr} is calculated according to the number of node generates the random backoff period and the number of suspended times during the backoff procedure. The MLCC will tune the wireless link's drop probability according to the p_{sfr}. The goal is to let TCP operate in the contention avoidance region. Simulation results show that the algorithm can increase the network throughput and control the network congestion in the MAC layer.

The rest of the paper is organized as follows. Section 2 describes the MLCC algorithm. Section 3 gives a model to analyze the relationship between the sensing failure ratio and the network throughput. Simulation results and the performance evaluation are presented in Section 4. Section 5 concludes this paper.

2   MLCC Algorithm

Due to the contention for the shared channel, only one node can capture the channel at one time. So nodes in multihop wireless networks will always be interfered with its neighbors and go into the backoff procedure[9-10]. This motivate us to take advantage of the backoff state to indicate congestion and tune the probability of packet loss, so as to control the source sending rate, and thus solve the congestion problem.

2.1   Checking the Congestion Status

The binary exponential backoff algorithm is used by the IEEE 802.11 DCF to control the access to shared medium among contending nodes. This is done through adjusting the contention window size based on the current medium status. When a node has some data to send, it senses the channel to determine whether it is idle. If the medium remains idle for a time interval equal to DIFS (DCF Interframe Space), the node is allowed to transmit. If the medium is busy, the transmission is postponed until the ongoing transmission concludes. Meanwhile, a slotted binary exponential backoff procedure takes place: the number of such slots is determined by a random value uniformly chosen in [0, CW-1], where CW (Contention Window) is the current contention window size.

The backoff procedure shall be invoked for a node to transfer a frame when finding the medium busy as indicated by either the physical or virtual CS (carrier sensing) mechanism. The backoff procedure shall also be invoked when a transmitting node infers a failed transmission as described in last paragraph.

According to the IEEE 802.11 DCF, we can record the number of one node entries the backoff algorithm during one packet transmission procedure:

1) Denotes n_{fb} is the number that the medium is determined by the CS mechanism to be busy when a node desires to initiate the initial frame.
2) Denotes n_{cb} is the number that after sending the RTS frame the sender does not receive the CTS frame successfully.
3) Denotes n_{ab} is the number that after sending the DATA frame, the sender does not receive the ACK frame successfully.
4) After a successful transmission, the node will also entry the backoff algorithm, say n_s.

Thus we calculate p_{sfr} as follows:

$$p_{sfr} = \frac{n_{fb} + n_{cb} + n_{ab}}{n_{fb} + n_{cb} + n_{ab} + n_s} \tag{1}$$

2.2 Description of the MLCC

In MLCC, the MAC layer maintains the average ratio of the p_{sfr}, so the congestion metric can be expressed as:

$$p_{sfr} = a \times p_{sfr} + (1 - a) \times p_{sfr}^{old} \tag{2}$$

where the p_{sfr}^{old} was the previous value of the congestion metric.

Algorithm 1. EACC

1: **if** $p_{sfr} < min_{th}$ **then**
2:     $p_d = 0$
3: **else if** $min_{th} < p_{sfr} < max_{th}$ **then**
4:     $p_d = (p_{sfr} - min_{th}) / (max_{th} - min_{th})$
5: **else if** $max_{th} < p_{sfr}$
6:     $p_d = 1$
7: **end if**
8: when a node has packets to transmit
9: calculate $n_{fb}, n_{cb}, n_{ab}, n_s$
10: calculate $p_{sfr} = \dfrac{n_{fb} + n_{cb} + n_{ab}}{n_{fb} + n_{cb} + n_{ab} + n_s}$
11: $p_{sfr} = a \times p_{sfr} + (1 - a) \times p_{sfr}^{old}$

The head-of-line packet is dropped from the MAC queue buffer with a probability based on the average sensing failure ratio. At each node, if the average p_{sfr} is small, say less than min_{th}, which means that the node is rarely congested, packets in the buffer are not dropped. When it is get larger, the dropping probability p_d is computed according to (3). If the average p_{sfr} is larger than max_{th}, all of the packet should be dropped since the network suffered serious congestion, that is $p_d = 1$. The MLCC pseudocode is shown in algorithm 1.

$$p_d = (p_{sfr} - \min_{th})/(\max_{th} - \min_{th}), \qquad \min_{th} < p_{sfr} < \max_{th} \tag{3}$$

Our algorithm relies only on local information, which a node can derive from its own experience without exploiting the content of the packet it receives nor the packet it can listen on the medium. There are many advantages in using such local information. For example, such information is always available and reliable and if no message is exchanged, the protocol overhead is reduced. Thus locality is an important property for wireless networks protocols, especially for MAC protocols.

3   Analytical Model

In this section, we propose the analytical model of the IEEE 802.11 DCF protocol with RTS/CTS frame. To simplify the model, this paper does not consider the channel error on the impact of the transmission. The Equation (1) can be expressed as

$$n_{fb} + n_{cb} + n_{ab} = n_s \frac{p_{sfr}}{1 - p_{sfr}} \tag{4}$$

In the transmission process, each packet needs retransmission N times, thus we have $n_s = 1$ and

$$N = n_{fb} + n_{cb} + n_{ab} = p_{sfr}/(1 - p_{sfr}) \tag{5}$$

Let $\overline{T_{RTS}}$ is the average time required to transmit the RTS frame during one successful transmission, so we have

$$\overline{T_{RTS}} = (1 + N)T_{RTS} \tag{6}$$

where T_{RTS} is the time required to deliver a RTS frame. According to the RTS/CTS access mode, the average RTT time between any adjacent nodes can be expressed as

$$\overline{T_{RTT}} = 2(\text{DIFS} + \overline{T_{RTS}} + T_{CTS} + T_{ACK} + 3\text{SIFS} + 4\delta + \overline{T_{CW}}) + T_{TCP\text{-}DATA} + T_{TCP\text{-}ACK} \tag{7}$$

The terms DIFS, SIFS are the time durations introduced by IEEE 802.11 DCF. T_{CTS}, T_{ACK} are the time required to deliver the CTS, ACK frame. $T_{TCP\text{-}DATA}$, $T_{TCP\text{-}ACK}$ are the durations of the transmission of the 802.11 data frames carrying the TCP DATA and the TCP ACK packet. δ is the propagation delay. $\overline{T_{CW}}$ is the average backoff time.

Now, let us try to estimate the average contention window size. Let m is the maximum retry times of one transmission. Since the backoff time is uniformly distributed over [0, CW-1], where $CW = 2^m CW_0$, CW_0 is the initial value of contention window. We assume that the backoff time chosen each time is equal to $CW/2$. Note that the p_{sfr} happens when two or more nodes transmit at the same slot, or when the

MAC frame is corrupted by medium contention. So the average contention window size $\overline{CW}$ is given by

$$
\begin{aligned}
\overline{CW} &= (1-p_{\text{sfr}})(\text{CW}_0/2)+(1-p_{\text{sfr}})p_{\text{sfr}}\cdot(2\text{CW}_0/2)+(1-p_{\text{sfr}})p_{\text{sfr}}^2\cdot(2^2\text{CW}_0/2)+\cdots+ \\
&\quad (1-p_{\text{sfr}})p_{\text{sfr}}^m\cdot(2^m\text{CW}_0/2)+p_{\text{sfr}}^{m+1}\cdot(2^m\text{CW}_0/2) \\
&= \frac{\text{CW}_0(1-p_{\text{sfr}}-p_{\text{sfr}}(2p_{\text{sfr}})^m)}{2(1-2p_{\text{sfr}})})
\end{aligned}
\tag{8}
$$

Hence, the average backoff time $\overline{T_{\text{CW}}}$ is expressed as

$$
\overline{T_{\text{CW}}} = \overline{CW}\cdot\text{T}_{\text{slot}}
\tag{9}
$$

where T_{slot} is a slot time in IEEE 802.11 DCF. Let *length_frame* denote the average data length at the application layer. The expected throughput *Th* for a TCP connection over IEEE 802.11 wireless link is given by

$$
Th = \frac{length\_frame}{\overline{T_{\text{RTT}}}}
\tag{10}
$$

According to (5)-(10), we then have the throughput function with p_{sfr}.

4   Performance Evaluation

In this section, we use the network simulator NS-2[11] to conduct the simulations. We use DSR protocol for routing. The transport layer protocol we used is TCP NewReno. We do not consider the node's mobility, which is the future work for us. The transmission range is about 250m and the sensing range is about 550m. We set the channel bandwidth as 2Mbps and use 1000 bytes as the payload size of each DATA packet. The threshold min_{th} and max_{th} are set 0.3 and 0.6. The parameters used in MAC layer are described in Table 1.

Table 1. Simulation parameters

MAC Header (bits)	224	DIFS (μs)	50
PHY Header (bits)	192	SIFS (μs)	10
RTS (bits)	160	SLOT (μs)	20
CTS (bits)	112	CW_{min}	31
ACK (bits)	112	CW_{max}	1023
δ (μs)	1		

First, we analyze the experiment to verify the validity of p_{sfr} as the congestion metric. We use a two-chain network topology with 10 nodes, similar with Fig.1, in which nodes are separated by 200m. The simulation time is 200s. During this time, TCP flow is injected at time 0s, 50s, 100s, 150s, the addition of each TCP flow will increase the medium competition. We statistic the times of node C enters BEB algorithm. The result is shown in Table 2. From Table.2 we can see that the number of successfully transmitted packets from 2689 down to 2219, the p_{sfr} increased from 0.111 up to 0.178. This indicates that with the increase of TCP flows, network congestion becomes more serious and p_{sfr} becomes bigger. Thus it is feasible to use p_{sfr} to describe the MAC layer congestion status.

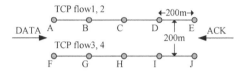

Fig. 1. An example network topology with two chains

Table 2. Correlation   between sensing failure ratio and TCP Congestion

	TCP	2TCP	3TCP	4TCP
n_s	2689	2550	2432	2219
n_{fb}	23	29	37	58
n_{cb}	245	261	292	323
n_{ab}	68	73	81	101
p_{sfr}	0.111	0.125	0.144	0.178

The relationship between the throughput and the sensing failure ratio (p_{sfr}) has shown on the Fig.2. The simulation result was slighter lower than the theoretical value. The simulation curve almost matches the theoretical value. When the p_{sfr} became bigger, the throughput became lower, so the p_{sfr} could indicate the network congestion status. Due to the inflection point on the curve, we set the threshold min_{th}, max_{th} are 0.3 and 0.6.

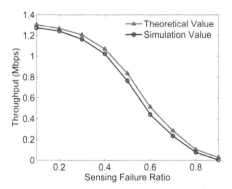

Fig. 2. The relationship between the throughput and the sensing failure ratio

The throughput of our scheme was tested over the cross topologies on Fig.3. We have run every simulation 10 times using different seeds and got the average value. The TCP throughput results are compared in Fig.4. We observe that our MLCC scheme enhanced link layer is able to boost 802.11 in throughput up to 5%. This is because our algorithm reduces the channel contention, and helps to improve spatial channel reuse, the heavier the contention, the more it benefits from the channel reuse.

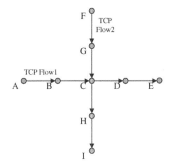

Fig. 3. An example network topology of cross traffic

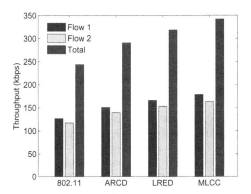

Fig. 4. Network throughput in the simulation

We only simulated the proposed scheme in a simple scenario, but the scheme can be extended to a complex scenario with more nodes, which is our future work. However, the results of the simulation indicate that the p_{sfr} can assist in controlling the network overload and accurately reflect the degree of wireless network congestion.

5   Conclusion

The performance of multihop wireless networks declined when using IEEE 802.11 MAC protocol. This is because nodes need to contend for shared channel with their neighbors, which leads to congestion and decreases throughput of the network. The paper presents a MAC layer solution based on the binary exponential backoff algorithm, MLCC. In this algorithm, we propose a new MAC layer metric for congestion, i.e., p_{sfr}. A node monitors the intensity of wireless channel competition and records the times it generates the backoff period, then it figures out p_{sfr}. During the transmission, nodes need to estimate the current level of the network congestion, and computes drop probability to discard its packet. Next, we give a function of p_{sfr} and throughput, and prove the effectiveness of p_{sfr} as the congestion metric. Simulation results show that MLCC can accurately estimate the network congestion status, improve the TCP throughput.

Acknowledgement. This work was supported in part by the Foundation for Innovative Research Groups of the National Science Foundation of China (Grant No. 60921001), the National Basic Research Program of China (Grant No. 2011CB707000), the National High Technology Research and Development Program of China (Grant No. 2011AA110101).

References

1. Khurshid, A., Kabir, M.H., Prodhan, M.A.T.: An improved TCP congestion control algorithm for wireless networks. In: 13th IEEE Pacific Rim Conference on Communications, Computers and Signal Processing, Canada, pp. 382–387 (2011)
2. Huang, Y.-C., Chu, C.-H., Wu, E.H.-K.: A novel congestion control mechanism on TFRC for streaming applications over wired-wireless networks. In: 7th ACM Workshop on Wireless Multimedia Networking and Computing, United States, pp. 9–15 (2011)
3. Deng, D.-J., Li, B., Huang, L., et al.: Saturation throughput analysis of multi-rate IEEE 802.11 wireless networks. Wireless Communications and Mobile Computing 8, 1102–1112 (2009)
4. Yun, J.-H.: Cross-layer explicit link status notification to improve TCP performance in wireless networks. EURASIP Journal on Wireless Communications and Networking 2009, 15 pages (2009)
5. Fu, Z., Zerfos, P., Luo, H., et al.: The impact of multihop wireless channel on TCP throughput and loss. In: Proc. of IEEE INFOCOM 2003, San Francisco, pp. 1744–1753 (2003)
6. Wu, W., Zhang, Z., Sha, X., et al.: Auto rate MAC protocol based on congestion detection for wireless ad hoc networks. Information Technology Journal 8, 1205–1212 (2009)
7. Armaghani, F.R., Jamuar, S.S., Khatun, S., et al.: An adaptive TCP delayed acknowledgment strategy in interaction with MAC layer over multi-hop ad-hoc networks. In: Proc. of CSA 2008, Hobart, pp. 137–142 (2008)
8. Wang, J., Wen, J., Zhang, J., et al.: TCP-FIT - A novel TCP congestion control algorithm for wireless networks. In: 2010 IEEE Globecom Workshops, GC 2010, United States, pp. 2065–2069 (2010)
9. Kliazovich, D., Granelli, F.: Cross-Layer Congestion Control in Ad Hoc Wireless Networks. IEEE/ACM Trans. on Ad Hoc Networks 4, 687–708 (2006)
10. ElRakabawy, S.M., Klemm, A., Lindemann, C.: TCP with Adaptive Pacing for Multihop Wireless Networks. In: Proceedings of the 6th ACM International Symposium on Mobile Ad Hoc Networking and Computing, pp. 288–299 (2005)
11. The network simulator ns-2, http://www.isi.edu/nsnam/ns

An Active Service Protocol Based on the Co-evolutionary Algorithm for Supply Chain Management

Rui Wang

School of Management Science and Engineering,
Shandong University of Finance and Economics, Jinan, China
kingkeen@126.com

Abstract. An active service protocol called ASP for supply chain management was proposed. This protocol exploits stable relation and resourceful nodes, called acquaintances, which perform active services in the supply chains. The experimental results show that the new protocol proposed offers better performance than other protocols. This work using the adaptable co-evolution algorithm can provide global optimization and continuously develop services for the supply chain management.

Keywords: active service, supply chain management, co-evolutionary.

1 Introduction

In recent decades, the service economy has always been the driving force of economic growth of every developed nation. Indeed, the transformation of industrialized economies from a manufacturing base to a service orientation is a continuing phenomenon. Supply chain management (SCM) is a common practice across manufacturing industries from both the practical and academic standpoints. the emphasis in SCM is still strongly skewed toward the manufacturing sector. This is because effective SCM can lead to a lowering of the total amount of resources required to provide the necessary level of customer service to a specific segment and improving customer service through increased product availability and reduced order cycle time while reducing costs. Although, it is believed that service industry can benefit applying some best practices from manufacturing industry, the indifferences between service and manufacturing industries could create a need for specific service supply chain performance measures reflecting service supply chain practices. Thus, there has been little research to date on service supply chain performance measurement. For this reason, it is necessary for researchers to measure the service supply chain processes.

The rest of the paper is structured as follows: §2 presents the related work; §3 details an active service protocol based on the co-evolutionary algorithm; §4 presents experimental analysis, §5 gives the conclusion.

M. Zhao and J. Sha (Eds.): ICCIP 2012, Part I, CCIS 288, pp. 615–622, 2012.
© Springer-Verlag Berlin Heidelberg 2012

2   Related Work

SCM has been defined to explicitly recognize the strategic nature of coordination between trading partners which would improve the performance of an individual organization, and to improve the performance of the entire supply chain. The goal of SCM is to create sourcing, making and delivery processes and logistics functions seamlessly across the supply chain as an effective competitive weapon. The concept of SCM has received increasing attention from academicians, consultants, and business managers alike[1-3]. Many organizations have begun to recognize that SCM is the key to building a sustainable competitive edge for their products or services in an increasingly crowded marketplace[4].

In an attempt to manage service supply chain processes, Giannakis [5] explores the utility of the manufacturing biased SCOR model in services and develops a reference model for use in service organizations. Boonitt and Pongpanarat [6] apply the Q-sort technique to the scale development process in order to address the reliability and validity problems caused by subjectivity of the supply chain management in service. Studies so far focus on application of existing SCM models to the management of service supply chains [7]. Few researchers have been interested in how traditional supply chain functions can be defined in services [8-9], and investigated the dyadic relationship between the service providers and the end consumer of a service [10]. In an attempt to develop a service SCM framework, Ellram [11]defined service supply chain management as the management of information, processes, capacity, service performance and funds from the earliest supplier to the ultimate customer. An important message in SCM is that a differentiation of tasks should take place[12]. Such a differentiation can be practiced through different types of relationships with customers, as well as suppliers. Like the research of Giannakis [13], they view capacity management as a key to understanding the service, by considering the process of providing a service as the transfer of capacity for the purposes of providing value to the customer.

3   ASP(Active Service Protocol)

3.1   The Active Service Protocol

The active service protocol we propose involves an active service agent (ASA), a set of potential contractors-service organization agent (SOA), and a set of client managers-migrating instance (MI). ASA's global perspective is modeled as a set of recommender policies. When a potential SOA registers with ASA, it becomes a alliance member and then can provide services on behalf of the alliance. These recommendations are applied to the list of proposals sent back by the potential contractors. In this way MI selects the proposals that are optimized from a goal-oriented perspective.

In this case the recommender policies may include: 1) minimize the number of available services by co-evolving the applications that imply the activation of available service organizations alliance and 2) minimize the total MI mobile distance by selecting the recommender service proposals.

3.2   Data Structures and Message Formats

Let ORG={org_1, org_2,···, org_n} be a mass of service organizations, and ASA={ASA_1, ASA_2,···, ASA_n} be a group of active service agents. A service alliance can be defined as Alli(ORG,ASA_i)={ org_j| org_j ∈ ORG ∧ ServiceRecommder(Alli)= ASA_i }, where i,j∈{1,...,n} and ASA_i is the active service agent of the ASA.

3.2.1   Goal Token Format
There is only one goal token for the each supply chain management instance. A goal hierarchy can be used to produce a schema comprising a set of nested sub works, where each sub work is aimed at achieving a corresponding goal in the goal hierarchy. By using the goal token, we can implement goal-oriented mechanism for recommender messages and contract messages that have been eventually delivered to MI.

A goal token GT is a tuple: GT={GID,G_{Time}, G_{Cost}},where

- GID is the ID of the Goal.
- G_{Time} is the valid time of the goal.
- G_{Cost} is cost of the goal.

3.2.2   Format of Messages
Our protocol employs two types of messages: recommender message and contract message.

(1) Recommender message
A recommender message (RM) is a tuple: RM=(AID,Qua,Goal,Recipient,Time), where

- AID is the ID of the service alliance.
- Qua is the qualification description of the service alliance.
- Goal is goal specification of the service alliance.
- Recipient is the desired MI receiving message RM.
- Time is the valid time of message RM.

(2) Contract message
Contract messages are used for confirming the competency to acquire service when MIs are moving between service alliance. A contract message (CM) is a tuple: CM=(CID, Task, Time),where

- CID is the ID of the CM.
- Task is the description of the task to be executed.
- Time is the expiration time of CM.

3.3   The Co-evolutionary Algorithm

As shown in algorithm 1, our service alliance recommendation generation algorithm is applicable to both designs: Expand Influence (EI) and Enforce Energy (EE). Given that two service organizations, $org_1=\{p_1,p_2,\cdots,p_n\}$ and $org_2=\{q_1,q_2,\cdots,q_n\}$. Because they do not achieve MI goal respectively, one new org^v is determined by cooperating strategy to expand influence or enforce energy. If fitness(org_1)<1 and fitness(org_2) <1 , then the new org^v is determined by Cooperating Strategy1, otherwise it is determined by Cooperating Strategy2, where fitness(org_i) $\in$ (0,1) is a evaluation criterion of organizational service capability.

The aim of Cooperating Strategy1 is to improve the capability of organizational service; however, Cooperating Strategy2 is to polymerize capability of organizational service. org^v_{EI} and org^v_{EE} are determined by (2) and (3), respectively:

$$org^v_{EI} =\{p_1, \cdots, p_{i-1}, p_{i+1}, \cdots, p_n, q_1, \cdots, q_{i-1}, q_{i+1}, \cdots, q_n, q_i+p_i\} \tag{1}$$

$$org^v_{EE} =\{p_1, \cdots, p_{i-1}, p_{i+1}, \cdots, p_n, q_1, \cdots, q_{i-1}, q_{i+1}, \cdots q_n, r\} \tag{2}$$

r = q_x+p_y (1<x,y<n) is the new individual .

Algorithm 1: service alliance co-evolutionary algorithm:

Step 1: $t=0$, initialize $Alli_0$ with one or more org.
Step 2: If the number of organizations in $Alli_t$ is less than two, go to 5.
Step 3: Randomly select two organizations, org_i and org_j from $Alli_t$. Perform Cooperating Strategy on them to produce a new organization org^v_t, delete org_1 and org_2 from $Alli_t$, and add org^v_t to $Alli_{t+1}$.
Step 4: Move the organizations left in $Alli_t$ to $Alli_{t+1}$, t=t+1, go to step 2.
Step 5: The service recommendation is $\Re = \{org_1, org_2, ..., org_i, org^v_t\}$

4   Experimental Analysis

The ASP is simulated on the well-known simulator Glomosim[14,15] under different mobility scenarios. Several interesting experiments are carried out to test the scalability and the efficiency of ASP in Supply Chain Management. Experiments are carried out ranging from a topology consisting of 25 sites to 100 sites. To evaluate the improvement of ASP, these two protocols are implemented: a traditional flooding scheme for service discovery (BASIC) and ODMRP[16].

4.1   Performance Metrics

Three performance metrics are considered in our experiments.

1) First-Response-Time: It is the interval between the generation of the MI's request packet and the arrival of the corresponding SOA's first reply packet. It measures the promptness of these service protocols.

2) Success-Scope: It is the scope of protocol sessions in which SOA has received at least one reply packet. It reflects the effectiveness of these service protocols.

4.2   Experimental Results

Three experiments are performed which use the two selected service discovery protocols and ASP, respectively, where request number is set to 20, 40, 60, 80, and 100. Each set consists of 100 similar simulations. Experiment results are shown in the following 3 figures.

Fig. 1 shows the effect of request number on first-response time metric. It can be seen that ASP improves the systems performance in terms of first-response time. The first-response time of ASP is significantly lower than that of BASIC. The ODMRP is relatively poor. When the number of service request packet is 40, the first-response time of ASP is only 4.9s, while that of BASIC reaches 8.9s. In BASIC and ODMRP, this metric keeps almost constant. However, in ASP, this metric decreases gradually along with the increase of request packet number. As request packet number increases, more service requests will be matched in fewer groups. Hence, first-response-time will be reduced.

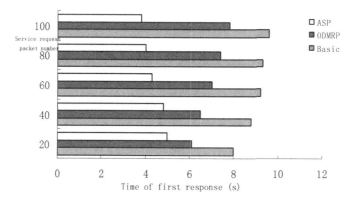

Fig. 1. First-Response-Time under different request packet number

Fig. 2 shows the effect of request packet number on Success-Scope metric. It can be seen that ASP effectively improves the Success-Scope of mobile transactions. When the number of service request packet is 20, the Success-Scope of ASP is 49.1%, while that of BASIC only reaches 30%. Request number increase leads to the packet transmission failures, which can greatly decrease the Success-Scope since that reply packets are very few. Therefore, in BASIC and ODMRP, Success-Scope decreases along with the increase of request packet number. However, in ASP, group-based service recommender operation makes up for the negative effect of request packet number on this metric. Hence, Success-Scope is not decreased in ASP.

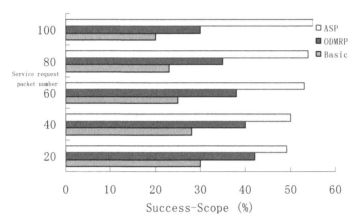

Fig. 2. Success-Scope under different request packet number

Fig. 3 shows the effect of request packet number on SPN2TPN metric. This metric is determined by request packet number, service recommendation/advertisement packets and reply packet number. Hence, the results in this figure are intelligible. It can be seen that the SPN2TPN of ASP is significantly higher than that of other protocols. When the number of service request packet is 20, the SPN2TPN of ASP reaches 0.08, while that of BASIC is only 0.022. Basing on the results, a conclusion can be made. ASP is almost the most efficient protocol under different request packet number. The superiority of ASP over BASIC and ODMRP protocols in this metric is more remarkable with higher request packet number.

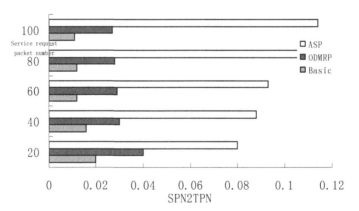

Fig. 3. SPN2TPN under different request packet number

5　Conclusions

This paper motivates the need for a goal-oriented active service protocol in a heterogeneous supply chain management. We propose a co-evolutionary algorithm.

offering better performance than other protocols. The process of active services is discussed allowing runtime selection, integration and coordination of distributed resources. Future work will be directed to conducting more MIs' engagements, and to enhancing existing QoS standards.

Acknowledgment. This work is supported by the Shandong Province Higher Educational Science and Technology Program: (grant Nos. J10LG29).

References

1. Croom, S., Romano, P., Giannakis, M.: Supply chain management: an analytical framework for critical literature review. European Journal of Purchasing and Supply Management 6(1), 67–83 (2000)
2. Tan, K.C., Kannan, V.R., Handfield, R.B.: Supply chain management: supplier performance and firm performance. International Journal of Purchasing and Materials Management 34(3), 2–9 (1998)
3. Van Hoek, R.I., Voss, R.I., Commandeur, H.R.: Restructuring European supply chain by mplementing postponement strategies. Long Range Planning 32(5), 505–518 (1999)
4. Boddy, D., Cahill, D., Charles, M., Fraser-Kraus, H., Macbeth, D.: Success and failure in implementing partnering. European Journal of Purchasing and Supply Management 4(23), 143–151 (1998)
5. Giannakis, M.: Management of service supply chains with a service oriented reference model: The case of management consulting source. Supply Chain Management: An International Journal 16(5), 120–128 (2011)
6. Boonitt, S., Pongpanarat, C.: Measuring service supply chain management processes: The application of the Q-sort technique. International Journal of Innovation, Management and Technology 2(3), 217–221 (2011)
7. Arlbjørn, J.S., Freytag, P.V., de Haas, H.: Service supply chain management: A survey of lean application in the municipal sector. International Journal of Physical Distribution & Logistics Management 41(3), 277–295 (2011)
8. Ellram, L., Tate, W., Billington, C.: Understanding and managing the services supply chain. Journal of Supply Chain Management 40(4), 17–32 (2004)
9. Kahraman, C., Cebeci, U., Ruan, D.: Multi-attribute comparison of catering service companies using fuzzy AHP: The case of Turkey. International Journal of Production Economics 87(2), 171–184 (2004)
10. Sampson, S.E.: Customer-supplier duality and bidirectional supply chains in service organizations. International Journal of Service Industry Management 11(4), 348–364 (2000)
11. Ellram, L., Tate, W., Billington, C.: Services supply management: The next frontier for improved organisational performance. California Management Review 49(4), 44–66 (2007)
12. Autry, C.W., Golicic, S.L.: Evaluating buyer-supplier relationship -Performance spirals: A longitudinal study. Journal of Operations Management 28(2), 87–100 (2010)
13. Giannakis, M.: Management of service supply chains with a service oriented reference model: The case of management consulting source. Supply Chain Management: An International Journal 16(5) (2011) (on-line print)

14. Feeley, M., Hutchinson, N., Ray, S.: Realistic Mobility for Mobile Ad Hoc Network Simulation. In: Nikolaidis, I., Barbeau, M., An, H.-C. (eds.) ADHOC-NOW 2004. LNCS, vol. 3158, pp. 324–329. Springer, Heidelberg (2004)
15. Kato, T., Ono, M., Higaki, H.: Parallelization of GloMoSim wireless network simulator. IPSJ SIG Technical Reports 2(1), 55–58 (2006)
16. Bae, S.H., Lee, S.J., Su, W., Gerla, M.: The design, implementation, and performance evaluation of the on-demand multicast routing protocol in multihop wireless networks. IEEE Network 14(1), 70–77 (2000)

Interactive Dynamic Influence Diagrams Modeling Communication

Bo Li and Jian Luo

Department of Automation, Xiamen University, Xiamen, Fujian, China
jianluo@xmu.edu.cn

Abstract. Communication embodied the social characteristic of multi-agent systems. Agents could benefit from exchanging information. When communication incurs a cost, whether to communicate or not also becomes a decision to make. In this paper, we study communication decision problems with an extension framework of interactive dynamic influence diagrams (I-DIDs), we assume a communication sub-stage where all communication complete before deciding the regular action. In our framework, agent at higher level has a choice of performing a communication action just after the previous action finishes and before the next action is chosen. The purpose of communication is for higher level agent to send its current observation (real or deceptive) to other agent at lower level. Agent initiates communication so as to optimize the benefit it obtains as the result of the interaction. An example problem is studied under this framework. From this example we can see the impact communication policies have on the overall rewards of agents.

Keywords: Multi-Agent Systems, Communication, Interactive Dynamic Influence Diagrams.

1   Introduction

Though growing up long before the concept of an intelligent agent was conceived, decision-theoretic modeling has gained increasing interest as a technique for communication in multi-agent systems. Huber and Durfee suggest using a probabilistic plan recognizer[1] to deduce the status of the commitments of other agents involved in a joint plan. Gmytrasiewicz et al. developed a rigorous approach for modeling the utility of communication, based on decision and game-theoretic methods[2]. Pynadath et al. present a formal framework based on the game theory with incomplete information for modeling the coordination and communication problem among a team of collaborative agents[3]. Xuan and Lesser present a multi-agent extension to Markov Decision Process (MDP) to optimize both actions and communication[4]. Decentralized partially observable MDP communication(Dec-POMDP-Com)[5] and its extreme form of decentralized MDP model with communication (Dec-MDP-Com) [6]with joint full observability, is a theoretic model for decentralized control of multiple decision-makers that share a common set of objectives.

In the tradition of cognitive science and related field[7,8] , the fundamental function of communication is to confer some advantage to speaker by influencing

M. Zhao and J. Sha (Eds.): ICCIP 2012, Part I, CCIS 288, pp. 623–630, 2012.

what the hearer(s) knows and intends to do. Communication enables agents to base their decisions on more complete knowledge of the overall situation. However, when communication incurs a cost, the computational complexity of finding the optimal communication policy ranges from NP-complete to NEXP-complete which depending on the specific characteristics of the domain[9-10]. The main objective of this work is thus to develop cost-effective methods[11] or value of communication[12] for deciding when to communicate in decentralized settings. A common approach to factor this into the model is to assign communication a negative reward or cost.

In this paper, we present a communicative extension to interactive dynamic influence diagrams[13], which to optimize both actions and communication. We model communication as an explicit action that incurs a cost. We will use the *tell* model of communication[4]. That is, one agent at higher level simply tells its current observation to other agent at lower level. We consider agents' decision-making from the perspective of an individual agent in a self-interested environment. An agent that is considering sending a message should base its decision on an estimation of whether the message's recursive impact on the sender and receiver's beliefs will improve the expected outcome of its decisions. We add communication into the framework of I-DID, and assume a communication sub-stage where all communication complete before deciding the regular action. We embody decision-theoretic techniques to select the communication and regular action with the highest expected utility.

2   Related Work

We outline interactive influence diagrams(I-IDs) for two-agent interactions followed by their extensions to dynamic settings, I-DIDs[14].

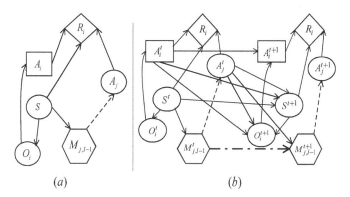

(a)   (b)

Fig. 1. Models of I-ID and I-DID [13]

I-IDs(Fig.1 (a)) are represented by directed acyclic graphs (DAGs) with four types of nodes: Chance nodes, shown as circles, represent random variables; Decision nodes, shown as squares, represent choices or actions available to the decision maker; Value nodes, shown as diamonds, represent local utility functions; Finally, model nodes, shown as hexagon, represent the model sets of other agents. The arcs in a I-ID have a different meaning based on their target. Furthermore, I-IDs have a chance node, A_j, that represents the distribution over the other agent's actions, and a dashed link, called a policy link. I-DIDs extend I-IDs to allow sequential decision making over several time steps. We depict a general two time slice I-DID in Fig.1 (b). For more detail and I-DID see references [13,14].

3   I-DID Model with Communication

We add a communication sub-stages in I-DID between two time slices.

3.1   Level $l > 0$ I-DID with Communication Sub-stage

We assume an agent at level l ($l > 0$) has a choice of performing a communication action just after the previous action finishes and before the next action is chosen. The purpose of communication is for one agent to send its current observation to other agents at level $l-1$, so as to influent receivers' beliefs and what tend to do. We show a general level l I-DID with communication for action sub-stage at t time slice to communication sub-stage, and communication sub-stage to action sub-stage at $t+1$ time slice.

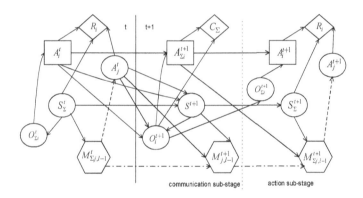

Fig. 2. I-DID with communication sub-stage($l > 0$)

As shown in Fig.2, the means of chance nodes A_j, hexagonal nodes M_j, dash-dot links and dotted links are as same as in I-DID. In action sub-stage, agents implement joint action $< a_i^t, a_j^t >$, and physical states S_Σ^t transit to S^{t+1} with probability $Pr(s^{t+1} \mid s^t, a_i^t, a_j^t)$, agent i will get observation o_i^{t+1} with probability $Pr(o_i^{t+1} \mid s^{t+1}, a_i^t, a_j^t)$. Message that agent i will share with other agents is stored in node $A_{\Sigma i}$, $A_{\Sigma i} = \{Null, \Omega\}$. That is agent will send its current observable information (real or deceptive) or *Null* message to other agents, which message that agent will choose to send determined by its expected utility. In order to make agent send its real observation information to others, we give a high cost for behaviors that transmit false information. To simplify the model, we assume agent j implement *accept information* form higher level agent.

There are many communication types, such as *tell*, *query* and *sync.*. In our model, we assume agent at higher level shares its current observation information with other agents at lower level, that is to say agent simply tells its current observation to other agent. In this type of communication, an agent knows other agent's observation information only when the other agent lies in the higher level and voluntarily decides to tell.

The update of the model node over time involves three steps: First, given the candidate models $M_{\Sigma j}^{t}$ at action sub-stage for time t, we identify updated set of models that reside in the model node at communication sub-stage for time $t+1$. Then, update each model in model node M_{j}^{t+1} after agents receive communication information from higher level agents. Finally, compute the new distribution over the updated models in $M_{\Sigma j}^{t+1}$ given the original distribution and the probability of the agent performing the action and receiving the observation on environment and communication information from other agents that led to the updated model.

In Fig.3, we show how the dash-dot model update link in Fig.2 could be implemented. If the model level $l-1$ model ascribed to j at time step t results in one action, agent i and j could make one of two possible observations, then the model node at communication sub-stage for time step $t+1$ contains two updated models $(m_{j,l-1}^{t+1,1}, m_{j,l-1}^{t+1,2})$, then j will receive three possible information from agent i, then the model node at action sub-stage for time step $t+1$ contains six updated models, as shown in Fig.3.

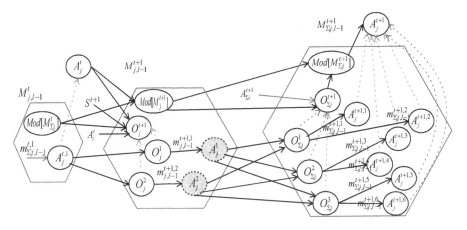

Fig. 3. Representing the model update link between model nodes using chance nodes and dependency links between them

Expansion of the I-DID with communication over more time steps, we note that the possible set of models of the other agent j grows exponentially with the number of time steps.

3.2   Level $l = 0$ DID with Communication

0 level as the bottom layer, agent can not send its observation information to other agents, but it can simply receive information from agents at level 1. The action of receiving information does not change the physical state, but affect agent's belief on physical state. Fig.4 is I-DID model with communication at level 0.

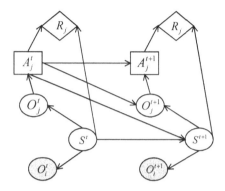

Fig. 4. I-DID model with communication ($l = 0$)

4   Solving a I-DID with Communication

The solution to a level l I-DID with communication for agent i expanded over T time steps proceeds in a bottom-up manner and may be carried out recursively. Generally speaking, solving a I-DID with communication will experience the same process with solving an I-DID[13], the difference is communication decision-making. Communication cost can be denoted as $C(a_{\Sigma i}, o_i)$, and $C(a_{\Sigma i} = Null, o_i) = 0$.

Optimal utility is:

$$U(\theta_i) = \max_{a_i \in A_i} \{ \sum_{is} ER_i(is, a_i) b_i(is) - C(a_{\Sigma i}, o_i)$$
$$+ \gamma \sum_{o_i \in \Omega_i} Pr(o_i \mid a_i, b_i) U(< SE_{\theta_i}(b_i, a_i, o_i), \hat{\theta}_i >) \} \qquad (1)$$

I-DID with communication that contains t time slices, optimal policy of agent i can be denoted as $OPT^t = \{a_i^{1*}, o_i^2, a_{\Sigma i}^{2*}, a_i^{2*}, \cdots, o_i^t, a_{\Sigma i}^{t*}, a_i^{t*}\}$, which:

$$OPT(\theta_i) = arg \max_{a_i \in A_i, a_{\Sigma i} \in A_{\Sigma i}} \{ \sum_{is} ER_i(is, a_i) b_i(is) - C(a_{\Sigma i}, o_i)$$
$$+ \gamma \sum_{o_i \in \Omega_i} Pr(o_i \mid a_i, b_i) U(< SE_{\theta_i}(b_i, a_i, o_i), \hat{\theta}_i >) \} \qquad (2)$$

5   Solution of the Multi-Agent Tiger Problem

The single agent tiger game was first introduced in [15]. In our model for multi-agent tiger problem[13], $A_{\Sigma i} = \{Null, GLcom, GRcom\}$ respectively denote agent i don't share information with other agent, or i tell j about its current observation on physical environment is GL or GR. $O_{\Sigma j} = \{Null, OGL, OGR\}$, corresponds to the set of $A_{\Sigma j}$. Agent receive information from other agents has an accuracy of 90%, or that agent believe what it receive is other agents' real observation with 90% accuracy. We solve a I-DID with communication ($l = 1$) model for multi-agent tiger problem.

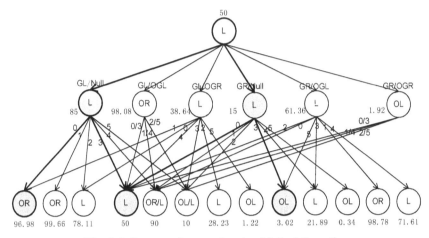

Fig. 5. Policy tree of agent j at level 0 for 3 time slices

Fig.5 gives optimal policy tree of agent j at level 0 for 3 time slices (0-GL/Null; 1-GL/OGL; 2-GL/OGR; 3-GR/Null; 4-GR/OGL; 5-GR/OGR). We note that the correspondence between nodes in the policy tree and model nodes in our framework. Policy tree with three levels do not match five model nodes in the graph of I-DID with communication on 3 time slices. The main reason is that we do not establish communication sub-stage for agent j. To this end, we extend the policy tree. Fig.6 gives the extended policy tree on first and second time-slice.

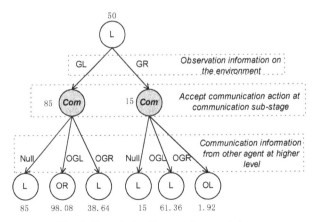

Fig. 6. Extended policy tree for agent j

In cooperative multi-agent tiger problem, we assume i's belief state on tiger location is $Pr(TL,TR) = (0.95, 0.05)$ at time t, and i will pursue highest expected reward $R(b, a_i = a_j = OR)$, so i hopes j will choose action OR. We assume there are one model $m_{\Sigma j} = < (0.5, 0.5), \hat{\theta} >$ in model node $M_{j,0}^t$. Agent i predicts j's action when receiving information from other agent. j's belief on tiger location is (0.5, 0.5), (0.9, 0.1) or (0.1, 0.9), if j has received message *Null*, *OGL*, *OGR* respectively, and j will choose action *L*, *OR* or *OL*. In this case, j's action depends on the received message from i. The content of the message passing by agent i is determined by the difference between reward and communication cost. i will pass message with greatest difference.

6   Conclusion

The centerpiece of our framework is the representation of communication. This has to include extending the framework of I-DID to study agents' communication in uncertain environment. We use tell style in our model. The fact that communication is behavior between agents, and is generally a two-way, when agent send message to others, other agents could take a similar approach gives their information to other agents. So we will rich our framework with more communication styles in our further work.

References

1. Huber, M., Durfee, E.: Deciding when to commit to action during observation-based coordination. In: Proceedings of the First International Conference on Multi-Agent Systems, pp. 163–170 (1995)
2. Gmytrasiewicz, P.J., Durfee, E.H.: Rational communication in multi-agent environments. Autonomous Agents and Multi-Agent Systems 4, 233–272 (2001)
3. Pynadath, D., Tambe, M.: Multi-agent teamwork: Analyzing the optimality and complexity of key theories and models. In: Proceedings of the First Autonomous Agents and Multi-Agent Systems Conference, pp. 873–880 (2002)
4. Xuan, P., Lesser, V., Zilberstein, S.: Communication decisions in multi-agent cooperation: model and experiments. In: Proceeding of the Fifth International Conference on Autonomous Agents, pp. 616–623. ACM Press (2001)
5. Goldman, C., Ziberstein, S.: Optimizing information exchange in cooperative multi-agent systems. In: Proceedings of the Second International Joint Conference on Autonomous Agents and Multi-Agent Systems, pp. 137–144 (2003)
6. Seuken, S., Zilberstein, S.: Formal models and algorithms for decentralized decision making under uncertainty. Journal of Autonomous Agents and Multi-Agent Systems 17(2), 190–250 (2008)
7. Machennan, B.: Synthetic ethology: An approach to the study of communication. In: Langton, C.G., Taylor, C., Farmer, J.D., Rasmussen, S. (eds.) Artificial Life II. SFI Studies in the Sciences of Complexity, pp. 631–658. Addison-Wesley (1991)

8. Dunbar, R.: Theory of mind and the evolution of language. In: Hurford, J.R., Studdert-Kennedy, M., Knight, C. (eds.) Approaches to the Evolution of Language, pp. 92–100. Cambridge University Press (1998)
9. Pynadath, D.V., Tambe, M.: The communicative multiagent team decision problem: Analyzing teamwork theories and models. Journal of Artificial Intelligence Research 16, 389–423 (2002)
10. Goldman, C.V., Zilberstein, S.: Decentralized control of cooperative systems: Categorization and complexity analysis. Journal of Artificial Intelligence Research 22, 143–174 (2004)
11. Becker, R., Carlin, A., Lesser, V., Zilberstein, S.: Analyzing myopic approaches for multi-agent communication. Computational Intelligence 25(1), 31–50 (2009)
12. Carlin, A., Zilberstein, S.: Value of communication in decentralized POMDPs. In: AAMAS 2009 Workshop on Multi-Agent Sequential Decision-Making in Uncertain Domains (2009)
13. Doshi, P., Zeng, Y.F., Chen, Q.: Graphical models for interactive POMDPs: representations and solutions. Journal of Autonomous Agents and Multi-agent Systems 18(3), 376–416 (2009)
14. Polich, K., Gmytrasiewicz, P.: Interactive dynamic influence diagrams. In: 6th International Joint Conference on Autonomous Agents and Multi-Agent Systems, pp. 147–149. ACM Press (2007)
15. Kaelbling, L.P., Littman, M.L., Cassandra, A.R.: Planning and acting in partially observable stochastic domains. Artificial Intelligence 101(2), 99–134 (1998)

A Complete Axiomatisation of Bisimulation in Polymorphic π-Calculus

Feng Yan, Zhoujin Cui, and Zisen Mao

College of Science, PLA. University of Science and Technology,
Nanjing, China
{Nudtyf,maozisen}@163.com, cuizhoujin@126.com

Abstract. The type system is playing an increasingly important role in the theory of distributed systems. Polymorphism constrains the power of observers by preventing them from directly manipulating data values whose types are abstract, leading to notions of equivalence much coarser than the standard untyped ones. In this paper, we study the impact of polymorphism on the algebraic theory of the π-calculus. Precisely, we give an axiomatisation of the polymorphic asynchronous π-calculus which is both sound and complete on the closed finite terms firstly.

Keywords: type system, π-calculus, polymorphism, bisimulation, axiomatisation.

1 Introduction

Concurrent computation model which is the formal characterization for concurrent computation is one of the most important fields in theoretical computer science. There are several traditional models of concurrent computation such as CSP [1], CCS [2], etc. The π-calculus which is the extension of CCS increased by formal characterization for mobility, proposed by Milner, Parrow and Walker, have been a paradigmatic calculus for mobile processes. The current study for the π-calculus focused on the algebraic theory and the type systems. For the algebraic theory, untyped π-calculus has been thoroughly investigated. The main results include various axiomatisations for the main behavior equivalences such as late and early bisimulation, late and early congruence [4], open bisimulation [5] and test equivalence [6]. For the type systems, the research focused on their impact on the behavior equivalences and algebraic theories [7][8][9][10][11]. In this paper, we study the impact of polymorphism types on the algebraic theory of the π-calculus.

The type system plays an important role in the theory of the distributed system. Essentially, the type system is a static analysis tool that ensures the correctness of the program. A common disadvantage of simple type systems is that, although they prevent common programming errors, they also disallow many useful and intuitively correct programs. The polymorphic type system overcome much of this problem by allowing generic operations, that is, operations which can be safely applied to many different types of argument. The polymorphic type allows three modes: Ad-hoc, Subtyping, parametric polymorphism. In this paper, we consider the third type.

M. Zhao and J. Sha (Eds.): ICCIP 2012, Part I, CCIS 288, pp. 631–639, 2012.

After the type system has been introduced into the π-calculus, there have been some new characteristics that need to be explored in depth. One of the most important things is to study the changes in equivalence relations between the two processes. Pierece and Sangiorgi first proposed the concept of capability types by allowing us to distinguish the capability of using a channel in input from that of using the channel in output in [7]. The equivalent relation between the two processes has been changed after introduced capability types mainly because the capability of communication of channels has been imposed restrictions. To see why, consider

$$P \overset{def}{=} (vc)\overline{b}c.a(y).(\overline{y} \mid c) \qquad Q \overset{def}{=} (vc)\overline{b}c.a(y).(\overline{y}.c + c.\overline{y})$$

These processes are not behaviorally equivalent in the untyped π-calculus. However, if we require that only the input capability of channels may be communicated at b, the P and Q are indistinguishable in any (well-typed) context. The behavior equivalence in the polymorphic π-calculus was investigated for the first time in [10]. In [11], a sound and complete bisimulation model for a polymorphic π-calculus have been established. The main contribution of this paper is that we give an axiomatisation of the polymorphic π-calculus which is both sound and complete on the closed finite terms for the first time. It should be pointed out that the π-calculus discussed in this paper is asynchronous, because asynchronism is much closer to the distributed system in reality and easier to implement. In [12], an axiomatisation of the asynchronous π-calculus is introduced without the type system. The situation was getting more complicated with the type system.

2   An Asynchronous Polymorphic π-Calculus

2.1   Syntax

We assume a potentially infinite set of channels C, ranger over by $a,b,\ldots$, and an infinite set of variables V, ranged over by $a,b,\ldots$. Channels, variables are the names, ranged over by $u,v,\ldots$. Below is the syntax of finite π-calculus processes.

$$P,Q ::= \overline{u}\langle T;v \rangle \mid P \mid Q \mid (va:T)P \mid G,$$
$$G ::= 0 \mid u(X;x:T).P \mid \tau.P \mid G+G.$$

Where the syntax makes use of types, ranged over by T, U, V, W and type variables, ranged over by X, Y. The distinction between channels and variables simplifies certain technical details. We write $fn(P)$, $fv(P)$ and $ftv(P)$ for the set of free names, the set of free variables and the set of free type variables, respectively, in P.

2.2   Type System

The type system is given in Table 1. We use Δ and Γ for type environments and write $dom(\Delta)$ for the channels and variables on which Δ is defined. We call type T is generative when T is a type with the form $\updownarrow[X;T]$.

The difference with the type system in [10] is the presence of polymorphism.

Table 1. Type System

$$X, Y, Z$$

$$T, U, V, W ::= X \mid \updownarrow[X;T]$$

$$\Gamma, \Delta ::= X;\, n{:}T$$

$$\frac{X \in \Gamma}{\Gamma \vdash X} \qquad \frac{X,\Gamma \vdash T \quad X \notin dom(\Gamma)}{\Gamma \vdash \updownarrow[X;T]}$$

$$\frac{X \vdash T}{X;n{:}T \vdash \Diamond} \qquad \frac{\Gamma \vdash \Diamond \quad (n{:}T) \in \Gamma}{\Gamma \vdash n{:}T}$$

$$\frac{\Gamma \vdash n{:}\updownarrow[X;T] \quad X,\Gamma,x{:}T \vdash P \quad \{X,x\} \cap dom(\Gamma) = \varnothing}{\Gamma \vdash n(X;x{:}T).P}$$

$$\frac{\Gamma \vdash n{:}\updownarrow[X;U] \quad \Gamma \vdash m{:}U[T/X]}{\Gamma \vdash n\langle T;m\rangle}$$

$$\frac{\Gamma \vdash \Diamond}{\Gamma \vdash 0} \qquad \frac{\Gamma \vdash P \quad \Gamma \vdash Q}{\Gamma \vdash P|Q} \qquad \frac{\Gamma \vdash G \quad \Gamma \vdash G'}{\Gamma \vdash G+G'}$$

$$\frac{T \text{ is generative} \quad \Gamma,a{:}T \vdash P \quad a \notin dom(\Gamma) \quad ftv(T) \subseteq dom(\Gamma)}{\Gamma \vdash (va{:}T)P}$$

2.3 Typed Bisimulation

Untyped labeled transition system does not respect the type system. We therefore investigate a restricted labeled transition system which respects types: this is defined in Table 2. The transition system is given by a relation:

$$(\Gamma \vdash [\sigma]P) \xrightarrow{\alpha} (\Gamma' \vdash [\sigma']P')$$

between configurations of the form $(\Gamma \vdash [\sigma]P)$. These comprise three constitute parts:

- P is the process being observed: after the transition, it becomes process P'.

- Γ is the *external* view of the typing context P operates in.

- σ is a type substitution, mapping the external view to the internal view.

A configuration $\Gamma \vdash [\sigma]P$ is closed whenever $\Gamma[\sigma] \vdash P$ and $\Gamma[\sigma]$ is closed. There are three kinds of transitions:

- *Silent transitions* which are inherited from the untyped transition system.

- *Receptivity transitions* which allow the environment to send data to the process.

- *Output transitions* which allow the process to send data to the environment.

We now formalize our notion of bisimulation equivalence. A typed relation on closed configurations $\mathcal{R}$ is a set of 5-tuples $(\Gamma, \sigma, P, \rho, Q)$ such that $\Gamma\sigma \vdash P$, $\Gamma\rho \vdash Q$ and both $\Gamma\sigma$ and $\Gamma\rho$ are closed.

For convenience, we will write $\Gamma \vDash [\sigma]P\mathcal{R}[\rho]Q$ whenever $(\Gamma, \sigma, P, \rho, Q) \in \mathcal{R}$.

Definition 1 (Bisimulation). A simulation $\mathcal{R}$ is a typed relation on closed configuration such that if $\Gamma \vDash [\sigma]P\mathcal{R}[\rho]Q$ and $(\Gamma \vdash [\sigma]P) \overset{\alpha}{\longrightarrow} (\Gamma' \vdash [\sigma']P')$ then we can show $(\Gamma \vdash [\rho]Q) \overset{\alpha}{\longrightarrow} (\Gamma' \vdash [\rho']Q')$ for some $\Gamma' \vDash [\sigma']P'\mathcal{R}[\rho']Q'$. A bisimulation is a simulation whose inverse is also a simulation. Let $\sim$ be the largest bisimulation.

Table 2. Typed Labeled Transitions

$$\frac{P \overset{\tau}{\longrightarrow} P'}{(\Gamma \vdash [\sigma]P) \overset{\tau}{\longrightarrow} (\Gamma \vdash [\sigma]P')}$$

$$\frac{\Gamma, \vec{a}:\vec{T} \vdash \overline{c}\langle \vec{U}; \vec{b} \rangle, \{\vec{a}\} \cap dom(\Gamma) = \varnothing, \vec{T} \text{ is generative}}{(\Gamma \vdash [\sigma]P) \overset{(\nu \vec{a}:\vec{T})c[\vec{U};\vec{b}]}{\longrightarrow} (\Gamma, \vec{a}:\vec{T} \vdash [\sigma]P \mid (\overline{c}\langle \vec{U}; \vec{b} \rangle \sigma))}$$

$$\frac{P \overset{(\nu \vec{a}:\vec{T})\overline{c}\langle \vec{U}; \vec{b} \rangle}{\longrightarrow} P', \Gamma \vdash c(\overline{X}; \vec{x}:\vec{V}).0, \{\vec{a}, \overline{X}\} \cap dom(\Gamma) = \varnothing}{(\Gamma \vdash [\sigma]P) \overset{(\nu \vec{a}:\vec{T})\overline{c}\langle \overline{X}; \vec{b}:\vec{V} \rangle}{\longrightarrow} (\overline{X}, \Gamma, \vec{b}:\vec{V} \vdash [\vec{U}/\overline{X}, \sigma]P')}$$

3   Axioms for Typed Bisimulation

3.1   Axiom System

The axiom system for polymorphic typed bisimulation is given in Table 3. Whenever we write $P =_{\Gamma}^{\sigma, \rho} Q$ to denote the equivalence between P and Q under type environment Γ. If the two type substitutions are the same we denote it by $P =_{\Gamma} Q$ simply.

Definition 2. If $\Gamma \vdash c : \updownarrow [X; T]$, we call $\overline{c}\langle U; b \rangle$ can be deduced from the type environment Γ if one of the following conditions are satisfied:

- $b \in dom(\Gamma)$, such that $\Gamma \vdash \overline{c}\langle U; b \rangle$;
- $b \in dom(\Gamma)$, $\Gamma \nvdash \overline{c}\langle U; b \rangle$, there exists $d \in dom(\Gamma)$, such that $\Gamma \vdash \overline{d}\langle V; b \rangle$ and $\Gamma \vdash d : \updownarrow [X; T]$;
- The type T is generative and $b \notin dom(\Gamma)$, then $\Gamma, b : T\{U/X\} \vdash \overline{c}\langle U; b \rangle$.

The definition is proposed due to the presence of the phenomenon that a name can be given to two or more types in this paper's environment.

3.2 Normal Form and the Completeness of the Axiom System

In this part, our main work is the proof of completeness of the axiom system. Our proof method largely based on the work of [12]. But due to the presence of type systems and the differences between the two axiom systems, the proof also has obvious difference.

Let $\Pi_{i \in I} \bar{a}_i b_i$ denote a product of outputs. We define now the set $Fire(v\vec{c}\Pi_{i \in I}\bar{a}_i b_i)$ of indices of firable outputs of $\Pi_{i \in I} \bar{a}_i b_i$ when all names in $\vec{c}$ are restricted.

Definition 3. Let $P \equiv (v\vec{c} : \vec{T}) \prod_{i \in I} \bar{a}_i \langle T_i, b_i \rangle$, $\Gamma \sigma \vdash P$, Then $Fire(P) = \bigcup_{n \in \omega} Fire_n(P)$, where $Fire_n(P)$ is the set of indices of outputs that can be fired after exactly n steps, given by:

$$Fire_0(P) = \{ i \mid a_i \notin \{\vec{c}\} \text{ and } \Gamma(a_i) \text{ is generative} \}$$
$$Fire_{n+1}(P) = \{ i \mid \exists k \in Fire_n(P), b_k = a_i, \Gamma(a_i) \text{ is generative} \} \setminus F_n$$

Where $F_n = \bigcup_{m \le n} Fire_m(P)$.

Definition 4 (Normal Form). A normal form is a term defined up to this process of the form:

$$(v\vec{c} : \vec{T}) \left(\Pi_{i \in I} \bar{a}_i \langle T_i, b_i \rangle \mid \left(\sum_{j \in J} \tau.P_j + \sum_{k \in K} a_k(X_k ; x : T_k).P_k \right) \right)$$

Where the sets I, J, K are pairwise disjoint, each P_j, P_k is a normal form and the following conditions are satisfied:

- $\forall c \in \{\vec{c}\}, \exists i \in I, b_i = c$;

- $Fire((v\vec{c} : \vec{T})\Pi_{i \in I}\bar{a}_i \langle T_i ; b_i \rangle) = I$

- $\forall k \forall j$, if Γ can deduce $\bar{a}_k \langle U_k ; b_k \rangle$ and for all type substitution σ, ρ,

$$P_k \{ U_k \sigma / X_k ; b_k / x \} \neq_{\Gamma}^{\sigma, \rho} \left(\bar{a}_k \langle U_k \rho; b_k \rangle \mid P_j \right)$$

For convenience, we will write $P_k \neq_{\Gamma} \left(\bar{a}_k \langle U_k ; b_k \rangle \mid P_j \right)$ for the third item. We will show that each finite term P can be reduced to a normal form using axioms in Table 3. The proof of normalization uses nested induction on the depth and on the structure of P.

Definition 5. The depth of a process P, $d(P)$, is defined inductively by:

$$d(0) = 0; \quad d(\bar{a}\langle T; b \rangle) = 1;$$
$$d(a(X : x : T).P) = d(\tau.P) = 1 + d(P);$$
$$d(P \mid Q) = d(P) + d(Q); \quad d((va : T)P) = d(P);$$
$$d(G + F) = \max\{d(G); d(F)\}.$$

The following lemma proves that each finite process P can be reduce to a normal form.

Lemma 1 (normalisation lemma). For any finite process P there exists a normal form:

$$\lceil P \rceil \equiv (v\vec{c}:\vec{T})\left(\Pi_{i\in I}\,\overline{a}_i\langle T_i,b_i\rangle \,|\!\left(\sum_{j\in J}\tau.P_j + \sum_{k\in K}a_k(X_k;x:T_k).P_k\right)\right)$$

Such that $P =_\Gamma \lceil P \rceil$ and $d(\lceil P \rceil) \le d(P)$.

Proof. Given in [13].

In the proof of our completeness result, we shall use also the following:

Lemma 2 (separation). Let P and Q be two normal forms:

$$P \equiv (v\vec{m}:\vec{T})\left(\prod_{i\in I}\overline{a}_i\langle T_i;b_i\rangle \Big| P_\Sigma\right),$$

$$Q \equiv (v\vec{n}:\vec{U})\left(\prod_{h\in H}\overline{c}_h\langle U_h;d_h\rangle \Big| Q_\Sigma\right)$$

Where $P_\Sigma \equiv \sum_{j\in J}\tau.P_j + \sum_{k\in K}a_k(X_k;x:T_k).P_k$,

$Q_\Sigma \equiv \sum_{l\in L}\tau.Q_l + \sum_{m\in M}c_m(Y_m;y:U_m).Q_m$.

If $\quad \Gamma \vDash [\sigma]P \sim [\rho]Q \quad,\quad |I| = N \quad,\quad \forall i\in I, \quad \Gamma \vdash \quad a_i(X_i;x:V_i) \quad$ and $\forall h\in H, \Gamma \vdash c_h(Y_h;y:W_h)$, then there exists an injective substitution γ such that:

$$\prod_{i\in I}\overline{a}_i\langle T_i;b_i\rangle \equiv \left(\prod_{h\in H}\overline{c}_h\langle U_h;d_h\rangle\right)\gamma$$

and $\qquad\qquad \Gamma_N \vDash [\sigma_N]P_\Sigma \sim [\rho_N]Q_\Sigma\gamma.$

Where $\Gamma_i = \Gamma, b_1:V_1,\cdots,b_i:V_i$, $\theta_i = T_1/X_1,\cdots,T_i/X_i$, and $\sigma_i = \sigma,\theta_i$, $\rho_i = \rho,\theta_i$, $i = 1, \ldots, N$.

Proof. Given in [13].

Theorem (the Completeness of the Axiom System). Let P, Q be two finite processes, then $\Gamma \vDash [\sigma]P \sim [\rho]Q \Leftrightarrow P =_\Gamma^{\sigma,\rho} Q$.

Proof. (Soundness): $P =_\Gamma^{\sigma,\rho} Q \Rightarrow \Gamma \vDash [\sigma]P \sim [\rho]Q$. This is the easy part: it is proved by exhibiting appropriate bisimulations for each axiom.

(Completeness): $\Gamma \vDash [\sigma]P \sim [\rho]Q \Rightarrow P =_\Gamma^{\sigma,\rho} Q$.

Given the Lemma 1 and the soundness of the axioms, it is enough to prove the statement for normal forms. So assume $P \equiv (v\vec{m}:\vec{T})\left(\prod_{i\in I}\overline{a}_i\langle T_i;b_i\rangle \Big| P_\Sigma\right)$,

$Q \equiv (v\vec{n}:\vec{U})\left(\prod_{h\in H}\overline{c}_h\langle U_h;d_h\rangle \Big| Q_\Sigma\right)$, where

$P_\Sigma \equiv \sum_{j\in J}\tau.P_j + \sum_{k\in K}a_k(X_k;x:T_k).P_k$; $Q_\Sigma \equiv \sum_{l\in L}\tau.Q_l + \sum_{m\in M}c_m(Y_m;y:U_m).Q_m$.

By the Lemma 2 we know that there exists a substitution γ such that $\gamma(\vec{n}) = \vec{m}$, $\gamma(w) = w$ if $w \notin \vec{n}$, and

$$\prod_{i \in I} \overline{a}_i \langle T_i ; b_i \rangle \equiv \left(\prod_{h \in H} \overline{c}_h \langle U_h ; d_h \rangle \right) \gamma \text{ and } \Gamma_N \vDash [\sigma_N] P_\Sigma \sim [\rho_N] Q_\Sigma \gamma .$$

We will show, by induction on the sum of depths of P and Q, that $P_\Sigma =^{\sigma_N, \rho_N}_{\Gamma_N} Q_\Sigma \gamma$,
This will imply the required result, namely

$$P_\Sigma =^{\sigma_N, \rho_N}_{\Gamma_N} Q_\Sigma \gamma$$
$$\Rightarrow (\nu \overline{m_N} : \overline{T_N}) \left(\overline{a}_N \langle T_N ; b_N \rangle \middle| P_\Sigma \right) =^{\sigma_{N-1}, \rho_{N-1}}_{\Gamma_{N-1}} (\nu \overline{m_N} : \overline{T_N}) \left(\overline{c}_N \langle U_N ; d_N \rangle \gamma \middle| Q_\Sigma \gamma \right)$$
$$\Rightarrow \ldots$$
$$\Rightarrow (\nu \overline{m} : \overline{T}) \left(\prod_{i \in I} \overline{a}_i \langle T_i ; b_i \rangle \middle| P_\Sigma \right) =^{\sigma, \rho}_{\Gamma} (\nu \overline{m} : \overline{T}) \left(\prod_{h \in H} \overline{c}_h \langle U_h ; d_h \rangle \gamma \middle| Q_\Sigma \gamma \right)$$

So $P =^{\sigma, \rho}_{\Gamma} (\nu \overline{m} : \overline{T}) \left(\prod_{h \in H} \overline{c}_h \langle U_h ; d_h \rangle \gamma \middle| Q_\Sigma \gamma \right) \equiv Q$

To this end it is enough to prove

(i) $P_\Sigma =^{\sigma_N, \rho_N}_{\Gamma_N} P_\Sigma + \tau.Q_l \gamma$; (ii) $P_\Sigma =^{\sigma_N, \rho_N}_{\Gamma_N} P_\Sigma + \left(c_m(Y_m ; y : U_m).Q_m \right) \gamma$

Then $P_\Sigma =^{\sigma_N, \rho_N}_{\Gamma_N} P_\Sigma + Q_\Sigma \gamma =^{\sigma_N, \rho_N}_{\Gamma_N} Q_\Sigma \gamma$.

(i)Suppose $(\Gamma_N \vdash [\sigma_N] P_\Sigma) \overset{\tau}{\longrightarrow} (\Gamma_N \vdash [\sigma_N] P_j)$.

Since $\Gamma_N \vDash [\sigma_N] P_\Sigma \sim [\rho_N] Q_\Sigma \gamma$, there exist $l \in L$ such that $(\Gamma_N \vdash [\rho_N] Q_\Sigma \gamma) \overset{\tau}{\longrightarrow} (\Gamma_N \vdash [\rho_N] Q_l \gamma)$ and $\Gamma_N \vDash [\sigma_N] P_j \sim [\rho_N] Q_l \gamma$. By induction $P_j =^{\sigma_N, \rho_N}_{\Gamma_N} Q_l \gamma$ and thus also $\tau.P_j =^{\sigma_N, \rho_N}_{\Gamma_N} \tau.Q_l \gamma$. Then $P_\Sigma =^{\sigma_N, \rho_N}_{\Gamma_N} P_\Sigma + \tau.Q_l \gamma$.

(ii)Let now

$$(\Gamma_N \vdash [\sigma_N] P_\Sigma) \overset{a_k[U_k ; b_k]}{\longrightarrow} (\Gamma_N \vdash [\sigma_N] P_\Sigma \mid \overline{a}_k \langle U_k ; b_k \rangle \sigma_N) \overset{\tau}{\longrightarrow} (\Gamma_N \vdash [\sigma_N] P_k \{ U_k \sigma_N / X_k ; b_k / x \}),$$

We show first that $Q_\Sigma \gamma$ is forced to match this move by a transition of the form
If there exists $m \in M$, such that $c_m \gamma = a_k$ and then

$$(\Gamma_N \vdash [\rho_N] Q_\Sigma \gamma) \overset{a_k[U_k ; b_k]}{\longrightarrow} (\Gamma_N \vdash [\rho_N] Q_\Sigma \gamma \mid \overline{a}_k \langle U_k ; b_k \rangle \rho_N) \overset{\tau}{\longrightarrow} (\Gamma_N \vdash [\rho_N] Q_m \gamma \{ U_k \rho_N / X_k ; b_k / x \}).$$

If there exists $l \in L$, such that

$$(\Gamma_N \vdash [\rho_N] Q_\Sigma \gamma) \overset{a_k[U_k ; b_k]}{\longrightarrow} (\Gamma_N \vdash [\rho_N] Q_\Sigma \gamma \mid \overline{a}_k \langle U_k ; b_k \rangle \rho_N) \overset{\tau}{\longrightarrow} (\Gamma_N \vdash [\rho_N] Q_l \gamma \mid \overline{a}_k \langle U_k ; b_k \rangle \rho_N),$$

and then $\Gamma_N \vDash [\sigma_N] P_k \{ U_k \sigma_N / X_k ; b_k / x \} \sim [\rho_N] Q_l \gamma \mid \overline{a}_k \langle U_k ; b_k \rangle \rho_N$
By induction on the depth, we have

$$P_k \{ U_k \sigma_N / X_k ; b_k / x \} =^{\sigma_N, \rho_N}_{\Gamma_N} Q_l \gamma \mid \overline{a}_k \langle U_k ; b_k \rangle \rho_N \text{ and } \Gamma_N \vDash [\sigma_N] P_\Sigma \sim [\rho_N] Q_\Sigma \gamma$$

Then there must be $j \in J$ such that

$$\Gamma_N \vdash [\sigma_N] P_\Sigma \overset{\tau}{\longrightarrow} \Gamma_N \vdash [\sigma_N] P_j \text{ and } \Gamma_N \vDash [\sigma_N] P_j \sim [\rho_N] Q_l \gamma$$

By   induction   this   implies $P_j =_{\Gamma_N}^{\sigma_N,\rho_N} Q_l\gamma$ and   hence
$P_k\{U_k\sigma_N/X_k;b_k/x\} =_{\Gamma_N}^{\sigma_N,\rho_N} P_j\,|\,\bar{a}_k\langle U_k\rho_N;b_k\rangle$, contradicting the hypothesis that P is a normal form.

Thus the transition is always matched by a former transition

$$\Gamma_N \vDash [\sigma_N]P_k\{U_k\sigma_N/X_k;b_k/x\} \sim [\rho_N]Q_m\gamma\{U_k\rho_N/X_k;b_k/x\}$$

By induction on the depth

$$P_k\{U_k\sigma_N/X_k;b_k/x\} =_{\Gamma_N}^{\sigma_N,\rho_N} Q_m\gamma\{U_k\rho_N/X_k;b_k/x\}$$

and therefore also

$$a_k(X_k;x:T_k).P_k =_{\Gamma_N}^{\sigma_N,\rho_N} a_k(X_k;x:T_k).Q_m\gamma =_{\Gamma_N}^{\sigma_N,\rho_N} (c_m(Y_m;y:U_m).Q_m)\gamma$$

Then $P_\Sigma =_{\Gamma_N}^{\sigma_N,\rho_N} P_\Sigma + (c_m(Y_m;y:U_m).Q_m)\gamma$.   □

4   Conclusion and Related Works

This paper gives the first axiom system for a polymorphic asynchronous π-calculus. Polymorphism is popular in programming languages, but the equivalence between processes in polymorphic π-calculus differs from the equivalence without polymorphism. Pierece and Sangiorgi first proposed the concept of capability types by allowing us to distinguish the capability of using a channel in input from that of using the channel in output in [7]. Then in [10] they investigated the behavior equivalence in the polymorphic π-calculus for the first time. But they only established a sound model. In [11], a sound and complete model for a polymorphic π-calculus was developed. Based on these results, we present a complete axiomatisation for the behavior equivalence above firstly.

Note that the process we considered is just a finite one. The future work of this paper is that the complete axiomatisation for the general processes in the polymorphic environment. When the process cannot guarantee finiteness property, the situation is complicated and need to do more work on this study.

References

1. Hoare, C.A.R.: Communicating Sequential Process. Prentice Hall (1985)
2. Milner, R.: Communication and Concurrency. Prentice Hall (1989)
3. Milner, R., Parrow, J., Walker, D.: A Calculus of Mobile Process, part I/II. Journal of Information and Computation 100, 1–77 (1992)
4. Parrow, J., Sangiorgi, D.: Algebraic theories for name-passing calculi. Information and Computation 120(2) (1995)
5. Sangiorgi, D.: A theory of bisimulation for the π-calculus. Acta informatica 33, 69–97 (1996)
6. Boreale, M., De Nicola, R.: Testing equivalences for mobile processes. Journal of Information and Computation 120, 279–303 (1995)

7. Pierce, B.C., Sangiorgi, D.: Typing and subtyping for mobile processes. Mathematical Structures in Computer Science 6(5), 409–454 (1996)
8. Hennessy, M., Rathke, J.: Typed behavioural equivalences for processes in the presence of subtyping. Mathematical Structures in Computer Science 14, 651–684 (2004)
9. Deng, Y., Sangiorgi, D.: Towards an Algebraic Theory of Typed Mobile Processes. In: Díaz, J., Karhumäki, J., Lepistö, A., Sannella, D. (eds.) ICALP 2004. LNCS, vol. 3142, pp. 445–456. Springer, Heidelberg (2004)
10. Pierce, B.C., Sangiorgi, D.: Behavioural equivalence in the polymorphic pi-calculus. J. ACM 47(3), 531–584 (2000)
11. Jeffrey, A.S.A., Rathke, J.: Full Abstraction for Polymorphic Pi-Calculus. Theoretical Computer Science (2008)
12. Amadio, R., Castellani, I., Sangiorgi, D.: On Bisimulations for the Asynchronous π-Calculus. In: Sassone, V., Montanari, U. (eds.) CONCUR 1996. LNCS, vol. 1119, pp. 147–162. Springer, Heidelberg (1996)
13. Yan, F., Cui, Z., Mao, Z.: A Complete Axiomatisation of Bisimulation in Polymorphic π-Calculus. Technical Report, Depart. of applied physics and mathematics, College of Science, PLA. University of Science and Technology (October 2011)

Secure Login for Web-Based Embedded Systems

Bo Qu

School of Mathematics and Information Technology
Nanjing Xiaozhuang College, Nanjing, China
Mr.QuBo@126.com

Abstract. This paper describes the technical details of design and implementation of secure login system for Web-based embedded systems, including secure Web server, verification code, password getting back by mail, and login IP binding, etc. A real example is given to demonstrate the application of it.

Keywords: Secure login, verification code, password getting back, login IP binding, Web-based embedded systems.

1   Introduction

With the rapid technical developments on Internet and Web, it is almost been become a standard form for embedded systems to communicate with users by using Web service via HTTP protocol [1, 2]. In this way, users can use a browser to login the remote embedded host to access or control the remote system. How to realize the secure login to Web and how to protect the system from being invaded by malicious users [3, 4], therefore, becomes a key consideration of the embedded system design.

By this reason, a secure login system for Web-based embedded systems is designed and implemented by the author of this paper, which uses the techniques of secure Web server, verification code, password getting back by mail, and login IP binding, etc. This paper gives a deep description of the technical details of it.

The contributions of the secure login system described in this paper are as following:

1) The program to generate graphical verification codes, including distortion of the digits image without needing any graphics library.
2) The program to realize mails for password getting back and login IP binding.
3) Using C as the programming language to design and implement the entire system [5].

2   Secure Web Server

As we all know, the communications between users and Web servers are realized with HTTP protocol which transmits the message in plaintext. However, the plaintext will

M. Zhao and J. Sha (Eds.): ICCIP 2012, Part I, CCIS 288, pp. 640–647, 2012.

decrease the security of the system seriously. A simple but practical alternative is by using a secure Web server based on SSL protocol [3, 4].

The secure login system described in this paper does use such a method. The design and implementation of secure Web server for embedded systems is described in reference [6]. To use such a secure Web server, the corresponding SSL library, named openssl, needs to be installed in the embedded system. It is an open source library and the source code can be downloaded from its official Web site: http://www.openssl.org/source. The porting method is also described by reference [6].

It is worthy noted that the version of openssl source code is depended upon the gcc version which will vary the porting procedures. At the same time, there are also some differences for each version while porting. Take the one mentioned in this paper as the example. The development platform used for this paper is Redhat 9.0 and the version of gcc on it is 3.4.1. By testing, we can know that the version of opensll should be 0.9.8, corresponding to the gcc version. The porting procedure is briefly described as following.

After downloading the source code package, the first job to do is creating script file, Makefile, with the command "config":

config no-asm shared --prefix=/usr/local/arm/openssl,

in which, "no-asm" means don't use assembler code, "shared" means generate shared (dynamic linked) library files, and "--prefix" set destination's installation directory.

Then, modify the compiling script file, Makefile, as following:

```
#CC=gcc
CC= arm-linux-gcc
#AR=ar $(ARFLAGS) r
AR= arm-linux-ar $(ARFLAGS) r
#RANLIB=/usr/bin/ranlib
RANLIB= arm-linux-ranlib
```

Next, compile and install it (make, and make install).Then the openssl target files are installed into preset installation directory, /usr/local/arm/openssl. Finally, download the command file, openssl in /usr/local/arm/openssl/bin, and the shared (dynamic linked) library files, i.e. libcrypto.so.0.9.8 and libssl.so.0.9.8 in /usr/local/arm/openssl/lib, into the ARM host, where command file openssl is in directory /bin, and the dynamic linked library files are in directory /lib.

3   Verification Code

In common ways, both username and password is required in a login form appeared in user's browser. When the Web server on the embedded system receives the information from the user, it will check the information with the user's profile to see whether or not the user is a valid one. If yes, the user's requested page is sent back to user's browser, otherwise a rejected page is sent to require the user login again using the right username and password. Although the way can work well for normal users, it is easy for embedded system to be attacked by so called auto password detectors.

That will obviously debase the security of the system therefore need some other ways to remedy the defect.

The popularly used method to do so is by using verification code during login procedure. That means not only the right username and password but also the correct verification code is needed to be sent to Web server. Such a verification code is typically a numeric or character string within an image in the login form. In general-purpose Web servers, verification codes are commonly generated by some kinds of graphics libraries, for example, the open source image processor, named GD. However, such graphics libraries are not suitable for commonly used embedded systems because the sizes of them are too large to fit into the small memory space of an embedded system.

For this reason, a simple and practical verification code generator is programmed by the author, which can form an image consisting of a numeric string. In order to increase the anti-recognize strength, each digit is distorted randomly. The program is written in C and does not need any graphics library therefore suitable for embedded systems.

The program consists of two parts, generating digits image and send it to user, in which the former generates a digit number by random function and processes the corresponding bitmap array of the digit to generate the distorted image, while the latter forms a response page to send the bitmap image back to user's browser. The format of the image is bitmap with monochromatic color.

3.1 Generating Digits Image

The number of the verification code is generated by expression (unsigned)(rand() * time(NULL)) while the random seed is set by seed(time(NULL)). The character string of the verification code is generated by above number.

The original bitmap for each numeric character (0, 1, ..., 9) is designed as a 8×12 (8 columns by 12 rows) array.

The normal digits image is shown as in Fig. 1.

Fig. 1. The normal digits image

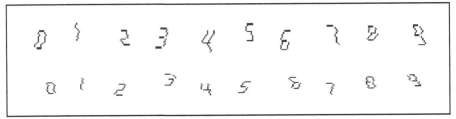

Fig. 2. The distorted digits image

The algorithm of distortion is very simple by modifying the pixel in two directions. In horizontal direction, a pixel will be randomly shifted 1 dot to left, 1 dot to right, or not changed. In vertical direction, a row of pixels will be randomly duplicated or not. By this way, the original digits image will be distorted randomly in both horizontal and vertical directions as show in Fig. 2.

The key code to implement the task is shown in Fig. 3. Note that the size of processed digit image is 32×32 thus each pixel row can be represented by one unsigned integer. But the order of the four bytes in an integer is reversed therefore the function cvt() is used to convert the order of the four bytes in a pixel row.

```
void hshift(char *str, char *bmp)
{
    int i, k = 12 + (my_rand() % 8);
    unsigned int bit[12], *p = bit;

    p = (unsigned int *)bmp + 31 - (my_rand() % 12);
    for (i = 0; i < sy; i ++) {
        bit[i] = str[i];
        k += (my_rand() % 3) - 1;
        bit[i] <<= k;
        bit[i] = cvt(bit[i]);
        *p -- = bit[i];
        if (my_rand() % 2)
            *p -- = bit[i];
    }
}
```

Fig. 3. The key code to distort a digit image

3.2   About Bitmap Format

For bitmap image file, the header consists of 54 bytes including the file header (14 bytes) and image header (40 bytes).The palette of monochromatic color is simply a 2×4 array in which the first four bytes represent the background color and the second four bytes the foreground color. The bitmap pixels come next in which the rows of pixels are stored from bottom to up.

3.3   Generating Web Page

In order to generate a response Web page including the verification code image, the first thing to do is forming the HTTP response header as shown in Fig. 4. The first statement represents the status is OK, the second statement set a cookie corresponding to the verification code, and the last statement define the content type of the page as a bitmap image file. Note that the second "\n" in the last statement means the blank line as the boundary between the page header and the body.

```
printf("Status:200\n");
printf("Set-Cookie: vcode=%s; expires=12-31-2038\n", crypt(str, salt));
printf ("Content-type: image/bmp\n\n");
```

Fig. 4. The HTTP response header

The body of the page consists of above mentioned bitmap file header, image header, palette, and the pixels array, sequentially.

4   Mail Program for Password Getting Back

Password getting back is a useful function in case a user lost his or hers password. There are several ways to get back the lost password for user, for example, by system administrator, by defining a new password after the user answers predefined questions correctly, or by sending a new password via email to user's preset email box.

The first way needs manual operation thus not a good one. The second needs user to answer some questions while these questions' answers are also easy to be forgotten. Therefore, the third way is most popularly used. In order to implement the password getting back function for the secure login system described in this paper, a simple email program is designed in C by the author of this paper.

4.1   Sending an Email

The core operations for sending message via email are following the steps specified by SMTP protocol. The pseudo codes are shown in Fig. 5.

```
send "HELO SERVER\r\n";
receive the response from server;
send "AUTH LOGIN\r\n";
receive the response from server;
send encoded username;
receive the response from server;
send encoded password;
receive the response from server;
send "MAIL FROM: sender\r\n";
send "RCPT TO: receiver\r\n";
receive the response from server;
send "DATA\r\n";
receive the response from server;
send "From: <sender>\r\n";
send "TO: <receiver>\r\n";
send "Subject: xxxxx\r\n\r\n";
send message of the email;
send "\r\n\r\n.\r\n";
send "QUIT\r\n";
```

Fig. 5. The pseudo codes of the mail program

4.2   Base64 Encoding

The purpose of base64 encoding is to transmit the binary data as numeric-alpha characters. The basic method of encoding including following steps:

First, divide a character string into groups of three bytes.

Second, divide each group (three bytes) into four parts of six bits. Third, take the six bits as an index for searching the encoding array to get the corresponding encoded character. The general expressions for converting three characters into four parts are as following:

(a>>2), ((a&0x03)<<4 | (b>>4)), ((b&0x0f)<<4 | (c>>6)) and (c&0x3f).

Take the string "abc" as an example. Before encoding, the bits of the three characters are: 01100001 01100010 01100011.

Now divide them into four parts of six bits: 011000 010110 001001 100011.

Thus, values of them are 24, 22, 9 and 35, respectively.

Using them as the indexes of encoding array, the corresponding encoded characters are obtained as: YWJj.

The encoding array is shown in Fig. 6.

```
table[ ] =
{"ABCDEFGHIJKLMNOPQRSTUVWXYZabcdefghijklmnopqrstuvwxyz01234
56789+/"}
```

Fig. 6. Character array for base64 encoding

4.3   Getting Back Password

First, randomly generate a new password. Second, send it via email program mentioned above to users' preset mail box.

After receiving the new password by email, the user can use it to login and then modify the password by him or her self.

5   Login IP Binding

The purpose of login IP binding is to restrict the host used by user to login. Although this way can protect the remote embedded system from being attacked by malicious users, the system may be failed if the bound IP unusable unexpectedly. To avoid such a case, the following method is used by the author.

If the current IP address is bound to be login IP, a new activation code is generated and sent via email to the user's mail box. In case the user's host IP changes, the login system will prompt the user entering this activation code. Only if the code is entered and verified to be correct, can the user login successfully with the new host IP.

In this case, the IP binding flag is cleared and the login IP must be re-bound, if necessary.

6   An Application Example

The functions of the secure login system described in this paper can be presented by the following example. The hardware platform used is an ARM development board, named FL2440. The operating system platform is ARM-Linux.

Since the restriction of the preinstalled Web server on the board, boa, is too rigid for the remote embedded hosts to control the system by CGI programs, and also for the reason of secure login, a secure Web server, named QWeb designed by the author, is used instead of boa. The software system is an embedded remote control system, named ERC, the functions of which are to start or stop the FTP server, named vsftpd, modify admin password, configure the system including setting user mail box and binding login IP, etc.

All of the programs including secure Web server, QWeb, embedded remote control system, ERC are developed on Linux platform with C [5] and needed to be downloaded into the ARM host. The method is described in reference [6] therefore it will not be mentioned here for saving page space.

The Fig. 7 (a) shows the secure login interface in which both username and password as well as verification code are requested to enter. The super-link, "Try a new code", on the left of verification code image is used to refresh the code image, while the one on the right, "Forget password?", is used to get back password when forgetting it. In this case, ERC will generate a new password for user and send it via email to user's mail box.

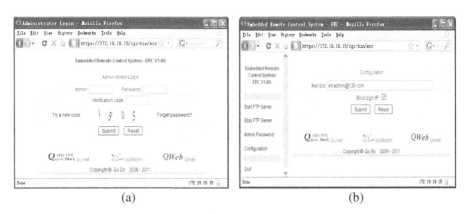

(a)   (b)

Fig. 7. The secure login form and the Web page for configuration of ERC

The functions of ERC are shown in Fig. 7 (b). The left column in the figure is the menu of ERC created by a page frame apart from the main frame on the right. As a demonstration system, ERC has simply four functions: Start FTP server, Stop FTP server, Modify admin password and Configure ERC system.

All the programs of ERC are written in C as CGI module invoked by Web server. In order to accomplish the control task of starting and stop FTP server, the CGI program must have the running right of root user, therefore the permission mode of the CGI file must be set to 755 in which the 7 means that it has all the rights of reading, writing, and running as root user.

The first two functions of ERC are controlling the FTP server implemented by invoke the daemon program of FTP, vsftpd, in the CGI module. It is not the focus of this paper then not be described further. Modifying admin password is a necessary function commonly used for the system and there is no special description needed.

Configuration is an important function for ERC in which the email box of the user can be set and the login IP can be selected to be bound or not. The corresponding page is shown in the right part of Fig. 7 (b). If the check box for binding login IP is selected, it means the IP address of the current host used by user is recorded and only this host can be used to login the system.

Each time when user selecting to bind login IP, ERC will send an activation code by email to the user's mail box. When user needs to use the login host with other IP, the activation code must be used as verification code for login.

Confined to the length of the thesis, some of technical details are omitted, for example, about cookie setting, login error processing, etc.

7   Conclusion

Embedded systems have been being used in a variety of difference fields, and at the same time the Browser/Server mode has already become a standard way for embedded systems to communicate with users. Therefore, how to make embedded systems more efficient and more secure has become an important issue on the field.

Lots of work for Web security and MIS security, especially on embedded systems, has been done by the author in recent years. The secure login system described in this paper is just one of them. It is simple, efficient, secure and reliable, therefore has great practical value.

References

1. Tanenbaum, A.S.: Computer Networks, 4th edn. Prentice Hall, Inc. (2008)
2. Comer, D.E.: Computer Networks and Internet with Internet Applications, 4th edn. Prentice Hall (2004)
3. Kahate, A.: Cryptography and Network Security. McGraw-Hill Companies, Inc. (2003)
4. Stallings, W.: Network Security Essentials: Applications and Standards, 3rd edn. Prentice Hall, Inc. (2007)
5. Rochkind, M.J.: Advanced UNIX Programming, 2nd edn. Addison-Wesley (2006)
6. Qu, B., Wu, Z.: Design and implementation of embedded secure web server for ARM platform. In: Proceedings of 2011 International Conference on Electronic and Mechanical Engineering and Information Technology, EMEIT 2011, vol. 1, pp. 359–362 (2011)

A Priority-Based Grid Scheduling Algorithm P-M-M and Its Modeling and Simulation with Colored Petri Net

Xiao-jing Meng and Li-li Wang

College of Information Science and Engineering,
Shandong University of Science and Technology,
Qingdao, China
`jack.meng@263.net, mengyue310@126.com`

Abstract. Grid task scheduling has been an important part of grid computing due to the heterogeneity, dynamic and autonomy of resource and the diversity of the task under grid computing environment. Therefore, the efficiency of task scheduling algorithm determines the efficiency of grid computing, the scheduling algorithm should be designed perfectly[1]. Using graphical math tools to complete formal description, correct testing, performance evaluation and testing of the algorithm and system is very important and necessary. In this paper, two classical grid scheduling algorithms (Min-Min and Max-Min algorithm) were analyzed, and the result is that the maximum completion time (makespan) is relatively long and the loads are obviously unbalanced in Min-Min algorithm, but Max-Min algorithm has a smaller makespan. Based on the above study, there is a need to improve the grid scheduling algorithm, making that the task scheduling algorithm has a smaller makespan and balanced load between the entire system machines. Therefore, this paper proposes a priority-based grid scheduling algorithm P-M-M. In order to solve the problem of load balancing between machines, the algorithm uses the group method by the average expected execution time; to make a smaller makespan of the algorithm, each group runs in accordance with the Max-Min algorithm.

Keywords: Colored Petri Net, stop and wait protocol, Modeling, Verification.

1 Algorithm Analysis on Two Classical Grid Scheduling Algorithms

Formal description of grid task scheduling is as follows: total number of tasks needed to schedule is n, and the total available resources are m in grid environment. Where tasks are: T = {T1, T2, ..., Tn} and resources R = {R1, R2, ..., Rm}. The n tasks are scheduled to m resources (host or clusters)through a suitable way to make the minimum maskspan and as far as possible to improve the utilization rate of resources and the overall performance of the network, this is the essence of grid task scheduling, the suitable way called scheduling algorithm. The ultimate goal of grid task scheduling is to achieve optimal scheduling of tasks submitted by users, and try to improve the overall throughput of the grid system.

M. Zhao and J. Sha (Eds.): ICCIP 2012, Part I, CCIS 288, pp. 648–656, 2012.

1.1   Min-Min Algorithm

Min-Min algorithm completes the selection of resources by calculating twice minimum value, it is intended to schedule tasks to resources which performs it fast, so that the completion time (Makespan) of all task is minimum. Min-Min algorithm selects the earliest complete time for each task, and then selects the task which has minimum completion time from all the earliest complete time[3]. Min-Min algorithm is still the base of current grid scheduling algorithm; the main idea of the algorithm is as follows:

M is a set for all unscheduled tasks - resources - time.

(1) To determine whether the set M is null, if M is not null, execute (2); else skip to step (7)
(2) To calculate the earliest complete time cij on all available machines for each task.
(3) According to the results of (2), find out the task Ti and the corresponding machine Rj which has the minimum earliest complete time.
(4) Mapping Ti to Rj; and delete the task Ti from M.
(5) Update the expected ready time of Rj .
(6) Update the completion time of other tasks in machine Rj; go back to (1).
(7) The mapping incident is end, and we can exit the program.

1.2   Max-Min Algorithm

Max-Min algorithm is very similar to the Min-Min algorithm. The earliest complete time for each task in any available resources is also calculated. Unlikely, Max-Min algorithm first schedules long task, the mapping from task to the resource is to choose the maximum maskspan [4].

Min-min algorithm firstly executes the shortest completion time of tasks, and the long task is waiting, so that extended the total completion time of tasks; Max - min algorithm firstly schedules long task, the short and long tasks are executed in parallel, so it shorten the total completion time of tasks.

2   An Improved Algorithm Description for Grid Task Scheduling

In the grid computing, A good task scheduling algorithm is not only to consider the maximum completion time of all tasks, making it as small as possible, it also should consider the load balance between whole system machines. From the above analysis we can see that:

(1) Without considering the priority of the task, that is the task execution emergency degree. Under the environment of grid, some tasks have higher priority and must execute precede the other tasks as soon as possible.

(2) Maximum completion time of tasks is relatively long in Min-Min algorithm, but the main disadvantage is the unbalanced load.

(3) Max-Min algorithm has less completion time (makespan).

According to the above three problems, this paper presents a grid task scheduling algorithm P-M-M based on the priority of tasks, the priority tasks should be firstly considered and assigned to resource that executes it fast. When the task does not have priority, using the algorithm that has less maskspan and load balancing. The Max-Min algorithm has less maskspan, so the algorithm is improved based on Max-Min algorithm.

Assume that the execution time of each task in each resource is known. In order to describe conveniently we adopt the following symbols [5]:

T: {T1, T2, ... , Tn} set of tasks

R: {R1, R2, ... , Rm} set of resources

ETC: nxm matrix, ETC (i,j) is the expected execution time of task Ti in resource Rj

P-M-M algorithm is described as follows:

(1) Firstly judge whether task flag(tflag) is greater than 0, if tflag > 0, showed that the task has priority right to execute, assigned it to the machine that executes it fastest; if there are multiple tasks with priority, the tasks should have a descending sort according to the tflag. If tflag is larger, it has priority to execute.

(2) if tflag = 0,showing the task does not have priority. We calculate the average expected execution time of each independent task in grid system computers, and then do a descending sort according to this average value of scheduling tasks. This sequence is divided into equal sections; each section is scheduled using Max-Min algorithm. Firstly scheduled task has larger average execution time, the task may have large execution time in each resource and also have greater time difference, because each section is used Max-Min scheduling algorithm, which can ensure that the relatively long task is assigned, let it executed with other smaller tasks in parallel, and can avoid the disadvantages in Min-Min algorithm with too long maskspan and bad load balance. When calculating the initial ranking values of avgetci of each task is to compute ETC matrix for average value of each line:

$$avgtci = (\sum_{j=1}^{m} ETC(i, j))/m \tag{1}$$

3   Modeling and Simulation with Colored Petri Net of P-M-M Algorithm

Simulating execution progress of P-M-M algorithm through an example, the expected execution time of task in resource is shown in Table 1.

Table 1. The expected execution time distribution

	R1	R2	Flag
T1	1	11	0
T2	2	3	0
T3	3	7	0
T4	6	24	0
T5	5	1	1
T5	5	1	1

3.1   Design of Color Set

In the CPN Tools based on grid scheduling algorithm, defined the color set of Task, its value is T1, T2, T3, T4, T5, T6, where T1, T2, T3, T4, T5 is five tasks in Table3.1 , T6 is not the task to schedule, it is set to compare the model. Variable ta represents task, mta represents the earliest execution task. Color set Re represents resource node, according to the table, its value is R1, R2, variable re represents resource, re1 represents resource firstly assigned to task. INT is an integer color set, which represents the time. Here, the variable rtime1, rtime2 represents the ready time of resource R1 and R2 respectively; itime represents the expected execution time and the earliest completion time of task; t41, t42 represents the completion time of task T4 in R1 and R2 respectively. Similarly, t31, t32 represents the completion time of task T3 in R1 and R2 respectively, t21, t22 represents the completion time of task T2 in R1

```
▼Standard declarations
  ▼colset INT=int;
  ▼colset TFlag=int;
  ▼colset Task = with T1|T2|T3|T4|T5|T6;
  ▼colset Re = with R1|R2;
  ▼colset TRIT= product Task*Re*INT*TFlag;
  ▼colset TRI= product Task*Re*INT;
  ▼var t1,t2,t3,itime:INT;
  ▼var tp1,tp2:INT;
  ▼var t41,t42,t31,t32,t21,t22,t11,t12,u1,mti:INT;
  ▼var ta,mta:Task;
  ▼var re,re1:Re;
  ▼var rtime1,rtime2:INT;
  ▼var avet1,avet2,avet3,avet4,avet:INT;
  ▼var tflag:TFlag;
  ▼colset RI =product Re*INT;
  ▼colset TRII =product TRI*INT;
```

Fig. 1. Definition of Color Set in P-M-M Algorithm

and R2 respectively; t11, t12 represents the completion time of task T1 in R1 and R2 respectively. Avet1, avet2, avet3, avet4 represents the average expected execution time of task T1, T2, T3, T4 in resources respectively. Color set Tflag is the flag of task priority, if tflag> 0, that indicates the task has a priority right to execute, if tflag = 0, that indicates the task does not have the priority to execute. TRIT is the product of the color set, which is a tuple (ta, re, itime, tflag), it represents the expected execution time of marked task in resource. TRI is a product of the color set, which is triple (ta, re, itime), it represents the completion time of task in resource. Color set RI is the tuple (re1, mti), which represents the earliest completion time of firstly executed tasks. TRII is product color set of TRI and INT, which indicates the average expected execution time of each task in all available resources. Specific color set is shown in Fig.1.

3.2   Modeling and Simulation of P-M-M Algorithm

From the Table 1, the initial value in place begin is:

1`(T1,R1,1,0)++1`(T1,R2,11,0)++1`(T2,R1,2,0)++1`(T2,R2,3,0)++1`(T3,R1,3,0)+ +1`(T3,R2,7,0)++1`(T4,R1,6,0)++1`(T4,R2,24,0)++1`(T5,R1,5,1)++1`(T5,R2,1,1).O nly the task T5 has priority, firstly T5 is executed. Initial value of P34 is 1 `((T6, R1, 0), 0) and set to compare model. The task with the maximum average completion time is selected firstly which is stored in the place P34. Before running the arc from P34 to T37 is off, after finding the maximum completion time the arc is linked. Transition T41 is the twice comparison seeking the maximum value. After twice comparison, P45 is the two tasks with larger average completion time, the remaining tasks in the P42. This is the realization of the task group. Group model of P-M-M algorithm is as follows:

Transition T1-> T2 (T3) -> T4-> T5-> T6 assigns the priority task T5 to resource executed it fastest, that is (T5, R2, 1).Place P8 stores tasks with no priority (tflag = 0) by transition T7. Next, the tasks in P8 are divided into two groups based on the average expected execution time. The reason is that there are four tasks in P8, it needs to divide into average groups, and the length of each group is neither too long nor too short, so two groups are divided. The idea of group is that the average execution time of each task is calculated and then finds the two tasks with maximum average execution time, these two tasks are in place P45, and the remaining tasks are into place P42. P11 and P12 stores the tasks in R1 and R2 respectively. P13, P14, P15, P16 stores the completion time of task T1, T2, T3, T4 respectively, P29, P30, P31, P32 stores the average completion time of task T1, T2, T3, T4 in both resources respectively. In Figure 2, In order to simplify the process, the average execution time of each task is translated into the sum execution time in resources. As shown in Figure 4.2, P29, P30, P31, P32, stores the sum execution time of T1, T2, T3, T4 respectively. P33 stores the set of tasks and the average completion time.

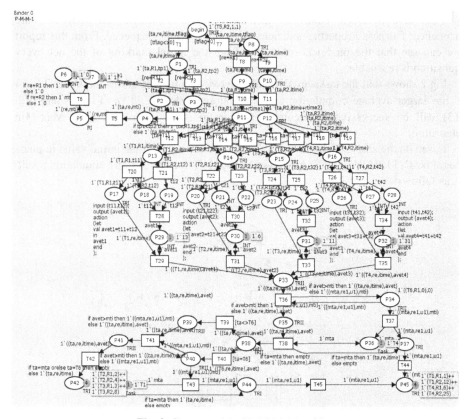

Fig. 2. Group model of P-M-M Algorithm

State space can be calculated when the model has run and not found error, and similarly, state space bar is dragged to the right panel. The operation step is: Enter SS (State Space), Calculate State Space, Calculate SCC Graph, and finally save Report[2]. We can also use the CPN Tools to generate reachability tree while generating simulation report, we can save the generated report as a text (. txt) format, and then copy it to Word for reading and analysis. The following shows part of the analysis:

Home Properties

　Home Markings
　　None
Liveness Properties

　Dead Transition Instances
　　None
Fairness Properties

　No infinite occurrence sequences

The value of Dead Transition Instances is None indicates all transitions are happened; Fairness Properties indicates there is no infinite sequence. From this report we can see that the model is reachable, from the initial marking of the net every transition is reachable.

Fig.2 shows that the tasks are divided into two groups, P45 stores the tasks (T1, T4) has larger average completion time, P42 stores tasks (T2, T3). (T1, T4) and (T2, T3) will be successively executed, each group is in accordance with Max-Min algorithm.

Based on the above analysis, firstly T4 and T1 is executed, the initial value in place begin is: 1`(T1,R1,1)++1`(T1,R2,12)++1`(T4,R1,6)++1`(T4,R2,25), simulation result is as follows:

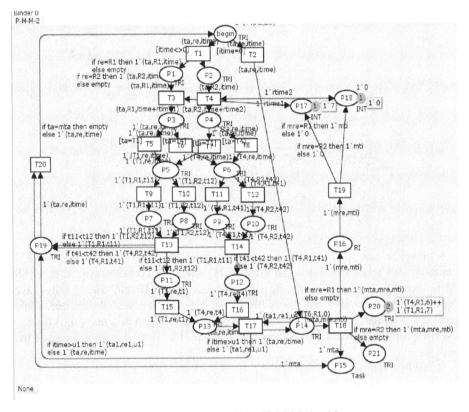

Fig. 3. Simulation result 1 of P-M-M algorithm

After the simulation, execution order is （T4, R1, 6）-> (T1,R1,7). The set （T2, T3）is on execution. The initial value in place begin is:

1`(T2,R1,2)++1`(T2,R2,4)++1`(T3,R1,4)++1`(T3,R2,8).The initial value in P17 and P18 is 7 and 0 respectively, simulation result is as follows:

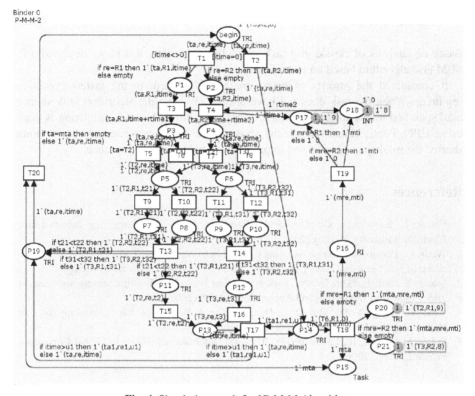

Fig. 4. Simulation result 2 of P-M-M Algorithm

3.3 The Results Contrast

Taking Table 1 as an example, the completion time of Min-Min and Max-Min scheduling algorithm is 17 and 15 respectively, and the improved P-M-M is 9, so the P-M-M algorithm has the shortest maskspan; Min-Min has bad load balanced, the P-M-M grid scheduling algorithm is relatively more balanced. Experimental comparison is shown below:

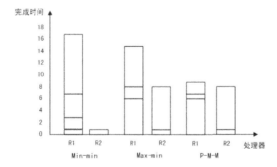

Fig. 5. Simulation result of grid scheduling Algorithms

4   Conclusion

Based on analysis of classic grid task scheduling algorithm, this paper designed a P-M-M grid algorithm based on task priority.

It considered the priority of tasks, and assigned them to the fastest execution resources. When the task does not have priority, We use the algorithm with shorter maskspan and load balance between the machines. Modeling and simulation is done using CPN Tools, simulation results show that P-M-M grid scheduling algorithm shorted the maskspan of tasks and improved load balancing performance.

References

1. Foster, I., Kesselman, C.: The Grid 2:Blueprint for a new Computing Infrastructure. Electronics Industry, Beijing (2004)
2. Wells, L.: Performance Analysis Using Colored Petri Nets (July 31, 2002), http://citeseer.ist.psu.edu-lindstrm99performance.html
3. Ma, J.-Y., Sui, B., Shu, W.-N.: Task scheduling based on Min-Min genetic algorithm in grid. Computer Engineering and Applications 44(23) (2008)
4. Luo, H., Wang, X.-D., Mu, D.-J., Deng, Z.-Q.: A Review of Job Scheduling for Grid Computing. Application Research of Computers 22(5) (2005)
5. Baker, M., Buyya, R., Laforenza, D.: The Grid: International Efforts in Global Computing. Proeeed, Rome (2000)

System for Online Patent Information Analysis Based on Data Mining

Nan Guo, Hongwei Hao, Xu-Cheng Yin[*], and Li Song

School of Computer & Communication Engineering, University of
Science and Technology Beijing, Beijing, China
dinvxin@163.com, {hhw,xuchengyin}@ustb.edu.cn,
lilysong_chen@sina.com

Abstract. In order to provide valuable technical information for technological innovation and business strategy, it is important to analyze implicit law from large amounts of patent data. We designed and implemented an online patent analysis system using rich analytical indexes with data mining techniques. This article describes the key techniques of our system, e.g., system framework, functional structures, index analysis, and visual and interface design. We performed experiments on the Derwent Innovations Index (DII) database. The results show that our system can help to mine and analyze an immense amount of patent data rapidly, conveniently and effectively. Moreover, the user can understand the patent value more profoundly to study, formulate and implement relative patent strategies.

Keywords: data mining, technical information, online patent analysis, visualization, patent strategy.

1 Introduction

With the development of computer and network techniques, the accumulated data becomes larger and larger in all walks of life. Patent information set is the largest technical information set which almost includes all the technology achievements in the applied areas [1].

As we all know, patent information is the result of human intelligence. It records the achievements and the track of human invention. It contains all the crucial information resources for economic development, scientific innovation and strategic decisions. Patent information is the most comprehensive and updated resource for technical intelligence[2]. According to the survey data from World Intellectual Property Organization(WIPO), we know that 90% to 95% of the innovation every year can be found from the patent literature.If those patent information can be made full use, 60% of research cycle and 40% of research fund can be saved [3]. However, people have not made full use of such rich information resources.

It seems that text analysis and simple statistical analysis for patent intelligence analysis has been outdated. Instead, advanced computer techniques took their place to

---

[*] Corresponding author.

M. Zhao and J. Sha (Eds.): ICCIP 2012, Part I, CCIS 288, pp. 657–665, 2012.

be the analytical method. Through the intelligent way, it can deeply analyze the implicit law of an immense amount of patent data which is sporadic and isomerous, it can provide decision support and intelligence security for technological innovation and the development of a company. Thus, the patent analysis technique based on data mining emerged as the times require.

Combining with project research and practice and taking Derwent Innovations Index(DII) for instance, we design and implement the patent analysis technique based on data mining. This article will introduce our study and the analysis of the research results.

2   Data Mining Technology

Data mining[4,5] is to extract the hidden, implicit, valid, novel and interesting spatial or non-spatial patterns or rules from large-amount, incomplete, noisy, fuzzy, random, and practical data.

The process of data mining, can be regard as knowledge discovery in databases(KDD),which generally includes steps as Fig. 1 shows: data clearing–eliminating noise or discrepant data; data integration–assembling data from different data resources; data selection–extracting and analyzing related data from databases; data conversion–transforming or unifying data to suitable format for data-mining by, for instance, summarization or aggregation; data mining–extracting data patterns in an intelligent way; pattern recognition– recognizing the real useful pattern which provides information according to interestingness measurement; and knowledge representation–providing mined knowledge to users by visualization and knowledge representation techniques.

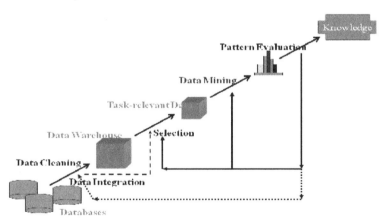

Fig. 1. General steps of KDD

Data mining enables people to extract interesting knowledge, law or high layer information from databases, and to observe or browse information from different perspectives. These knowledge and information can be helpful in decision making, process control, information management and query processing etc. Due to the above advantages, data mining is considered as one of the most cutting edges of database systems in information industry. It is the most promising interdisciplinary subject in this industry as well.

With respect to the perspective of patent information, the amount of patent information is enormously large in current situation. In addition, it grows faster and faster. Patent data includes rich technological, legal and economic information. Analyzing the patent information correctly can greatly contribute to seize and predict the most updated technology frontier, mine more information from patent data profoundly and deeply, and study, draw up and implement patent strategies. Mining patent information usually means counting and analyzing the information with certain index, in certain field or year, which is position relevant. All this shows that data mining technique can solve the issue of patent information analysis with effect.

3   Design and Implementation of System

This system implements online patent data analysis, based on online information retrieval and data marking of the patent assignee, as well as the feature item and the index item, and presents the visualized product to users.

3.1   System Framework

On the whole, this system is based on .NET2010 framework, adopting the B/S(Browser/ Server)mode and employing C# language in ASP.NET4.0. Under the framework of .NET4.0, it takes SQL Server2005 as the database. The entire system framework includes three parts, namely resource layer, service layer and presentation layer. The presentation layer is the Web interface of users; the service layer provides the business processing logic; using the database server as the core platform, the resource layer provides patent information analysis online service, the system framework is presented as the Fig. 2.

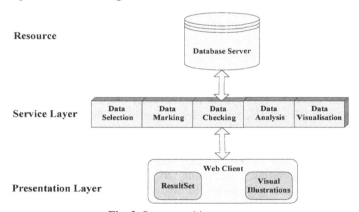

Fig. 2. System architecture

The specific software system framework mainly includes three parts, namely Web layer, business logic layer and data access layer. Web layer provides the accession to application program for users; business logic layer consists of business façade tier and business rules tier, the two logic sub-layers finishing in collaboration the logic processing business which the user submits to the server; data access layer serves business façade tier and business rules tier with online information.

3.2   System Function Structure

In terms of function module, there are three functions of this system, which are patent data marking, patent data checking and patent data analysis. With reference to the basic design principles of website, this system is mainly made of the following modules, as shown in the function structure Fig. 3.

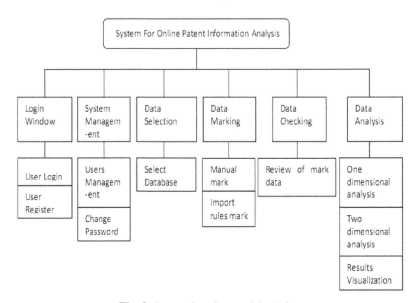

Fig. 3. System function module design

(1) Login Window: Users can apply the module function only after authentication log-in.

(2) System Management: System administrators can administrate by adding or deleting users, and setting or modifying users permission; all users can modify their own authentication information.

(3) Database selection: This system automatically obtains the entire database list in the database server. Users can select a particular theme database to their own need; meanwhile build or delete marking record table of the designated subject database for the convenience of following operations.

(4) Data Marking: Data Marking, which consists of manual marking and automatic marking by importing rules, aims to further regulate related patent data information in order to facilitate the analysis result which users need during data analysis. Manual marking provides the function of similarity retrieval. Users can select relevant patent data on the basis of search results and conduct on-demand marking. Automatic marking automatically update data according to the pre-existing rule base. Users need to submit the marking results for checking.

(5) Data Checking: It is to check the marking data submitted by users. Those approved will be passed to database for modification, those unapproved not passed to database for modification.

(6) Data Analysis: Data Analysis consists of one-dimensional and two-dimensional characteristic analyses. Users select analysis index, then qualify related

conditions, and by means of a series of data mining process, produce and present online analysis results data and the according analysis charts. Users can save the final analysis results.

3.3   Patent Information Analysis Index System

The patent information analysis system (PIAS), which is based on the feature item and the index item, first designs a set of relatively complete analysis index system. Second it implements the function of index analysis in the Web environment. At last, it visualizes the results online. This system puts forwards one-dimensional and two-dimensional analyses for index design, as manifested in the Fig. 4.

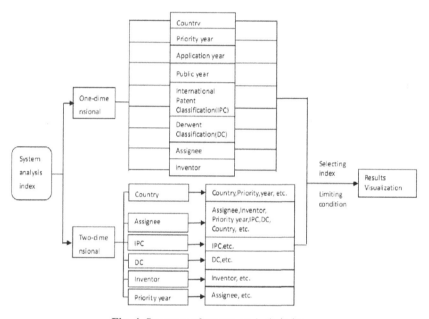

Fig. 4. Structure of system analysis index

The analysis of every layer all contains specific analysis index. One-dimensional analysis is designed to satisfy users' need to know about a certain feature of patent information and then present the result; two-dimensional analysis to know about the correlation between two certain features and present the result. Users only designate one-dimensional feature analysis index or two-dimensional feature correlated analysis index. Then this system automatically mine out feature analyses result which users need from the large amount of original patent information in database according to related features and present online, which facilitates users.

3.4   Data Visualization Technology

In consideration of interaction, network transmission capacity and the client browser performance, the design and development of visualization of this system adopts hybrid client/server visualization. Balancing the load during visualization can be realized by dynamic allocating tasks between the client and the server. It allocates the data conversion from original data to geometrical data to the server. The client is responsible for processing geometrical data into visualized pictures by means of "view mapping" and "conversion process".

In order to better provide user interaction, this system uses SilverLight as the tool to realize data visualization. According to the features of SilverLight and the actual necessity of visualization module, as well as the object oriented technology, visualization module is mainly composed of the following several parts: data processing class library, drawing class library and a SilverLight application program. Data processing class library is responsible for processing received datasets and transforms geometrical data which can be processed for drawing class library; drawing class library for visualized graphics rendering according to different needs of analysis index, namely data visualization. In the design of drawing class library, this system introduces the third part open-source component Visfire and on this basis according to actual necessities make the corresponding expand change. The SilverLight application program is responsible for controlling the entire process of visualization and user interface etc.

Rendering algorithms of visual illustrations plays an important role in visualizing illustrations. In consideration of the large analysis index system, different analysis index results data need to be presented with different visualized illustrations. Also every illustration needs its corresponding rendering algorithm, so a series of problems of rendering algorithm will arise during the data visualization. Take the cooperative association map as the example to elaborate rendering algorithm as Algorithm1 shows.

Algorithm1: Draw the cooperative association map

input: ResultDS, including the value$\{P_1,...,P_n\}$of all association nodes and the associated value $\{L_1,...,L_m\}$ between two different nodes;

  pLower, the floor level of the value of association nodes which need to show;

  lineLower, the floor level of the associated value between two different nodes which need to show.

output: M, the cooperative association map, including PointSet$\{P_{a1},...P_{ak}\}(a_k=<n)$ and $\{L_{b1},...L_{br}\}(b_r=<m)$.

1 for $i\in[1,n]$ DO
2 if P_i>=**pLower** then
3   **Show node i;**
4   **Add i to PointSet;**
5 for $j\in[1,m]$ DO
6 if L_j >=**lineLower** then
7   if **nodes of L_j in PointSet**
8   **Show L_j**
9 **Show map title.**

---

4   Running Effect of the System Test

The analysis result of patent information achieved by data mining technique in this system would finally be presented to users in the form of result data lists and online illustrations. Visualized illustration includes not only common histogram, bar chart, line graph and pie chart, but also some relatively complex figures like relation figures. Take the test data of Derwent patent information provided by Beijing WanFang Data Limited Company as an example; following is part of the running effect of the system test.

(1) Choose the one-dimensional index, patent family country, and generate the result of an analysis on distribution of patent families. The online visualized illustration is showed as Fig. 5. From this figure, patent application in different countries can be seen clearly, which is helpful for the comparison of technical strength of different countries.

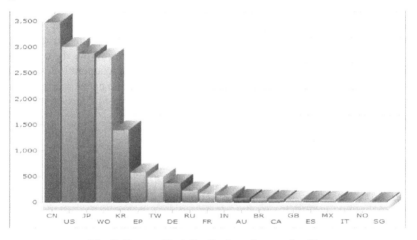

Fig. 5. Geographical distribution of patent families

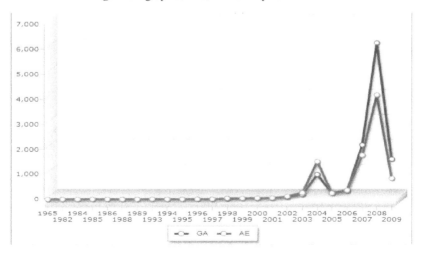

Fig. 6. Technology life cycle

(2) Choose the two-dimensional index, priority year + patent assignee, and generate the result of technology life cycle of patent. The online visualized illustration is showed as Fig. 6. By defining countries and years, we can see the condition of patent application and the variation of relevant patent assignee year by year in a certain area. This helps to understand the technological development in one area.

(3) Choose the two-dimensional index, IPC part + IPC broad heading, and generate the result of technology level map of IPC part–broad heading. The visualized illustration is showed as Fig. 7. In Fig. 7, level 1 shows patent distribution of each IPC part. By clicking each IPC part, one can understand the distribution of each IPC broad heading, the accordingly subordinate part of IPC part (as showed in level 2). All these can help to get knowledge of patent application in different fields or industries, which are the important factors in making patent strategies.

(4) Choose the two-dimensional index, DC part + DC part, and generate the result of Technology association map of DC part. The visualized illustration is showed as Fig. 8. In Fig. 8, the size of points represents the quantity of patent application in one single DC part; while the thickness of the lines represent the quantity of patent application cooperated by two DC parts. This figure shows the comparison between patent application among each DC part and the cooperation association among different DC parts clearly. This helps to understand patent's application in each field, which provides references for market investment decision making for an enterprise.

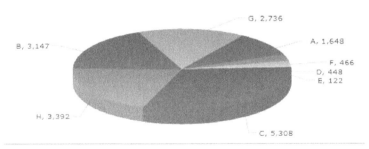

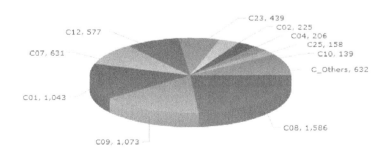

Fig. 7. Technology level map

Fig. 8. Technology association map

5   Conclusion

This article introduced the design and implementation of a system for online patent information analysis based on data mining. This system is provided rich analytic index, which can help users process and analyze an enormous amount of patent information quickly, conveniently and effectively. The data result lists and visualized illustration it provides online can assist users to dig out and search for the valuable information more profoundly and comprehensively. In one word, this system is conducive to the study, draft and implementation of patent strategy.

Acknowledgements. This work is supported by the National Natural Science Foundation of China (61105018, 61175020) and the R&D Special Fund for Public Welfare Industry (Meteorology) of China (GYHY201106039, GYHY201106047). Also, we would like to express my deep gratitude to Beijing WanFang Data Co., Ltd. for providing experimental data.

References

1. Dou, H., Leveillé, V., Manullang, S., Dou, J.J.: Patent analysis for competitive technical intelligence and innovative thinking. Data Science Journal 4, 209–237 (2005)
2. Stembridge, B., Corish, B.: Patent data mining and effective patent portfolio management. Intellectual Asset Management, 30–35 (October/November 2004)
3. Ma, F., Wang, X.-Y.: Analysis of patent intelligence based on data mining. Information Science 11, 1672–1675 (2008) (in Chinese)
4. Cao, L., Zhang, H., Zhao, Y., et al.: Combined mining: discovering informative knowledge in complex data. IEEE Trans. Systems, Man, and Cybernetics, Part B: Cybernetics 41, 699–712 (2011)
5. Yan, C., Ming, Y., Lin, Z.: General data mining model system based on sample data division. International Symposium on Knowledge Acquisition and Modeling 2, 182–185 (2009)

Color Image Inpainting Based on Multichannel-MCA and K-SVD

Haofeng Huang[1,2] and Nanfeng Xiao[1]

[1] School of Computer Science and Engineering, South China University of Technology,
Guangzhou 510641, China
[2] Department of Computer Science, Zengcheng College of South China Normal University,
Guangzhou, 51 1363, China
haofeng_huang@163.com

Abstract. The Morphological Component Analysis (MCA) is a decomposition method based on sparse model. MCA assumes that signal is linear combined of different components, it can decompose image into texture and cartoon part. MCA can solve the inpainting problem. Multi-channel MCA (mMCA) which is extension of MCA and better represents multichannel data. In general, the dictionaries of MCA are chosen by artificial. In this paper, a method for adaptive dictionary choice base mMCA is proposed, the color image is considered as multi-channel data which composed of three channels, and combine K-SVD to adaptive choose the dictionary. The experiment results show that the method can well restore the damaged image.

Keywords: Sparse Model, Image Inpainting, MCA, K-SVD, Total Variation.

1 Introduction

Image inpainting, an important part of image processing, was first introduced Bertalmio et al [1], is used for restore old photos, films. Its purpose is to reconstruct the missing parts of images.

In the past few years, several different methods have been proposed to solve the complex image processing tasks. Non-textured images inpainting is traditionally approached by diffusion Equations [26], Bertalmio et al[1] created image inpainting algorithm based on the partial differential equations (PDEs), Chan and Shen proposed the Total Variation algorithm [2](TV) and the Curvature-Driven Diffusion (CDD) [3] algorithm. Following their work, several inpainting methods base high partial differential equations have proposed [24, 25].

With the development of sparse model, Morphological Component Analysis (MCA) [4, 6] is a decomposition method based on sparse model of signals. MCA can separate images into texture and piecewise smooth (cartoon) parts and solve the inpainting problem [8]. Extension of MCA, a method MCA (mMCA) [9, 10] was proposed, which to take into account m-dimensional observations [11].

mMCA must search the morphological layers's sparse representations by the overcomplete dictionaries [11, 19]. Therefore, the choice of the dictionary is a key step. Generally, the dictionary select by artificial.

M. Zhao and J. Sha (Eds.): ICCIP 2012, Part I, CCIS 288, pp. 666–674, 2012.

In this paper, a method for adaptive dictionary choice base mMCA is proposed, the color image is considered to be made of three channels, which corresponding to each color layer. Also, Minimum Energy [18, 19] method is used to adaptive choose the dictionary, and the result show that the method performs well in image inpainting.

2   Sparse Representation Model

Linear inverse problems arise lots of application areas. Mostly, these problems are under determined. There are many solutions of the underdetermined equation, among these solutions, the few nonzero entries will be seek, and it referred to as sparse representation.

Sparse representation is a powerful tool for acquiring and representing high-dimensional data [14], which can be regarded as a linear combination of atoms from over complete dictionary [21]. It's useful in statistics, signal processing, machine learning, and approximation theory.

The sparse decomposition framework can be described as follow. Consider the linear system:

$$x \in R^n \ x = \Phi \alpha \tag{1}$$

where, $\Phi \in R^{n \times m}$ is the over complete dictionary, α is the decomposition coefficients of x. There are many solutions of $x = \Phi \alpha$, and the least number of non-zero coeffcients α_i would be found.

Donoho [15] proposed to solve such minimization problem:

$$\hat{\alpha} = \arg \min \|\alpha\|_0 \ \ s.t. \ x = \Phi \alpha \tag{2}$$

where $\|\alpha\|_0$ is l^0 norm (i.e, the nonzero elements in α)

If the signal is contaminated with noise, the constraint equation will be relax with error tolerance $\varepsilon > 0$,

$$\hat{\alpha} = \arg \min \|\alpha\|_0 \ \ s.t. \ \|x - \Phi \alpha\|_2 \leq \varepsilon \tag{3}$$

The problem (3) is NP-hard, because of its nature of combinational optimization .Donoho [15] proposed to relax the non-convex sparsity equation to convex problem:

$$\hat{\alpha} = \arg \min \|\alpha\|_1 \ s.t. \ \|x - \Phi \alpha\|_2 \leq \varepsilon \tag{4}$$

3   K-SVD

The goal of K-SVD is to find the overcomplete dictionary Φ which can sparse representation for the training signals [16]. The K-SVD algorithm is used to construct the overcomplete dictionary, flexible with pursuit algorithm (MP, BP). The model of K-SVD is described as follow[13]:

$$\min_{\Phi,\alpha}\|X - \Phi\alpha\|_2^2 \quad s.t \forall i, \|\alpha_i\|_0 < T_0 \tag{5}$$

where, T_0 is given sparsity level, $X = \{x_i\}_{i=1}^n$ is the training signals, α is the relevant coefficient, Φ is the dictionary to be found.

Figure 1 shows the flow chart of K-SVD, there are two stages in K-SVD algorithm [17],

(i) Sparse Coding Stage: Using MP or BP.
(ii) Dictionary Update Stage: update one atom at a time.

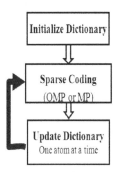

Fig. 1. K-SVD Algorithm

4   Inapinting Base mMCA

4.1   Overview MCA and mMCA

For an input signal x, in the MCA setting, x is the linear combination of n different morphologies,

$$x = \sum_{i=1}^n x_i \tag{6}$$

the MCA model assumes [8]:

i) For every signal x_k, there exists a dictionary $\Phi_k \in M^{N \times L_k}$, and the solve

$$\hat{\alpha_k} = \arg\min\|\alpha\|_0 \quad s.t. \quad x_k = \Phi_k \alpha \tag{7}$$

has a very sparse solution.

ii) For every signal x_l, solving for $k \neq l$

$$\hat{\alpha}_l = \arg \min \|\alpha\|_0 \quad s.t. \quad x_l = \Phi_k \alpha \tag{8}$$

has a very non-sparse solution.

According to MCA model, the different Φ_k can be seen that signals are discriminating between the different components, thus we need to solve

$$\min_{\alpha_1,...,\alpha_n} \sum_{i=1}^{n} \|\alpha_i\|_0 \quad s.t. \quad x = \sum_{i=1}^{n} \Phi_i \alpha_i \tag{9}$$

The Basis Pursuit (BP) method suggests replace l_0 with l_1 and relax the equality constraint, the MCA algorithm will turn to be:

$$\arg \min \sum_{i=1}^{n} \|\alpha_i\|_1 + \lambda \left\| x - \sum_{i=1}^{n} \Phi_i \alpha_i \right\|_2^2 \tag{10}$$

Figure 2 shows MCA separation result for the pepper image, the original Barbara pepper (left), the separated texture (middle), and the separated cartoon (right).

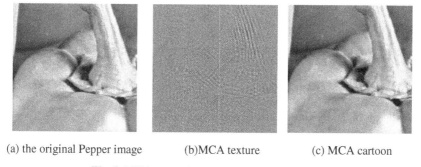

(a) the original Pepper image   (b)MCA texture   (c) MCA cartoon

Fig. 2. MCA separation result for the Pepper image

MCA (mMCA) is extension of MCA, in the mMCA setting, assume that multichannel data is linear mixture model, it can be described as follow [22]:

$$X = AS \tag{11}$$

where, $S = [s_1, s_2,..., s_m]$ is the multichannel data, A is the   is the   mixing matrix. And each source s_i is modeled as the linear combination of K morphological components,

$$s_i = \sum_{k=1}^{K} x_{ik} = \sum_{k=1}^{K} \alpha_{ik} \Phi_k, \forall i \in \{1,...,m\} \tag{12}$$

where, s_i are sparse in the dictionary Φ. Therefore, the mMCA is expressed by the following optimization problem:

$$\min_{A,\alpha} \sum_{i=1}^{m} \sum_{k=1}^{K} \left\| \alpha_{ik} \right\|_1^1 \ s.t \ \left\| X - A\alpha\Phi \right\|_2 \le \delta, and \ \left\| \alpha^i \right\|_2 = 1, \forall i = 1,...,m \quad (13)$$

4.2   Choose the Dictionary

In the image processing, it assumes that images are mostly composed of a piecewise smooth (cartoon-like) and a texture part. Image = Cartoon + Texture. The overcomplete dictionary is an important key for MCA, choose appropriate dictionary can represented sparsely cartoon and texture components. Generally, dictionary choices are used the wavelets, curvelets, bandlets, contourlets or ridgelets basis for the cartoon components and the local discrete cosine transform (DCT) basis for the texture components. In this paper, Minimum Energy [18, 19] method is used to adaptive choose the dictionary.

To the texture part's dictionary Φ_t, we also use DCT basis. And to the cartoon part's dictionary Φ_c, follow the Minimum Energy method, we have:

$$\min_{\Phi_c} \left\| X_{cartoon} - \Phi_c \alpha_c \right\|_2, s.t \begin{cases} \forall i, \left\| \alpha_t \right\|_0 \le s \\ \forall k, \left\| \Phi_t \right\|_2 = 1 \end{cases} \quad (14)$$

This model is a non-convex problem and it can be solved using K-SVD.

4.3   Image Inpainting Process

The model of image inpainting can be described as follow:

$$Y = MX + N \quad (15)$$

wher X is the original data, Y is the observed data, M is a binary mask that multiplies the data matrix X and N models noise.

Suppose the missing pixels are described by 'mask' matrix $M \in \{0,1\}^{N \times N}$, M take the value with '1' for existing pixels, and '0' elsewhere.

Now consider the case that color image inpainting. The color image is considered to be made of three channels, which corresponding to each color layer. To each channel, the combination of two morphological components is considered: cartoon part and a texture part. Therefore, the mMCA model can be modified to estimate the missing entries as follows:

$$\min_{A,\alpha} \sum_{i=1}^{3} \sum_{k=1}^{2} \left\| \alpha_{ik} \right\|_1^1 \ s.t \ \left\| Y - M(A\alpha\Phi) \right\|_2 \le \delta, and \ \left\| \alpha^i \right\|_2 = 1, \forall i = 1,...,3 \quad (16)$$

Solve this problem, the missing pixels could be recovered, because the existing pixel is just consider. Once A, Φ, α are restored, the whole image is recover.

5   Experimental Results

5.1   Image Pixel Missing

The random pixel missing is often observed in spread the image. The color Pepper is uses as a test image, figure 3 shows the 'Pepper' image and its inpainted results for three random mask of 30, 50, 75 percent missing pixels.

(a) 30% pixels missing   (b) 50% pixels missing   (c) 75% pixels missing

Fig. 3. Image pixel missing inpainted

5.2   Chessboard Mask

Figure 4 shows the 'Pepper' image and its inpainted results for chessboard mask. Chessboard mask is a very serious damage to the image, and the method can get a well visually.

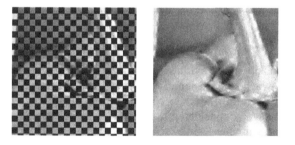

Fig. 4. Chessboard mask inpainted

5.3   Removal of Text

In some image processing, request to remove the redundant text. Figure 5 shows the 'Pepper' image and its inpainted results for text mask.

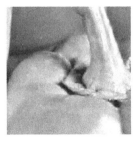

Fig. 5. Removal of text

5.4   Comparison Results

Table 1 shows the comparison result between TV and this method,   using PSNR as the measure. It shows that this method is better than TV method. To this method , the inpainting result of Barabara is better than other images,   because DCT basis are well represented the texture components.

Table 1. Result of TV inpainting and this method(PSNR)

Image	Mask Type	75% Pixels Missing	Chessboard Mask	Text Mask
Barbara	TV	25.57	26.99	31.71
	This method	27.57	28.54	33.69
Pepper	TV	25.62	26.16	31.05
	This method	26.40	26.97	31.55
Boats	TV	24.82	25.01	29.07
	This method	25.82	25.08	29.64
Baboon	TV	23.04	24.08	28.43
	This method	25.14	26.08	29.82
Lena	TV	23.21	23.81	29.02
	This method	23.70	23.79	29.15

6   Conclusion

MCA is a decomposition method based on sparse model, it can solve the inpainting problem. mMCA which is extension of MCA and better represents multichannel data. Image inpainting based on mMCA needs choose the dictionary by artificial. In this paper, the color image is considered to be a multichannel data which composed of three channels, and combine K-SVD to adaptive choose the dictionary. This method can choose the dictionary by image content, and the experiment result shows that it can well recover the damaged   image.

Acknowledgments. This work was supported by the National Natural Science Foundation of China (61171141), the National Natural Science Foundation of China and Civil Aviation Administration China (No. 6077681 6),   the Nature Science Foundation of Guangdong Province (No. 8251064101000005).

References

1. Bertalmio, M., Sapiro, J., Caselles, V., et al.: Image inpainting. In: Proceedings of SIGGRAPH, pp. 417–424 (2000)
2. Chan, T., Shen, J.: Mathematical models for local non-texture inpaintings. SIAM Journal on Applied Mathematics 62(3), 1019–1043 (2001)
3. Chan, T., Shen, J.: Non-texture Inpainting by Curvature-Driven Diffusions (CDD). Journal of Visual Communication and Image Representation 12(4), 436–449 (2001)
4. Elad, M., Starck, J., Donoh, D., Querre, P.: Simultaneous cartoon and texture image inpainting using morphological component analysis (MCA). ACHA 19(3), 340–358 (2005)
5. Guleryuz, O.: Nonlinear approximation based image recovery using adaptive sparse reconstructions and iterated denoising-part I: theory. IEEE Trans. On Image Processing 15(3), 539–554 (2006)
6. Starck, J.L., Elad, M., Donoho, D.: Redundant multiscale transforms and their application for morphological component analysis. Advances in Imaging and Electron Physics 132(82), 287–348 (2004)
7. Starck, J.L., Elad, M., Donoho, D.: Image decomposition via the combination of s parse representation and a variational approach. IEEE Transactions on Image Processing 14(10), 1570–1582 (2005)
8. Starck, J., Moudden, Y., Bobin, J., Elad, M., Donoho, D.: Morphological component analysis. In: Proceedings of SPIE Conference on Wavelets, vol. 5914 (2005)
9. Bobin, J., Moudden, Y., Starck, J., Elad, M.: Multichannel Morphological Component Analysis. In: Proceedings of Spars 2005, pp. 103–106 (2005)
10. Bobin, J., Moudden, Y., Fadili, M.J., Starck, J.: Morphological diversity and sparsity for Multi-channel data restoration. Journal of Mathematical Imaging and Vision 33(2), 149–168 (2009)
11. Backer, A., Rolfs, B., Felix, Y.: Video Restroation Using Multichaael-Morphological Component Analysis Inpainting,
http://cs229.stanford.edu/proj2009/BackerRolfs~Yu.pdf
12. Bobin, J., Starck, J., Moudden, Y., Fadili, Y.: Blind Source Separation: the Sparsity Revolution. Advances in Imaging and Electron Physics 152, 221–298 (2008)
13. Aharon, M., Elad, M., Bruckstein, A.: The K-SVD: An algorithm for designing of overcomplete dictionaries for sparse representations. IEEE Trans. Image Process. 54(11), 4311–4322 (2006)
14. Elad, M., Aharon, M.: Image denoising via learned dictionaries and sparse representation. In: IEEE Computer Vision and Pattern Recognition, New York, USA (2006)
15. Donoho, D., Huo, X.: Uncertainty principles and ideal atomic decomposition. IEEE Trans. on Inf. Theory 47(7), 2845–2862 (2001)
16. Aharon, M., Elad, M., Bruckstein, A.: K-SVD: design of dictionaries for sparse representation. In: Proc. SPARS 2005. IRISA, Rennes (2005)
17. Aharon, M., Elad, M., Bruckstein, A.: K-SVD: An algorithm for designing overcomplete dictionaries for sparse representation. IEEE Transactions on Signal Processing 54(11), 4311–4322 (2006)
18. Gabriel, P.: Manifold model s f or signals and images. Computer Vision and Image Understanding 113(2), 249–260 (2009)
19. Zhang, T., Hong, W.X.: Image inpainting based on MCA featured adaptive dictionary selection. Optical Technique 36(5), 672–676 (2010)

20. Li, Y., Zhang, Y., Xu, X.: Advances and Perspective on Morphological Component Analysis Based on Sparse Representation. Acta Electronica Sinica 37(1), 146–152 (2009)
21. Mallat, S., Zhang, Z.: Matching pursuits with time-frequency dictionaries. IEEE Transaction on Signal Processing 41(12), 3397–3415 (1993)
22. Bobin, J., Moudden, Y., Starck, J.L., Fadili, J.: Sparsity and morphological diversity for hyperspectral data analysis. In: ICIP 2009: 2009 IEEE International Conference on Image Processing, pp. 1481–1484. IEEE, Piscataway (2010)
23. Elad, M., Figueiredo, M., Ma, Y.: On the Role of Sparse and Redundant Representations in Image Processing. Proceedings of the IEEE 98(6), 972–982 (2010)
24. Aujol, J., Aubert, G., Feraud, L., Chambolle, A.: Image decomposition into a bounded variation component and an oscillating component. Journal of Math. Image and Vision 22, 71–88 (2005)
25. Ballester, C., Bertalmio, M., Caselles, V., Sapiro, G., Verdera, J.: Filling-in by joint interpolation of vector fields and gray levels. IEEE Trans. Image Processing 10, 1200–1211 (2001)
26. Peyré, G., Fadili, M., Starck, J.L.: Learning adapted dictionaries for geometry and texture separation. In: Wavelet XII, San Diego (2007)

Mine Risk Assessment Based on Location and Monitoring Emergency Communication System

Hongde Wang and Han Deng

School of Civil and Safety Engineering, Dalian Jiaotong University
116028 Dalian, China
whdsafety@126.com, hand1982@qq.com

Abstract. Mine emergency communications are poor by general industry standards, and generate significant risks in the lack of information available from underground areas. Coal mines often employ multiple incompatible systems for communication. The paper concludes that an improved communications system would allow real time risk assessment to be carried out at the coal mine, and the requirements for monitoring, assessment and decision making have been investigated for some common hazards. These include ventilation issues, strata control and emergency response. This would incorporate the latest technologies in safety management and real time risk assessment, using computer-based assessment, assisted decision making, and virtual reality. Results show that the greatest needs are for an emergency communication system that has a common standard, has wide band capacity, and allows for easy connectivity for sub-networks which are customized for specific applications.

Keywords: Mines risk assessment, emergency communication system, locating and monitoring, information integration.

1 Introduction

Mining is a dynamic operation system, with a continuous stream of timely information needed to monitor trends which indicate a change in risk status. This is producing increasing larger data outputs for mine communication systems. Mine operators are also expecting to have access to all the information in real time, increasing demand for communications bandwidth. Equipment manufacturers provided the monitoring and communication equipment to suite their individual applications. This has resulted in multiple communications systems operating in most mines. [1-2]. New technologies make a significant contribution to mine safety, particularly in risk management, by improving the monitoring and communication capabilities available to mine operators. This paper focus on the present status of mine communications for risk analysis, analyses what may be possible in the future.

M. Zhao and J. Sha (Eds.): ICCIP 2012, Part I, CCIS 288, pp. 675–682, 2012.

2   Communication System in Mine

Improved mine communications can assist in safety management in mines. In addition to communication technology developments, other new technologies which can contribute include: new sensors to collect information not currently available, communication interface modules, computer assisted decision making methods, visualization of mine data, risk assessment and safety management procedures.

2.1   The Status of Mine Communication

Many systems are used for communications in mines and it is common for a number of information systems. These communications technologies include fixed wire telephones, leaky feeder, cellular radio, low frequency through infrastructure, magnetic induction through personal emergency device (PED). PED uses a large loop on the surface to propagate signals through the rock to devices carried by underground workers [2-4]. The low data rate allows for communications equivalent to a messaging system.

2.2   Emergency Communication Capabilities

An emergency mine communications system is required to support self escape, aided rescue and mine recovery. Underground staffs need to be made aware of safe exit paths for self escape. In the aided rescue phase, the emergency management teams need to know where people are trapped in a mine by a physical impediment or injury. Finally, in the mine recovery phase, data about prevailing conditions is desired to minimize risk to workers while attempting to recover the situation. It follows that the emergency communications requirements include sending evacuation messages to underground personnel, personnel location monitoring and mine sensor monitoring. It is desirable that, if the mine power system fails, the communication system should remain active for up to a week and the system should be able to survive a section being lost in a roof fall.

2.3   Location and Monitoring Emergency Communication System

Location and Monitoring Emergency Communication System (LMECS) has three types of components: tags (also known as personal transponders), readers (also known as network beacons) and control / monitoring. Tags will be built into cap-lamp battery covers and routinely transmit a unique identification number. A network of readers will provide staff location information and communication through to a control / monitoring facility.

A LMECS network is depicted in Fig.1. Eight readers are shown, which provide communications along multiple, redundant paths within underground tunnels. The figure also depicts a personnel transponder, reporting vital signs data to nearby readers. A separate control and monitoring subsystem at the surface monitors the communications traffic and displays the staff location information. In emergencies, the control and monitoring subsystem serves to communicate escape route information to the individual transponders.

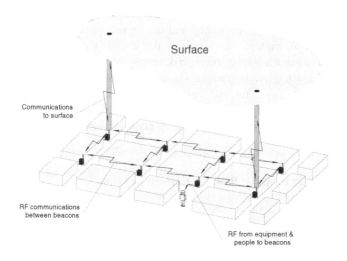

Fig. 1. Depiction of an underground LAMPS network

2.4   A Total Mine Communication System

A total mine communications system has both an integrated communications systems for operational functions of the mine, and an emergency mode of operating which allows for basic communications between the surface and underground even after an incident has damaged the main communications carrier.

The main communication system has a high bandwidth, and a common interface such as Ethernet for all devices.

The LMECS is unique, in that it becomes part of the everyday network of the mine. Under normal conditions it is connected via Ethernet to the main communications carrier, and any data it provides can be accessed from any other Ethernet connection in the system. In addition to this "operational" function, if the main communications are lost, it has an inherent capability to maintain a reduced level of functionality, connecting to the surface stations through radio links passed between the LMECS modules.

By making the LMECS emergency part of everyday mine communications; it will be regularly maintained, and much more likely to be available at times when its emergency capabilities are required. Its cost can also be justified as it contributes to normal production activities in the mine, whereas special emergency systems are not usually given a high priority by mine management.

3   Mine Risk Assessment

Risk assessment has been adopted as the basis of safety management for mines. It is a generic process that is applicable to any situation, and standard processes have been developed which can be applied in any industry.

Risk management systems all develop a risk level assessment by consideration of the likelihood of a situation developing and the impact of the event occurring [3-5]. Common events with high impact represent the highest risk levels, and uncommon events with low impact have the lowest risk levels. By applying numerical values to likelihood and impact, quantitative assessment of risk can be determined.

This can be done on a one-off basis to determine where the risks are in an operation, which leads to safe operating procedures being developed to manage the risk. The level of risk will dictate the priority given to the safe operating procedures within the mine operations.

3.1   Technologies to Assist Risk Assessment in Mine

In mining, conditions underground change continuously, and hence risk profiles change as mining progresses. This dynamic process is accommodated in the safety management system, but requires:

- Data on the changes to be measured and available.
- Analytical processes that determine the significance of the changes.
- Lines of communication which convey data and responses around the mine.
- Decisions for appropriate action.
- A method of intervene to manage the risk.

3.2   Decision Making Processes

Decisions are made at appropriate times in the safety management process. These can be made by the intervention of a nominated person who considers the evidence and reacts according to agreed guidelines. It is also possible to develop computer programs which take in data and automatically determine a response from a set of pre-programmed options. It is common for there to be some mix of these procedures, where a person is advised of a set of options with the implications of each action predicted. The choice remains with the responsible person.

For complex situations, the implications of new data may only be able to be assessed by using specialist modeling programs [6-8]. The output from these programs may still be ambiguous, and require considerable judgment on the part of mine staff.

3.3   Presentation Using Visualizations

Virtual reality is a new technology which can be a powerful tool in conveying the significance of events, as part of safety management. Its use can be incorporated into procedures adopted by a mine. It is particularly powerful for real-time assessments. To achieve this, the visualization programs need access to capable communications systems that can deliver data immediately, and modeling programs that determine the effects of the changes, which are then fed to the visualization program for presentation to users.

4   Examples of Risk Situations in Mine

The following discussion explores some possibilities of typical hazards which could be addressed in a research and development program to improve mine safety management systems.

4.1   Mine Atmospheres

The control of mine atmospheres is essential to
- Provide safe air/oxygen for miners underground by controlling the level of methane, other noxious gases, dust and particulates from sources such as diesel vehicles, and temperature in work places.
- Remove seam gas emitted into the workings from exposed coal.
- Control spontaneous combustion/heating in the workings or goafs.

Ventilation Fans. The main method of maintaining safe working atmospheres in the mine is by ventilation with fresh air. The fans in an average Chinese underground coalmine (3 to 5 million tons of coal per annum) will move from 200 to 300m3/s of air and will run at constant speed, with monitoring of mechanical performance, power consumption, air moved and gas composition. It is necessary to balance air flows in different parts of the mine, and a mixture of flow controls (doors and brattice) and supplementary auxiliary fans are used.

Ventilation flow models are being used to analyze and design ventilation systems. There is usually not enough information gathered in the mine to measure ventilation performance in real time and to implement any necessary changes. If real time modeling of the ventilation is to be developed, there will need to be better sensing of gas concentrations, and air pressure and air velocity throughout the mine, and improved mine ventilation models capable of real time output.

Air Quality. Sampling of underground air is carried out routinely in Australian mines and tube bundles are used to collect samples continuously for analysis at a central laboratory located on the surface. Depending on the length of the sample tubes, there may be more than half an hour delay in getting an analysis. Instantaneous readings are sometimes collected from electronic gas sensors distributed through the mine. Most mines use tube bundles and analytical systems attached to a computer system which has set warning levels to alert the mine at the onset of high risk conditions.

Monitoring for Heating's and Fires. The first indications of heating's or fires in mines are seen in gases measured in the ventilation air. Gaseous products of heating's and fires are related to the temperature of the coal and an initial heating will be indicated by an increase in carbon monoxide. At higher temperatures hydrogen and higher hydrocarbons are generated, and the percentages of different gases give a reliable indication of the temperature at the seat of a fire. It cannot be assumed that normal ventilation flow continues once a fire commences, as buoyancy effects can reverse flow directions. Better data collection, communications and analysis are required to determine what is happening in the mine.

Monitoring Gas Drainage. Drill holes are used within gassy underground mines to reduce the amount of gas flowing into mine workings. The effective performance of gas drainage systems is critical to maintaining a safe mine atmosphere, but there is very little monitoring of details of different parts of the system. Monitoring systems to determine gas pressure, composition and flow rates could be developed which could be used to control individual sections of the system remotely.

4.2   Strata Control

Strata control remains one of the major areas for specialized safety activity in mines In contrast to normal industrial activity, mines expend most of their effort on maintenance of their working environment. Mining creates openings in the ground, and these must remain stable for the period that access is required to them. This might range from a few hours to access a specific ore resource, or decades in the case of access roads in long term mines. Inadequate rock support will lead to failures which interrupt the mining operation and generate risks to operators, and too much support is wasted effort. Rock deformation is a time dependent process, so mining engineering is a process of balancing the level of strata control engineering to just keep the mine functioning, and wasting money doing things which are not necessary.

In-situ Ground Conditions. A prerequisite for geotechnical assessments is the geology of a mine site. Information is compiled into geological models, and full 3D models are created with computer programs. These use data from boreholes, outcrop and geophysics to model the coal seams, and also the interseam rocks that affect the performance of the mine openings. Faults and fractures are a major control of strata behavior, but are difficult to both measure and incorporate into models. New techniques are being developed to assist rapid collection of fracture data. Seismic and other geophysical methods can be used to build 3D images of the rock mass.

All types of 3D information about the mine can be combined by virtual reality computer techniques. Data of different types can be displayed together in correct spatial relationship. In a predictive model information ahead of workings in a particular area of the mine could be combined to present an "X-ray view" of the ground about to be mined.

Monitoring Mining Effects. Monitoring changes in rock conditions during mining poses many challenges with respect to access to install instruments, the availability of intrinsically safe instruments, maintaining communication with instruments through the operation, the adequacy of models to interpret data being collected, and communication of integrated conclusions to operators.

Physical measurement of mining induced movements can be made with extensometers or lasers monitoring displacements on exposed rock faces. Deformations are associated with microseismic events, which can be monitored. Analysis of the small microseismic waves can indicate the location of the deformation and the type of rock fracture involved. By mapping these through time, any variation that might pose special risks can be identified by anomalous microseismic activity.

These data can be compared with computer modeling of anticipated strata performance. They can be used to update the model of site characteristics, and hence make adjustments to mine designs to make allowance for previously undetected hazards.

4.3   Mine Operations and Machine Monitoring

There are many areas of mine operations which might be selected as examples of activities for safety management. They might be related to a specific machine, or an area of works such as a longwall face. The data required from each of these situations would be integrated in an appropriate way with the communication system. New generation smart sensors will combine an analogue sensor with a microcontroller to give serial data output directly to the front-end computer.

4.4   Emergency Response Capabilities

When a mine emergency occurs, each mine has a management plan which takes over the running of the mine, and organization of escape and rescue operations. Traditional mines rescue brigades are becoming restricted in what they can do, as duty of care responsibilities prevents them being used in circumstances where it cannot be demonstrated that it is safe to work. A prime requirement is that adequate information is available on conditions in the mine following an incident.

LMECS Communication. This system has been specifically designed for these conditions, and can provide:

- A robust communications system which will survive even if the main mine services are lost.
- Links to individual miners underground that can provide information from personal monitors indicating the person is alive and their location.
- Send simple instructions to trapped workers if a suitable unit for workers to carry is developed.

Emergency Response Decision Support Program. When data from a mine is integrated into a Virtual Mine system using the virtual reality techniques, all relevant information for analyzing an emergency and planning escape and rescue operations could be immediately available [5, 9-11].

5   Conclusions

The Location and Monitoring Emergency Communication System (LMECS) can be customized to provide the data in a format which is most relevant to emergency management. These can be tested in training exercises. A typical scenario would be to present the whole layout of the mine and indicate where services relevant to emergency workers were, to help plan rescue activities. It could show the position of relevant equipment, location of people, or in the worst case, their location immediately prior to the incident. In the case of explosive gases being released the gas levels throughout the mine could be displayed, along with the output of analytical programs that tracked compositional variations through time and their significance. The source of fires could be identified and the state of the fire determined from gas analysis trends. The progress of any rescue efforts could be monitored.

References

1. Ke, J.H., Wei, X.Y.: Research on underground mine personnel tracking system base on RFID and CAN. Coal Engineering 11, 104–106 (2006) (in China)
2. Li, J., Fan, X.M.: Application of Underground Personnel Position and Management System Based on RFID Technology. Industry and Automation 37, 57–61 (2011) (in China)
3. Addinell, S.J., Rowan, G., Matsuyama, S.: Nexsys™ Real Time Risk Management System and Demonstration at Kushiro Coal Mine. Coal and Safety (26), 7–10 (2005)
4. Einicke, G.A., Rowan, G.: Real-time Risk Analysis and Hazard Management. In: Proc. 6th Australian Coal Operator's Conference, pp. 299–306 (2005)
5. Haustein, K., Rowan, G., Beitz, A., Widzyk-Capehart, E.: The Nexsys™ Realtime Risk Management System for Advanced Decision Support. In: Proceedings from the 12th World Multi-Conference on Systemics, Cybernetics and Informatics, pp. 254–259 (2008)
6. U.S. Department of Labor: Mine Safety and Health Administration (internet), http://www.msha.gov/stats/charts/mnm2007yeayend.asp
7. Tu, J.: Safety Challenges in China's Coal Mining Industry. China Brief 7(1), 6–8 (2007) (in China)
8. Haustein, K., Rowan, G.: The enhanced mine communications and information systems - the development of the Nexsys real-time risk management system. Coal and Safety Journal (30), 42–50 (2007)
9. Kissell, F.N.: Handbook for Dust Control in Mining U.S. Department of Health and Human Services. Public Health Service, Centers for Disease Control and Prevention, National Institute for Occupational Safety and Health, DHHS (NIOSH) Publication No. 2003-147, Information Circular 9465, pp. 1–131 (2003)
10. Sapko, M.J., Weiss, E.S., Harris, M.L., Man, C.K., Harteis, S.P.: Centennial of mine explosion prevention research. In: 2010 SME Annual Meeting and Exhibit, Phoenix, Arizona, pp. 1–13. Society for Mining, Metallurgy, and Exploration, Inc. (2010)
11. Coal Mines Technical Services, http://www.cmts.com.au/gasanalysis.htm

Gender Determination from Single Facial Image by Utilizing Surface Shape Information

Dongjun Yu[1,2], Xiaowei Wu[1], and Weiwei Yang[1]

[1] School of Computer Science and Technology,
Nanjing University of Science and Technology, China
[2] Changshu Institute, Nanjing University of Science and Technology, China
njyudj@njust.edu.cn

Abstract. This paper investigates the feasibility and the effectiveness of performing gender determination from single 2D facial intensity image for each subject by utilizing recovered 3D facial surface shape information. The 3D facial surface shape in the form of needle-map, the fields of facial surface normals, is recovered from single 2D facial intensity image by using principal-geodesics-based shape-from-shading technology (PGSFS). An important fact is that the original 2D facial image is implicitly encoded into the 3rd component of the recovered 3D needle-map. The recovered needle-maps lying on high-dimensional Riemannian manifold are projected onto a lower-dimensional sub-manifold space by applying a special manifold learning technology - Principal Geodesics Analysis. Liner discriminant analysis is then performed on the projected needle-maps to find the optimal discriminant direction(s) for gender determination. Experimental results on FERET database demonstrate that the proposed method, PGA+LDA on the recovered 3D needle-maps, outperforms the classical method, PCA+LDA on 2D facial intensity images.

Keywords: Gender Determination, Shape-from-Shading, Needle-map, Principal Geodesic Analysis.

1   Introduction

Face images convey rich information, such as identity, age, gender, ethnicity and expression etc, which play important roles in human social interactions. Based on the information the face convey, different levels of categorization can be performed: identity identification, gender determination and ethnicity determination etc, amongst which identity identification has been widely and deeply investigated as a typical problem in pattern recognition circles. Many commercial products on face identity identification have emerged. Gender determination, as one of most important sub-problems of face identity identification, has attracted significant attention of researchers in both psychology and Computer Science. Developing effective and robust machine gender determination methodologies can enhance the communication between machine and human and will do great contribution to the performance improvements of machine face identity identification.

M. Zhao and J. Sha (Eds.): ICCIP 2012, Part I, CCIS 288, pp. 683–692, 2012.
© Springer-Verlag Berlin Heidelberg 2012

Many researchers have done contributions to machine gender determination: Gollomb [1] proposed a neural network model SEXNET in 1991 for face gender classification under lower resolution (30×30). Brunelli and Poggio [2] utilized the geometrical features extracted from 2D intensity face images to train a HyberBF neural network. Independent Component Analysis (ICA) was performed on 2D intensity images to extracted features for gender classification in A. K. Jain's [3] work. Buchala et al. [4] used Principal Components Analysis (PCA) to reduce the dimensionality of long image vector, and then applied Linear Discriminant Analysis (LDA) on the projected data to find the optimal discriminant directions for gender determination. They also found that the gender encoding abilities of different principal components are different. Recently, Cootes [5] proposed Active Appearance Models (AAM), which can also be applied on gender classification. Lu [6] proposed a multi-modal integrating scheme, which fuses the different modalities - 2D intensity images and 3D range images, for gender determination. They reported that range modality provides competitive discriminative power on gender determination to intensity modality.

Researches [7] have shown that 3D shape information on human face surface plays important role in human gender determination. However, up to date, most of works on machine gender determination are conducted on 2D intensity images. The reason is that there exist many disadvantages such as 1) expensive capture devices, 2) time-consuming, 3) high complexity in computation and 4) large volume of storage, in capturing 3D shape of faces. So, if the 3D face shape information can be recovered directly from 2D intensity images, it will do great contribution to the gender determination.

Shape-from-Shading (SFS) is the kind of technology that can recover 3D shape information of the object contained in a 2D image. However, the classical SFS technologies are not reliable since there are problems due to concavity/convexity inverse, self-shadowing and albedo variation. Applying the classical SFS to recover the shape of faces and then performing gender determination is not feasible, if not impossible.

Recently, Smith & Hancock proposed a new PGASFS [8, 9]technology based on principal geodesics analysis (PGA) and robust statistics, which overcome the aforementioned problems elegantly and effectively. With PGASFS, we can recover the shape information of face, either in the form of the field of facial surface normals (Needle-map) or in the form of the facial height function, from just single face image.

In this paper, we proposed a gender determination approach based on PGASFS which utilizing shape information recovered from single 2D face image. In addition, the proposed approach also utilizes the information contained in the 2D face image implicitly. We also compare the performance between the proposed approach and the classic approach PCA+LDA.

2   Principal Geodesic Analysis

In PCA, data in high-dimensional Euclidean space are projected to a low-dimensional linear sub-space spanned by principal components while maximizing the variance of the projected data in Euclidean distance metric. Likewise, PGA projects data lying on high-dimensional manifold onto a low-dimensional sub-manifold spanned by principal geodesics while maximizing the variance of the projected data in Riemannian distance metric. Each principal component axis in PCA is a straight line whilst in PGA each principal geodesic axis is a geodesic curve.

More formally, let M be a Riemannian manifold and $\{X_1, X_2, \cdots, X_N\}$ be a set of points lying on M. The purpose of PGA is to find a set of geodesic sub-manifolds $\{H_i\}$ ($\{H_i\}$ are also called principal geodesic sub-manifolds, analogy to the principal components in PCA) of M, which maximize the variance, under Riemannian distance metric, of the transformed data obtained by projecting data $\{X_i\}$ onto $\{H_i\}$.

2.1   Riemannian Log Map and Exp Map

Let I be a point lying on Riemannian manifold M, $T_I M$ be the tangent plane to M at point $I \in M$, v be a non-zero vector on the tangent plane $T_I M$ ($v \in T_I M$, $v \neq 0$), γ_I^v be the geodesic curve that pass through I in the direction of v. The Riemannian Log map of v at base-point I, denoted by $Exp_I(v)$, is the point $I^* \in M$ along the geodesic curve γ_I^v at distance $\|v\|$ from I, i.e.,

$$I^* = Exp_I(v) \text{ and } d(I, I^*) = \|v\|$$ (1)

Riemannian Exp map is the inverse of Riemannian Exp map:

$$v = \log_I(I^*)$$ (2)

It is easy to find that the distance between two points, I and I^*, on M is:

$$d(I, I^*) = \|\log_I(I^*)\|$$ (3)

The intrinsic mean of the N points $\{X_1, X_2, \cdots, X_N\}$ lying on the Riemannian manifold M is defined as:

$$\overline{X} = \arg \min_{X \in M} \sum_{i=1}^{N} d(X, X_i)$$ (4)

Unfortunately, there do not exist any analytic solutions to the aforementioned optimization equation. An iterative gradient-descending approach was presented in paper [10], the uniqueness of the solution can be guaranteed when the data is well localized [10]:

$$\overline{X}_{t+1} = Exp_{\overline{X}_t}\left(\frac{\tau}{N}\sum_{i=1}^{N}\log_{\overline{X}_t}(X_i)\right)$$ (5)

After defining intrinsic mean, the variance can be defined as:

$$\sigma^2 = \frac{1}{N}\sum_{i=1}^{N}\left(d(X_i, \overline{X})\right)^2 = \frac{1}{N}\sum_{i=1}^{N}\left\|\log_{\overline{X}}(X_i)\right\|^2$$ (6)

For the purpose of clarity, here we restate the main idea of PGA: ① Obtaining the mapped vectors by mapping (Riemannian Log map) the points lying on manifold M to tangent plane at base-point $\overline{X}$ - the intrinsic mean of all points on M; ② Performing standard PCA to the mapped vectors on the tangent plane and finding principal components of the mapped vectors; ③ Principal geodesic sub-manifolds are the geodesic curves that pass through the intrinsic mean and have the same direction with principal components of the mapped vectors. The key step in PGA is to define accurate and efficient Riemannian Log map and Riemannian Exp map. Riemannian Log and Exp map are different in different manifolds. In next section, we will define Riemannian Log and Exp map for a specific manifold $S^2(n)$ and detail the algorithm of PGA on Needle Maps.

2.2   Performing PGA on Needle-Maps

As stated in above section, given face images set $\{\mathbf{X}_i \mid 1 \leq i \leq N\}$, the corresponding needle-maps set $\{\mathbf{NX}_i \mid 1 \leq i \leq N\}$ can be obtained by applying SFS, where $\mathbf{X}_i \in R^{n \times 1}$ is a long image vector, $\mathbf{NX}_i \in R^{n \times 3}$ is the corresponding needle-map matrix of $\mathbf{X}_i$. The p-th ($1 \leq p \leq n$) row of $\mathbf{NX}_i$, denoted by $\mathbf{NX}_i^p \in R^{1 \times 3}$, is a unit vector representing the unit normal vector on the recovered facial surface at the point corresponding to the pixel p in image $\mathbf{X}_i$.

Unit vector $\mathbf{NX}_i^p \in R^{1 \times 3}$ can be considered as a point X_i^p lying on a unit 2-Sphere manifold, i.e., $X_i^p \in S^2$. Likewise, $\mathbf{NX}_i \in R^{n \times 3}$ describing a facial surface shape can be considered as a point X_i lying on a manifold $S^2(n)$, where $S^2(n) = \prod_{i=1}^{n} S^2$.

Let point $I = (0,0,1)$ be the base-point on a unit 2-Sphere manifold S^2, then the vector on tangent plane $T_I S^2$ can be written in the form of $\mathbf{v} = (v_1, v_2, 0)$. Thus the Riemannian Exp map on S^2 at base-point I can be formulated as

$$Exp_I(\mathbf{v}) = \left(v_1 \frac{\sin\|\mathbf{v}\|}{\|\mathbf{v}\|}, v_2 \frac{\sin\|\mathbf{v}\|}{\|\mathbf{v}\|}, \cos\|\mathbf{v}\| \right) \tag{7}$$

Likewise, the corresponding Riemannian Log map for a point $I^* = (x, y, z)$ on S^2 is given by

$$Log_I(\mathbf{x}) = \left(x \frac{\theta}{\sin\theta}, y \frac{\theta}{\sin\theta} \right) \tag{8}$$

where $\theta = \arccos(z)$.

Under real circumstance, the coordinates of base-point $I = (x, y, z)$ is not always equal to $(0,0,1)$. If that's the case, we can first transform the coordinates of point I to

$(0,0,1)$ by two successive rotations (first around x-axis, then around y-axis, vice versa), and then the Log and Exp map can be obtained by applying the aforementioned two formulas. The Exp and Log maps on the manifold $S^2(n)$ are simply the direct products of n copies of the maps for S^2 given above.

In summary, here we present the detailed algorithm for performing PGA on Needle-maps as follows:

Input: points set $\{X_i \mid 1 \le i \le N\}$ on manifold $S^2(n)$

Output: $\{\mathbf{w}_k, \lambda_k\}$, $\overline{X}$, $\mathbf{w}_k \in T_{\overline{X}} S^2(n)$, $\lambda_k \in R$

Begin

$$\overline{X}_p \leftarrow \arg\min_{X \in S^2} \sum_{i=1}^{N} d(X, X_i^p) \quad \overline{X} \leftarrow \left(\overline{X}_1^T \mid \overline{X}_2^T \mid \cdots \mid \overline{X}_p^T \mid \cdots \mid \overline{X}_n^T \right)^T$$

$$\mathbf{v}_i^p \leftarrow \log_{\overline{X}_p} \left(X_i^p \right)$$

$$\mathbf{v}_i \leftarrow \left(\mathbf{v}_i^1 \mid \mathbf{v}_i^2 \mid \cdots \mid \mathbf{v}_i^p \mid \cdots \mid \mathbf{v}_i^n \right)^T$$

$$\mathbf{D} \leftarrow \left(\mathbf{v}_1 \mid \mathbf{v}_2 \mid \cdots \mid \mathbf{v}_N \right)$$

$$\mathbf{S} \leftarrow \frac{1}{N} \mathbf{D} \mathbf{D}^T$$

$\{\mathbf{w}_k, \lambda_k\} \leftarrow$ the first k eigenvectors and eigenvalues of $\mathbf{S}$

End □

Constructing transformation matrix $\mathbf{W}^{PGA}$ by taking the m leading eigenvaectors of $\mathbf{S}$:

$$\mathbf{W}^{PGA} = \left(\mathbf{w}_1 \mid \mathbf{w}_2 \mid \mathbf{w}_3 \mid \cdots \mid \mathbf{w}_m \right) \in R^{2N \times m} \tag{9}$$

Given a needle-map X, its PGA parameter vector $\mathbf{Y}$ can be obtained by

$$\mathbf{v} = \log_{\overline{X}} \left(X \right) \tag{10}$$

$$\mathbf{Y} = (\mathbf{W}^{PGA})^T \mathbf{v} \tag{11}$$

More clearly, we first map X to a vector $\mathbf{v} = \left(\mathbf{v}^1 \mid \mathbf{v}^2 \mid \cdots \mid \mathbf{v}^n \right)^T \in R^{2n \times 1}$ on tangent plane $T_{\overline{X}} S(n)$ using Log map, where $\mathbf{v}^p = \log_{\overline{X}^p} \left(X^p \right), 1 \le p \le n$; Then, we project the obtained vector to the transformation matrix $\mathbf{W}^{PGA}$.

Contrarily, when the PGA parameter vector $\mathbf{Y}$ is known, the procedures to get back original needle-map are:

$$\mathbf{v} = \mathbf{W}^{PGA} \mathbf{Y} \tag{12}$$

$$X = Exp_{\overline{X}} \left(\mathbf{v} \right) \tag{13}$$

3   Experiments and Analysis

3.1   Datasets and Pre-processing

Our experiments were conducted on the subsets of FERET. FERET [11] - the outcome of FERET program sponsored by DARPA - has become a standard face image database in face recognition circles. There are large amount of subjects in FERET and each subject has different face images with variety in pose, angle of view, illumination, expression and age etc. Different gender and ethnicity categories are also well delivered in FERET. In our experiments, a subset of FERET named as Dataset-I which consists of 200 subjects (100 females and 100 males) and each subject has only one face image, is used.

Each image in Dataset-I is pre-processed to a resolution of 142×124 by cropping, rotating, scaling and aligning. Face images are aligned with each other based on the central points of left eye and right eye. More specifically, the central point of left eye locate at (27, 34) and the central point of right eye locate at (98, 34). In addition, the intensity contrast of each image is linearly stretched to normalize the ambient illumination variations.

3.2   Recovering Needle-Maps from Face Images Using SFS

We use the PGASFS [12] to recover the needle-map for each face image in Dataset-I and name the set of recovered needle-maps as Dataset-II. The statistical model of facial needle-maps used in our PGASFS is built on the ground-truth facial needle-maps obtained from Face Video Database of the Max Planck Institute for Biological Cybernetics.

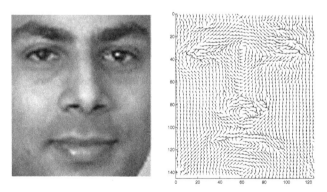

Fig. 1. An example of recovered facial needle-map

Fig. 1 depicts an example of the recovered facial needle-map. Note that the recovered needle-map is viewed along the z-axis and for the purpose of clarity to view, only 1/3 sampled surface normals are plotted.

An important characteristic of PGASFS is that the recovered 3D needle-map encodes implicitly the 2D intensity image. We view each component (x, y and z) of the recovered needle-map as an image as shown in Fig. 2. It is clear that the needle-map encapsulates the original 2D intensity image in the 3rd component. That is to say the recovered needle-map contains both the shape information of facial surface and the original face intensity information. The extreme right image is a rendered result by re-illuminate the recovered needle-map with a different light source $s = [1 \quad 0 \quad 2]$.

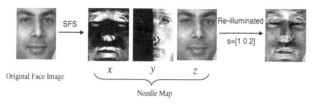

Fig. 2. Viewing x, y and z components of the recovered needle-map and re-illumination

3.3   Results and Analysis

We use 2 different schemes to perform gender determination: (1) PCA+LDA: PCA is first performed on 2D intensity images to find principal components, and then LDA is applied to find the optimal discriminant direction. (2) PGA+LDA: PGA is performed on 3D needle-maps recovered from original face images using SFS, as opposed to PCA on intensity images, to find principal geodesics; then LDA is applied on the principal geodesics to obtain optimal discriminant direction. The simple nearest neighbour classifier is used in both schemes. We try to compare the performance between two schemes and unveil whether the shape information delivered by needle-map is important and effective in gender determination.

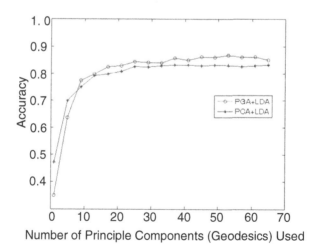

Fig. 3. The influences of the reduced dimensionality

First, we investigate the influence of the reduced dimensionality to the accuracy by using 30% samples as training samples and the remaining 70% used as testing samples, as shown in Fig. 3. It is found in Fig. 3 that the accuracies of both PGA+LDA and PCA+LDA are increasing with the increment of the number of the principle components used. In addition, the accuracy of PGA+LDA is consistently higher than that of PCA+LDA.

Table 1 presents the recognition results when 50% samples as used as training samples.

Table 1. Performance comparison of GPA+LDA and PCA+LDA

	Accuracy
PCA+LDA	85.7%
PGA+LDA	92.4%

From table 1, we can easily draw conclusions that 1) it is feasible to perform gender determination using face shape information and 2) PGA+LDA on 3D needle-maps outperforms PCA+LDA on 2D intensity images. We speculate the intrinsic reason for PGA+LDA outperforming PCA+LDA is that the recovered 3D needle-map contains more information than that in 2D intensity image. More clearly: one the one hand, the recovered needle-map contains the shape information, delivered in the form of surface normal, of the face surface; on the other hand, 2D intensity image information is directly encoded in the 3rd component of the recovered needle-map.

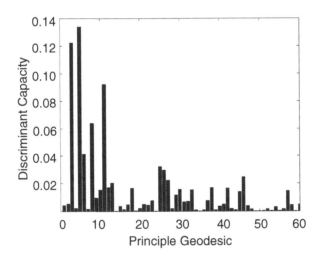

Fig. 4. Discriminant capacities of the 60 leading principal geodesics

We measure discriminant capacity of the i-th principal geodesic with the following metric:

$$S_i = \frac{(Diag\{\mathbf{S}_b\})_i}{(Diag\{\mathbf{S}_w\})_i} \tag{14}$$

where $Diag\{\bullet\}$ is the diagonal matrix of matrix $\bullet$, $(\bullet)_i$ it the i-th entry of vector $\bullet$.

Fig. 4 shows the discriminant capacities of the 60 leading principal geodesics in an experiment. Compared with other principal geodesics, the 3rd, 5th, 8th and 11th principal geodesics are extremely prominent.

Why are the discriminant capacities of some principal geodesics more prominent than that of other principal geodesics? Not losing generality, taking the 5th principal geodesic as an example, we investigate the gender encoding capacity in the 5th principal geodesic direction by intuitively viewing the effectiveness of the vector $\mathbf{w}_5$ on tangent plane $T_{\bar{X}} S^2(n)$. More specifically, we first map the vector $\alpha \sqrt{\lambda_5} \cdot \mathbf{w}_5$ $(\alpha = 0, \pm 1, \pm 2, \pm 3)$ on tangent plane $T_{\bar{X}} S^2(n)$ to a point (needle-map) lying on manifold $S^2(n)$; then view the 3rd component of mapped point (needle-map) in the form of image. When $\alpha = 0$, the mapped point (needle map) is just the intrinsic mean $\bar{X}$. We gradually modify the coefficient α from -3 to 3 with a fixed step of 1 and Fig.5 shows the results corresponding to different coefficient α.

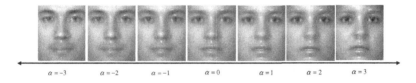

$\alpha = -3 \qquad \alpha = -2 \qquad \alpha = -1 \qquad \alpha = 0 \qquad \alpha = 1 \qquad \alpha = 2 \qquad \alpha = 3$

Fig. 5. Viewing the gender encoding capacity in the 5th principal geodesic

From Fig. 5, we can clearly observe that the images gradually, from left to right, changed from masculine to feminine. The left face images corresponding to $\alpha < 0$ contain much more masculine features such as thicker eyebrows and dark region around mouth – this is because most men are with beards. We can also find that left images with a mouth closed while the mouths in right images tend to be opened. The reason my be that women are more likely to smile compared with men. The face corresponding to $\alpha = 0$ is really a very neutral face, it is very difficult for even human to decide its gender. We also viewed gender encoding capacities of some other non-prominent principal geodesics in the same way, and find subjectively their gender encoding capacities are not as notable as that of the prominent principal geodesics.

4   Conclusions

We proposed a gender determination method PGA+LDA based on 3D face surface shape information and 2D face intensity information.   Needle-maps, which encapsulate both 3D face surface shape information and 2D intensity information, are recovered from 2D face images by using Shape-from-Shading technology; Principal geodesic analysis is then performed on the recovered needle-maps to obtain principal geodesics; finally, linear discriminant analysis is applied on the reduced sub-manifold spanned by the principal geodesics to find the optimal discriminant direction. Gender information encoding capabilities of different principal geodesics are illustrated in an intuitionistic style. We also compared the performance of the proposed method with that of the classical method PCA+LAD on 2D intensity images. Experimental results show that the proposed method consistently outperformed the classical method PCA+LDA.

Acknowledgments. This work was supported by the Natural Science Foundation of Jiangsu (No. BK2011371) and the NUST Research Funding (No. 2011YDXM19).

References

1. Golomb, B.A., Lawrence, D.T., Sejnowski, T.J.: SEXNET: A neural network Identifies sex from human faces. Advances in Neural Information Processing Systems, 572–577 (1991)
2. Brunelli, R., Poggio, T.: HyberBF Networks for Gender Classification. In: Proc. DARPA Image Understanding Workshop, pp. 311–314 (1992)
3. Jain, A., Huang, J.: Integrating independent components and linear discriminant analysis for gender classification. In: Proceedings Sixth IEEE International Conference on Automatic Face and Gesture Recognition, pp. 159–163 (2004)
4. Buchala, S., Davey, N., Gale, T.M., Frank, R.J.: Principal Component Analysis of Gender, Ethnicity, Age, and Identity of Face Images. In: IEEE ICMI 2005 (2005)
5. Cootes, T.F., Edwards, G.J., Taylor, C.J.: Active appearance models. IEEE T. Pattern Anal. 23(6), 681–685 (2001)
6. Lu, X., Chen, H., Jain, A.K.: Multimodal Facial Gender and Ethnicity Identification. In: Zhang, D., Jain, A.K. (eds.) ICB 2005. LNCS, vol. 3832, pp. 554–561. Springer, Heidelberg (2005)
7. Bruce, V., Burton, A.M., Hanna, E., Healey, P., Mason, O., Coombes, A., Fright, R., Linney, A.: Sex discrimination: how do we tell the difference between male and female faces? Perception 22, 131–152 (1993)
8. Smith, W.A.P., Hancock, E.R.: Recovering facial shape using a statistical model of surface normal direction. IEEE T. Pattern Anal. 28(12), 1914–1930 (2006)
9. Smith, W.A.P., Hancock, E.R.: Facial shape-from-shading and recognition using principal geodesic analysis and robust statistics. Int. J. Comput. Vision 76(1), 71–91 (2008)
10. Fletcher, P.T., Lu, C.L., Pizer, S.A., Joshi, S.: Principal geodesic analysis for the study of nonlinear statistics of shape. IEEE T. Med. Imaging 23(8), 995–1005 (2004)
11. Phillips, P.J., Moon, H., Rizvi, S.A., Rauss, P.J.: The FERET evaluation methodology for face-recognition algorithms. IEEE T. Pattern Anal. 22(10), 1090–1104 (2000)

Research of Reconfigurable Servo Architecture Based on Component Technology

Wen Meng[1,2], Yue Ma[2], Zhicheng Wang[2], and Yilin Zheng[1,2]

[1] Graduate University of Chinese Academy of Sciences, Beijing, China
[2] Shenyang Institute of Computing Technology, Chinese Academy of Sciences, Shenyang, China
mwlinux@hotmail.com,
{mayue,wangzc,zhengyl}@sict.ac.cn

Abstract. Traditionally, there are high coupling heavily against the effectiveness of Servo development between hardware and software of Servo device. This paper discovers the defects of existing component model and proposes an improved component model for embedded system and formalizes it. Based on the model and following suitable architecture convention and system acting convention, reconfigurable servo system is constructed in software level. Result of simulation and experimental verification shows that the reconfigurable servo architecture could meet basic demands of servo about real-time feature and runtime overhead.

Keywords: software architecture, embedded component, reconfiguration, servo-system.

1 Introduction

Traditionally, in Servo System with AC motor, control algorithm and structure of hardware and software will change a lot, with alteration of control objects and methods. High coupling between software and hardware and irrationality of software architecture will make development from scratch be common practice. For reuse is hardly ever heard of in embedded area, a lot of manpower is wasted. Open systems have become the trend in Control Field [1]. This paper discards the traditional and lagging methods of servo development, and puts forward a new development methodology based on component technology. According to actual demand, develop new components and reuse existing components to implement a reconfigurable architecture of Servo-system.

Today although component technology has been more and more mature in the traditional software development method [2], popular common component models require lots of the underlying support at run time which is not suitable for the embedded system. Existing embedded component models, due to self-defects, are not fully applicable to high performance servo system. Considering the functional properties and structure characteristics of servo, this paper proposes a new component model used in reconfigurable servo system.

M. Zhao and J. Sha (Eds.): ICCIP 2012, Part I, CCIS 288, pp. 693–702, 2012.

2   Component Model

Although processors are more and more powerful and memory capacity is growing in embedded system, considering the cost and real-time requirements in Servo, existing component models [5, 6] cannot be applied directly to the servo system development process. This paper puts forward a component model for servo system.

2.1   Model Definition

The model formalizes various aspects of basic components, properties set, interface and relationships among them. The structure chart of basic component is given in Fig.1.

Definition 1: component X is a tuple <P(X), C(X), PF(X), RF(X)> where:

- P(X) is properties set of component X.
- C(X) is sub-components set of X, $C(X) = \{C_0, C_1, \ldots, C_n\}$.
- PF(X) is interface provided by X, named "provide interface".
- RF(X) is interface required by X, named "require interface".

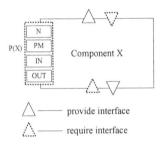

Fig. 1. Basic component model

Definition 2: P(X) is a tuple < N(X), PM(X), IN(X), OUT(X)> where:

- N(X) is a sign of the component X, $N(X) = \{N_0, N_1 \ldots N_n\}$. For example, there are component names, component id, and component description and so on.
- PM(X) is parameter set of component X, for modifying configuration of X.
- IN(X) is input of X.
- OUT(X) is output of X.

There are data sharing between IN(X) and OUT(X) to construct data flows among components.

Introduction of interface types ensure the separation between definition and implementation of component. Users do not have to care about the interface's implementation details. In component model, there are two types on interface: "provide interface" and "require interface". "Provide interface" is the one that component has implemented while "require interface" is not implemented. "Provide interface" provides services to other components or non-component modules and "require interface" requires implementation from other components and non-component modules.

Definition 3: PF(X) is a tuple <Fp(X), Dp(X)>, similar with PF(X), where:

$Fp(X) = \{f0, f1 \ldots fn\}$, is operations set contained in the "provide interface".

Dp(X) is data set contained in the "provide interface".

2.2   Execution Model

There are two separated data flow and control flow in component model. The data flow describes data sharing between IN(X) and OUT(X) in P(X), which is shown by Fig 2. OUT(X) represents writing shared data while IN(X) represents reading. The control flow describes interface calls between components and non-components modules shown by Fig.3.

Considering data flow in Fig.2, IN and OUT are elements of P(X), which shares the data block. The result of calculation in component is transferred into data block by OUT for being read by other components and non-component modules.

It shows that control flow contains three scenarios in components: direct connection, selective connection, and connection with non-component module. In Fig.3 C1 and C2 is direct connection. It is not sure that whether C3 is connected with C1 or C2, which is decided by middleware M [3], probably happening in the code trimming period or run time. The "provide interface" provided by C3 is called by non-component modules.

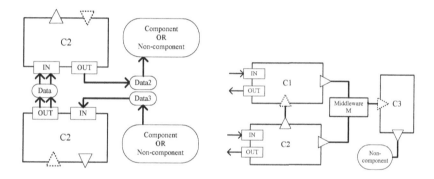

Fig. 2. Data flow in model   **Fig. 3.** Control flow in model

2.3   Composite Component

The components extracted from system according to some requirements need to be combined together to meet some new demands. The component model presented in this paper can achieve the same effect. As shown in Fig.4, the composite component contains three sub-components, C(X)={ C0, C1, C2}. The properties set P(X) and the interface set PF(X) and RF(X) are composed of three sub-components.

3   Reconfigurable Servo Architecture

The hardware platform of servo device is the basis of software architecture. This paper designs a modular servo device hardware structure and proposes reconfigurable software architecture for servo system based on component technology. In the process of development of Servo, some components are reused. According to different requirements, a new Servo system is reconstructed through the component assembly.

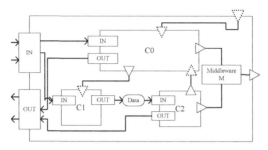

Fig. 4. Composite component

3.1   Hardware Architecture

There are two independent energy flow and data flow in Servo device. Energy flow is from the perspective of energy conversion. Servo device converts electrical energy absorbed from power network into motor of mechanical energy. Data flow means that instructions sent by the controller and feedback data. According to the rationality of energy and data flows and following a good architecture statute, servo device is divided into five independent function modules: power-supply module, power drive module, control unit, communication unit and encoder unit, as shown in Fig.5.

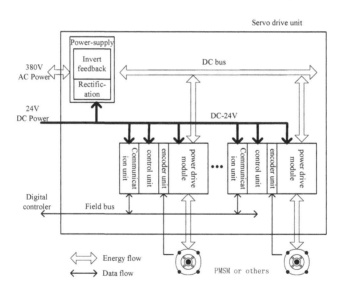

Fig. 5. Servo device hardware architecture

Power-supply module converts electrical energy absorbed from AC power network into DC bus voltage, which impacts motor's running performance directly. Power-supply module centrally manages DC bus, improving stability of DC bus voltage and energy utilization. Power drive module converts DC bus voltage into voltage of driving motor and collects data of current, voltage, position, rate and so on. Control unit is responsible for driving motor and controlling the current ring, speed loop and position loop of the axis. Encoder unit is responsible for calculations of motor's speed and position feedback data. Communications Unit ensures reliability of the information flows in Servo system.

3.2   Servo Software Architecture

Based on component model proposed above, and taking Servo features into account, this section describes how to build reconfigurable architecture of Servo software system on three layers respectively, which are drive layer., control layer, and application layer. Layered architecture is conducive to the scalability and stability of system [4].

Having taken Servo structure properties and Servo features into account, some components are extracted from system to guarantee servo functions. These components are USB component, PWM component, QEP component, Meter component, Oscilloscope component, Control algorithm component and communication protocol component. The first three components are in the driver layer. The next three are in the control layer. And the last one is in the application layer. The architecture is shown in Fig.6.

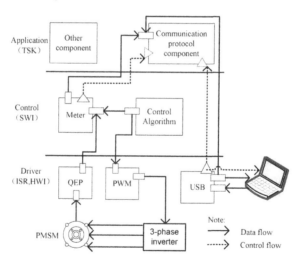

Fig. 6. Servo Software Architecture

The followings are details of the three layers.

1)   Driver layer

This layer's role is encapsulating hardware access and achieving isolation between control layer and hardware to reduce the coupling between software and hardware. There are three components:

a) *USB component:* It plays an important role in ensuring data transferring between Servo device and PC computer. PDIUSBD12 produced by Philips is used as USB controller chip, and the USB chip driver based on DSP/BIOS is packaged in the component to provide the data R/W interface to the external components and non-component modules. When the I/O demand changes, as long as the data R/W interfaces remain same forms, it's not necessary to modify upper modules where the interfaces are invoked, which guarantees the expansibility and low coupling among components.

b) *PWM component:* PWM pulse modulation control method is used in motor control. PWM waveforms are produced by peripheral circuits in DSP chip, TMS320F28335. There are six PWM waves whose dead-time and polar is programmable, to make three-phase AC induction motor work. PWM driver is encapsulated in the component.

c) *QEP component:* It is used to measure rotation and speed of motor. Working with Incremental Photoelectric Encoder and other rotation measurement, Peripheral circuits of QEP in F28335 are used to calculate speed and position feedback of motor. QEP driver is encapsulated in the component.

2) Control layer

This layer is mainly used for controlling and management of motor. There are three components too.

a) *Meter component:* It is used to monitor component output variables in real time. There are four pointers to observe four variables simultaneously. While using the component, users modify control parameters to output variables of components they want to observe. The monitored variables will be saved in corresponding internal ones.

b) *Oscilloscope component:* It is also used to monitor component output variables in real time. However, the variables observed will be saved in buffers to draw waveforms with debugging tools.

c) *Control algorithm component:* With Field Oriented Control method, Electromagnet torque of PMSM is strictly proportionate to the amplitude of Stator Current. In order to obtain appropriate electromagnet torque, the amplitude of Stator Current must be precisely controlled. The principle of permanent magnet synchronous motor speed control system is introduced other literatures.

3) Application layer

In this layer, only one communication component is implemented, which is mainly responsible for parsing the commands which come from controller. There are starting byte, instruction code, data length, data content, CRC code and ending byte field in communication frame. The protocol is good at self–describing and expansibility. Controller and PC send commands to servo device with unified format on the agreement.

4   Analysis of Reconfigurable

According to the connection method which has defined by component models, the servo system can be assembled shown by Figure 6. The unity of component model provides guarantee for the reconfigurable servo system. Before running of the system, the meter component in Control Layer can be replaced by the Oscilloscope component. This paper implements a control algorithm component, which is based on the PMSM control strategy. Control algorithms encapsulated in components make it easier to use other kinds of motor controlling strategy components to replace the PMSM control strategy.

In order to ensure the reconfigurable characteristic of the architecture, component models must meet the following three conditions:

1)   Consensus of component structure

Components design method is based on the model presented in Section II, which could ensure the consensus of components and facilitate realization of components re-assembly and make it easier to reconstruct a new system.

2)   Low coupling between components

In the process of extracting components, taking functional features and structural characteristics into account, it could reduce the coupling between components as much as possible. The lower coupling between components, the easier to achieve re-contracture target in the process of components reassembling.

3)   Open architecture

Open architecture demands a good partition of system architecture. In response to new development needs, an open architecture is designed in this paper, which could reduce the complexity of re-constructing a new system.

5   Key Techniques

During the system design process, developers must first complete decomposition of system architecture to extract reusable components they wanted. It is a major problem that how to ensure system is open and sequence behavior is also taken into account, and that how to guarantee reactivity and conversions of system behavior to be simultaneously reflected in the process of reconstructing system with components. Given both of architecture and acting statute of system, ease of reconstruction is guaranteed.

5.1   Statute of Architecture

Mostly, embedded system development is process-based, which illustrates uniformly time series statically and dynamically. Decomposition based on system structure is not taken seriously; it kills the openness and reconstruction of system, while this way can focus on decomposition based on system function. On the contrary, object-based statute pays attention to decomposition based on structure, to guarantee the openness and reconstruction of system. But this statute often overlooks sequence behavior and timing analysis which are quite important to real-time system. Taken all these characteristics into consideration together, and adopt design method which based on approach mixed with process-based and structure-based, this paper decomposes Servo system into a complete set of reusable components, ensuring that reconstructed system is open.

5.2   Statute of System Acting

There are not only continuous and periodic events, but also discrete events in servo system. Unfortunately, there is no one system reflecting reactivity and conversions of system behavior simultaneously. To meet this remand as much as possible, the architecture proposed in this paper considers both of the two software structures, one emphasizes the relationship between components is driven by events and control flows, the other emphasizes the relationship between components is driven by timing and data flows. These are reflected by data flows and control flows in component model.

6   Results

When implementing servo system, the Control Circuit Board, DSP chip, TMS320F28335, is used. Software environment is:

- Integrated Development Environment on DSP: Code Composer Studio Version 3.3.81.6
- Real-time OS: DSP/BIOS Version 5.41.09.34
- Code   Generation Tool: C2000 Code Generation Version 5.0

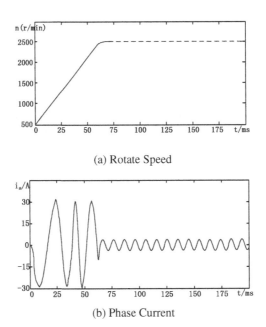

(a) Rotate Speed

(b) Phase Current

Fig. 7. Speed waveforms starts from zero to a given value

1) *Simulation Results:* Waveforms depicts motor speed increasing from zero to a given value (2500r/min) are shown in Fig.7, where Fig.(a) depicts Rotate Speed and Fig.(b) depicts wave of Phase Current.

2) *Actual Running Results:* PWM waveforms are shown in Fig.8. Difference between the top waveform and bottom waveform is called Dead Zone. Phase Current and Voltage waveforms, captured from Servo System when it running steadily, are shown in Fig.9 and Fig.10.

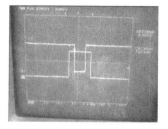   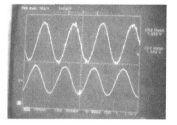

Fig. 8. PWM waveforms   **Fig. 9.** Phase Current waveforms

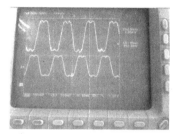

Fig. 10. Phase Voltage waveforms

7   Related Work

Several approaches to the composition of software from components have been proposed in the literature. In [5] van Ommering et.al. introduce a component model that is used for embedded software in consumer electronic devices. But it is only implemented in dedicated OS. PECOS is a collaborative project between industrial and research partners that seeks to enable component-based technology for a certain class of embedded systems known as "field devices" by taking into account the specific properties of this application area[6]. But component in this model is black box for users, not conducive to the openness of the system. Also there is CCOM model in the project of SEESCOA funded by IWT association in Italy.

8   Conclusion and Future Work

Based on existing component models, this paper proposes an improved model that is applicable to Servo System development. And based on the component model, this paper designs and implements a reconfigurable architecture to make it easier to reconstruct different Servo systems. If there are enough components in component library, developers can reconstruct the different Servo system without implementing new components. In this way, we can reduce the cost of research and development and further unify development process.

Considering the specific properties of software systems for embedded devices, the level of component reuse in this paper is in the source code level. So, system developers could understand the component inside-situation clearly, there will be no risk of losing control of system behavior. These source code level components allow the unused parts of component to be tailored before and during compiling period [7], to save system running-time overhead. In this paper, only one PMSM motor driver component is designed and implemented, and other types of control algorithms will be implemented in the next work.

Acknowledgment. These research works of this dissertation are supported by National Basic Research Program of China (973 Program, No. 2011CB302400).

References

1. Yu, D., Hu, Y., Xu, X.W., et al.: An Open CNC System Based on Component Technology. IEEE Transactions on Automation Science and Engineering 6(2), 302–310 (2009)
2. Szyperski, C.: Component Software: Beyond Object-Oriented Programming. Addison-Wesley Longman Publishing Co., Inc., Amsterdam (2002)
3. Lagaisse, B., Joosen, W.: Component-Based Open Middleware Supporting Aspect-Oriented Software Composition. In: Heineman, G.T., Crnković, I., Schmidt, H.W., Stafford, J.A., Szyperski, C., Wallnau, K. (eds.) CBSE 2005. LNCS, vol. 3489, pp. 139–154. Springer, Heidelberg (2005)
4. Pessemier, N., Barais, O., Seinturier, L., Coupaye, T., Duchien, L.: A three level framework for adapting component-based systems. In: Second International Workshop on Coordination and Adaptation Techniques for Software Entities (WCAT 2005), Glasgow, Scotland (July 2005)
5. van Ommering, R., van der Linden, F., Kramer, J., Magee, J.: The koala component model for consumer electronics software. IEEE Computer (2000)
6. Genßler, T., Nierstrasz, O., Schönhage, B., et al.: Components for embedded software: the PECOS approach. In: Proceedings of the 2002 International Conference on Compilers, Architecture, and Synthesis for Embedded Systems, October 8-11 (2002)
7. Suvée, D., Vanderperren, W., Jonckers, V.: JAsCo: an aspect-oriented approach tailored for component based software development. In: Proceedings of the 2nd International Conference on Aspect-Oriented Software Development (AOSD 2003), pp. 21–29. ACM Press, New York (2003)

Research on Data Compatibility of PMU/SCADA Mixed Measurement State Estimation

Lei Wu and Li Xia

Institute of Electrical and Information Engineering,
Naval University of Engineering
Wuhan, China
wulei840127@163.com

Abstract. Aiming at the problem that how to make use of mixed data of PMU(Phasor Measurement Unit) and SCADA (Supervisory Control and Data Acquisition) to improve the traditional state estimation in power system, a new method to solve the compatibility problem of PMU/SCADA mixed data is proposed. Firstly, the differences between PMU and SCADA are analyzed, and the model of PMU/SCADA mixed data is built. We can conclude that time synchronization and measure weights are the main factors which affect the compatibility of mixed data. Therefore, data relevance analysis is used to implement the synchronization of PMU and SCADA data, and the measure weights are re-quantified by considering the delay distribution of measure data. The simulation results of ship integrated power system show the accuracy of compatibility analysis and the validity of compatibility method.

Keywords: power system, mixed measurement, state estimation, compatibility.

1 Introduction

In order to ensure security and reliability of power system, power system state estimation is an important part of modern energy management system (EMS), and is the basis of running other advanced computing software. Mixed measurements composed of PMU (Phasor Measurement Unit) and SCADA (Supervisory Control and Data Acquisition) is an effective method to improve traditional state estimation by single SCADA. As PMU and SCADA using different technology platforms, there are many differences between two kinds of measurements. There will be a series of data compatibility when mixed measurements are combined without been treated. It will lead to the introduction of PMU measurements will not be able to play its full role, or even reduce the performance of the traditional state estimation. So we must pay attention to data compatibility issues of mixed measurement state estimation.

PMU and SCADA data have the following four major differences:(1)data elements,(2)refresh rate, (3) transmission delay,(4)accuracy. Different data elements determine different combining methods of mixed measurements. Three other differences determine the compatibility of mixed measurement. The current study mainly focus on data integration methods [1]-[10], but there are few research on

M. Zhao and J. Sha (Eds.): ICCIP 2012, Part I, CCIS 288, pp. 703–712, 2012.
© Springer-Verlag Berlin Heidelberg 2012

analysis of data compatibility and compatibility method. So data compatibility must be solved first for it is preliminary work of mixed data state estimation.

Data refresh rate and transmission delay can be combined into a unified issue of time synchronization. SCADA and PMU measurement have different delay on the part of sample, sending, communication, reception, storage and applications, and refresh rate is different, so it lead to poor time synchronization of mixed measurement. The time synchronization must be guaranteed if you want to apply the mixed measurement. The research of time synchronization is divided into two categories, (1)passive use of a particular state estimation method to reduce the impact of data synchronization [11]-[12], (2) to establish the mathematical model, and application of compatibility method to improve the time synchronization [13]-[14]. Second type of research can reveal the nature of data synchronization, and it can solve problem more favorably.

Differences in measurement accuracy also affect data compatibility. Mixed measurement accuracy is far too different for it is two generations of technology, and differences reach an order of magnitude in the technical specifications [15]-[16]. Accuracy determines weights in state estimation, so PMU have high weight. Sometimes it also brings risk of high weight. High weight of PMU will reduce the state estimation performance. At present, most studies only consider the measurement error without involving error caused by not synchronization of time.

In this paper, mathematical model of mixed data   compatibility is established. Influence to state estimation of time synchronization and weight is analyzed. We make data of PMU and SCADA synchronize by data relevance analysis. Weight of the mixed data is re-quantified by considering impact of time difference. A viable data compatibility method is formed to ensure stability and accuracy of mixed measurement state estimation.

2   Impact of Data Synchronization

SCADA data refresh rate is currently 1 to 5 frames/s due to communication technology limitation, but PMU refresh rate is 50 frames/s, even 100/s [16]. In addition, SCADA and PMU have different delay in all aspects, so control center receives data from different time. Both cases of these two effect time synchronization. Impact of time synchronization to state estimation is discussed below through results inversion. The estimated error of measurement can be expressed as

$$z - \hat{z} = z - h(\hat{x}) \approx H(\hat{x})(x - \hat{x}) \tag{1}$$

z and $\hat{z}$ are the true value and estimate value, $H(x)$ is jacobian matrix of measurement function $h(x)$, x and $\hat{x}$ is true value and estimated value of state variables. The estimated variance of measurement can be obtained from (1)

$$E[(z - \hat{z})(z - \hat{z})^T] = E\{[H(\hat{x})(x - \hat{x})][H(\hat{x})(x - \hat{x})]^T\} = H(\hat{x})E[(x - \hat{x})(x - \hat{x})^T]H^T(\hat{x}) \tag{2}$$

$E[(x - \hat{x})(x - \hat{x})^T]$ is information matrix. Substance of information matrix is estimated variance of state variables.

$$E[(x - \hat{x})(x - \hat{x})^T] = [H^T(\hat{x})R^{-1}H(\hat{x})]^{-1} \tag{3}$$

R is error variance matrix. If taking into account the measurement error and data time synchronization error, R can be expressed as

$$R = R_m + R_t \tag{4}$$

R_m is measurement error variance, R_t is error variance generated by time sync. So information matrix (3) can be expressed as

$$E[(x - \hat{x})(x - \hat{x})^T] = \Sigma_m(x) + \Sigma_t(x) \tag{5}$$

$$\Sigma_m(x) = [H^T(\hat{x})R_m^{-1}H(\hat{x})]^{-1} \tag{6}$$

$$\Sigma_t(x) = [H^T(\hat{x})R_t^{-1}H(\hat{x})]^{-1} \tag{7}$$

Σ_m and Σ_t are state phasor estimated variance caused by measurement error and time synchronization. Take equation (5) into equation (2),

$$E[(z - \hat{z})(z - \hat{z})^T] = H(\hat{x})\Sigma_m(x)H^T(\hat{x}) + H(\hat{x})\Sigma_t(x)H^T(\hat{x}) \tag{8}$$

Make $F = I - H(\hat{x})[H^T(\hat{x})H(\hat{x})]^{-1}H^T(\hat{x})$, I is unit matrix, $F^2 = FF = F$ can be verified, so F idempotent matrix [17].

$$diag[H(\hat{x})\Sigma_m(x)H^T(\hat{x})] < R_m \tag{9}$$

To determine the effect of state estimation filter, estimated error variance is compared with measurement error variance R_m.

$$\begin{aligned} diag\{E[(z - \hat{z})(z - \hat{z})^T]\} &< R_m \\ diag\{E[(z - \hat{z})(z - \hat{z})^T]\} &= R_m \\ diag\{E[(z - \hat{z})(z - \hat{z})^T]\} &> R_m \end{aligned} \tag{10}$$

When the estimated error variance is less than the original measurement error variance, state estimation has played a filtering effect, Equal time shows no effect.

Since equation (8) contains error variance respect to time not synchronized $H(\hat{x})\Sigma_t(x)H^T(\hat{x})$, so estimated variance $diag[H(\hat{x})\Sigma_m(x)H^T(\hat{x})]$ is not necessarily smaller than the original measurement error variance. So filtering effect of state estimation can not be ensured.

The following conclusions can be drawn. When time synchronization of PMU and SCADA is poor, $diag[H(\hat{x})\Sigma_m(x)H^T(\hat{x})]$ will increase, which would weaken the filtering effect. When $E[(z - \hat{z})(z - \hat{z})^T] > R_m$, mixed measurements do not improve performance of state estimation based on SCADA, but even lower.

Theoretical weight should be error variance reciprocal to the true value. Mixed variance is composed of device variance itself and error variance caused by time synchronization. The current value of weight is determined based solely on the accuracy of measuring equipment, but time synchronization is ignored which lead to inappropriate of weight selection. Known by the state estimation theory [18], improper selection of weight will undermine filtering effect.

Foregoing analysis shows that, the worse of time synchronization, the greater negative impact on state estimation. While weight deviate from the actual farther, it weaken the role of state estimation.

3   Data Compatibility Method

3.1   Reference Time

While PMU measurements have time scale, but SCADA measurements have not, the first step is time synchronization. We make data relevance of PMU and SCADA maximum applying data relevance analysis theory, so as to achieve the purpose of synchronization.

Measurement in a short time can be considered relatively stable. Common method to measure synchronous relationship of different signals is to get different relevance coefficient [19].

$$\rho_{SP}(t_1, t_2 - \tau) = \frac{C_{SP}(t_1, t_2 - \tau)}{\sqrt{C_{SS}(t_1, t_1) C_{PP}(t_2 - \tau, t_2 - \tau)}} \qquad (11)$$

ρ_{SP} is relevance coefficient of z_S (SCADA) and z_P (PMU), t_1 is measurement time for the current SCADA, because SCADA measurement is not uniform to each other, so t_1 value is unknown. t_2 is cut-off time of current PMU measurement sequence. τ is time series of current PMU measurement sequence. C is cross-covariance function. Take C_{SP} for example, its expression is

$$C_{SP}(t_1, t_2 - \tau) = E\{[z_S(t_1) - \mu_s][z_P(t_2 - \tau) - \mu_P]^T\} = R_{SP}(t_1, t_2 - \tau) - \mu_s \mu_P^T \qquad (12)$$

μ_s and μ_P are means of z_S and z_P for a period of time, R_{SP} is cross-relevance coefficient of z_S and z_P

$$R_{SP}(t_1, t_2) = E\{z_S(t_1)[z_P(t_2)]^T\} \qquad (13)$$

$\rho_{SP}(t_1, t_2 - \tau)$ is relevance coefficient matrix of PMU and SCADA vectors. PMU measurement time corresponds to column vector of most relevant is the current reference time.

$$\rho_{SP}(t_1, t_2 - \tau_t) = \max[\rho_{SP}(t_1, t_2 - \tau)] \qquad (14)$$

$$t = t_2 - \tau_t \qquad (15)$$

τ_t is the time corresponds to column vector of most relevant, t is reference time.

3.2   Weight Considering Time Synchronization

Accuracy of the data decides size of weight, so accuracy of mixed state estimation is decided by accuracy of unit and deviation from data to reference time.

$$\varepsilon = e_t + e_m \tag{16}$$

Error caused by time synchronization e_t is decided by rate of change and deviation from the reference time.

$$e_t = kt_d \tag{17}$$

Device measurement error is known, so we must get the error caused by time synchronization. We can see by time synchronization, SCADA measurement delay t_d can be considered subject to the following probability density.

$$f(t_d) = \frac{1}{\sigma_t \sqrt{2\pi}} e^{-(t_d - t)^2 / (2\sigma_t^2)} \tag{18}$$

σ_t^2 is variance of t_d, t is reference time.

Device measurement error and synchronization error are independent. Therefore, the variance of overall error can be expressed as

$$E[\varepsilon\varepsilon^T] = E[e_m e_m^T] + E[e_t e_t^T] = E[e_m e_m^T] + k^2 E[t_d t_d^T] \tag{19}$$

$k^2 E[t_d t_d^T]$ is synchronization error variance σ_t^2, $E[e_m e_m^T]$ is device measurement error variance σ_m^2, these two variance can be obtained through experiments

So weight matrix considering time synchronization can be expressed as

$$R^{-1} = \frac{1}{E[\varepsilon\varepsilon^T]} \tag{20}$$

4   Simulation Example

4.1   Evaluation Index and Simulation System

We use equation(21) and (22) to evaluate simulation results. Equation(21) characterize the filtering effect in k time. Equation(22) characterize the filtering effect to overall measurement in state estimation.

$$\rho_k = \frac{\sum_{i=1}^{N} \left| \hat{z}_{i,k} - z_{i,k}^t \right|}{\sum_{i=1}^{N} \left| z_{i,k} - z_{i,k}^t \right|} \tag{21}$$

$$\rho = \frac{1}{M} \sum_{k=1}^{M} \rho_k \tag{22}$$

$z_{i,k}^t$ and $\hat{z}_{i,k}$ are true value and estimated value of measurement i in time k . N is dimension of measurement vector, M is the number of measurement samples.

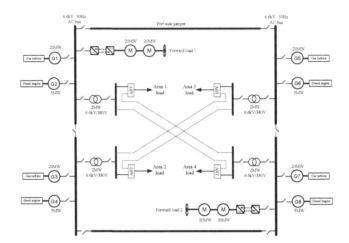

Fig. 1. Ship integrated power system

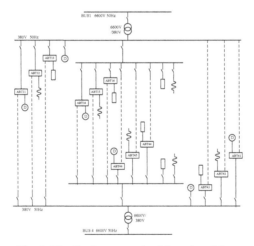

Fig. 2. Distribution network of Area 1 and Area

Example is the ship integrated power system, shown in Figure 1. Distribution network of Area 1 and Area 4 is shown in Figure 2. Distribution network of Area 2 and Area 3 is similar. SCADA measurements include all active and reactive power, bus voltage magnitude. Data refresh rate is set to 10 frame/min. Measurements subject to normal distribution of standard deviation 0.02 and average error 0. Measurement delay subjects to normal distribution of standard deviation 0.1 and average error 0.1. Part of the distribution board installed PMU. PMU measurements include bus voltage phasor and current phasor. Data transmission is set to 50 frames/s.

Least-squares algorithm is used in simulation. Voltage amplitude and phase angle of PMU are joined into state estimation measurement vector. The following three cases were compared and analyzed.

(1) CASE1-State estimation with only SCADA measurement.
(2) CASE2-Mixed state estimation without compatibility method.
(3) CASE3-Mixed state estimation with compatibility method.

4.2   Data Compatibility Simulation in Steady System

When simulation system is in steady state, is not disturbed, the generator and load power did not change. Simulation results for single node are shown in Table 1. Average standard deviation of voltage magnitude and phase angle error in single node to that period. As can be seen from the table, estimation accuracy of single node is very close, and better than CASE 1. Mixed measurement state estimation is not very different before and after the compatibility method when the system is stable. That is mainly due to the constant measurement in steady-state, not subject to the impact of time synchronization. For rate of change is zero, weight is unchanged, seen from equation (19).

Table 1. Estimated standard deviation

Bus number	CASE 1 standard deviation $/10^{-3}$	CASE 2 standard deviation $/10^{-3}$	CASE 3 standard deviation $/10^{-3}$
1	0.8114	0.5436	0.5411
2	1.0278	0.6947	0.6937
3	0.9263	0.6317	0.6324
4	0.9541	0.6213	0.6200
5	0.8321	0.5736	0.5728
6	0.8826	0.6201	0.6167
7	0.9412	0.6725	0.6714
8	1.0414	0.6554	0.6538
9	0.8761	0.6430	0.6411
10	0.9345	0.6389	0.6357
11	0.9233	0.5787	0.5799
12	0.8649	0.5850	0.5853

4.3   Data Compatibility Simulation in Dynamic System

When the load of simulation system changes, system is dynamic after 10 minutes. We select the part of measurement to describe process of computing reference time. Table 2 lists the relevance of the measured data. In Table 2, maximum value of each row almost is all in the fifth column. It explains that calculation of reference time is consistent with mean of 0.1s delay.

4.4 Impact of Time Synchronization to Compatibility

Time synchronization of PMU and SCADA is important factor to affect the measured data compatibility. Different time differences are set in dynamic Simulation. The estimated effects of applying compatibility method or not are compared. The simulation results are shown in Table 3.

Estimation accuracy of CASE 2 became lower with time difference increasing, but estimation accuracy of CASE 3 remained unchanged, as shown in table 3. Mixed state estimation is no longer affected by time synchronization with compatibility method applied.

Table 2. Dynamic data relevance

SCADA Data time /s	relevance to PMU data sequence					
	1	2	3	4	5	6
600	0.9754	0.9712	0.9645	0.8679	0.9871	0.9719
660	0.8784	0.8459	0.8813	0.8647	0.9997	0.8927
720	0.7165	0.8412	0.7954	0.8159	0.9471	0.8471
780	0.6987	0.7489	0.8147	0.8429	0.9874	0.8533
840	0.5417	0.6428	0.7125	0.8169	0.9327	0.8945
900	0.3984	0.4514	0.4893	0.7841	0.9023	0.7637
960	0.3968	0.4871	0.5563	0.5741	0.8499	0.7154
1020	0.2371	0.6487	0.5573	0.6391	0.9411	0.8442
1080	0.2189	0.3745	0.5893	0.8411	0.9337	0.7448
1140	0.3674	0.4587	0.5237	0.6693	0.9577	0.7395
1200	0.5428	0.8411	0.7436	0.6386	0.9981	0.7461

Table 3. Estimates in different synchronization

PMU and SCADA Time difference /s	Estimated effect in CASE2 $\rho/10^{-2}$	Estimated effect in CASE3 $\rho/10^{-2}$
1.0	8.98	4.27
0.9	8.87	4.27
0.8	8.63	4.27
0.7	8.39	4.27
0.6	7.89	4.27
0.5	7.74	4.27
0.4	7.54	4.27
0.3	7.13	4.27
0.2	6.75	4.27
0.1	6.23	4.27

5 Conclusion

Through the analysis above, we can get following conclusions, (1) time synchronization is the main factor of compatibility, (2) we should determine weights by considering synchronization, (3) rate of change is closely related with the compatibility issues, and the greater rate of change, the more serious compatibility issues are.

Compatibility method is proposed as follow, (1) taking relevance analysis can ensure the synchronization of mixed data, (2) re-quantify weights by considering probability distribution of time difference, so that weight is closer to reality. The simulation results of ship integrated power system show the accuracy of compatibility analysis and the validity of compatibility method.

References

1. Phadke, A.G.: Synchronized phasor measurements in power systems. IEEE Computer Applications in Power 6(2), 10–15 (1993); Clerk Maxwell, J.: A Treatise on Electricity and Magnetism, 3rd edn., vol. 2, pp. 68–73 Clarendon, Oxford (1892)
2. Phadke, A.G., Pickett, B., Adamiak, M., et al.: Synchronized sampling and phasor measurements for relay and control. IEEE Trans. on Power Delivery 9(1), 442–452 (1994); Elissa, K.: Title of paper if known (unpublished)
3. Thorp, J.S., Phadke, A.G., Karimi, K.J., et al.: Real time voltage-phasor measurements for static state estimation. IEEE Trans. on Power Systems 1(1), 233–241 (1986); Nicole, R.: Title of paper with only first word capitalized. J. Name Stand. Abbrev. (in press)
4. Yu, Q., Wang, X., You, J., et al.: Equality constraintstwo-step state estimation model based on phasor measurements. Power System Technology 31(10), 84–88 (2007) (in Chinese)
5. Zhao, H., Xue, Y., Wang, D., et al.: State estimation model with PMU current phasor measurements. Automation of Electric Power Systems 28(17), 37–40 (2004)
6. Qin, X., Bi, T., Yang, Q.: A new method for hybrid nonlinear state estimation with PMU. Automation of Power Systems 31(4), 28–32 (2007)
7. Ding, J., Cai, Z., Wang, K.: Mixed measurements state estimation based on WAMS. Proceedings of the CSEE 26(2), 58–63 (2006)
8. Lu, Z., Hao, Y., Kang, Q., et al.: Research of the structure of phase angle monitoring and controlling system in electric power system. Power System Technology 22(5), 18–20 (1998)
9. Wang, K., Mu, G., Chen, X.: Precision improvement and pmu placement studies on state estimation of a hybrid measurement system with PMUs. Proceedings of the CSEE 21(8), 29–33 (2001)
10. Wang, K., Mu, G., Han, X., et al.: Placement of phasor measurement unit for direct solution of power flow. Proceedings of the CSEE 19(10), 14–16, 41 (1999)
11. Su, C.L., Lu, C.N.: Interconnected network state estimation using andomly delayed measurements. IEEE Trans. on Power Systems 16(4), 870–878 (2001)
12. Su, C.L., Lu, C.N., Hsiao, T.Y.: Simulation study of internet based inter control center data exchange for complete network modeling. IEEE Trans. on Power Systems 17(4), 1177–1183 (2002)
13. Zhao, H., Xue, Y., Gao, X., et al.: Impacts of the difference between measurement transmission delays on state estimation and the countermeasures. Automation of Electric Power Systems 28(21), 12–16 (2004)
14. Mao, A., Guo, Z.: A practical placement of PMU in WAMS complemental to SCADA and data processing method. Power System Technology 29(8), 71–74 (2005)

15. Power System Relaying Committee of the IEEE Power Engineering Society. IEEE standard for synchrophasors for power systems. The Institute of Electrical and Electronics Engineers, Inc., New York(2005)
16. State Grid Corporation of China. Technical specification for WAMS. State Grid Corporation of China, Beijing (2006)
17. Horn, R.A., Johnson, C.R.: Matrix analysis, pp. 277–283. Cambridge University Press, London (1985)
18. Yu, E.: Power system state estimation, pp. 62–64. China Water Power Press, Beijing (1985)
19. Zhang, X.: Modern signal processing, pp. 7–18. Tsinghua University Press, Beijing (2005)

A Novel Feature Extraction Methods for Speaker Recognition

Muchun Zou[*]

School of Computer and Math
YiChun College
YiChun, 336000 China
zmclhj222@yahoo.com.cn

Abstract. Feature principal component selection and dimension reduction have been the key problem in speaker recognition, especially in acoustic processing by virtue of large scale sample data. We propose a new method that is based on the kernel K-means clustering and the SKPCA approach to tackle the above problem. Here kernel K-means clustering is to divide all the frames of each sample into a given amount of clusters; the resulted clustering centers are used as the input samples for the SKPCA since they can represent better the clusters they belong to. This method reduced store and compute complexity, it guarantee to reduced data well represent the original data and Information is lost minimum. The experimental results show the proposed approach is valid of for being applied to speaker recognition.

Keywords: Sparse KPCA, kernel K-means clustering, speaker recognition.

1 Introduction

Speaker recognition, including both speaker identification and verification, has been an active research area for several decades. The goal of speaker recognition is to automatically identify a particular person in a pre-specified set of speakers or to verify a claimed speaker identity from his/her own voice. Wide applications of speaker recognition have been tried, including: access control, telephone-based account transactions, automatic labeling of a talking speaker for indexing or archiving audio recordings of multi-party meetings, commerce and business, security etc. The focus of this study is on text-independent speaker recognition   applications.

Nonlinear principal components afforded better recognition rates than the corresponding linear principal components in speaker recognition. Nonlinear features are obtained by mapping data from the original feature space into a high-dimensional one through a nonlinear transformation chosen. As a result, those patterns that are linearly inseparable become separable in the new feature space (kernel space) [1].

---

[*] Muchun Zou (1970-), Male, Master, Associate Professor, The Main Research Directions: Computer Science and Its Application.

M. Zhao and J. Sha (Eds.): ICCIP 2012, Part I, CCIS 288, pp. 713–722, 2012.
© Springer-Verlag Berlin Heidelberg 2012

This approach was applied to speaker recognition. Some examples of kernel-based learning machines are Kernel Discriminative Analysis (KDA) [2], Kernel Principal Component Analysis (KPCA) [3-4] and Sparse KPCA [5-8]. The KPCA is a non-linear approach to PCA. It depends on the training data to evaluate the higher dimensional principal components and also to represent a certain input data in the feature space. Depending on the training data amount these evaluations could be unfeasible and/or cause a huge computational burden. Considering this, the training data reduction is fundamental to the KPCA realization. The standard frame reduction is performed by choosing frames randomly, however these choices do not guarantee that the reduced data well represent the original data set. The SKPCA [8] was developed to solve this problem by generating the reduced data set through a likelihood maximization criterion.

Although the SKPCA generates a reduced training data, it requires the full original training data to evaluate the maximization step, which could be computationally unfeasible, depending on the training data amount. In order to solve it, an approach is proposed, where the original training data is clustered and the SKPCA is applied to these clustering centers. Despite this approach does not guarantee that the overall data maximum is reached, it will be shown by experimental results that SKPCA could overcome the performance of KPCA and standard feature extraction approach.

We propose a new method that is based on the kernel K-means clustering (KKMC) [9] and the SKPCA approach to tackle the above problem. The goal for clustering analysis here is to divide all the frames of each sample into a given amount of clusters. As a result, the centers of all clusters can be used as the input for the SKPCA since they can represent better the clusters they belong to. The proposed method has proved to be an efficient performance for being applied to speaker recognition.

The paper is structured as follows. In Section 2, a detailed evaluation of kernel K-means clustering, KPCA and SKPCA approaches are described, emphasizing the main points to obtain SKPCA. In Section 3, the algorithm is proposed, and it comprises the feature clustering and the dimension reduction. In Section 4, experiments are presented assuring the efficiency of the proposed approach. Finally, Section 5 presents the conclusions of this work and ideas for future work, as well.

2   Feature Clustering and Dimension Reduction

2.1   Kernel K-Means Clustering

The goal of clustering analysis for speaker recognition is to divide all the frames of each sample into the given amount of clusters. Consequently, the centers of all the clusters, which can represent the data better, will be used as the input samples of the SKPCA. Therefore, it is very important for us to select a suitable and efficient clustering approach. Considering the clustering methods usually used in practice, there are fuzzy C-means clustering (FCMC), K-means clustering (KMC), kernel K-means clustering (KKMC) etc. Since there are a large number of Nonlinear feature included in speech data, therefore, the kernel K-means clustering approach is more suitable for the speech data analysis than the conventional clustering method. Thus we choose this KKMC approach to first process the speaker recognition in this paper. The KKMC approach can be described as follows.

A high dimensional space is denoted by H here which is called the feature space, whereas the original space R^n is called the data space. H is in general an infinite dimensional inner product space. A mapping $\phi : R^n \to H$ is employed and $x_k \in R^n$ is transformed into $\phi(x_1), \cdots, \phi(x_N)$. The explicit form of $\phi(x)$ is not known but the inner product is represented by a kernel: $\phi : x \bullet y \to \phi(x) \bullet \phi(y) = k(x, y)$

The kernel K-means clustering algorithm is based on the minimization of the following objective function in kernel space:

$$J = \sum_{k=1}^{K} \sum_{i=1}^{N_k} \left\| \phi(x_i) - m_k \right\|^2 \tag{1}$$

Where $m_k = \dfrac{1}{N_k} \sum_{i=1}^{N_k} \phi(x_i)$, $i = 1, \cdots, N_k$, $k = 1, \cdots, K$. N_k is the number of the kth cluster. $d_H(\phi(x), m_k)$ is the Euclidean distance between random sample $\phi(x)$ and m_k is defined as:

$$d_H(\phi(x), m_k) = \sqrt{\left\| \phi(x) - m_k \right\|^2}$$
$$= \sqrt{\phi(x) \bullet \phi(x) - 2\phi(x) \bullet m_k + m_k \bullet m_k} \tag{2}$$

Choose a kernel function in kernel learning method is key problem, kernel function affect ultimate clustering effect and affect algorithmic speed. From this example that use of the kernel function makes it possible to calculate the value of the dot product in the feature space H without explicitly calculating the mapping function ϕ. Three commonly used kernel functions are the polynomial kernel function[10]

$K(x, x_i) = [(x \bullet x_i) + 1]^q$; the radial basis function $K(x, x_i) = \exp(-\dfrac{\left| x - x_i \right|^2}{2\sigma^2})$; and

the sigmoid kernel function $K(x, x_i) = \tanh[b(x \bullet x_i) + c]$.

Generally, polynomial kernel function can be used as kernel function in speaker recognition, by using Mercer kernel method, where the original Euclidian distance in KKCM is replaced with the following kernel-induced distance measures:

$$d_H(\phi(x), m_k) = \sqrt{K(x, x) - 2\sum_{i=1}^{N_k} K(x, x_i) + \sum_{i,j=1}^{N_k} K(x_i, x_j)} \tag{3}$$

As a result, the steps of the kernel K-means clustering (KKMC) for speaker recognition can be described as follows:

(1) Set the initial centers of clustering $m_1, \cdots ; m_k$;

(2) For each sample $\phi(x)$ and centers of clustering m_k, calculate $d_H(\phi(x), m_k)$ using Equation (3). And then assign $\phi(x)$ to the closest clustering;

(3) Renewal centers of clustering, renewal Calculate $d_H(\phi(x), m_k)$ and J;

(4) Repeat (2) and (3) until J becomes stable or unchanged value.

2.2   KPCA

The Kernel PCA [8] is the approach which applies the kernel function to the PCA technique, in order to obtain the representation of PCA in a high-dimensional space.

Assuming that the data set consists of N dimensionality $X = (x_1, \cdots, x_N)$, the sample covariance matrix corresponding to this data set is given by

$$S = \frac{1}{N} \sum_{j=1}^{N} x_j x_j^T = N^{-1} X X^T \tag{4}$$

The mapping of the full data matrix X can be defined by a ($D \times N$) matrix $\Phi = [\phi_1, \cdots, \phi_N]$. Analogous to equation (4), the covariance matrix in a feature space is given by

$$S_H = \frac{1}{N} \sum_{j=1}^{N} \phi_j \phi_j^T = N^{-1} \Phi \Phi^T \tag{5}$$

And consequently the representation of the eigenvectors R in the feature space is $R_H = \Phi A_K \Lambda_K^{-\frac{1}{2}}$, where A_K and Λ_K contain the eigenvectors and eigenvalues of the kernel matrix K. The kernel matrix K is defined as the matrix whose indexes are

$$(K)_{ij} = k(x_i, x_j) \tag{6}$$

Finally, It is mathematically expressed as $T^{kpca} = R_H^T \Phi(x)$, where T^{kpca} is a D dimensional column vector, which gives the KPCA representation of $\Phi(x)$. The final representation is shown as follows:

$$R_H^T \Phi(x) = (\Lambda_K^{-\frac{1}{2}})^T A_K^T \Phi^T \Phi(x) = \Lambda_K^{-\frac{1}{2}} A_K^T k_t^T \tag{7}$$

Where k_t represents a N dimensional column vector formed by $k(x, x_i)$, for $i = 1, \cdots, N$.

2.3   SKPCA

The SKPCA approach [8] was developed in order to provide a solution for the previous mentioned disadvantage of the KPCA approach. It consists in estimating the feature space sample covariance for a noise component and the sum of the weighted outer products of the original feature vectors, which generate a sparse solution to KPCA. This is obtained by maximizing the likelihood of the feature vectors under a Gaussian density model $\phi - N(0, C_H)$, where the covariance C_H is defined by

$$C_H = \sigma^2 I + \sum_{i=1}^{N} \omega_i \phi_i \phi_i^T = \sigma^2 I + \phi W \phi^T \tag{8}$$

Where ω is a diagonal matrix composed by the adjustable weights $\omega_1, \cdots, \omega_N$, and σ^2 is an isotropic noise component, $N(0, \sigma^2 I)$, common to all dimensions of feature space. This approach was based on the probabilistic PCA (PPCA) formulation [11].The log-likelihood under the Gaussian model with covariance C_H given by (4), ignoring the terms independent of the weights, is denoted by

$$L = -\frac{1}{2}[N \log | C_H | + tr(C_H^{-1} \phi \phi^T)] \tag{9}$$

Differentiating (9) under the weights ω_i and making it equal to zero, means to maximize the log-likelihood with respect to ω_i. However, in order to reach better mathematical representation, (9) should be decomposed. The first term of (9) can be decomposed in $N\log|C_H| = N(D\log\sigma^2 + \log|W| + \log|W^{-1} + \sigma^{-2}K|)$ and the second term in $tr(C_H^{-1}\phi\phi^T) = \sum_{i=1}^{N} \sigma^{-2}k_{ii} - \sigma^{-4}k_i^T(W^{-1} + \sigma^{-2}K)^{-1}k_i$ where $k_{ii} = k(x_i, x_i)$.

Now evaluating $\dfrac{\partial L}{\partial \omega_i}$ by differentiating the two terms of (9) obtained above with respect to ω_i, the following expression is achieved

$$\frac{\partial L}{\partial \omega_i} = \frac{1}{2\omega_i^2}[N \Sigma_{ii} - N\omega_i + \sum_{j=1}^{N} \mu_{ji}^2] \tag{10}$$

$$\Sigma = (W^{-1} + \sigma^{-2}K)^{-1} \tag{11}$$

Where Σ_{ii} and μ_{ji} are respectively the diagonal components of the matrix   and the elements of the column vector $\mu_j = \sigma^{-2}\Sigma k_j$. Setting (10) to zero, which means to find the maximum of the function represented by the equation (9), generates the re-estimation update functions for the weights, $\omega_i^{new} = N^{-1}\sum_{j=1}^{N} \mu_{ji}^2 + \Sigma_{ii}$ According to [5], an equation for re-estimation update that converges faster than the one previously mentioned, can be obtained by rewriting (10) equal to zero as

$$\omega_i^{new} = \frac{\sum_{j=1}^{N} \mu_{ji}^2}{N(1 + \Sigma_{ii} / \omega_i)} \tag{12}$$

Equivalently to the KPCA representation, the projection of $\Phi(x)$ onto the principal axes $\tilde{R}_H$ is calculated by

$$T^{skpca} = \tilde{R}_H^T \Phi(x) = \tilde{\Lambda}_K^{-\frac{1}{2}} \tilde{A}_K^T \tilde{k}_t^T \tag{13}$$

$$\tilde{R}_H = \Phi \tilde{A}_k \tilde{\Lambda}_k^{-\frac{1}{2}} \tag{14}$$

Where $\tilde{A}_K$ and $\tilde{\Lambda}_K$ are defined, respectively, as the eigenvectors and eigenvalues of $W^{\frac{1}{2}} K W^{\frac{1}{2}}$, and $\tilde{k}_t$ represents the vector calculated by $k(x, x_i)$ where x_i corresponds to the non-zero weighted Vectors represented in X.

3   Speaker Recognition Algorithm

SKPCA was developed to solve standard frame reduction problem by generating the reduced data set through a likelihood maximization criterion, but this approach computationally complexity for a great number of samples. In order to overcome this limitation, it is proposed to first using the clustering approach to obtain the corresponding clustering centers for different targets of the speech data, the centers of all the clustering, which can represent the data better, will be used as the input samples of the SKPCA. Consequently, it reduced store and compute complexity in the kernel matrix. Here we using kernel K-means clustering (KKMC) approach application of clustering of speech data, it's obtain better effect of clustering and greatly improved of recognition rate, but it's compute quantity more than others clustering approaches. Overall consider we will choose the kernel K-means clustering approach. The SKPCA approach overcome the disadvantage of KPCA, it does not guarantee to reach the overall speech data maximization, just individual cluster maximization, but it guarantee to reduced data well represent the original data and Information is lost minimum, the corresponding fine features for speech data can be easily extracted. Then, rebuild speech data, which can represent the originality speech data better. Finally, we choose the Gaussian mixture model (GMM) as speech training model, which has been successfully used for both speaker identification and verification [12].GMM can be considered as one single-state HMM. The linear combination of Gaussian functions is capable of representing a large class of sample distributions of speaker's utterances. The basis of this approach is to represent the distribution of training vectors from each speaker with a weighted sum of several multivariate Gaussian functions the parameters in the model can be estimated using the iterative Expectation-Maximization (EM) algorithm. GMM is also computationally efficient and easily implemented, especially on a real-time platform. In principle, it is a compromise between performance and complexity.

In the light of the above analyses, the steps of extracting nonlinear features by the SKPCA approach after the KKMC can be summarized as follows:

(1) Choose polynomial function as kernel function, and the resulted clustering centers as the input samples of the SKPCA, then calculate the matrix K and Σ using Equations (6) and (11);

(2) Calculate ω_i^{new} and $\tilde{R}_H$ according to Equations (12) and (14);

(3) According to principal components $\tilde{R}_H$, project principal axes direction of the principal components using Equation (13). As a result, the speech data principal components can be obtained easily by a simple transformation for the projected data;

(4) Rebuild $\Phi(x)$ using Equation $\tilde{\Phi}(x) = \tilde{R}_H \tilde{R}_H^T \Phi(x)$, acquire the superior expression of speech data;

(5) Choose the GMM for speaker is obtained from the rebuild speech data;

(6) Adjust the number of clustering centers and the q of radial basis function, then go to (1), repeat the clustering analysis and the SKPCA.

As a result, by means of this method a certain number of nonlinear principal component Speech characteristic can be easily attained according to practical needs.

4   Experiment

4.1   Settings

The speech signal was sampled with 11,025 Hz and 16 bit quantified. After pre-emphasis $1 - 0.97z^{-1}$, each utterance's short-time frame analysis was over contiguous speech frames of 20.48 ms (256 points) and overlapping 10.24 ms (128 points). Multiplied by a Hamming window, each frame is extracted a 36-dimensional feature vector is extracted, comprised of 12-Mel-frequency cepstral coefficients (MFCC), which reflect the instantaneous Fourier spectrum, their corresponding deltas (which represent transitional spectral information) and maximum auto-correlation values (which represent pitch and voicing information). Features extracted from train set are used to build the GMM statistical model, and features extracted from test set are used to calculate the recognition error rate.

4.2   Results

To show the effectiveness of the proposed method, we performed two experiments using speech data. For the first experiment (Table 1), for each frame choosing 12dimensions, using KPCA & q=1, which represents the PCA with a reduced training data, KPCA & q=2and SKPCA & q=2, where the k-means clustering (KMC) and kernel K-means clustering (KKMC), the number of clustering is 20 or 25 or 30. The first experiment equivalent characteristics of the second experiment (Table 2), except that 24 dimensions for each frame.

Table 1. D=12d

	KPCA&q=1		KPCA&q=2		SKPCA&q=2	
N	kmc	kkmc	kmc	kkmc	kmc	kkmc
20	7.85	3.70	8.62	3.92	8.44	4.36
25	7.63	2.61	8.41	3.70	7.04	1.33
30	6.44	4.42	5.22	3.43	5.21	3.15

Table 2. D=24d

	KPCA&q=1		KPCA&q=2		SKPCA&q=2	
N	kmc	kkmc	kmc	kkmc	kmc	kkmc
20	8.15	3.03	7.54	2.35	5.31	2.14
25	7.09	3.42	7.88	2.59	4.02	1.30
30	6.02	4.67	5.61	2.47	3.88	2.38

In the Table 1, the best performances were respectively, 2.61% （kkmc & KPCA & q=1）,3.70%(kkmc & KPCA & q=2), 1.30%(kkmc & SKPCA & q=2). From the Table 1 we can see the kernel K-means clustering has proved to be valid than others clustering for being applied to speech data, and it is observed that the SKPCA overcame all the others approaches, which possibly was due to the data reduction for the SKPCA case. Thus, this approach was improved accuracy of speaker recognition.

Table 2 shows that the best performances were respectively, 3.03%(kkmc & KPCA & q=1),   2.35%(kkmc & KPCA & q=2),1.30%(kkmc & SKPCA & q=2) . The results presented in this table confirmed the efficiency of SKPCA over the PCA with full training data.

Comparing the best performances for KPCA and SKPCA in both tables, it is noticed that the performances degrade when the number of dimension is reduced, except for the KPCA & q=2 with KKMC. This could be explained by the elimination of important data information from the data set with 24 dimensions when it is reduced to 12 dimensions. The overall best performance was 1.30% of error rate using SKPCA & q=2with 24 dimensions and KKMC. The experimental results show the proposed approach was proved to be valid of for being applied to speaker recognition.

5   Conclusions

In this paper, using Sparse KPCA based on kernel K-means clustering approach was applied for feature extraction in speaker recognition. As it was expected the SKPCA provided a better representation of the reduced training data than the one obtained by the standard randomly chosen frames approach used in KPCA. The results confirmed the efficiency of the proposed approach for speaker recognition. Despite the approach presented in this paper has considerably improved the recognition performance of the analyzed task, it is required further research in order to observe carefully the effects of using different approaches to cluster the full training data to make the SKPCA re-estimation realizable. Besides the previous mentioned topic, further study on other kernel-based sparse approaches and different kernel-based learning machines are the natural future steps of this work.

References

1. Huang, L.-X., Zhang, X.-Y.: Speaker independent recognition on OLLO French corpus by using different features. In: Proceedings of Pervasive Computing, Signal Processing and Applications, pp. 332–335. IEEE, Harbin (2010)
2. Roth, V., Steinhage, V.: Nonlinear discriminant analysis using kernel functions. Advances in Neural Information Processing Systems, 568–574 (1999)
3. Sayoud, H., Ouamour, S.: Speaker clustering of stereo audio documents based on sequential gathering process. Journal of Information Hiding and Multimedia Signal Processing 1(4), 344–360 (2010)
4. Lima, A., Zen, H., Nankaku, Y., Miyajima, C., Tokuda, K., Kitamura, T.: On the use of KPCA for feature extraction in speech recognition. IEICE Trans. Inf. & Syst. E87-D(12), 2802–2811 (2004)
5. Tipping, M.E.: Sparse kernel principal component analysis. Advances in Neural Information Processing Systems, 256–262 (2010)
6. Tipping, M.E.: Sparse kernel principal component analysis. Advances in Neural Information Processing Systems 13, 334–341 (2001)
7. Smola, A.J., Mangasarian, O.L., Schölkopf, B.: Sparse kernel feature analysis. Tech. Rep., University of Wisconsin, 685–693 (2004)

8. Lima, A., Zen, H., Nankaku, Y., Tokuda, K., Kitamura, T., Resende, F.G.: Sparse KPCA for feature extraction in speech recognition. ICASSP, I353-I356 (2005)
9. Kong, R., Zhang, G.X., Shi, Z.S., Guo, L.: Kernel-based K-means clusterings. Computer Engineering 30(11), 78–80 (2004)
10. Kim, S.-W., John Oommen, B.: On Using Prototype Reduction Schemes to Optimize Kernel-based Nonlinear Subspace Methods. Pattern Recognition 37(2), 227–239 (2004)
11. Pal, N.R., Pal, K., Keller, J.M., Bezdek, J.C.: A possibilistic fuzzy c-means clustering algorithm. IEEE Transactions on Fuzzy Systems 13(4), 517–530 (2005)
12. Hu, J.-S., Cheng, C.-C., Liu, W.-H.: Robust Speaker's Location Detection in a Vehicle Environment Using GMM Models. IEEE Transactions on Systems, Man and Cybernetics-Part B: Cybernetics 36(2) (April 2006)

An Investigation of Image Compression Using Block Singular Value Decomposition

Yin-jie Jia[1], Peng-fei Xu[2], and Xu-ming Pei[3]

[1] Faculty of Computer Engineering, HuaiYin Institute of Technology,
223003, Huai'an, Jiangsu, China
[2] Center Research Institute, ZTE Corporation,
210012, Nan Jing, Jiangsu, China
[3] Research Center for Wireless Communications,
200335, Shanghai, China
jiayinjie@126.com, xu.pengfei1@zte.com.cn, xmpei@yahoo.cn

Abstract. The purpose of this paper is to discuss the usage possibility of singular value decomposition in image compression applications. Based on the basic principle and characteristics of singular value decomposition , combined with the image of the matrix structure. A block SVD-based image compression scheme is demonstrated and the usage feasibility of Block SVD-based image compression is proved.

Keywords: Singular Value Decomposition, Image Compression, Compression Ratio.

1 Introduction

With the further increase of the information society, the increasing amount of information people need, digital images contain an increasingly large amount of data, how to make these large data transfer across the network quickly and easily to become a hot issue of concern, Image compression is one of the key technologies to solve this problem[1]. Currently, image compression algorithms with different characteristics, thus forming a variety of specialized image formats, there are many kinds of sophisticated compression algorithms, such as DCT transform coding (for JPEG, MPEG) and wavelet transform coding (for JPEG2000), etc.

Image compression using SVD is also relatively new field of study, singular value decomposition (SVD) is one based on the feature vector matrix transformation method. it has been applied in signal processing, pattern recognition, digital watermarking technology fields. As the image has a matrix structure, some papers [2-3] proposed that apply singular value decomposition in image compression, it make success and is seen as an effective image compression method. This article is for still images, using block SVD singular value decomposition transform to achieve image compression.

The paper is organized as follows. In Section 2, the background of SVD is introduced following with SVD-based image compression described in section 3.

M. Zhao and J. Sha (Eds.): ICCIP 2012, Part I, CCIS 288, pp. 723–731, 2012.
© Springer-Verlag Berlin Heidelberg 2012

Section 3 provides two scheme for image compression and the calculation steps, Section 4 gives some experimental results to demonstrate the effectiveness of the block SVD-based image compression with conclusion and discussion on future works given in the last section.

2   Background on SVD

It's necessary to first introduce the conception of singular value for understanding SVD. SVD is said to be a significant topic in linear algebra by many renowned mathematicians. SVD has many practical and theoretical values, other than image compression. One special feature of SVD is that it can be performed on any real (m,n) matrix. It factors A into three matrices U, S, V, such that, $A = SVD^T$. Where U and V are orthogonal matrices and S is a diagonal matrix.

The matrix U contains the left singular vectors, the matrix V contains the right singular vectors, and the diagonal matrix S contains the singular values. Where the singular values are arranged on the main diagonal in such an order.

$$\alpha_1 \geq \alpha_2 \geq \alpha_3 \geq ... \geq \alpha_r \geq \alpha_{r+1} = ... = \alpha_p = 0$$

where r is the rank of matrix A, and where (p) is the smaller of the dimensions m orn.

They are based on the following theorem of Linear Algebra [4]: "*Any M x N matrix A whose numbers of rows M is greater than or equal to its number of columns N can be written as the product of an M x N column orthogonal matrix U , an N x N diagonal matrix S of singular values and the transpose of an N x N orthogonal matrix V*". Qualitatively the U matrix represents a vector basis for the most relevant information in the system while the eigenvalues s_i represents the variability in the information. Singular value decomposition is the numerical matrix diagonalization algorithm, the singular value demonstrated the essential characteristics of the image after the singular value decomposition of the image.

The singular value decomposition [5] can be defined as:

Let matrix $A \in R^{m \times n} (r \geq 1)$. Its nonzero singular values are $\alpha_1, \alpha_2, \alpha_3, ..., \alpha_r$, Therefore, a new diagonal matrix Σ_r can be defined as $\Sigma_r = diag(\alpha_1, \alpha_2, \alpha_3, ..., \alpha_r)$. Orthogonal Matrices $U^{m \times m}$ and $V^{m \times m}$ can make transformation of the singular value decomposition of matrix A as follows:

$$A = USV^T = \sum_{i=1}^{r} \alpha_i u_i v_i^T \tag{1}$$

Where

$$S = \begin{pmatrix} \Sigma_r & 0 \\ 0 & 0 \end{pmatrix}_{m \times n}$$

The α_i are termed the singular values of the matrix A , the u_i and v_i are the left and right singular vectors, respectively.

Then, we obtained the decomposition formula from the formula (1)

$$A = M_1 + M_2 + ... + M_r =$$
$$\alpha_1 u_1 v_1^T + \alpha_2 u_2 v_2^T + ... + \alpha_r u_r v_r^T \qquad (2)$$

The formula (2) shows the image A is the superposition of sub-images $u_1 v_1^T, ..., u_r v_r^T$ and the corresponding singular value is the the superposition factor. The smaller singular value , the smaller contribution to the image, most of the energy of image is concentrated in the larger singular value corresponding to the previous sub-image, singular values of matrix S are descending from top left corner to foot right corner. It isn't necessary to select all singular values to reconstruct image for getting preferably reconstructive image. After applying singular value decomposition to an image, there always be some small singular values in the diagonal matrix S . and these singular values are small enough that they can be ignored and don't affect the quality of the reconstructive image greatly. So, if we select $q(q < r)$ singular values in descending order to generate one matrix

$$\tilde{A} = \sum_{i=1}^{q} \alpha_i u_i v_i^T$$

which is an approximation of original matrix A , this achieved the purpose of image compression. The less the number of singular values of q , the smaller amount of data composed of matrix A , the higher the compression ratio. the closer q and r , the lower compression ratio, the restore image is more close to the original image.

3   Block SVD-Based Image Compression

The fundamental concept of the SVD-based image compression scheme is to apply the SVD directly to the matrix of the image. A further reduction on the singular values is subtracting the mean of the original image before performing the SVD. The mean is then added back to the SVD construction to obtain the reconstructed image. This process is called singular value subtracting one update, it essentially compacts the distribution of the singular values [6].

To facilitate the description, the matrix here is N×N phalanx matrix. Here are two kinds of algorithm, the first scheme steps are described as follows:

1) Get a new image X through subtracting the mean of the original image M .

2) Calculate the correlation matrix $A_{n \times n}$ of X .

3) Apply the SVD to $A_{n \times n}$ and get its eigenvalues and eigenvectors .

4) Select the n eigenvectors corresponding to the previous larger eigenvalue from the matrix $U_{N \times N}$ to form a matrix $T_{N \times n}$.

5) Calculate the equation $\hat{X} = T' \times X$, the matrix $\hat{X}$ here is $n \times N$ matrix. this step is the image coding, we just store $\hat{X}_{n \times N}$ and $T_{N \times n}$ and the total amount of storage is $2 \times n \times N$, so, the compression ratio here is $(N \times N)/(2 \times n \times N) = N/(2n)$.

6) We can get the restore image $\tilde{X}$ through this equation $\tilde{X} = T \times \hat{X} + M$.

Of course, this scheme is lossy compression as we discard the eigenvectors corresponding to the smaller singular values.

Instead of compressing the whole image at once, here we cut the $N \times N$ gray image into $K \times K$ sub-block image[7], there are total $M \times M$ sub-block images, $M = N / K$, then apply SVD to the martrixs corresponding to the sub-block images. the second scheme steps are summarized as follows:

1) Transform the $N \times N$ image into $K^2 \times M^2$ dimensional matrix X, as the two figures below shows.

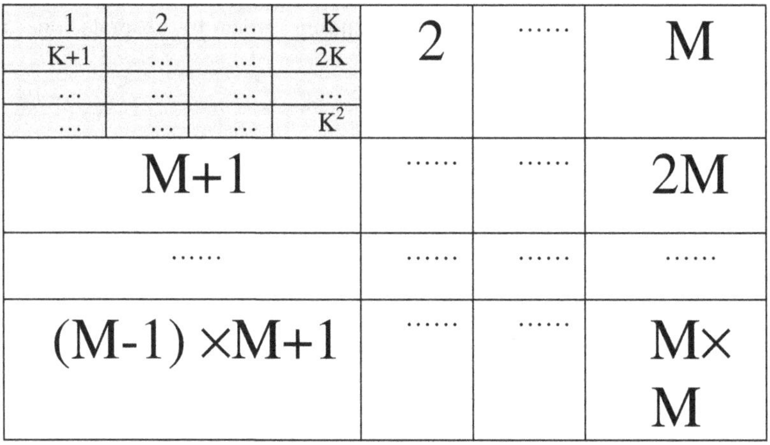

Fig. 1. Matrix of the whole original image

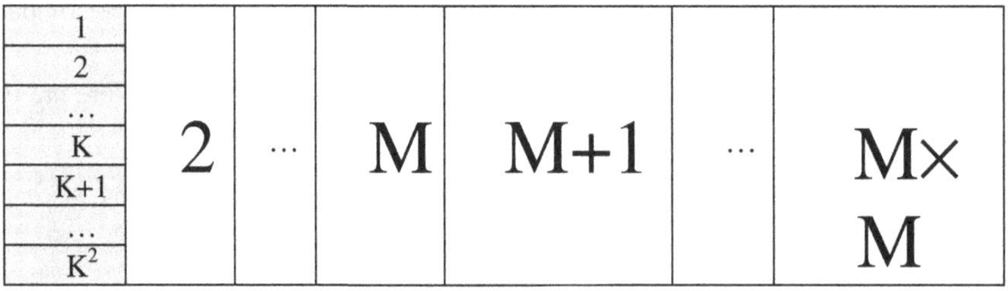

Fig. 2. Result of transforming matrix to sub-block images

The large font number in big box of the figure represent the serial number of sub-block image, each sub-block image has K^2 elements. The column of matrix stores the gray value of sub-block image.

2) Get a new image $\overline{X}_{K^2 \times M^2}$ through subtracting the mean of the original image $V_{1 \times M^2}$.

3) Calculate the correlation matrix $A_{k^2 \times k^2}$ of $\overline{X}_{K^2 \times M^2}$, where $A = \overline{X} \times \overline{X}'$.

3) Apply the SVD to $A_{k^2 \times k^2}$ and get its eigenvalues and eigenvectors.

4) Select the n eigenvectors corresponding to the previous larger eigenvalue from the matrix $U_{K^2 \times K^2}$ to form a matrix $T_{K^2 \times n}$.

5) Calculate the equation $\hat{X} = T' \times \overline{X}$, the matrix $\hat{X}$ here is $n \times M^2$ matrix. this step is the image coding, different from the first scheme, this need store $\hat{X}_{n \times M^2}$ and $T_{K^2 \times n}$ and the total amount of storage is $n \times (K^2 + M^2)$, so, the compression ratio here is $(K^2 \times M^2) / (n \times (K^2 + M^2))$.

6) The restore image $\tilde{X} = T \times \hat{X} + V$, note that the matrix $\tilde{X}$ here is $K^2 \times M^2$ matrix, so we need transform the $K^2 \times M^2$ matrix to $N \times N$ matrix (inverse process of step 1) and save it as an approximation of the original image.

4   Experimental Results

In order to investigate into using singular value decomposition as a method of image compression, the popular "Lena" image (512 x 512, gray value image) is tested for the two compression scheme described above. Quality of the compression is measured in term of Correlation Coefficient (CC), Compression Ratio (CR) and Execution Time (ET).

For scheme 1, there is only one adjustable parameter n, which is numbers of eigenvalues and eigenvectors selected, we can get different compression ratio by adjusting parameter n.

For scheme 2, there are two adjustable parameters, namely $K(M = N / K)$ and n.

First, we compare the two schemes under same compression ratio, for convenience's sake, $CR = 16, K = 8$.

the compression ratio of scheme 1 is $N / 2n_1 = 512 / 2n_1 = 16$, here $n_1 = 16$

the compression ratio of scheme 2 is

$$(K^2 \times M^2) / (n_2 \times (K^2 + M^2))$$
$$= (8^2 \times 64^2) / (n_2 \times (8^2 + 64^2)) = 16$$

here $n_2 = 3.9385 \approx 4$.

(a) result of scheme 1   (b) result of scheme 2

Fig. 3. Comparison of image restoration between two scheme under CR=16

Evaluating the performance of image restoration, there is a index named Correlation Coefficient.

$$C(s_1, s_2) = \text{cov}(s_1, s_2) \big/ \sqrt{\text{cov}(s_1, s_1) \cdot \text{cov}(s_2, s_2)}$$

Where $\text{cov}(\cdot)$ is   the   covariance   function. $\text{cov}(s_1, s_2) = E\{[s_1 - E(s_1)]^T [s_1 - E(s_2)]\}$. $E(\cdot)$ is   the   mean   operator. $C(s_1, s_2) = 0$ means that s_1 and s_2 are uncorrelated, and the image correlation increases as $C(s_1, s_2)$ approaches unity. The image become fully correlated as C becomes unity. s_1 here represent.

The original image, s_2 here represent the restore image.

Table 1. Comparison of scheme 1 and scheme 2

	Correlation Coefficient	Execution Time
scheme 1	0.9483	10.8270s
scheme 2	0.9842	0.5930s

As is shown in figure 3 and table 1, we can easily see that scheme 2 is obviously better than scheme 1 in the same compression ratio from the comparison results of two compression schemes. Although the two schemes are both applying SVD to matrix, the difference is that scheme 2 decompose the whole image into $M \times M$ sub-block images before using SVD. The singular value here is the average of sub-block images, As the adjacent pixels have a strong correlation, we can get better image quality under larger compression ratio by using a relatively few eigenvector. In other words, the compression ratio of the program 2 is far larger than that of scheme 1 under the premise of the same image restore quality.

Secondly, we take the same compression ratio for scheme 2, the image recovery effects are analyzed under different K values . Here for the sake of simplicity, $CR = 16$.

1) When $K = 4$, compression ratio here is

$$(K^2 \times M^2) / (n_1 \times (K^2 + M^2))$$
$$= (K^2 \times (N / K)^2) / (n_1 \times (K^2 + (N / K)^2))$$
$$= (4^2 \times (512 / 4)^2) / (n_1 \times (4^2 + (512 / 4)^2)) = 16$$

here $n_1 = 0.9990 \approx 1$

For this case here, if $n_1 = 0.9990$, the compression ratios can reach 16, but in fact the minimum of n_1 is 1, so the CR less than 16 when $K = 4$.

Follow the above calculation, we get the results under different K values.

2) When $K = 8$, compression ratio here is $(K^2 \times M^2) / (n_2 \times (K^2 + M^2)) = 16$

here $n_2 = 3.9385 \approx 4$

3) When $K = 16$, compression ratio here is $(K^2 \times M^2) / (n_3 \times (K^2 + M^2)) = 16$

here $n_3 = 12.8000 \approx 13$

4)   When $K = 32$ compression   ratio   here   is
$(K^2 \times M^2) / (n_4 \times (K^2 + M^2)) = 16$

here $n_4 = 12.8000 \approx 13$

Table 2. Comparison of image restoration of scheme 2 under different K values

	The number of required eigenvectors	Correlation Coefficient	Execution Time
K=8	n2=4	0.9842	0.4520s
K=16	n3=13	0.9835	0.8740s
K=32	n4=13	0.9643	70.0600s

(a) K=8   (b) K=16   (c) K=32

Fig. 4. Restoration of image restoration of scheme 2 under different K values

For scheme 2, How to select the value of K is also a relatively important issue. Theoretically, the smaller the K value, the more the number of sub-block images, the more image information the first eigenvector contains, the better the recovered image when select the same number of eigenvectors. The maximum compression ratio which scheme 2 can achieve theoretically is K^2, so, The smaller K value, the smaller the maximum compression ratio. Otherwise, the lager the value of K, the lager the maximum compression ratio, the requirement of $K = M$ may ensure the compression ratio achieve the maximum. Simple proof is as follows: the compression ratio

$$(K^2 \times M^2) / (n \times (K^2 + M^2))$$

$$< (K^2 \times M^2) / (K^2 + M^2) = \zeta$$

When $K < M$, $\zeta < K^2$;

When $K > M$, $\zeta < M^2 < K^2$

When $K = M$, $\zeta = K^2 / 2$

However, when the value of K is becoming larger than ever, the compression ratio is larger than ever too, thus we have to increase the number of eigenvectors n to ensure the quality of image restoration, this will lead to reduced compression ratio, Moreover, the lager the value of K, the greater the Computation, it is not desirable in terms of efficiency. Therefore, K value should be appropriate, from the figure 4 and table 2 above, we can see that K value is obtained around 10 is more appropriate.

If we do not consider the case of image quality, the maximum compression ratio of scheme 1 is $N/2$, here we take only one eigenvector. Namely, $n = 1$

the maximum compression ratio of scheme 2 is also $N/2$, here $K = M$, $n = 1$.

$$(K^2 \times M^2) / (n \times (K^2 + M^2))$$

$$= (K^2 \times M^2) / (K^2 + M^2) = K^2 / 2 = K \times K / 2$$

$$= K \times (N / M) / 2 = K \times (N / K) / 2 = N / 2$$

From this point of view, two solutions is equivalent.

But, the restore quality should be considered in the practical application, considering the relatively small distortion of restored images, the compression ratio of scheme 1 can only reach 2, while that of scheme 2 achieve at least 10. From this point of view, scheme 2 is better than scheme 1.

Scheme 2 can also applies to the compression decomposition of three-channel color image. After color image break down into three-channel RGB, the scheme 2 is applied to each channel separately. Finally, combination is made when restoring image.

5   Conclusions and Future Work

Singular Value Decomposition Method can be an extremely valuable and simple method of analyzing data . Using SVD for image compression can be a very useful tool to save storage space. We are able to get an image that is indistinguishable from the original image, but only using 45% of the original storage space. In this paper we investigate into using singular value decomposition as a method of image compression scheme. If we apply the SVD to the whole image, it is a large amount of computation, so, we can calculate the original image block. The application of block SVD-based image compression schemes has shown their effectiveness.

Although we have drawn some progress, some limitations of this study are still in existence. These limitations could be solved by our future work. We need more singular values to ensure the quality of the images. However, it is different for the number and size of value of each block of the singular, so we can consider for select the appropriate number of singular values adaptively for each sub-block. Moreover, the complexity of SVD transform operation is the main factor of calculation speed. The most difficult task is to search for a fast arithmetic of SVD. A more effective usage of adaptive singular value scheme can be achieved by dynamically select the block size to be compressed.

References

1. Amir, S., William, A.P.: An image multire mlution representation for lossless and lossy compression. IEEE Trans. Image Processing 5(9), 1303–1310 (1996)
2. Image Compression using Singular Value Decomposition. Adam Abrahamsen and David Richards, December 14 (2001)
3. Wu, J.Z.: A Method of Image Compression Based on Singular Value Decomposition. Computer& Digital Engineering 37(5), 136–138 (2009)
4. Press, W.H., Flannery, B.P., Teukolsky, S.A., Vetterling, W.T.: Singular Value Decomposition. In: Numerical Recipes in C, pp. 60–72. Cambridge University Press, Cambridge (1988)
5. Zhang, K.Y., Xv, Z.: Numerical algebra. Northwestern Polytechnical University Press (August 2000)
6. Tian, M.S., Luo, W., Liao, L.Z.: An Investigation into using Singular Value Decomposition as a Method of Image Compression. In: Proceedings of the Fourth International Conference on Machine Learning and Cybernetics, pp. 5200–5204 (2005)
7. Shnayderman, A., Gusev, A., Eskicioglu, A.M.: An SVD-based grayseale image quality measure for local and global assessment. IEEE Transactions on Image Processing 15(2), 45–52 (2006)

Design and Implementation of Four-Channel ENDAT2.2 Interface

Yilin Zheng[1,2], Hu Lin[2,3], Yaodong Tao[2,3], and Long Chen[1,2]

[1] Graduate University of Chinese Academy of Sciences, Yuquanstr.19,
Shijingshan Area, 100049 Beijing, China
[2] Shenyang Institute of Computing Technology, Chinese Academy of Sciences,
Nanping Eaststr.6, Dongling Area, 110168 Shenyang, Liaoning Province, China
[3] Shenyang Golding CNC Co., Ltd., Nanping Eaststr.6, Dongling Area,
110168 Shenyang, Liaoning Province, China
{zhengyl,linhu,taoyd,chengl}@sict.ac.cn

Abstract. Due to the wider application of ENDAT2.2 protocol in CNC systems, a four-channel ENDAT2.2 interface is proposed in this paper. By using SOPC technology, the paper designs and implements the custom logic for the four-channel ENDAT2.2 AVALON interface and the corresponding software driver. Through the verification, it turns out that the interface can support four-channel absolute encoders which implement the ENDAT2.2 protocol in high-precision CNC systems and can get the data from the servo motors quickly and accurately.

Keywords: ENDAT2.2, CNC system, absolute encoder, SOPC.

1 Introduction

CNC technology, an important industrial control technology, is developing to the trend of high precision and speed in recent years. Now, in order to process more complicated parts, five-axis and even six-axis machine tools are used for cutting. This requires several servo motors to drive the movement axes. And each servo motor requires an absolute encoder to obtain absolute position of the current process. ENDAT2.2 protocol, which is developed by the German company-HEIDENHAIN, accounts for more and more proportion in the domestic sensor protocol market for its advantages in simple connection and higher transmission rates [1]. Most domestic manufacturers of CNC production use original German import interfaces with a high cost and a limited number of channels (two channels). It becomes a hot issue to design and implement a multi-channel absolute encoder digital interface for ENDA2.2 in a multi-axis numerical control system.

System-On-Programmable-Chip (SOPC) technology, which can integrate micro-controller, memory and other hardware-specific circuits on a silicon wafer [2], overcomes the shortcomings of the traditional encoder digital interface including large chips, high power consumption and cost. Thanks to the advantages of high integration, flexibility and risk, SOPC turns into a mainstream technology of digital interface in numerical control system. With the widespread use of ENDAT2.2

M. Zhao and J. Sha (Eds.): ICCIP 2012, Part I, CCIS 288, pp. 732–739, 2012.

protocol and SOPC technology, the protocol-design company has provided the corresponding IP core which integrates the decoding and encoding functions of ENDAT2.2 protocol. This paper presents the design and implementation of the four-channel ENDAT2.2 interface digital system. This implementation has the advantages of modular structure, distinctive nuance, upgradable and low cost.

2   Construction of SOPC System

This design of the SOPC system is to send commands and receive the feedback data from the encoders through sending and receiving circuit. Then the feedback data is transferred to CNC PC and the control signals are sent to the SOPC system through the PCI bus. The core of the SOPC system is NIOS2 which is an embedded soft-core processor developed by ALTERA. The AVALON bus, the bridge for data transmission, is responsible for the communication between the processor and other modules. Dual-port RAM module is used to store the transmission data of ENDAT2.2 protocol. The overall structure of the SOPC system is shown in Fig. 1.

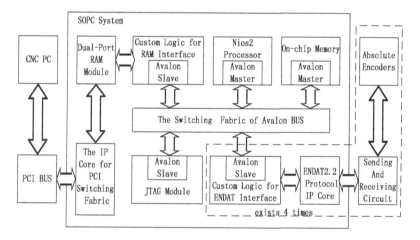

Fig. 1. The structure of SOPC system

The developers need to customize the logic for ENDAT interface and RAM interface. Thanks to the popularity of RAM interface, the corresponding custom logic technology is very mature. Readers can refer to the relevant articles and source code. This paper focus on the design and implementation of custom logic for ENDAT2.2 AVALON interface.

3   Custom Logic for ENDAT2.2 AVALON Interface

When developers construct the SOPC system with the ENDAT2.2 protocol IP core provided by vendors, they need to customize the logic for ENDAT2.2 AVALON interface by hardware description language (HDL). The custom logic for ENDAT2.2

AVALON interface can access AVALON bus so that NIOS2 embedded soft-core processor can handle the relevant signals from the ENDAT2.2 protocol IP core.

3.1   Design Method of Custom Interface

A FPGA-based SOPC system can be designed easily by the SOPC-BUILDER software of ALTERA. Its component library provides some modules that are used commonly, such as RAM and ROM, etc. Developers can easily call them to generate the SOPC system whose modules are connected by the AVALON bus.

The software offers two different methods for the ENDAT2.2 protocol IP core to access the AVALON bus. The IP core can access the AVALON bus directly or by the general IO ports. The former method needs to use the SOPC-BUILDER to edit features in the hardware module with the appropriate parameters for the timing constraints. The other method requires the appropriate timing signals as general IO ports to access the AVALON bus. And at the same time, the corresponding software drivers should be used for controlling the timing constraints.

Comparing the two methods mentioned above, we can draw the conclusion that the former achieves the timing control in the new module with fewer IO ports and easier software drivers. But the developers should deeply understand the timing of the AVALON bus peripherals. The latter method seems intuitive, but its software program is more complex because of the simulation of the timing. As the hardware runs the program faster than the software, we choose the first method for the rapid speed. And it can also avoid the errors of the timing simulation from the software. This method reflects the character of high level of integration of SOPC system, since it makes the timing control integrated in the new module.

3.2   Timing Requirements

Timing Requirements of the ENDAT2.2 Protocol IP Core.   When the developers make the IP core access the AVALON bus directly, they should learn the timing requirements of the IP core at first. The ENDAT2.2 protocol IP core provides a number of parallel IO ports for an external processor to control it. These interfaces include clock input signal CLK, chip select signal N_CS, 16-bit data output bus DOUT[15..0], 16-bit data input bus DIN[15..0], 7-bit address signal A[6..0], reset signal RST_N, reading strobe input signal RD_N, writing strobe input signal WR_N and ready signal READY_N. By reference to the relevant information [3], this paper summarizes the timing requirements shown in Fig. 2 and Table 1.

Table 1. Range of timing requirments

Time	Description	Range(ns)
T1	Address active before RD_N	$>=0$
T2	RD_N hold time	$>=3T_{CLK}+18$
T3	Address active after RD_N	$>=0$
T4	Address active before WR_N	$>=0$
T5	WR_N hold time	$>=3T_{CLK}+18$
T6	Address active after WR_N	$>=0$

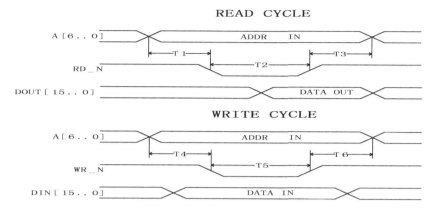

Fig. 2. The timing requirements of ENDAT2.2 protocol IP core

Timing Requirements of the AVALON Bus. AVALON bus, which interconnects the embedded processors and peripherals, is an on-chip bus invented by ALTERA. The AVALON bus does not require peripheral signals which must be used. It only defines many kinds of peripheral signals such as data, address, clock and so on. The reading and writing of the AVALON bus has many ways and the following only describes the relevant way. It is shown in TABLE I that the ENDAT2.2 protocol IP core reading and writing hold time longer than one cycle, and AVALON bus provides a multi-cycle waiting transfer specification for these IP cores. Fig. 3 is the AVALON slave port writing process of this transfer specification (2 waiting cycles).

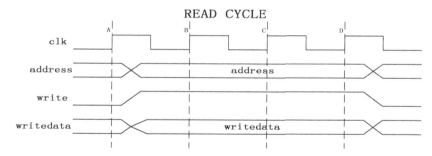

Fig. 3. The writing process timing with 2 waiting cycles

The first waiting cycle is active from Time A to B, and the second is active from Time B to C. The AVALON slave port captures the signals of writing, address and writedata at Time D. Then the writing process ends. The reading process is similar with the writing except that the active signal of readdata appears at Time C.

3.3   Design in SOPC-BUILDER

According to the frequent requirements of the IP core, SOPC system's operating frequency is set to 48MHz. So the time T2 and T3 of Fig. 2 should be greater than or equal to 4 cycles (1 cycle of about 20ns). We should make the reading set-up time, the reading waiting time, the reading hold time, the writing set-up time, the writing waiting time and the writing hold time of the custom AVALON interface consistent with Time T1, T2, T3, T4, T5 and T6 so that they could meet the two timing requirements mentioned above at the same time. Through the analysis we can find that the minimum time of the time T1, T3, T4 and T6 is 0 cycle and that of T2 and T6 is 4 cycles. Those kinds of time should be distributed greater than or equal to the minimum time. The final setting is shown in Fig. 4 (time unit: cycle).

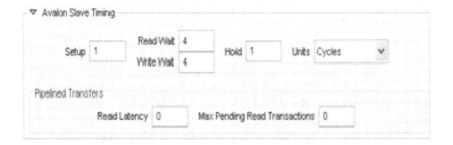

Fig. 4. The setting of the AVALON slave timing

3.4   Logic Design of Custom AVALON Interface

The function of custom logic for ENDAT2.2 AVALON interface is to make ENDAT2.2 AVALON bus access the ENDAT2.2 protocol IP core for the operation of NIOS2 kernel. In the case of single channel, the structure of the custom logic is shown in Fig. 5.

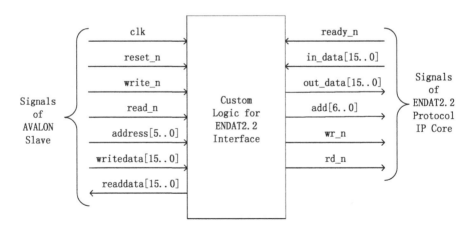

Fig. 5. The structure of the custom logic(signal channel)

The ready_n signal in Fig. 5 is the ready signal of the ENDAT2.2 protocol IP core. The falling of this signal indicates that the IP core has finished the last reading or writing operation and the feedback data has been sent to the data bus. According to the timing requirements of the IP core and the internal structure of the custom AVALON interface, the flow of the custom logic is designed as shown in Fig. 6.

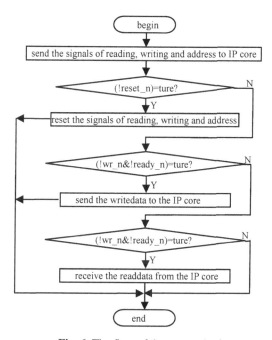

Fig. 6. The flow of the custom logic

4   Software Design of Sopc System

ENDAT2.2 protocol provides three different types of encoder feedback data: the encoder position values, the storage area parameters and the test values [4]. Therefore, the software design of the SOPC system needs to support not only four-channel operations but also three different kinds of data. The developers can write the system driver easily through the NIOS-IDE software which is a production of ALTERA. The general process of the system drive is shown in Fig. 7.

5   Results

The SOPC system is integrated in the EP3C16Q240 which belongs to the Cyclone III family chips of ALTERA. When the developers need to debug and verify the software driver, they should download the hardware logic on the chip through the QUARTUS2 software. Then the program can run on the hardware logic by NIOS-IDE software. In the case of reading the encoder position values of the first channel, we can use the SIGNALTAP logic analyzer to capture the waveform at the time of the ready_n signal falling. The result is shown in Fig. 8.

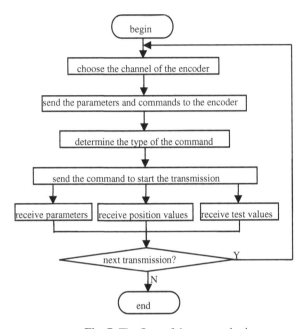

Fig. 7. The flow of the custom logic

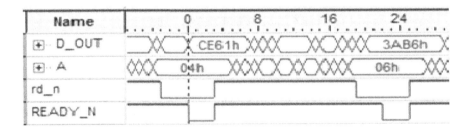

Fig. 8. The flow of the custom logic

From Fig. 8 we can find that the ENDAT2.2 protocol IP core sends the position data to the D_OUT bus when the rd_n signal from the custom AVALON interface has been active. Then the position data transmission of the IP core has been finished with the falling of the READY_N signal. The custom AVALON interface should read the 16-bit data from the D_OUT bus at this time so that the NIOS2 kernel can get the correct value of encoder position. The result proves the accuracy of the system driver and the custom logic for ENDAT2.2 AVALON interface.

6   Conclusions

This design and implementation of four-channel ENDAT2.2 interface achieves the real-time reception of four-channel absolute position values in CNC systems. It solves the problem caused by the traditional encoder interface such like only one channel or only supporting the incremental encoders [5]. This design can implement the reading of the position value and diagnostic information of the absolute encoders so that CNC systems could control the servo motors more rapidly and accurately.

Acknowledgment. The project is supported by the National Basic Research Program (or 973 Program) (No. 2011CB302400) and the Major National S&T Program (High-grade CNC Machine Tools and Basic Manufacturing Equipment-the Innovation Platform Construction for Supporting Technology of Open Numerical Control (ONC) System: No. 2011ZX04016-071).

References

1. EnDat2.2—Bidirectional Interface for Position Encoders. HEIDENHAIN GmbH, pp. 2–4 (2008)
2. Peng, C.L.: The NIOS-based Design and Practice of SOPC, pp. 1–2. Tsinghua University Publishing House, Beijing (2004)
3. EnDat2.2—Softmacro for Master Component. MAZeT GmbH, p. 38 (2008)
4. EnDat2.2—Master Component Program Samples. MAZeT GmbH, pp. 11–25 (2004)
5. Wang, G.H.: Absolute encoder for motion control of the superiority. OME Information 16, 11–13 (1999)

Hopf Bifurcation in a Three-Stage-Structured Prey-Predator System with Predator Density Dependent

Shunyi Li and Xiangui Xue

Department of Mathematics, Qiannan Normal College for Nationalities
Duyun, Guizhou, 558000, China
lishunyi19820425@163.com

Abstract. A three-stage-structured prey-predator model with delay and predator density dependent is considered. The characteristic equations and local stability of the equilibrium are analyzed, by applying the theorem of Hopf bifurcation, the conditions for the positive equilibrium occurring Hopf bifurcation are obtained. Finally, numerical simulations and brief conclusion are given.

Keywords: three-stage-structured, Hopf bifurcation, time delay, prey-predator system.

1   Introduction

A time-delay model of single-species growth with two stage structure was introduced by W.G. Aiello and H.I. Freedman in 1990 [1] and summarized by Liu et al [2]. In these papers, the authors assume that the life history of each population is divided into distinctive stages: the immature and mature members of the population, where only the mature member can reproduce themselves. However, in the nature many species go through three life stages: immature, mature and old. For example, many female animals lose reproductive ability when they are old.

A three-stage-structured single-species growth model was considered by S.J. Gao [3], the conditions for stability of equilibrium and the sufficient conditions for the existence of a globally asymptotically stable of positive equilibrium of the model are obtained. Delays play an important role in the dynamics of populations, which can cause the loss of stability and can bifurcate various periodic solutions. In this paper, we consider following three-stage-structured prey-predator model with time delay and predator density dependent

$$\begin{cases} x_1'(t) = \alpha x_2(t) - (\gamma_1 + \Omega)x_1(t) - \eta x_1^2(t) - Ex_1(t)y(t), \\ x_2'(t) = \Omega x_1(t) - (\theta_1 + a)x_2(t), \\ x_3'(t) = ax_2(t) - bx_3(t), \\ y'(t) = y(t)(kEx_1(t) - d - fy(t-\tau)), \end{cases} \tag{1}$$

where $x_i(t)(i = 1, 2, 3)$ are the densities of immature preys, mature preys and old preys at time t, $y(t)$ is the density of predator at time t, respectively. All of the parameters are positive, α is the birth rate of mature population, and γ_1, θ_1, b are the death rate of immature, mature and old prey population, respectively. Ω and a are

M. Zhao and J. Sha (Eds.): ICCIP 2012, Part I, CCIS 288, pp. 740–747, 2012.

the maturity rate and ageing rate of the prey population, respectively. η and f are the density dependent coefficients of immature prey population and predator population, respectively. k is the rate of conversing prey into predator and E is the predation coefficient. τ is the desinty dependent delay for predator population.

Note that in (1), the first and the second equations are independent of the third equation. It is easy to obtain that, if $x_2(t) \to x_2^*$ as $t \to \infty$, then $x_3(t) \to x_3^* = ax_2^*/b$ as $t \to \infty$, and if $x_2(t) \to 0$ as $t \to \infty$, then $x_3(t) \to 0$ as $t \to \infty$. That is, the asymptotic behavior of $x_3(t)$ is dependent on that of $x_2(t)$. Therefore, we just need to study following subsystem

$$\begin{cases} x_1'(t) = \alpha x_2(t) - \gamma x_1(t) - \eta x_1^2(t) - E x_1(t) y(t), \\ x_2'(t) = \Omega x_1(t) - \theta x_2(t), \\ y'(t) = y(t)(kE x_1(t) - d - fy(t - \tau)), \end{cases} \quad (2)$$

where $\gamma = \gamma_1 + \Omega, \theta = \theta_1 + a$, The initial conditions for (2) are
$x_1(t) = \phi_1(t) \geq 0, x_2(t) = \phi_2(t) \geq 0, y(t) = \phi_3(t) \geq 0, t \in [-\tau, 0]$.

2 Stability Analysis and Hopf Bifurcation

2.1 Local Stability Analysis

Obviously, (2) has two boundary equilibrium $E_0 = (0,0,0)$, $E_1(x_1, x_2, 0)$ (if condition C_1 holds), and a unique positive equilibrium $E_2(x_1^*, x_2^*, y^*)$ (if condition C_2 holds), where

$$x_1 = \frac{\alpha\Omega - \gamma\theta}{\eta\theta}, x_2 = \frac{\Omega}{\theta}x_1, (C_1 = \alpha\Omega - \gamma\theta > 0),$$

$$x_1^* = \frac{f(\alpha\Omega - \gamma\theta) + dE\theta}{\theta(kE^2 + \eta f)}, x_2^* = \frac{\Omega}{\theta}x_1^*, y^* = \frac{kEx_1^* - d}{f},$$

$$(C_2 = kEx_1^* - d > 0),$$

Let $\bar{E} = (\bar{x}_1, \bar{x}_2, \bar{y})$ be any arbitrary equilibrium. The linearized equations about $\bar{E}$ are

$$\begin{pmatrix} x_1'(t) \\ x_2'(t) \\ y'(t) \end{pmatrix} = A \begin{pmatrix} x_1(t) \\ x_2(t) \\ y(t) \end{pmatrix} + B \begin{pmatrix} x_1(t-\tau) \\ x_2(t-\tau) \\ y(t-\tau) \end{pmatrix} \quad (3)$$

where

$$A = \begin{pmatrix} -\gamma - 2\eta\bar{x}_1 - \bar{y}E & \alpha & -\bar{x}_1 E \\ \Omega & -\theta & 0 \\ k\bar{y}E & 0 & k\bar{x}_1 E - d - \bar{y}f \end{pmatrix},$$

$$B = \begin{pmatrix} 0 & 0 & 0 \\ 0 & 0 & 0 \\ 0 & 0 & -\bar{y}f \end{pmatrix},$$

and the characteristic equation about $\bar{E}$ is given by

$$\det(A + Be^{-\lambda\tau} - \lambda I) = 0 \tag{4}$$

(i) From (4), the characteristic equation about E_0 is given by

$$\det\begin{pmatrix} -\gamma-\lambda & \alpha & 0 \\ \Omega & -\theta-\lambda & 0 \\ 0 & 0 & -d-\lambda \end{pmatrix} = 0.$$

Namely

$$(\lambda+d)[\lambda^2 + (\gamma+\theta)\lambda + \gamma\theta - \alpha\Omega] = 0. \tag{5}$$

Then $\lambda_3 = -d < 0$, and λ_1, λ_2 are the two other roots of $\lambda^2 + (\gamma+\theta)\lambda + \gamma\theta - \alpha\Omega = 0$. By Routh-Hurwitz criterion, E_0 is local stable if $\gamma\theta > \alpha\Omega$, local unstable if $\gamma\theta < \alpha\Omega$ and E_1 exist.

(ii) From (4), the characteristic equation about E_1 is given by

$$\det\begin{pmatrix} -\gamma-2\eta x_1-\lambda & \alpha & -x_1 E \\ \Omega & -\theta-\lambda & 0 \\ 0 & 0 & kEx_1-d-\lambda \end{pmatrix} = 0,$$

Namely

$$(\lambda+d-kEx_1)[\lambda^2 + (\gamma+\theta+2\eta x_1)\lambda + \theta\eta x_1] = 0. \tag{6}$$

Then, λ_1, λ_2 are the two roots of $\lambda^2 + (\gamma+\theta+2\eta x_1)\lambda + \theta\eta x_1 = 0$, with negative real parts, and $\lambda_3 = kEx_1 - d$. By Routh-Hurwitz criterion, E_1 is local stable if $kEx_1 < d$, local unstable if $kEx_1 > d$ and E_2 exist.

From (i) and (ii), we have the following result.

Theorem 1. (i) E_0 is local stable if $\gamma\theta > \alpha\Omega$, local unstable if $\gamma\theta < \alpha\Omega$ and E_1 exist.
(ii) E_1 is local stable if $kEx_1 < d$, local unstable if $kEx_1 > d$ and E_2 exist.

2.2   Existence of Hopf Bifurcation

The characteristic equation about the positive equilibrium E_2 is given by

$$\det\begin{pmatrix} -\gamma-2\eta x_1^*-Ey^*-\lambda & \alpha & -Ex_1^* \\ \Omega & -\theta-\lambda & 0 \\ kEy^* & 0 & -e^{-\lambda\tau}fy^*-\lambda \end{pmatrix} = 0.$$

Namely

$$D(\lambda,\tau) = M(\lambda) + N(\lambda)e^{-\lambda\tau} = 0. \tag{7}$$

where

$$M(\lambda) = \lambda^3 + m_2\lambda^2 + m_1\lambda + m_0,$$

$$N(\lambda) = n_2\lambda^2 + n_1\lambda + n_0,$$

$$m_2 = \gamma + 2\eta x_1^* + Ey^* + \theta,$$

$$n_2 = fy^*,$$

$$m_1 = x_1^*(\theta\eta + kE^2y^*),$$

$$n_1 = fy^*(\gamma + 2\eta x_1^* + Ey^* + \theta),$$

$$m_0 = kE^2\theta x_1^* y^*,$$

$$n_0 = f\eta\theta x_1^* y^*,$$

When $\tau = 0$, (7) becomes to

$$\lambda^3 + (m_2 + n_2)\lambda^2 + (m_1 + n_1)\lambda + m_0 + n_0 = 0. \tag{8}$$

and

$$m_2 + n_2 = \gamma + 2\eta x_1^* + Ey^* + \theta + fy^* > 0,$$

$$m_1 + n_1 = x_1^*(\theta\eta + kE^2y^*) + fy^*(\gamma + 2\eta x_1^* + Ey^* + \theta) > 0,$$

$$m_0 + n_0 = \theta x_1^* y^*(kE^2 + f\eta) > 0,$$

Note that

$$(m_2 + n_2)(m_1 + n_1) - (m_0 + n_0) > \theta\{[2\eta fx_1^* y^* + Ey^*(d + 2fy^*)] - (f\eta + kE^2)x_1^* y^*\} > 0.$$

By Routh-Hurwits criterion, all roots of (8) have negative real parts. Then, the equilibrium E_2 is local stable.

Suppose $\lambda = i\omega(\omega > 0)$ is a root of (7) and separating the real and imaginary parts, one can get that

$$\begin{cases} m_2\omega^2 - m_0 = (n_0 - n_2\omega^2)\cos\omega\tau + n_1\omega\sin\omega\tau, \\ \omega^3 - m_1\omega = n_1\omega\cos\omega\tau - (n_0 - n_2\omega^2)\sin\omega\tau, \end{cases} \tag{9}$$

From (9), we get

$$(n_0 - n_2\omega^2)^2 + n_1^2\omega^2 = (m_2\omega^2 - m_0)^2 + (\omega^3 - m_1\omega)^2 \tag{10}$$

Namely

$$\omega^6 + p\omega^4 + q\omega^2 + r = 0, \tag{11}$$

where

$$p = m_2^2 - 2m_1 - n_2^2 > 0, \tag{12}$$

$$q = m_1^2 + 2n_2n_0 - n_1^2 - 2m_2m_0, \tag{13}$$

$$r = m_0^2 - n_0^2 = x_1^* y^* \theta(m_0 + y_0)(kE^2 - f\eta), \tag{14}$$

If $C_3 : kE^2 < f\eta$ hold, from (14) we know that (7) has a unique positive root . From (9), we have

$$\cos\omega_0\tau = \frac{(m_2\omega_0^2 - m_0)(n_0 - n_2\omega_0^2) + n_1\omega_0(\omega_0^3 - m_1\omega_0)}{(n_0 - n_2\omega_0^2)^2 + (n_1\omega_0)^2},$$

Thus

$$\tau_n = \frac{1}{\omega_0} \cos^{-1}\left[\frac{(m_2\omega_0^2 - m_0)(n_0 - n_2\omega_0^2) + n_1\omega_0(\omega_0^3 - m_1\omega_0)}{(n_0 - n_2\omega_0^2)^2 + (n_1\omega_0)^2}\right] + \frac{2n\pi}{\omega_0}, n = 0,1,2,\cdots \quad (15)$$

Let $\lambda(\tau) = v(\tau) + i\omega(\tau)$ be the roots of (7) such that when $\tau = \tau_n$ satisfying $v(\tau_n) = 0$ and $\omega(\tau_n) = \omega_0$. We can claim that

$$\frac{d(\mathrm{Re}\,\lambda)}{d\tau}\bigg|_{\tau=\tau_0} > 0.$$

In fact, differentiating two sides of (7) with respect to τ, we get

$$[(3\lambda^2 + 2m_2\lambda + m_1) + e^{-\lambda\tau}(2n_2\lambda + n_1) - e^{-\lambda\tau}\tau(n_2\lambda^2 + n_1\lambda + n_0)]$$
$$= \lambda(n_2\lambda^2 + n_1\lambda + n_0)e^{-\lambda\tau}d\lambda/d\tau$$

then

$$\left(\frac{d\lambda}{d\tau}\right)^{-1} = \frac{3\lambda^2 + 2m_2\lambda + m_1}{\lambda(n_2\lambda^2 + n_1\lambda + n_0)e^{-\lambda\tau}} + \frac{2n_2\lambda + n_1}{\lambda(n_2\lambda^2 + n_1\lambda + n_0)} - \frac{\tau}{\lambda}$$

Therefore

$$\mathrm{sign}\left[\frac{d(\mathrm{Re}\,\lambda)}{d\tau}\right]_{\lambda=i\omega_0} = \mathrm{sign}\left[\mathrm{Re}\left(\frac{d\lambda}{d\tau}\right)^{-1}\right]_{\lambda=i\omega_0}$$

$$= \frac{1}{\omega_0^2}\mathrm{sign}\left\{\mathrm{Re}\left[\frac{(m_0 + m_2\omega_0^2) + 2\omega_0^3 i}{(m_2\omega_0^2 - m_0) + (\omega_0^3 - m_1\omega_0)i} + \frac{n_2\omega_0^2 + n_0}{(n_0 - n_2\omega_0^2) + n_1\omega_0 i}\right]\right\}$$

$$= \frac{1}{\Psi}\mathrm{sign}\left[\begin{array}{l}(m_2\omega_0^2 - m_0)(m_0 + m_2\omega_0^2) + 2\omega_0^3(\omega_0^3 - m_1\omega_0) \\ +(n_0 - n_2\omega_0^2)(n_0 + n_2\omega_0^2)\end{array}\right]$$

$$= \frac{1}{\Psi}\mathrm{sign}[2\omega_0^6 + (m_2^2 - 2m_1 - n_2^2)\omega_0^4 - (m_0^2 - n_0^2)],$$

$$= \frac{1}{\Psi}\mathrm{sign}(2\omega_0^6 + p\omega_0^4 - r)$$

where $\Psi = \omega_0^2[(n_0 - n_2^2\omega_0^2)^2 + (n_1\omega_0)^2] > 0$. Since $p > 0$ and $r < 0$, then

$$\mathrm{sign}\left[\frac{d(\mathrm{Re}\,\lambda)}{d\tau}\right]_{\lambda=i\omega_0} = 1, \quad \frac{d(\mathrm{Re}\,\lambda)}{d\tau}\bigg|_{\tau=\tau_0} > 0,$$

according to the Hopf bifurcation theorem for functional differential equations [4], we have the following result.

Theorem 2. If $C_3 : kE^2 < f\eta$ holds, then (i) There exists a τ_0, when $\tau \in [0, \tau_0)$ the positive equilibrium E_2 of (2) is asymptotically stable and unstable when $\tau > \tau_0$.

(ii) System (2) can undergo a Hopf bifurcation at the positive equilibrium E_2 when $\tau = \tau_n (n = 0,1,2,\cdots)$, where τ_n is defined by (15).

Remark 1. It must be pointed out that Theorem 2 can not determine the stability and the direction of bifurcating periodic solutions, that is, the periodic solutions may exists either for $\tau > \tau_0$ or for $\tau < \tau_0$, near τ_0. To determine the stability, direction and other properties of bifurcating periodic solutions, the normal form theory and center manifold argument should be considered [5].

3   Numerical Simulation

We consider following three-stage-structured system with time delay

$$\begin{cases} x_1'(t) = 2x_2(t) - 0.8x_1(t) - 0.2x_1^2(t) - 0.5x_1(t)y(t), \\ x_2'(t) = 0.6x_1(t) - 0.8x_2(t), \\ y'(t) = y(t)(0.2x_1(t) - 0.1 - 1.2y(t-\tau)), \end{cases} \tag{16}$$

where $\alpha = 2, \gamma_1 = 0.2, \Omega = 0.6, \eta = 0.2, E = 0.5, \theta_1 = 0.2, a = 0.6, k = 0.4, d = 0.1, f = 1.2,$ $X(0) = (3,1.5,1)$.   System   (16)   has   unique   positive   equilibrium   point

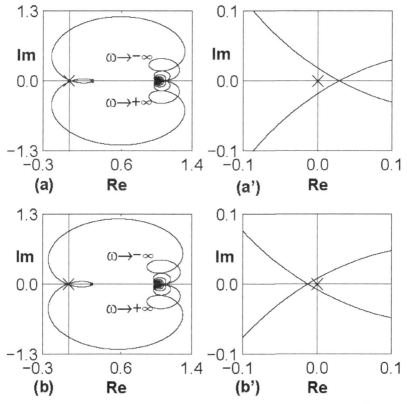

Fig. 1. The Nyquist plot of $D(i\omega, 3.4)/(1+i\omega)^3$ and $D(i\omega, 3.6)/(1+i\omega)^3$, show that positive equilibrium point of (16) are asymptotically stable for $\tau = 3.4 < \tau_0$ ((a) and (a)') and unstable for $\tau = 3.6 > \tau_0$ ((b) and (b)')

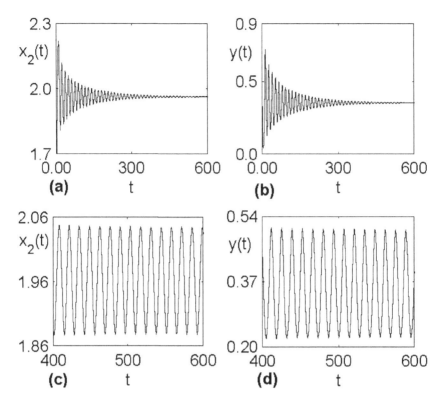

Fig. 2. The time-series plot show that positive equilibrium point E_2 of (16) are asymptotically stable for $\tau = 3.4 < \tau_0$ ((a) and (b)) and Hopf bifurcation for $\tau = 3.6 > \tau_0$ ((c) and (d))

$E_2 = (2.62, 1.96, 0.35)$. We evaluate that $p = 6.77, r = -0.026, \omega_0 = 0.47, \tau_0 = 3.53$. The the positive equilibrium point E_2 is asymptotically stable when $\tau = 3.4 < \tau_0$. Because the Nyquist plot [6] of $D(i\omega, 3.4) / (1 + i\omega)^3$ does not encircle the origin of the complex plane (Fig.1(a) and Zoom around the origin of the Nyquist plot (a')) and the time-series plot are showed (Fig.2 (a),(b)). When $\tau = 3.6 > \tau_0$, the positive equilibrium point E_2 is unstable. Because the Nyquist plot of $D(i\omega, 3.6) / (1 + i\omega)^3$ encircles the origin of the complex plane (Fig.1(b) and Zoom around the origin of the Nyquist plot (b')) and the Hopf bifurcation occurring around the positive equilibrium E_2 are shown (Fig.2 (c),(d)). The bifurcating periodic solution (limit cycle) of (16) are stable when τ from 4 to 7 and the amplitudes of period oscillatory are increasing as time delays increased. But, too large time delay would make the population to be die out, because the population very close to zero (Fig.3 (b)-(d)) as time delay increase to some critical value.

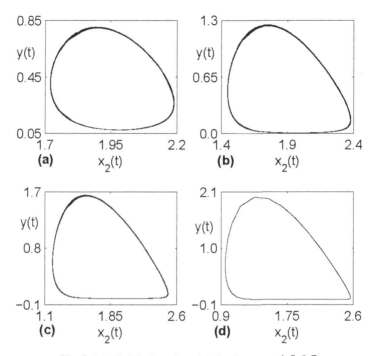

Fig. 3. (a)-(d): Limit cycles of (16) when $\tau = 4, 5, 6, 7$

Acknowledgments. This work was supported by the The Natural Science Foundation of Guizhou Province (No. [2011]2116) and Foundation of Key Supported Disciplines of Guizhou province (No. [2009]303).

References

1. Aiello, W.G., Freedman, H.I.: A time-delay model of single-species growth with stage structure. Math. Biosci. 101, 139–153 (1990)
2. Liu, S.Q., Chen, L.S., Agarwal, R.: Recent progress on stage structured population dynamics. Math. Comput. Model. 36, 1319–1360 (2002)
3. Gao, S.J.: Global Stability of Three-stage-structured Single-species Growth Model. J. Xinjiang Univ. 18, 154–158 (2001) (in Chinese)
4. Hale, J.K.: Theory of Functional Differential Equations. Springer, New York (1977)
5. Hassard, B.D., Kazarinoff, N.D., Wan, Y.H.: Theory and applications of Hopf bifurcation. Cambridge University Press, Cambridge (1981)
6. Fu, M.Y., Olbrot, A.W., Polis, M.P.: Robust stability for time-delay systems: The edge theorem and graphical tests. IEEE Trans. Autom. Contr. 34, 813–820 (1989)

Using Vector Mapping and Inverse Kinematics for Motion Retargeting

Shurong Ning, Linfang Wang,
Linjie Miao, and Chaoen Xiao

School of Computer and Communication Engineering
University of Science and Technology Beijing
Beijing, China
fancyning123@sina.com

Abstract. In order to reuse an object's existing behaviors and improve the efficiency of computer animation, a vector-mapping-based motion retargeting method is used in this paper. A virtual arm example is utilized to show the feasibility of this method in solving motion retargeting problem with similar structure and different bone model. Empirical results show that the position and orientation of each joint can be gained only by the end-effector's position and behavior. This method not only simplifies the control problem, but also realizes the motion retargeting for different roles more easily.

Keywords: vector mapping, motion retargeting, virtual arm.

1   Motion Retargeting

The current redirected technology is mainly used in two aspects [1]: role animation which has the characteristics of the joints and the face animation. Libo Sun[2] proposed a motion retargeting method of mapping movement data from a kind of role to another one with completely different joint structures. Based on middle joint, Suddhajit Sen[3] proposed a motion retargeting method for different joint structures. The method proposed by Kosit Nopvichai[4] was a hierarchical method of interactive editing motion data, and could change existing motion data to force the motion to meet a series of constraints. Choi[5] proposed an algorithm for real-time motion retargeting by using the intensive repetition of capturing the information, which achieves the goals to retargetable real-time computing. Seyoon[6] proposed a new constraint-based motion data editing technique and transformed the problem into a bound state problem. Min JePark[7] proposed a movement cloning technique based on the movement of sample cases; Hsieh[8] proposed an interactive system to transfer and connect the behaviors of different joint connection objects such as people and dogs. LuoZhongXiang[9] mainly researched the motion editing based on time and space constraints.

M. Zhao and J. Sha (Eds.): ICCIP 2012, Part I, CCIS 288, pp. 748–756, 2012.
© Springer-Verlag Berlin Heidelberg 2012

2   Model and Initialization

2.1   Associated Relationship between Virtual Arm Joints

In order to visually review the effect of vector - mapping method on redirection, the virtual arm of joint model is simplified as shoulder joint and elbow joint (Fig.1). Joint model of IK setting is characterized by: when a parent node is moving, the child node must follow the movement; when child node is moving, the parent node does not necessarily do the same action. Associated relationship between virtual arm joints are described as follows by tree-level model (Fig.1 (b)) and joint kinematic chain (Fig.2):

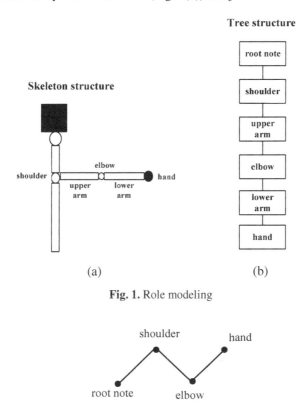

Fig. 1. Role modeling

Fig. 2. Articular moving chain of virtual arm

2.2   Initialize the Virtual Arm

Firstly, the movement skeleton objects of the virtual arms are initialized.

In Fig.3:

l1, l2: The length of the virtual bone

ex, ey: target position of the end-effector, Vertical and horizontal position coordinates angle1: Upper arm swing angle

angle2: Lower arm swing angle

angle3, angle4: Defined for facilitating the calculation of the value of angle1, angle3 value can be calculated in the triangle ACD and angle4 value can be calculated in the triangle ABC to calculate angle1

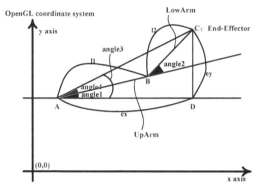

Fig. 3. IK setting schemes of virtual arm

2.3   Description of the Movement State for Virtual Arm

Suppose the virtual arm (right arm) movement from bottom to top as forward movement, from top to bottom as negative movement.

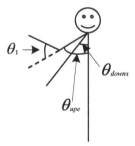

Fig. 4. Upper arm's state when it stops moving

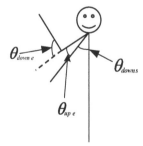

Fig. 5. Lower arm's state when it stops positive moving

The figure above:

θ_{up0} : The initial angle of the upper arm to the body.

ω_{up} : The initial angular velocity of the upper arm relative to the body.

$\theta_{down\ 0}$: The initial angle of the lower arm to upper arm.

$\theta_{down\ s}$: The critical angle of upper arm when lower arm began to move.

ω_{down} : The initial angular velocity when lower arm began to move.

$\theta_{up\ e}$: Upper arm stopped moving when it reached this angle.

θ_1 : The angle of lower arm relative to upper arm when upper arm stopped moving.

$\theta_{down\ e}$: Lower arm began to move in the opposite direction when lower arm reached this angle.

Angle of the upper arm in moving:

$$\theta_{up1} = \theta_{downs} + \omega_{up} \bullet \theta_{downe} / \omega_{up}\ . \tag{1}$$

Angle of the lower arm in moving:

$$\theta_{down1} = (\theta_{downe} - \theta_{downs}) / \omega_{up} \bullet \omega_{down}\ . \tag{2}$$

In the initial state, upper arm of the virtual arm moves positively, and lower arm resting.

$$\begin{cases} \theta_{up} = \theta_{up\ 0} \\ \theta_{down} = 0 \end{cases} \tag{3}$$

a) $\theta_{up} >= \theta_{upe}$ When the upper arm moves to a certain angle, upper arm stops movement. At this point, only the lower arm is moving. At this moment, the angle of the lower arm to the upper arm is θ_1 (Fig.4).

b) Lower arm began to move in the reverse direction when ($\omega_{down} > 0$ .AND. $\theta_{down} >= \theta_{downe}$) . OR. ($\omega_{down} < 0$ .AND. $\theta_{up1} <= \theta_{down0}$) namely the lower arm moved forward and reached a certain angle, now $\omega_{down} =- \omega_{down}$,lower arm moves, upper arm stops(Fig.5).

c) Upper arm began to move in the reverse direction when ($\omega_{up} > 0$ .AND. $\theta_{up} >= \theta_{upe}$).OR. ($\omega_{up} < 0$. AND. $\theta_{up} <= \theta_{up0}$) namely the movement angle of upper arm reached a certain angle of θ_{upe} , now $\omega_{up} = -\omega_{up}$ .In addition, when $\theta_{down} >= \theta_1$, namely the movement angle of lower arm in the reverse direction reached θ_1 , the upper arm began to move in the reverse direction, now $\omega_{up} = -\omega_{up}$, both upper arm and lower arm moves.

d) When $\theta_{down} >= \theta_{down0}$,namely the lower arm movement angle of reverse direction reached θ_{down0} ,at this point the lower arm stopped, only the upper arm moved.

e) The upper arm began to move forward when $\theta_{up} >= \theta_{up0}$, namely the upper arm movement angle of reverse direction reached θ_{up0} .

3   The Vector - Mapping Motion Retargeting of Virtual Arm

In the process of movement, the movement of virtual arm needs to meet accessibility; otherwise it will easily lead to distortion of the movement which does not meet the laws of nature.

3.1   The Acquisition of the Initial Motion Curve of the Virtual Arm

Take the movement virtual arm in a virtual scene as a reference, track and record the end-effectors trajectory, which are denoted as the initial motion curve.

The specific method is to record the animation sequence, obtain the end-effectors of the moving object by background subtraction technique, track the trajectory by moving object tracking technology, and obtain the moving curve of the moving object. Simultaneously record the size of the moving object and the joint chain. Joint chain is for the movement of joints associated information. To facilitate the redirection of the virtual arms of different backbone of the ratio, it is necessary to record the virtual arm as the standard model, set the size of the backbone as "1", compare the redirection objects and the moving objects when redirecting, adjust the ratio of the motion data accordingly, and then redirect the exercise.

3.2   Initial Motion Vector of the Curve

As the motion model and the target object model belong to different coordinate system, or the difference between the proportion of the backbone, it will result in the problem of movement distortion. For this problem, this paper will draw the data of movement into BMP bitmap image and then vector computing the initial motion curve based on the vector algorithm, namely transform the data into a standard coordinate system data, in order to facilitate the coordinate transformation when to redirect. For random, uncertain motion curves, vector-based algorithm is able to well preserve the data of the original motion curve, maximally maintain its characteristics, and ultimately to ensure the results of the motion retargeting of the target object.

As the initial movement of the curve with high randomness and uncertainty, in order to avoid losing its original characteristics, efficiently store critical features, vector-based calculation method is adopted, which is taken into sharp point extraction and fitting a straight line tangent vector calculation two steps to complete.

1) Sharp point extraction. In the vectorization process, the initial movement of the curve has high randomness and uncertainty, the method of seeking sharp points through the chord length ratio can maximally save the original movement curve data.

In Fig.6, $P_i(x_i, y_i)$, $P_{i-k}(x_{i-k}, y_{i-k})$, $P_{i+k}(x_{i+k}, y_{i+k})$ are the movement of points on the curve and the linear equation of P_{i-k} and P_{i+k} is $Ax + By + C = 0$, in which

$A = y_{i-k} - y_{i+k}$, $B = x_{i+k} - x_{i-k}$, $C = x_{i-k} y_{i+k} - x_{i+k} y_{i-k}$. The chord length and the distance between points and the chord are respectively:

$$L_{ik} = \sqrt{(y_{i-k} - y_{i+k})^2 + (x_{i-k} - x_{i+k})^2} = \sqrt{A^2 + B^2} \qquad (4)$$

$$d_{ik} = \frac{|Ax_i + By_i + C|}{\sqrt{(y_{i-k} - y_{i+k})^2 + (x_{i-k} - x_{i+k})^2}} = \frac{|Ax_i + By_i + C|}{L_{ik}} \qquad (5)$$

The curvature c_{ik} of the curve at point P_i :

$$c_{ik} = \frac{d_{ik}}{L_{ik}} \qquad (6)$$

The higher the value of c_{ik} , the higher the probability of sharp point is. If it is greater than or equal to the threshold, you can determine P_i as the cusp. In a range, the curvature of the point mutations are must be cusp. The main purpose of marking points on the tip is to prevent the cusp to be smoothed in the process of fitting the vector.

2) Fitting a straight line tangent vector calculation. During vectorization process, the motion curve varied, the method of fitting a straight line tangent curve fitting exercise can maximally reflect the different characteristics of the curve.

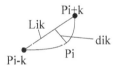

Fig. 6. Chord length ratio

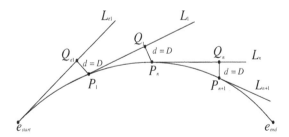

Fig. 7. Fitting a straight line tangent

Fig.7: e_{start} and e_{end} are the start and end points of movement curve respectively. On the curve L_{e1} over e_{start} tangent equation is $Ax + By + C = 0$, A (x_1, y_1) of any point on the curve obtained, the distance from point A to the tangent is

$$d = \frac{|Ax_1 + By_1 + C|}{\sqrt{A^2 + B^2 + C^2}} \qquad (7)$$

If d=D, marked point A as P_1, using the same method to draw a tangent at the point of P_1 , and then look for points P_2, so draw a tangent L_n over point P_n on the curve, Mark the point as P_{n+1} when d=D, until the last one tangent L_m , The distance $d \leq D$ between the end point e_{end} and the tangent L_m ; Points $\overline{e_{start}P_1}$, $\overline{P_1P_2}$, ...$\overline{P_ne_{end}}$ connected by straight lines, Vector of curve fitting is completed.

4   Motion Information Mapping

A series of motion data movement point information is obtained after the initial motion vector of the curve calculation. Firstly, the movement start and end point of the curve are determined, and then the connection of them is the movement vector of the curve. These movement data mapped to the target object to complete the motion retargeting. However, before data mapping exercise, you need to re-calculate the backbone of the ratio between the target object and the standard model. According to the proportion of the value of the backbone, correspondingly scaling the motion vector of the curve into the target object movement of the curve and then to map, so as to avoid the distortion problem of redirection of different backbone ratio of the scale model. Having the same topology, between the proportions of different models of the backbone, the amount of its motion displacement length ratio is equal to the ratio of the backbone length.

Apply scaling-based mapping to divide the vector motion of the curve and the target motion flat into the same grid plane. Divide the vector motion curve of the plane and the target movement curve into the same grid, so both of them have the same number of network, thus, the two have the same number of grid. After meshing, use the method base on three cases of the scaling in Fig.8.

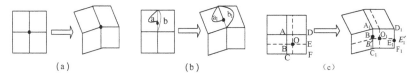

Fig. 8. Three cases of scaling transformation

a) Key points on the movement curve coincident with the network nodes. determine its number of rows and columns in the grid lines and find the mapping point on the target movement surface according to the same number of rows and columns;

b) Key points on the movement curve are above the line in the grid. Determine the origin of the number of rows and columns on the grid, find the target movement surface corresponding to the grid, calculate a, b and the arc length of b_1 according to the ratio $a/b = a_1/b_1$, and determine the mapping point on the target surface;

c) Key points on the movement curve are within the grid. Establish parametric curves on the surface according to the origin point (dashed line); traversal to determine which grid are the origin point and the mapping point belong to; calculate AB, AC ; DE, DF ; BO, BE ; A_1C_1 and D_1F_1 ; determine point B_1 and E_1 on the flattened map according to the ratio $AB/AC = A_1B_1/A_1C_1$ and $DE/DF = D_1E_1/D_1F_1$; Extract parameter values of point B_1 and E_1 on the flattened map. These two points have different general direction of v (figure vertical) parameter values. Calculate their average V_0 , and construct a new U (figure horizontal) curve through V_0 ,with the grid lines intersect at points $B_1^{'}$ and $E_1^{'}$;Calculate the arc length of $B_1^{'}E_1^{'}$;determine the corresponding point O_1 of point O according to the ratio $BO/BE = B_1^{'}O_1/B_1^{'}E_1^{'}$ on the U curve which through $B_1^{'}$ and $E_1^{'}$.

5   The Results

As shown in Fig.9, two virtual objects Model1 and Model2 in the environment are in the same coordinate system. End effector (i.e., hand) changed into hang down state from the suspended state. We know the movement state of each arm joint according to the inverse kinematics. By controlling the movement of each joint, Model1 completes a movement, and record the trajectory of Model1 during the process, and then the trajectory of this data is mapped to the same scene Model2, thus completing the two same structure but different roles model of the virtual arm motion retargeting.

For a more intuitive animation of arm movement, three view modes are designed.

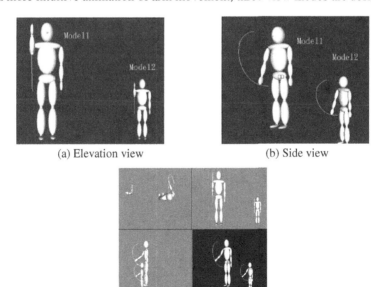

(a) Elevation view   (b) Side view

(c)   Sorted view

Fig. 9. Three modes to view the moving of virtual arm

6   Conclusions

Taking the virtual arm as an object, we study a motion retargeting method based on inverse kinematics of the vector-mapping.This method calculates the position of other joints and directions by the known movement way of the end effector, and applies inverse kinematics and geometric methods to calculate a set of state values of all the joints of the virtual arm, realizing to control the motion retargeting of the virtual arm. The core of the vector-mapping-based motion retargeting method is to get the initial movement curve, the initial motion vector of the curve and the maps of the moving information. Experimental results show that the method can effectively achieve the movement to redirect, and simplify the controlling problem in the process of motion retargeting.

References

1. Brand, M., Hertzmann, A.: Style Machines. In: Proceedings of the 27th Annual Conference on Computer Graphics and Interactive Techniques, pp. 183–192 (2000)
2. Lu, W., Liu, Y., Sun, J., Sun, L.: A Motion Retargeting Method for Topologically Different Characters. In: Sixth International Conference on Computer Graphics, Imaging and Visualization, pp. 105–108 (2009)
3. Sen, S., Abboud, R., Wang, W.: A motion simulation and biomechanical analysis of the shoulder joint using a whole human model. In: The 4th International Conference on Biomedical Engineering and Informatics (BMEI), pp. 11–19 (2011)
4. Nopvichai, K., Kanongchaiyos, P.: 3d HandMotion Retargeting From Video Image Sequence. In: The 2nd International Conference on Computer and Automation Engineering (ICCAE), pp. 39–48 (2010)
5. Choi, K., Ko, H.: Online Motion Retargetting. The Journal of Visualization and Computer Animation 11(5), 223–235 (2000)
6. Tak, S., Ko, H.: Example Guided Inverse Kinematics. In: The Proceedings of the International Conference on Computer Graphics and Imaging (CGIM), pp. 19–23 (2000)
7. Park, M.J., Shin, S.Y.: Example-based motion cloning. Computer Animation and Virtual Worlds 15(3-4), 245–257 (2004)
8. Hsieh, M.K., Chen, B.Y., et al.: Motion Retargeting and Transition in Different Articulated Figures. In: Proceedings of 2005 International Conference on Computer Aided Design and Computer Graphics, Hong Kong, China, pp. 457–462 (2005)
9. Luo, Z., Zhuang, Y., Liu, F., et al.: Space-Time Constraints Based Motion Editing and Motion Retargeting. Journal of Computer-Aided Design & Computer Graphics 14(12), 1146–1150 (2002)

Loss-Free Slotted OBS for Ring and Mesh Hybrid Networks

Hongkyu Jeong[1], Min-Gon Kim[2,*], and Hong-Shik Park[3]

[1] Department of High Tech. Medical System, Kyungil University
hongkyu.jeong@gmail.com
[2] Department of Electrical Engineering, KAIST
kmg0803@gmail.com, parkhs@ee.kaist.ac.kr

Abstract. This paper proposes a loss-free time-slot allocation (LTA) algorithm working on Optical Burst Switching (OBS) for ring and mesh hybrid networks. It preserves the number of time-slots for each source node, so that it avoids contention among time-slots fundamentally just by sacrificing acceptable delay at source nodes. In order to manipulate time-slots efficiently, it is suggested that an OBS superframe, which is a cyclic time duration. In addition, we propose a flow control scheme aiding the LTA algorithm, adjusting the number of time-slots allocated for source nodes so as to prevent loss of data bursts from buffer overflow of source nodes. Simulation results show that the LTA algorithm achieves zero blocking rate with acceptable queueing delay at moderate traffic loads. Moreover, the proposed flow control scheme supporting the LTA algorithm maintains a target upper-bound of queueing delay, and thus packet loss caused by buffer overflow is inhabited.

Keywords: Slotted Optical Burst Switching, Loss-free Time-Slot Allocation, Flow Control.

1 Introduction

Tremendous traffic increase caused by smart-phone like 'iPhone' becomes a hot issue in the network industry. To exemplify, AT&T is talking about 5,000 percent increase in their traffic in a span of three years from 2010 [1]. Traffic increase makes service providers spend more CAPEX in order to maintain the quality of service (QoS). Moreover, since most smart-phone applications require real-time response, delay requirements are incredibly tight. For that, ITU Y.1541 [2] defines 100 ms latency for real-time, jitter-sensitive, and highly interactive applications. Therefore, it is not avoidable for the service providers to adopt the most cost-effective and delay-guaranteed next generation network technologies.

To date, Optical Burst Switching (OBS) [3] has been received uncountable attention as a promising switching technology for the next generation Internet and has been studied for the last decade. Notwithstanding every effort for the study of OBS, contention problem has not been thoroughly resolved enough to

---

* Corresponding author.

M. Zhao and J. Sha (Eds.): ICCIP 2012, Part I, CCIS 288, pp. 757–764, 2012.
© Springer-Verlag Berlin Heidelberg 2012

guarantee QoS in terms of blocking rate and latency. In the meanwhile, a slotted OBS (SOBS) [4] was suggested as a promising solution to minimize blocking rate radically by synchronizing from the beginning until the end time of data bursts. However, this idea also remained unacceptable blocking ratio for the real-world services.

Moreover, in order to provide seamless application services, it is necessary to resolve a congestion problem caused at the link between metro area and backbone area. This happens normally owing to the different transport mechanism. Therefore, several ideas considering seamless data transport from ring network for metro area to mesh network for backbone area [5,6] are suggested in the domain of optical WDM networks. However, these ideas are not evaluated at the real-world networks such as NSFNET as well as not proposed, as far as we know, for OBS networks.

These situations have provided the motivation of this study; in order to achieve loss-free switching technology for the ring and mesh hybrid networks, we propose a novel loss-free time-slot allocation (LTA) algorithm. It avoids contention problem utterly just by sacrificing acceptable delay at the source node. In addition, a flow control scheme is also suggested to amend the number of allocated time-slots for the source nodes according to altered traffic amount, so that it enhances the network availability. The rest of this paper is organized as follows. Section 2 describes a proposing loss-free time-slot allocation (LTA) algorithm with a flow control scheme aiding the LTA algorithm. Performance of the proposing LTA algorithm will be evaluated with existing representative algorithms in Section 3. At last, this paper is concluded in Section 4.

2   Loss-Free Time-Slot Allocation (LTA) Algorithm

2.1   Slotted OBS

It is helpful to look over the Slotted OBS (SOBS) first since the proposing loss-free time-slot allocation (LTA) algorithm is designed based on the SOBS. SOBS divides a wavelength into time-units (or time-slots) at the time-axis, and transmits data bursts contained in a time-slot. For this, source nodes should aggregate incoming packets into data bursts suitable for a time-slot. SOBS can achieve at most a 50% lower blocking rate when compared to non-slotted OBS [7].

However, the blocking rate of general SOBS is not acceptable to satisfy QoS of real-world service, which is mostly under a 10^{-3} blocking rate at the transport networks [8]. Therefore, OBS should satisfy highly tight blocking rate at least under a 10^{-3} as well as delay under 100 ms so as to be a prefered next generation packet switching technology.

2.2   OBS Superframe for Ring and Mesh Hybrid Networks

In order to manage and allocate time-slots efficiently, a time-slot structure is necessarily required, and thereby we propose an OBS superframe (i.e., $OBS-Superframe_{BID,WL}^{D_k}$), which consists of time-slots and repeats cyclically with a

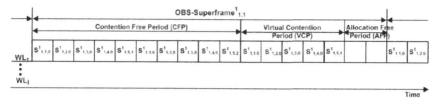

Fig. 1. Example of an OBS superframe on a link

given time duration (e.g., 10ms). The OBS superframe is identified by a desti-nation node number (D_k), a Branch ID (BID) of the node, and a wavelength (WL) number. BID is assigned to the source nodes, which transmits time-slots to the same destination via the same link, and the link is directly connected to the destination node. As shown in Figure 1, an OBS superframe consists of contention free period (CFP), virtual contention period (VCP), and allocation free period (AFP). The CFP consists of the time-slots allocated to the source nodes transmitting time-slots to the same destination node except the source node which is directly connected to the destination node. The time-slots within the CFP do not cause any contention among them because the time-slots are uniquely allocated to each source node.

Figure 1 illustrates the $OBS - Superframe_{1,1}^1$ consisting of the time-slots al-located to the source node $(S_{BID,NID,RID}^{D_k})$ at the CFP in a sequential manner of $S_{1,1,0}^1$, $S_{1,2,0}^1$, $S_{1,3,0}^1$, $S_{1,4,0}^1$, $S_{1,5,1}^1$, and $S_{1,5,2}^1$; the Node ID (NID) indicates the source nodes with the same BID, the Ring ID (RID) indicates whether the node is belonged to a ring network and is the solely farthest node from the core node in the tree based node structure. For example, if there are four nodes in a ring network, where one node is the core node connecting the core network with the metro net-work, the farthest node from the core node is sole. In that case, the farthest node can transmit data bursts evenly through bi-direction paths. This is because bi-direction path can be the shortest path in the tree structure. Thus, the farthest node (e.g., $S_{1,5,r}^1$) is logically located in two positions in the tree structure as shown in the Figure 2, and the RID can be '1' or '2' with the identical NID. However, the time-slots for the farthest node should be the same with that of the other nodes in the same ring network, and thereby the total number of allocated time-slots for the farthest node are the same as that for other nodes. On the contrary, if there are odd number of nodes in the ring network, the farthest nodes from the core node are two. Hence, the RID of the farthest nodes is zero. Also if the node is not belonged to a ring network, the RID will be zero.

On the other hand, the VCP consists of time-slots allocated to the source node (called it as First-Hop-Node), directly connected to a destination node. However, the First-Hop-Node has a lot of chances to utilize the unused time-slots of other source nodes with the same BID, and thereby it is affordable to virtually reallocate the time-slots at the VCP to other source nodes in the steady traffic condition. Moreover, since the time-slots in the VCP are originally allocated to the First-Hop-Node, the node has a right to get back and/or restrict to utilize the time-slots in the bursty traffic condition.

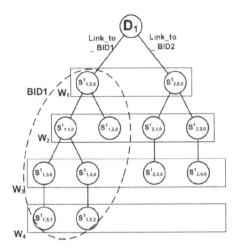

Fig. 2. Example of tree structure configuration

The time-slots in the AFP are not used for the source nodes in the same OBS superframe, but those can be utilized for multiplexing OBS superframes in order to minimize wavelength consumption.

2.3   Operation Mechanism of the LTA Algorithm

A control node operated based on the LTA algorithm, firstly, allocates the number of time-slots for source nodes based on the expecting traffic volume, and then recalculates them according to the weight policy of network operator. Secondly, the control node optimizes the number of wavelengths consumed by OBS superframes so as to achieve high utilization of network bandwidth resource. The following will describe the specific process of operating the LTA algorithm for ring and mesh hybrid networks.

For the remainder of the paper, the following symbols and notations pertain. N is the number of nodes, which are source nodes, intermediate nodes, and destination nodes. D_k is destination nodes ($k \in N$). $S_{i,j,r}^k$ is a source node generating traffic, where k is the destination node, i is the Branch-ID (BID), j is the Node-ID (NID) in the same branch, and r is the Ring ID (RID) in the same ring network. $TS_{i,j,r}^k$ is pre-calculated number of time-slots for traffic of $S_{i,j,r}^k$ delivered to D_k in an OBS superframe. W_h is a weight used in the time-slot allocation, where h is the number of hops to arrive at the destination node from a source node. $TS_{i,j,r}^k$ allocated to each $S_{i,j,r}^k$ is calculated by

$$TS_{i,j,r}^k = \lceil (P_{traffic} \times Cycle_{OBS-Superframe}/DB_{size}) \rceil_{time-slot} \qquad (1)$$

where $P_{traffic}$ is expecting incoming peak traffic rate (bps) of $S_{i,j,r}^k$ toward destination node k, $Cycle_{OBS-Superframe}$ is the cycle period (ms) of the OBS superframe, DB_{size} is the fixed size (bits) of the data burst calculated from the time-slot size after subtracting the guard-time size.

The LTA algorithm assigns a weight to each source node according to the policy of network operator, so that it can not only improve network utilization but support fairness among the source nodes. This is because the source nodes close to the destination node easily can utilize the time-slots allocated to but not used by other source nodes. However, the source nodes far from the destination node mostly come to utilize the time-slots allocated just for them. The weight value is a parameter deciding the number of allocating time-slots by increasing or decreasing a proportional quantity compared to the original $TS_{i,j,r}^k$. In this paper, the weight value is classified by the hop-count. A weighted time-slot is calculated by

$$WTS_{i,j,r}^k = \lfloor TS_{i,j,r}^k \times W_h \rfloor_{time-slot} \tag{2}$$

where the range of W_h is $0 < W_h < 2$ in this paper. The summation value of $TS_{i,j,r}^k$ having the same BID and k should be the same as the summation value of $WTS_{i,j,r}^k$ having the same BID and k as shown in Eq.3. For this, if some number of time-slots in the CFP is lacking or left over in the progress of recalculating number of time-slots based on Eq.2, such time-slots are taken from or added to the VCP.

$$\sum_{\forall j} \sum_{\forall r} WTS_{i,j,r}^k = \sum_{\forall j} \sum_{\forall r} TS_{i,j,r}^k \tag{3}$$

Moreover, if the number of time-slots allocated to a source node is more than one, the time-slots will be evenly distributed over the CFP and the VCP in order to minimize delay variation. A control packet is transmitted ahead of a time-slot with some amount of offset-time like conventional OBS. Since a control packet has enough offset-time for the processing delay, we assume that time-slots will not overtake its control packet.

If network traffic pattern is altered, it is pivotal to adjust the allocated time-slots in order to avoid packet loss from the buffer overflow. For example, if a source node has 256 Kbits memory with a 70% upperbound rate and the arrival rate is 250 Mbps, the upper-bound becomes 5.7 ms based on the following:

$$Upperbound = (Buff_{size} \times R_{upper})/R_{arrival} \tag{4}$$

For flow control, if the First-Hop-Node requests more time-slots assuming no time-slots in the AFP, the control node lets the node utilize the time-slots in the VCP first and prohibits the time-slots from other source nodes. On the other hand, if a source node beyond the First-Hop-Node requests time-slots, the control node lets the node utilize the time-slots in the VCP, where the time-slots already should not be prohibited by the First-Hop-Node. After allocating time-slots in the VCP, if the source node still requests more time-slots, the control node takes the time-slots from other source nodes based on the time-slot usage ratio.

3   Performance Evaluation

In this section, we evaluate the performance of the loss-free slot allocation (LTA) algorithm (below we call it LTA-OBS) from the simulation tests using an event-driven simulator. We first describe the blocking rate of LTA-OBS compared with JET-OBS [3] and TS-OBS [4]. We then evaluate the queueing delay of LTA-OBS with and without the flow control scheme. Simulation environments are assumed as follows; a two-step tree architecture is utilized. First, ten source nodes generate data bursts with 100 kbits size and the inter-arrival time of the data bursts is exponentially distributed with a mean of (1/arrival rate). And then the outgoing data bursts are contending with the data bursts generated by other nine source nodes in order to emulate the blocking situation of 14-node NSFNET (averagely 2.32 links) assuming low blocking in the metro networks. The time-slot size is the same as the data burst size and we assume that the guard-time is negligible. The OBS superframe cycle is ten ms. The source nodes deliver the data bursts contained in a time-slot to an intermediate node which is directly connected to a destination node. The time-slots delivered by the source nodes content at an output port of the intermediate node towards the destination node. Each link has one wavelength with 2.5 Gbps bandwidth. The FDL is not utilized for all cases.

Figure 3 shows the blocking probabilities of JET-OBS, TS-OBS, and LTA-OBS. Performance of TS-OBS is better than that of JET-OBS because TS-OBS can avoid contention between the data bursts through aligning start points of the data bursts. Nevertheless, the blocking rate of TS-OBS is still unacceptable at most offered loads to support Quality of Service (QoS) for commercial services. On the contrary, LTA-OBS does not experience blocking among the time-slots since each source node has reserved the number and the position of the time-slots. Such a high benefit of LTA-OBS comes from the sacrifice in the queueing delay of the data bursts at the source nodes. And the queueing delay of LTA-OBS is minimized by evenly distributing the time-slots in the CFP for a source node and by increasing the available time-slots via the VCP. Moreover, it is controlled by a flow control scheme in order not to exceed predefined upper-bound.

For the evaluation of the proposed flow control scheme, we have chosen a system environment (i.e., 5 ms) as the output port buffer upper-bound where the memory size is 256 Kbits and the arrival rate is 250 Mbps. We also deemed that 5 ms is somewhat the acceptable upper-bound as the maximum queueing delay at the source nodes in order to support interactive application services.

Figure 4 shows the average maximum queueing delay of the data bursts at various traffic loads in the time line. When we adopt 5 ms as the output port buffer upper-bound, packet loss caused by buffer overflow can occur at more than 0.7 offered load. Therefore, the source node requests the additional time-slots to avoid buffer overflow as the offered load increases more than 0.7. In LTA-OBS case without the flow control, as expectedly, the average maximum queueing delay exceeds the buffer upper-bound at more than 0.7 offered load. When the source node receives 10% additional time-slots (i.e., W=1.1), the average maximum queueing delay decreases up to about 4 ms at 0.8 offered load. However, if

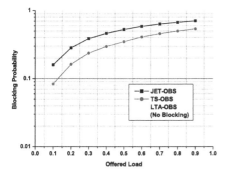
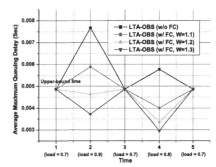

Fig. 3. Blocking probability of the data burst in JET-OBS, TS-OBS, and LTA-OBS at 14-node NSFNET

Fig. 4. Average maximum queueing delay of the data bursts in LTA-OBS supported by the proposed flow control algorithm

the offered load increases up to 0.9 with 10% additional time-slots, the average maximum queueing delay eventually exceeds the buffer upper-bound. On the contrary, when the source node receives more than 20% additional time-slots, the average maximum queueing delay does not exceed the buffer upper-bound at any traffic loads. In addition, the source node returns additionally allocated time-slots when the offered load decreases lower than 0.8 offered load. Therefore, it is possible to keep the delay upper-bound by making use of the proposed flow control at the fluctuating high offered loads.

4   Conclusion

In this paper, we proposed a loss-free time-slot allocation (LTA)-Optical Burst Switching (OBS) with a flow control scheme for ring and mesh hybrid networks. The LTA-OBS is first designed to preserve time-slots for each source node in the OBS superframe cycle duration, so that the time-slots transmitted from the source node can arrive safely at the destination node by sacrificing only the acceptable delay at the source node. Putting into consideration the unpredictable case that the source nodes can receive more traffic than their expectation in the network planning stage, the LTA-OBS additionally adopts a flow control scheme that adjust the number of the allocated time-slots for the source nodes according to altered traffic amount. Through the performance evaluation, it is proved that the LTA-OBS does not suffer from contention among the time-slots. Moreover, the LTA-OBS does not exceed the target queueing delay, so that the data bursts are not dropped by buffer overflow at the fluctuating high offered load (up to load 0.9) condition. As a consequence, the LTA-OBS can be one of the promising next generation optical switching technologies, due to fundamental resolution of blocking problem and network availability enhancement with a flow control scheme.

Acknowledgment. This work was supported in part by (1) the Kyungil University Grant, (2) the KCC, Korea, under the R&D program supervised by the KCA (KCA-2011-(09913-05003)) and (3) the MKE(The Ministry of Knowledge Economy), Korea, under the ITRC(Information Technology Research Center) support program supervised by the NIPA(National IT Industry Promotion Agency)" (NIPA-2011-(C1090-1111-0013)).

References

1. http://saintpetersblog.com/2010/09/19/
   att-forecasting-a-5000-increase-in-their-traffic/
2. Network Performance Objectives for IP-based services, ITU-T Rec. Y.1541 (May 2002)
3. Qiao, C., Yoo, M.: Optical Burst Switching (OBS) - A New Paradigm for an Optical Internet. Journal of High Speed Networks 8(1), 69–84 (1999)
4. Ramamirtham, J., Turner, J.: Time-Sliced Optical Burst Switching. In: Infocomm 2003, vol. 3, pp. 2030–2038 (2003)
5. Hermann, K.: Ring-Mesh Networks. United State Patent, Patent No. US 6,848,006 B1, January 25 (2005)
6. Bourduas, S., Zilic, Z.: A Hybrid Ring/Mesh Interconnect for Network-on-Chip Using Hierarchical Rings for Global Routing. In: Proceeding NOCS 2007, pp. 195–204 (2007)
7. Zhang, Z., Liu, L., Yang, Y.: Slotted Optical Burst Switching (SOBS) Networks. Journal of Comp. Comm. 30(18) (December 2007)
8. 3GPP TS 23.203 V10.1.0, 3rd Generation Partnership Project; Technical Specification Group Services and System Aspects; Policy and charging control architecture (Release 10) (September 2010)

Author Index

Printed in the United States
By Bookmasters